Loading...

曹斐

CAO FEI

欢迎登陆

章魚

RMB City

MY CITY IS YOURS

Credits.txt

EDITED BY RUBY ARROWSMITH-TODD AND YIN CAO

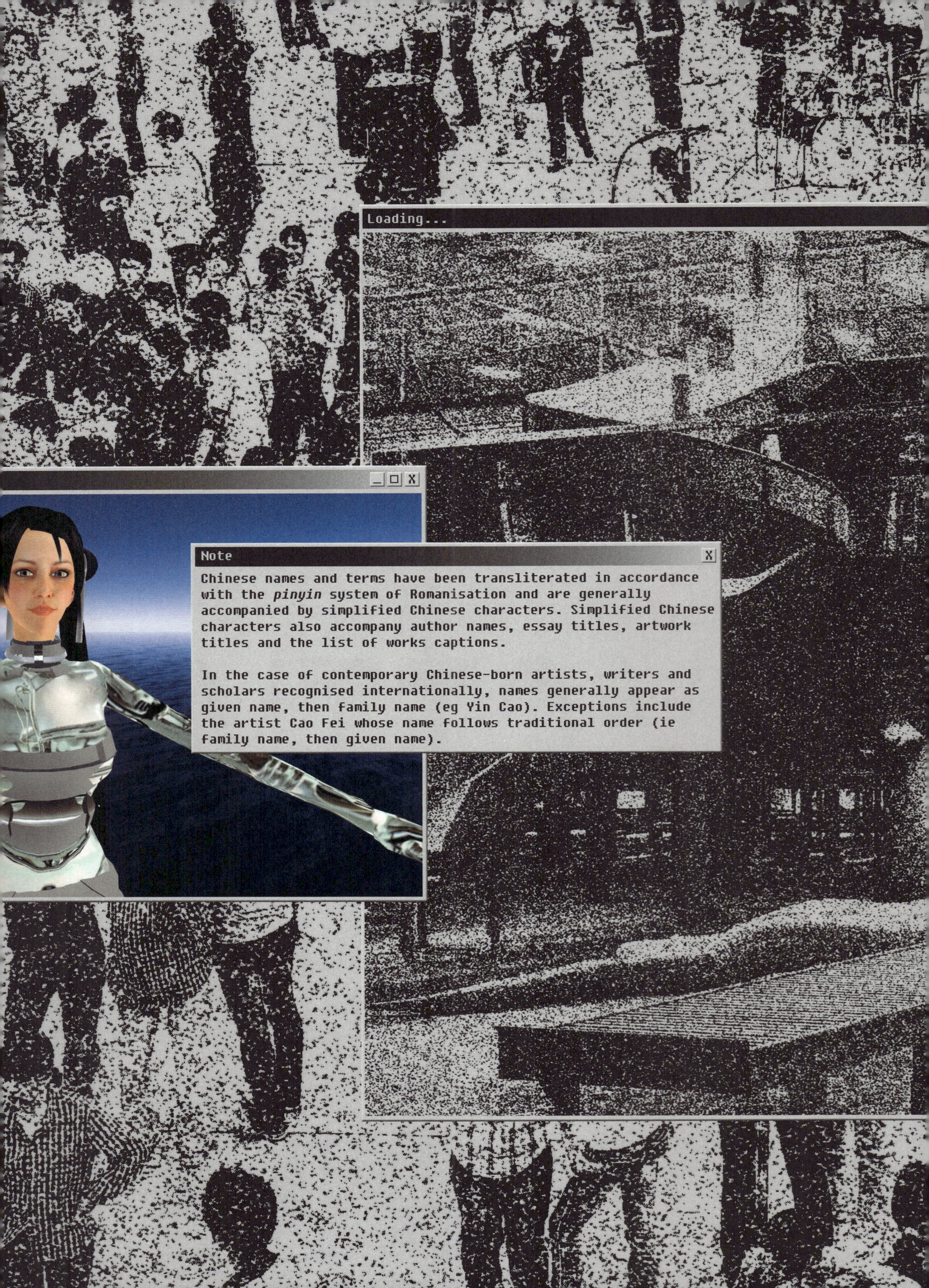

Note

Chinese names and terms have been transliterated in accordance with the *pinyin* system of Romanisation and are generally accompanied by simplified Chinese characters. Simplified Chinese characters also accompany author names, essay titles, artwork titles and the list of works captions.

In the case of contemporary Chinese-born artists, writers and scholars recognised internationally, names generally appear as given name, then family name (eg Yin Cao). Exceptions include the artist Cao Fei whose name follows traditional order (ie family name, then given name).

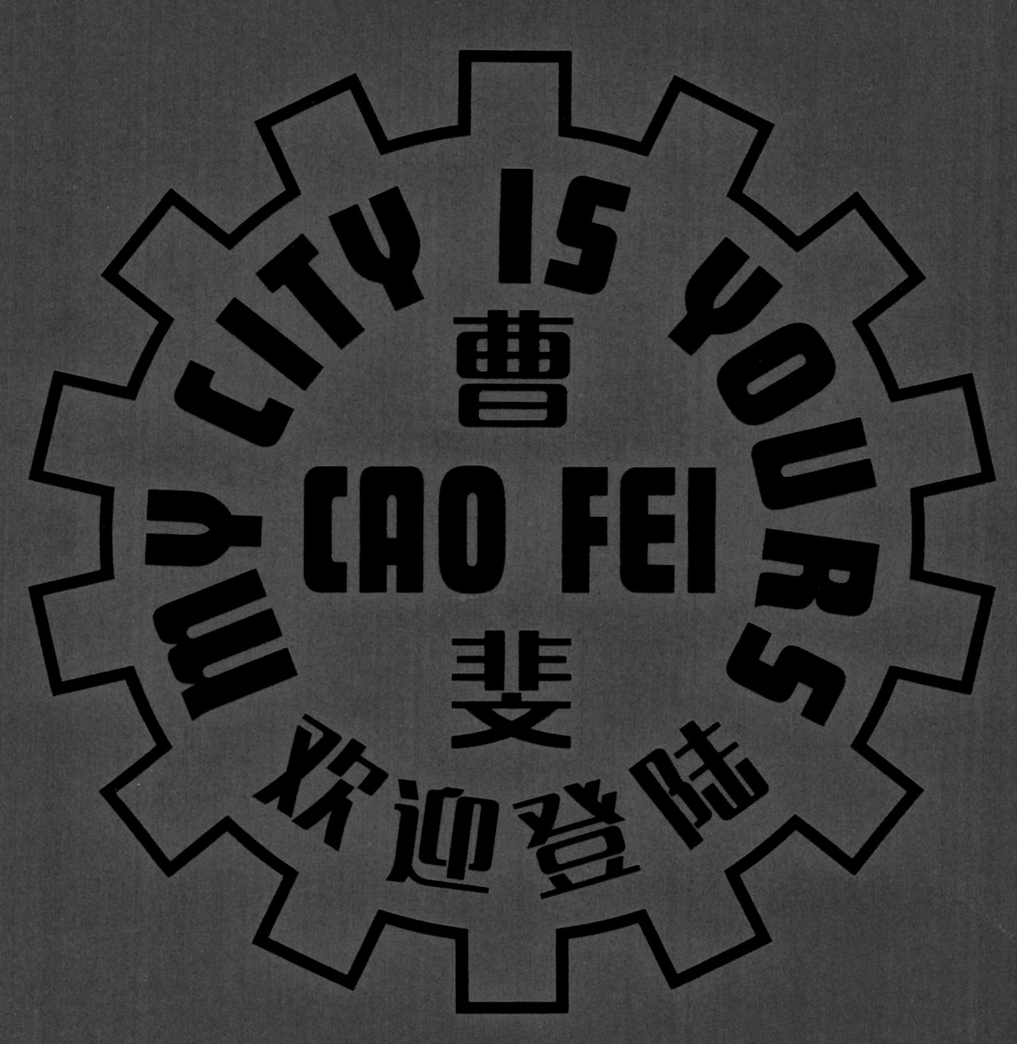
MY CITY IS YOURS
曹
CAO FEI
斐
欢迎登陆

Access Registration [X]

MY CITY IS YOURS 曹 CAO FEI 斐 欢迎登陆

MY CITY IS YOURS™
v6.15
CAO FEI

[Start]

Visit Cao Fei world at: http://www.caofei.com

Acknowledgement of Country

The Art Gallery of New South Wales acknowledges the Gadigal of the Eora Nation, the traditional custodians of the Country on which it stands.

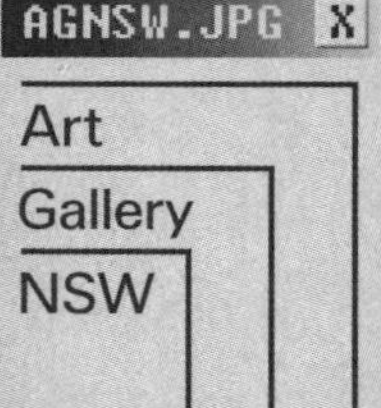

Minister's message

On behalf of the NSW Government, it is my pleasure to welcome you to the Art Gallery of New South Wales for the Sydney International Art Series exhibition *Cao Fei: My City is Yours*.

This remarkable showcase marks the first major retrospective of the pioneering artist Cao Fei in Australia. Cao Fei's artistry serves as a powerful lens through which we can examine urbanisation, globalisation and technological advancement.

I commend Cao Fei and her studio, alongside the dedicated team at the Art Gallery, for their commitment in bringing this exhibition to fruition. *Cao Fei: My City is Yours* is presented as part of the Sydney International Art Series – a collaboration between the NSW Government's tourism and major events agency, Destination NSW; the Art Gallery of New South Wales; and the Museum of Contemporary Art Australia – which brings the world's most outstanding artists and their works exclusively to Sydney.

I am sure you will enjoy this exhibition and its accompanying publication, and I invite you to take some time to experience our beautiful city's unique combination of vibrant cultural precincts and natural wonders.

The Hon John Graham MLC
Minister for Jobs and Tourism
Minister for the Arts
Minister for Music and the Night-time Economy

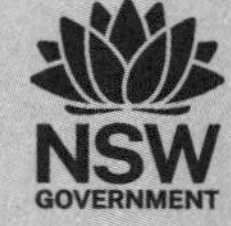

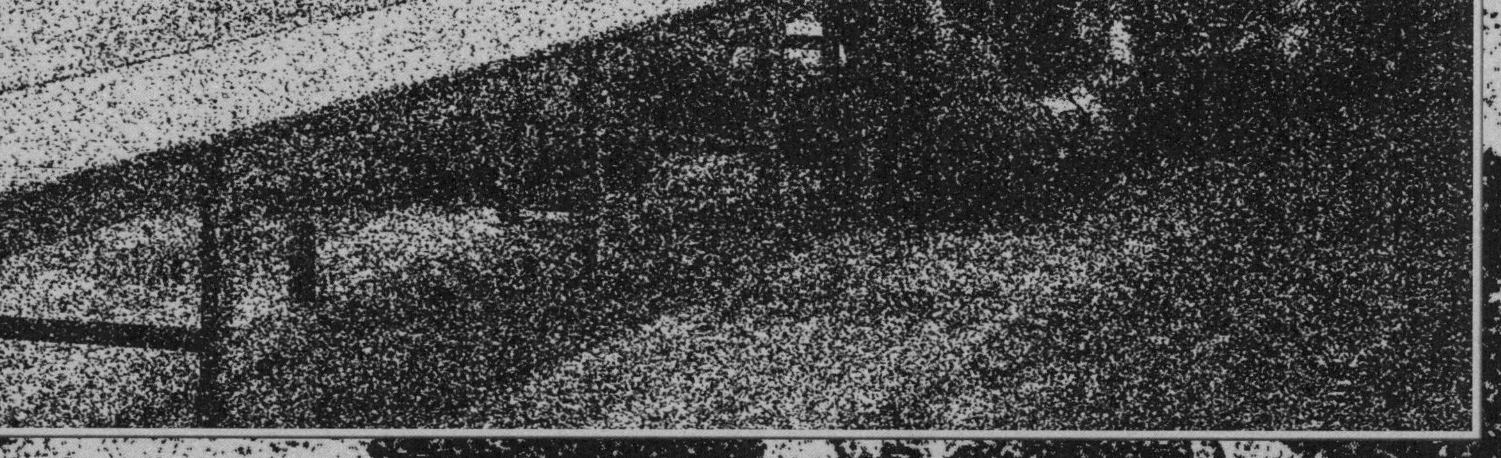

DIRECTOR'S FOREWORD

The Art Gallery of New South Wales is honoured to present Cao Fei's *My City is Yours*, the first major solo exhibition of this internationally renowned Chinese artist in Australia. This exhibition builds upon the Art Gallery's history of staging exhibitions of Chinese art since the 1940s and its commitment to promoting Australia's engagement with China in the field of art, both past and present. Our earlier major Chinese exhibitions have predominantly focused on ancient China and historical artforms. With this exhibition and its accompanying publication, we aim to highlight our dedication to introducing startling new art experiences to the public at our recently transformed art museum in Sydney, situated on Gadigal Country.

Cao Fei is one of the most dynamic contemporary artists on the world stage. She was born in 1978, the same year Chairman Deng Xiaoping instigated the 'Reform and Opening-up' (*gaige kaifang* 改革开放) program in China. Cao's birthplace of Guangzhou, in China's southern Guangdong province, was at the forefront of these emerging economic strategies. The gate was opened and fresh waves of popular culture poured into the city. She has witnessed and continues to experience drastic changes in China, which she examines in her art with insight and audacity.

The artworks in this exhibition, dating from the 1990s until the current day, provide Australian audiences with an understanding of the impacts of urbanisation, globalisation, popular culture and technological development on people's lives, both in China and worldwide. Cao's extraordinary ability to navigate the intersection of documentary and fictional forms is visible in a practice that encompasses photography and film, new digital artforms and virtual reality, as well as sculptural installations – all of which are presented at the Art Gallery's new building, Naala Badu, in an environment that emulates a cityscape. Together, Cao's works invite visitors on an immersive journey, where we feel the struggles of individuals in an ever-changing world and sense the uncertainty of a future in which AI will play a dominant role.

Cao's connection to Sydney also marks this retrospective exhibition as particularly special. Her hometown Guangzhou is

Sydney's official sister city and Sydney is also the place her own sister Cao Xiaoyun (1971–2022) called home for many years. For this exhibition, she has created two commissioned works that pay tribute to these links: *The golden wattle* and *Hip hop: Sydney*. The former is dedicated to her late sister, who migrated to Sydney in 1998. In it, she explores the lives and experiences of migrants who form an integral part of our multicultural society. The latter work is a continuation of the *Hip hop* video series that Cao began in 2003. With the generous involvement of members of the public who have embraced the joy of dance, it showcases the cultural diversity of contemporary Sydney and the myriad influences that shape our vibrant cultural landscape.

I congratulate Cao Fei and her studio, who have worked closely with the team at the Art Gallery led by curator of film Ruby Arrowsmith-Todd, curator of Chinese art Yin Cao and senior exhibitions manager Danielle Earp to deliver this stimulating exhibition. I also warmly acknowledge and thank architects Charlotte Lafont-Hugo and Gilles Vanderstocken of Beau Architects in Hong Kong for an exceptional exhibition design that conceptually merges the city and the Art Gallery to enhance the visitor experience.

For their contributions to this exhibition book, I am deeply grateful to Hou Hanru, Michael Sun and Pao-chen Tang for their scholarship; Amy Reigle Newland for her expertise and thoughtful editing; and Evi O for her extraordinary book design that captures the essence of Cao's art.

I wish to thank our major exhibition patrons, The Robert H.N. Ho Family Foundation Global and the Turnbull Foundation for their extraordinary support of this remarkable venture, as well as the Art Gallery's VisAsia, for their significant philanthropic commitment. I also acknowledge the support of bequest patron, the Neville Holmes Grace Exhibition Endowment. Such benefaction is vital to the success of our exhibition program. Additionally, we are immensely grateful to the NSW Government for their invaluable support through tourism and events agency Destination NSW, which has been instrumental in bringing this exhibition to life.

In presenting *Cao Fei: My City is Yours*, we celebrate the innovative work of this globally acclaimed artist as well as the boundless possibilities that art offers for deeper understanding and connection.

MICHAEL BRAND
DIRECTOR
ART GALLERY OF NEW SOUTH WALES

Directory

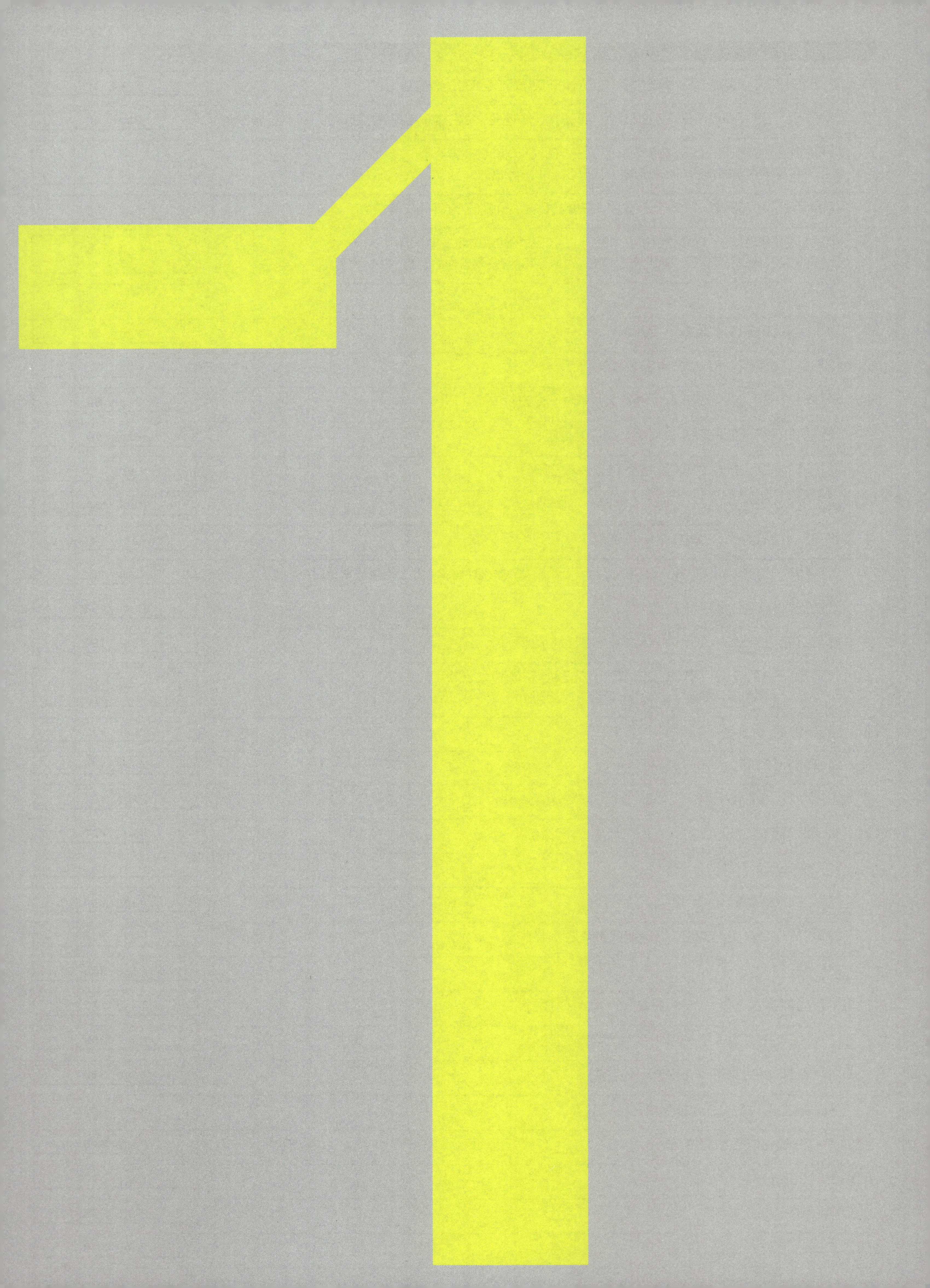

RUBY ARROW SMITH-TODD

THROUGH THE WORMHOLE

穿越虫洞

曹茹碧

穿越虫洞穿越虫洞穿越虫洞穿越虫洞脱离时间线

In science fiction, wormholes – tunnels through space and time – have long been the go-to means of travel across the universe. Astronauts and adventure seekers voyage through shimmering passageways from our solar system in search of other galaxies. Wormholes are a prediction of Einstein's theory of general relativity, which has also revealed proven phenomena such as black holes – regions so dense they obliterate light. One simple version of the wormhole, known as an Einstein-Rosen bridge, consists of two black holes, each facing out into its own realm of the universe and joined by a 'throat'. This cosmic tunnel folds the fabric of space-time, facilitating faster-than-light travel between two distant points and even regions of time. In some sci-fi narratives, wormholes are gateways to intergalactic exploration and the discovery of new worlds. In others, these vortexes beckon as escape hatches from an ailing planet: shortcuts to survival and reinvention. No-one knows if wormholes exist. Theoretically possible, yet never proven, they inspire fantastical speculation.

Wormholes offer one way into the worlds of Cao Fei. The daring postulate that space and time can bend resonates with an artistic practice forged in 21st-century networked China. For over two decades, Cao has watched as far-out fantasies have become everyday realities. The artist was born in 1978, the same year that then Chairman of the People's Republic of China Deng Xiaoping first introduced sweeping political and economic reforms. Under the spell of 9.6 per cent yearly economic growth, China's urbanisation and technological advancements occurred at a discombobulating speed and scale. Villages turned into suburbs, turned into cities, turned into high-rise megalopolises. Former security guards have reinvented themselves as e-commerce couriers. Robotic trucks sell ice cream at art parks in Beijing.

Since the late 1990s, Cao has documented and dreamt alongside these 'top-down, earth-shaking changes' through videos, photography and multimedia installations.[1] She has herself gravitated to the concept of the wormhole – a shorthand for warp-speed connectivity – to make sense of her historical era. As the artist recalls in an interview with *My City is Yours* co-curator Yin Cao, 'When I was building *RMB City* and the Second Life platform was quite new, I very much believed in the wormhole theory and the forms of life living in it, as well as the idea seen in science fiction of folded space'.[2] Cosmic tunnels feature as plot devices in several of her films, including *Nova* 2019 and *La Town* 2014. And the wormhole is also a telling metaphor with which to understand Cao's work in its entirety. Hers is a cinematic universe where time is out of joint, reality slips into fantasy, people tap in and out of virtual realms, and radical, disjunctive upheavals are an everyday fact of life. This essay trips down the wormhole to survey 20 years of practice, traversing, in Cao's words, 'a history of fiction and reality folding a maze of small people and dreams, daily life and miracles, reality and fables'.[3] We begin at the threshold of the artist's retrospective in Naala Badu, the Art Gallery's new north building, with a pink and pistachio Sino-Soviet cinema foyer.

ESCAPING THE TIMELINE

Visitors enter this exhibition through a time capsule: a re-creation of the lobby of a now-demolished cinema in Beijing's north-eastern Jiuxianqiao neighbourhood. The Hongxia (Red Dawn) Theatre was constructed in 1957 as a cultural space for workers employed at nearby factories in China's first advanced electronics district. This 'autonomous electronics city', a proto-Silicon Valley, grew from the 1940s to the 1960s as part of the Five-Year Plan with aid from the Soviet Union. Engineers tasked with building China's first computers could visit a gaming parlour, dance at a ballroom and end the night with a free film screening at the Hongxia,

脱离时间线脱离时间线脱离时间线脱离时间线脱

all courtesy of the state. The prospect of an early Sino-computer revolution was ultimately dashed as transistors replaced electronic tubes and the state-run company failed to keep pace with overseas competitors. When the theatre finally shut its doors, it remained untouched: a dream palace, a white brick portal to an earlier era of techno-optimism. Between 2015 and 2020, Cao transformed the space into a studio-cum-research laboratory. The artworks created as part of the Hongxia project twist time. They retrieve unrealised narratives and neglected utopian dreams from China's technological past to spin speculative visions of the future. Or, in Cao's words, 'I just built a stage on top of the ruins, raised the curtains, and did some magic tricks'.[4]

Trick one: a computer scientist subjects his son to 'Hongxia Time Software', an experiment to turn humans into digital matter in the lush feature film *Nova*. Transmission fails between point A and B. Things go awry in the wormhole. The young boy becomes lost in cyberspace, a spectre haunting the past, present and future worlds that overlap throughout the video. Stuck in limbo, this 'lonely electronic phantom' floats through tableaux where material culture from the past (tin rocket ships, Soviet-era film posters) merge with visions of a neon-lit future.

Trick two: visitors are invited to put on a VR headset and teleport to the kitchen of the old Hongxia in *The eternal wave* 2020. With its vintage television, tea thermos and yellowed newspapers, the kitchen appears as a frozen moment, a perfect replica captured when the artist 3D scanned the entire building. But look closer. Some of these are contemporary props that Cao bought on the e-commerce platform Taobao. There's a sleek poster for the artist's latest film hanging in the corner. Open the kitchen window and you discover that you're in the middle of an asteroid field. This virtual reality experience disorients. Against the relentless churn of Beijing's razing and redevelopment in the name of 'progress', Cao describes the Hongxia project as an attempt to 'destroy linear time'.[5] She is keenly aware that in some theoretical scenarios wormholes enable time travel. If movement at one end of the wormhole accelerates to the speed of light, the portal might undergo time dilation such that the internal 'clock' of the passageway would run slower than the rest of the universe. The two ends of the wormhole would no longer be synchronised: you could walk in one side and end up in the past. 'Time, for us, is too real, it's hard to escape', Cao reflects. 'That's why the scientist sends his son into the machine, maybe I want to escape the timeline, you know? And just swim across it'.[6]

FOLDING SPACE

As visitors cross through the red-velvet curtains of the Hongxia foyer, they land, in the next section of the exhibition, in the realm of the Pearl River Delta. As much as Cao is interested in time travel, she is also a poet of place. Cao grew up in Guangzhou, the sprawling port city of 19 million that was a laboratory for China's technological revolution, a test case for the country's rapid urbanisation and a gateway to global exchange.[7] As a young artist in the 1980s and 1990s, she gorged on Cantopop and Japanese anime, bootlegged tapes and MTV. 'After China's open-door policy, all these moving images, films, pop culture arrived. I naturally wanted to use the digital camera to express myself', she remembers.[8] Material flows – and China's transformation into the world's factory – became the focus of one of her earliest breakout works.

Whose utopia 2006 was created in collaboration with employees at the OSRAM (Siemens) lightbulb factory in the industrial Foshan zone in the Pearl River Delta, which at the time was ground zero for the global manufacture of consumer goods. The 20-minute video

离时间线脱离时间线脱离时间线折叠空间折叠空

间折叠空间折叠空间折叠空间幻象能量幻象能量

attends to the human stories of young production-line recruits, members of China's 'floating population' of migrant labourers, who flocked from farms to the big smoke in what has been described as the largest internal migration in human history.[9] Even as a young artist Cao noticed the commodity chains linking her hometown to remote places. She zooms in on the hands of workers, showing how repetitive labour here in the Pearl River Delta transforms raw materials into objects with exchange value elsewhere. In one lightbulb, a radiating web of connections links southern China to the world. *Whose utopia* was the culmination of a six-month-long residency that began with Cao distributing a survey to employees that asked questions like, 'What are you doing here?' and 'What are you dreaming'? She captures the responses in strange and moving scenes of eruptive dance. The workers moonwalk, strut like peacocks and strum electric guitar on the factory floor, briefly freed of the routines that structure their days.

In *Whose utopia*, we find the enduring features of Cao's practice. A tonal slippage between the fantastic and the mundane. A collaborative ethos. And, above all, a sensitivity to contemporary China's global interdependencies. As art critic Philip Tinari notes, Cao's vision has never been parochial: 'She was, even at this early moment, working through China to the much larger idea of a fundamentally neoliberal subjectivity, perhaps common to her generation, the first to be globally networked'.[10] Another iconic series, the *Hip hop* videos (2003–06, 2024), illustrates this point. Inspired by her own love of rap, the artist filmed everyday people – shopkeepers, elderly residents, passers-by – dancing to hip-hop music across the globe. The series of short, dynamic music videos considers the global export of African American culture and its reimagining on the streets of Guangzhou, Fukuoka, New York and Sydney. The animating energy behind this and many of the artist's early works is close to that found in music sampling – the practice of bringing disparate elements together to revelatory effect. In a lightbulb or a hip-hop track, Cao folds space, bridging distant coordinates at the dawn of the new millennium.

PHANTOM ENERGY

Wormholes are said to require negative energy or exotic matter so that they don't collapse under the force of gravity. This image from speculative science once again resonates with Cao's idiosyncratic practice. For she has always injected her explorations of contemporary social structures with doses of the surreal, using her sharp eye for the weird and the improbable to keep bleakness at bay and also keep us fascinated. As an artist, Cao is attuned to the presence of wayward energies in everyday life. Critic, curator and contributor to this book, Hou Hanru calls it a distinctively 'Southern' vision. A Cantonese predilection for irony and satire. A cutting humour.

Since the early 2000s, Cao has turned her gaze to the question of how digital transformations – newfound proximities between the 'real' and the 'virtual' – have generated novel subjectivities, bristling against existing social conventions. In 2004 Cao created *Cosplayers*, a landmark video and photography series capturing the escapades of a generation of Chinese youth raised on the internet. On the outskirts of Guangzhou, Cao filmed and photographed cosplay (or 'costume' play) aficionados who roleplay as characters from popular Japanese anime and manga series. With aqua wigs and gold capes, Cao's protagonists pose amid the rubble of construction sites and half-built mansions. These striking tableaux capture young genies, knights and fairy princesses – representatives of one of China's earliest online subcultures. Already Cao was preoccupied with how networked media – here, online video games – could manifest in reality, in strange

幻象能量幻象能量幻象能量幻象能量幻象能量幻

eruptions on the street. As she remarks, 'the culture of the cosplayers has brought this group of young people out of the cyber community inside the computer and into the everyday life in the real world'.[11] For Cao, cyberspace has never been a separate realm, an abstract sphere of ones and zeroes. In her practice, the 'physical' and the 'digital' are not opposed but rather 'two trajectories constantly in flux – often indistinguishably close, sometimes intersecting'.[12] Indeed, from this early work through to *Meta-mentary* 2022, a recent video where she asks passers-by to point to the physical location of the metaverse on a map, Cao makes the virtual tangible. As a critic, she analyses how technological change interplays with the surreal effects of China's urban growth. The fantastic quality of *Cosplayers* derives not only from the cosplayers' theatrics but from the backdrop of a rapidly expanding Guangzhou, where fake zebras and cows stand in for animals displaced by sprawl.

Cao's eye for the bizarre collisions of globalised culture is at its sharpest in another video, *East wind* 2011. A dump truck with the face of Thomas the Tank Engine rides around Beijing, transporting waste from a demolition site to landfill. Shot with droll matter-of-factness, the ten-minute travelogue shows bemused onlookers observing this hybrid vehicle on the highway: cartoon cuteness as a beneficent front for the razing of lifeworlds. In this work, Cao juxtaposes familiar objects in discordant settings to convey some of the stunned disbelief that has greeted China's hyper-urbanisation. The sight of an AI vacuum cleaner rolling over rubble or a Frankenstein Thomas truck on the highway offers wry commentary on the churn of 'progress'. Though the reality behind these images is often demoralising or dismaying, the strangeness of Cao's images opens space for laughter and its transformative magic. In the artist's words, 'Reality is too heavy and time is too long. The surrealism in my practice allows people to escape'.[13]

ESCAPE HATCH

It's a familiar trope in many sci-fi stories: space travellers trip down the wormhole in search of replacement planets for a worn-out Earth. The cosmic vortex presents a way out. It's a shortcut, an urgent fix, an exit plan. But do such dreams of technologically aided escape from our troubles hold any true hope today? An early adopter of new media, Cao Fei has always been both fascinated by and critical of escapist techno-narratives. In 2006 she began work on a landmark project using the virtual reality platform Second Life, an online universe where users could roam the 'commons' and communicate via instant messaging. Unlike multiplayer games whose worlds came fully built, Second Life represented the emancipatory aspirations of Web 2.0: an early unregulated form of the internet where users had the agency to shape their own shared virtual space. A new arrival to Beijing, Cao turned to Second Life as her own kind of escape hatch. The platform offered a reprieve from the city's cold winters and, more importantly, a means of experimenting with the construction of a digital landscape from the ground up. Outside, a rapacious building boom was underway in preparation for the 2008 Beijing Summer Olympics. Inside, Cao spent eight hours per day behind the keyboard as China Tracy, a cyberpunk avatar who dabbled in romance with other users (eg *i.Mirror* 2007) and became the mayor of a metropolis. As the artist recalls, 'I was interested in virtual cities, and at the time I just had the sensation that this virtual reality would have notable consequences in the future, I could just feel it in the air'.[14]

The *RMB City* project 2007–11 was forged in an era of greater techno-optimism. 'Hand in hand, move forwards, make a virtual future!' proclaimed the digital city's prospectus. 'There are no nationalities or borders here; we are all world citizens in a future world where

象能量幻象能量幻象能量逃生舱口逃生舱口逃生

舱口逃生舱口逃生舱口逃生舱口逃生舱口逃生舱

everyone lives his second life and creates his own values', declared its citizenship guidebook. Described by the artist as a 'condensed incarnation of contemporary Chinese cities', *RMB City* reimagined iconic landmarks, including the National Stadium (Birds Nest) and CCTV building in Beijing and the Buddhist Feilai Temple in Qingyuan. Users from around the world teleported across vaporwave skylines to attend groundbreaking ceremonies, dance parties, feng shui lessons and karaoke. Identity was anonymous, avatars were infinitely customisable. Everything was 'much more unbridled and wild'.[15] On Second Life, as Cao tells her lover in *i.Mirror*, 'you can just be yourself'.

The Second Life project, and the series of video works that remain as its major legacy, represent a period of striking idealism in Cao's practice. *RMB City* was a landmark of early internet art, a laboratory for testing the utopian potentials of placemaking and community-building on a participatory online server. Already, however, Cao was alert to spurious promises of technological utopias and to the susceptibility of virtual worlds to cooption by market forces. Rather than shy from digital art's complicity with a neoliberal economic system, Cao sought to expose it. She actively courted funds from art institutions and held real-estate auctions, encouraging donors and major galleries to exchange cash for virtual land deeds. The project illuminated the rapaciousness of Chinese real-estate development and the fiscal opportunism of the global art industry. A literal translation of the project's title, drawing from the abbreviation of China's official currency (renminbi), could read simply as 'money town'. As critic Xin Wang has noted, while *RMB City* may have seemed like an otherworldly fiction, it was more documentary-like than it appeared. The project was 'a most accurate expression of China's schizophrenic contemporaneity, precarious and fabulous, simultaneously at the threshold of prosperity and collapse; a place where Mao, Marx and a Lehman brother were literally in dialogue'.[16] In other words, the digital wormhole did not open to a utopia but to an accelerated, overdeveloped version of the megalopolises of early 2000s China.

In the wake of the *RMB City* project, Cao created a new work about a city that was small scale and handmade. *La Town* is a stop-motion dystopia spun from plastic and figurines. Again, Cao fashions a tale of folded space. As the narrator begins:

> Everyone has heard the myth of La Town. The story first appeared in Europe, but after travelling through a space-time wormhole, reappeared in Asia and Southeast Asia. It was last seen near the ocean bordering the Eurasian tectonic plate, vanishing in its midst as if a mirage. La Town, struck by unknown disaster – where without sunlight, time froze.

The video surveys scenes of post-apocalyptic ruin, where axe murderers run loose among the wreckage of car crashes and train pile-ups. These chaotic, violent tableaux glow under the light of McDonalds billboards and the neon scallop of Shell oil and gas. Again, as these vignettes suggest, here the wormhole does not lead to a fantasy getaway. Rather, it delivers us into a world of compressed and accelerated social forces – a diorama that does not sell a 'new development' but distils the costs of late-stage capitalism.

La Town inaugurated a distinct shift towards a mood of cyber-scepticism in Cao's recent practice. As she tells Yin Cao, 'I do wonder if cyberspace is still a safe haven, a space for further development and a tool paralleling our real world'.[17] The artist's disillusionment with new technologies is evident in the 2018 feature drama *Asia one*. Set in the first fully automated distribution centre in Shanghai, the video follows the factory's two remaining employees and their robotic assistant. Scenes within the flagship warehouse of

口逃生舱口逃生舱口逃生舱口逃生舱口逃生舱口

Jingdong Logistics (JD.com), one of China's most profitable, Amazon-like companies, are dystopian. Torrents of stuff – nappies, nerf guns, eggs, vitamins – roll down the conveyor belt, packed and scanned by robotic hands, ready for dispatch. The two lonely workers struggle to communicate, estranged from each other and the products of their own hands. In this major work, Cao captures China's transition from a manufacturing powerhouse (eg *Whose utopia*) to a global leader in smart logistics and automated distribution. She meditates on what has been lost as technology has been streamlined and privatised, becoming a mechanism of surveillance, a generator of mega profit, and an alienating substitute for human labour. *Asia one* is a cautionary tale from China to the wider world, a warning shot from the horizon of a fast-approaching technocratic-capitalist future-present.

SISTER CITIES

Exiting *My City is Yours*, you pass through another time capsule: a re-creation of a soon-to-be-demolished Cantonese yum cha restaurant. Originally located in Sydney's CBD Chinatown, the Marigold was an iconic space for community events and family gatherings. It closed its doors in 2021 after 39 years of service, a casualty of the downturn of trade in the Haymarket area following several years of COVID-19 pandemic restrictions. When the artist travelled to Sydney for an initial site visit in late 2023, she was immediately drawn to its 1990s Canto-decor: all red-velvet curtains, gold fittings and fake crystal chandeliers. More tellingly, she gravitated to its lingering energy as a now-abandoned social space that lives on in the cultural memory of the city and the local Chinese diaspora. Encountered within the Art Gallery, the lovingly salvaged red carpet and dim sum trolleys in a white box setting are classic Cao: objects of surreal displacement. The Marigold zone is a generous offering by an artist who has borne witness to her own country's upheavals and now seeks to retrieve the physical intimacy, the 'joy and collective feeling' of lost communal spaces on the other side of the world.[18]

So, although it emerges from the folded virtual spaces of a hyper-connected world, Cao's work also speaks to enfoldment in a slower, more intimate sense: of linked hands and entwined limbs.

Think of the father and son desperate for reunion in *Nova*, of the lovers in *La Town*, or the couriers returning home to their families after long days on the road in *11:11* 2018. Despite all the chilly CCTV cameras and drones that populate her recent films, Cao's vision is empathetic, attuned to flesh, erotics, romance and love. She's always had skin in the game. She's a fan, an avatar, a participant observer. In her words, 'I feel that it's really important that art has this social aspect, this function of trying to reach out to society, not just to be making something beautiful in your studio but to actually function as a bridge'.[19]

The exhibition's title affirms this ethos of hospitality and reciprocity. Sydney and Guangzhou are designated sister cities. On the edge of Sydney's CBD Chinatown, the Chinese Garden of Friendship was built in 1988 to officially mark the two cities' interconnections and diplomatic relations. Since the 19th century, flows of people and trade have linked the southern port towns.[20] One of Australia's earliest Chinese migrants, Guangzhou-born Mak Sai Ying, arrived in Sydney as a free settler in 1818 and purchased land at Parramatta. Generations of Cantonese have followed a similar migration pathway ever since. Indeed, this exhibition features a new commission, *The golden wattle* 2024, dedicated to Cao's late sister Cao Xiaoyun, an artist who migrated from Guangzhou to Sydney in the late 1990s. She loved the Opera House and the nearby Botanic Gardens and painted local flora such as the acacia. Visitors are invited to reflect on one woman's

逃生舱口姐妹城市姐妹城市姐妹城市姐妹城市姐

personal migration story through artefacts and watercolours that provide evidence of what Cao describes as a life 'filled with beauty'.[21] This work, perhaps more than any Cao has made, bears out her assertion that 'what moves me is human'.[22]

Visitors enter Cao's retrospective via an old Sino-Soviet cinema foyer and they exit through a re-creation of an iconic Sydney yum cha joint: two portals each facing outward, far-flung coordinates drawn together, as if through a wormhole. *My City is Yours*, it's a pledge and a promise. It's an invitation into an acclaimed practice that traverses the fantastic imaginaries of 21st-century China, an era of accelerated time and revelatory proximities, slippages between the physical and the virtual, radiating from Guangzhou to Sydney, folding one place into another.

---

1. 'Conversation I: Cao Fei and Susanne Gaensheimer, Kathrin Beßen, Agnieszka Skolimowska' in Susanne Gaensheimer & Kathrin Beßen (eds), *Cao Fei*, Kunstsammlung Nordrhein-Westfalen, Dusseldorf & Hirmer Verlag GmbH, Munich, 2018, p 54.
2. See 'Utopian promises and future nostalgia', Cao Fei in conversation with Yin Cao, p 54.
3. Gaensheimer & Beßen (eds) 2018, p 62.
4. Zack Hatfield, 'Cao Fei on the limits of truth and virtuality', *Artforum*, 15 Mar 2020, artforum.com/columns/cao-fei-on-the-limits-of-truth-and-virtuality-246875, accessed 2 Feb 2024.
5. Günseli Yalcinkaya, 'Artist Cao Fei uses Soviet sci-fi to explode time and space as we know it', *Dazed*, 10 Mar 2020, dazeddigital.com/art-photography/article/48301/1/artist-cao-fei-blueprints-soviet-sci-fi-to-explode-time-and-space-as-we-know-it, accessed 2 Feb 2024.
6. Yalcinkaya 2020.
7. Guangzhou's proximity to Hong Kong saw it designated a Special Economic Zone in the 1980s, intended to attract foreign investment and create new jobs.
8. Farah Nayeri, 'Shining a light on Chinese workers', *The New York Times*, 8 Mar 2019, nytimes.com/2019/03/08/arts/cao-fei-china-woman-artist.html, accessed 12 Jan 2024.
9. Heidi Østbø Haugen and Tabitha Speelman, 'China's rapid development has transformed its migration trends', *Migration Policy Institute*, 28 Jan 2022, migrationpolicy.org/article/china-development-transformed-migration, accessed 13 Jan 2024.
10. Philip Tinari, 'Cao Fei, or, the art of exuberant ambiguity' in Susanne Gaensheimer & Kathrin Beßen (eds), *Cao Fei*, Kunstsammlung Nordrhein-Westfalen, Dusseldorf & Hirmer Verlag GmbH, Munich, 2018, p 24.
11. Cao Fei, '*Cosplayers* artist statement' in *Portfolio of Cao Fei's video works*, Vitamin Creative Space, Guangzhou, nd, np.
12. Klaus Biesenbach (ed), 'Cao Fei in conversation with Klaus Biesenbach,' *Kaleidoscope Asia* 3, spring/summer 2016, pp 138–43.
13. Cao Fei in Hannah Abel-Hirsch, 'Any Answers: Cao Fei', *British Journal of Photography*, 6 Jul 2021, 1854.photography/2021/07/any-answers-cao-fei, accessed 2 Feb 2024.
14. Cao Fei & Monia Trombetta, 'Interview' in Hou Hanru & Monia Trombetta (eds), *Cao Fei. Super Nova*, MAXXI, Rome & Nero, Rome, 2022, p 128.
15. 'Cao Fei in "Fantasy"', *Art in the twenty-first century*, season 5, *art21*, 14 Oct 2009, art21.org/watch/art-in-the-twenty-first-century/s5/cao-fei-in-fantasy-segment, accessed 12 Jan 2024.
16. Xin Wang, 'Cao Fei: Urban legend', *Blanc Dexin*, 31 Mar 2016, blancdexin.com/2016/03/31/cao-fei-urban-legend, accessed 12 Jan 2024.
17. Cao Fei in conversation with Yin Cao, p 54.
18. Shraddha Nair, 'Gamescapes: Cao Fei recalls "RMB City", the virtual world, and its future', *STIRworld*, 25 Aug 2020, stirworld.com/think-opinions-gamescapes-cao-fei-recalls-rmb-city-the-virtual-world-and-its-future, accessed 12 Jan 2024.
19. Jordan Strom, 'Your utopia is ours – Fillip', *Cao Fei.com*, fall 2006, caofei.com/texts.aspx?id=50&year=2006&aitid=1, accessed 12 Jan 2024.
20. Earlier connections of Chinese contact with Australia were on the north-east coastline, with the trade in sandalwood and trepang.
21. Cao Fei in conversation with Yin Cao, p 56.
22. Cao Fei in conversation with Yin Cao, 23 Jan 2023, unpublished.

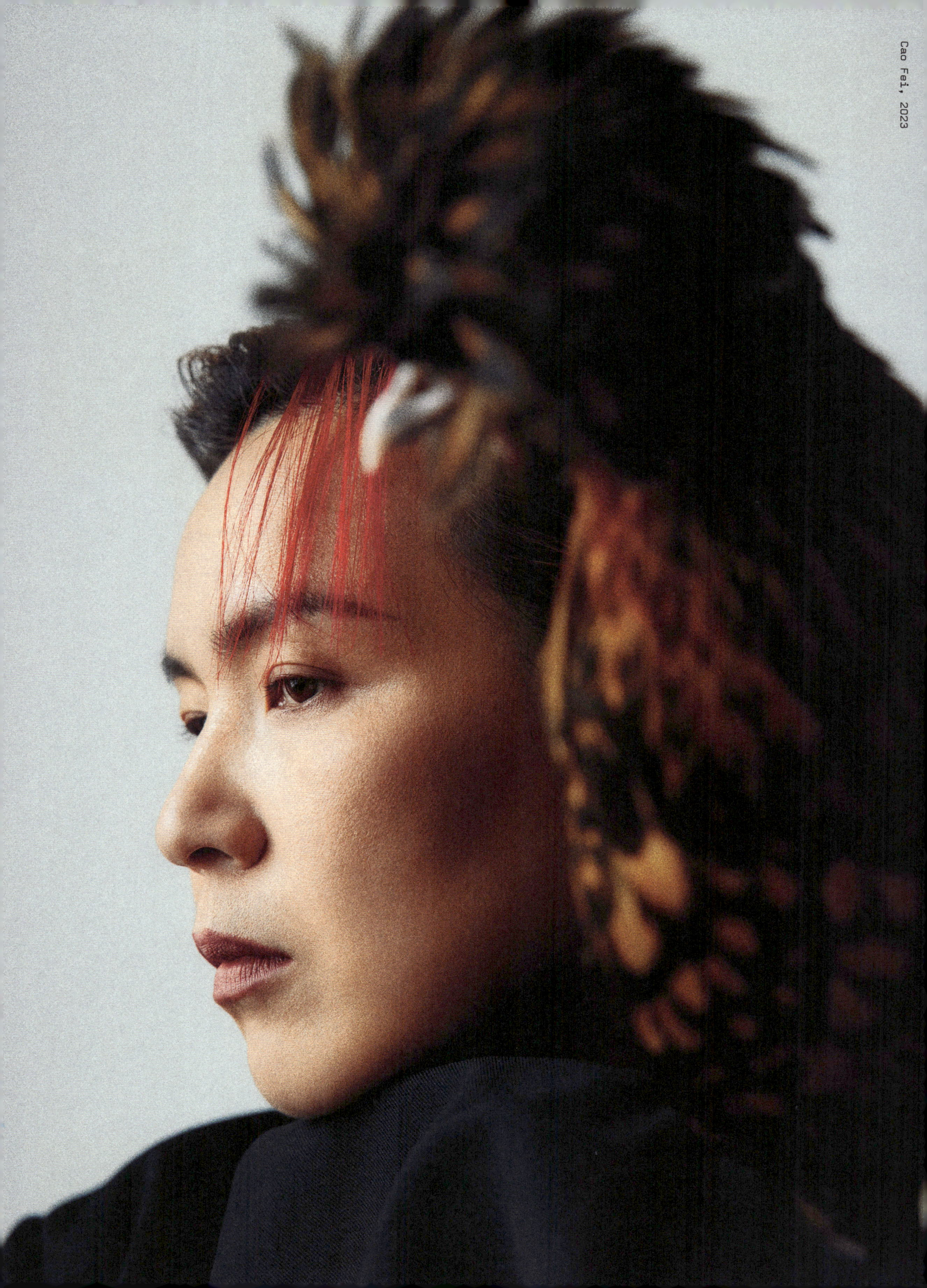

Cao Fei, 2023

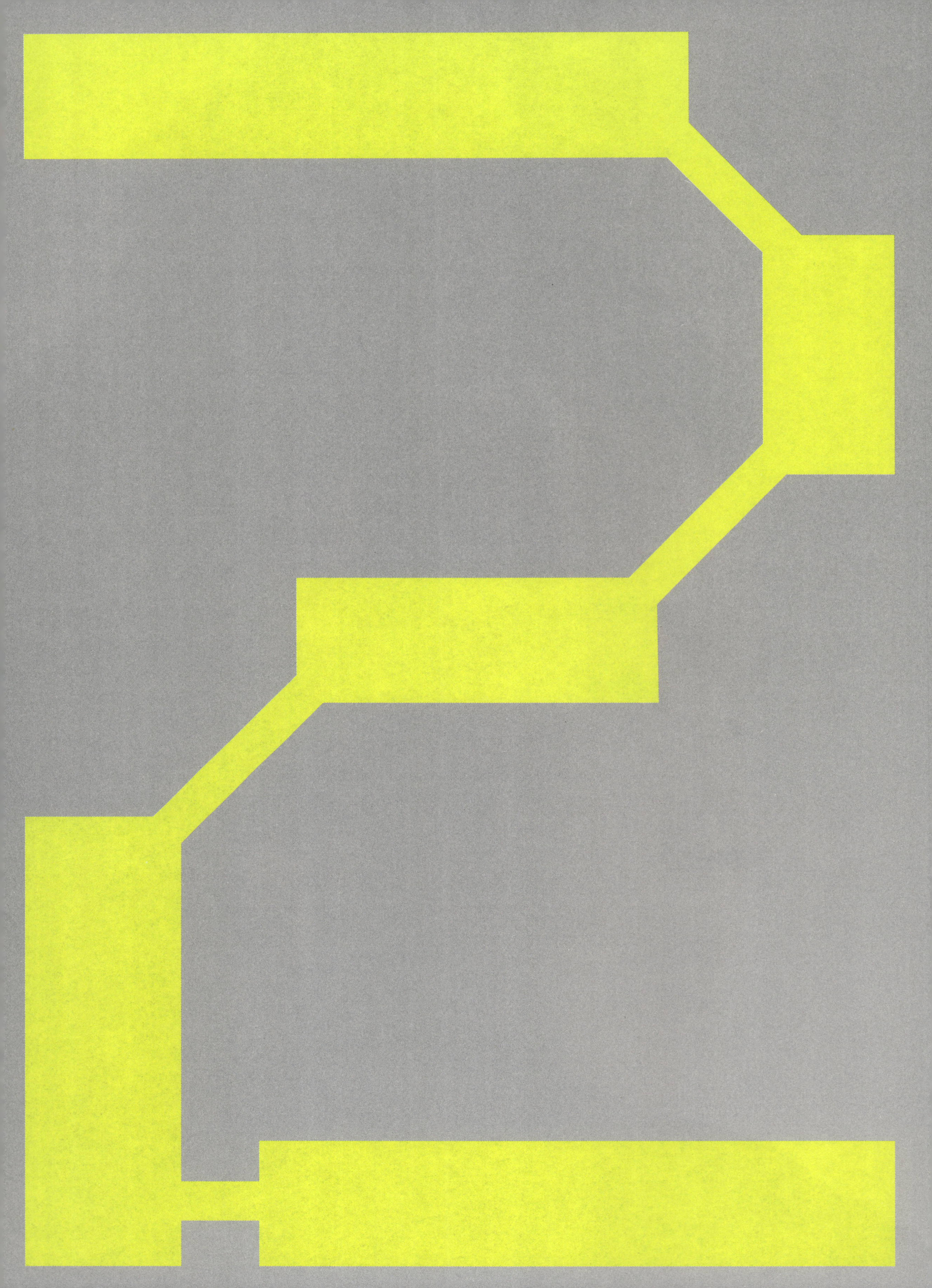

HOU HANRU

CAO FEI, OR THREE NEVER—ENDING QUESTIONS

侯瀚如

曹斐，或三道永远无解之题

三道永远无解之题三道永远无解之题三道永远无

1

WHO IS CAO FEI?

One of Cao Fei's recent projects, *Screen autobiography (Shanghai)* 2023, turns out to be a perfect summary of her career from the past 20 years. One can say that it divulges the red line that has connected all her works, realised in highly diverse media and languages ranging from photography, video, film, installation, performance, theatre, online projects, virtual reality and more. Unfolding in complex systems, her works represent an incessant and permanent enquiry of the artist's autobiography. They are multiple forms of self-portraits. But they are also the results of Cao's efforts to distance herself from what she is supposed to 'naturally' be. She always seeks to conceive and produce 'another' of her own image and personality, evolving and metamorphosing into 'someone else' according to and against the changing conditions of life – social, cultural, economic and political realities as well as technological 'landscapes'. Among the most outstanding inventors (not only in art) of her generation, she is determined to become a free and happy person, 'relieved' of all burdens of playing social roles imposed by the established moral norms, or 'officialdom'. Cao has hence become an open but mysterious incarnation, or various incarnations, of the Rimbaldian expression: '*je est un autre*' ('I is somebody else'), namely, her own avatars... In our time, for almost everyone, an 'other', generated by the digitalisation of material life and immaterial thoughts, has become a part of the self. The 'true self' has ultimately been diminished into a secondary role that submits to the order of the 'virtual self'... Then, an unknown world opens and one has to ask, 'Who am I now?'. '*Je est un autre*', in a departure from Rimbaud's embracement of a new self as a romantic poet, now serves as a crudely challenging answer to the question of our common existence as humans... Cao always tends to take this entanglement actively and even positively, with joy and playfulness. Her art sets out on a totally open journey from a totally new departure point.

Retrospectively we can write up a long list of avatars created by Cao in her works. They are in constant transformation, shrewdly responding to how new norms of socialisation have been shaped by economic, cultural and technological, therefore political, activities. This is the reality in which the artist and her contemporaries live and grow – in Chinese society – breaking away from the stagnation of the hardcore 'proletarian dictatorship' in an uncertain process of integrating-disintegrating the world system of modernisation for the last three decades. *Screen autobiography*, with pop-ups of video clips of Hong Kong films from the ex-colony's 'golden age' (1980–90s) and Shenzhen's cityscapes in its boomtown years (from the foundation of the Special Economic Zone in the early 1980s to its establishment as a symbol of a global success story in the 2000s) is the latest manifestation of a long metamorphosis.

Interestingly, the installation reappropriates the format of *daihuo zhibo* 带货直播 (live streaming sales by online celebrities) that has become one of the most popular modes of doing business in the post-COVID-19 pandemic period. By resorting to such a 'ready-made' of our age, Cao puts forward that the 'screenisation' of image and life itself has become the very norm of representation of the real, a biopolitical rendering of what we are turned into today. At the same time, Cao voluntarily embraces such a game of self-flattening in order to generate a new avatar of herself or of a generation that has grown up in the most 'seamless' interaction and integration with digital technologies. Yet she has never forgotten to add a dose of irony, self-derision and, therefore, critique in the play...

Cao began her work early in the 1990s, surfing the wave of China's opening to the globalising world. Her city is Canton, or Guangzhou (the current official spelling), in the Pearl River Delta, China's frontier of contact with the outside world due to its historical status of being a relatively autonomous region far from the centre in Beijing and close to Hong Kong, the then British colony (until 1997). Along with her contemporaries, her living world, as well as cultural sensibilities, has been widely influenced and formatted by the entertainment culture of Hong Kong and multicultural expressions of modernity, epitomised by Cantopop, together with the

解之题三道永远无解之题三道永远无解之题三道

永远无解之题三道永远无解之题三道永远无解之

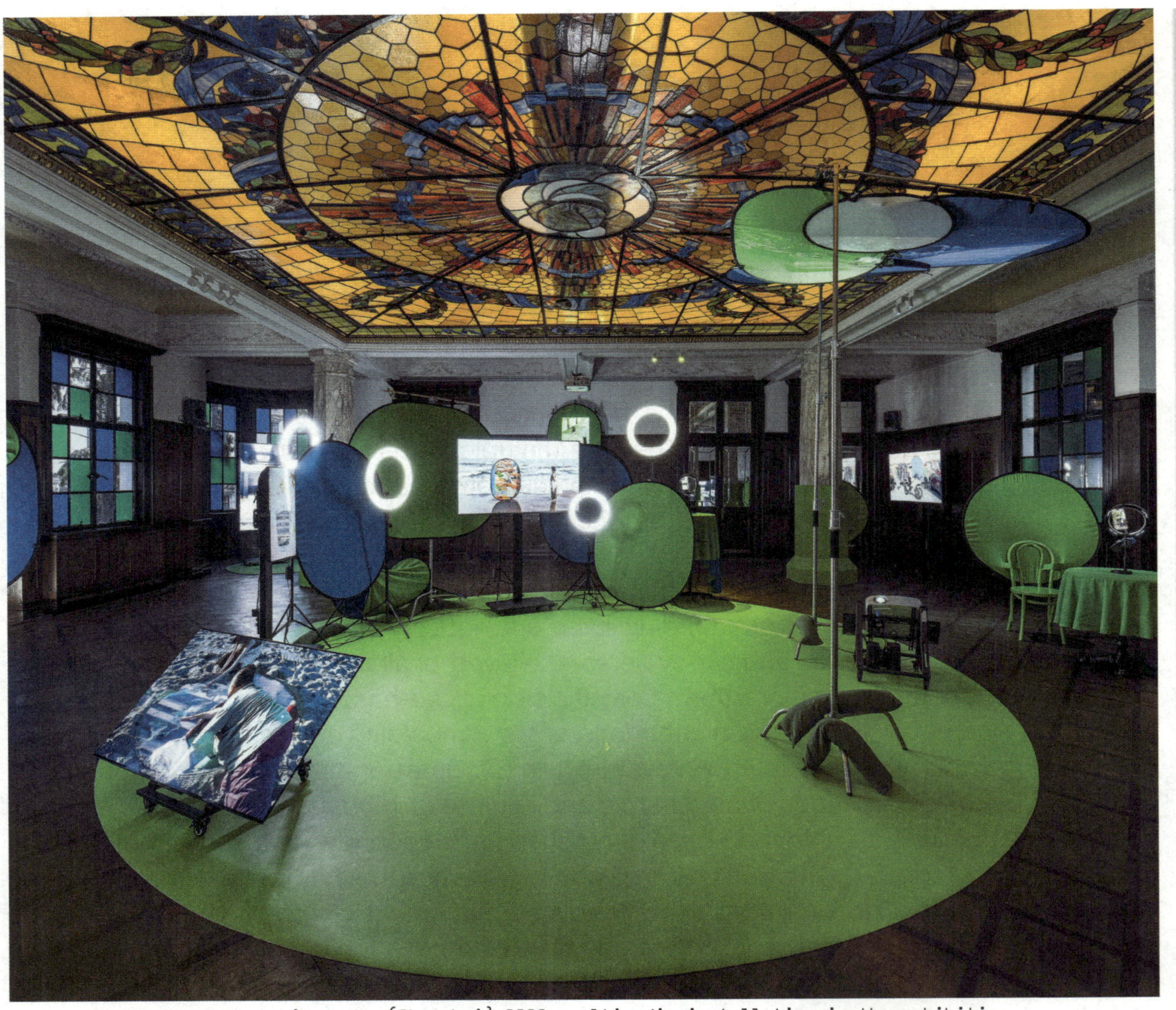

Screen autobiography (Shanghai) 2023, multimedia installation in the exhibition *Paraventi*, Prada Rong Zhai, Shanghai, 3 November – 21 January 2024

experimental films of directors such as Wong Kar-wai, Christopher Doyle, Tsui Hark and others. This all unfolded amid the dynamic cityscape of the 'Oriental Pearl', as Hong Kong was known. At the same time, the rise of commercial advertisements and the proliferation of fashion have generated a totally new world of imagery, value and lifestyles for the younger generation. Trying to reinvent their own expressions that incorporate entirely new visual experiences prompted by fluid and 'flashy' movements of images and the body, they claim to be *xin xin renlei* 新新人类, or a 'new new humankind'. Cao's early works represented such a claim in a radically spectacular way by blending excitement and transgression, joy and humour. Disguising her own body and outlooks in different roles, in photography, video and performance, she realised her work as a kind of 'publicity' for this 'new species'. She obtained a new identity completely detached from a standard 'good schoolgirl' imposed by the established education system. She became a joyful but critical 'heretic'…

Early in the new millennium, the trend of cosplay, promoted by Japanese anime, manga and video games, flourished among youngsters in Chinese cities. The game offered an amusing but provocative way for them to transgress conventional social norms and acquire a temporary alternative identity. By merging theatre, game and real life, they managed to invent and live in a utopian 'free world'. 'However,' Cao has noted, 'in the moment when they are turned into genies, chivalrous knights, fairy princesses, or geeks, the pains of reality are assuaged, even if the "real" world they are standing in has not changed to the slightest'.[1] In a series of video and photography works, she played the antagonist in various scenes of cosplay games set against the backdrop of everyday life in her city.

The rapid rise of digital technology and the predominance of the internet has offered her a new motivation to bring this playful experiment into a much more audacious adventure. She moved to explore the then brand-new world of virtual reality. In 2007 Cao was selected to be one of the four women artists to 'represent' China at the Chinese pavilion in the Venice

题三道永远无解之题三道永远无解之题三道永远

无解之题三道永远无解之题三道永远无解之题三

道永远无解之题三道永远无解之题三道永远无解

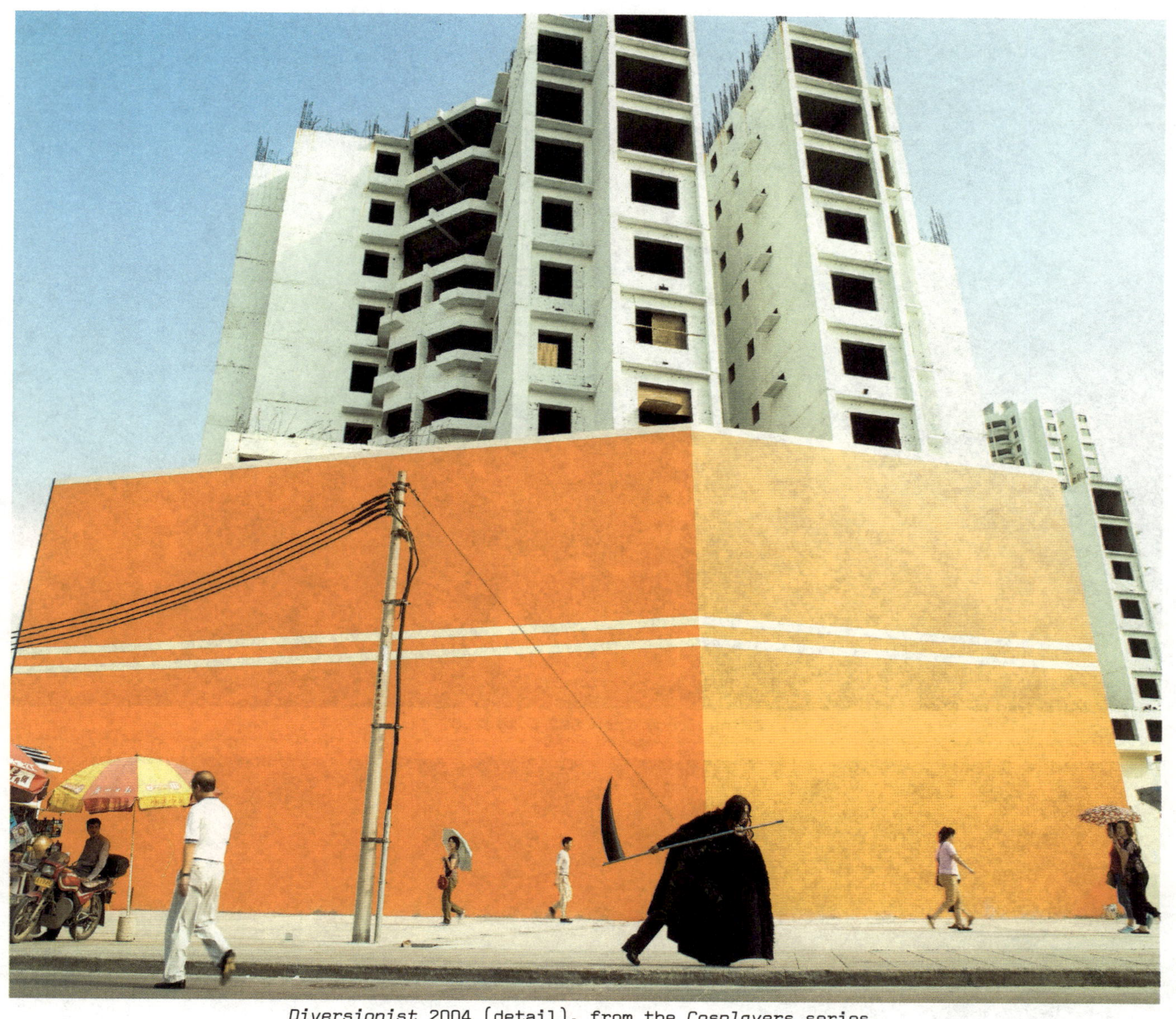

Diversionist 2004 (detail), from the *Cosplayers* series, C-print, 75 × 100 cm

Biennale. That year virtual reality became a hot topic, prompted by the rise of online platforms such as Second Life, the predecessor of the metaverse. Cao was among the first artists, not only in China but also globally, to react to the trend with fascination and she incorporated it as an innovative toolbox of art production and, more importantly, as a new conceptual and existential foundation. She came up with *i.Mirror* 2007, a transnational and trans-temporal love affair directed by China Tracy, her first virtual incarnation or avatar. The same year, China Tracy began unfolding her life in the online space of Second Life by building the utopian-dystopian *RMB City* 2007–11. In this virtual city, encounters and 'crashes' were designed and realised among historic figures and art-world actors. They instigated tragicomic events that predicted the future of the world. Art and online games were merged while the real body of the artist and the virtual image of the avatar became one. Cao became China Tracy, and vice versa . . . In the virtual skin of China Tracy, she flew across oceans and skies like a free bird . . .

Recently, Cao has transformed into another virtual creature, combining robotic AI and an octopus in *Oz* 2022. Oz crawls across the unfathomable space of the 'metaverse'. This time, she appears more as a ghostlike goddess, combining beauty, justice and evilness . . . Has this got something to do with the way the world is being transformed today?

Along with her *Screen autobiography*, Cao intends to demonstrate a dilemma of human efforts to create, train and 'improve' AI so it will be endowed with a certain human identity to become a new 'social human'. Eventually we are running the risk of turning AI into the master of human life in a 'totalised world' run by it. Cao seems to reveal that by merging our physical body with the flat screen, the border between human and machine is blurred. We are swiftly losing our control over the machine that we designed. We are no longer masters of our own thoughts and actions. We are dismantled and dissolved into the safe, sterile, smooth, transparent and risk-free cyber-society as we are trying to expand our 'selves' . . . [2]

Then, who is Cao Fei? She is unique but always an 'other' . . .

曹斐何人？曹斐何人？曹斐何人？曹斐何人？曹

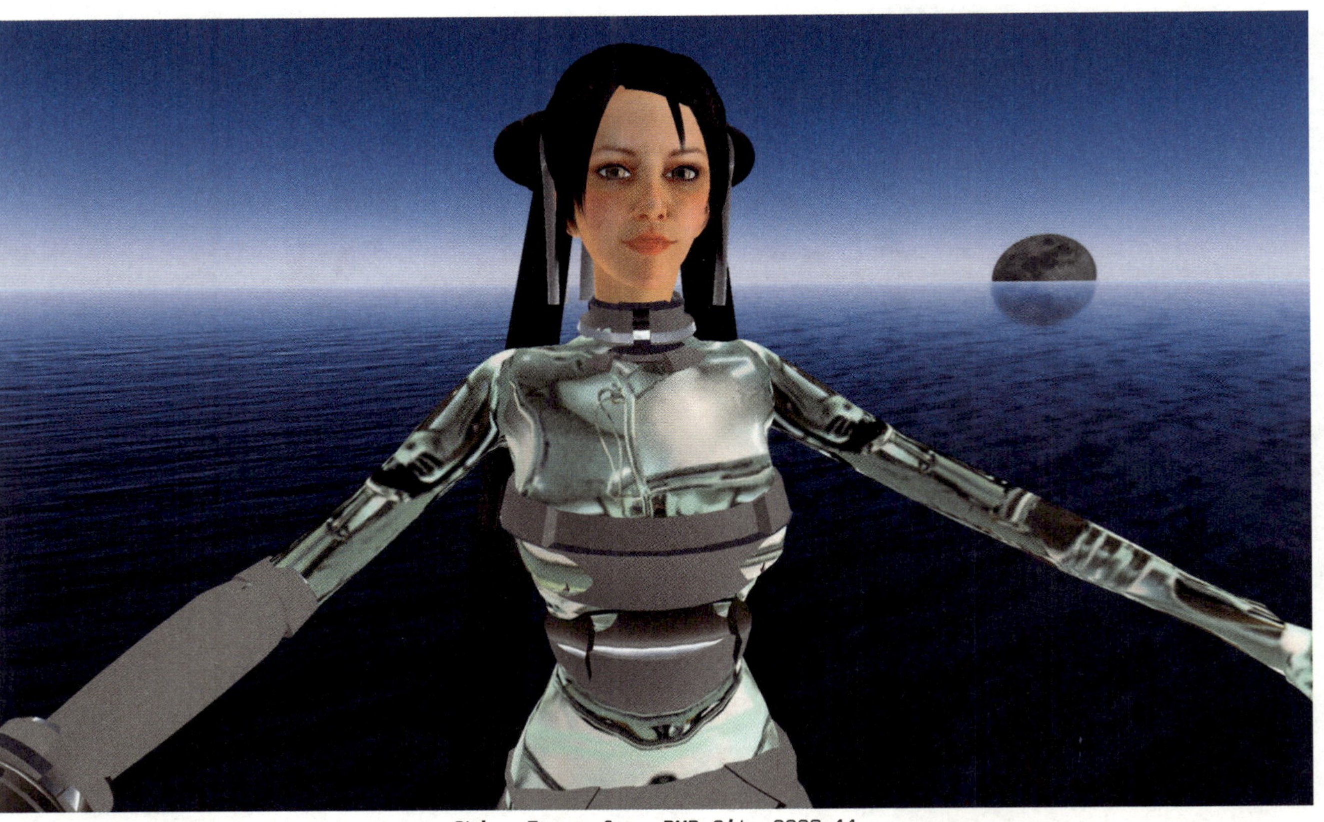

China Tracy from *RMB City* 2007–11

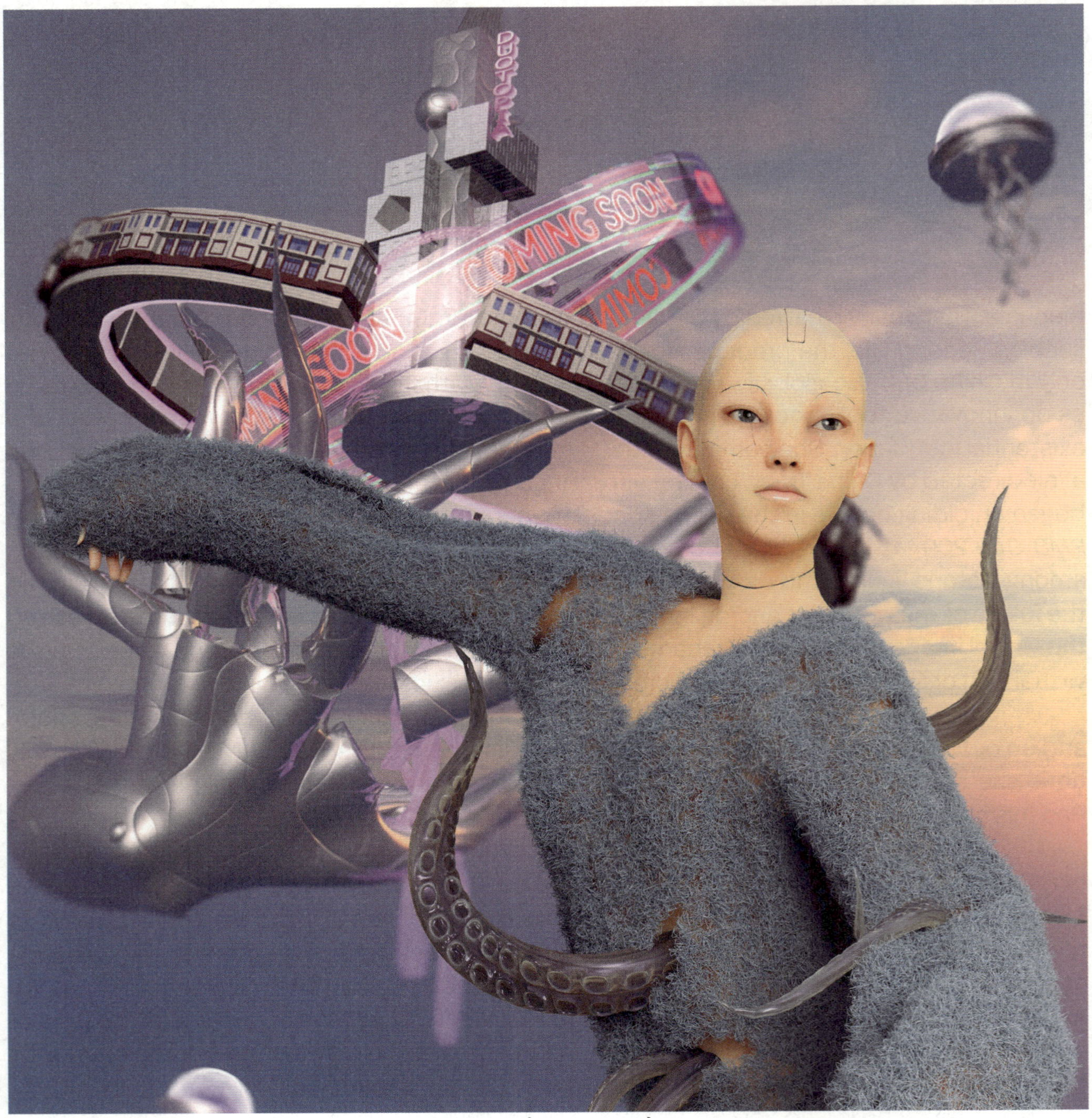

Oz 2022 (video still)

斐何人？曹斐何人？曹斐何人？曹斐何人？曹斐

谁的乌托邦？谁的乌托邦？谁的乌托邦？谁的乌

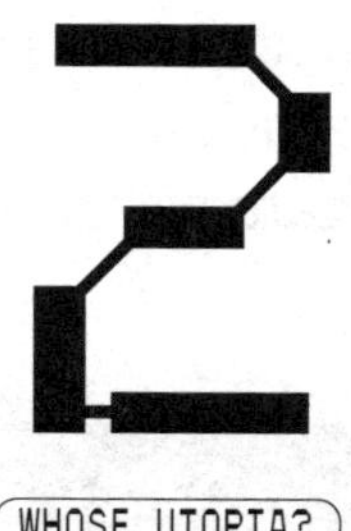

WHOSE UTOPIA?

Cao is a maker of fiction, a 'mother' of avatars. In the earthly real life, she is a daughter, sister, mother, lover, artist, professor, theatre and film director, stage designer, social activist, hip-hop dancer and kickboxer… And she has been excellent in all those roles. Her works are closely related to her direct experiences of living in a swiftly changing Chinese society in the process of 'integrating' itself into a globalising world, struggling between idealistic, optimistic and even utopian visions of the future and the pragmatic, occasionally pessimistic and even dystopian reality. It all started with a life of permanent movement and mutation in the Pearl River Delta. This region has, from the 1980s, become a 'world factory', the largest base of industrial and technological production for the global market. It is the most dynamic engine that has fuelled the 'miraculous' development and modernisation of China for the last four decades.

Instead of being attracted by the middle-class dream of self-enrichment, Cao has focused her attention and care on the world of work – and more precisely of workers – most of whom are migrants from the countryside rushing to the rapidly expanding cities for work in construction sites or factories producing clothing, plastics and electronics for the global market. She has a particularly strong interest in the condition of the younger generations who are looking for their futures in China's booming economy.

From the early 2000s Cao developed a body of work that not only engaged with the working-class situations of survival but also their imaginings and inventions regarding the meaning of life. After *Rabid dogs* 2002, in which she exposed, sarcastically, the dog-like conditions of the rising white-collar youth, Cao investigated the world of the 'urban villages' in which migrant workers found their homes in the metropolitan centre of Guangzhou (*San Yuan Li* 2003, co-directed with Ou Ning).

Inspired by Soviet director Dziga Vertov's avant-garde film *Man with a movie camera* 1929, Cao and Ou sought to render the spaces and the people living in the dire conditions of the urban edge – villages in the city – somehow poetic and, more significantly, dignified. They dream of and struggle for their own 'better-off' through hard work. They are optimistic and somehow utopists… This condition has been embodied and expressed most radically in her work *Whose utopia* 2006. Turning the Pearl River Delta into a 'world factory' was an economic project decided at the state level. It was also perceived by many 'normal people' as an opportunity for emancipation. They have not only participated in improving their quality of life through hard labour but also collectively 'cooking up' together a better society in which they may have some say regarding their own destinies. *Whose utopia* attempted to provide a test ground to achieve such a success story, albeit temporally. In this project, Cao incited the workers of an OSRAM (Siemens) lightbulb factory in the industrial Foshan zone in the Pearl River Delta to take over the control of the production process and freely express their personal wishes by transforming the company motto (TPM) from 'Total productive maintenance' to 'Team, people, motivation'. The workers – most in their early twenties – were encouraged to learn various kinds of artistic skills, such as playing guitar, ballet, painting and design. They ended up organising a large art festival. The factory campus became a temporary art institution. Once the festival was over, however, they had to recognise that 'our future is not a dream'.

Utopia is never far from disillusion, just like the utopian projects of China's modernisation and those of other countries across the contemporary world. There has always been a revolutionary impulse that has driven billions of people under 'great leaders' to pursue a utopia, a paradise of full happiness. But every time, the reality proves it to be a mere disillusionment. In spite of that, this impulse has become the DNA of society in general, keeping it at once alive and failed. Cao's more recent works such as *Asia one* 2018 and *Nova* 2019 uncover and expose this inerasable 'DNA of revolution' through an exploration of the fetishist frenzy for scientific and technological progress as the engine of today's program of

托邦？谁的乌托邦？谁的乌托邦？谁的乌托邦？

谁的乌托邦？谁的乌托邦？谁的乌托邦？谁的乌

the nation's dream. This is another utopian joint venture of top-down political powers, one deeply rooted in a certain ideology and a vision of an 'ideal world'. The fact is that a neoliberal capitalist global economy boosted by 'state will' always ends up demonstrating that workers can never be the real bosses!

Whose utopia is it?

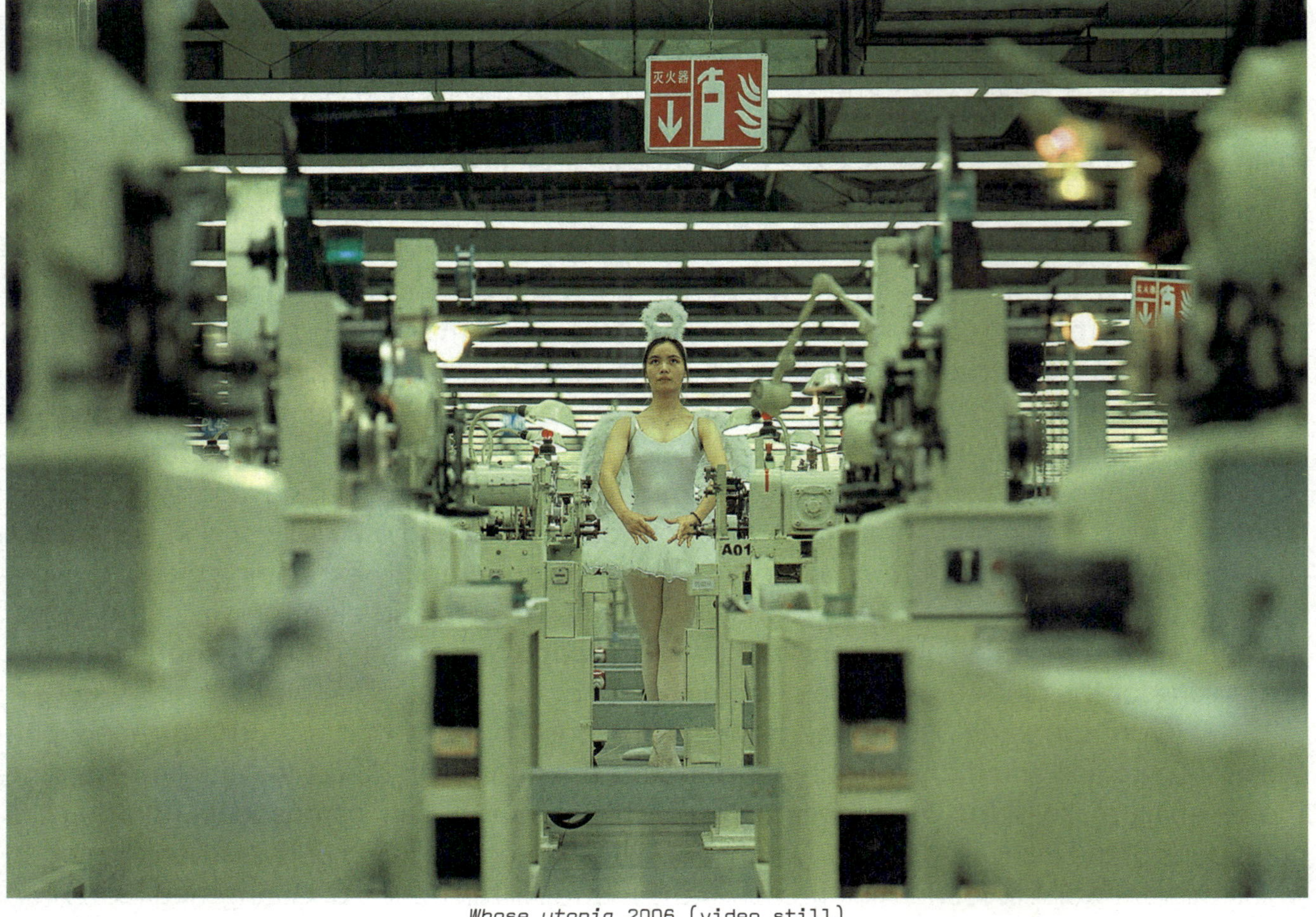

Whose utopia 2006 (video still)

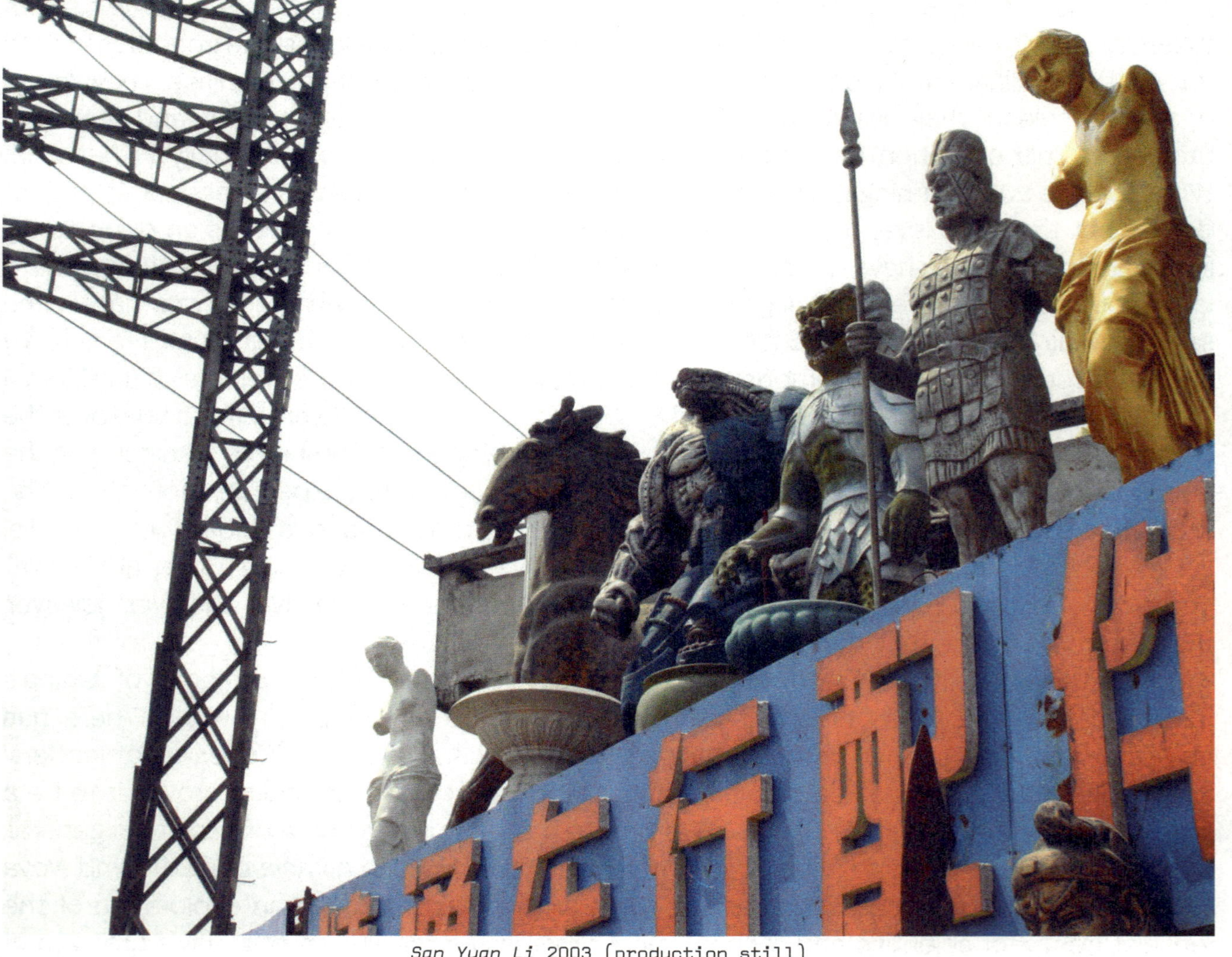

San Yuan Li 2003 (production still)

托邦？谁的乌托邦？谁的乌托邦？谁的乌托邦？

谁的乌托邦？谁的乌托邦？谁的乌托邦？谁的乌

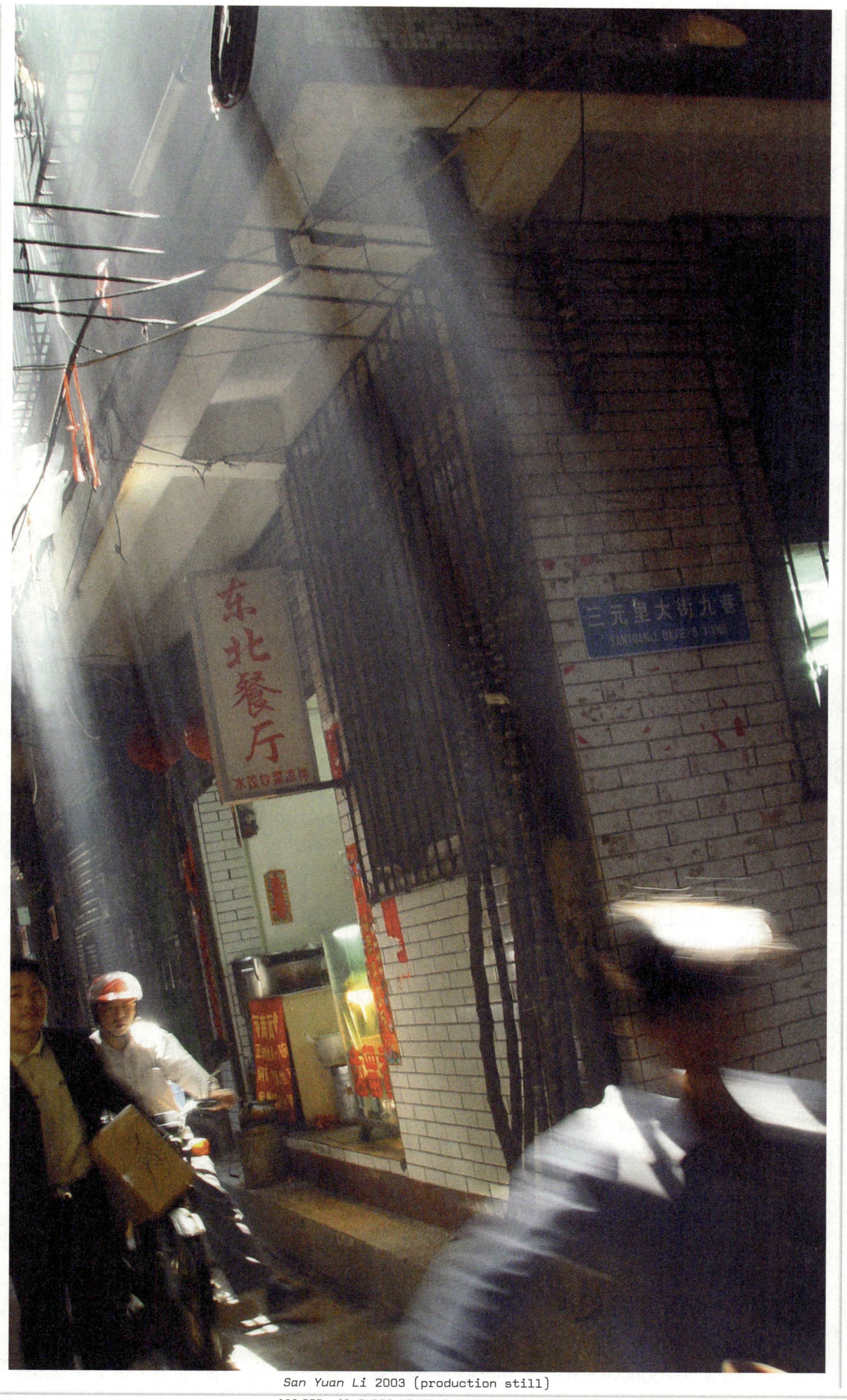

San Yuan Li 2003 (production still)

托邦？谁的乌托邦？谁的乌托邦？谁的乌托邦？

广式技术？广式技术？广式技术？广式技术？广

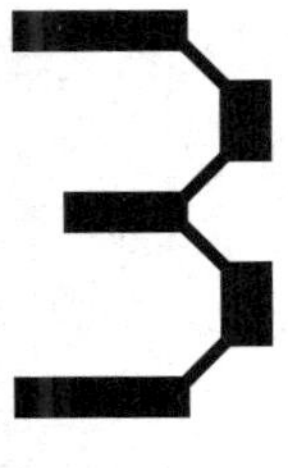

CANTOTECH?

Cao stands out as one of the most versatile artists working with new media. She has resorted to the latest technologies for the last two decades: photography, video, installation, live performance, theatre, literature, cinema, and all sorts of online exploration, from Second Life to virtual reality... Lately she has shown an obsessive interest in science fiction. Her recent major solo exhibition at UCCA Center for Contemporary Art in Beijing (Mar–Jun 2021) was designed as a 'fun palace', while another at the MAXXI – National Museum of 21st Century Art in Rome (Dec 2021–May 2022) incorporated a multistage cinema. In 2023 she took up the artistic directorship for the concert of the Canton-based music band Wu Tiao Ren 五條人, who sing in Teochew dialect. Cao's engagement with media art in such an enthusiastic and multifaceted manner reflects how artists of her generation consider new technologies as the main route towards the globalised world. In her practice, Cao always manages to add a sense of irony, sarcasm and self-derision. Her work tastes bittersweet. Despite the range of emotion and criticality she employs, ultimately she asserts that the most important thing is to have fun – the most pungent weapon to resist all ideological and economic dominations!

Back to her *Screen autobiography*. Cao's use of technologies has been intimately rooted in her interest in the cultural sphere at the turn of the millennium, a momentum built upon the synergy of rapid urbanisation and the importation of cultural expressions from the outside world, especially those from Hong Kong, marked by the rise of Cantopop music, Cantonese films and TV shows... This has fostered a sense of pride in being Cantonese, characterised by an independence from the communist mandarin and a view of individual freedom as an ethical life goal. Over time, this trend has evolved into a widely disseminated national fashion that has shaped the collective vision of a modern world to be constructed across the country.

Cao's approach of developing her creative career represents a fundamentally Cantonese way to embrace technologies and the world of the future. This approach is playful, amusing and somewhat sarcastic, hence critical. It echoes what the kung-fu master Bruce Lee stated, 'Be water, my friend!' But like many who have grown up in the fast transition towards modernisation, Cao is always pragmatic and inventive in adapting to trends and the rise of new technologies. *Shanzhai* 山寨 – 'illegal' counterfeits of technological products, including music CDs, film DVDs, computer programs and electronic chips, among other things – have helped 'developing countries' such as China to evolve speedily and catch up with the developed world. This manner of appropriating technological innovation has demonstrated various alternative strategies to open up new grounds for competing with the dominant powers in the global capitalist market. It displays a genuine astuteness in a David-versus-Goliath battle. The cultural zone of the Cantonese (from Guangdong to Shenzhen, Hong Kong and Macau or the Pearl River Delta, lately rebaptised The Great Bay Area) has been the most active and efficient laboratory of such a strategy. In a number of ways, the practices of artists in the 'developing world' using new technologies are echoing vigorously this strategy and becoming highly creative. Eventually this generates new categories of media that lead to new avenues in writing global art history. Cao's appropriation of the largest possible range of media, especially digital, is a perfect example of the strategy of *wandao chaoche* 弯道超车 – to take a shortcut to surpass the more advanced rival. Now she has managed to turn herself into a global leader in the exploration of new technologies in the arts...

This very 'Cantonese' or 'Southern' vision and strategy to survive in an uncertain world is perfectly relevant in the context of the current North-South negotiation. Both the North and South (China versus Australia, Guangzhou versus Sydney) are trying to find their positions of dominance in this frantic power game, driven by the battle for the newest technologies, not only in industrial, economic, social and political realms but also in culture and art. Cao is acutely aware of the significance of this technological war. In her recent

式技术？广式技术？广式技术？广式技术？广式

技术？广式技术？广式技术？广式技术？广式技

projects, she seeks to employ various sources for the origins of technological developments in different contexts in history and the present-day in order to expose the geopolitical raisons d'être and implications. She is alert to and critical about the potentially alienating effects of 'technological progress' over human life and society. China is today the country where the most advanced digital technologies are omnipresent. There, people live in a truly 'brave new world' without the slightest consciousness about its existence. Living in such a reality, Cao's works – including *Whose utopia*, *La Town*, *Asia one*, *Nova* and the entire Hongxia project – blend together excitement, hope, optimism, poetry, humour, irony, desperation, disillusion and even fury. By doing so, Cao invites us to look closely at how the overwhelming domination of digital technologies has fundamentally transformed our ways of seeing the world and of interweaving socio-political relationships – thereby transforming how we live. Her works form an ontologically contradictory condition of biopolitics that forces us to face the impossible choice between comfort and passiveness, surveillance and freedom. We have to admit that we are mobilising our best intellectual capacities to create machines that alienate us as humans. Our love for technological progress is now threatening our own destiny as masters of the world. Can any alternative ways to use technologies, such as Cantotech, save us?

HONG KONG
25 DECEMBER 2023

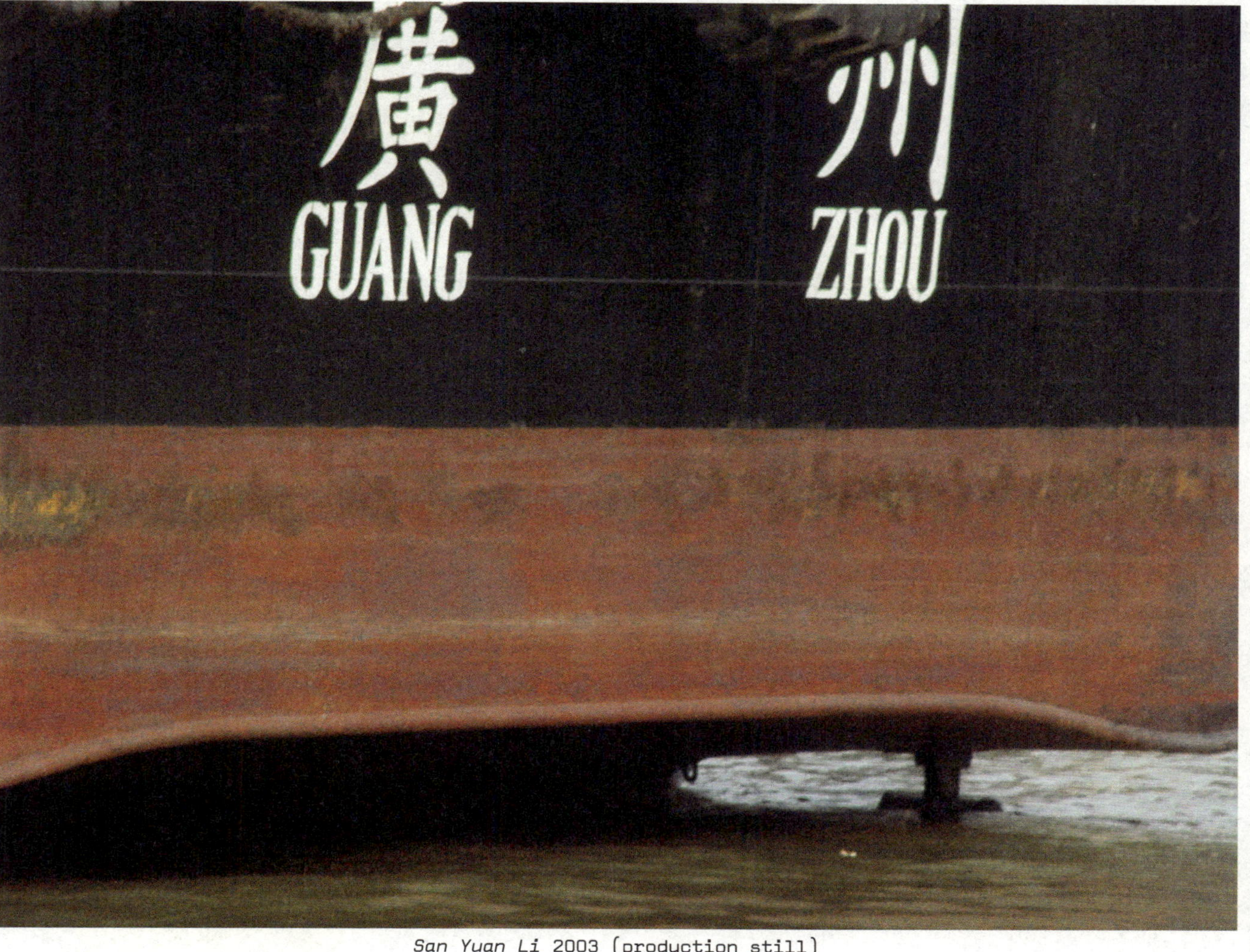

San Yuan Li 2003 (production still)

1 Cao Fei, Stijn Huijts & Auke van den Berg, *PRD anti-heroes*, Museum Het Domein, Sittard, 2006. 'PRD' refers to the Pearl River Delta.

2 Cao Fei's recent interview on *Screen autobiography (Shanghai)* 2023, presented at *Paraventi: Folding Screens from the 17th to 21st Centuries*, Fondazione Prada, Milan, 26 Oct 2023 – 22 Feb 2024.

术？广式技术？广式技术？广式技术？广式技术

前后的梦想和幻想

MICHAEL SUN

孙启喆

FREAKING OUT: DREAMS AND FANTASIES IN CHINA CIRCA Y2K

抓狂：中国千禧年

<tommyilgb>
ASL?
<mikezzsun>
17/male/ottawa
<mikezzsun>
you?
<tommyilgb>
16/male/illinois
<mikezzsun>
cool
<tommyilgb>
yeah, u wanna know something?
<mikezzsun>
yeah
<tommyilgb>
ive always wanted to talk to a stranger online
<mikezzsun>
is that why you started talking to me on exitreality
<tommyilgb>
yeah
<mikezzsun>
ok well same
<tommyilgb>
oh nice, can i ask you something?
<mikezzsun>
ive never rly talked to anyone online before
<tommyilgb>
like...never ever?
<mikezzsun>
yeah
<mikezzsun>
what did u wanna ask
<tommyilgb>
like, are you ever worried that you could meet like a bad stranger online?
<mikezzsun>
haha not really
<tommyilgb>
oh... i mean there can be a lot of bad ppl online and some of them can be really good at hiding it
<mikezzsun>
i mean like there was no one even on exit reality
<tommyilgb>
yeah im surprised no one really goes on there anymore
<mikezzsun>
if u were trying to be a bad person on exit reality then ur not doing a very good job lolol
<tommyilgb>
lol. i feel like most of the ppl on exit reality are nice, but a little weird. like the other day i met this weird guy in this other game and he kept asking me my age and personal info
<mikezzsun>
hahahahHAAHAHAHAHAHAHAHA
<tommyilgb>
yeah... he's probably like middle aged and stuff too
<mikezzsun>
oh my god
<mikezzsun>
i promise i am 17
i am not sum middle aged creep
<tommyilgb>
are you like one of the few ppl on there that actually are teenagers?
<mikezzsun>
literally ur the only other person i've met on there so yes 2 out of 2 people on exit reality i have seen so far are teenagers
<mikezzsun>
what's illinois like

1

By now we are all tired of diasporic literature about yearning, alienation, et cetera but – with apologies – here is another addition to the canon. The year was 2009 and it had been exactly one decade since we came to this country that people referred to as 'the largest island in the world', which is actually a euphemism for 'place where everything closes at three in the afternoon and it is always too hot'. Both these things were doubly true that summer: one of those febrile summers that made everyone scurry indoors, inflamed and panting like lolling pooches. I stared, slack-jawed, at the ceiling fan that reflected the sunbeams beyond my window and concentrated on them until they became one single spotlight whose effulgence seemed infinite, cosmic. I longed for the apocalypse. Days went by like this.

The laptop beckoned. My dad – like every other father who had journeyed across the seas, citing words like 'sacrifice' and 'opportunity' so often they began to take on a cultish sheen – was working in an industry bearing little relation to what he had studied in the old country. Here, in this terrible, idle place, he was an IT man forever beholden to the chunnering ineptitudes of others. But in all his hours spent probing the mysteries of the computer, he had made a discovery: a virtual reality platform that touted itself as the latest innovation in online technology.

I clicked into the platform. In actuality, there was nothing innovative about it. It felt like Second Life on benzos. It was built from stuttering 3D graphics and tyrannised by the perpetual lag of the adolescent internet. Its streets were haunted by a permanently crepuscular sky and emptied of pedestrians. There was none of the clamour of Second Life or the jaunty overtures of something like The Sims. I was completely enamoured.

It was not a good platform. There was no-one to talk to. You could click and click for hours until your buttocks were fused to the furniture and fail to encounter a single other user of the site. But I persisted. It was sufficiently diverting – a serviceable distraction from the heat. It was close enough to the apocalypse. On day four, my persistence paid off: in the distance, I glimpsed a fellow traveller swaggering through the deserted city. In the inky twilight I could make out a pixelated mohawk and a motorcycle jacket. I thought this was extremely punk because I was twelve. I approached.

ASL? he asked. It was the internet's earliest, corniest proposition. *17/male/Ottawa*, I typed back, even though I was a tweenaged boy living in suburban Sydney. Soon we began talking on MSN. We traded surface-level queries like insider secrets. He told me his favourite band was Death Cab for Cutie and I immediately pirated all of their albums and began proselytising their virtues to anyone who would listen, which was no-one. I read the Wikipedia entry titled 'Culture of Canada' like a sacred scroll and repeated garbled facts back to him. I said the words 'ice hockey' so often they began to take on a cultish sheen. His name was Tommy and his age was an enigma. This was a time when parents still allowed their children to fall in love with strangers on the internet. I imagined my heart exploding. I imagined our futures unravelling before us like a vacant street. Months passed. The summer ended and we never spoke again.

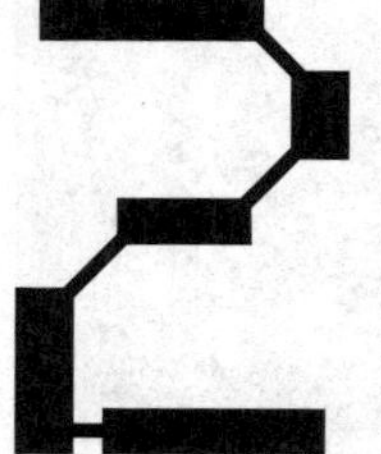

I have thought about Tommy over and over in the intervening years. It is craven, humiliating. He appears whenever the weather grows unseasonably warm. The kind of weather that drives people loopy, that makes people enter a fugue state where all of their past indiscretions tumble towards the present to elicit an

<tommyilgb>
it's alright... most of the time boring tbh, and it gets super cold during winter... but there's some pretty nice parks and stuff
<mikezzsun>
i've always wanted to go to the US
<tommyilgb>
you live in canada right?
<mikezzsun>
yeah
<tommyilgb>
oh yeah, i've always wanted to go to canada
<mikezzsun>
it gets super cold here too
<tommyilgb>
yeah i've heard
<mikezzsun>
i just bought earmuffs last week
<tommyilgb>
oh nice, were they expensive?
<mikezzsun>
bc my ears were so cold they were freezing
<mikezzsun>
nah they weren't expensive, they were from like the $2 shop
<tommyilgb>
$2 is pretty cheap i'd say
<mikezzsun>
but can i tell you something
<tommyilgb>
yeah, what is it?
<mikezzsun>
and this is kinda embarrassing
<tommyilgb>
its alright, you can tell me
<mikezzsun>
the only earmuffs i could find were orange and fluffy
<mikezzsun>
like FULLY fluffy
<mikezzsun>
idk if i can wear them at school
<tommyilgb>
omg that sounds really cute actually
<mikezzsun>
but they are soooo comfortable
<tommyilgb>
and the fact they're $2 is good too
<mikezzsun>
100%
<tommyilgb>
bro imagine they made them with that soft fabric that plushies are made of, omg thatd be the best thing ever
<mikezzsun>
i think they kinda are
<tommyilgb>
OMG WHAT... i never thought i'd ever feel jealous over someone elses earmuffs until now...
<mikezzsun>
teehee
<mikezzsun>
stay jealous
<tommyilgb>
oh believe me, i will...
<mikezzsun>
if you ever come to ottawa i'll make sure you are ear muffed UP
<tommyilgb>
omg u're so nice... i've always wanted to go to canada, it seems like such a cool place!

<mikezzsun>
it's ok but i feel
like when u live here
it's kinda boring
<tommyilgb>
thats actually how i
feel about illinois, its
boring most of the time
<mikezzsun>
everyone's just always
talking about ice hockey
<tommyilgb>
yeah, that's the biggest
sport in canada, right?
<mikezzsun>
yeah and it SUCKS
<tommyilgb>
i mean, it can't suck
that bad right?
<mikezzsun>
the uniforms are
kinda hot though
<tommyilgb>
wait the players
are attractive too?
<mikezzsun>
i get it
<tommyilgb>
now you've got
me interested
in hockey lmao
<mikezzsun>
LMAOOOOOO
<tommyilgb>
maybe i should actually
watch a hockey match...
<mikezzsun>
we can watch one
together sometime
<tommyilgb>
omg yes
<mikezzsun>
do you go to school btw
<tommyilgb>
yeah, im in my second
year of high school.
wbu?
<mikezzsun>
yah same but in last
year of high school
<tommyilgb>
oh cool, so you're
probably gonna go on
to college soon after
this year right?
<mikezzsun>
sooooo much studddyyyyy
<tommyilgb>
lol, well i mean college
has more freedom which
is kinda better
<mikezzsun>
idk yet
<tommyilgb>
i mean its your choice,
but like college would
be a lot less boring
than high school
<mikezzsun>
i rly want to go to
college in the us
<mikezzsun>
but that's because
i listen to too much
vampire weekend and
wanna move to new york
soooo bad
<tommyilgb>
honestly new york seems
really nice and it seems
like there's a lot of
stuff to do there... but
i've seen pictures of
the nyc subway and it
looks like hell
<mikezzsun>
please never show
me i need to keep
romanticising
<tommyilgb>
i mean, there are plenty
of other nice things
in nyc... but yeah,
probably shouldn't
show you the subway
<mikezzsun>
have you heard
vampire weekend
<tommyilgb>
i've heard bits and

indiscriminate surge of nervous breakdowns across the land. Call it open season for analysts.

I saw Tommy recently in Cao Fei's *Cosplayers* 2004, one of the artist's early video works. Tommy is a ghost confined to digital ephemera; *Cosplayers* manifests digital ephemera into the physical world with spectral results. In the beginning, all is quiet. A river shivering in the breeze. A house by the water with spires vaulting towards the firmament. But then the landscape ruptures. Emerging from the bucolic haze are figures in elaborate robes and gleaming armour. Adorning them are outsized wings and lurid tresses that do not so much fall as float far past their waists, aqueous and buoyant.

Cao conducts an act of transubstantiation: forging materiality from myth. She films her young subjects – cosplayers, each assuming the guise of a fictional, fantastical avatar – in and among Guangzhou. It is the locus of China's industrialisation, a megacity powered from the late 20th century by the centripetal force of the nation's workers leaving their agrarian roots for the allure of the metropolitan. You can hear the mantra: 'sacrifice', 'opportunity', et cetera.

In *Cosplayers*, Cao refashions Guangzhou into alien territory. A space that feels eerily removed from time itself. It may be a mystical past. It may be a dystopian future. Like the online platform upon which Tommy and I first met under a rutilant sky, the setting of *Cosplayers* is profoundly uncanny. Like the site of my tween love affair, the city of Cao's work is a fabrication. An urban environment glazed with the lore and longing of its inhabitants. Cao shrouds each image in a bluish mist. There is a lustre laminating each surface. Eventually, remnants of reality leak in. They infiltrate this alternate dimension. The hum of machinery echoes in the distance. A herd of cows stamps past a cadre of gilded guards. The ugly din of traffic bleeds in from the edges, threatening to collapse this hermetic fantasy.

Cao's actors strain against the weight of the world. Their fictions redouble. *Cosplayers*' editing grows increasingly frantic, unleashing a salvo of fight scenes. Leather-clad assassins sprint down concrete corridors; a team of golden warriors incite a fracas at a soccer game, counting everyone from elderly passers-by to policemen as collateral. The soundtrack leans into its hammiest instincts, a symphony of foley effects accompanying each flesh-on-bone impact. Thump. Thwack. Oof. Kapow!

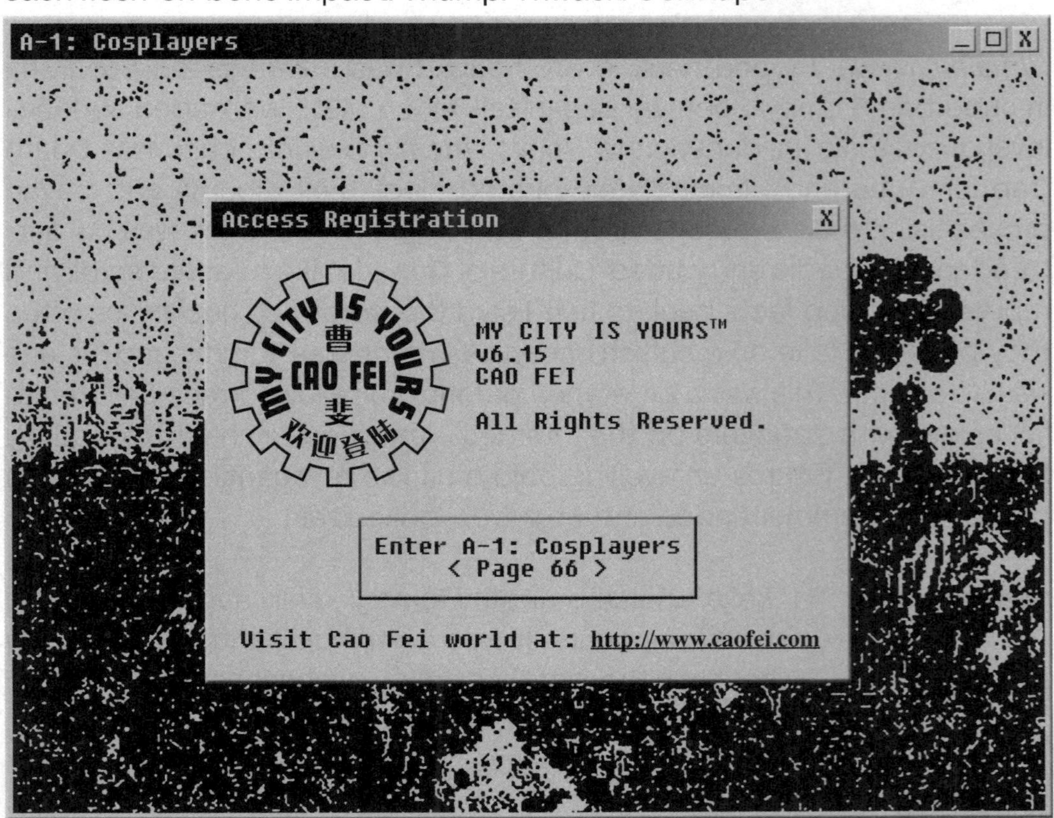

pieces of some of their
songs but i dont really
listen to them tbh,
should i?
<mikezzsun>
it's transcendental
<mikezzsun>
you def should
<tommyilgb>
alr, i'll listen to them
later... which songs do
u recommend?
<mikezzsun>
they just came out
with an album which is
amazing, there's this
song called campus
<tommyilgb>
oooh, sounds good...
you want me to listen
to it rn?
<mikezzsun>
which makes me wanna
be in american SOO bad
<mikezzsun>
yeah :) listen and
tell me if you like
<tommyilgb>
omg this is really
good actually
<mikezzsun>
wait
<tommyilgb>
ok
<mikezzsun>
should i listen
to something too
<tommyilgb>
yeah!
<mikezzsun>
tell me one of
ur fav songs
<tommyilgb>
uhhh, idk i have a lot
of favorite bands, like
death cab for cutie, you
should listen to them
<mikezzsun>
ooooh i love death
cab for cutie
<tommyilgb>
oh my gosh really?
i didnt expect that
actually
<mikezzsun>
so sad
<mikezzsun>
so angst
<tommyilgb>
yes very angst... i'm
all about that angst
<mikezzsun>
what do you have
to be angsty about
<tommyilgb>
literally nothing,
i hate when ppl say
teenage angst cos they
just think teenagers
are always moody or
something
<mikezzsun>
let it all out
<tommyilgb>
ok fine, i get all angsty
about my parents getting
mad at me sometimes but
like... they don't even
understand me, you know?
<mikezzsun>
LITERALLYYYYYY
<tommyilgb>
and like... my mom
always threatens to take
away my computer and
stuff because she thinks
i'm "addicted to it",
even though like...
its not because im
addicted to it, its
because its kinda my
only escape and if she
took it away, i wouldn't
have anything....
<mikezzsun>
no i feel the exact
same way
<tommyilgb>
its like, they dont
understand that this

computer is everything
for me...
<mikezzsun>
my parents also threaten
to take away my computer
and my nintendo ds :(
<tommyilgb>
NINTENDO DS?!
<mikezzsun>
my dad actually
confiscated my ds
and broke one of
my games recently
<tommyilgb>
NOOOOOO not ur ds!!!
<mikezzsun>
i was SO SAD
<tommyilgb>
i would be devastated
if my parents took
away my DS...
<mikezzsun>
like... how else am
i gonna play mario kart
at 2am while trying not
to make a single sound
so no one else wakes up
<tommyilgb>
LMAO THATS SO REAL
<mikezzsun>
I KNOW :-(
<tommyilgb>
i remember the time i
used to take my DS under
the covers just so i
could play some Pokemon
when i was younger lol
<mikezzsun>
ok classic
<tommyilgb>
my DS is probably one
of my most used things
i own tbh... i have sooo
many memories playing it
<mikezzsun>
anyway im listening to
death cab for cutie
now and just feeling
depressed for no reason
<tommyilgb>
i can relate to that...
the lyrics are so
comforting tho
<mikezzsun>
soul meets body
<tommyilgb>
yesssss
thats probably my
favourite song by them
<mikezzsun>
perfect song
<tommyilgb>
my second favourite song
is i will follow you
into the dark
<mikezzsun>
i said that song title
to one of my friends the
other day and she was
like EW!!!! get away
from me you creep!!!!
<tommyilgb>
lmao really??? i mean,
the lyrics aren't creepy
if u understand them...
<mikezzsun>
nah but she didn't
realise it was a song
title, she thought i was
just saying it to her
<tommyilgb>
LMAOOOOO i cant believe
she thought u were the
creep for saying that
<mikezzsun>
lololol
<tommyilgb>
i mean tbh, if u had
no context of the song,
u could interpret that
as pretty creepy lmao
<mikezzsun>
and she diddddddd
<tommyilgb>
well yeah, imagine ur
just walking around and
some random dude walks
up to u and says, "i
will follow you into the
dark", i mean i'd get

The video is oneiric. In its most striking sequence, a pair of cosplayers perch in a field, both atop life-sized replicas of zoo animals. One is holding a bouquet of black balloons, which drift upwards towards an endless pale expanse. I watch this sequence on repeat. Each time, it plays like a half-remembered dream, already slipping away upon waking, ceding to the demands of the day.

3

'My early work is about freaking out, about going against the system', Cao tells *The White Review* in 2016.[1] The cosplayers in her 2004 video perform a kind of subversion that could be called delusion. To freak out is to reject the mores that bind, to replace the dreadful violence of existence with a concoction of one's own. Tommy, with his serrated mohawk and his leather jacket, was donning his own manner of cosplay. So was I: cosplaying as a Canadian who listened to Death Cab for Cutie. Like Cao's subjects, we could not bottle our rapture. It could not linger offline.

Cosplayers' denouement is shorn of Cao's initial stylisation. Day breaks and each gaudily costumed character must now confront a city impervious to their spectacles. They ride the train. They traipse down highways. They languish in apartments as family members sew, read and clean. The video's earlier frenzy slips away upon waking. A dream, after all, is a fragile condition. It is exiled as easily as it materialises – by a chilly metropolis, by the departure of summer.

But here is another thing about dreams: they are persistent. They may retreat to the recesses, subjugated as they are under the conditions of living. And yet they are resistant to extirpation. At the end of Cao's work, we peer into a grated window, glimpsing a young cosplayer – now disrobed of their fanciful attire – loitering in a kitchen. There is a certain malaise to the image, though I prefer the optimistic reading: a dream delayed, rather than a forced re-entry into reality. The video's prior fantasy thrums beneath this scene of domestic ambience. Through their windows, the city's residents might imagine streets of overflowing bounty, a populace of gods and monsters. In my bedroom, down pixelated boulevards, I imagined a romance that could alter my fate, that could pluck me from the suburban heatwave and thrust me skywards instead. In both instances, an environment transfigured by the sheer will of yearning alone.

Cling on hard enough and a dream can be vitalising. It seems trite to vocalise this; it is, of course, the organising principle behind all change: counterculture, revolution, migration. The fragrance of possibility spiralling in the air. It is why people freak out. It is why people leave far-flung villages to toil in industrial cities. It is why my parents left their icy hometown in north-eastern China two years after I was born; three weeks after a vague recommendation by a streetside psychic. The story sounds apocryphal but so do most things from the 1990s. They had wanted to move to the United States but they lacked the qualifications. They had wanted to move to Canada but the visa officer had merely laughed. By some celestial misfortune they ended up in this terrible, idle place instead.

Whose utopia 2006 – the video work that made Cao an art-world cynosure – understands the lure of a dream. A cast of factory workers mimes a series of glamorous professions: ballerinas, rockstars, performers. It is tempting to graft a critical reading onto Cao's work – labour is exploitative, pity the poor factory worker, et cetera. But to do so would be an oversimplification. 'It's not an exposé', Cao avers in an interview shortly after *Whose utopia* is released. Among other things, she says, it is about 'the opportunity to survive'.[2]

scared as hell lmao
<mikezzsun>
honestly it'd be
pretty sick
<tommyilgb>
i mean, it'd be kinda
cool if someome was
like really smooth with
it, but if it was just
like some random dude
following me in an alley,
then id be like nah wtf
<mikezzsun>
i'd be like ok so now i
finally have a boyfriend
<mikezzsun>
well what do you
call this
<tommyilgb>
if some random dude was
following me into a dark
alley, i might just call
that stalking tbh
<mikezzsun>
what if some random
dude was messaging you
on msn after you met
on a random virtual
reality game
<tommyilgb>
LMAO THAT WOULD BE
SOOO CREEPY
if some random 30 year
old dude was dm'ing me
on exit reality, i would
block him immediately
<mikezzsun>
ok what if some random
17 year old was dm'ing
you on exit reality
<tommyilgb>
well... if he's nice
like you, then he's
probably just being
nice but if he was like
"you're so hot omg" or
sending weird pictures,
then thatd be creepy
<mikezzsun>
ok noted
<tommyilgb>
but yeah, i wouldnt
block you just bc ur
messaging me and being
nice haha
<mikezzsun>
i will not say 'you're
so hot omg' or send
weird picutres
<tommyilgb>
yeah definitely dont
do that lol, some ppl
online just have no
shame
<mikezzsun>
well considering that
i dont even know what
you look like i would
have no reason to say
'you're so hot'
<tommyilgb>
lmao, imagine if in
ur first message u were
just like "OMG UR SO
HOT AND FINE"
<mikezzsun>
honestly i would feel
complimented if someone
said that to me
<tommyilgb>
LOL, yeah, i suppose
i would too XD
<mikezzsun>
AM IJ UST LONELYYYYYY
<tommyilgb>
ME TOO, IM SO LONELY...
I JUST WANT SOMEONE TO
HOLD ME IN THE NIGHT,
IS THAT TOO MUCH TO
ASK?!?!???!
<mikezzsun>
ok wow this is
kinda deep
<tommyilgb>
sorry... i got carried
away... but i am really
lonely tho
<mikezzsun>
all i want is someone to
sleep next to at night

<tommyilgb>
me too . . . it would be so nice to just cuddle up in bed with someone at night . . .
<mikezzsun>
and yes cuddles
<tommyilgb>
omg yes, just cuddling up with someone and listening to them breathing and feeling them slowly fall asleep in ur arms, omg, i cant imagine something more perfect tbh . . .
<mikezzsun>
its ok
<tommyilgb>
its my literal dream at this point tbh
<mikezzsun>
we can just
<tommyilgb>
imagine if we just like met up and just cuddled all night . . .
<mikezzsun>
pretend
<tommyilgb>
pretend i was laying with my head on ur chest while i hugged you close and u ran ur hand through my hair . . .
<mikezzsun>
to be cuddling tonight
<tommyilgb>
imagine it's a cold night, and when I fall asleep i snuggle close to you for warmth . . .
<mikezzsun>
who needs ear muffs when they have you falling asleep close to me
<tommyilgb>
and then you're laying in my arms and we're all cuddled up together, and my fingers are brushing through ur hair and i'm slowly falling asleep
<mikezzsun>
need my hair brushed right now
<tommyilgb>
i could brush ur hair while we cuddled . . .
oh my god, imagine this actually happened
<mikezzsun>
sigh
<tommyilgb>
like, we dont even have to talk, we just cuddle together and be quiet . . . like, thered be no awkward silence or anything, it'd just be us in peace
<mikezzsun>
my dream
<tommyilgb>
i could literally see it rn . . . us laying in a bed together, its 11:57pm . . . we're just laying there and we hear thunder . . . and ur warm breath is slowly brushing over me . . .
its the most comforting feeling in the world
<mikezzsun>
i wish we could make it happen
<tommyilgb>
sameeee, it'd be so nice if we could just fall asleep together or smth
<mikezzsun>
once i actually get a JOB
<tommyilgb>
same, once i get a JOB I'd totally have the funds to visit u . . . and if thats too expensive,

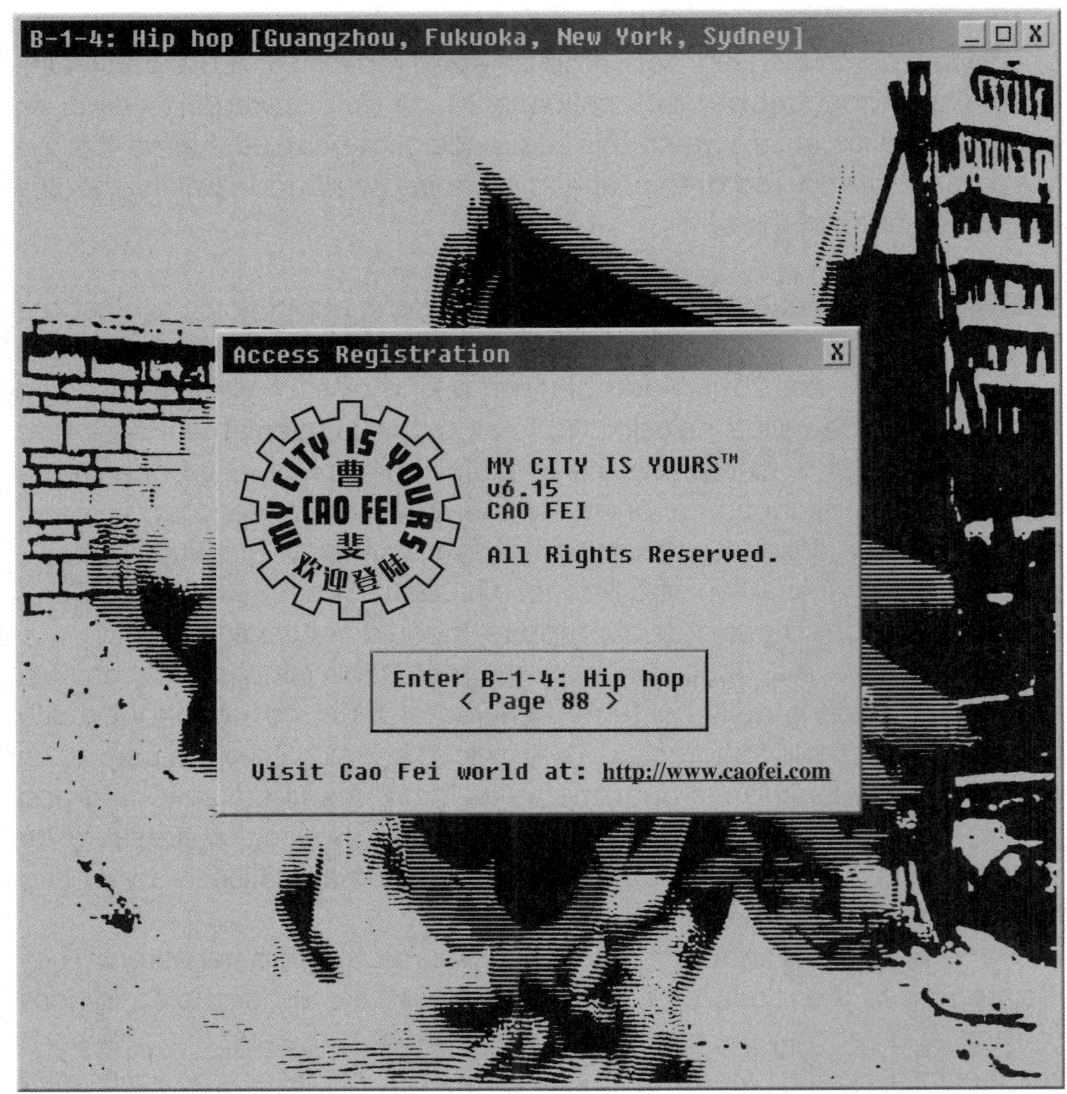

A dream, then, is a lifeline. A dream is an antidote to drudgery, as it is in Cao's *Hip hop* series initiated in 2003. In a trio of short videos shot in Guangzhou 2003, Fukuoka 2005, New York 2006 – each scored by the genre that lends the series its name – Cao films a cross-section of civilians dancing and capering about public spaces.[3] The choreography is kitschy: a smear of waving arms, restless feet, the occasional glimpse of breakdancing, executed with varying degrees of success. Like *Cosplayers*, the *Hip hop* videos transfigure their geography. Cao imbues otherwise unremarkable sites – a thoroughfare, a business building – with talismanic value. They become stages for momentary ebullience.

The *Hip hop* series is often indistinguishable from fable. In Guangzhou, a beat cop and a small-time crim join forces, wrists linked by a set of handcuffs, punching the sky with their free arms. They are gangly. They are graceless. I am completely enamoured.

In Fukuoka, an office cleaner emerges behind a janitor's trolley, fingers splayed in a pair of deuces. Elsewhere in the video, Cao returns to a familiar sight: a cosplayer in a peroxide wig and greatcoat bouncing and swaying. With a little panache, any street can be a runway. These are surreal images; each amateur performer punctures their surroundings with stabbing elbows, shuddering knees. We might call them freaks. We might call their behaviour freaking out: swapping the expansionist principles of the city for an unburdened play, a bizarro grammar of legs akimbo and blundering pirouettes. A language that zips from person to person, perforating the brutality of industrialisation with a communal rhapsody. For a moment, each performer is united in clownish zeal. Their effulgence seems infinite, cosmic. A sunburst.

we could just go on exit reality together if that was fine with you
<mikezzsun>
and can afford flights to illinois
<tommyilgb>
yeah, i could . . . and then if money was still an issue, we could always just wait like a few years until im in college myself and have a bigger budget
<mikezzsun>
yeah we could fall asleep under the sky on exit reality <3
<tommyilgb>
omg yes, we can just lie on the grass and watch the stars . . .
<mikezzsun>
feel the pixels etc
<mikezzsun>
LMFAO
<tommyilgb>
LMAO, but yeah, we could watch the stars, we could talk about music and movies, we could talk about death cab for cutie and vampire weekend, and maybe after we could just go back to our respective houses and text each other, and maybe like a year later, i could visit again and we could cuddle all night again . . .
<mikezzsun>
WHY IS THIS SOOO DREAMY
<tommyilgb>
IDK BUT ITS SO AMAZING, ITS LITERALLY MY PERFECT SCENARIO
we'd have to like . . . be really quiet tho so our parents dont hear us lmao
<mikezzsun>
hahahahahahahaha
<tommyilgb>
you know, we're just being all romantic and cheesy together on MSN rn
<mikezzsun>
ugh my heart genuinely hurts so much
<mikezzsun>
bc i can also smell my mum baking brownies from the kitchen
<tommyilgb>
OMFG THEY MUST SMELL SO GOOD IM A LITTLE jealous ngl
<mikezzsun>
they smell sooooo good
<tommyilgb>
OMG I WANT SOME SO BAD RN
<mikezzsun>
a little nostalgic
<tommyilgb>
now I want my mom to bake brownies rn . . . but it's almost midnight and
<mikezzsun>
i will . . . . mail you some ;)
<tommyilgb>
OMG REALLY? THEYRE MY FAVOURITE
I WOULD LITERALLY MARRY YOU IF U DID THAT, OMG
<mikezzsun>
ok im sending some on the plane as we speak . . . goodbye brownies, safe travels
<mikezzsun>
now what will our wedding look like
<tommyilgb>
omg . . . i feel like we should have a beach wedding, i don't know,

it just feels right . . . but we'd also need to decide if we should invite people or just do a small wedding . . . idk i dont think we have a lot of like . . . friends or family we'd want to invite anyways . . .
<mikezzsun>
i mean since we're both like I'M SOOO LONELY im gonna assume a small wedding
<tommyilgb>
yeah, probably, who would we invite tho???
<mikezzsun>
couple friends, couple family, my mum's BROWNIES
<tommyilgb>
OH YEAH, THE BROWNIES ARE A MUST, THEY COULD BE LIKE OUR WEDDING CAKE?
<mikezzsun>
we can invite vampire weekend lololol
<tommyilgb>
omg yeah totally, i'll be honest, i feel like they'd probably say no but like, just them being there with us would be like, amazing . . .
<mikezzsun>
wedding band!
<tommyilgb>
oh yeah!!! wedding band, also, death cab for cutie could write a like . . . special song just for our wedding???
<mikezzsun>
HAHAHAHA
<mikezzsun>
ok stop im gonna cry
<tommyilgb>
aww, nooooo, dont cry :(
<mikezzsun>
that is the power of death cab for cutie baybeee
<tommyilgb>
OMG I WANT MY WEDDING ALBUM TO JUST ALL HAVE DEATH CAB FOR CUTIE IN IT, LIKE I NEED TO PLAY THE SONG THEY SING WHEN WE FIRST KISS OMG OMG I WANT MY WEDDING TO BE SO ROMANTIC
<mikezzsun>
yessssss
<tommyilgb>
omg if we like . . . got our own apt after we get married, we could just like listen to death cab for cutie and vampire weekend all night every night while cuddling . . .
<mikezzsun>
ok confession time
<tommyilgb>
OMG SAY ITT
<mikezzsun>
i fully used to watch wedding videos on youtube
<tommyilgb>
SAME OMGGGGGGG
<mikezzsun>
like OTHER PEOPLES WEDDING VIDEOS
<tommyilgb>
SAME, i would sometimes watch like these couples channels and like, im embarrassed to
<mikezzsun>
AND THEN
<tommyilgb>
i would be like fantasizing about having my own wedding . . . but i guess i never really

5

I am reminded of another work set in Japan: Shunji Iwai's film *All about Lily Chou-Chou* (*Rirī Shushu no subete*) 2001, a Homeric saga of juvenile delinquency located among fields so verdant they could make anyone religious. It doesn't matter what happens in the film, only that the teenaged inhabitants of Iwai's world – marred as it is by depravity and danger – assign grand meaning to a pop idol named Lily Chou-Chou. She is never seen, barely heard, and yet exerts an oracular power. In interstitial sequences, her devotees message breathlessly in an online chat room. It is the only 'free space in the ether', one user types. It is a sort of utopia.

Like Lily Chou-Chou's disciples, the performers in the *Hip hop* series craft private utopias by submitting to the magnetism of pop culture, where progress trumps tradition, where an artificial bliss conceals the machinations of survival. It is an allure that Cao Fei knows well. By the late 1980s and early 1990s, Western media had long disseminated across China – especially in Cao's native Guangzhou, one of the mainland's pioneers in international trade. 'I spent my entire adolescence captive to music video culture', she writes in a 2009 *Artforum* feature. 'I would listen to pop music on my Walkman on the way to and from school, and the fruits of my diligent study were obvious every time I hit the dance floor'.[4] The music video's influence is overt in Cao's *Hip hop* series but its traces are evident from her first video, *Imbalance 257* 1999, made as a student at art college (p 58). It is a bricolage of squalor and mayhem. Cao's university peers run amok in bathrooms and narrow corridors. They languish and smoke and spar. Like a classic MTV clip, the video is dictated by absurdity over logic, mood over narrative. These are also the traits of a dream.

Dance and cosplay: both offer respite from reality. Like a fervid romance forged over dial-up. Like an evanescing dream. The fantasy sours at the end of *Hip hop: New York*, the raucous choreography replaced by a lone figure by the Hudson River as dusk falls. Fade to black. But give it a few seconds, and the music saunters in again with the breeze. A hand oscillates in time with the beat. The urban in Cao's work is an anonymous, anonymising place where the endless pursuit of novelty is prioritised above all else. It is a place that preys on base desire. A place where a dream may slip away, unnoticed. To freak out, then, is to capture the dream, live in its anarchy a little longer. Pretend to be somewhere – or someone – else, if only for one languorous summer.

1. Izabella Scott, 'Interview with Cao Fei', *The White Review*, Jun 2016, thewhitereview.org/feature/interview-with-cao-fei, accessed Feb 2024.
2. Philip Tinari, 'Coming up hip-hop and questioning utopia', interview Dec 2008, trans Xiaotong Wang, art21.org/read/cao-fei-coming-up-hip-hop-and-questioning-utopia, originally published on Art21.org, Dec 2013, accessed Feb 2024.
3. Cao's *Hip hop* series now includes the recently filmed *Hip hop: Hong Kong* 2024 and *Hip hop: Sydney* 2024, the latter work being commissioned for the *My City is Yours* exhibition at the Art Gallery of New South Wales.
4. Cao Fei, 'Cao Fei', trans Philip Tinari, *Artforum*, vol 47, no 7, 2009, artforum.com/features/cao-fei-2-190348, accessed Feb 2024.

thought anyone would like me enough to . . . marry me lol
<mikezzsun>
I WOULD START CRYING?????
<tommyilgb>
I WOULD TOO TBH LMAO
<mikezzsun>
HAHAHAHAHA
<tommyilgb>
AND LIKE, WE WOULD HAVE THIS BEAUTIFUL WEDDING BUT LIKE A LOT OF PEOPLE WOULD PROBABLY BE THINKING, "WHO ARE THEY??" AND LIKE, I WOULD BE SO EMBARASSED
<mikezzsun>
imagine we meet for the first time in real life and its our WEDDING
<tommyilgb>
LOL THAT'D BE SO HILARIOUS
i can imagine a bunch of people there's thinking "who are these people??" and then we kiss and everyone's just like "what the hell, did they even know each other???" and then we're just like, "WE LOVE EACHOTHER SO MUCH WE DECIDED TO MARRY ON THE SPOT"
<mikezzsun>
ROM-COM MOMENT
<tommyilgb>
LITERALLY THE PLOT TO ONE OF THE MOST ROMANTIC ROMCOMS EVER WE NEED TO WRITE A SCREENPLAY
<mikezzsun>
lolol i have always dreamed of writing a screenplay
<tommyilgb>
omg same . . . maybe we should collab on one "Two Lonely Souls, in desperate need of a life, discover a website which promises a way out of their loneliness with an online reality. They decide to log on, and their world changes for the better"
we could call it "Exit Reality" or something like that? It sounds kinda corny but its just a basic idea lol
<mikezzsun>
HAHAHA
<mikezzsun>
yeah if we don't get sued by the actual exit reality
<tommyilgb>
LMAO "Exit Reality, the most romantic dating site 2000"
maybe we could make the app name like "Entrance Reality" to kinda avoid copyright issues
<mikezzsun>
you know i feel like i do wanna write about this but i just have no screenplay skills
<tommyilgb>
it's ok, i feel like the hardest part would be like . . . getting into the film industry. we'd prolly need some money or something to shoot like a small demo to convince someone to actually make it
<mikezzsun>
maybe someday in the future
<tommyilgb>
yeah, who knows? we're still young

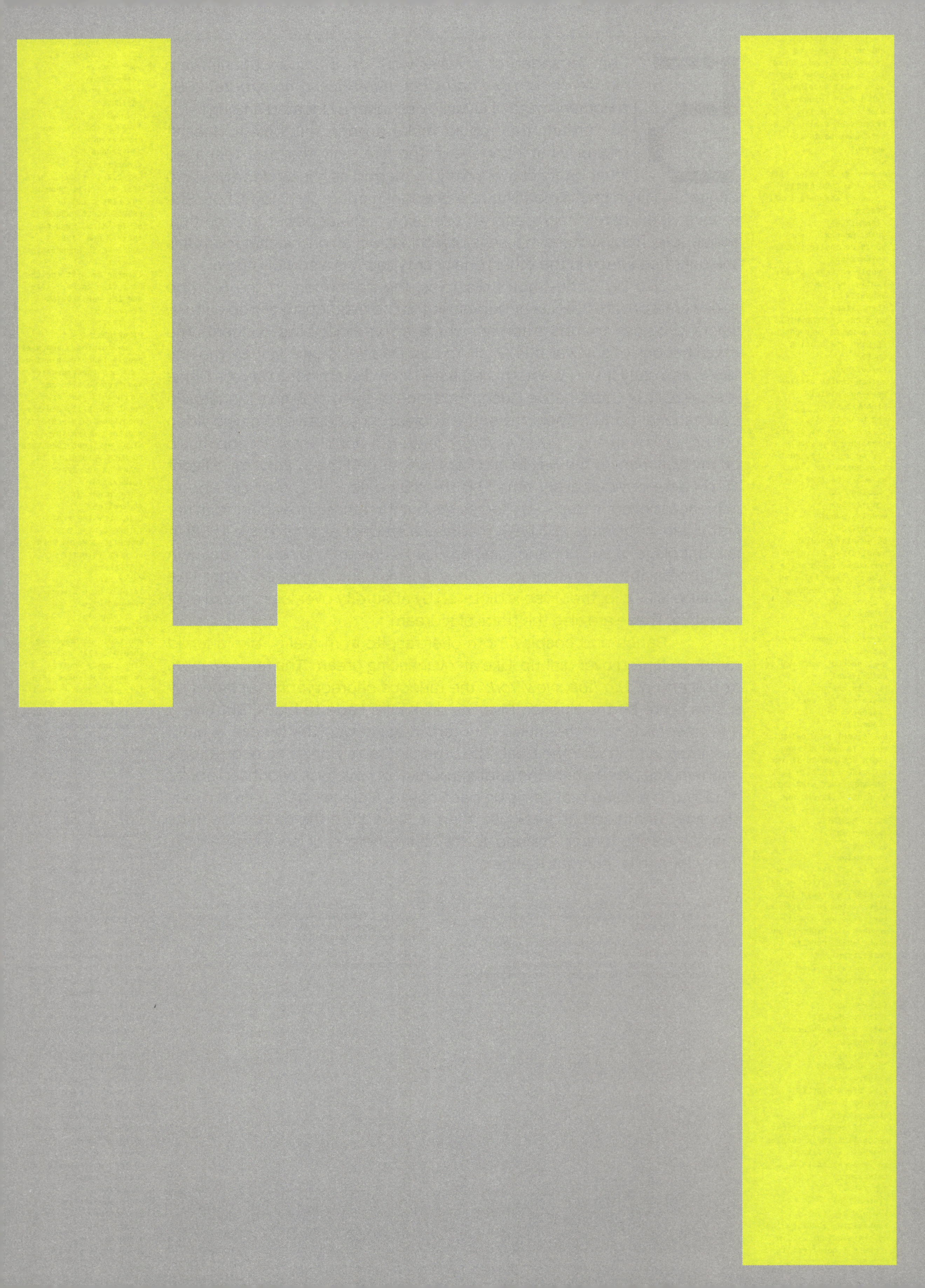

PAO-CHEN TANG

TOWARDS A UTOPIAN ARCHIVE

唐葆真

走向乌托邦的档案

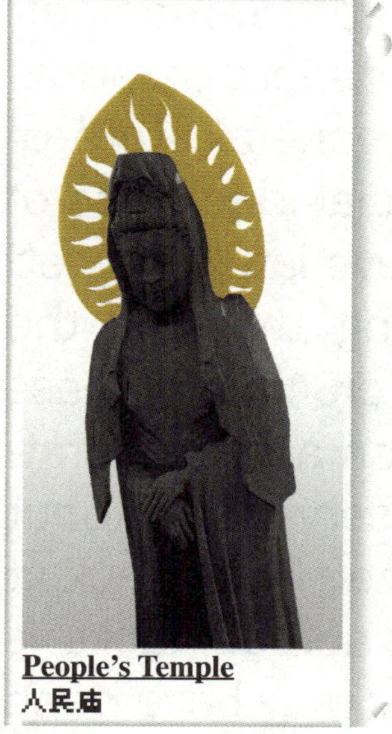
People's Temple
人民庙

A girl of enigmatic origin teleports amid boundless virtual spheres. Her cascading locks and her ensemble shift in colours and styles, transitioning from the innocence of a schoolgirl in a uniform to the futuristic allure of a platinum-blonde cyberpunk. Yet ever-present is the embrace of her radiant, welcoming smile. Behold China Tracy, Cao Fei's avatar in Second Life, a multi-user online platform developed by Linden Lab and launched in 2003, which serves as a canvas upon which denizens craft their own worlds and interact with each other. At its zenith from the late 2000s to the early 2010s, the platform boasted nearly one million regular users. Cao emerged as a luminary through China Tracy, designing a city, experiencing a romantic affair with another avatar and even delivering a digital baby.

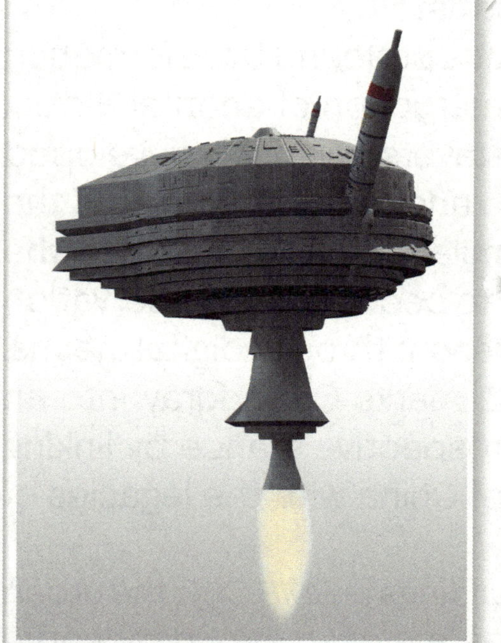
People's Aerial Castle 人民空港
RMB City boasted a range of civic spaces where citizens could gather and connect. Resembling a metal spaceship, the People's Aerial Castle was used as an online exhibition space by the Beijing-based art gallery Ullens Center for Contemporary Art. The nearby People's Temple served as the spiritual heart of this digital metropolis, allowing avatars to experiment with religion.

The sojourns of China Tracy come to life in Cao's video works, notably *i.Mirror* 2007 and *Live in RMB City* 2009. The eponymous city of the latter is perhaps Cao's most famous project, constructed from 2007 to 2011. Within its pixelated expanse, structures akin to iconic landmarks from Chinese metropolises rise with compelling force to convey nuanced historical consciousness in the lead-up to the 2008 Beijing Summer Olympics. The virtual cityscape unfolds in glitchy vaporwave aesthetics. Flat planes intersect under the glow of artificial lighting, wildly refashioning and juxtaposing newly erected architectural marvels, including the Beijing National Stadium (Bird's Nest), the National Centre for the Performing Arts and the CCTV Headquarters building. In its intricate design, *RMB City* also features various transportation infrastructures, such as the People's Wharf, which evokes the bustling ports in the Pearl River Delta, one of the country's principal export-oriented manufacturing and industrial hubs.

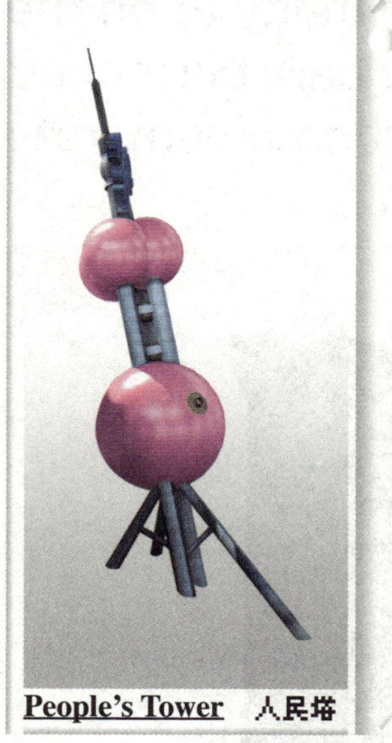
People's Tower 人民塔

As Cao's creation captures the vibrancy, paradoxes and absurdities of China's rapid urbanisation, the threads of local narratives are woven into the fabric of the broader globalised world, shaped by interconnected flows of capital and commerce. In this era marked by an unprecedented pace of development, all that is solid melts into air – change becomes the sole constant. The manifesto accompanying *RMB City* encapsulates this ethos and presents virtuality as the teleological destination of Chinese modernity: '... let all the virtual-real conflicts vanish in *RMB City*... try reversing all the discussions about realness by shifting them into the virtual light year'.[1] A sense of technological optimism prevails, as the seemingly limitless potential of Second Life serves as a suitable vehicle through which to sculpt the country's unbounded future.

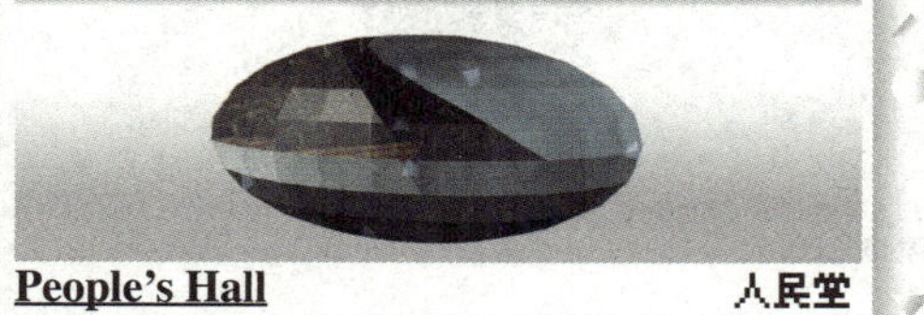
People's Hall 人民堂

Seen from the vantage point of 2024, *RMB City* can be understood as a historical document capturing the fervour when post-1980s China embraced the tenets of a market economy. Indeed, 'RMB' not only denotes China's official

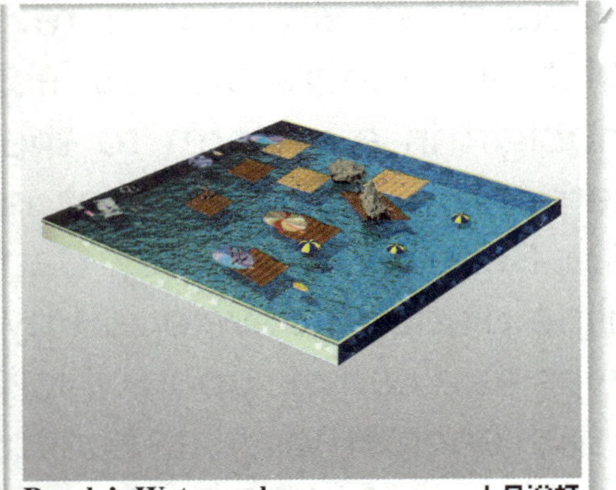

People's Waterpark 人民浴场
Translated as 'people's bathhouse' in Chinese, this aqua fun-park evoked the history of Chinese public bathhouses as spaces of democratic commune at a time when private bathrooms were luxuries for working-class people. Just as bars and coffee houses were key to the emergence of 'public spheres' in the West, bathhouses were central to the formation of new kinds of collectivity and the development of free speech in China.

currency (renminbi) but also contracts the word 'remember'. But if *RMB City* serves as a record of this period, paradoxically, it also stands as a memorial to a general state of disappearance, for the then dominant social ideologies of developmentalism and accelerationism have lately yielded negative consequences. Foremost among these is the erosion of once-public spaces – the very crucible of mass culture – through the forces of privatisation and corporatisation. In a 2020 interview, Cao voiced reservations about the utopian vision of *RMB City*: 'But now when I look back at that idea, and see what the city nowadays actually lacks, is a sense of cohesion and intimacy, which all may have been snatched by these online platforms'.[2]

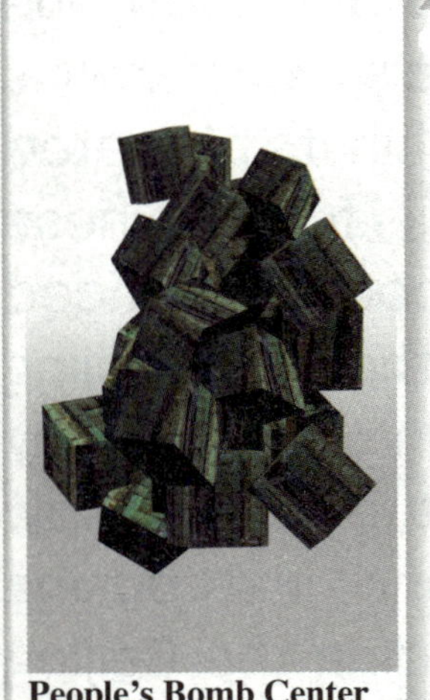

People's Bomb Center
人民阵

The purpose of Cao's endeavours underwent a profound transformation when she was invited to undertake the construction of another virtual metropolis within Yuanbang Mega City, a metaverse platform developed by the Chinese media company Meta Media and tech giant Baidu. If the previous focus was on the proposed assimilation of the real into the virtual, now the vector had reversed course to become the preservation of indices from the past and the vanishing present through digital means. The resulting creation, *Duotopia vol 1* 2022, marks Cao's foray into an archaeology of the everyday. It takes a retrospective stance by linking the contemporaneity and even the future of China with the legacies of its socialist era from the 1950s to the 1970s.

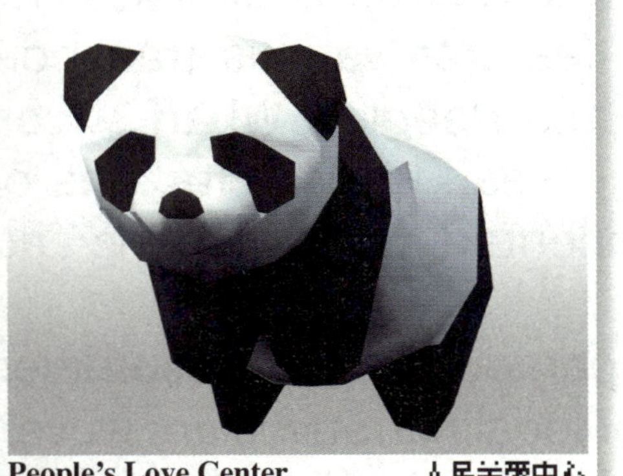

People's Love Center 人民关爱中心
Find your way into the panda-shaped Love Center through a secret entrance and experience intimacy in the big city!

Unlike the jungle of assembled buildings in *RMB City*, the urban landscape of *Duotopia* assumes a systematic, concentric form: a suspended silver entity reminiscent of a fragmented cyborg octopus with ascending tentacles that support a vertically stacked skyscraper. This central element is encircled by a rotating, two-storey, circular space station. These designs bestow an aura of monumentality upon the city that resemble a public sculpture strategically positioned in a serene setting. What does it want to commemorate and immortalise?

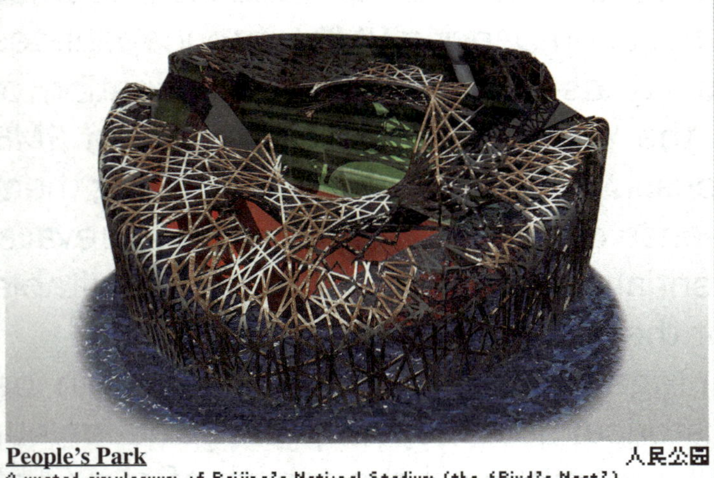

People's Park 人民公园
A rusted simulacrum of Beijing's National Stadium (the 'Bird's Nest'), People's Park was a sports venue in RMB City where users could engage in various 'social competitions'.

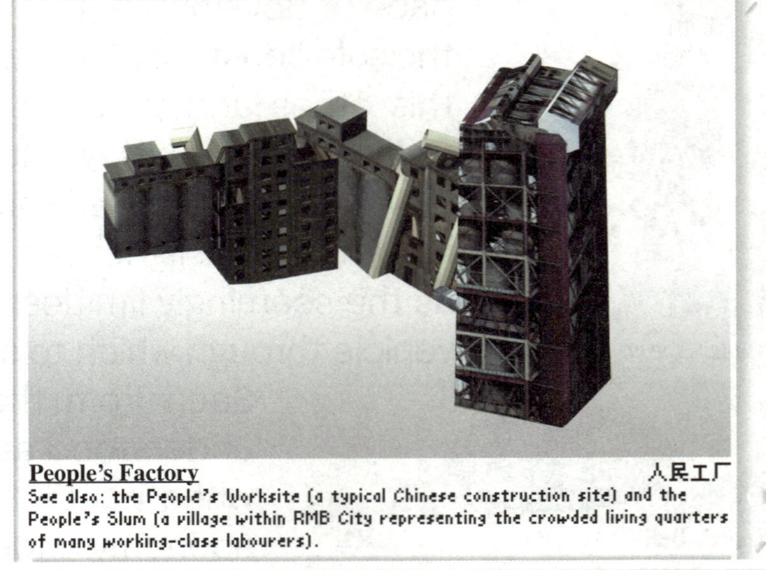

People's Factory 人民工厂
See also: the People's Worksite (a typical Chinese construction site) and the People's Slum (a village within RMB City representing the crowded living quarters of many working-class labourers).

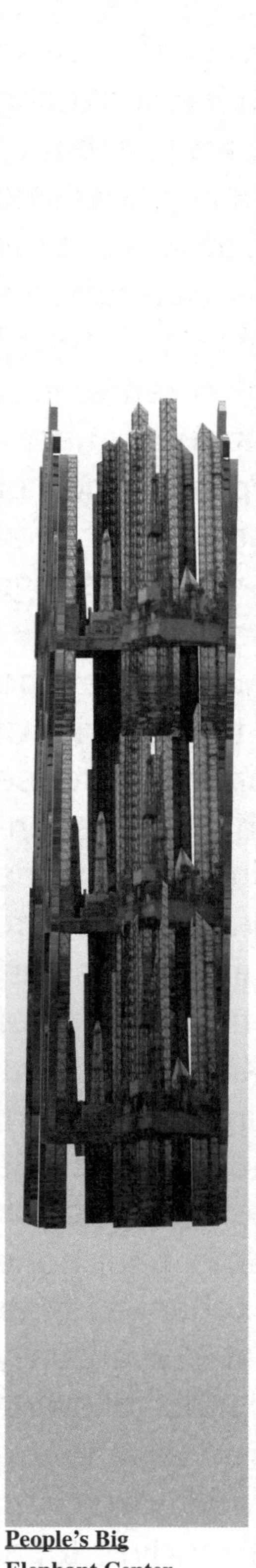

People's Big Elephant Center
人民大厦

Mimicking one of the unfinished buildings that are ubiquitous in Chinese cities (due to investors' pulling out halfway through construction), this dystopian structure reflects upon the relentless churn of capitalism and rampant urbanisation.

A nearby landmark was the People's Bank (人民银行), a skyscraper resembling the Hong Kong headquarters of a Chinese state-owned bank. Towering in the digital sky, this building was composed of (virtual) gold bricks. Gold – a material prised for its stability – contrasts with the cold randomness and wild speculation of the global financial markets which bankroll risky new construction projects.

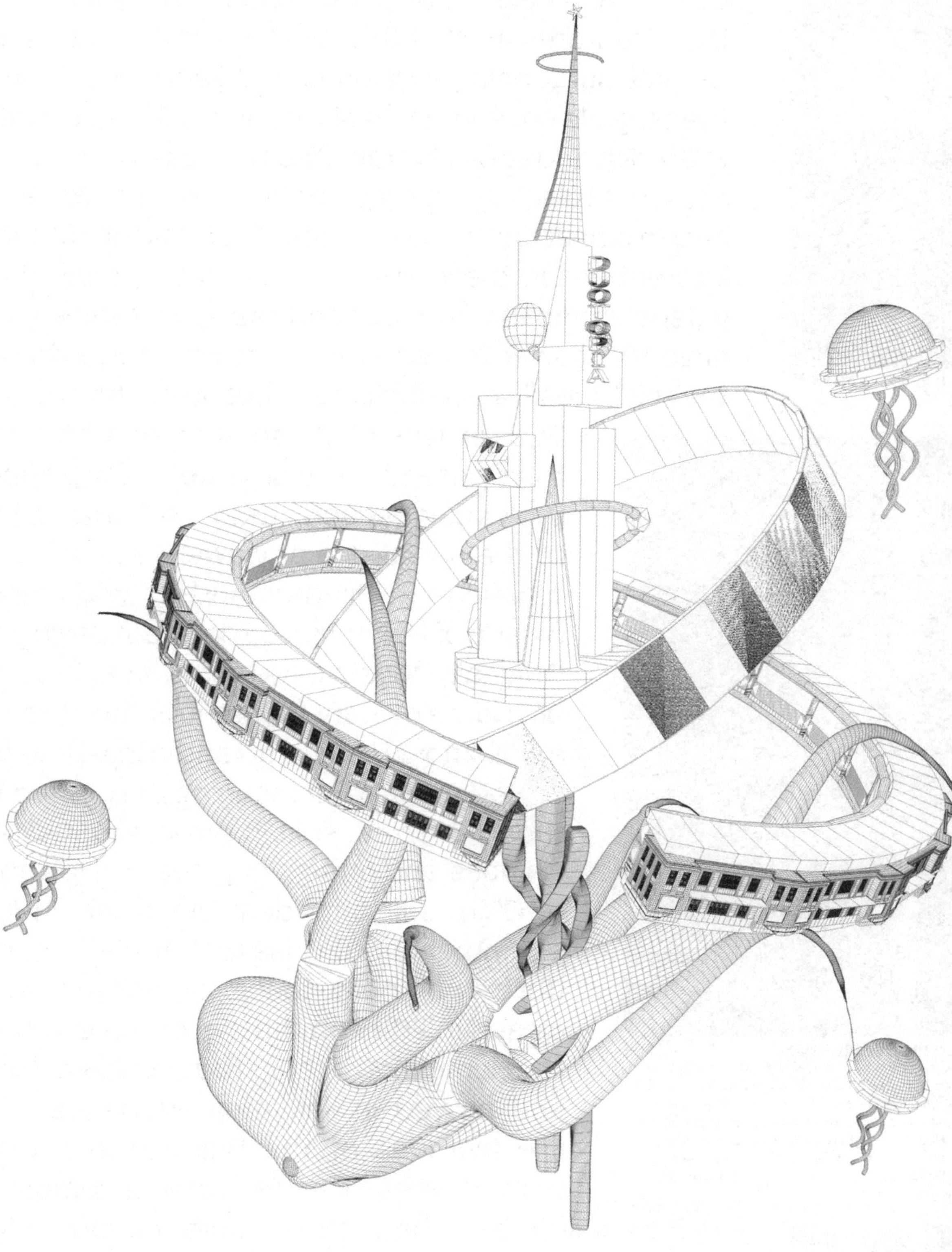

Duotopia vol 1 model sketch, 2022

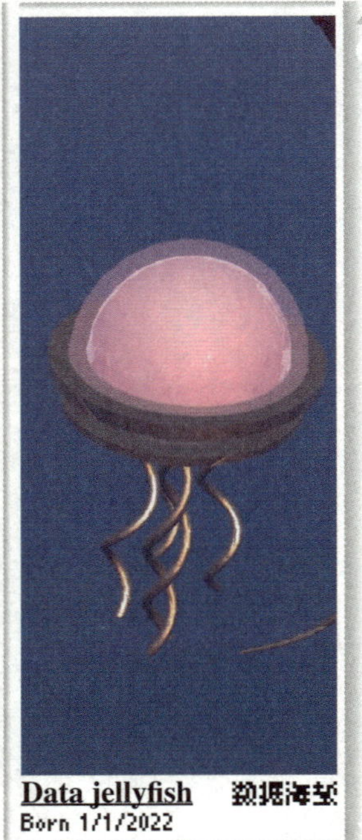

Data jellyfish 数据海蜇
Born 1/1/2022

Duotopia exhibits a notably futuristic ambience compared to *RMB City* and aligns with the sentiments Cao expressed in her 2020 interview. It also incorporates recognisable settings and cultural institutions, including a cinema, a cafe, small shops and an art gallery. In contrast to most of the structures in *RMB City*, which mimic urban landmarks symbolising China's burgeoning economic and geopolitical reach, *Duotopia* evokes the tangible environments of the physical world. Here, individuals navigate with ease and sociality transpires at a casual, intimate scale. Could these sites establishing community be what *Duotopia* seeks to remember and reconstruct? The increase of Cao's documentation of users' interactions in these spaces – perhaps paralleling the proliferation of videos stemming from Second Life – may allow us to determine if they have the power to become virtual counterparts of real-world settings that historically have facilitated public exchange and discussion.

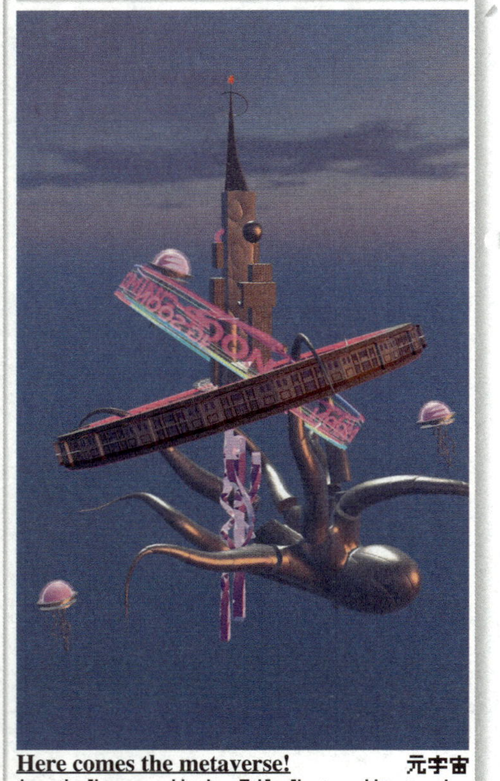

Here comes the metaverse! 元宇宙
Aquatic figures orbit Cao Fei's first architectural creation in the metaverse. Displayed on a horizontal screen, the video is experienced by lying on the floor and looking upward at a range of hypnotic forms floating in a digital ether. A 3D scan of the Hongxia Theatre, a neon pink 'coming soon' sign, jellyfish and octopi tentacles orbit a spinning steel skyscraper.

The designs of these sites carry historical weight beyond their potential social value. Many, especially the exterior of the circular space station in *Duotopia*, reflect the influence of the socialist era. Viewers acquainted with Cao's recent creations will understand its wellspring of inspiration: the facade of the Hongxia Theatre in Beijing's Jiuxianqiao district. Originally constructed in the late 1950s, the building was part of 'a large military-industrial factory complex modelled after a well-known Leningrad enterprise, known as Krasnaya Zarya, or Red Dawn' (the meaning of Hongxia in Chinese).[3] Before the Sino-Soviet split in the late 1950s/early 1960s, numerous Chinese and foreign engineers involved in the construction of China's first modern electronic industry and telephone equipment enterprise met at the factory to exchange ideas. Built as a social space for workers, the theatre eventually closed in 2008 on the eve of the Olympics. In 2015, following the demolition of her studio, Cao Fei discovered the theatre and moved in, initiating five years of fieldwork exploring the histories of the building and the surrounding local communities. (The theatre was demolished in late 2023.)

Red star horizons
红星塔
Born 1/1/2022

As if to ensure that the theatre would not fade into collective oblivion, Cao has consistently positioned this social space as the primary backdrop for her recent work, such as the documentary *Hongxia* 2019, the sci-fi feature film *Nova* 2019 and the VR work *The eternal wave* 2020. A replica of the lobby was also erected in her 2021 retrospective at the UCCA Center for Contemporary Art in Beijing. Various items, including filmstrips, a projector and movie tickets, were brought to the gallery to conjure the ambience of this bygone dream palace. This archive fever further extends into *Duotopia*, which functions as a data repository designed to store and showcase Cao's painstakingly scanned representation of the theatre. Cao hopes that this digital platform will enable younger users to immerse themselves in the lived realities that

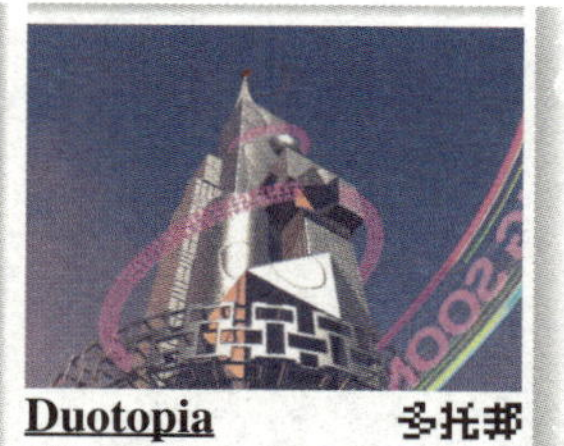
Duotopia 多托邦

this space once signified. Moreover, in the event that Beijing authorities consider reconstructing the theatre – a prospect not entirely implausible given the fluid and occasionally self-contradictory urban planning strategies in contemporary China – the virtual data may play a pivotal role in facilitating its re-materialisation.

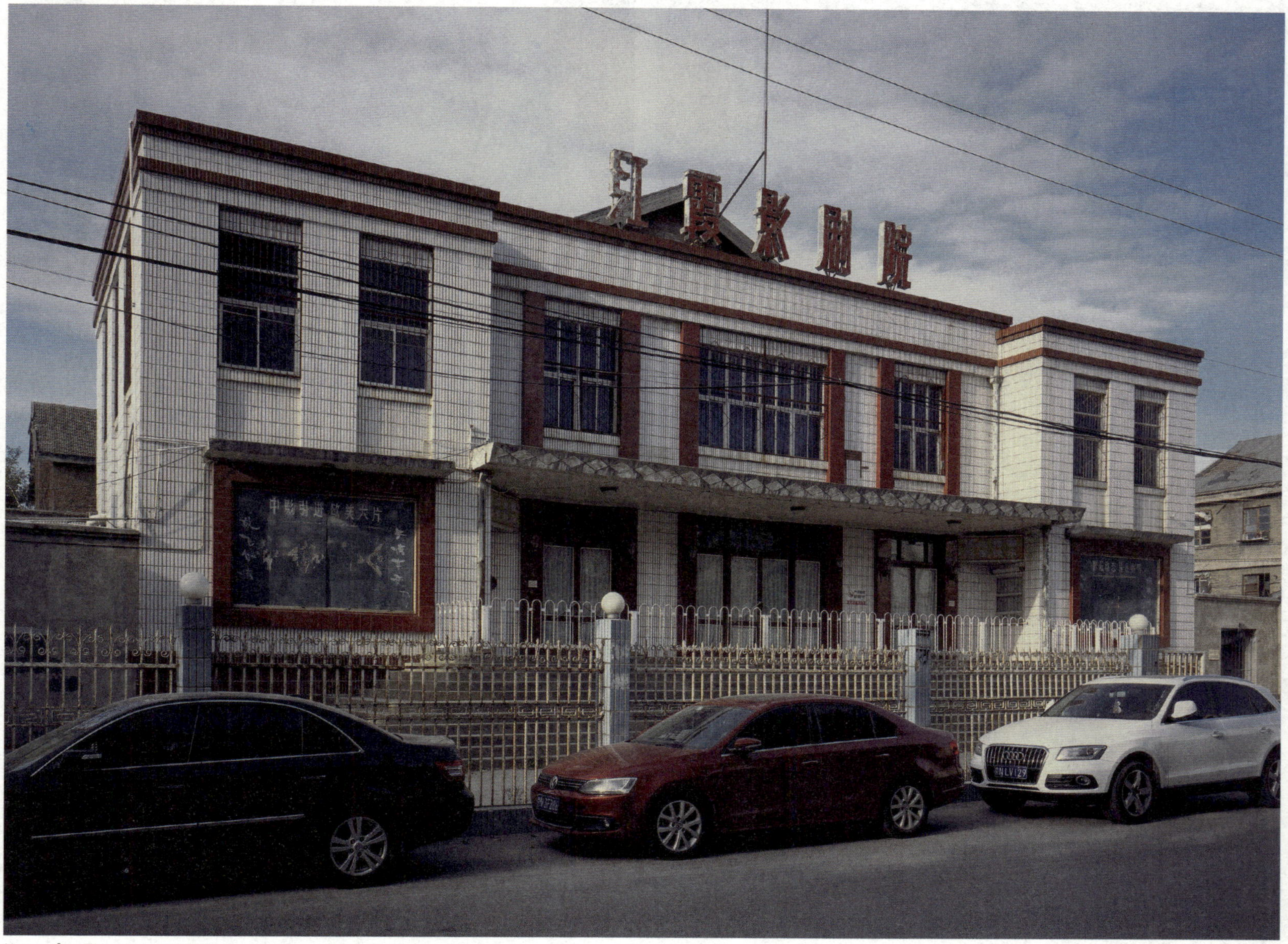

Hongxia Theatre 01 2019, photo, 105 x 150 cm

Interlacing the past with the future, *Duotopia* uncovers a complex conception of temporality, reflected in its title, which combines the words 'duo' and 'utopia'. 'Duo', meaning 'multiple' in Chinese, signifies more than just the multiplicity of diverse spaces, identities and perspectives embraced within the social space that this utopian city aspires to create. Cao's deepening historical consciousness enriches the temporal dimension of this project. The digital reconstruction of Hongxia, for instance, simultaneously mirrors the changing cityscape of a subdistrict in Beijing and revisits the alternative modernity cultivated in the 1950s – a period when the then recently established People's Republic of China envisioned its own techno-utopian possibilities. Through this archaeological tracing, the importance of 'duo' expands to encompass not only an amalgamation of the many but also the multifaceted aspects of a singular entity.

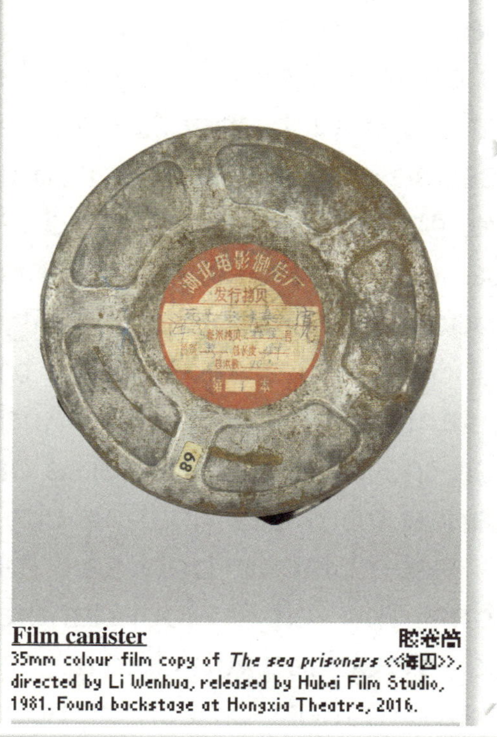
Film canister 胶卷筒
35mm colour film copy of *The sea prisoners* <<海囚>>, directed by Li Wenhua, released by Hubei Film Studio, 1981. Found backstage at Hongxia Theatre, 2016.

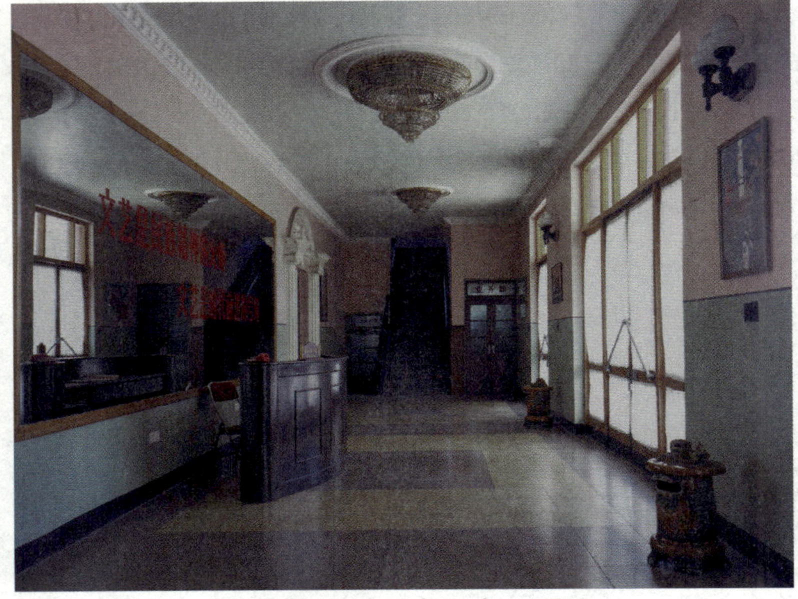

Hongxia Theatre interior, 2019

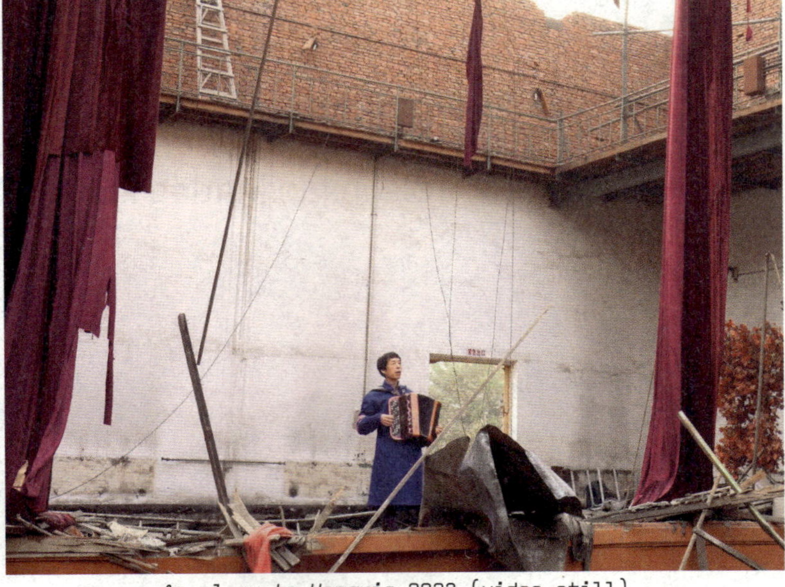

An elegy to Hongxia 2023 (video still)

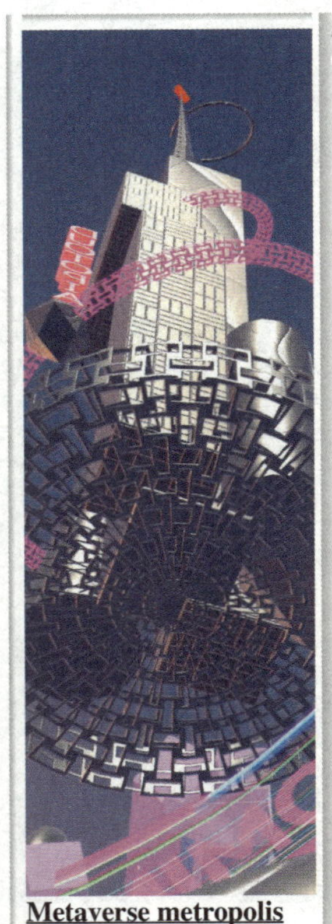

Metaverse metropolis
多托邦都市
Born 1/1/2022
Resident

The contextualisation of *Duotopia* within Cao's Hongxia archive – as a physical site *and* an ideal – accounts for the changing media of her recent creations. It becomes evident that Cao's primary enquiry does not revolve around specific platforms, techniques or technologies. Instead, film, photography, video, multimedia installation, VR and social media have all been mobilised to interrogate the historicity of the site. Cao's prior reliance on a singular digital medium (ie Second Life) for *RMB City* has now evolved into an exploration of how each of the several media can distinctly contribute to the remembrance of things past. Collectively they beckon the viewer to a historical tableau, retroactively brought to life with the emergence of each latest tech trend. (Indeed, the once-buzzy metaverse has been declared obsolete in less than three years, now upstaged by AI.) As Cao has regularly engaged with various media since the early 2000s, the significance of medium specificity and transmediality in her work warrants reconsideration. A new term is needed to capture Cao's identity as a multimedia artist. Given the temporal awareness implied by 'duo', a fitting alternative might be 'duo-media'.

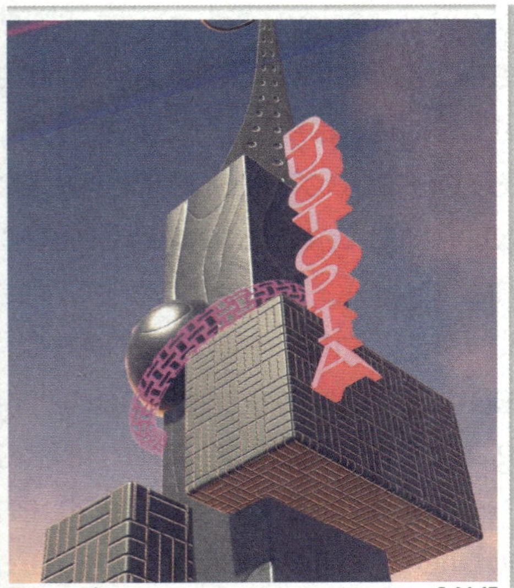

Duotopia 多托邦
The 'duo' in *Duotopia* refers to the mandarin word duō, meaning many – evoking a multiplicity of possible worlds, slipping between the 'real' and the 'virtual.' The video quotes Filippo Marinetti's 'Manifesto of futurism', declaring: 'Time and space died yesterday. We already live in the absolute since we have created eternal, omnipresent speed.'

Oz, the new avatar created by Cao to accompany *Duotopia*, offers an impression quite distinct from China Tracy. While China Tracy is delineated in relation to such specificities as gender and nationality, the essence of Oz – as its name indicates – is much more elusive. An androgynous hybrid of a human and an octopus, suspended in midair with bionic tentacles extending from its body, Oz embodies fluidity across gender and species boundaries. Cao's reference to *The Wizard of Oz* also alludes to fantasy and escapism. And unlike China Tracy, who navigates the pixelated universe of *RMB City*, Oz maintains a distance from the floating city. Judging by the morphological resemblance between its tentacles and those supporting the city's foundation, Oz might be more aptly described as a poised guardian at the border of this space rather than as a restless citizen therein.

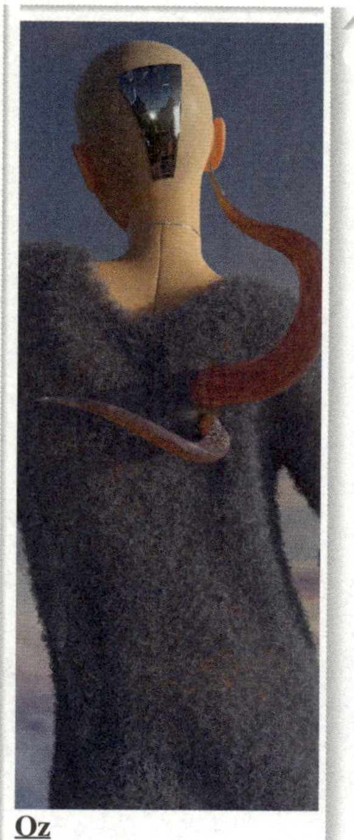

Oz
Born 1/6/2022

The loose connection of Oz to the virtual city might serve as a model for our engagement with the metaverse in general, a perspective that is much more measured and sobering than the earlier invitation to construct new selves within, as once exemplified by China Tracy. Over a decade after Cao's Second Life series, a confluence of global factors, including the COVID-19 pandemic, warfare, ecological debts and economic recession, has significantly disrupted the processes of urbanisation. Simultaneously, the trajectories of technological development have shifted, not least in recent years with the deteriorating conditions for below-the-line workers across digital industries. Confronting this uncertain and insecure world, *Duotopia* prompts us to recognise that the projection of utopian desires into the virtual future cannot continue without delving into the material histories of what was and what has been – long-gone and disappearing worlds that might already hold the key to their fulfilment.

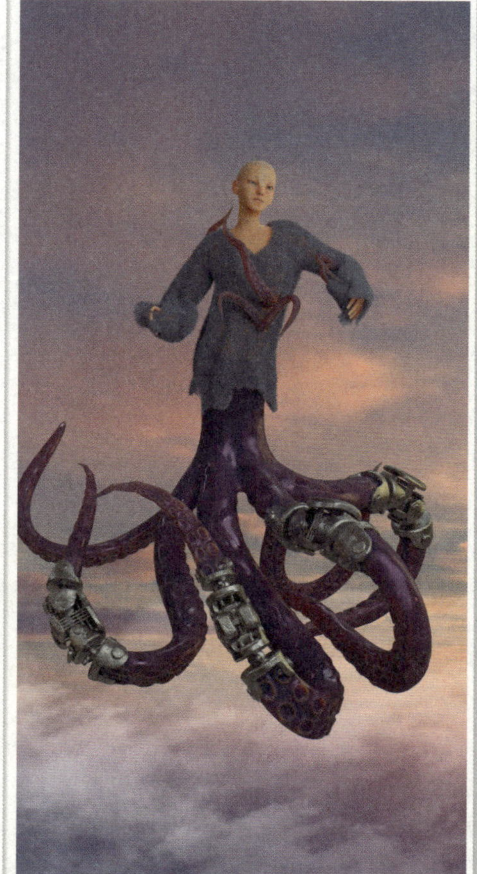

Avatar 2.0 虚拟化身 2.0
Sixteen years after the birth of China Tracy, Cao Fei has imagined a new avatar for the metaverse. Part squid, part machine, part humanoid, Oz hovers serenely on high-definition screens.

'Like a gust of wind from *The Wizard of Oz*, Oz carries spectators into a universe beyond the realm of physical reality.' – Cao Fei

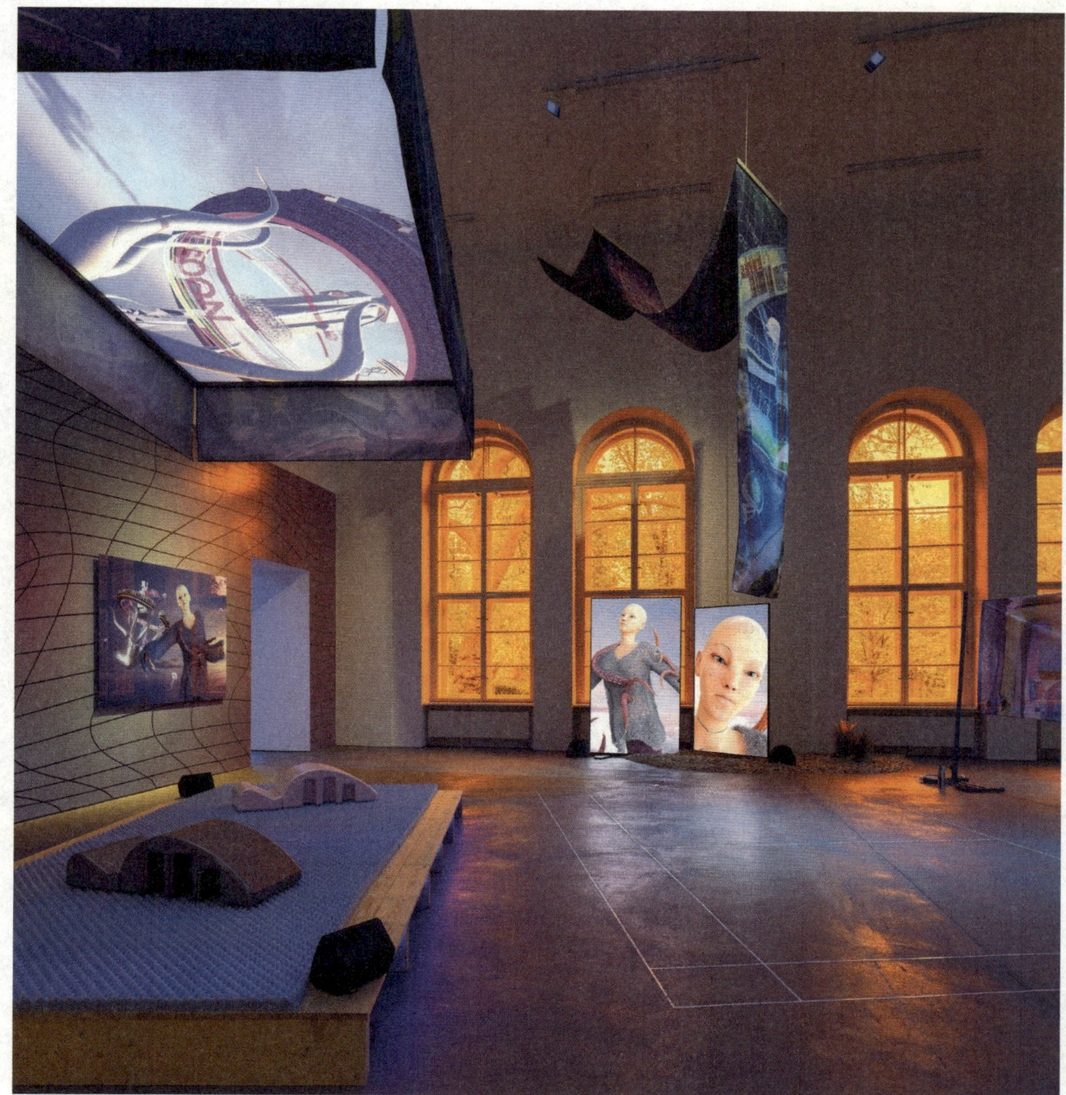

Oz 2022 and *Duotopia vol 1* 2022 in the exhibition *Duotopia*, Sprüth Magers, Berlin, 2023

1. 'RMB City Manifesto', *RMB City*, 26 May 2009, rmbcity.com/about/city-manifesto, accessed 30 Jan 2024, no longer active. See pp 140–41 for the *RMB City* manifesto.
2. Shraddha Nair, 'Gamescapes: Cao Fei recalls "RMB City", the virtual world, and its future', *STIRworld*, 25 Aug 2020, stirworld.com/think-opinions-gamescapes-cao-fei-recalls-rmb-city-the-virtual-world-and-its-future, accessed 30 Jan 2024.
3. Deborah Kaple, 'The Soviet Union of today is China's tomorrow!' in *Cao Fei: HX*, The Pavilion, Serpentine Galleries, London, 2020, pp 89–90.

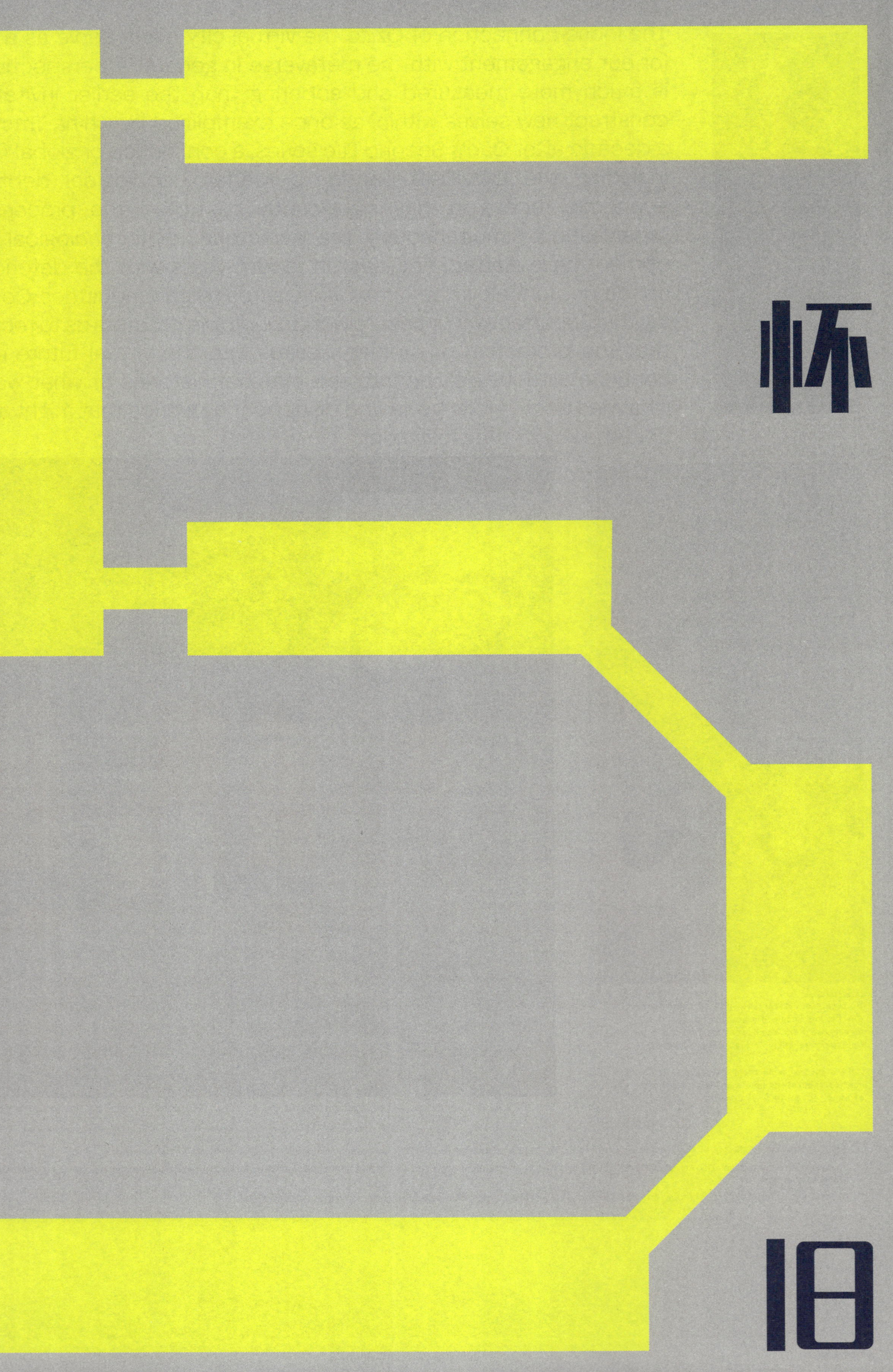
怀
18

CONVERSATION BETWEEN CAO FEI AND YIN CAO

UTOPIAN PROMISES AND FUTURE NOSTALGIA

乌托邦承诺和未来

曹斐和曹音的对话

THE FOLLOWING EDITED CONVERSATION TOOK PLACE IN CHINESE VIA ZOOM ON 23 JANUARY 2024, WITH CAO FEI SPEAKING FROM BEIJING AND YIN CAO FROM SYDNEY.

YC First, I would like to congratulate you on being ranked no 10 in the 'Power 100' list of the journal *ArtReview* in 2023. Since 2018 your name has appeared six times on this prestigious list, which was selected by a panel of forty international art-world insiders. How do you feel about this accolade?

CF When I entered the list's top 10, I did not care that I was the only Chinese artist – I was more interested in finding out who the other nine artists ahead of me were, what kind of art they made and where I fit into this vision. I wanted to know how their works reflected their concerns about the world, whether it was an individual artist or as artistic groups, critics or architects. This benchmark also makes me think what contemporary art is about, what is needed from an artist today and how to dig deeper in a direction of artistic creation outside the art market.

YC You are described as a multimedia artist exploring new technologies and digital culture. But you were a student of decorative art and design, and your first job was working in advertising. Could you please talk about the development of your artistic practice in the past two decades?

CF I was born into an artistic family in 1978, a significant year not only for me but also for my country. That year Deng Xiaoping enacted his policy of 'Reform and Opening-up' (*gaige kaifang* 改革开放). I feel that I boarded this 'Reform and Opening-up' express train as soon as I was born, and the city of my birth, Guangzhou, had an important place in this new policy and strategy. The floodgates were opened and the popular culture of Hong Kong, Macao, Taiwan and the West poured into the city. We were able to see a world completely different from the rest of China – in entertainment, perspectives, pop music and in other ways that pictured and revealed life outside ours. So I experienced two forms of education that greatly clashed with each other: on the one hand, I was taught socialism, patriotism and collectivism in public school; on the other, this 'screen world' showed me a new capitalist and highly entertaining realm. Just as Deng Xiaoping claimed that China should build 'a socialism with a Chinese characterisation', so too these two parallel spheres and two parallel ideological systems – at times intertwining – planted a seed in my heart from a very early age and helped to form my own worldview.

Back then in mainland China you would go to museums to see historic objects, such as at the Museum of the Western Han Dynasty Mausoleum of the Nanyue King, as a sort of cultural tourism. But no official museums or galleries displayed contemporary art that related to our everyday lives. The experience of contemporary art in Hong Kong had a great impact on me, however, and I never realised that one could find such expression. It inspired my imagination and led me to create short theatrical works at college.

In 1999, working with my fellow classmates at the Guangzhou Academy of Fine Arts, I made *Imbalance 257,* a film that used a stream-of-consciousness style. It was met with great excitement and Professor Luo Ka, a leading scholar in Hong

Kong who studied French and Hong Kong new wave films in the 1980s, commented that, 'It contains the language of French new wave films and is very free in style'. Later, in 2000, Hou Hanru, originally from Canton but who has become a well-known curator in the West, liked it very much. He presented it at several of the exhibitions that he curated outside China. I always say that my entrance onto the world art scene was by accident or, as we say in Chinese, '*mangda wuzhuang*' 盲打误撞. Back then, not many artists were making video art and it was hard to categorise the kind of work I made. I tried to tell a story that represented the state of mind of young people in the new millennium, but I also filled these pieces with complicated emotions such as rebellion and displacement. Around the time I made *Imbalance 257*, I was asked to assist in setting up scenes for advertising film shoots. Working with directors, theatre and costume staff and others added to my understanding of how to make a film.

YC You were an early user of the internet in your art practice in China. Tell us about your memories of surfing the web in China in the late 1990s, writing a blog, and your reflections on the utopian promise of the World Wide Web during that period.

CF The main reason I moved to Beijing in 2006 was because of the Beijing Summer Olympics to be held in 2008, when all the country's resources and energies were concentrated in the capital. This energy also sucked me in. At the same time, northern China, which I hadn't explored before, started to appeal to me. I felt I should give it a try and experiment in different spaces. My move to Beijing occurred when the internet was rapidly developing. Because I did not know many people in this huge metropolis and also was not used to the cold winters there, I spent a lot of time on the internet where I encountered Second Life, a vast virtual space that helped me to escape the unfamiliar city. I built my own paradise and utopia and created a virtual lifestyle. *RMB City* was made around the time of the Olympics and coincided with an era of phenomenal Chinese economic growth. My work coincidentally echoed this period of 'digital optimism'.

YC You have created a rich body of work that covers a wide range of topics, from China's urbanisation to globalisation and digitisation. It covers historical events, contemporary moments and evokes futuristic imaginations. You seem to possess a sensitivity in detecting the 'hot topics' before anyone else. How do you choose the topics and subjects for your projects?

CF I do think I possess the sensitivity of an artist who is quite close to the era in which he/she/they live, while also having the ability to keep some distance. I am also called a new media artist, but I think I am equally a new material artist. My materials include people, factories, social change, and I try to show the relationships between these as they connect to our times, our history and our human feelings, whether it be memory, hope, disappointment, despair and frustration. If you look at my work from this angle, it is no longer screen or digital. Depending on the subject, I will use VR, photography or even an entire cinema. If you are a traditional painter, you could express a great many things in your paintings, but you still have to return to your canvas and then you have to make a frame for the work.

I am not making a negative comment about [painting], rather I mean to compare painting with my practice in terms of materials. The contemporary world is very complicated and technical yet it can be revealed through the use of diverse materials: a tricycle, a train and boxes in *Asia one* 2018; in *Hongxia* 2019 it required a wholistic environment that provided an immersive experience that transported you into the past; a sandy beach taking you into the film *Nova* 2019. Occasionally [the choice of topics and materials] felt accidental. I think you need courage.

When a particular theme or subject attracts me, my imagination creates a narrative. I am especially interested in how the technological environment shapes and changes us. *Whose utopia* 2006 asks the questions: 'Who makes what we consume?', 'Who supports our system?', 'Who makes us have certain desires?' Workers also have dreams, yet have we paid attention to their lives? *Asia one* is actually the continuation of my interest in these questions: 'Where does consumerism come from?' We click on the invisible shops on the internet but, behind the scenes, who is sending the merchandise you find on the internet? One Chinese word for online shopping is *taobao* 淘宝, literally 'panning treasures'. We are seeking something from the ocean of our desires; perhaps these things are not really necessities.

YC

I find your method and your approach to subjects fascinating. It is as if you are artist, archaeologist and sociologist. Could you describe your process from conducting in-depth research and examination to the final presentation of the artwork?

C·F

As an artist, you have to combine many roles. Fundamentally you are a human being. *Hongxia* does feel like an archaeological project, but most of the time I place myself in various dimensions. As a living artist, I live in the here and now, although I am also fascinated by the past. That said, the subjects and themes of my art all relate to my life. I consume and I '*taobao*'. I grew up in Guangzhou in the Pearl River Delta. The factory where I made *Whose utopia* was close by. Hongxia Theatre was not far from my home. *RMB City* was at my fingertips. I am not searching for something remote. I am not doing research on Sanxingdui [a 3000-year-old archaeological site in Sichuan province] or going to Xi'an for an archaeological dig. I feel like a dot. When things are within one's grasp, you press the button, you open a Pandora's box – naturally I become interested.

Another dimension comes from my love for life and pop culture. I don't imagine archaeologists like idols or hip hop, do they? [My experience of temporality] has more elasticity, which can be stretched very far or brought near and in the present, giving a different energy to my work. For example, in *Asia one*, there is all of a sudden a blast-from-the-past moment, with disco music and dancing with an octopus. In *Hongxia*, there is an unexpected dance party and a scene of travelling through time. My interest in the past, the present and the imagination of the past has led me to create multiple narratives.

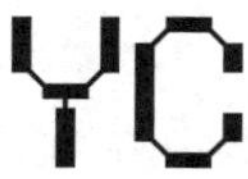

Your works have often been described as travel between two worlds: the real and the virtual. Could you explain how you deal with the entanglement of these two worlds in your artistic creations?

CF

When I was building *RMB City* 2007–11 and the Second Life platform was quite new, I very much believed in the wormhole theory and the forms of life living in it, as well as the idea seen in science fiction of folded space. During the making of *RMB City*, a new online community, I believed in its impact and future influence. Of the two worlds – the real and the virtual – I was more enthusiastic about the virtual world because dimensions in the real world are quite limiting. The sky-scrapers in this real world are only those in front of my eyes. But when I entered the newly created virtual world, I met different people with whom I chatted every night in English. I felt the virtual world is much richer than the real world, more constructive, more future-oriented.

I am more sceptical than pessimistic about the internet compared to how I was during the *RMB City* period. I do wonder if cyberspace is still a safe haven, a space for further development and a tool paralleling our real world. The depression and disappointment [of many young people] seem to be the opposite to the openness promised by cyberspace.

Have you noticed how humans are transforming the unlimited into the limited instead of opening up more broadly? After a period of excessive opening up to the internet, we are retreating to a smaller space. On social media, the most popular thing now is the streamlined short video and story. Due to privacy concerns, we edit our contents, because we are not willing to meet openly and honestly in the virtual realm. We have photo apps to make us look prettier and apps to shorten our videos to fifteen seconds – even five seconds – because otherwise people won't watch them. We have a limited story in 24 hours but we don't want to live in a virtual 24-hour world.

Almost a century ago, we longed for a future in which robots would help us, like the Tin Man in *The Wizard of Oz*. Our imagination about an era of mechanical industry was very shallow: if a robot stood before you, it was scary. Now there is AI: Tesla is creating robots who can walk like humans and deliver coffee. Nonetheless, it feels weird. Robots appear even before you find a lover!

YC

You are an acute observer of things and people around you but you also have an emotional engagement with your subjects. In an interview from 2023, you mentioned the emotional aspect of a project is very important to you.[1] Could you speak a bit more about that?

CF

I believe that I have very strong sense of empathy. Whenever I like a subject, I pay attention to the individual involved. In *Whose utopia*, for instance, the focus is on the factory, one link in the production chain with its productivity tied into the macro-economic strategy of the era. It also marked an era of suffering in the history of China's successful development. But an artist who places themselves in that environment meets the individual worker, gazes into their eyes, and learns their life stories. This means you can't use an overview lens to see the entire scene from an elevated position, as seen in photographs of the German artist Andreas Gursky.

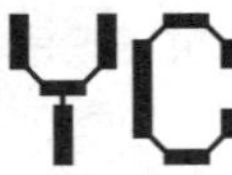

While most of your works are full of playfulness and humour, they also evoke a sense of melancholy, such as *East wind* 2011 and *La Town* 2014 in this exhibition.

There are also a great many contradictions in some of your works, as seen in *RMB City* or *Meta-mentary* 2022. Are you optimistic or pessimistic about the future of humankind? Do you think an artist has a role in lifting the public's spirit?

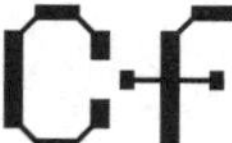

Artistic creation represents the expression of a personal world. When an artist's work is displayed in a public institution, it is inevitable that they take on a public role. I follow the complicated human emotions attached to each subject with great interest and that, together with my strong empathy with the people involved, naturally results in my art possessing this kind of publicity. I simply move to my own rhythm in conveying feelings towards the subject. *Hongxia*, for example, is a historical topic, but when it was shown in different countries people can feel the universal joys and sorrows associated with reunion and separation, even though it was an imaginary space in China's past.

I reveal the complexity in different topics with passion and full energy: there is sadness, hope and despair, exactly the emotions that we see in human beings. But we see hope in despair, optimism in pessimism. People ask me, 'Why you are doing Muay Thai and jiu-jitsu?' 'To learn new things', I say. I think new things give me power to live in our world. I also have the need to have something to lift me up.

YC

You have become a world-renowned artist who has had solo exhibitions in major international museums. Have you ever thought of leaving China and establishing your artistic career in the West?

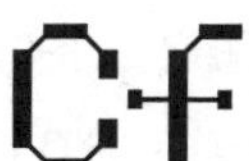

I have not thought of leaving China. To me, my projects and their themes closely relate to the space and environment in which I live. I feel that I rely on these themes. I have yet to live totally in the metaverse. I could move to Singapore or Sydney, living in a new environment to get to know the local culture and immersing myself in a new setting where I could look for new topics and subjects. Many Chinese artists, both past and present, have moved to the West, either taking up artist residencies or through marriage. Perhaps they think it is more comfortable abroad or that they can focus more on their art in foreign countries. I feel that I have a 'down-to-earth' life here in China, deeply rooted in an environment that I am familiar with, in my own country that is necessary for my artistic creation. I live on this land, which is the foundation of my creation and from which questions emerge. Even within the limitations here one can still find directions and motivations to explore themes for discussion. I believe audiences of later generations – be they national or international – would find my artworks well grounded in solid arguments and evidence. Film director Andrei Tarkovsky never left Russia but he made powerful works enjoyed by generations of audiences internationally. He expressed his anxiety poetically. Does one really have to go to the West to build an artistic career? I think differently. The art environment here might seem quite difficult. I sometimes feel that people loom large in an imperfect environment. The decision to stay can be seen as a gesture of wanting to improve things. I don't want to appear aloof; however, for me it is more important to transcend and to probe certain topics as one pursues truth, and then to present them. I feel this endeavour is much bigger and more significant.

For a long time now my works have been mostly shown in public museums and galleries since many commercial galleries no longer show video works. But what you choose to pursue is what you believe in and what real art is. This takes me back to the 'Power 100' list. Their recognition nonetheless reminds you that your work is seen and valued.

YC A more light-hearted question: it seems that you are quite fond of the octopus, which appears in a number of your works. Why?

CF The octopus first appeared in *Asia one*. The reason I used this creature is that there was hardly anybody in the factory where I made this work. The tentacles of the octopus resemble the invisible system or invisible hands that distribute the factory goods. In our world, there are many things that one can't control and there is also unpredictability that controls us. The work *Oz* 2022 also has an octopus body, floating in an uncertain environment. The octopus can easily escape – you want to capture it but sometimes it can get on top of you. This is very similar to our relationship with the world. We invented AI for humans. Then we say we do not need it, as it might hurt us, and so we now are trying to launch a counterattack. For me, the octopus is capricious, almost like the fate of humans, our destinations arbitrary and unknown. This animal makes me feel as if some invisible hands, or something bigger beyond our universe, is looking at us like in the American film *Arrival* 2016, which I like a lot. Human civilisation, as we know, seems to have reached its limit. Is there another dimension? No-one knows. I mention this because my work deals with different dimensions. For example, the metaverse is another parallel world being squeezed by technology. I am also interested in other invisible worlds because when you examine history – just like a wormhole – it requires a space to time travel when you encounter uncertainty and unpredictability, myth, quantum mechanics, materialism, idealism and Darwinism. It reminds me of the recent cinema box-office hit *Oppenheimer* 2023, another example of the contest between humans and the universe.

YC For your first major retrospective exhibition in Australia, you have produced a commissioned work *The golden wattle* 2024 based on the story of your late sister. Could you expand on how this project explores themes of home and migration?

CF *The golden wattle* is a very personal work. My sister, like me, was born in Guangzhou and later migrated to Sydney. She was an artist who painted many works relating to her life in Australia – her 'new world' – and of its national flower, the golden wattle, which she so liked. She was optimistic and loved Australia; her life was filled with beauty. Her paintings are like poetry and music that distil the essence of the Chinese migration experience, uplifting the people who saw them. My sister was like a window through which Australian life was opened up to me.

Later, I went to [Sydney's CBD] Chinatown to do some research in the surroundings where my sister lived in order to get more materials for *The golden wattle*. Talking to an elder leader in Chinatown, I learned of his life story and how he gained respect in white society. He now feels that protecting Chinese tradition in Sydney is both his duty and mission. This has also influenced his son and grandsons, who are adamant about protecting and continuing Chinese cultural traditions in Sydney.

> There appears to be two parallel threads running through the lives of many older generation Chinese migrants. In one, they feel it is their mission to establish their cultural dignity, to set up a Chinatown with a symbolic archway, a space where their voice can be heard and their migration stories – often ignored by mainstream society – can be told. And in the other, they also make charitable contributions to organisations such as schools and temples in their hometowns back in China.

All of this helps me to understand how Chinese migrants put down roots overseas, from the individual, the group to the community. The Chinese expression '*jiren lixia*' 寄人篱下, or 'living under someone else's roof', refers to migrants leaving their countries of origin to settle in another land where they establish their own communities, such as Little Italy, Chinatown or Vietnam town, and where they can assist each other – after all, we are social animals. Within Chinatown itself, there are also different communities, including those from Chaozhou, Wenzhou and Zhongshan. When people in certain vulnerable groups struggle to survive, they often form an underground order that runs according to its own rules and customs. For migrant groups, it is not clear if their voices can be heard. They want the essence of their spirits to be transmitted down through future generations.

> I feel that my sister is like a small satellite floating in the outskirts of Chinatown – at the heart of Sydney.

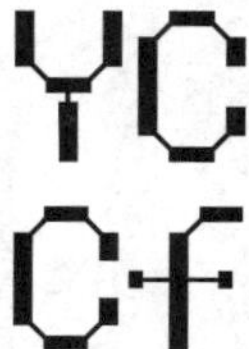

What do you hope that Sydney audiences will take away from this retrospective?

I hope that through this exhibition Sydney audiences can 'land' in the 'world' I present. What awaits them after travelling through the wormhole is a city that is no longer restricted by physical boundaries. It will feel like a platform where we can visit and communicate with one another. Can we meet in the past and greet each other in the future? Perhaps, at the end of the wormhole, we can exchange and share our respective understandings of emotions, identities and views of such a complex and ever-changing world.

TRANSLATED FROM THE CHINESE BY YIN CAO, FEB 2024

(1) An interview in Chinese (English translation link available) by He Min, 26 Apr 2023, freewechat.com/a/MjM5MjUzMjUwMw==/2662499727/1, accessed Feb 2024.

C:/

I spent my entire adolescence captive to music-video culture, as well as to Hollywood movies, Western television programs, and so on. These media were an explosive cultural stimulus for my generation in China. I fell in love with MTV for a time, imitating the dances and fashions I saw in the videos. I would listen to pop music on my Walkman on the way to and from school, and the fruits of my diligent study were obvious every time I hit the dance floor.[1]

CAO FEI

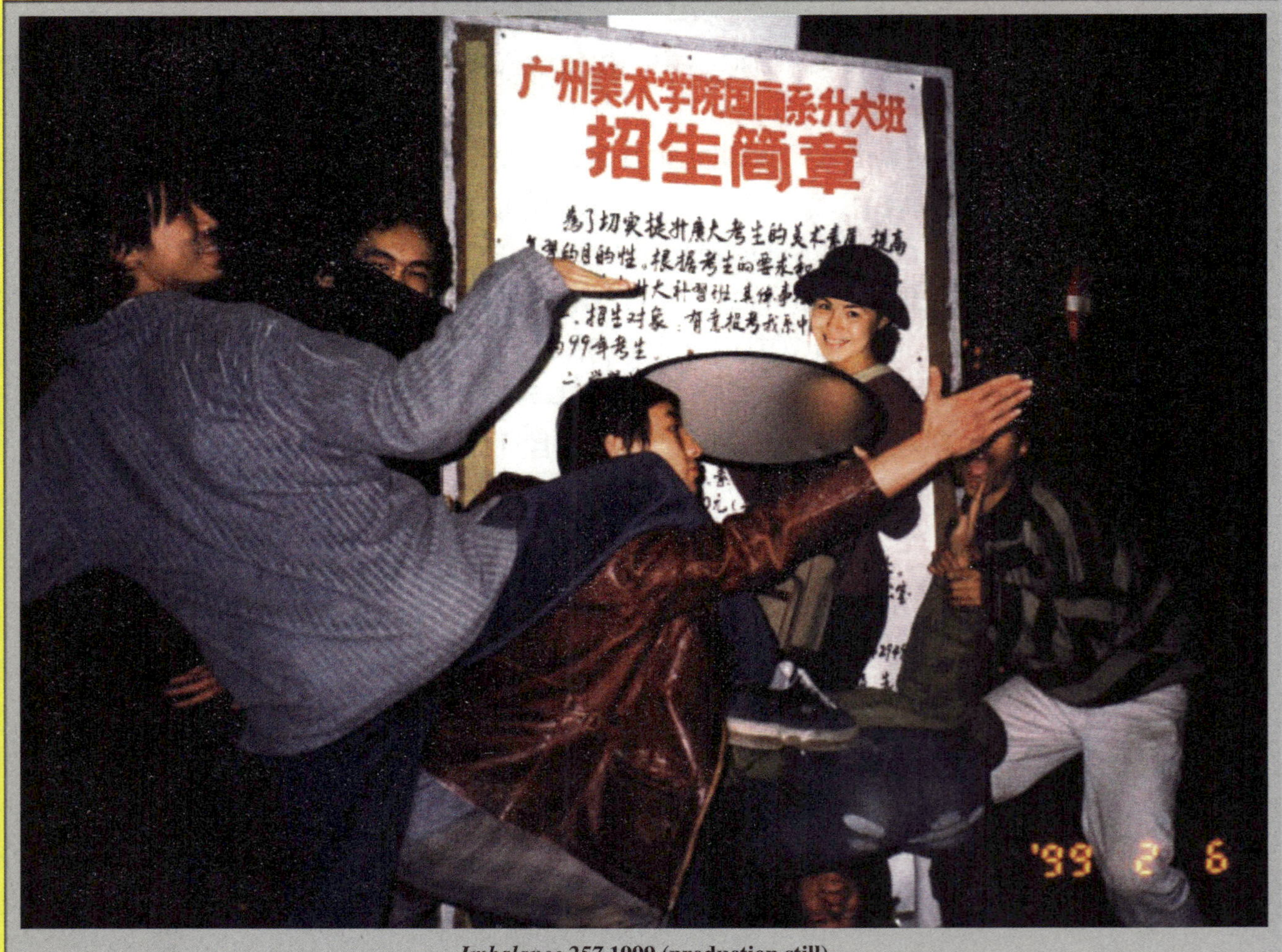

Imbalance 257 1999 (production still)

[1] Cao Fei, 'Cao Fei', trans Philip Tinari, *Artforum*, New York, 2009, artforum.com/features/cao-fei-2-190348, accessed 25 Jul 2024

Background: Celebrity stickers from the 1990s, from Cao Fei's collection

C:/

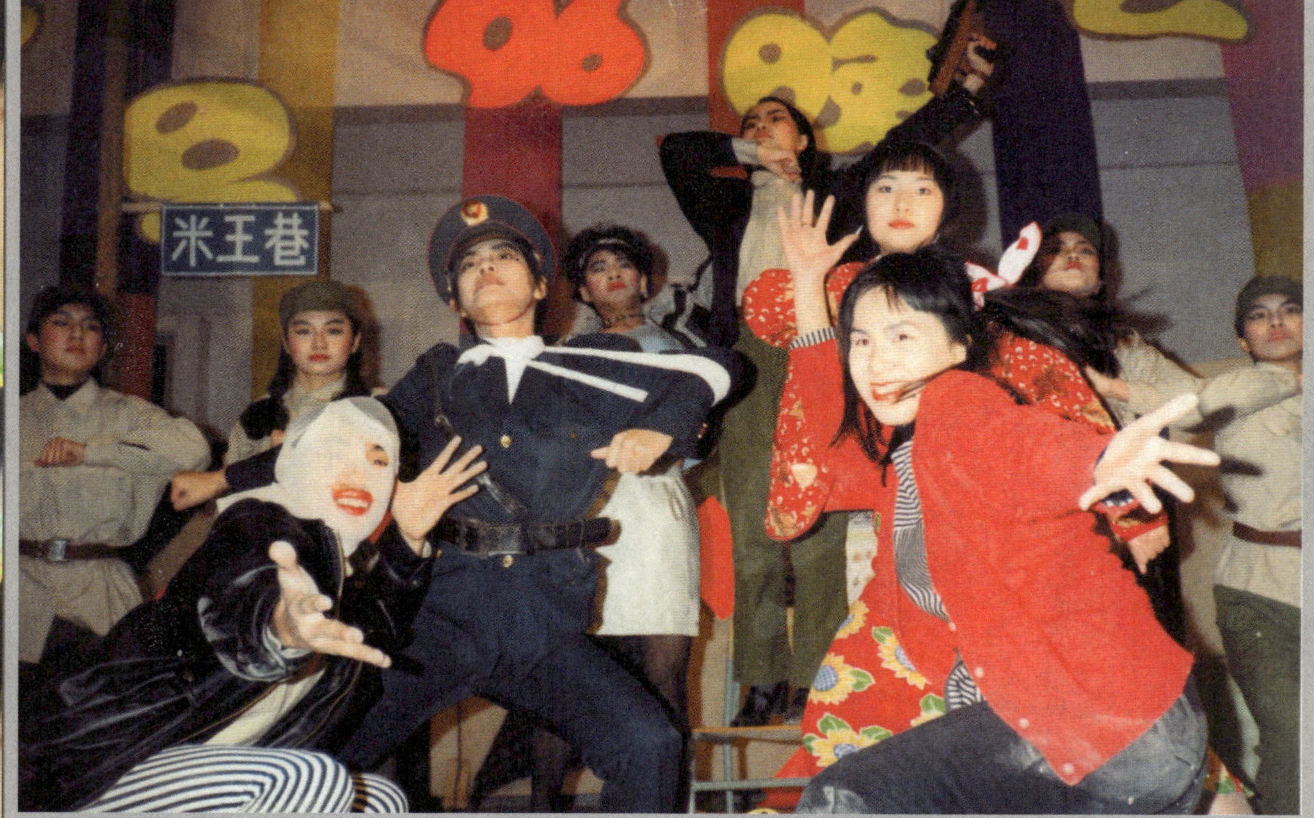

The little spark 1995 (production still)

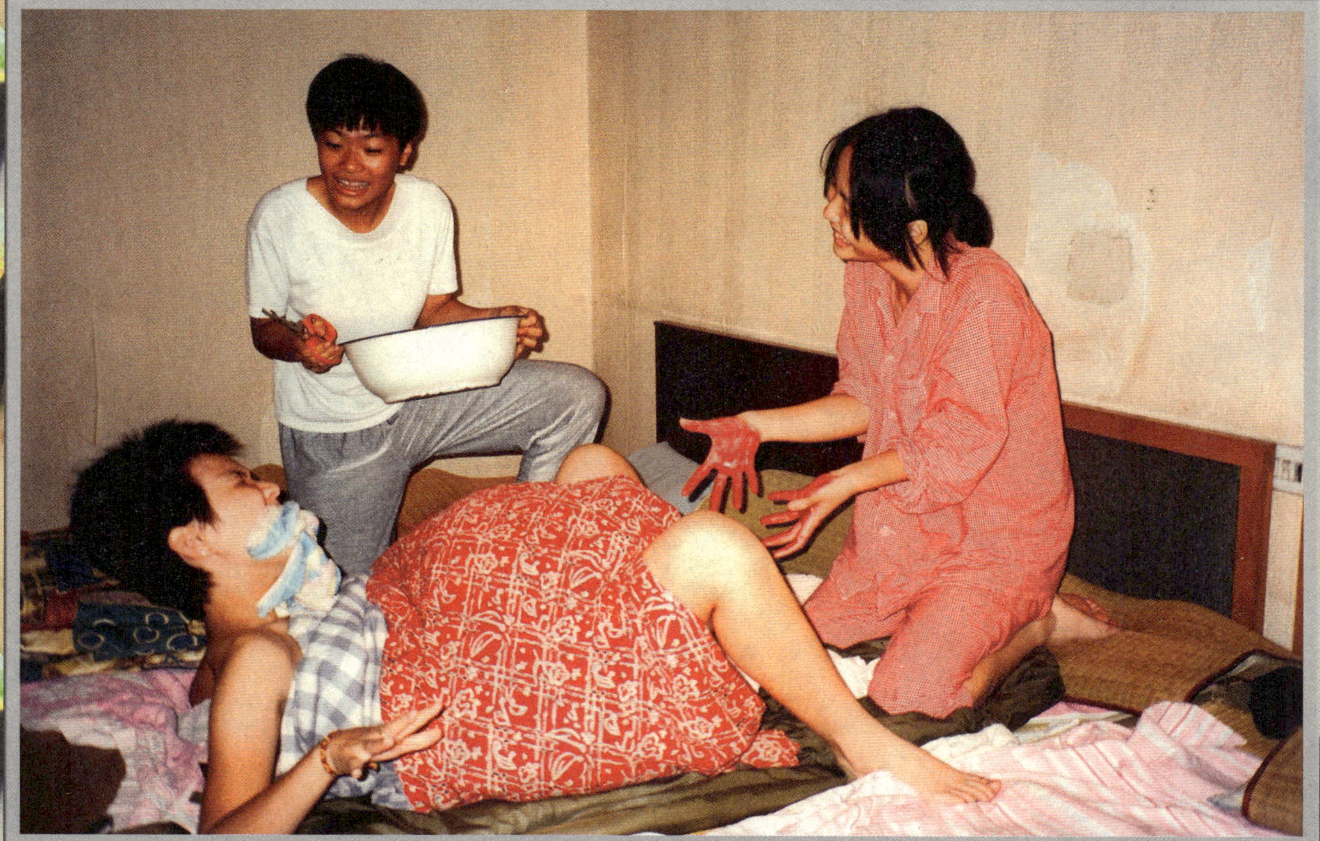

Deliver 1996 (production still)

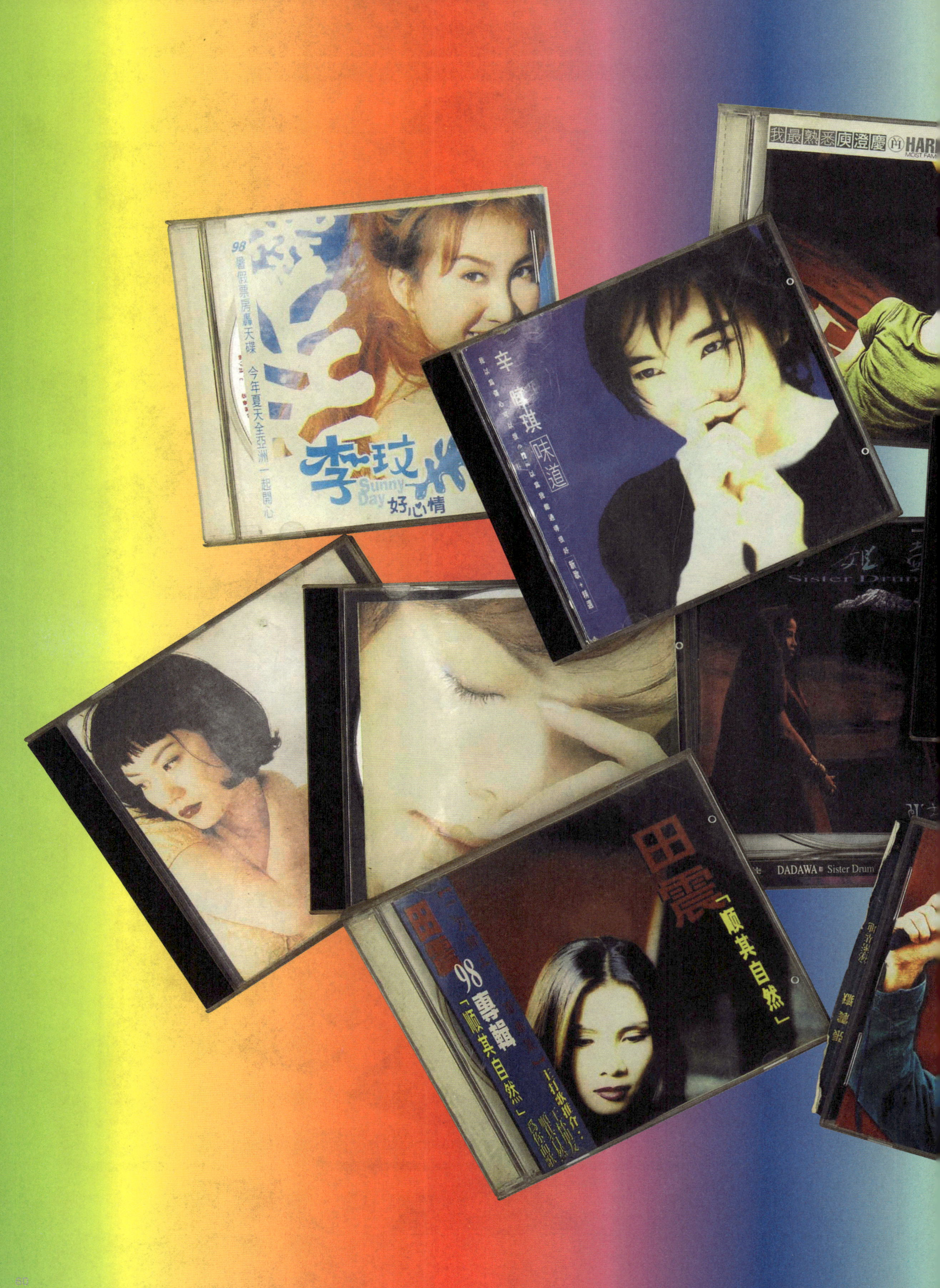
我最熟悉庾澄慶
98
暑假票房轟天碟
今年夏天全亞洲一起開心
李玟
Sunny Day
好心情
辛曉琪
味道
新歌＋精選
Sister Drum
DADAWA
Sister Drum
田震
「順其自然」
98
專輯
「順其自然」

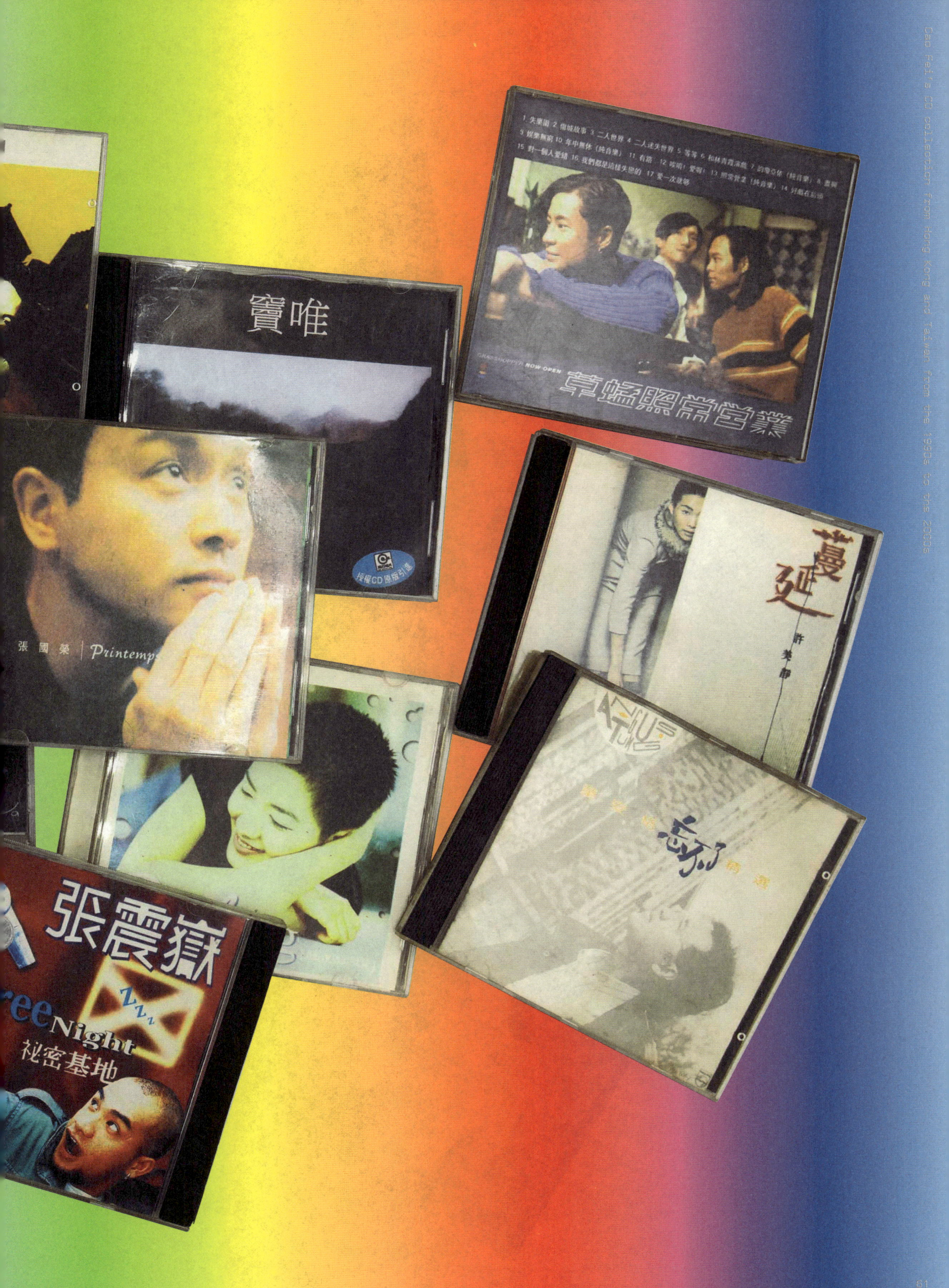

Cao Fei's CD collection from Hong Kong and Taiwan from the 1990s to the 2000s

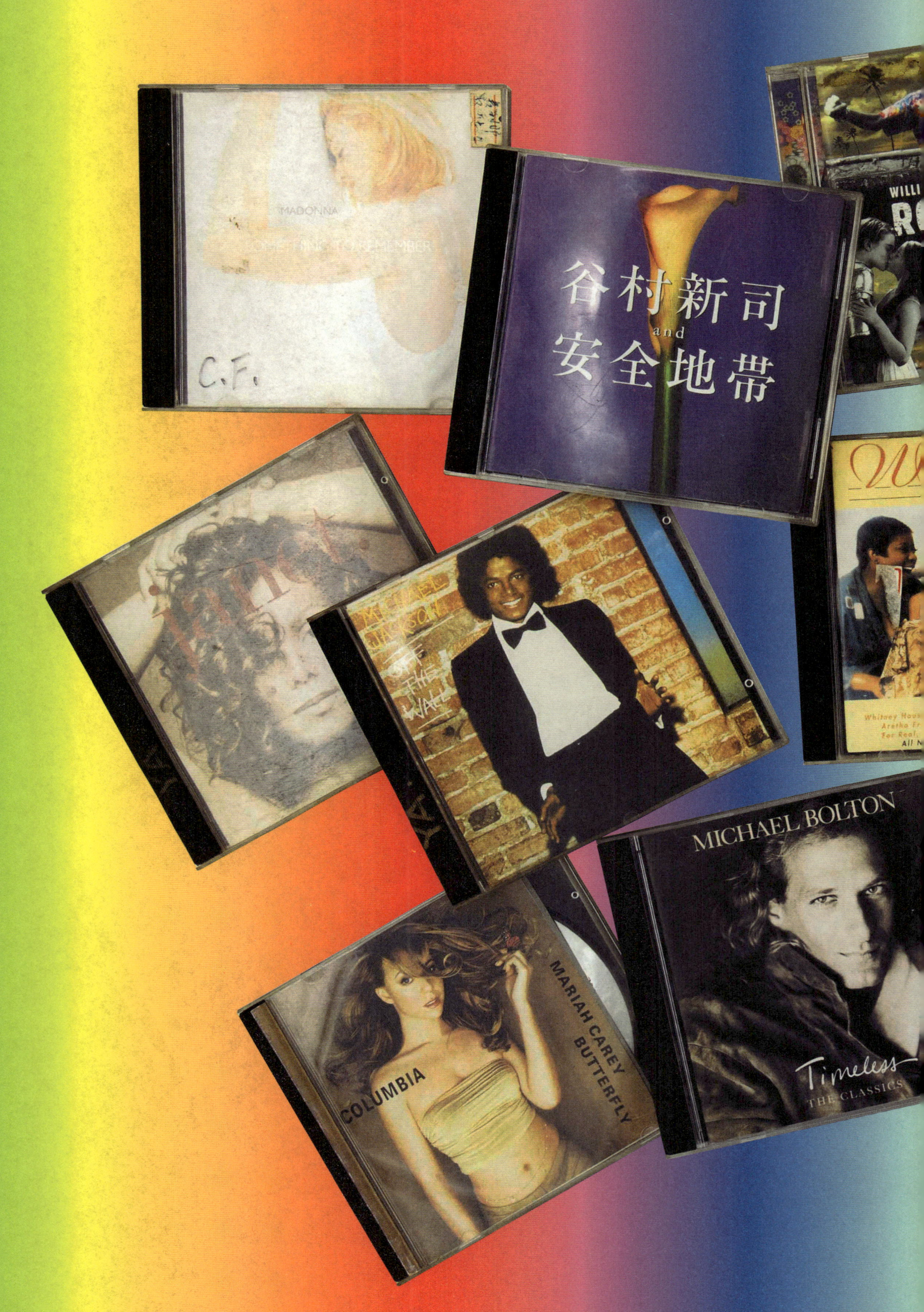
MADONNA
C.F.
谷村新司
and
安全地帯
MICHAEL JACKSON
OFF THE WALL
MICHAEL BOLTON
Timeless
THE CLASSICS
MARIAH CAREY
BUTTERFLY
COLUMBIA

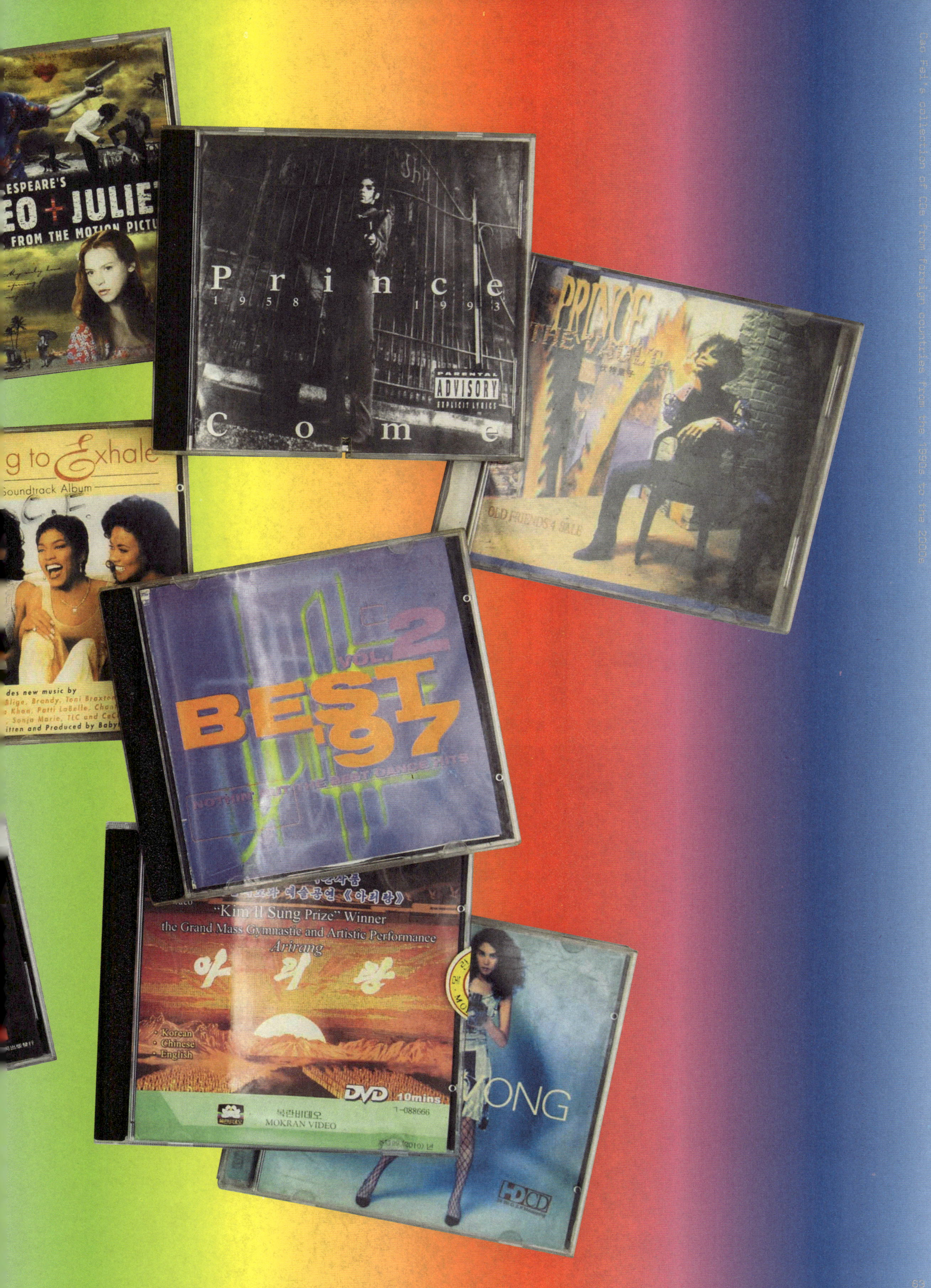

Gao Fei's collection of CDs from foreign countries from the 1990s to the 2000s

C:/

SELECTE

WORKS

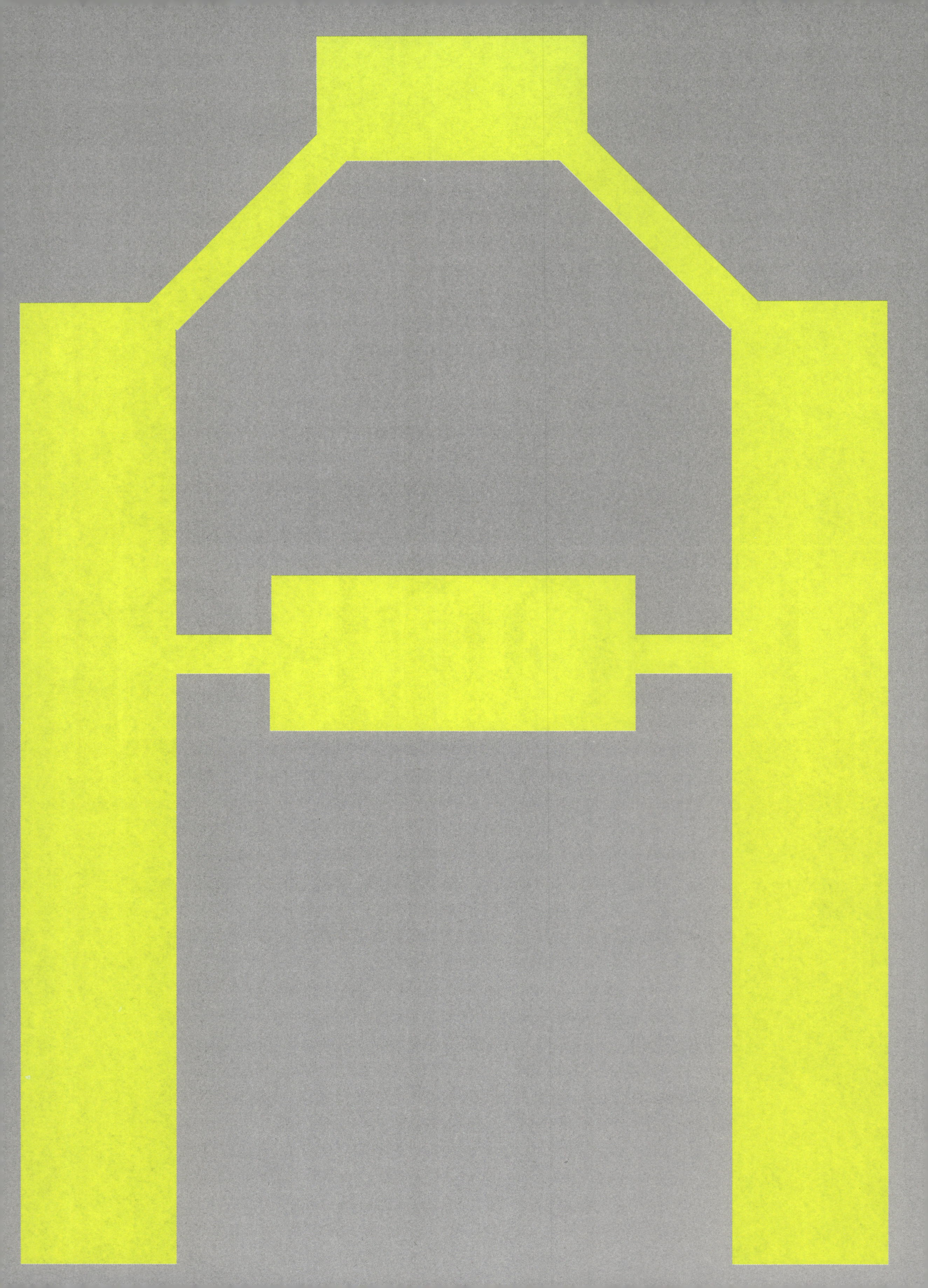

1 COS PLAYERS 2004 角色

2 UN-COS PLAYERS 2006 非角色

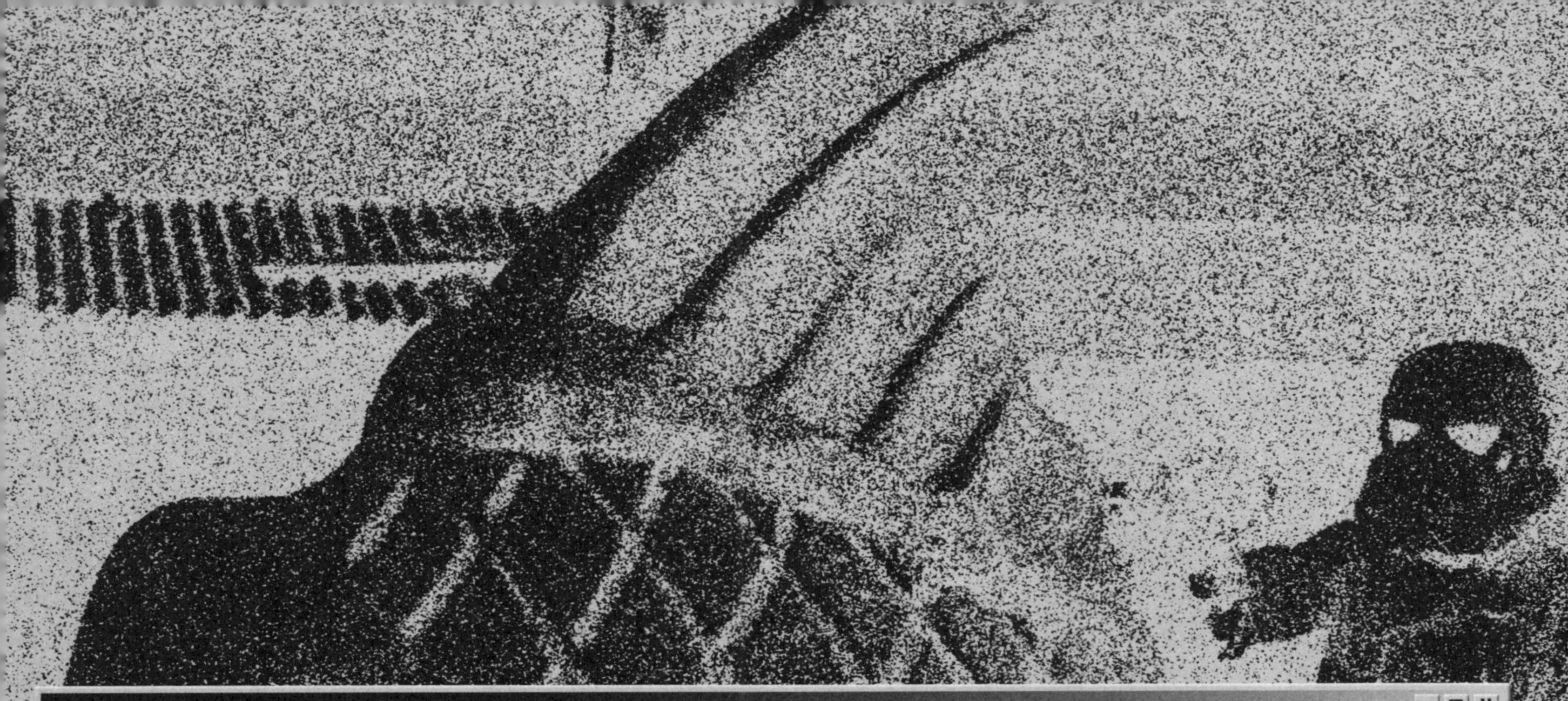

A[1-2]: Cosplayers / Un-Cosplayers

In fantastic tableaux, Cao portrays the escapades of one of the earliest generations of Chinese youth raised on the internet. Cloaked in gold capes, plumed wings and pixie ears, young cosplayers cavort as Japanese anime and manga characters. These avatars of a new subculture appear against the equally surreal backdrop of rapidly urbanising Guangzhou. As a generation playacts wild digital identities, a new city is being dreamt up: virtual and physical dreamworlds converge. Genies and fairy princesses run amok in half-built McMansions as empty underpasses and fields are encroached upon by high-rises. *Cosplayers* celebrates freewheeling self-invention while also counting its costs. These landscapes are vanishing. The grasslands where two characters release black balloons is now Zhujiang New Town, a sprawling central business district with luxury condos and steel skyscrapers.

Artwork specification

Cosplayers 2004
single-channel digital video, colour, sound
9:12 min, 4:3

《角色》2004
4:3 彩色有声单频影像
9分12秒

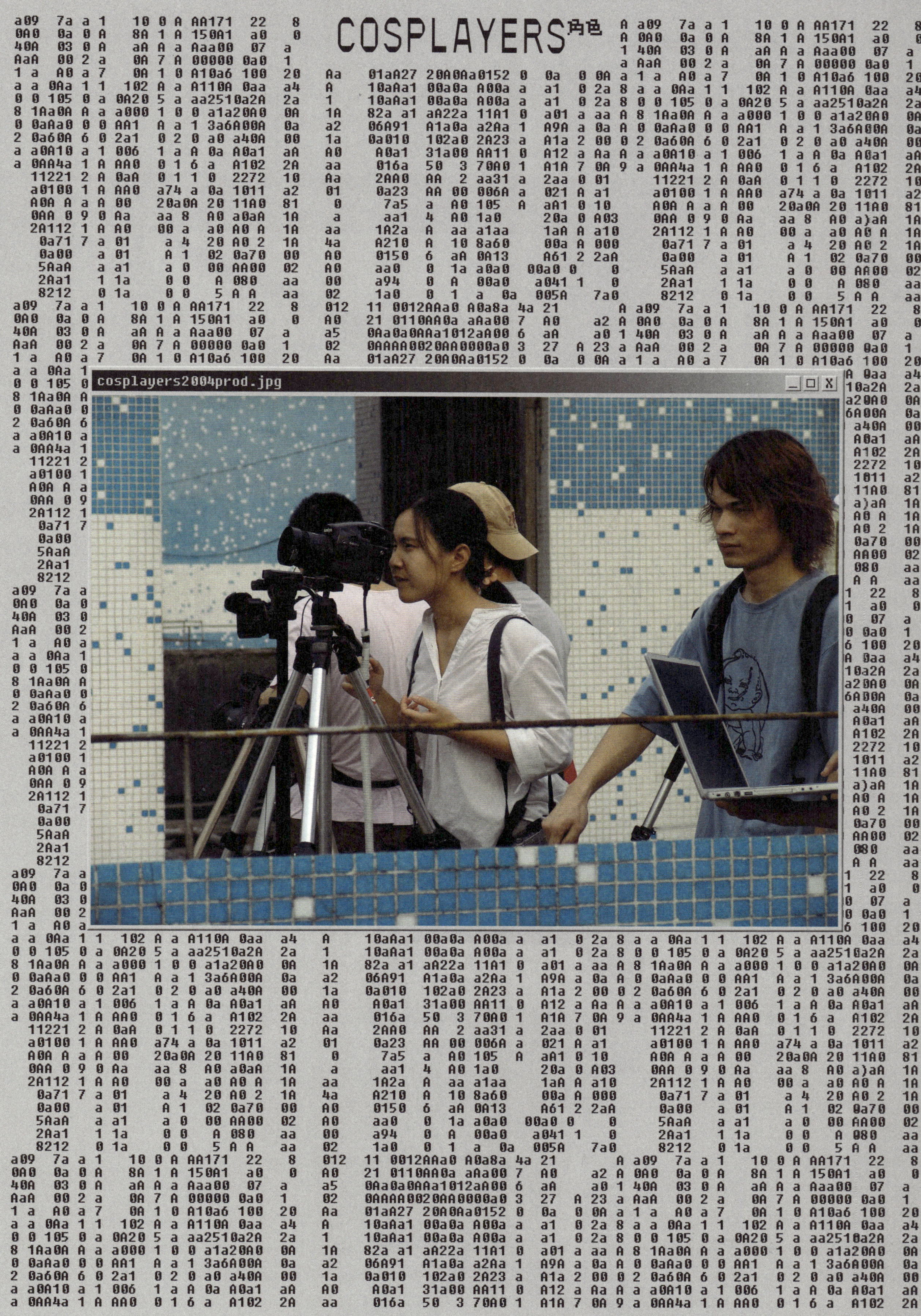
COSPLAYERS 角色
cosplayers2004prod.jpg

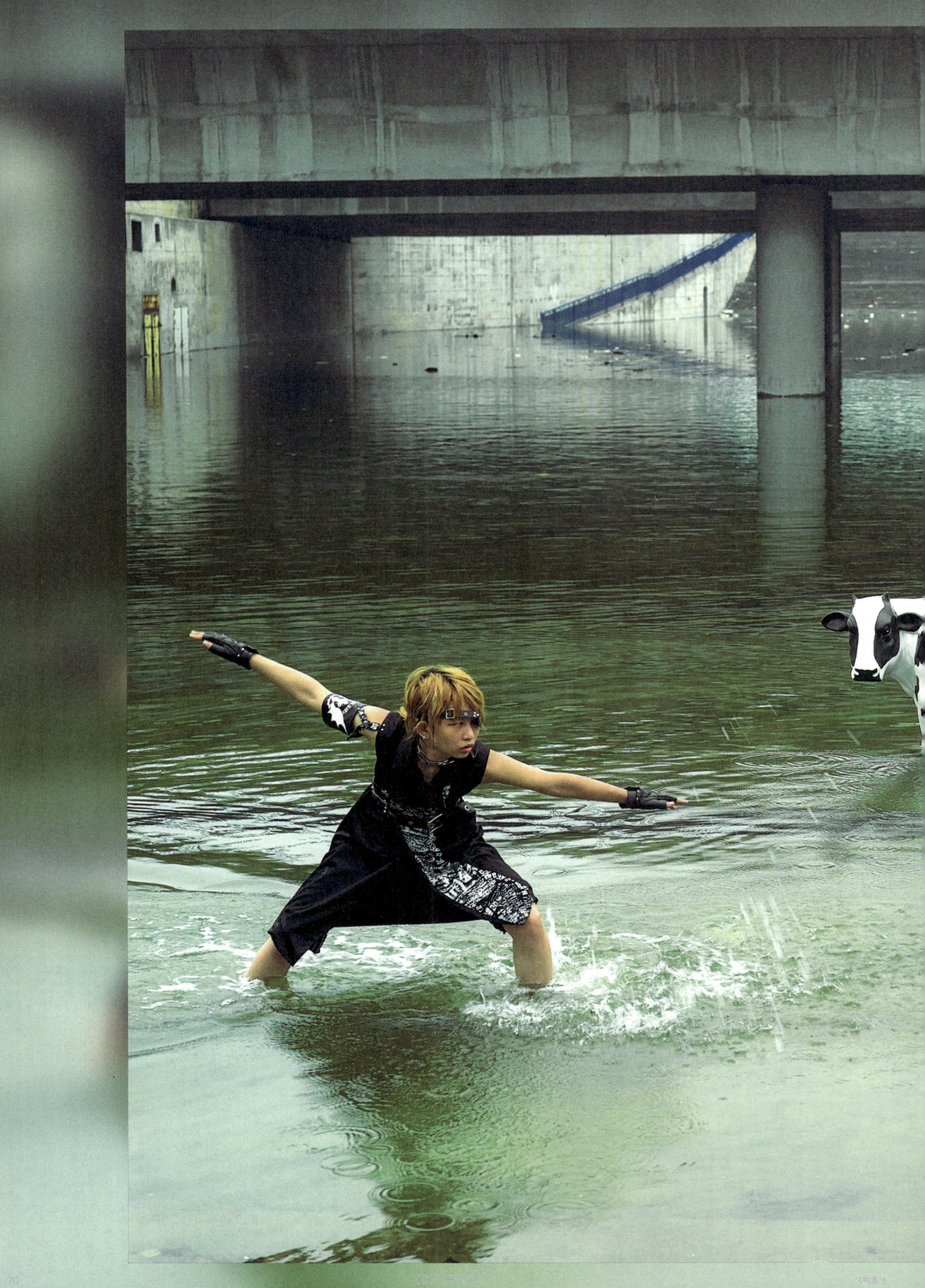

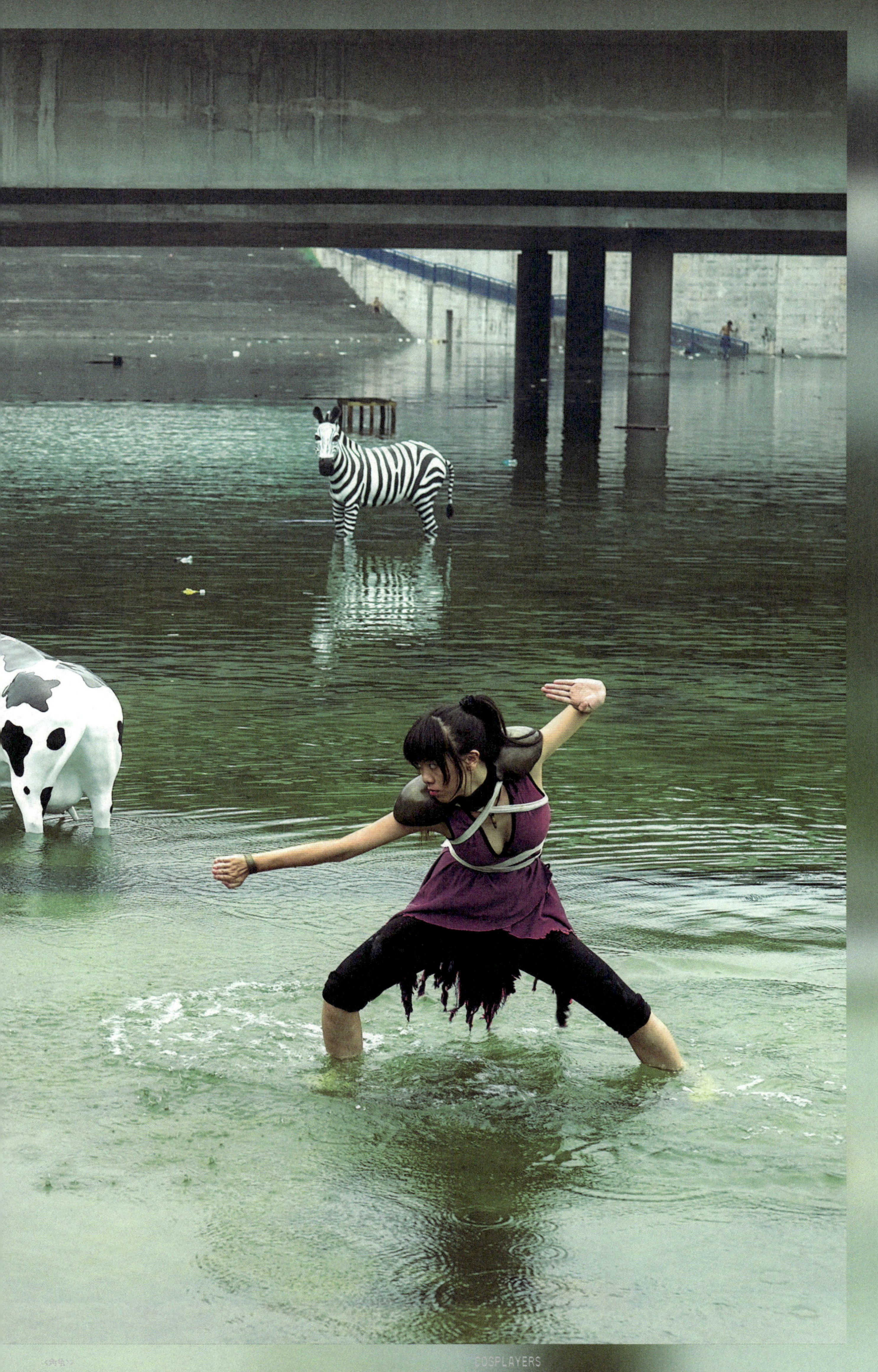

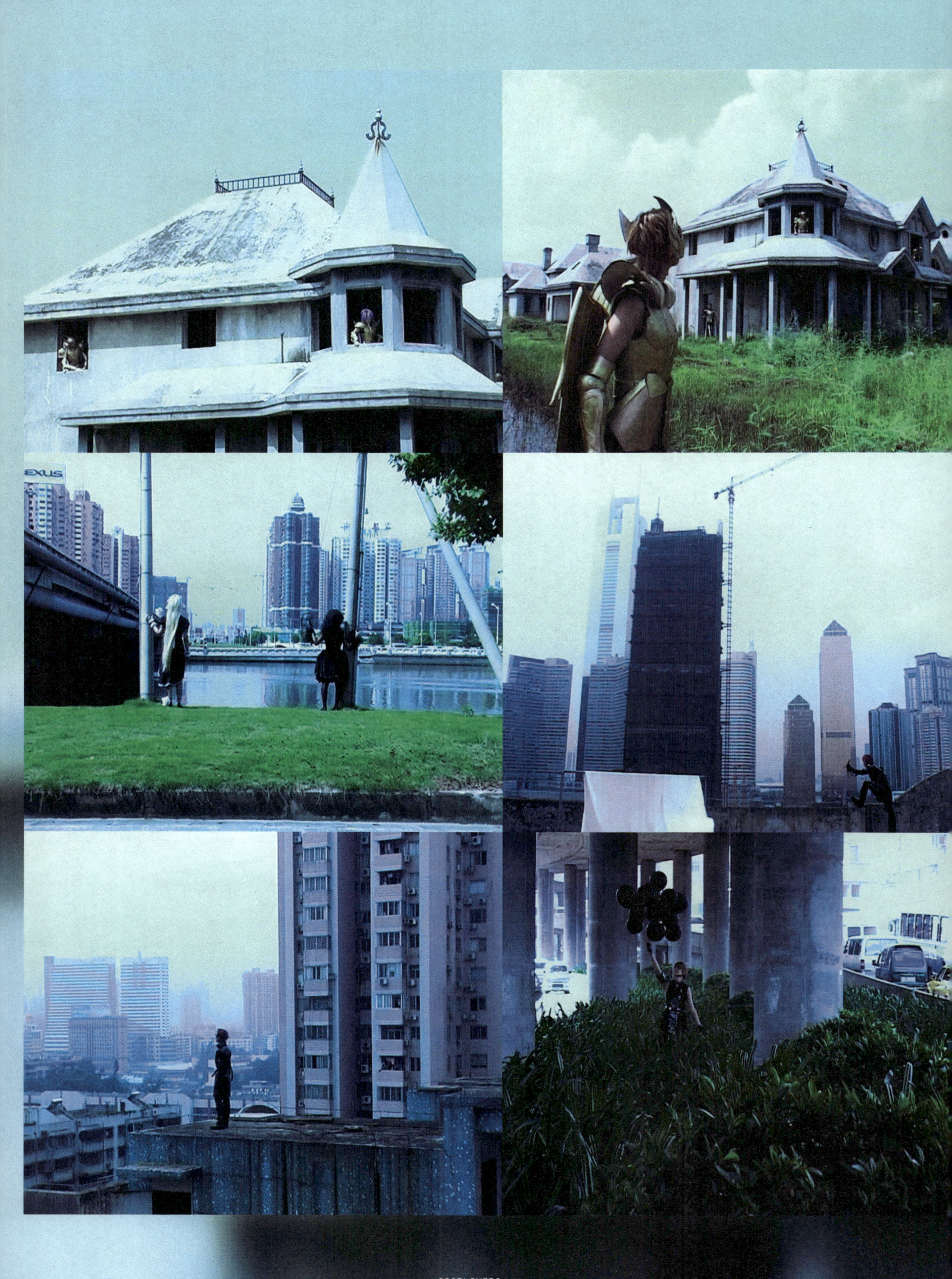

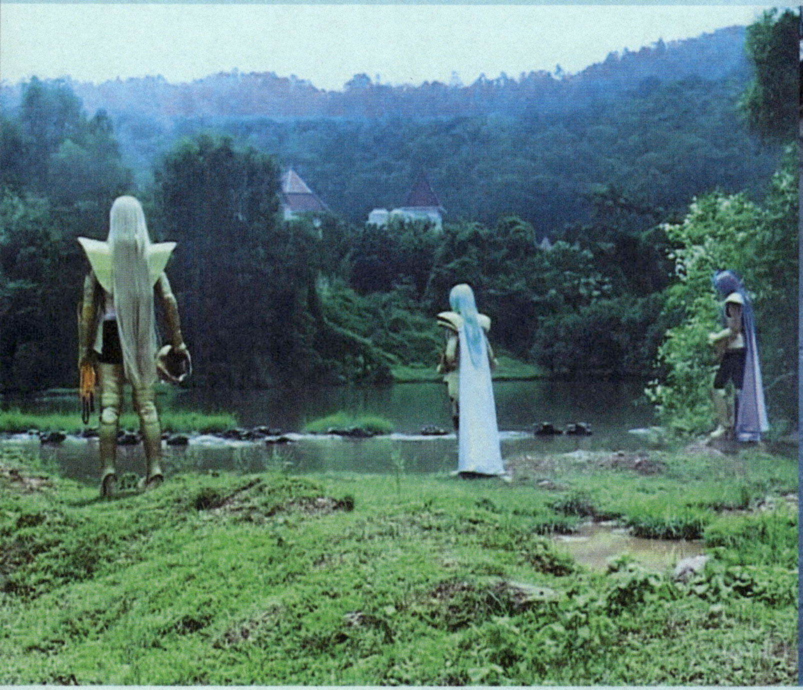

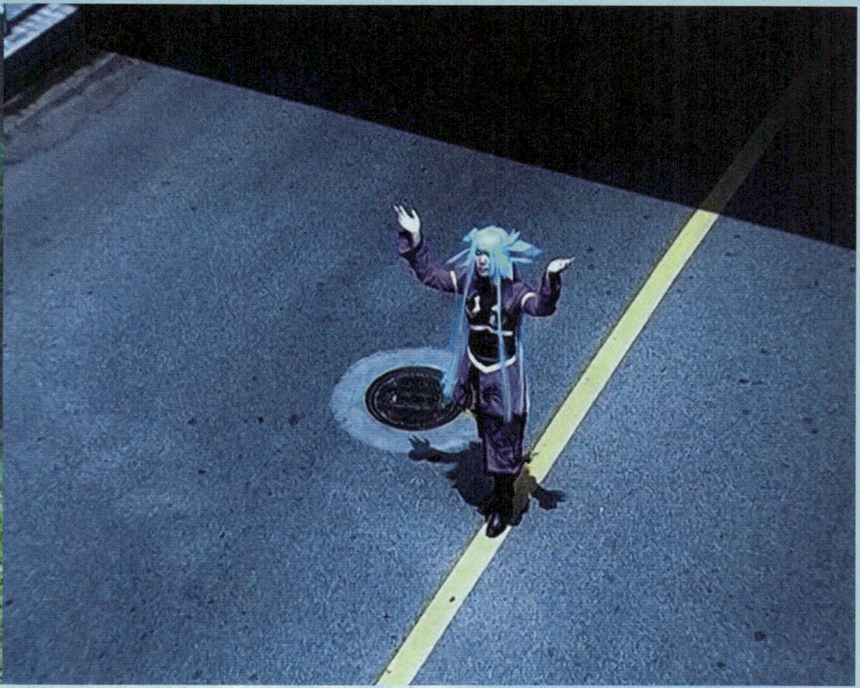

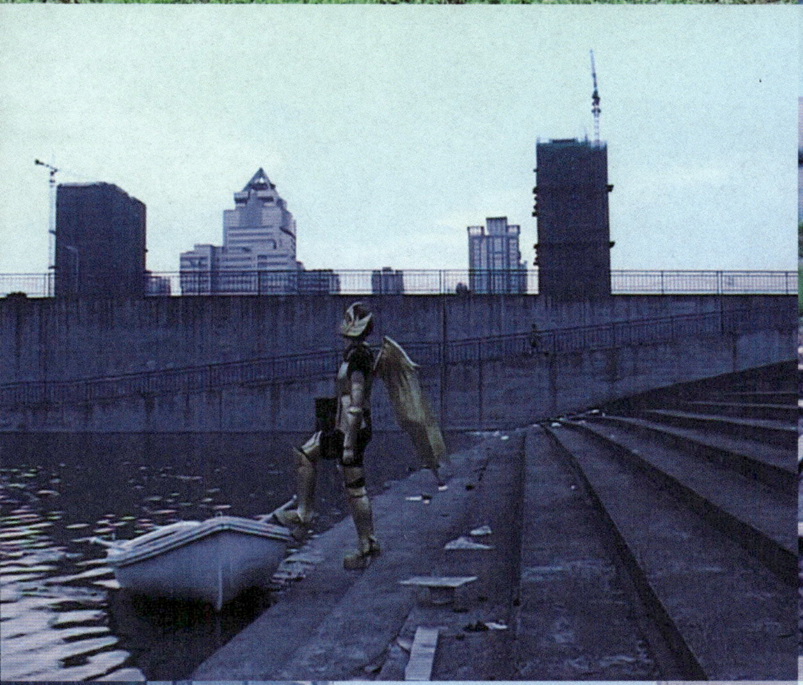

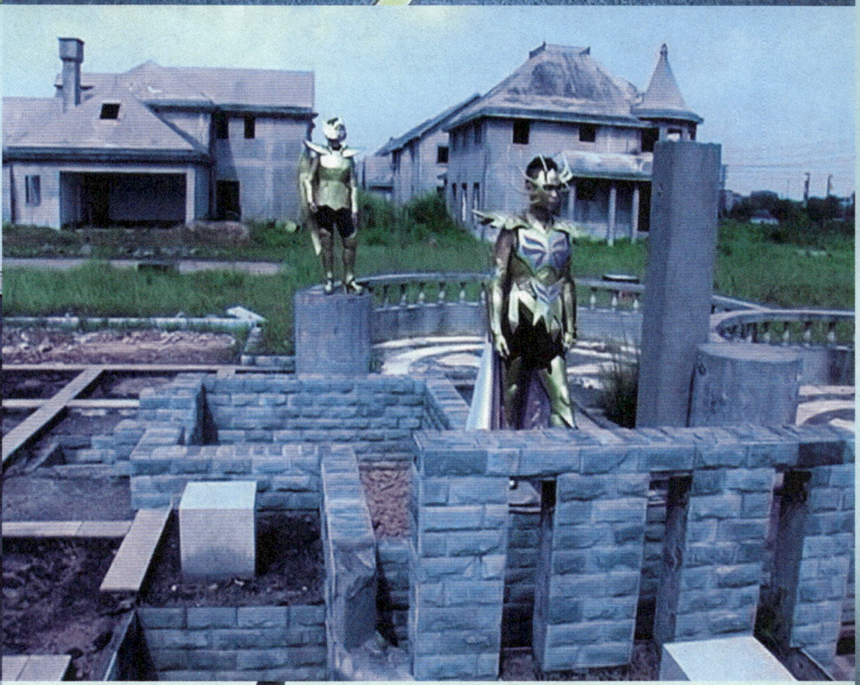

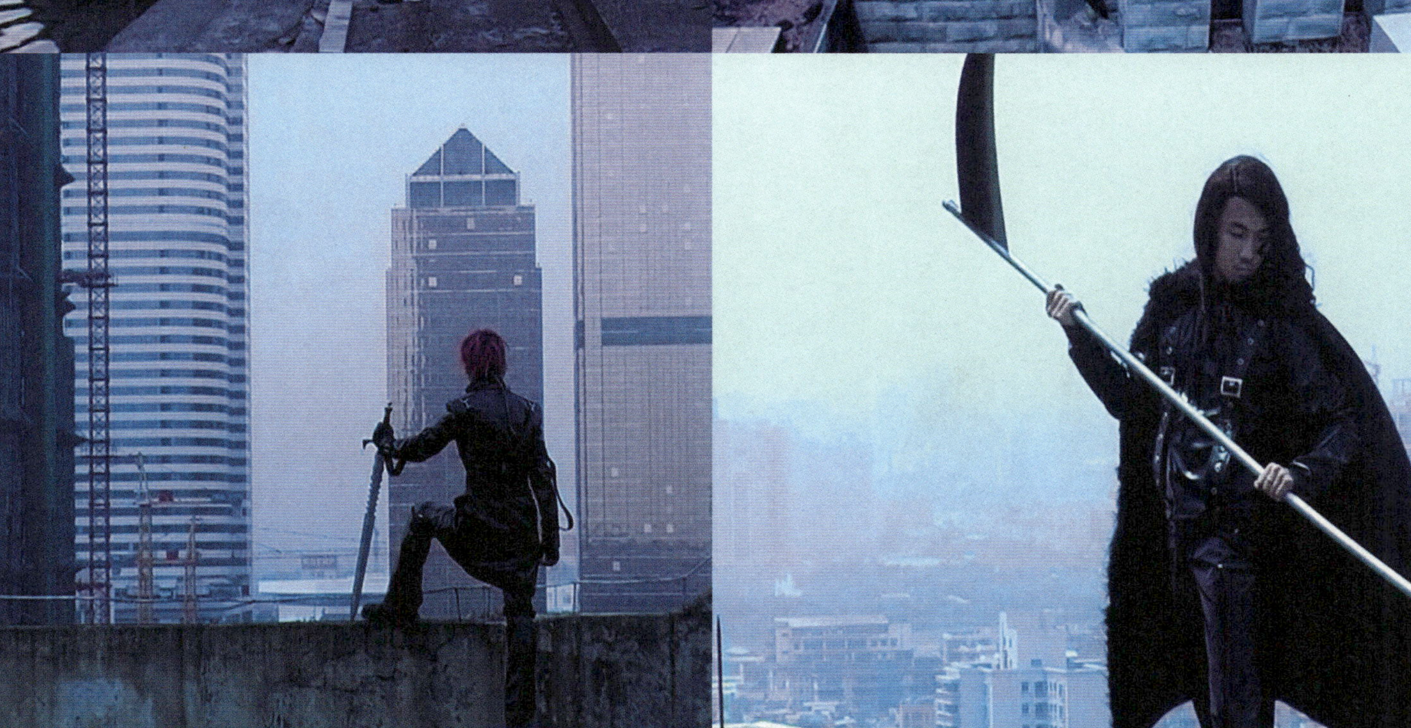

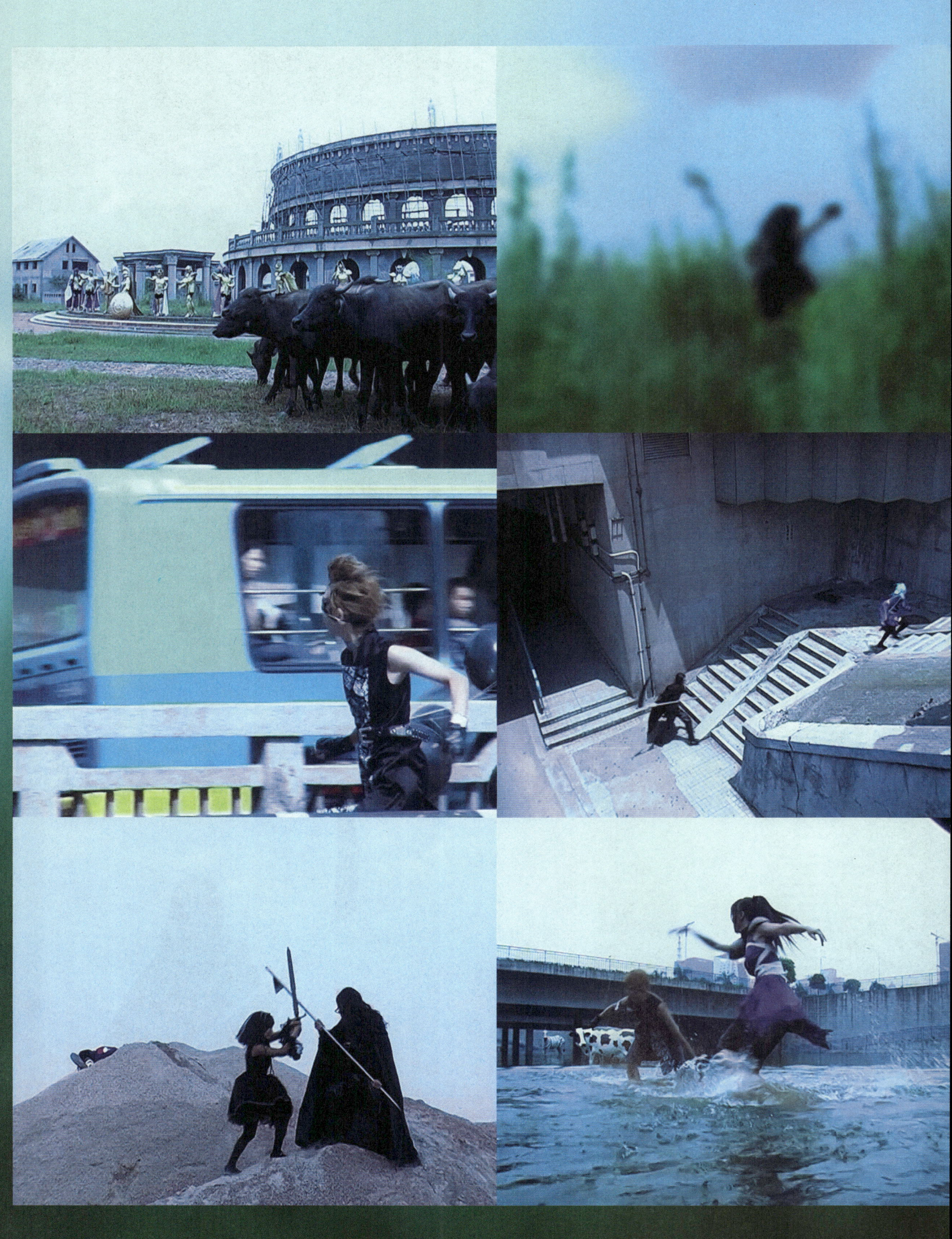

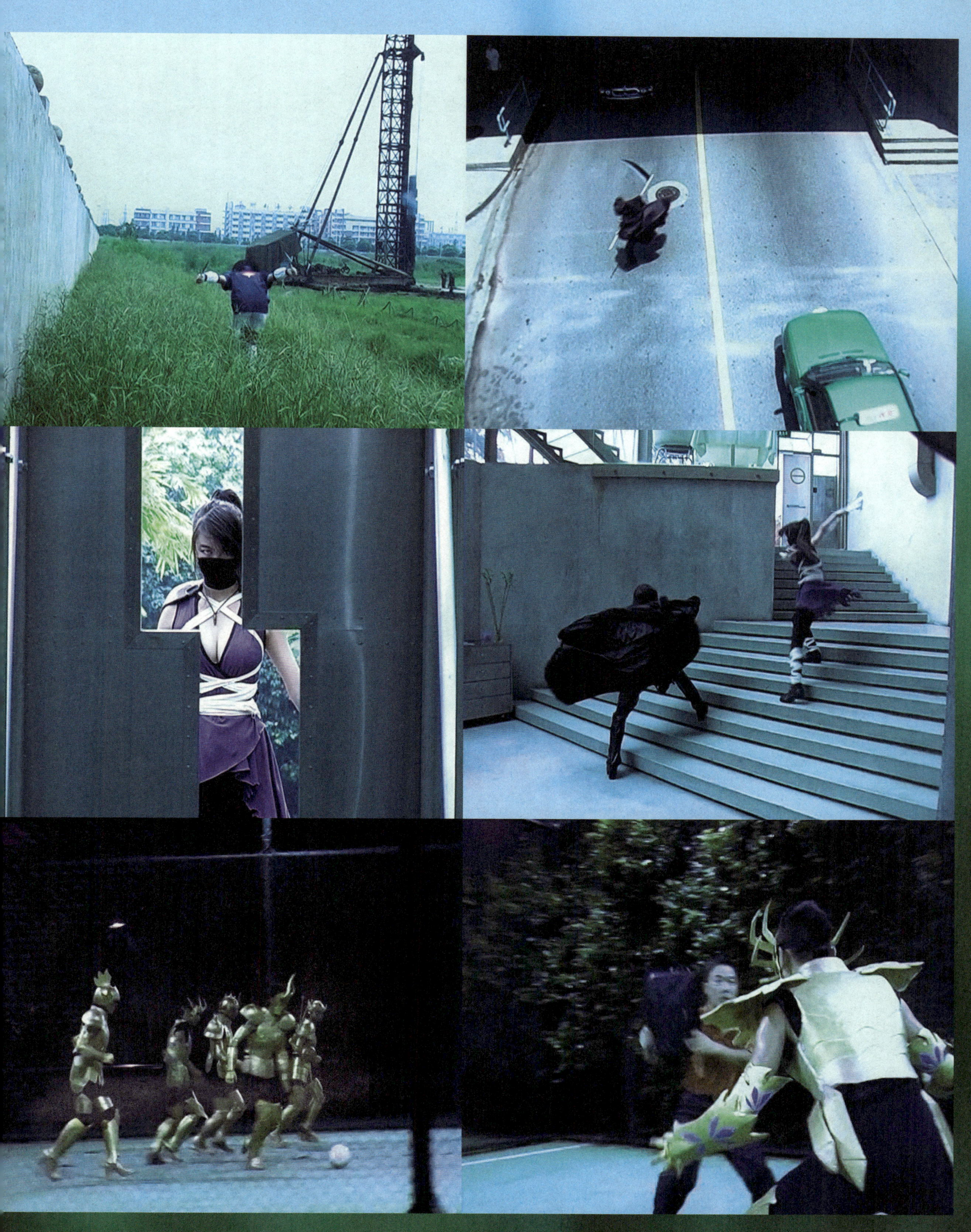

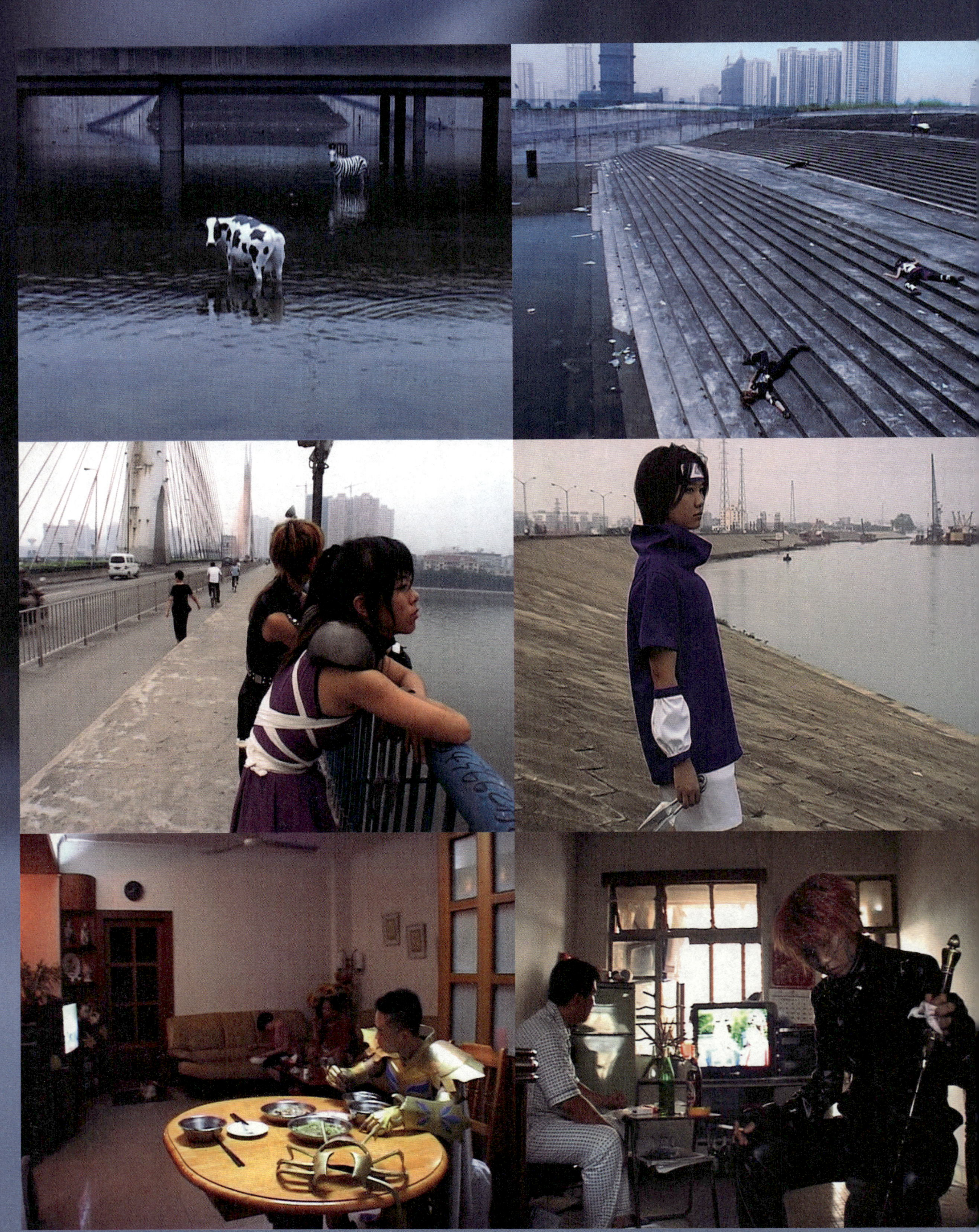

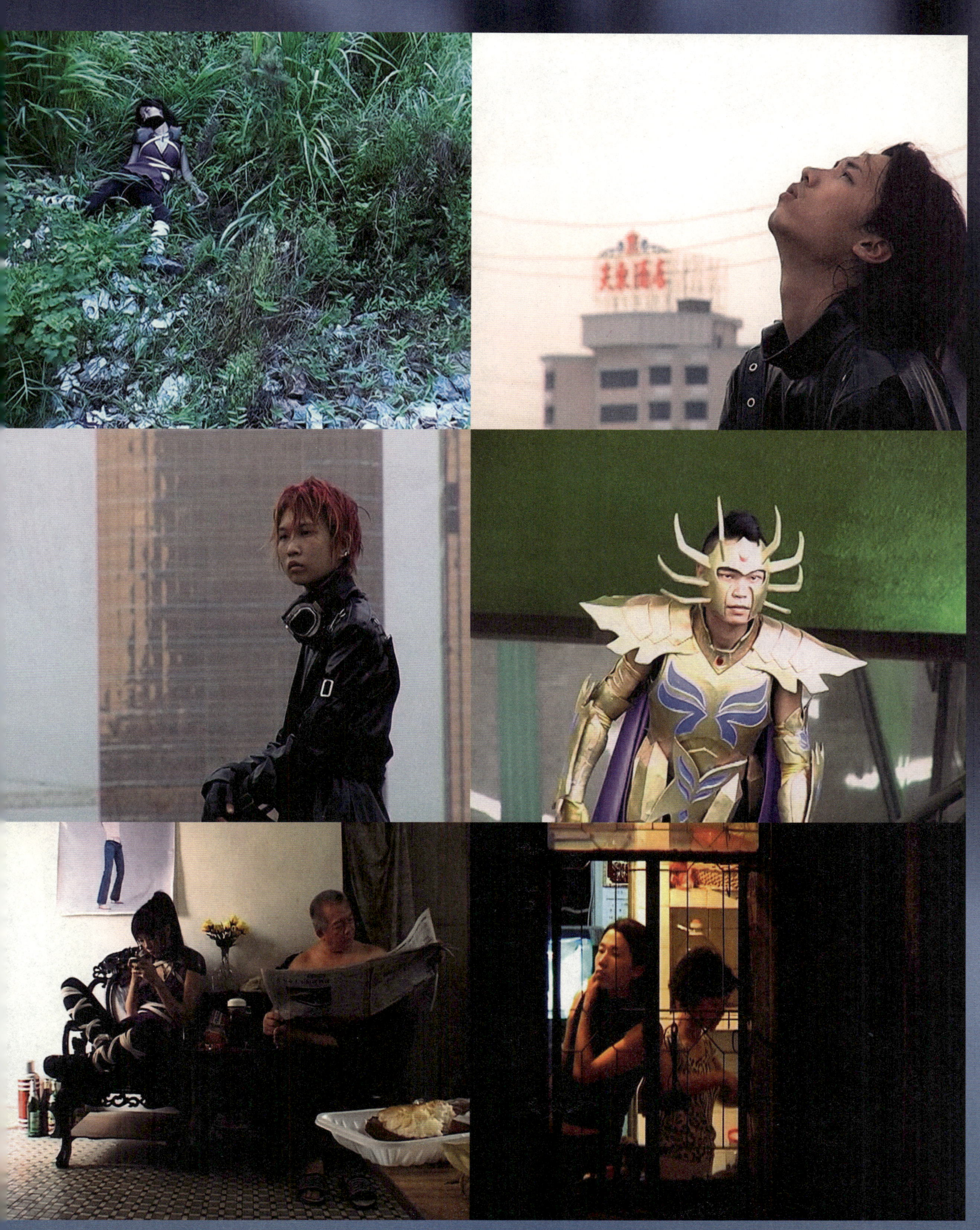

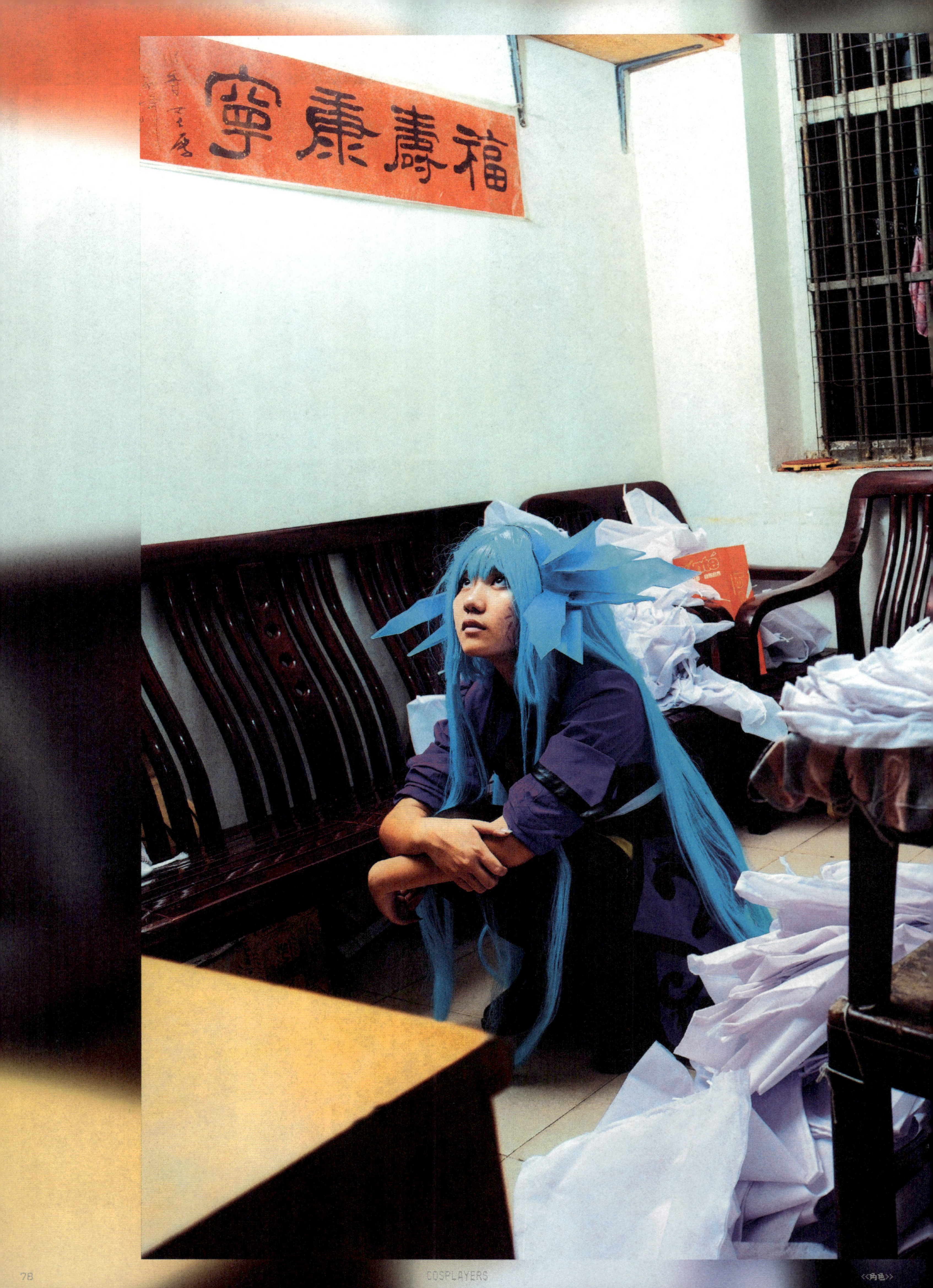
福壽康寧

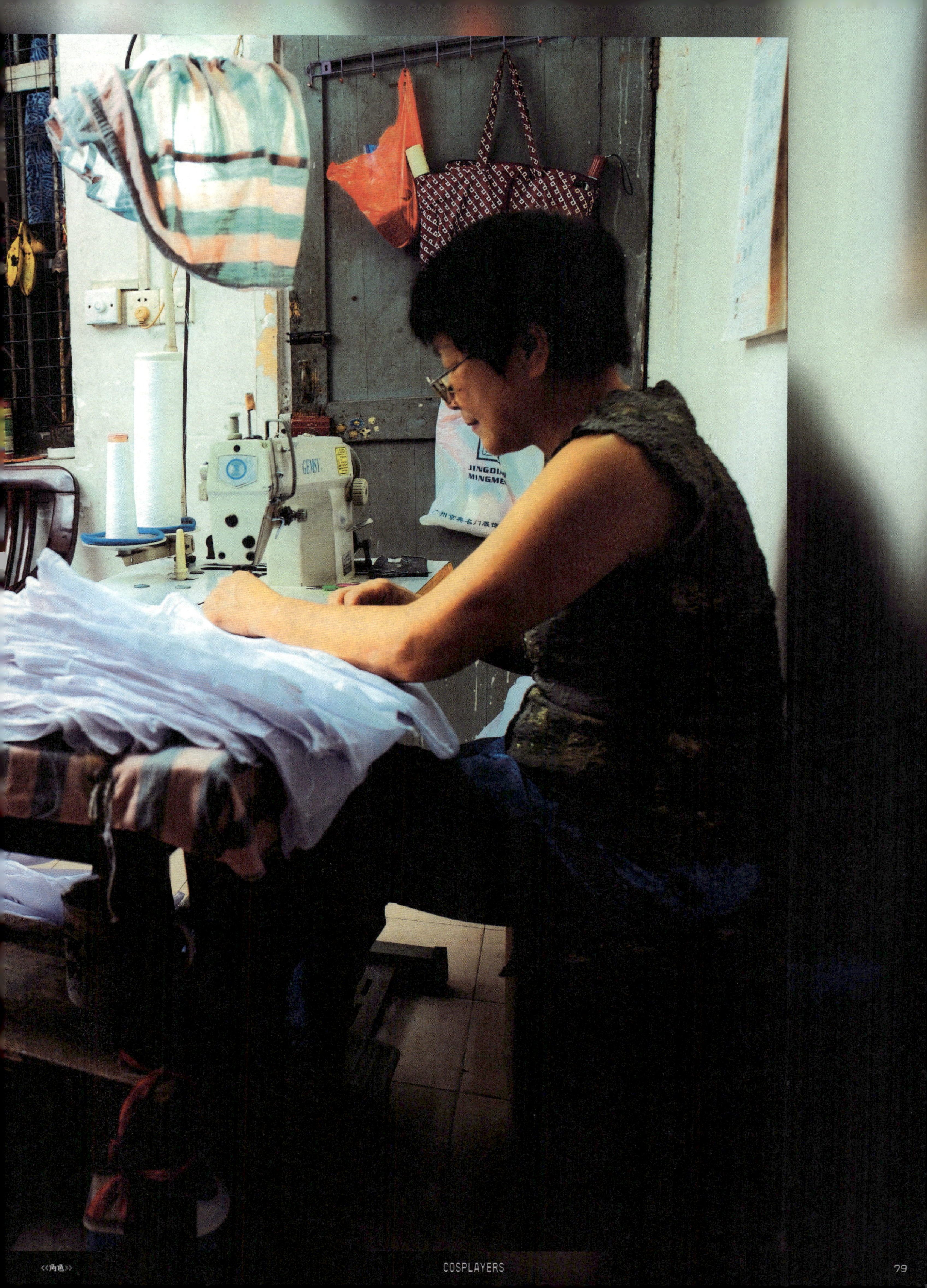
GEMSY

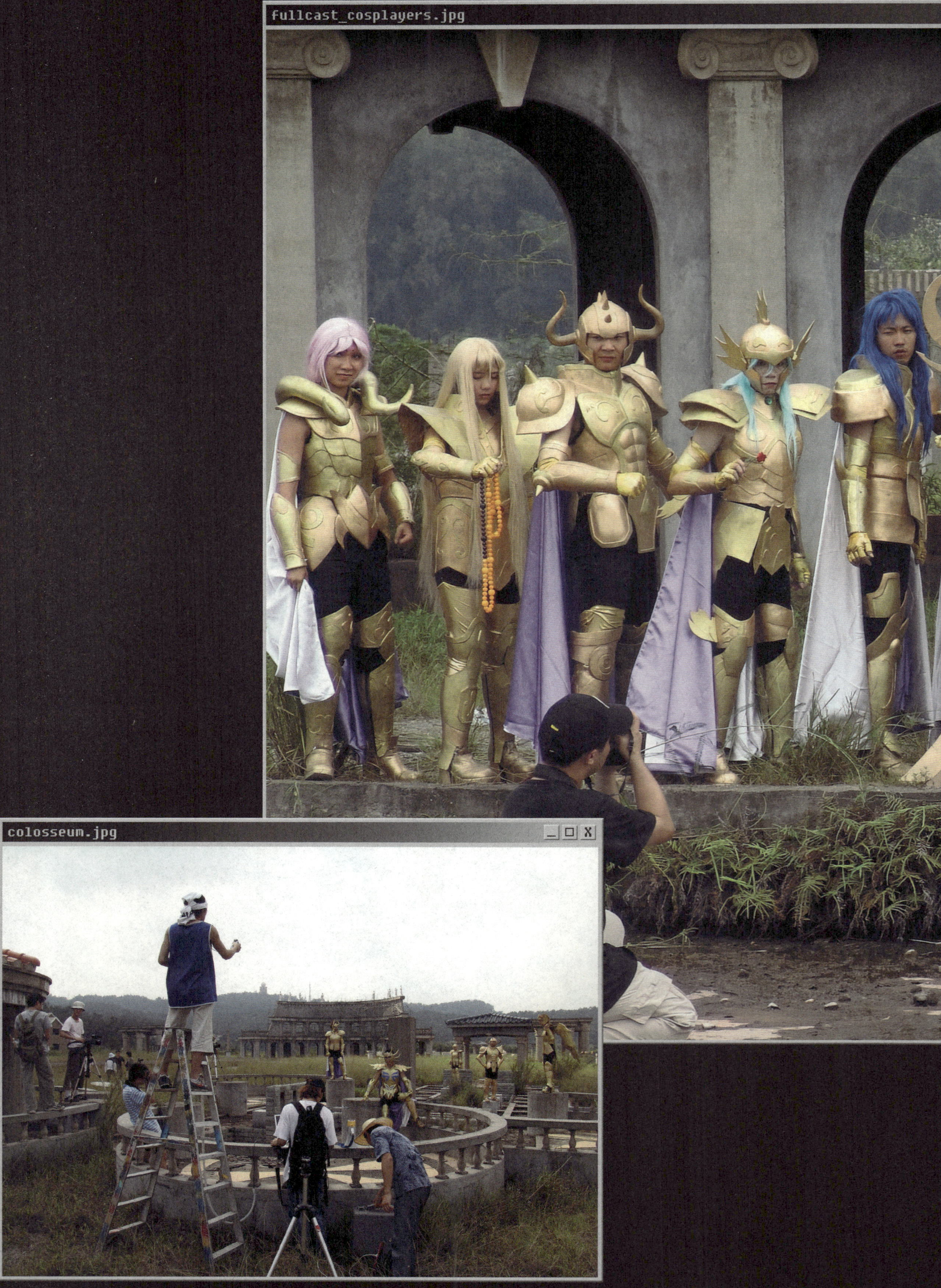
fullcast_cosplayers.jpg
colosseum.jpg

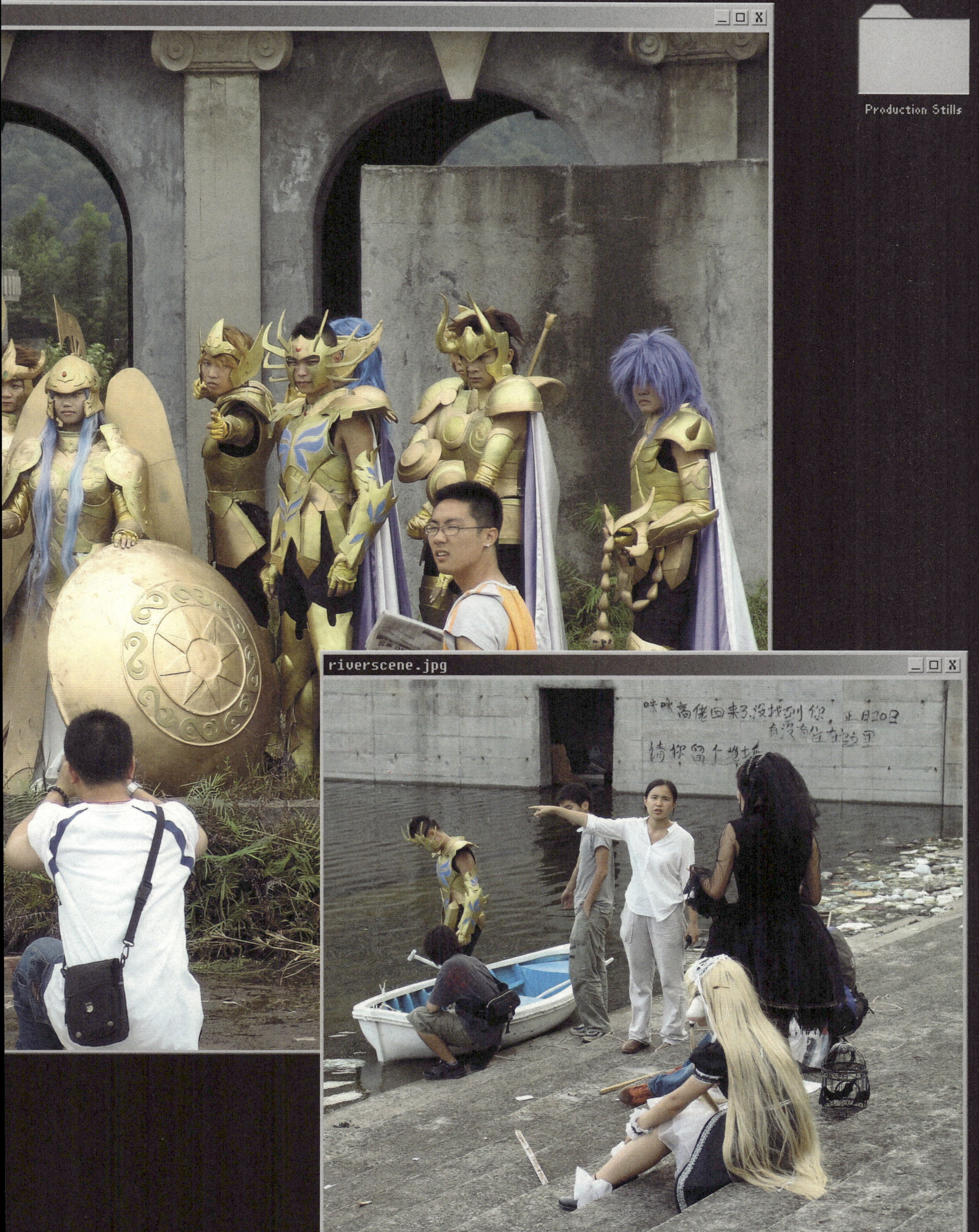
Production Stills
riverscene.jpg
咪咪高佬回来了,没找到你, 正月20日

UN-COSPLAYERS 非角色

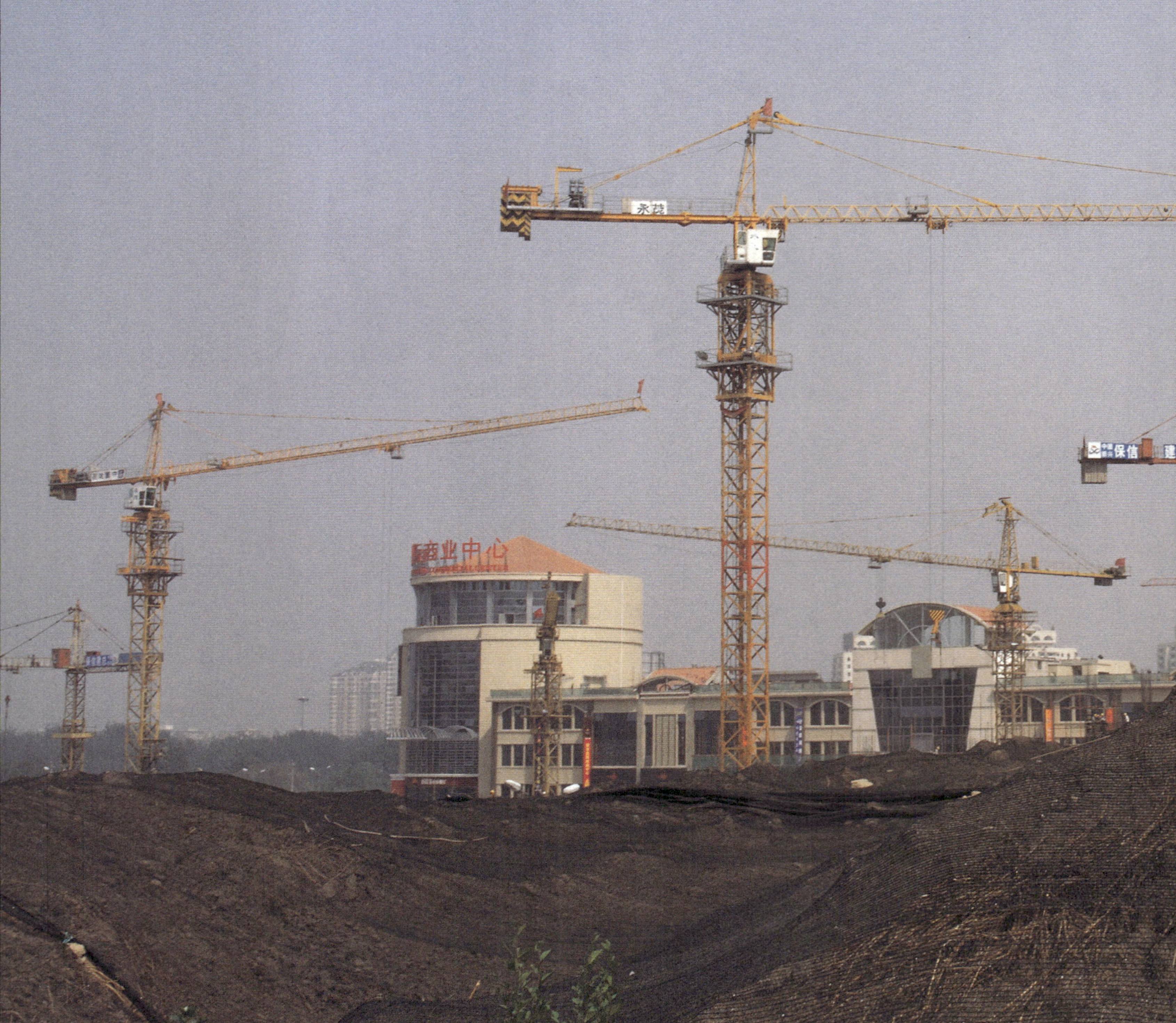

Artwork specification

Un-Cosplayers series 2006
inkjet prints on paper
dimensions variable

"非角色"系列摄影 2006
纸本艺术微喷
尺寸有别

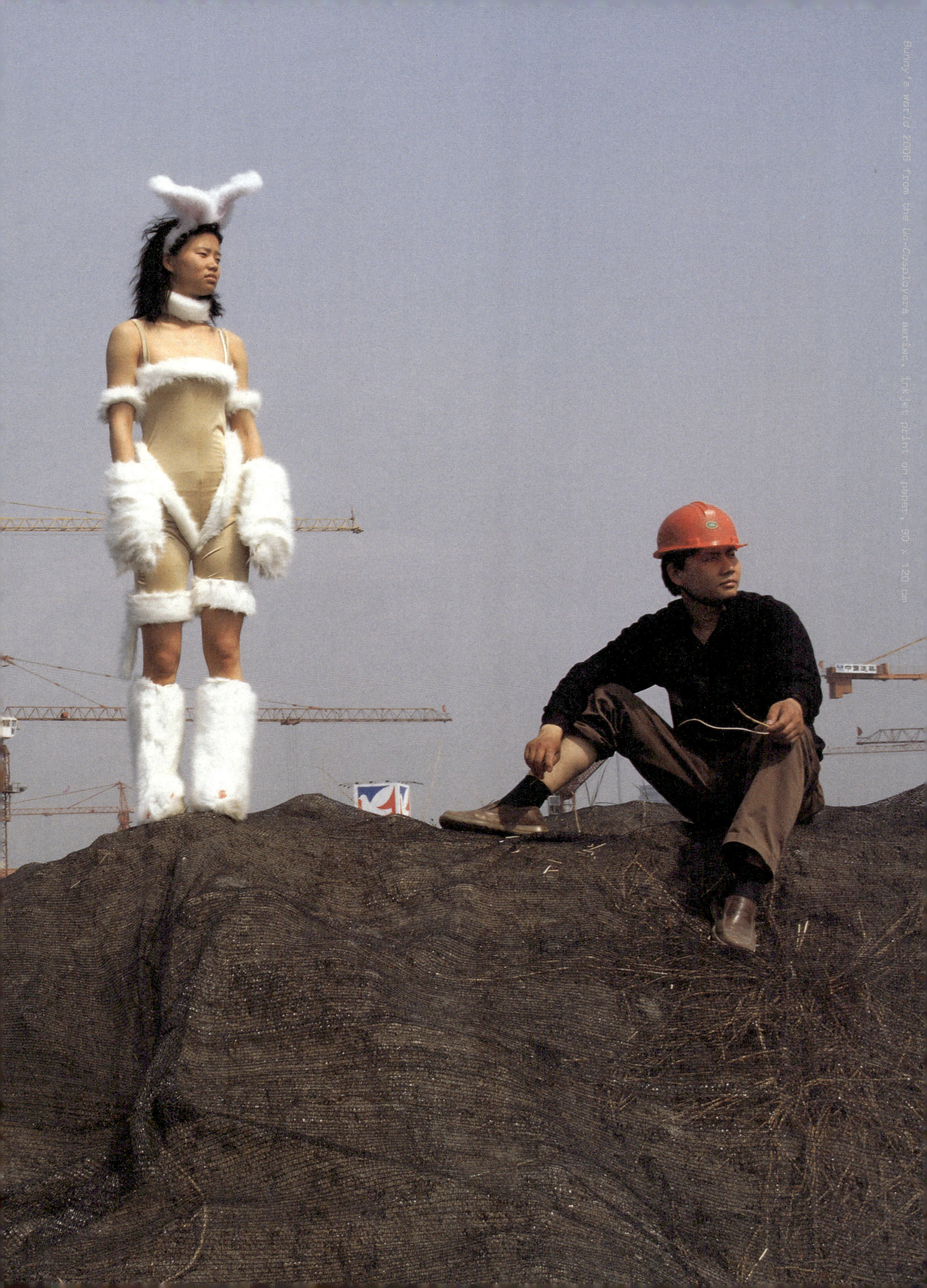

Bunny's world 2006 from the Un-Cosplayers series, inkjet print on paper, 90 x 120 cm

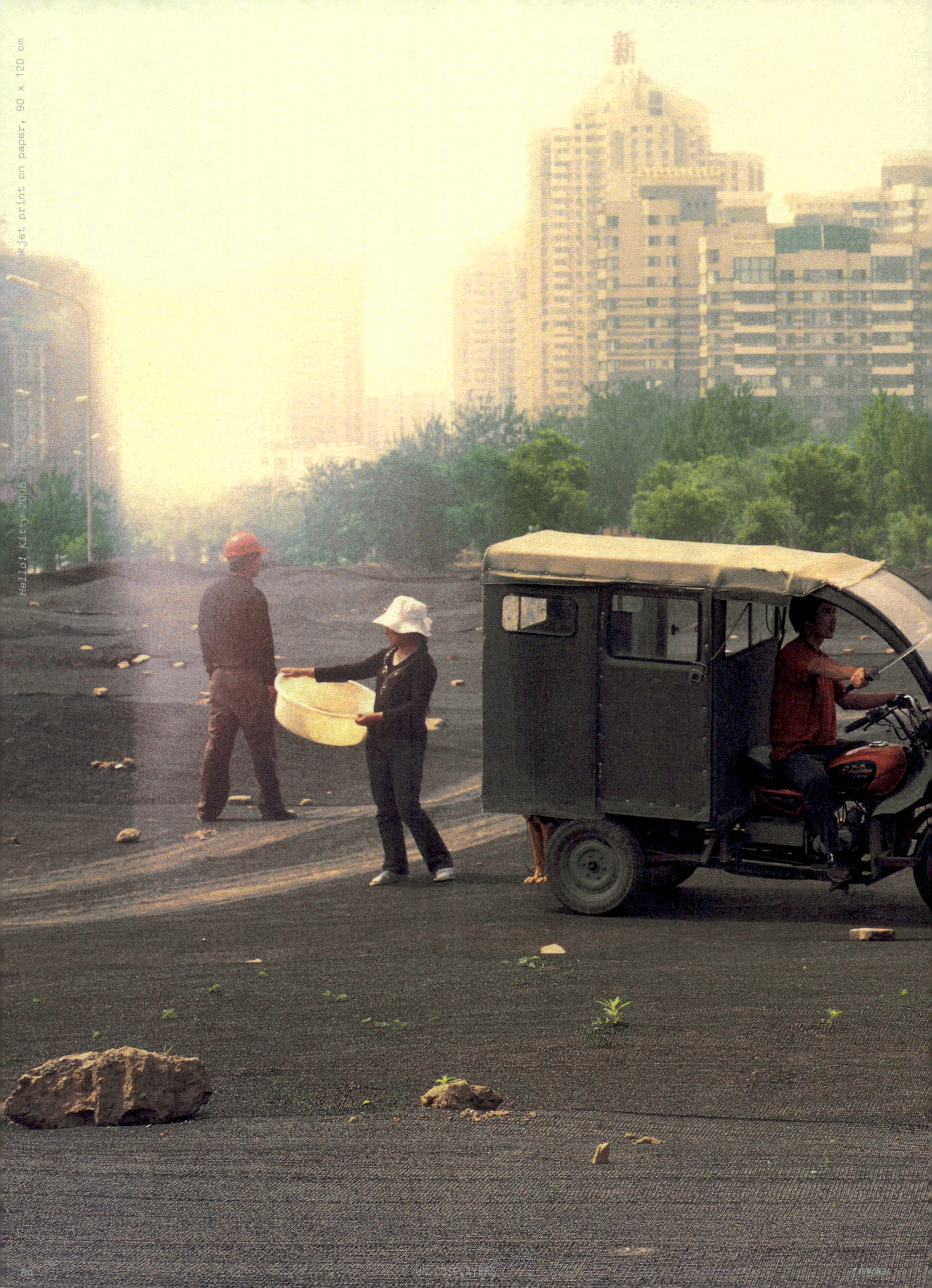

Hello! Kitty 2006 from the Cosplayers series, inkjet print on paper, 90 x 120 cm

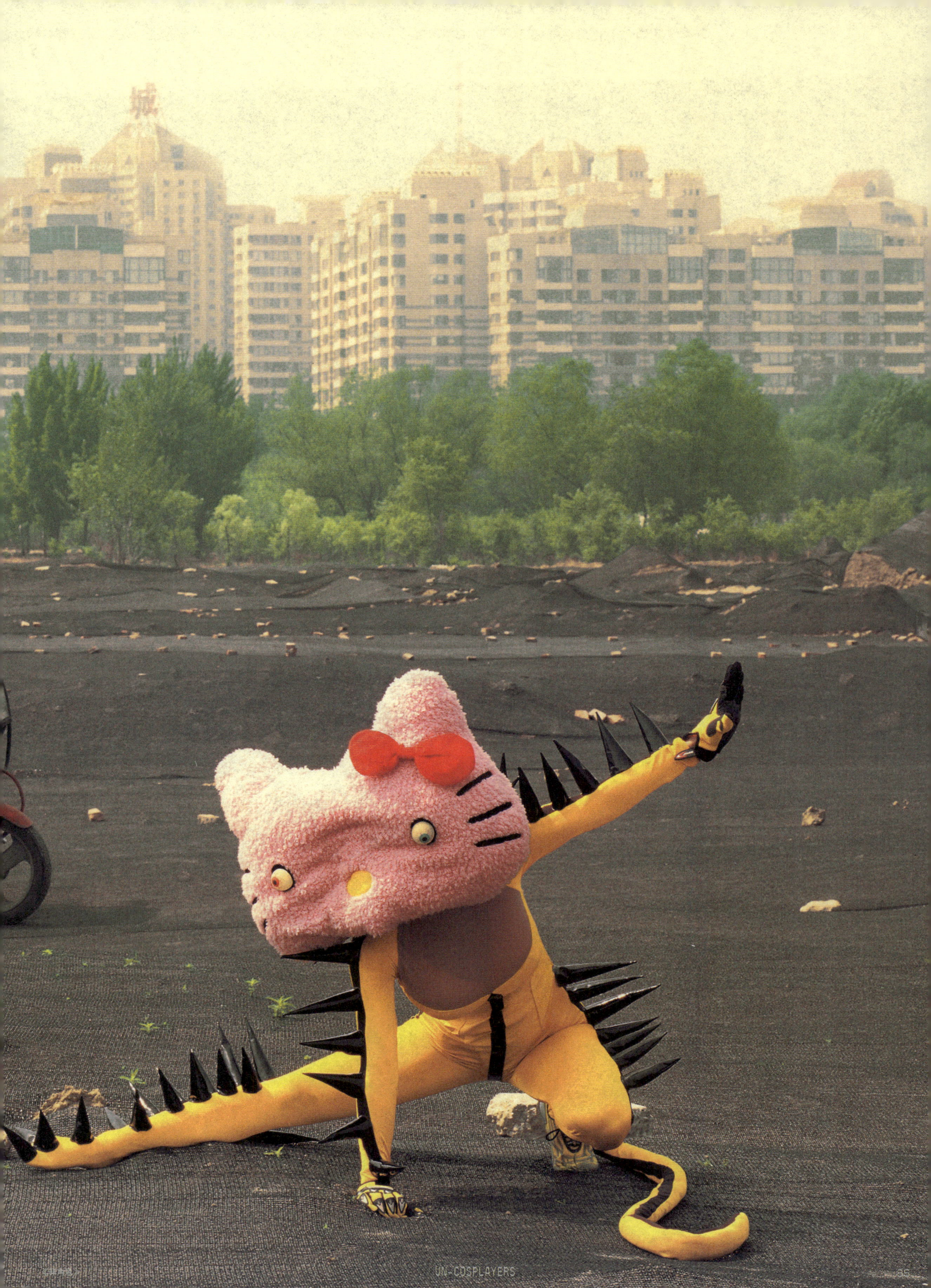

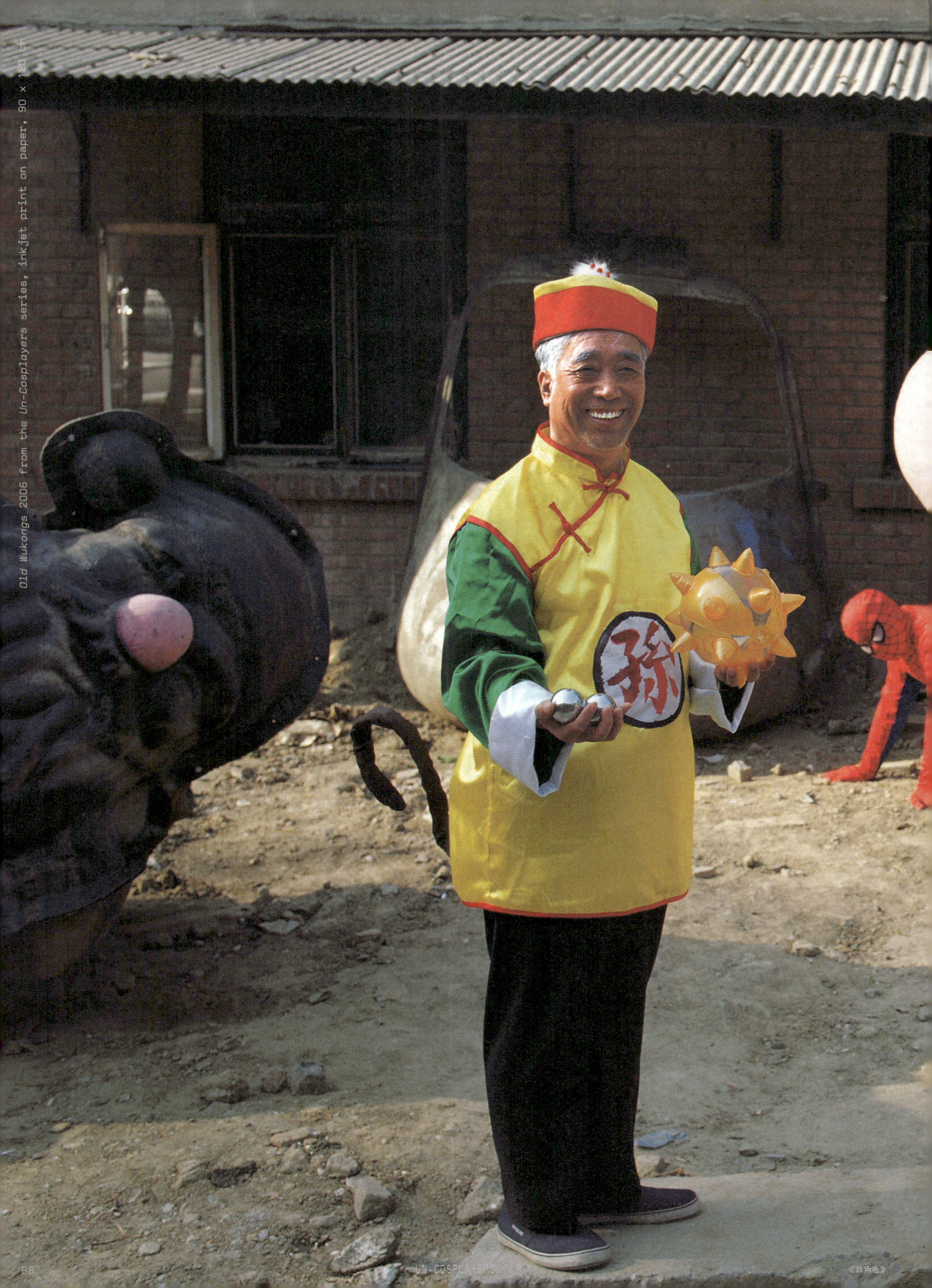

Old Wukongs 2006 from the *Un-Cosplayers* series, inkjet print on paper, 90 x 120 cm

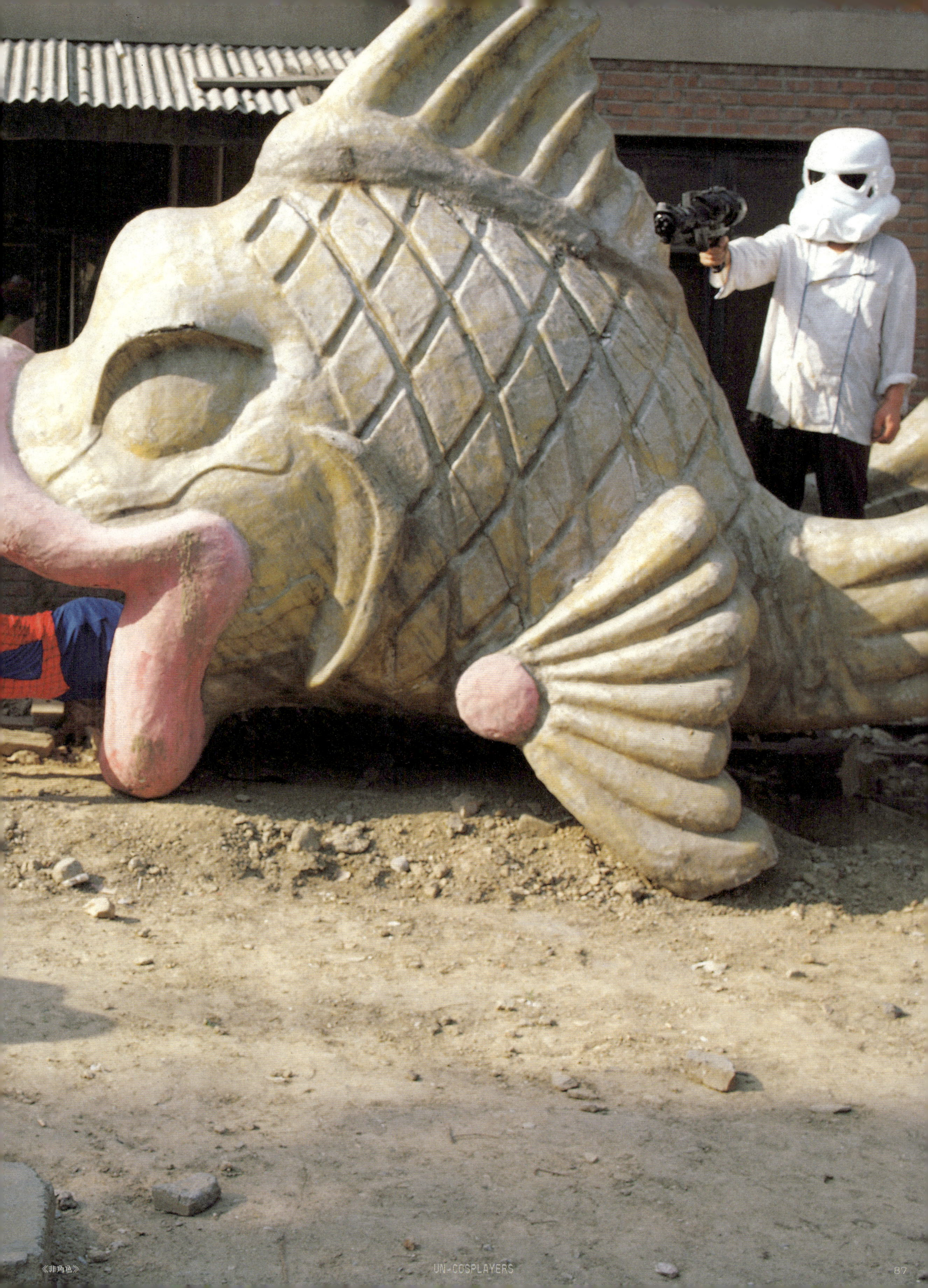

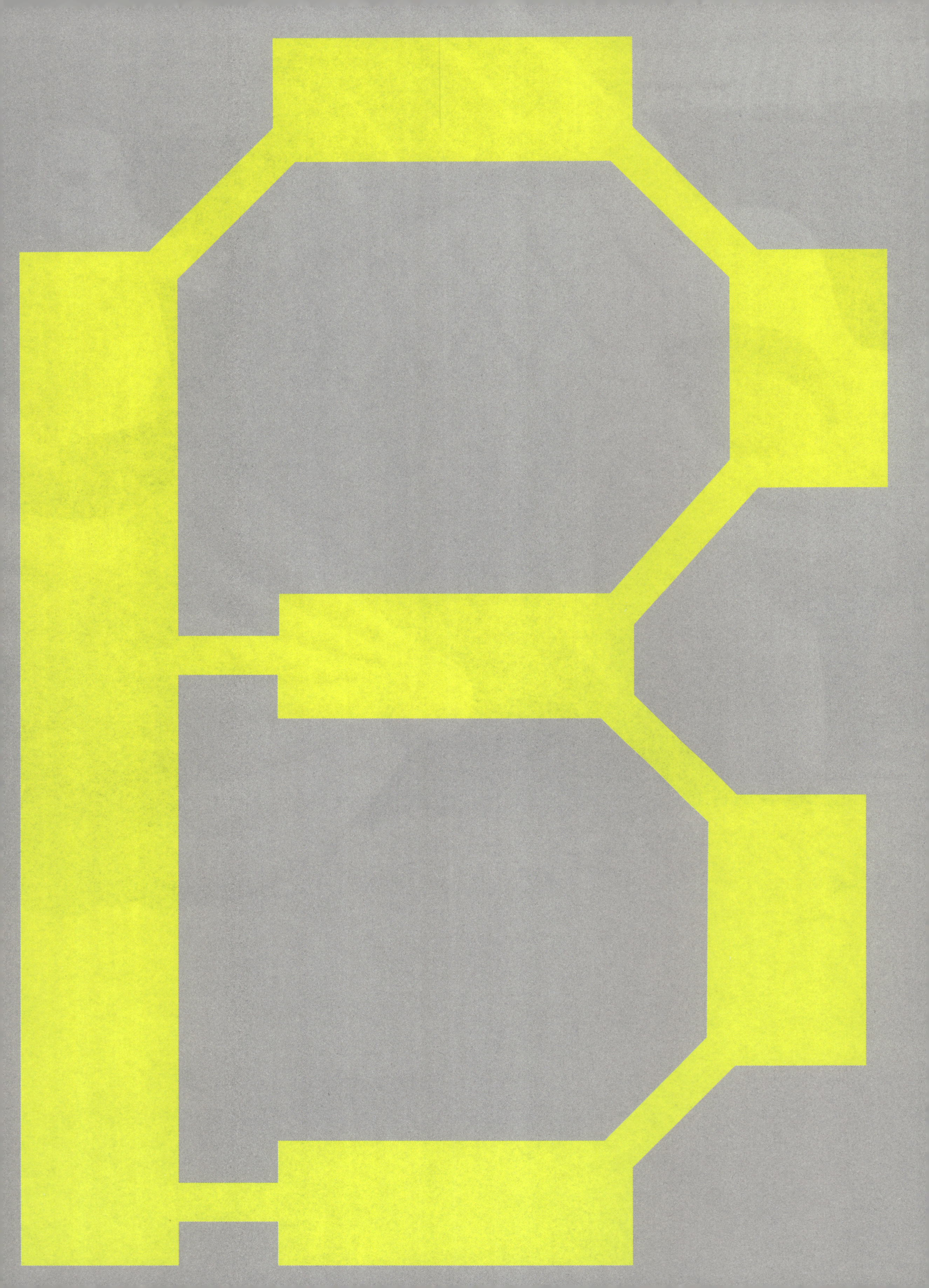

1 HIP HOP: GUANGZHOU 2003

嘻哈：广州

2 HIP HOP: FUKUOKA 2005

嘻哈：福冈

3 HIP HOP: NEW YORK 2006

嘻哈：纽约

4 HIP HOP: SYDNEY 2024

嘻哈：悉尼

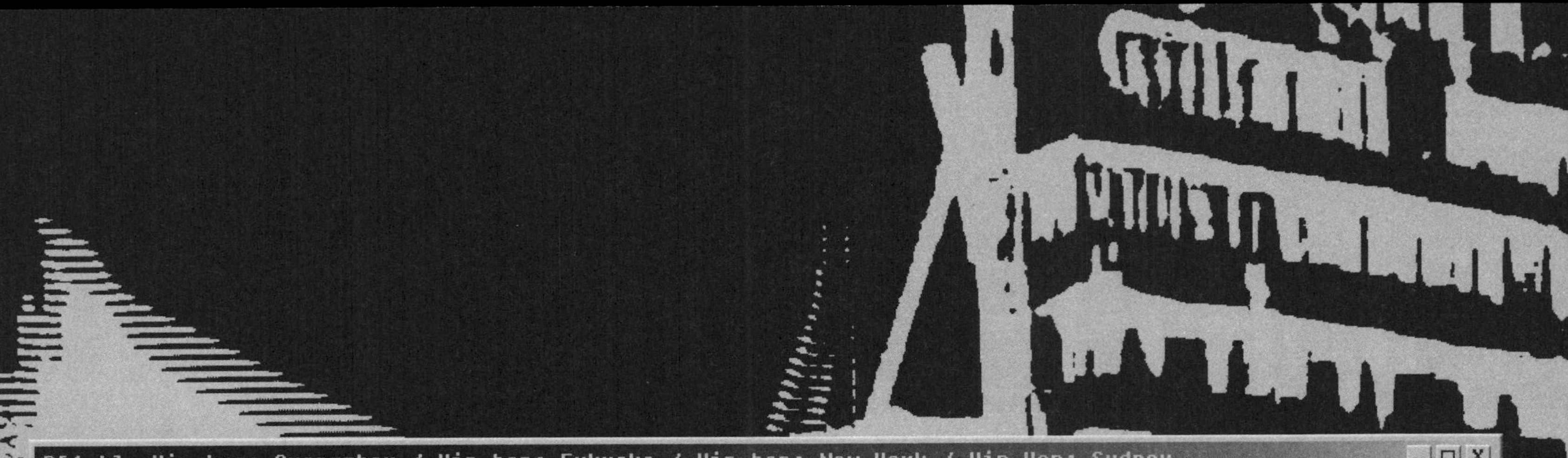

B[1–4]: Hip hop: Guangzhou / Hip hop: Fukuoka / Hip hop: New York / Hip Hop: Sydney

Shopkeepers, construction workers and grannies dance to hip hop on streets across the world. The *Hip hop* series celebrates Cao Fei's early pop cultural influences: MTV, bootlegged tapes and pirated cassettes of Cantopop and American rap. Taking over sidewalks, shop fronts and parking lots, the stars of her lo-fi music videos enact the utopian promise of cities as spaces of play and self-reinvention. All of these works highlight the hybrid nature of contemporary global culture, but the New York and Sydney films intentionally look to diasporic Chinese enclaves for their distinctive subversive energy and spirit of rebellion. In the artist's words:

> Chinatowns give rise to modalities of social organization not quite the same as the mainstream order of their 'host' countries. They run according to an underground order, providing a safe haven for Chinese and other similarly situated immigrants as well as the disadvantaged generally. Out of this grows a kind of resistant power.[1]

For *My City Is Yours*, Cao has filmed a new instalment of the *Hip hop* series in Sydney's Chinatowns with local community members including Yuan Liu, Eddie Ma and George Wing Kee.

[1] *Cao Fei: Hip Hop*, exhib cat, Lombard-Freid Projects and CourtYard Gallery, New York, 2006, np

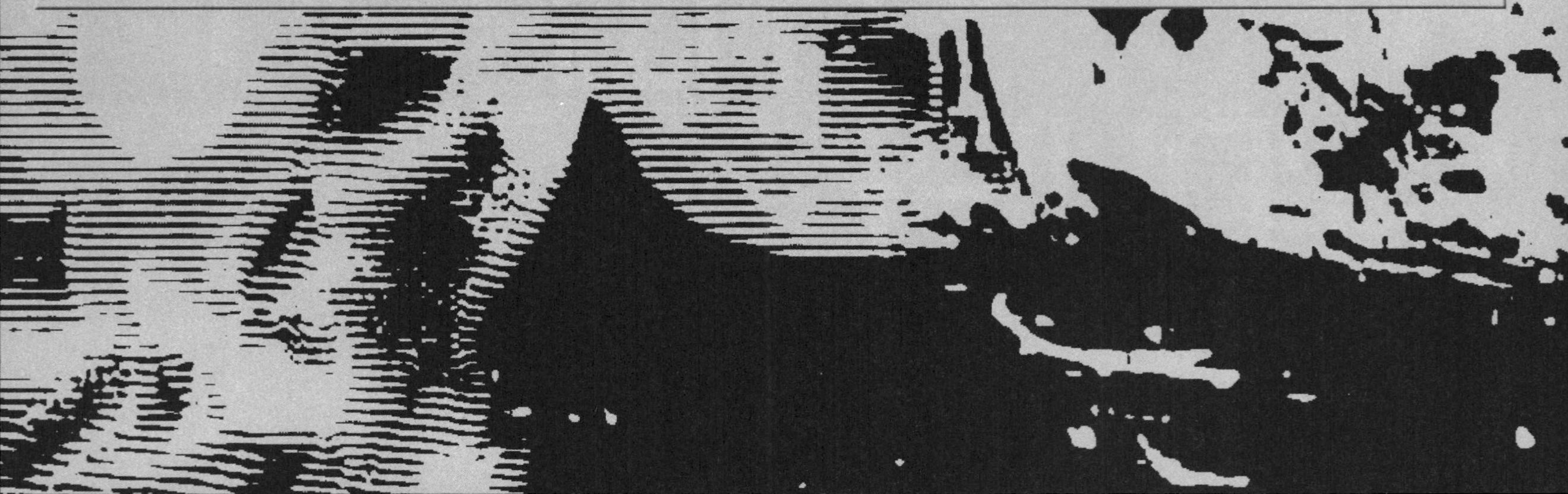

HIP HOP: GUANGZHOU 嘻哈：广州

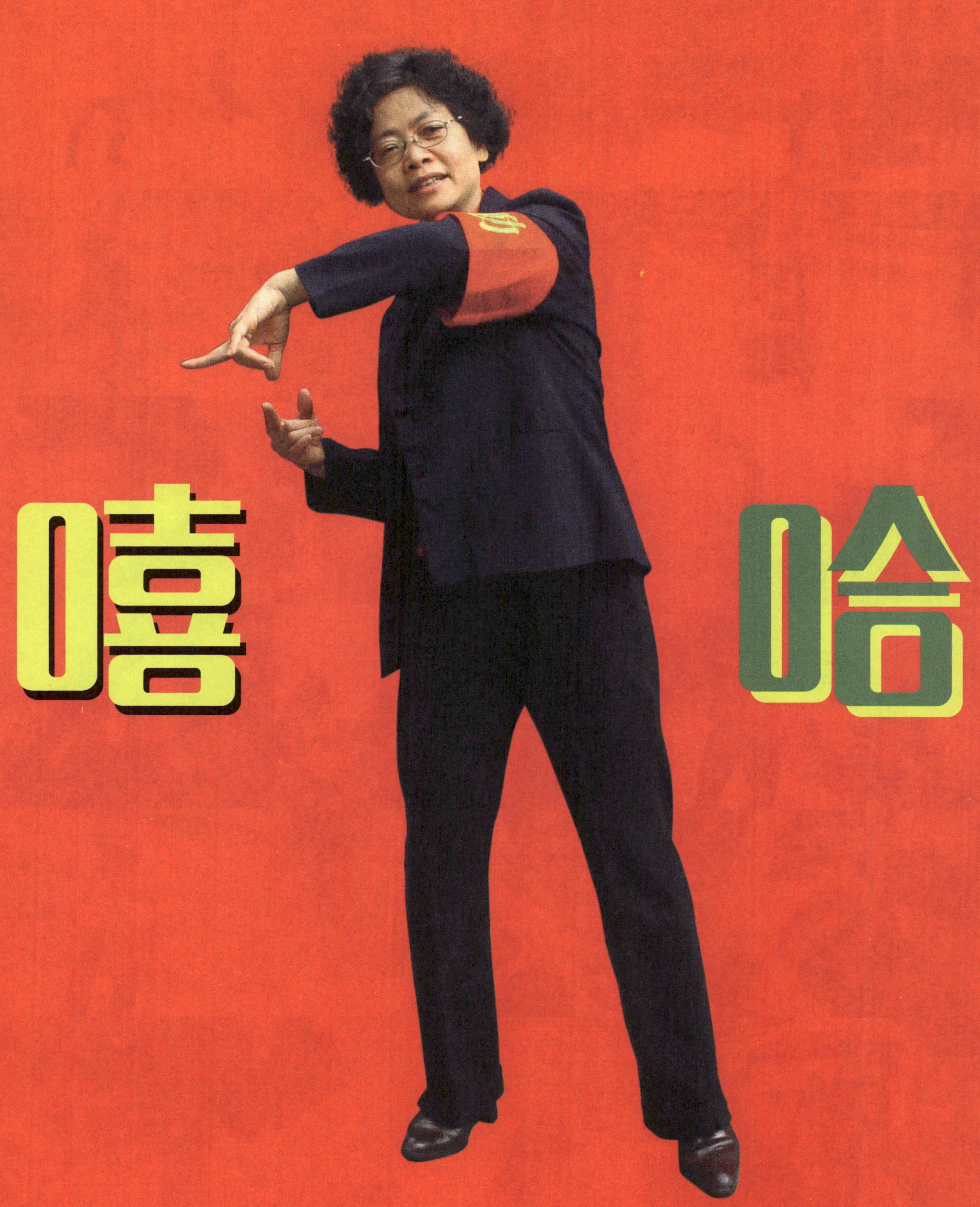

Artwork specification

Hip hop: Guangzhou 2003
single-channel digital video, colour, sound
3:28 min, 5:4

《嘻哈：广州》2003
5:4 彩色有声单频影像
3分28秒

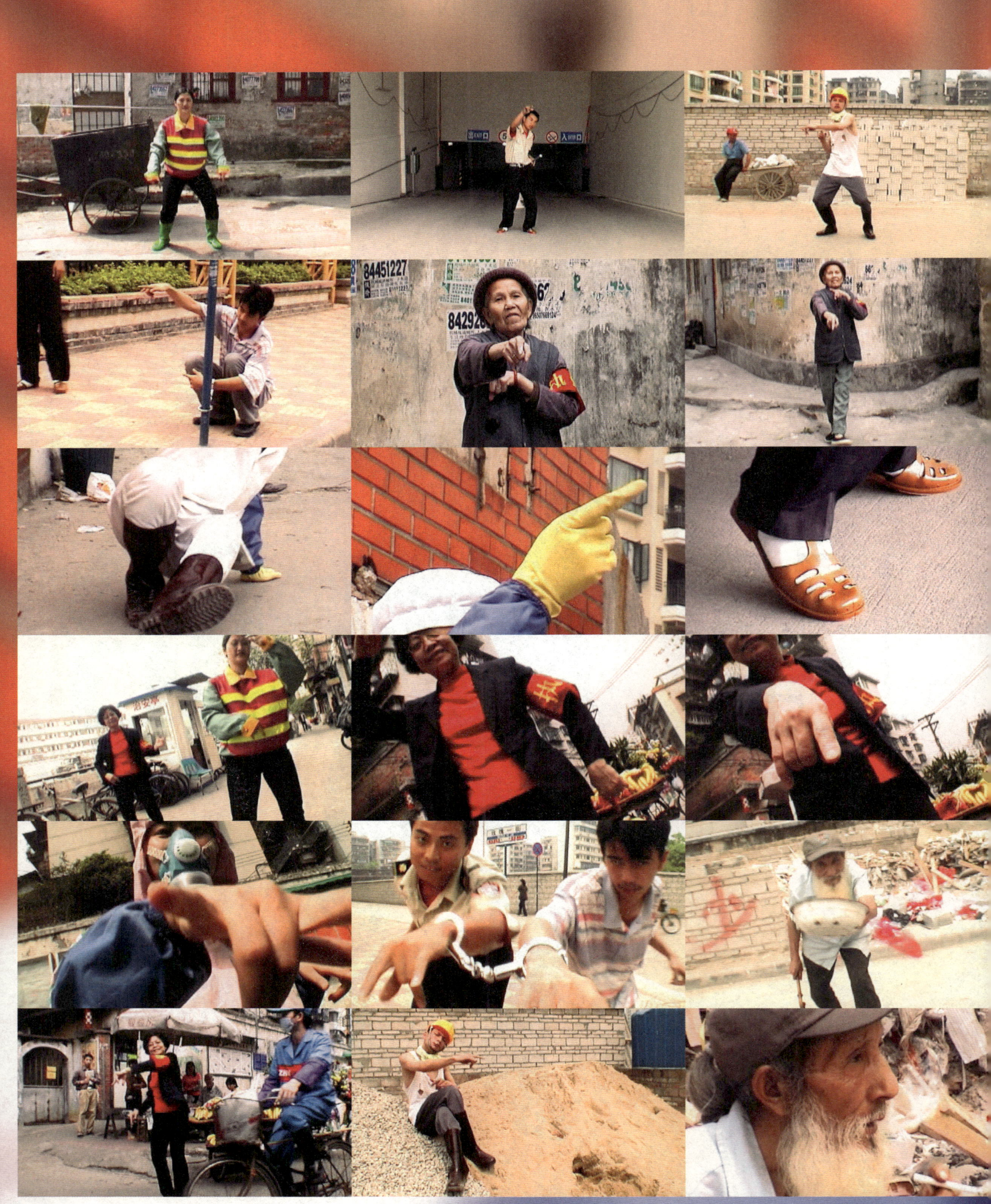

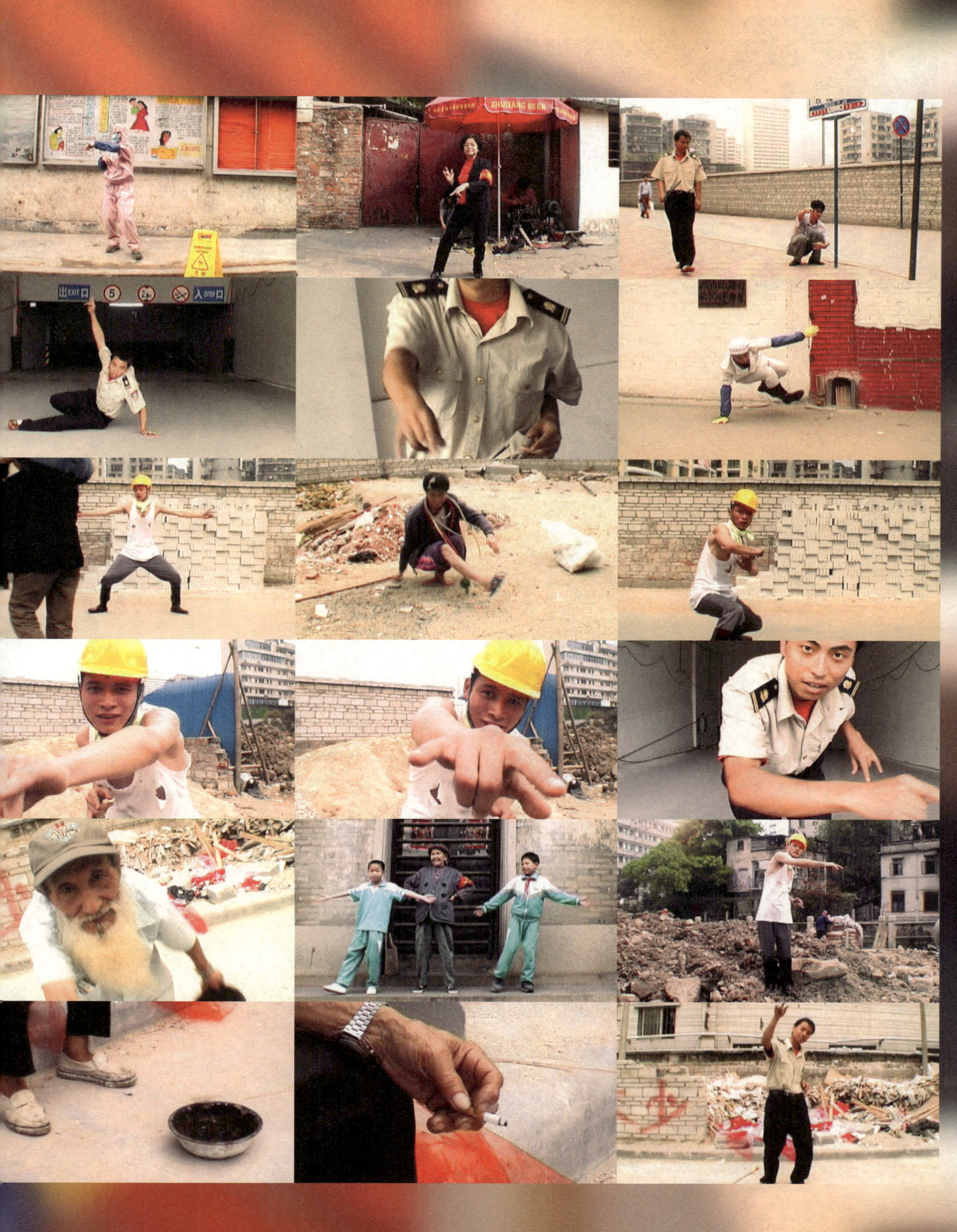
ZHUJIANG BEER

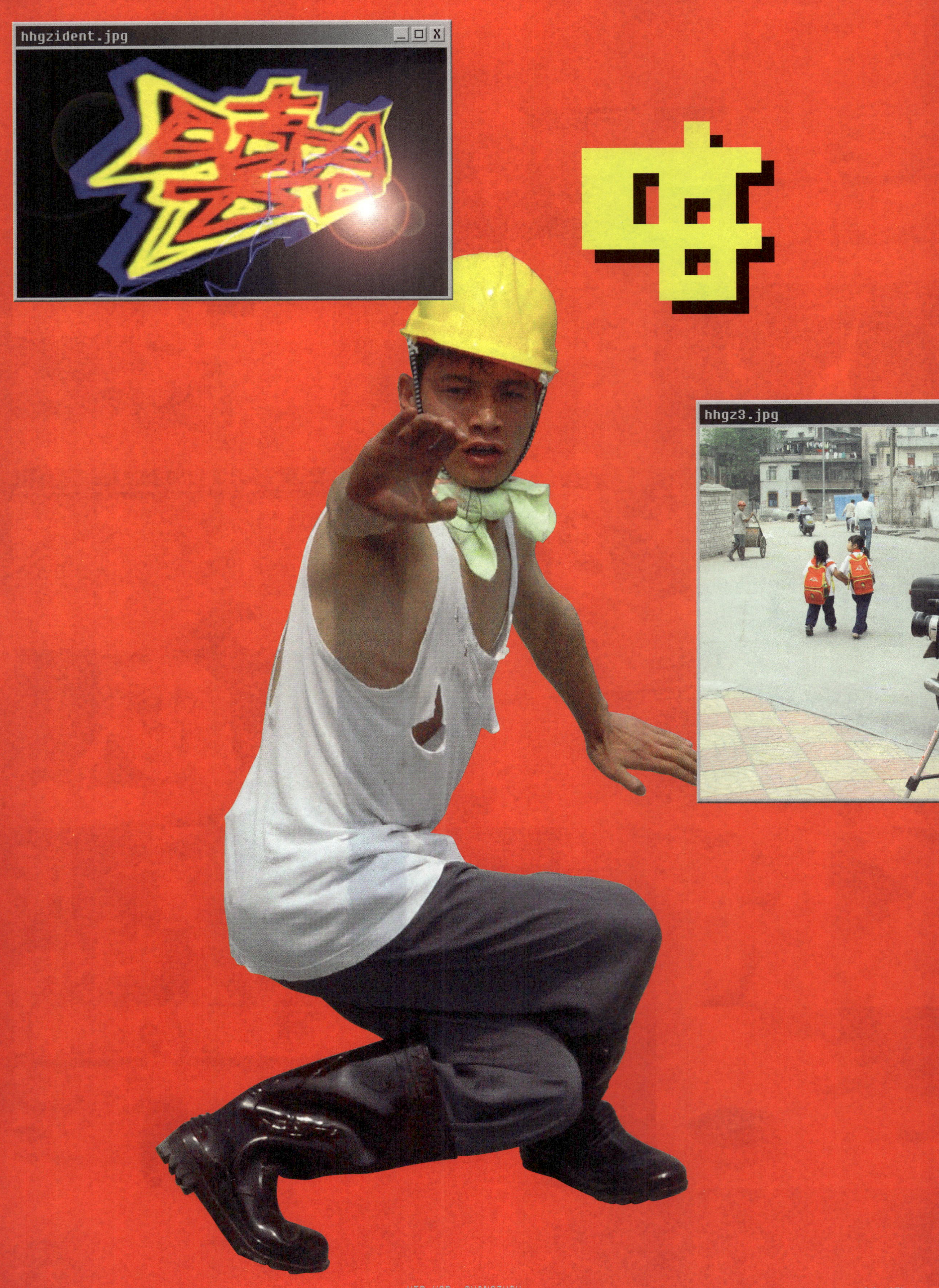

hhgzident.jpg
hhgz3.jpg

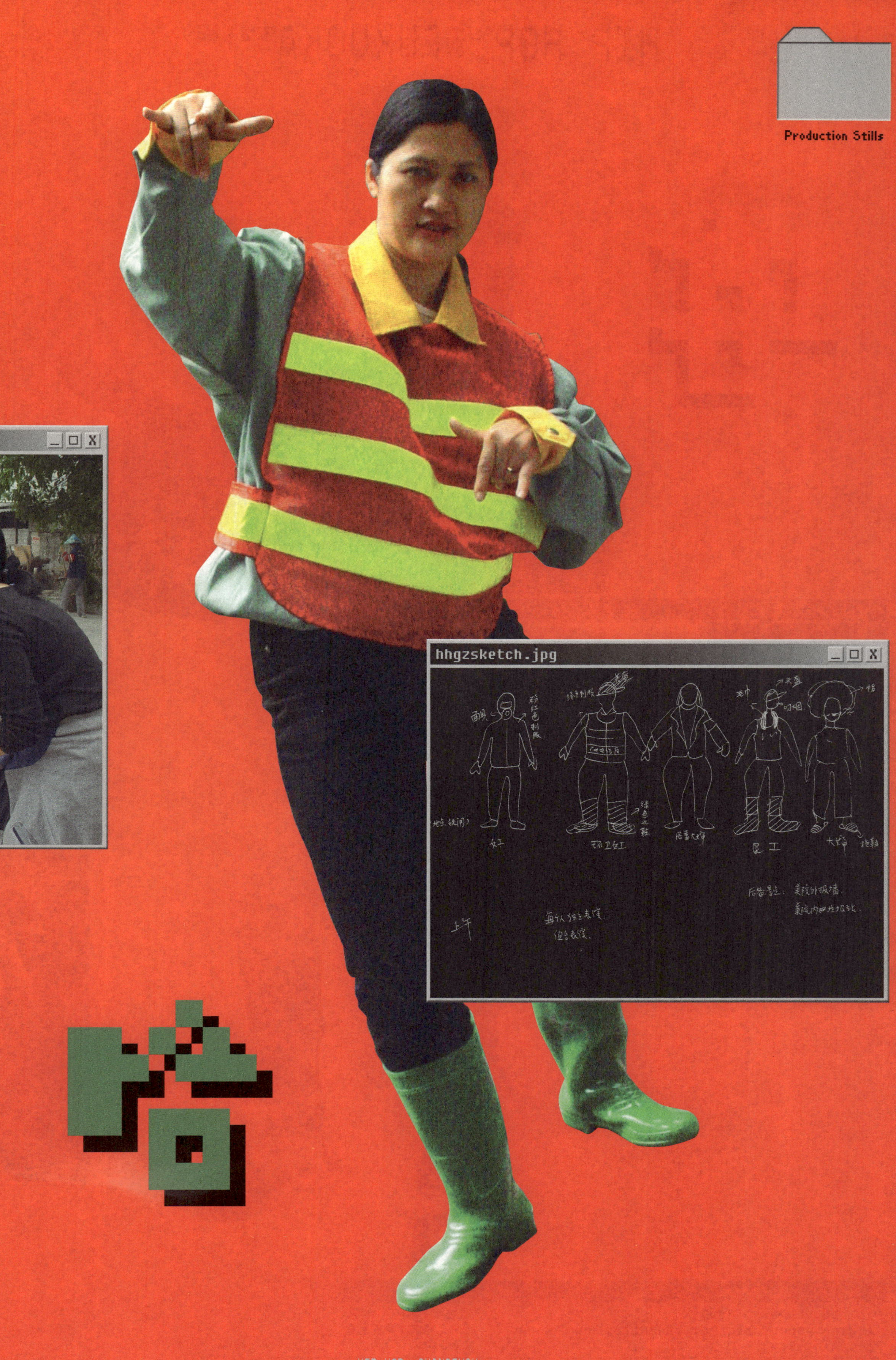
Production Stills
HONDA
hhgzsketch.jpg
面具
粉红色制服
绿色制服
绿色水鞋
女工
环卫女工
毛巾
叼烟
民工
帽
大妈
拖鞋
上午
每个人独立表演
组合表演

HIP HOP: FUKUOKA 嘻哈：福冈

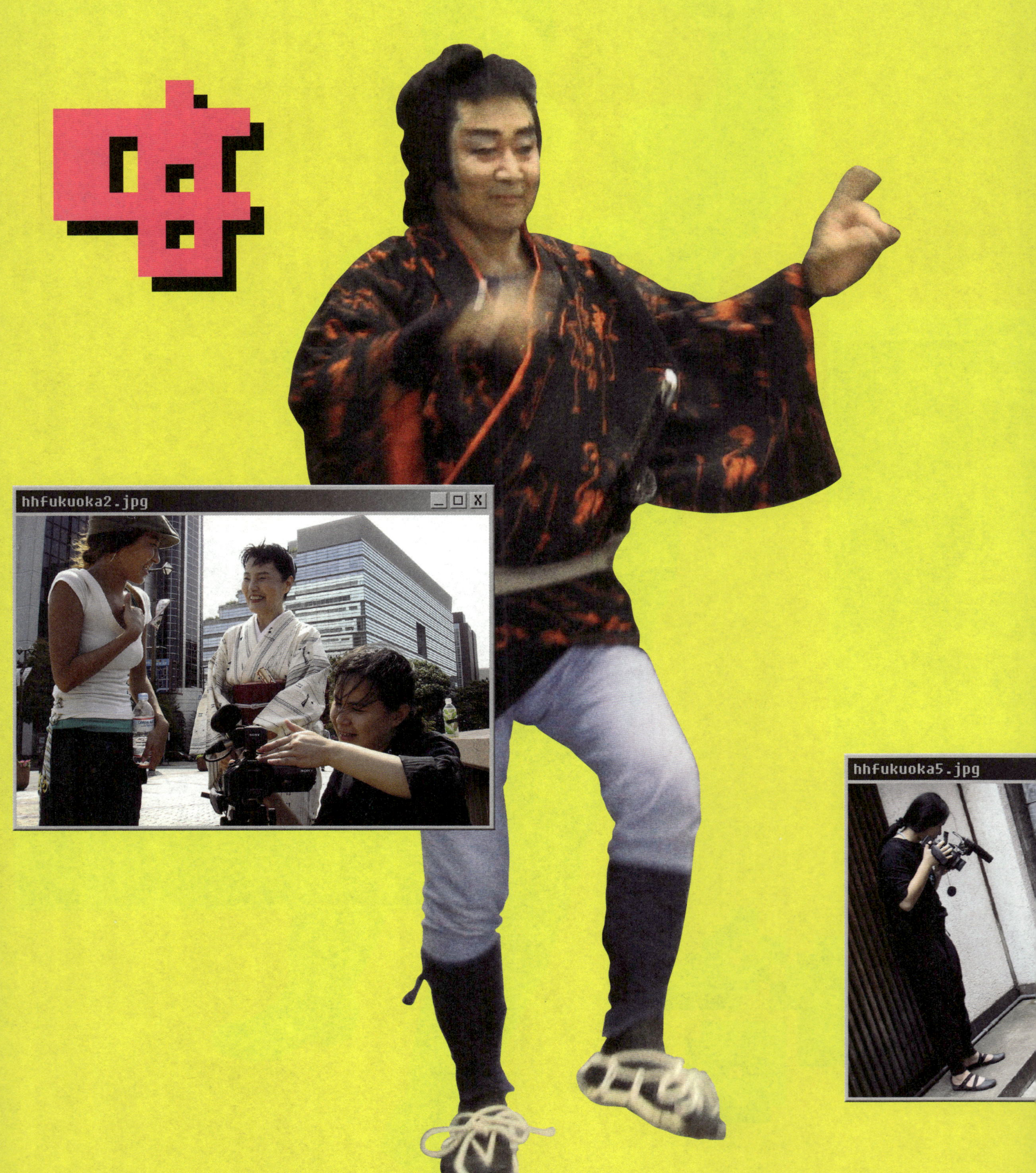

Artwork specification

Hip hop: Fukuoka 2005
single-channel digital video, colour, sound
7:40 min, 5:4

《嘻哈：福冈》2005
5:4 彩色有声单频影像
7分40秒

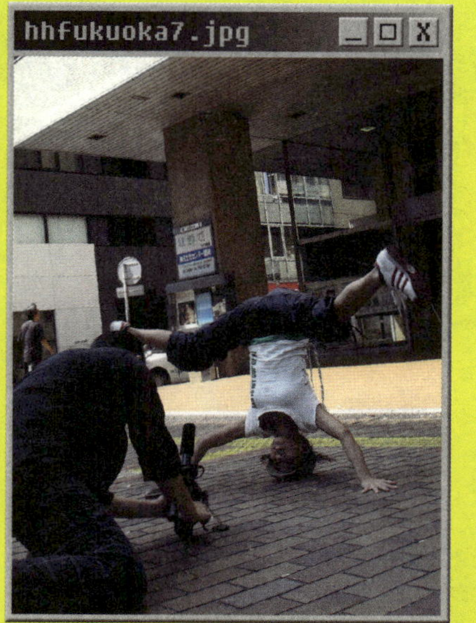

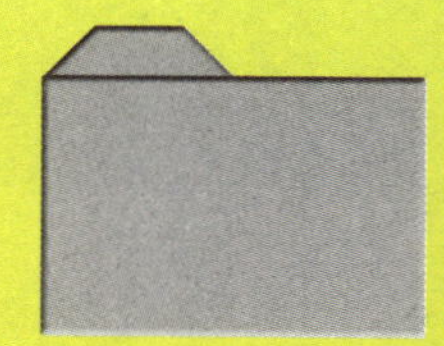

Production Stills

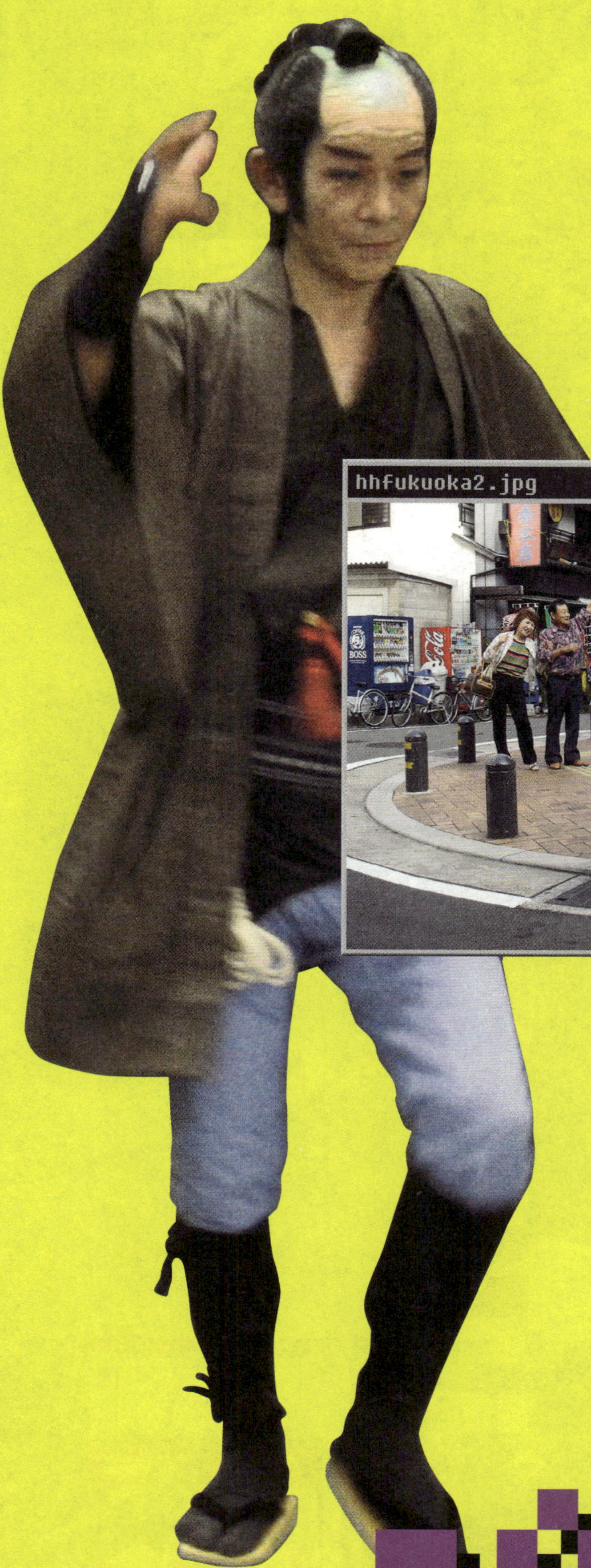

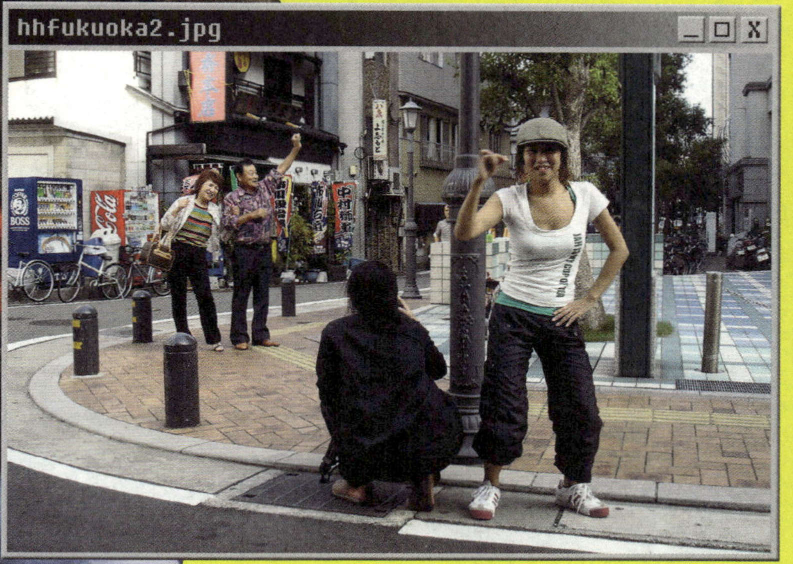

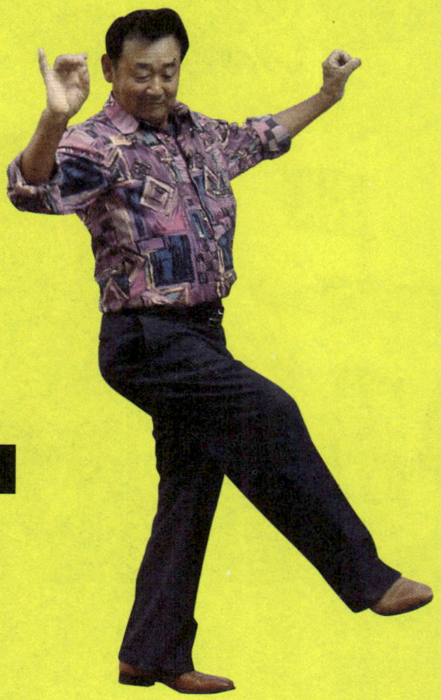

hhfukuoka2.jpg

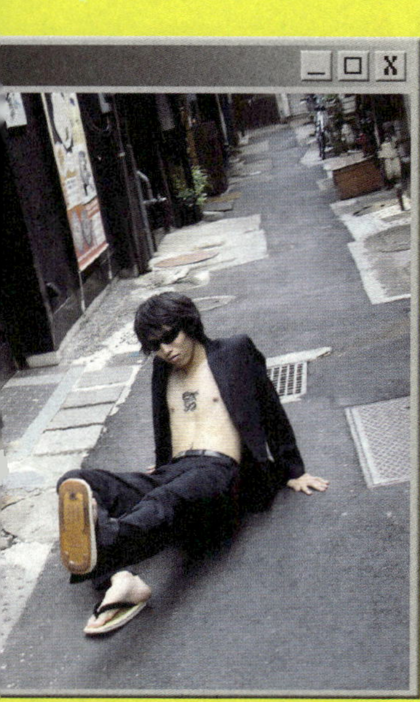

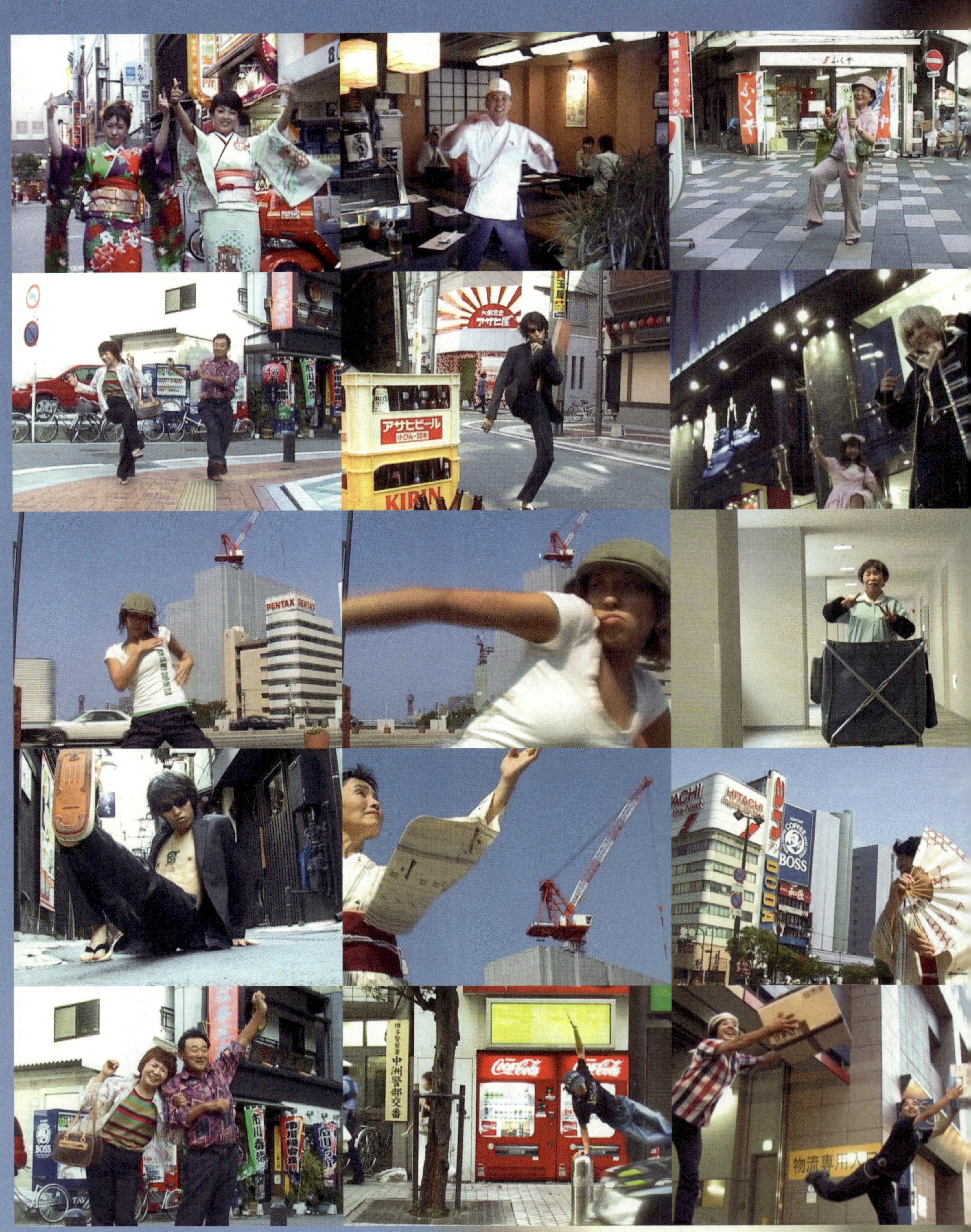

アサヒビール
KIRIN
PENTAX
HITACHI
BOSS
DODA
Coca-Cola
中洲警部交番
物流専用入口

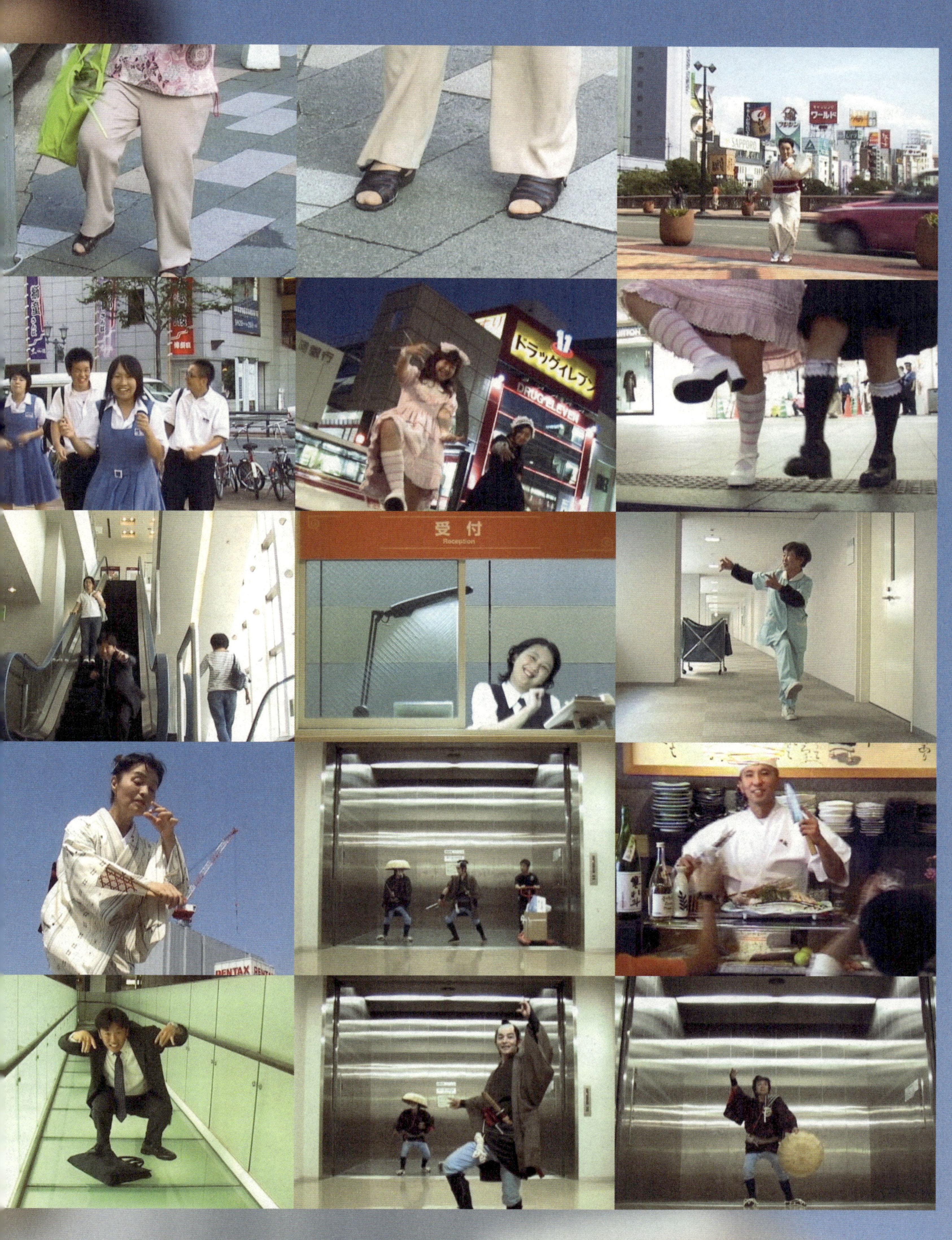
SAPPORO
ワールド
ドラッグイレブン
DRUG ELEVEN
受付
Reception
PENTAX

HIP HOP: NEW YORK 嘻哈：纽约

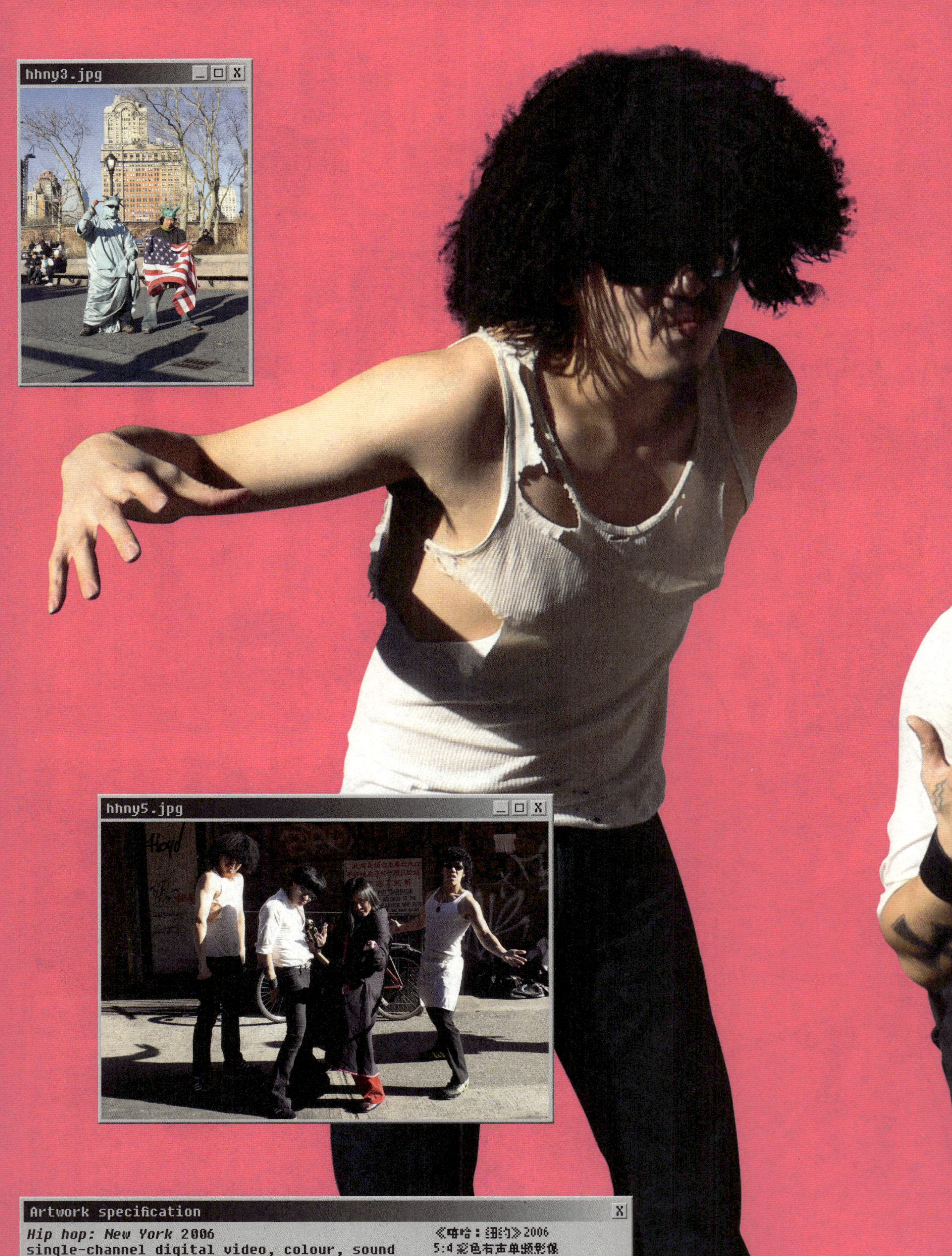

Artwork specification

Hip hop: New York 2006
single-channel digital video, colour, sound
5:15 min, 5:4

《嘻哈：纽约》2006
5:4 彩色有声单频影像
5分15秒

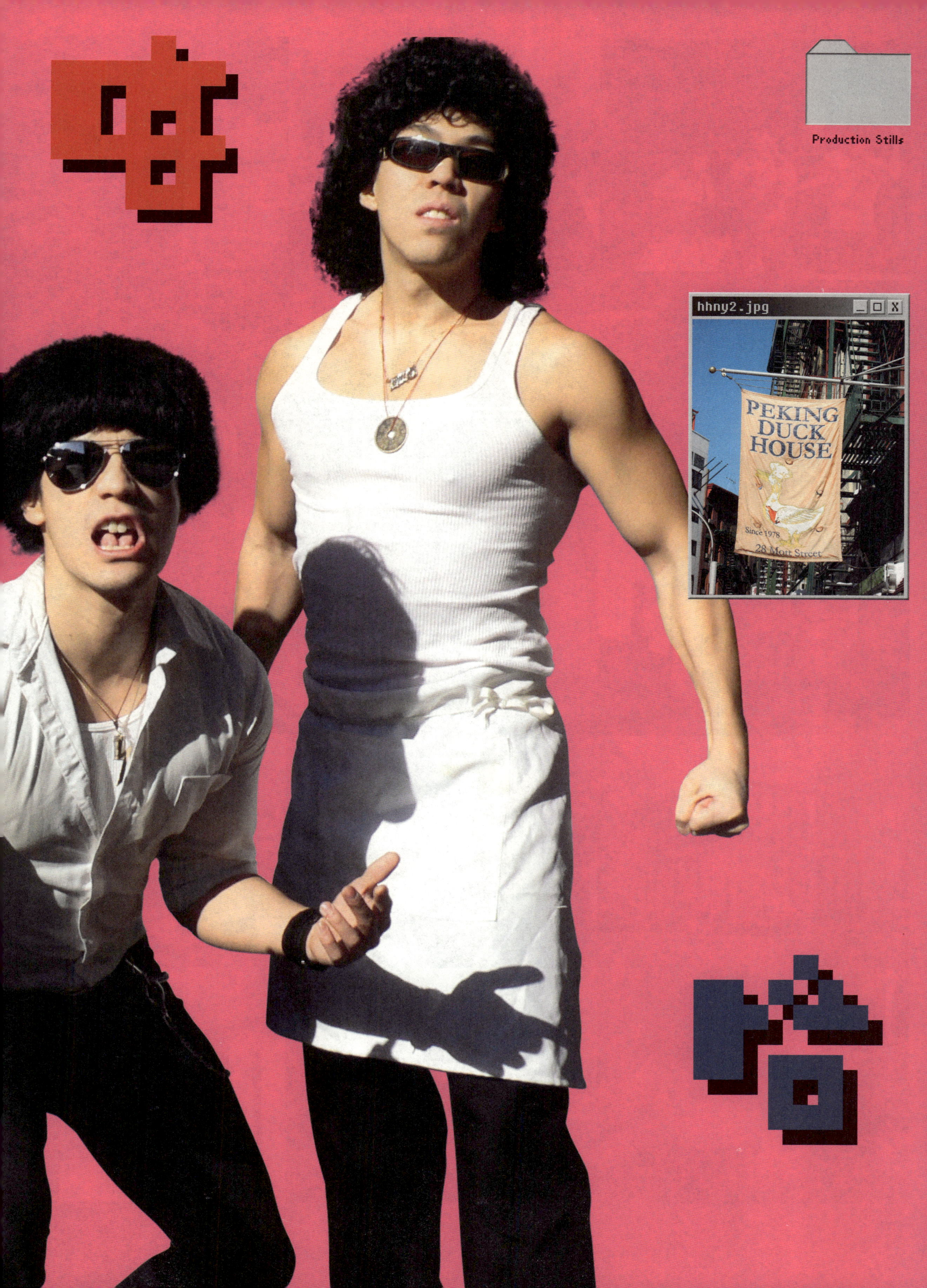
Production Stills
hhny2.jpg
PEKING
DUCK
HOUSE
Since 1978
28 Mott Street

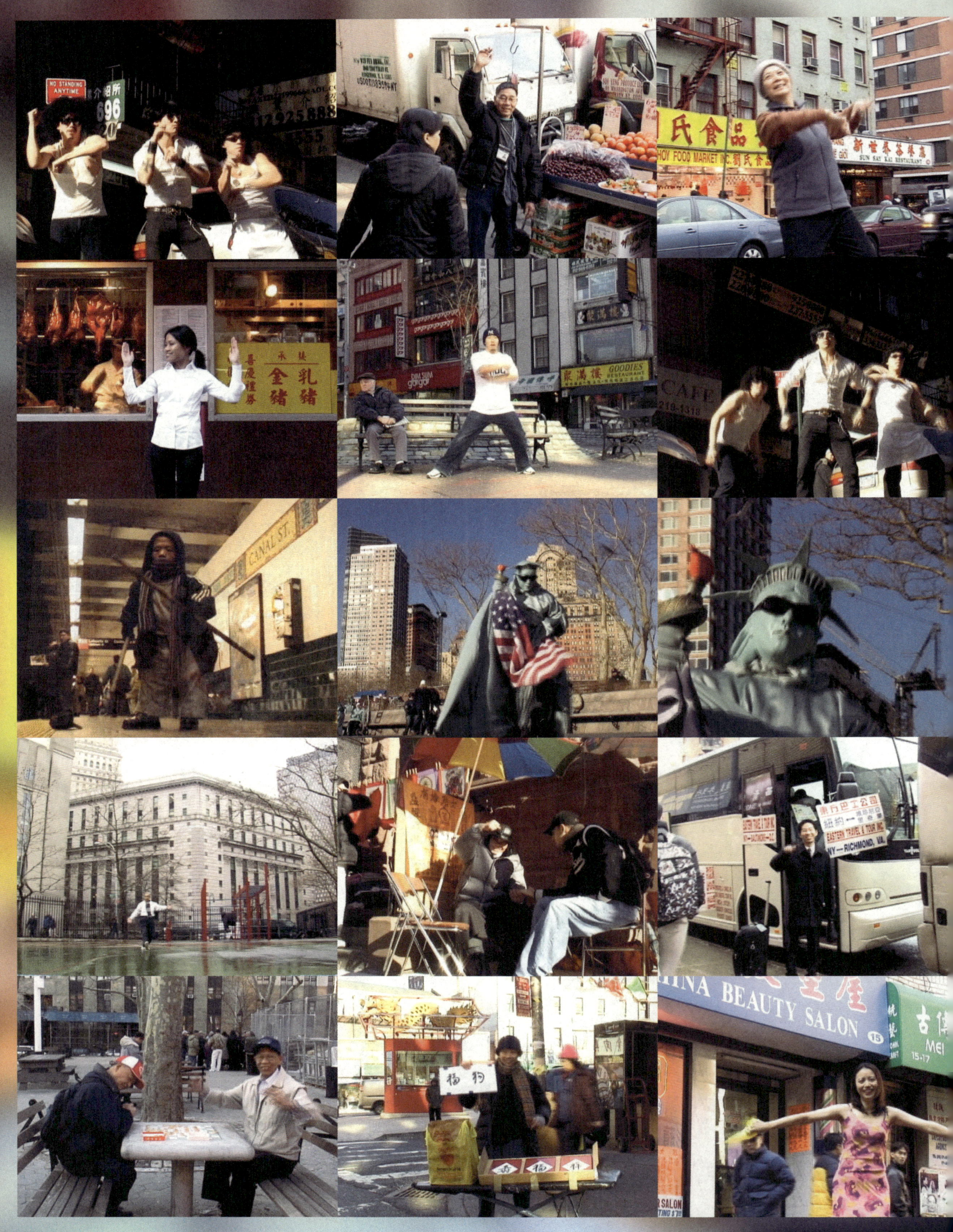
NO STANDING ANYTIME
696
CANAL ST.
GOODIES
CAFE
EASTERN TRAVEL & TOUR INC
NY — RICHMOND, VA.
HINA BEAUTY SALON
MEI
SUN SAY KAI RESTAURANT
全乳猪

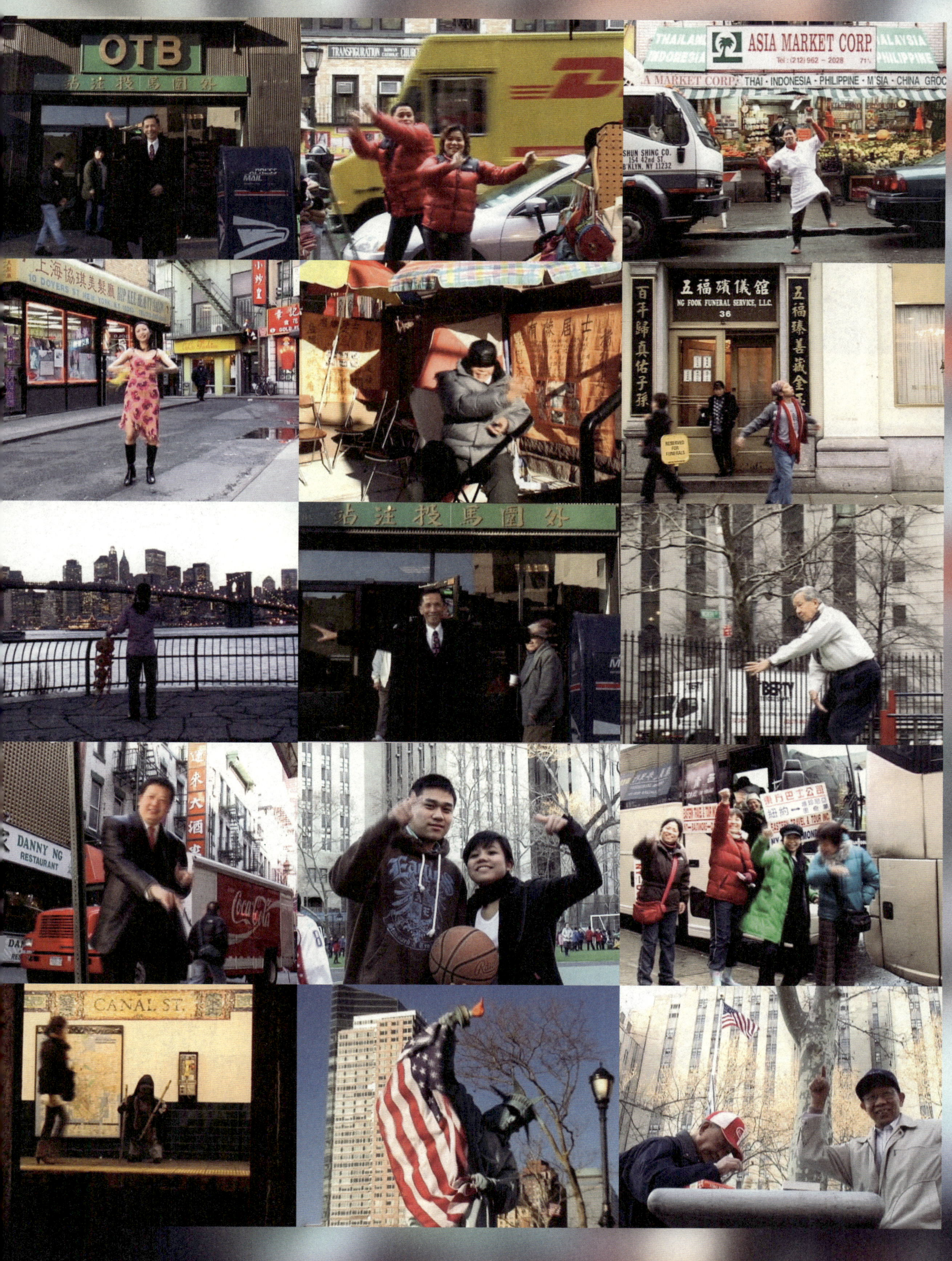
OTB
ASIA MARKET CORP
Tel : (212) 962 ~ 2028
THAI · INDONESIA · PHILIPPINE · M'SIA · CHINA GROC
SHUN SHING CO.
五福殯儀館
NG FOOK FUNERAL SERVICE, LLC.
36
DANNY NG
RESTAURANT
Coca-Cola
CANAL ST.

HIP HOP: SYDNEY 嘻哈：悉尼

Location shots from Sydney's CBD Chinatown, 2024

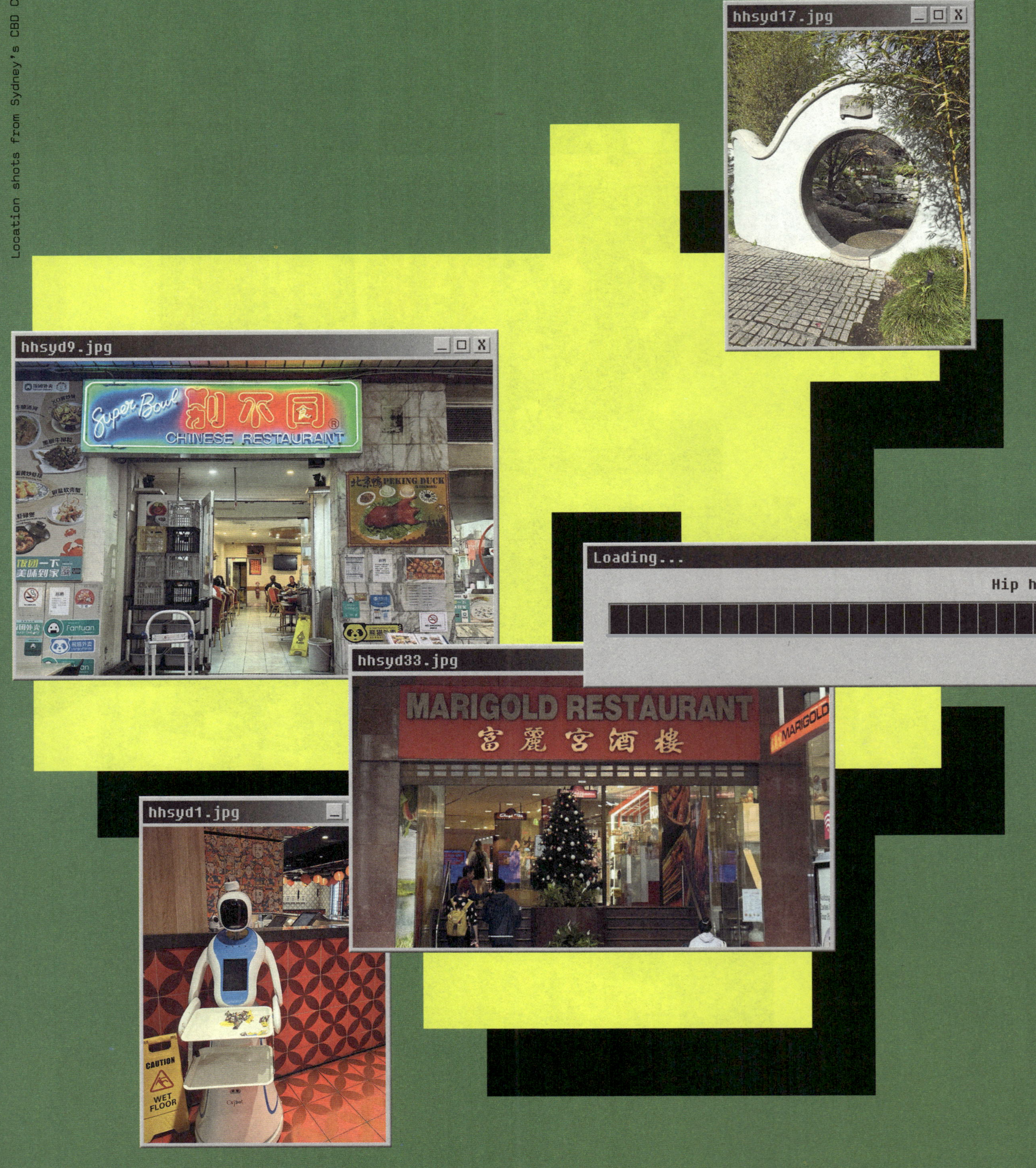

Artwork specification

Hip hop: Sydney 2024
three-channel digital video, colour, sound
work in progress at the time of publication
Commissioned by the Art Gallery of New South Wales

《嘻哈：悉尼》2024
彩色有声三频影像
图录截稿时仍在制作中
受新南威尔士艺术博物馆委托创作

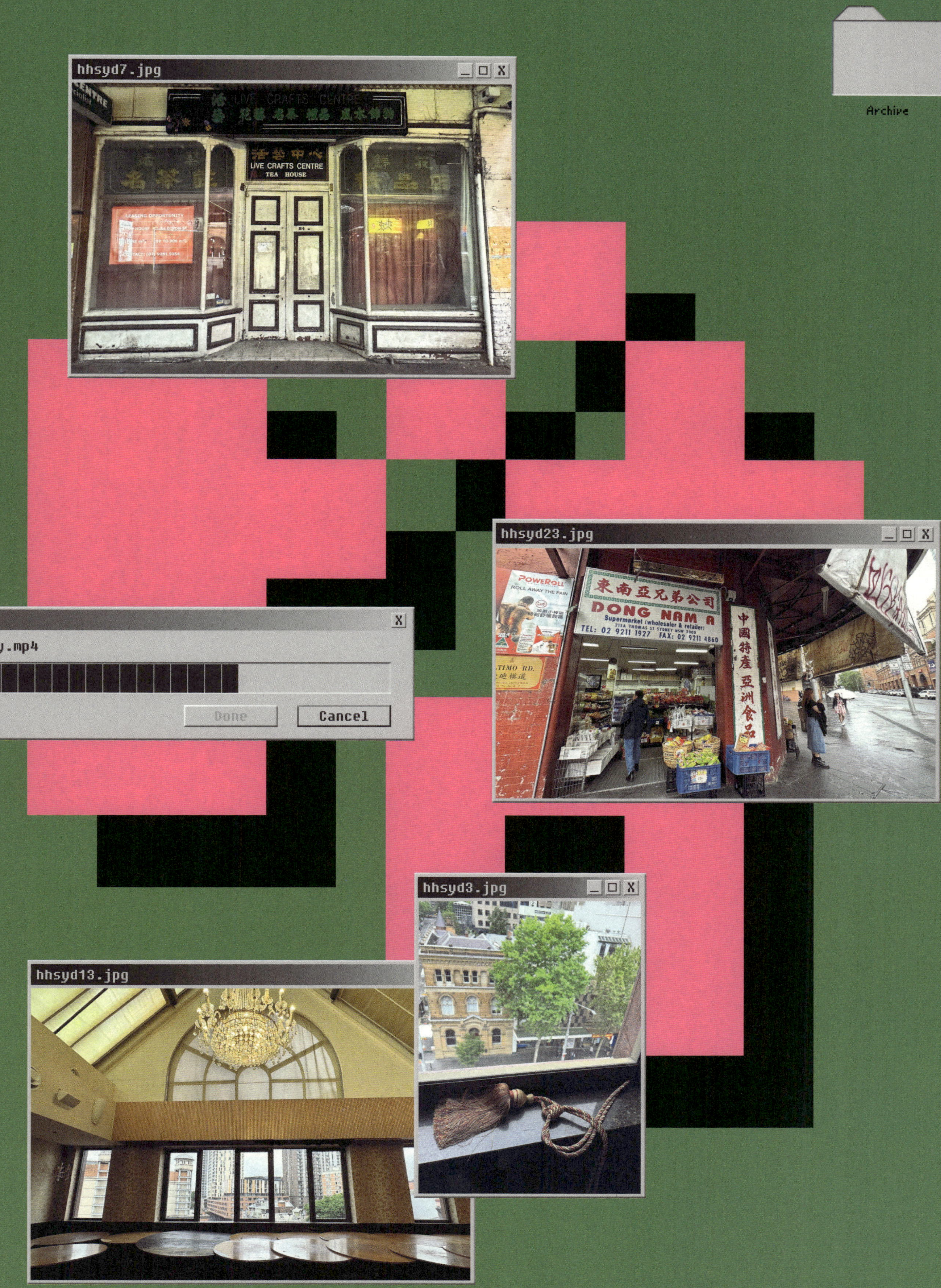
Archive
hhsyd7.jpg
LIVE CRAFTS CENTRE
TEA HOUSE
hhsyd23.jpg
POWEROLL
ROLL AWAY THE PAIN
東南亞兄弟公司
DONG NAM A
Supermarket (wholesaler & retailer)
TEL: 02 9211 1927 FAX: 02 9211 4860
中國特產 亞洲食品
ey.mp4
Done
Cancel
hhsyd3.jpg
hhsyd13.jpg

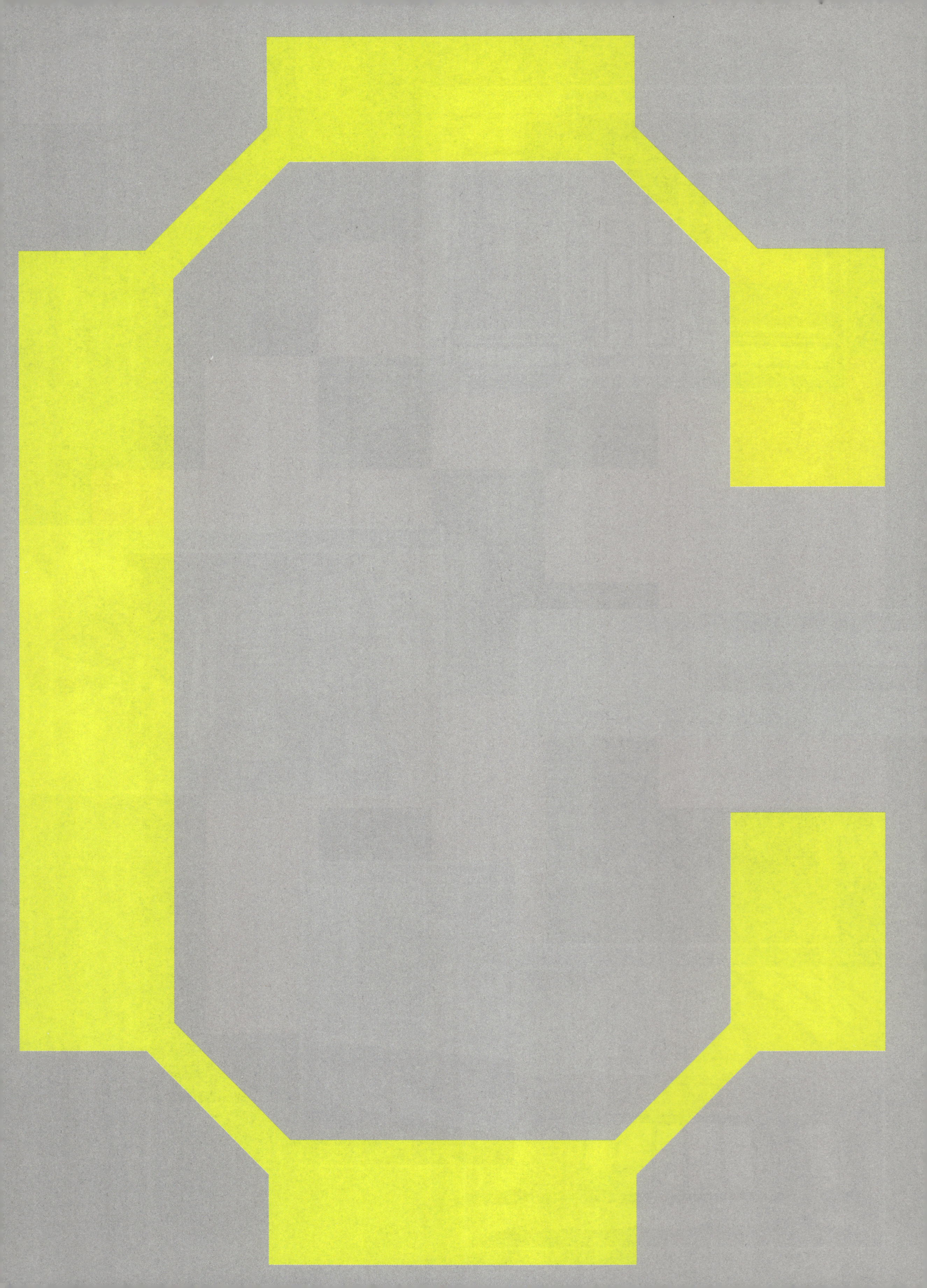

WHOSE UTOPIA

2006

谁的乌托邦

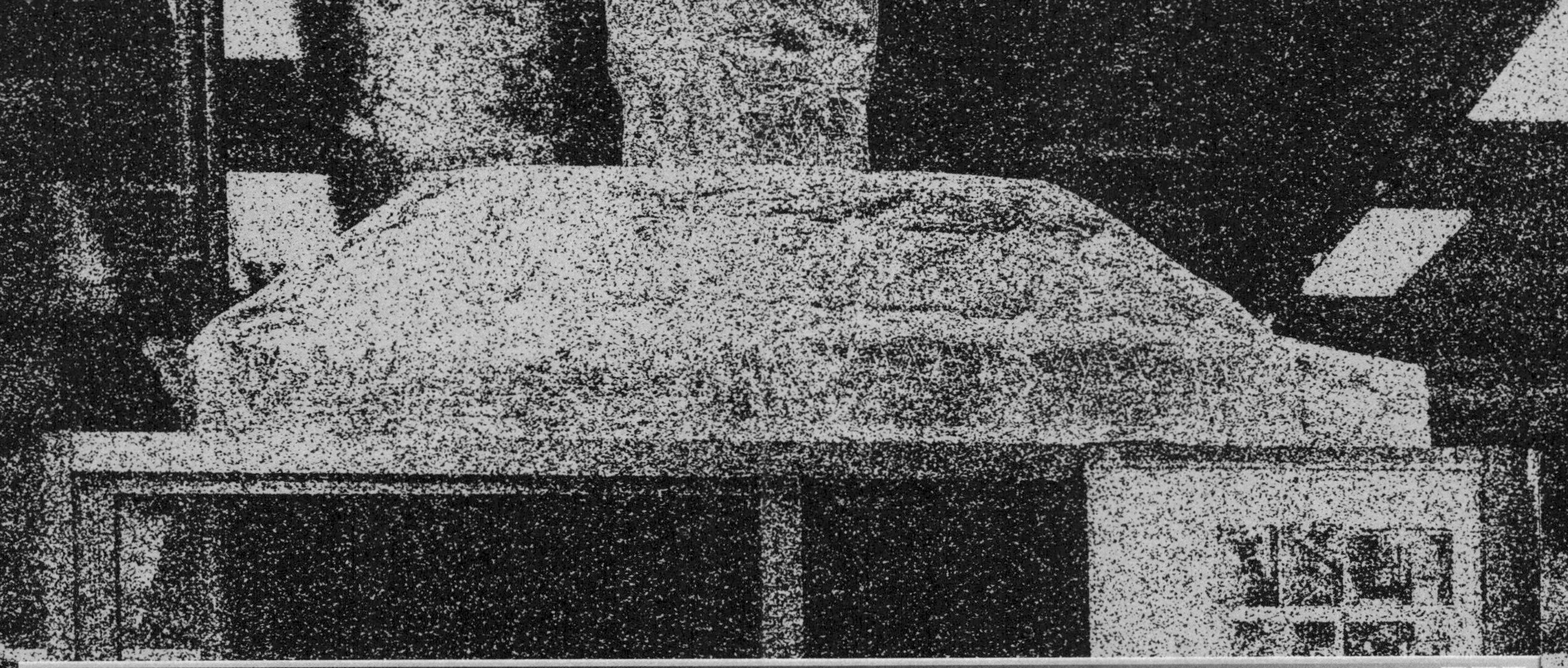

C: Whose utopia

What do you hope for the future? Why did you decide to leave your home? How do you feel about the factory? In 2005 Cao Fei posed these questions to migrant workers during an artist residency at the OSRAM (Siemens) lightbulb factory in Foshan, an industrial zone of the Pearl River Delta. The artist invited employees to channel their ambitions and dreams into art-making, a collective newspaper and a song contest called ‘Utopia Idol’. A rock band was formed. The company motto (TPM), ‘Total productive maintenance’ became ‘Team, people, motivation’. And the production line turned into a dance floor, with workers moonwalking and pirouetting throughout Cao’s breakout film, *Whose utopia*.

This three-part video vividly reveals the working and living environment of individual employees, delving into their innermost feelings as they contemplate their role within the system and glimpse possibilities for utopian change.

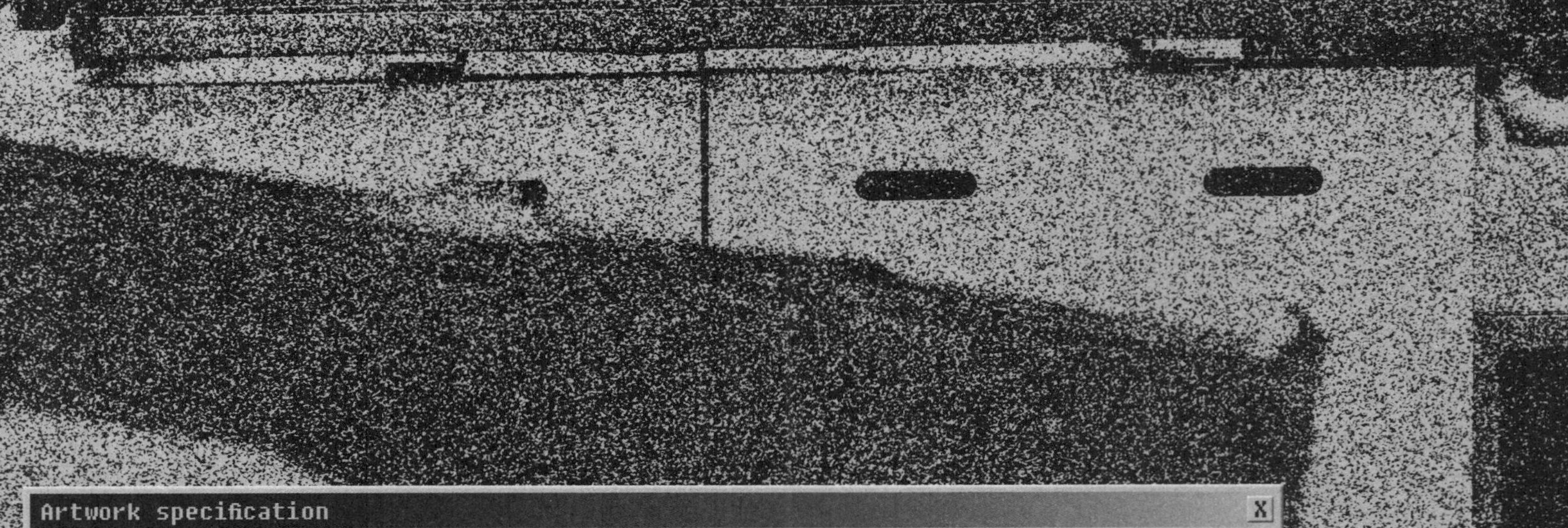

Artwork specification

Whose utopia 2006
single-channel digital video, colour, sound
20:20 min, 5:4

《谁的乌托邦》2006
5:4 彩色有声单频影像
20分20秒

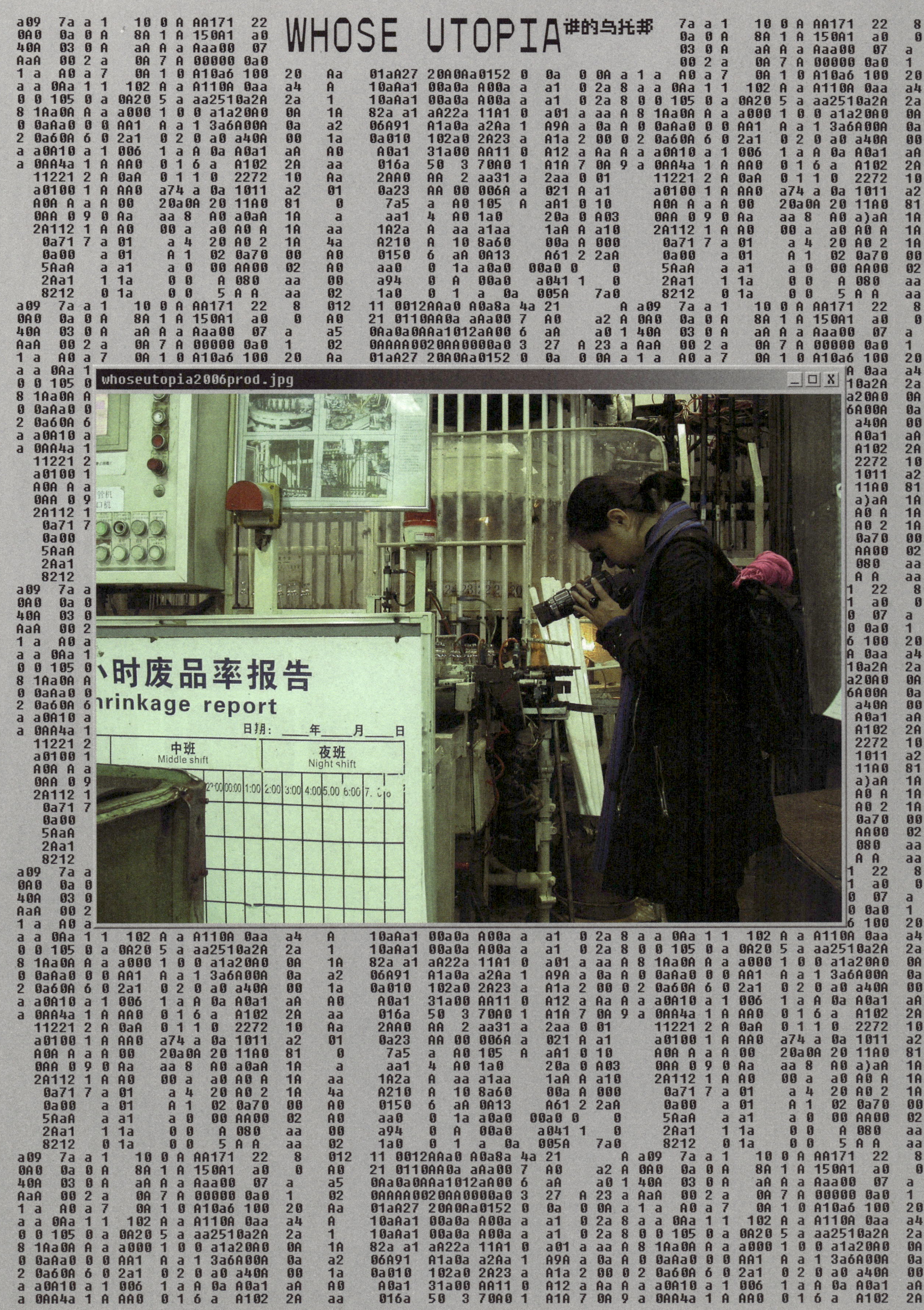
WHOSE UTOPIA 谁的乌托邦
whoseutopia2006prod.jpg
时废品率报告
hrinkage report
日期：____年____月____日
中班
Middle shift
夜班
Night shift

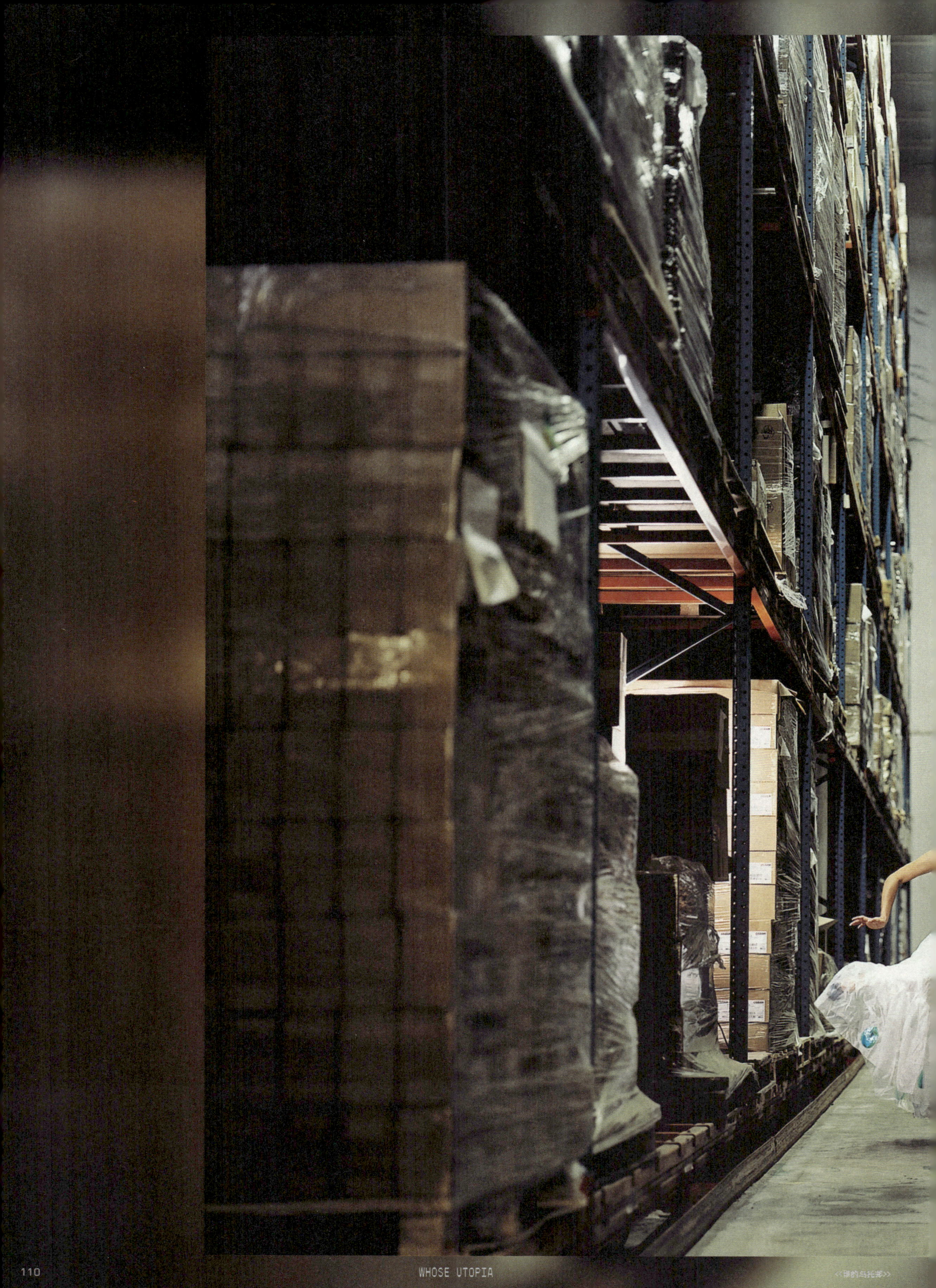

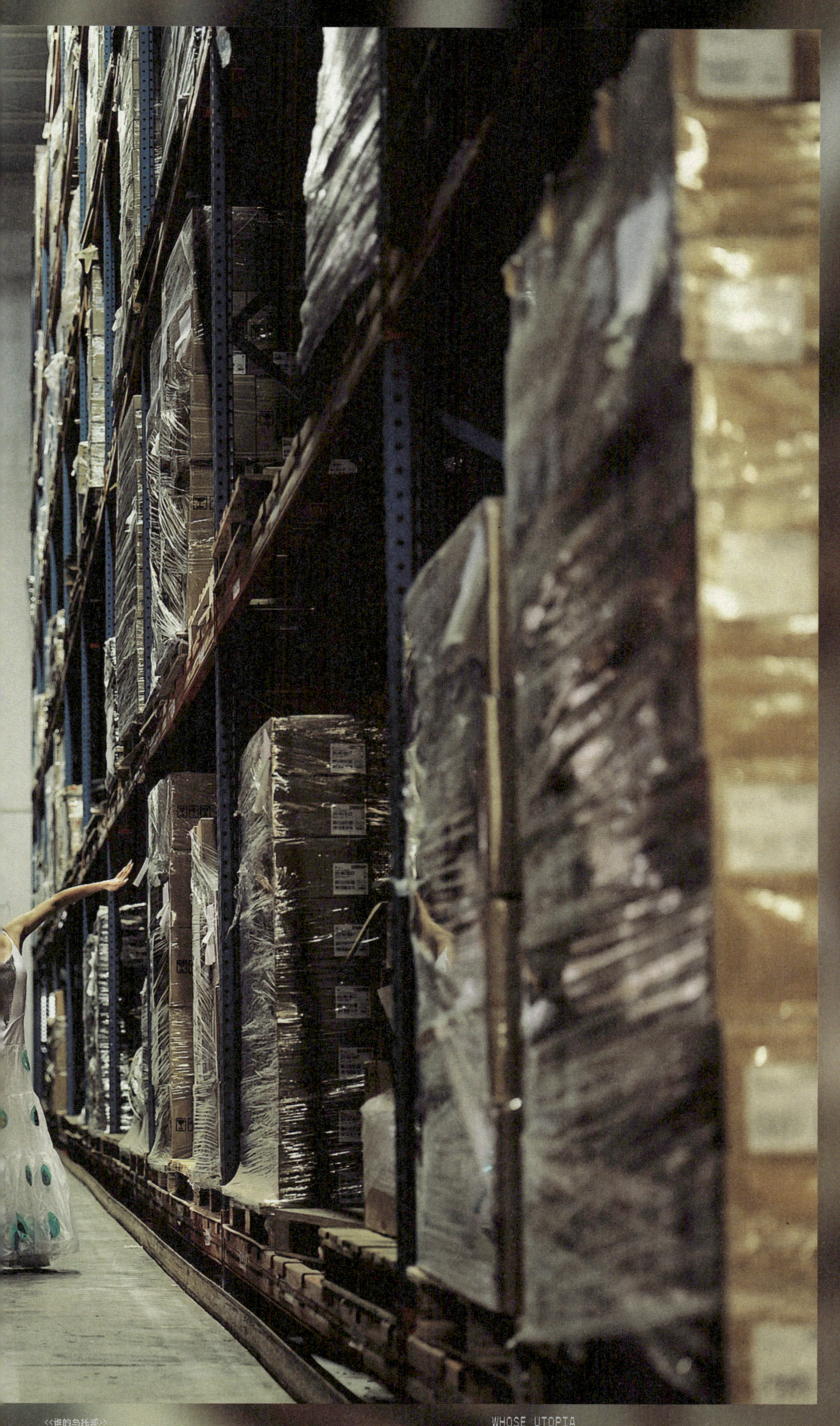

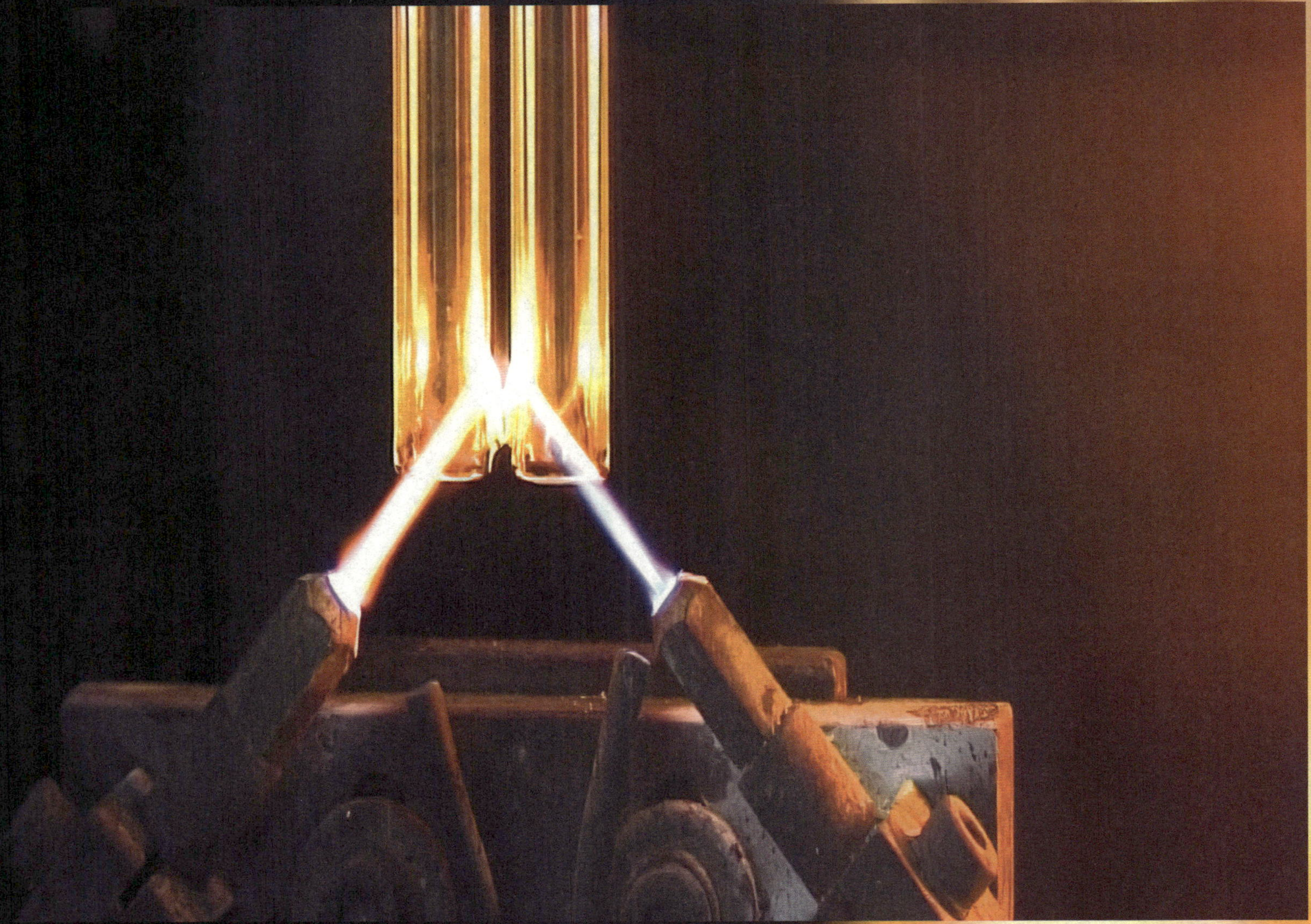

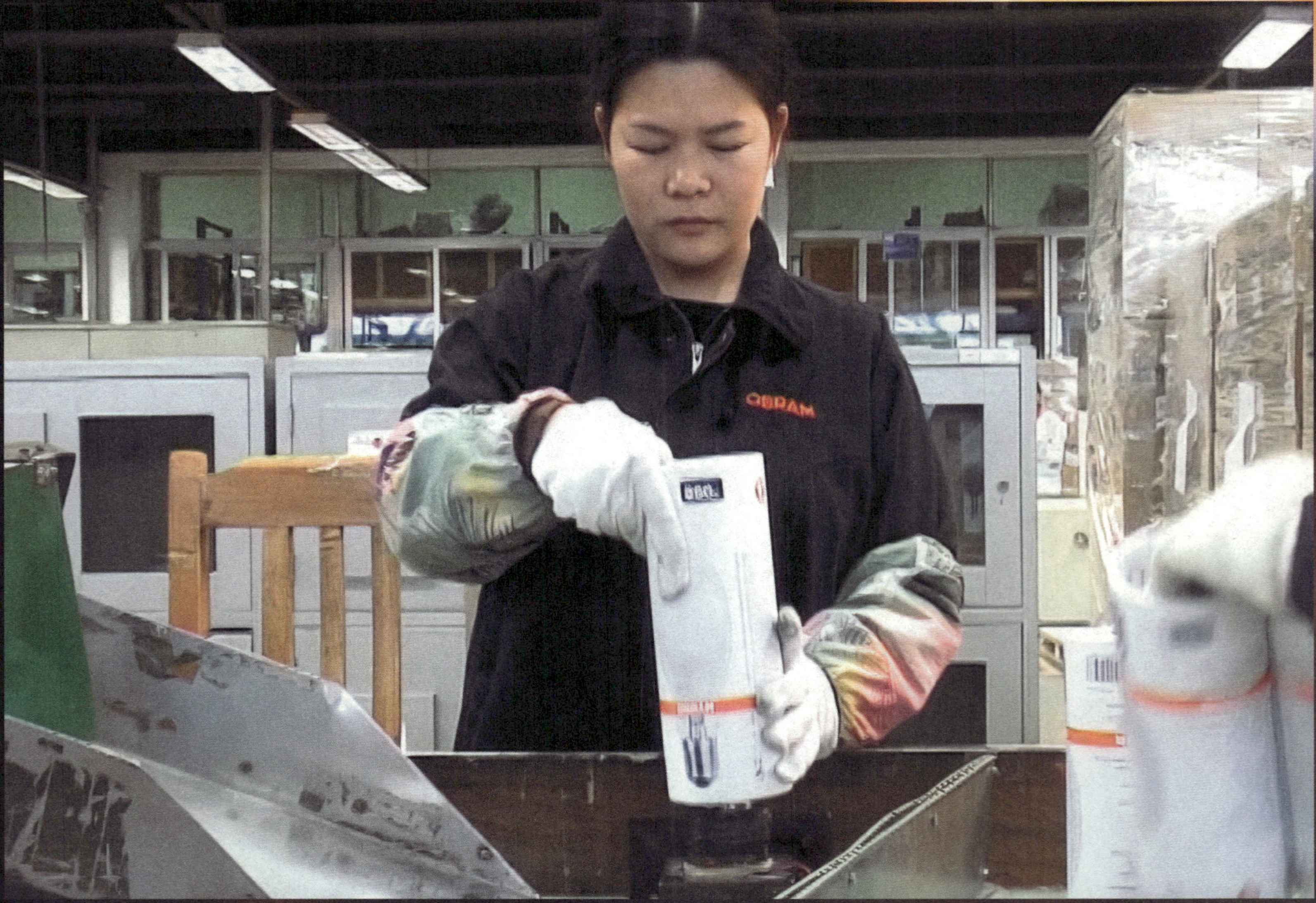

OSRAM

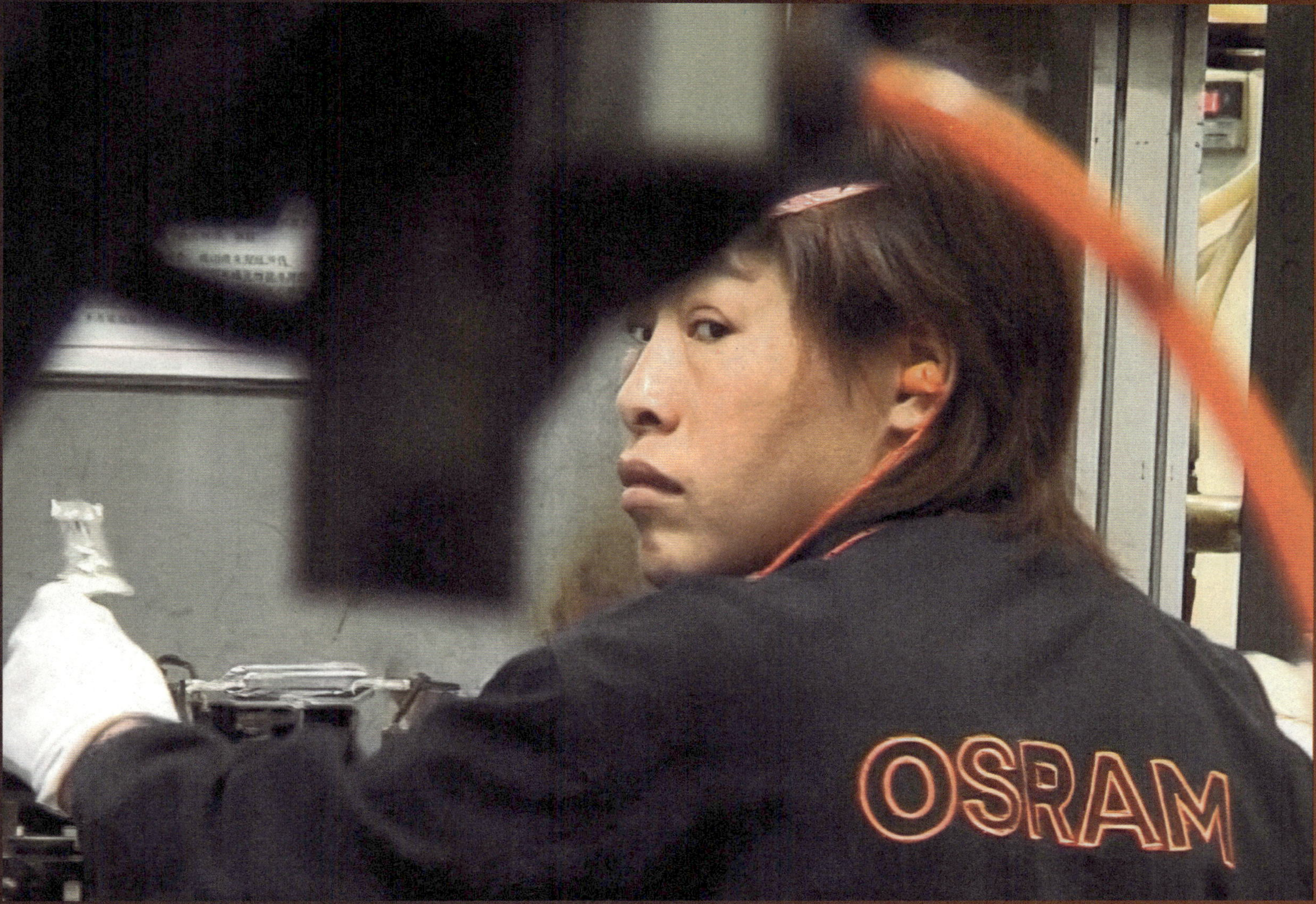

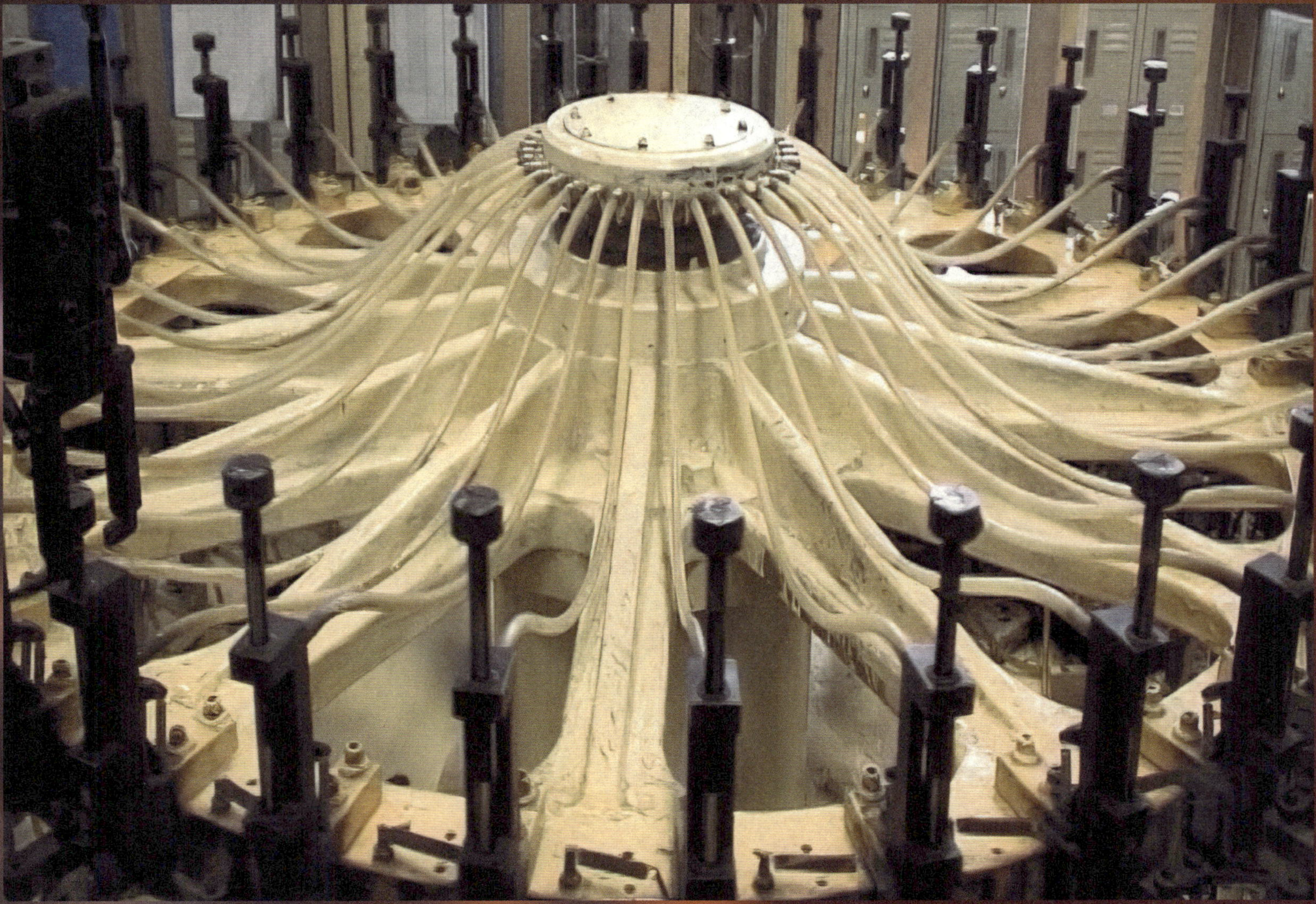

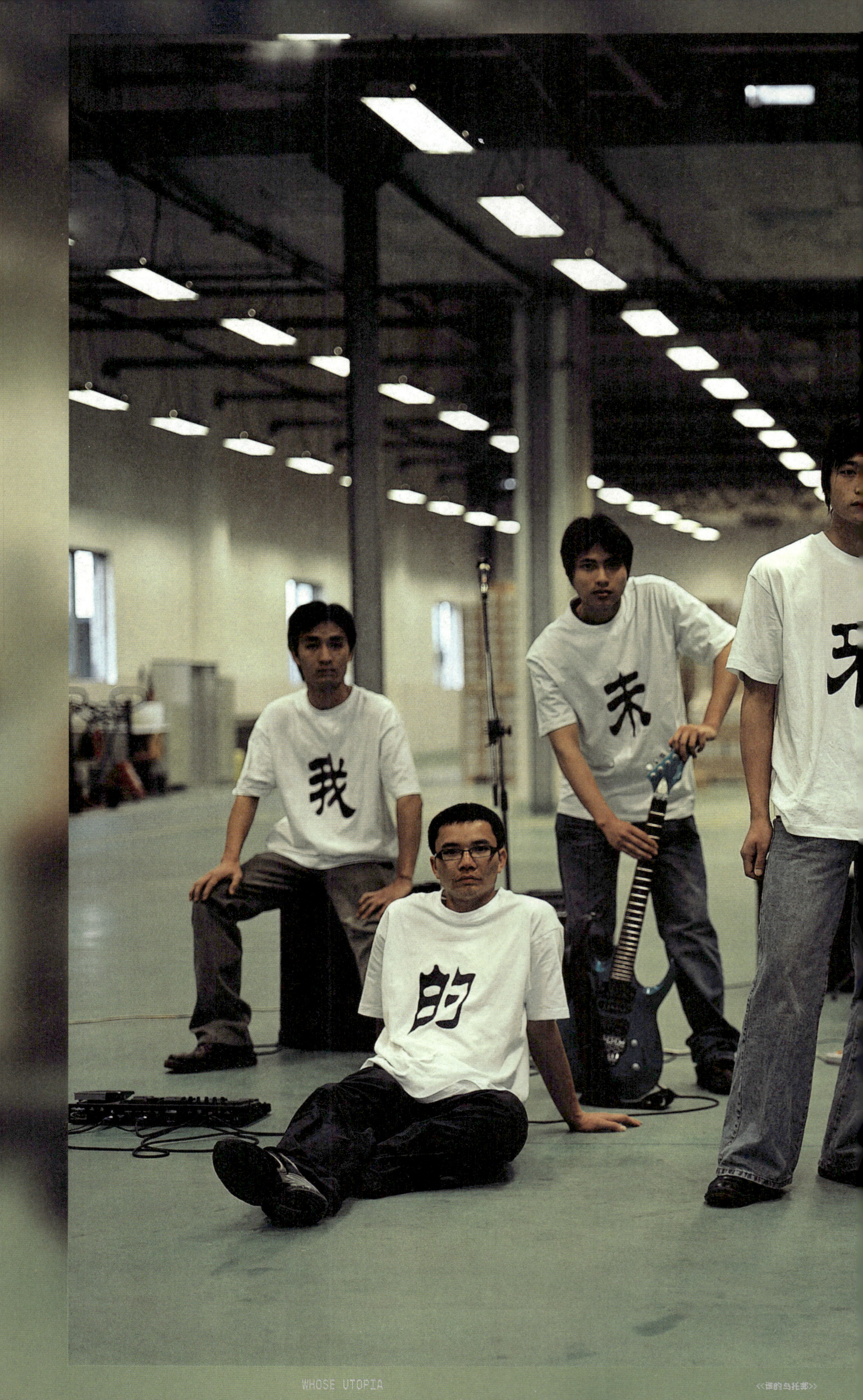
我
的
未

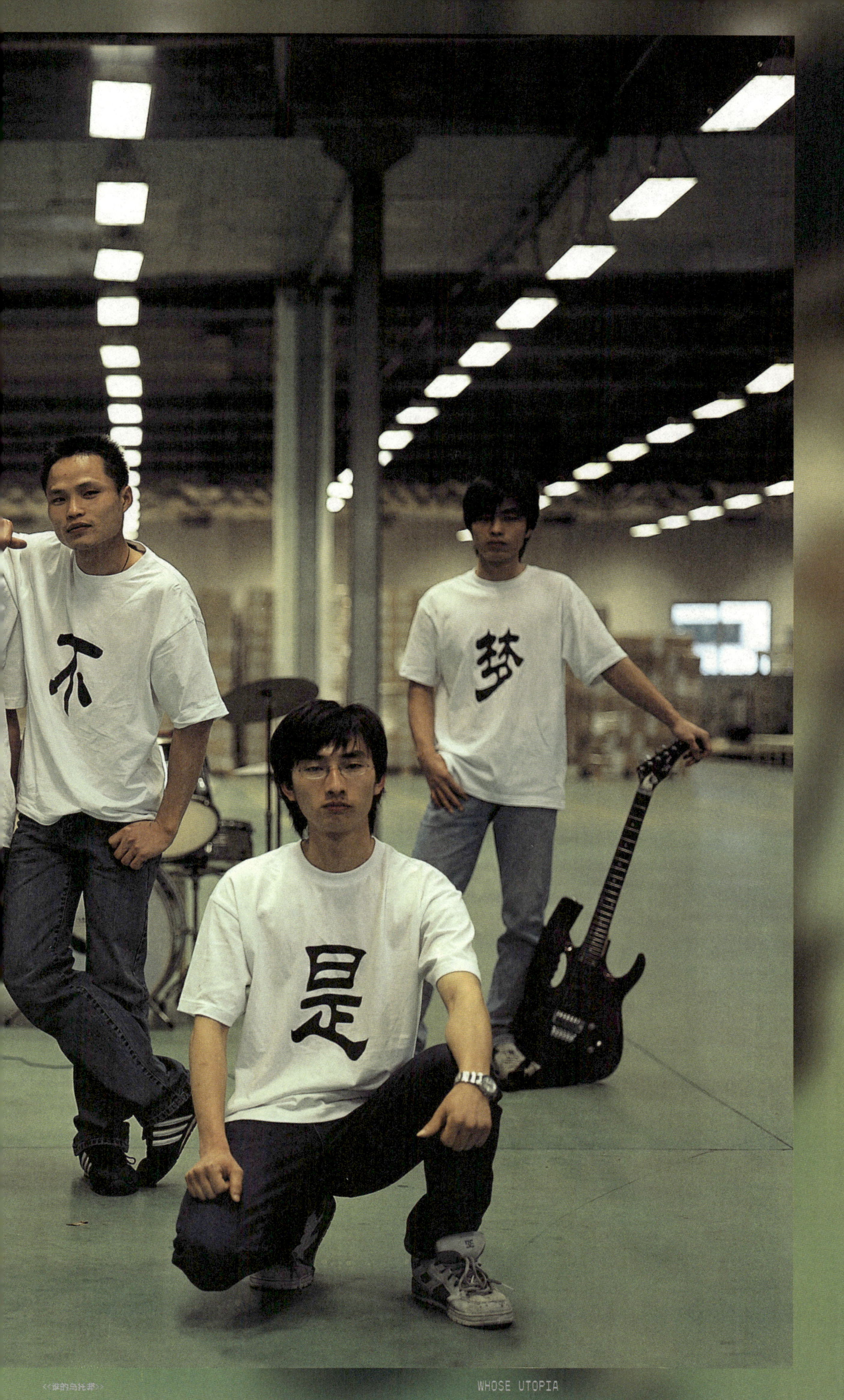
不
梦
是

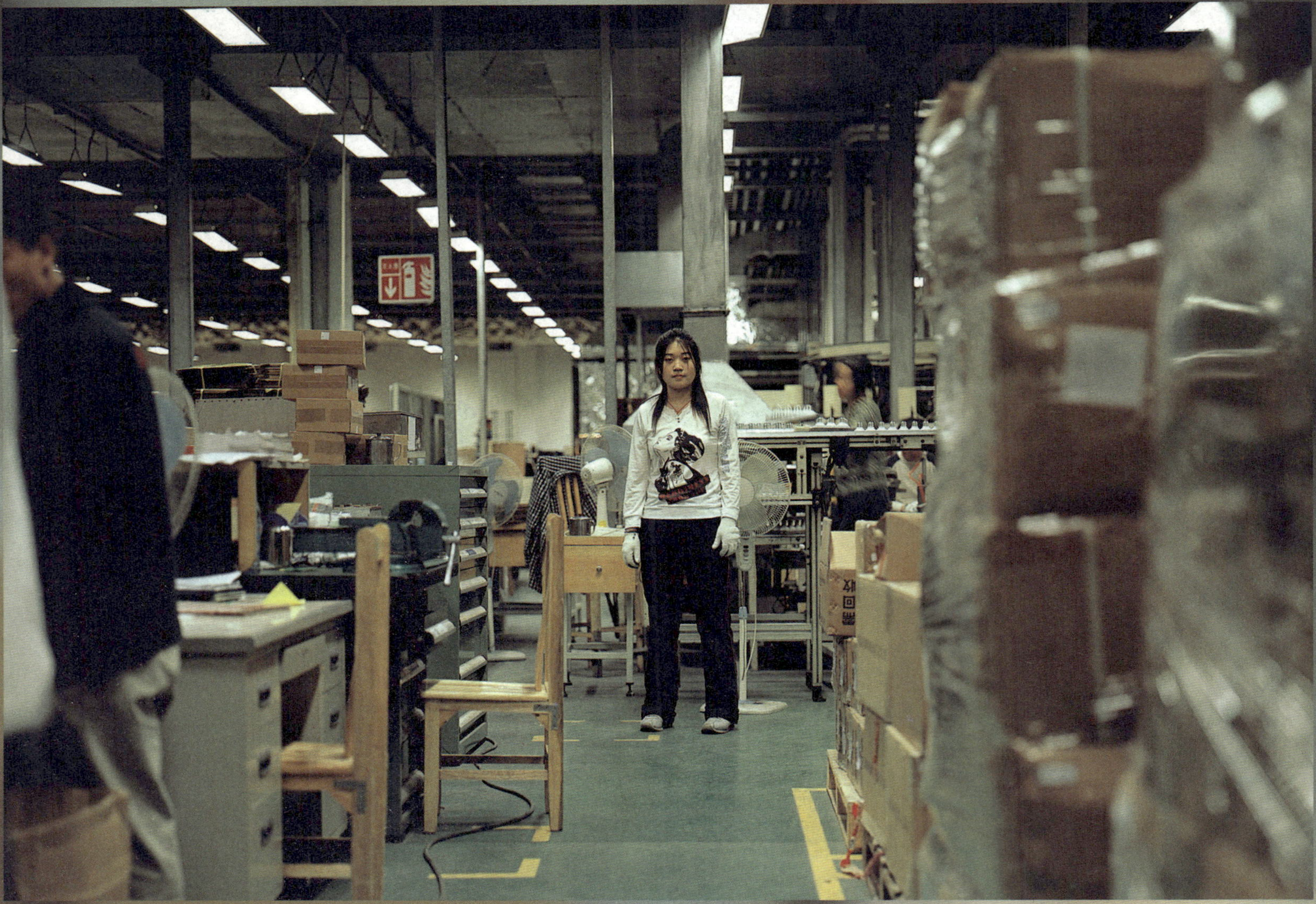

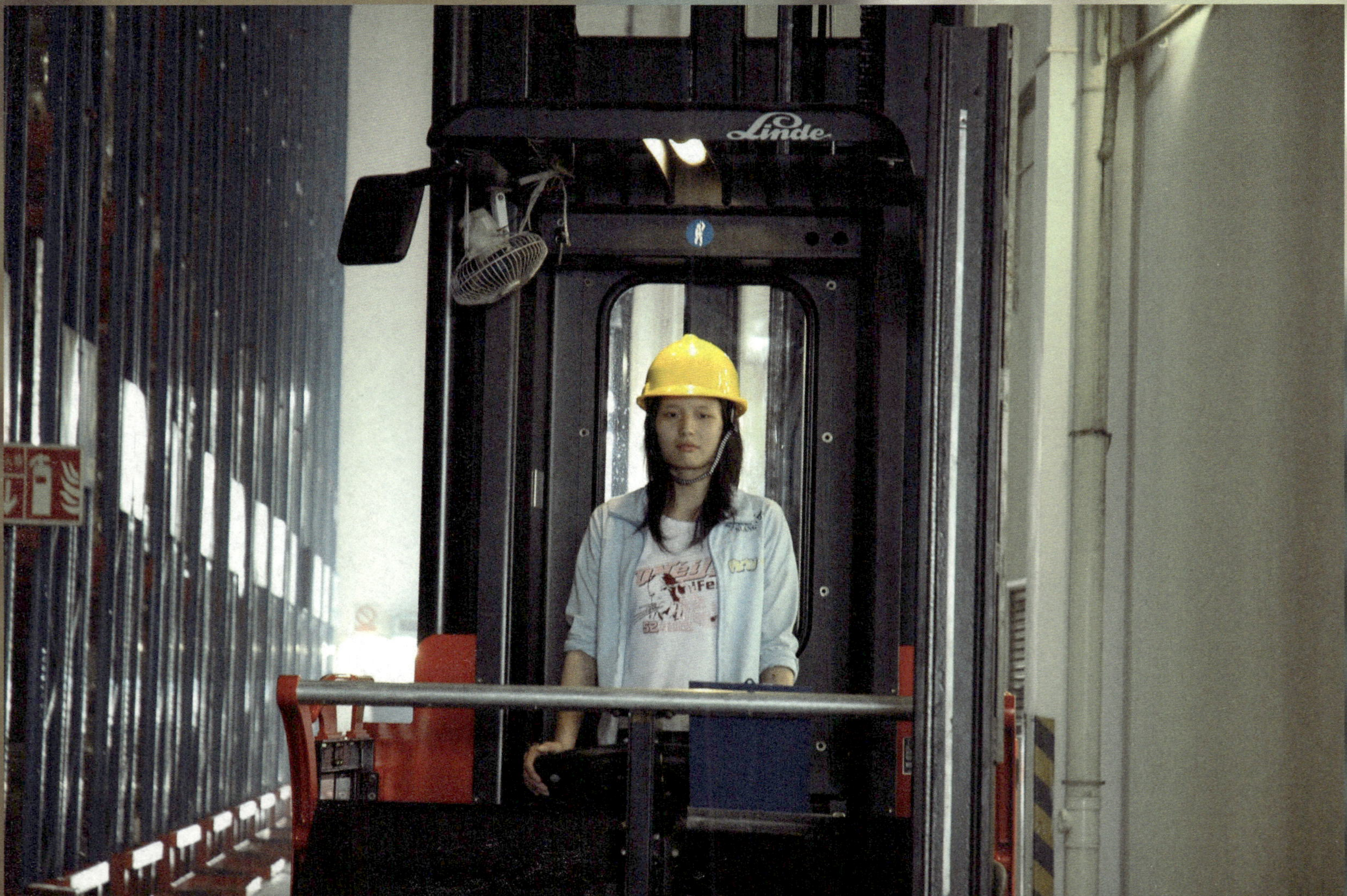

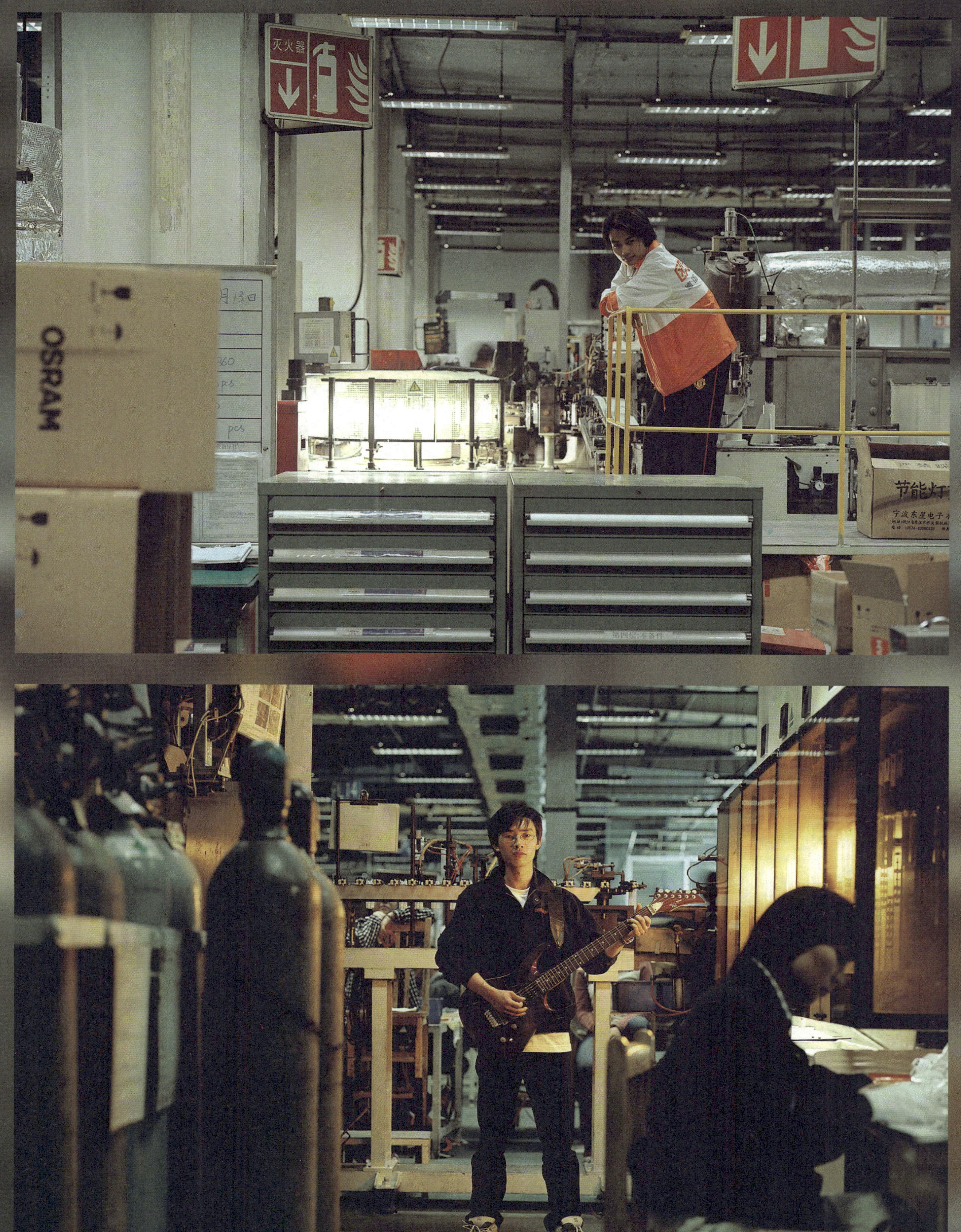
灭火器
OSRAM
节能灯

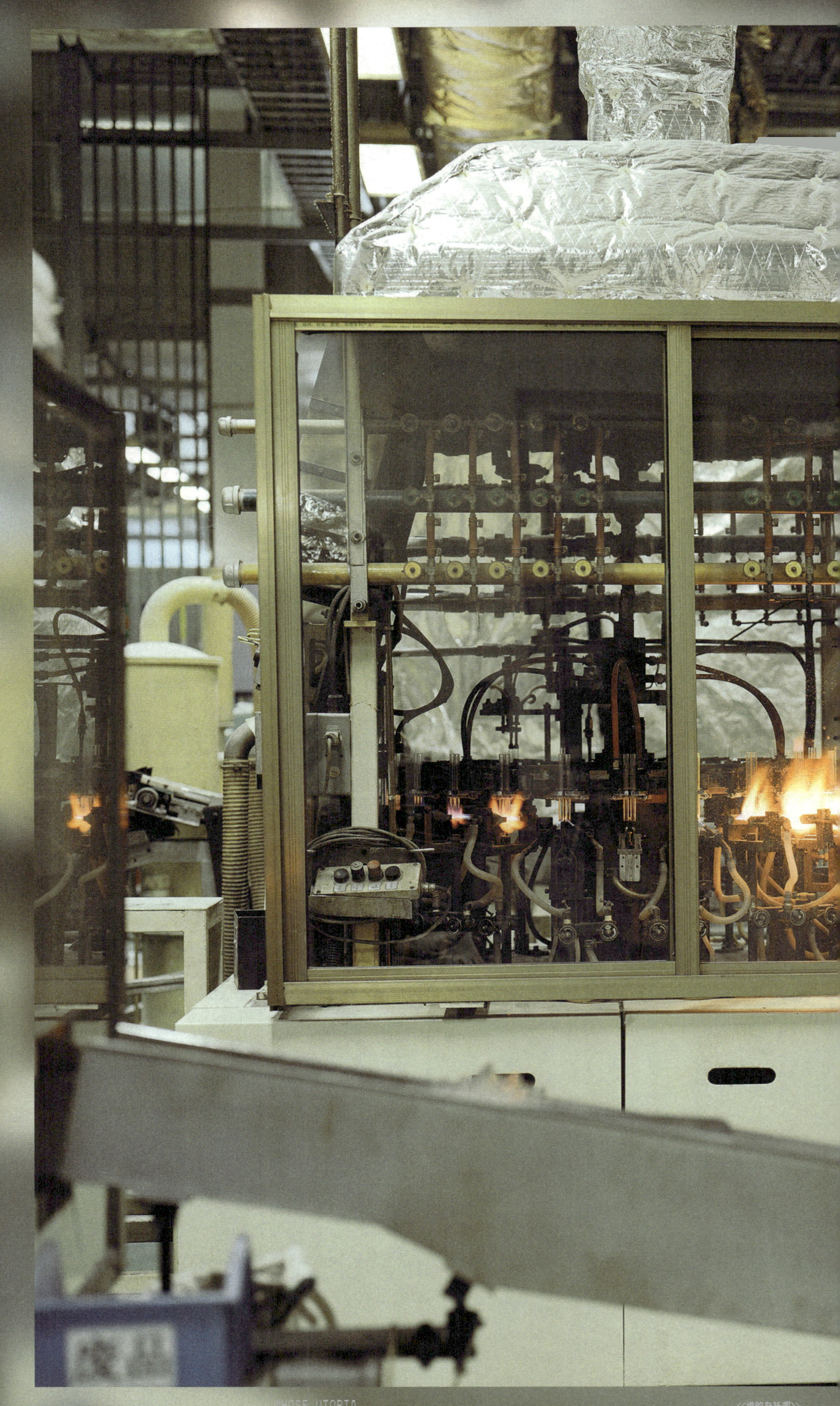

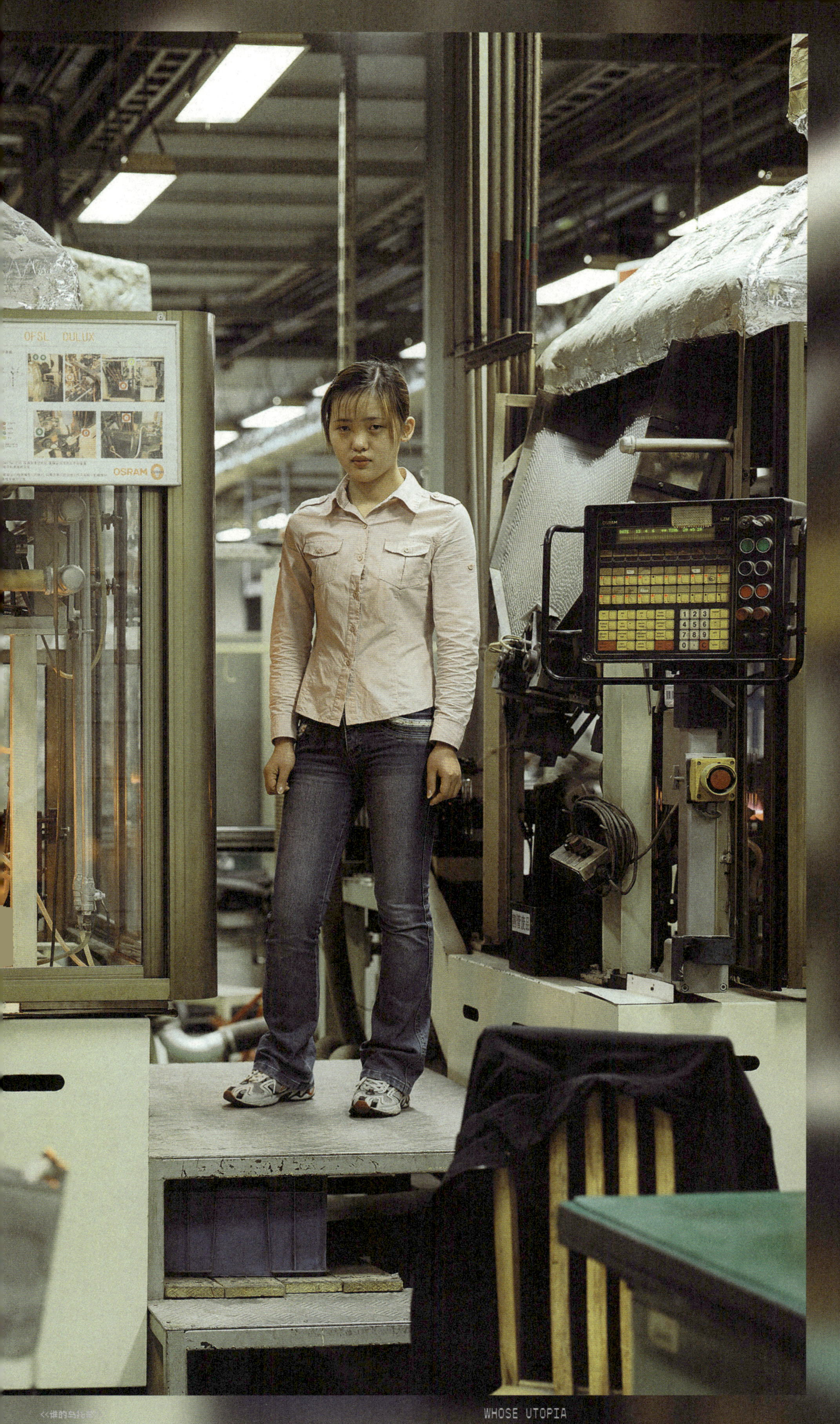
OFSL DULUX
OSRAM

Utopia Daily newspaper, produced as part of *Whose utopia* 2006

Archive

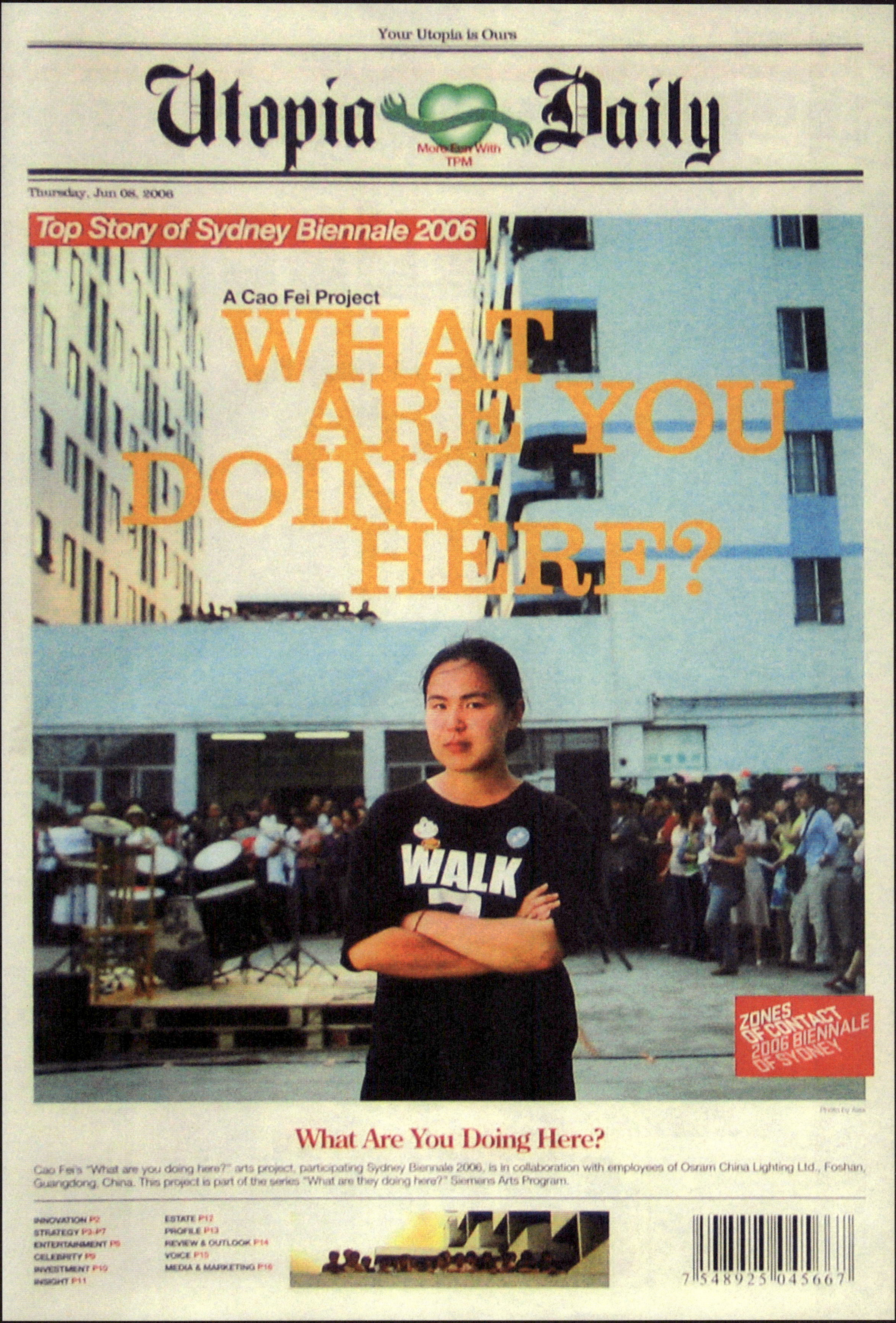

Your Utopia is Ours

Utopia Daily

More Fun With TPM

Thursday, Jun 08, 2006

Top Story of Sydney Biennale 2006

A Cao Fei Project

WHAT ARE YOU DOING HERE?

ZONES OF CONTACT 2006 BIENNALE OF SYDNEY

Photo by Alex

What Are You Doing Here?

Cao Fei's "What are you doing here?" arts project, participating Sydney Biennale 2006, is in collaboration with employees of Osram China Lighting Ltd., Foshan, Guangdong, China. This project is part of the series "What are they doing here?" Siemens Arts Program.

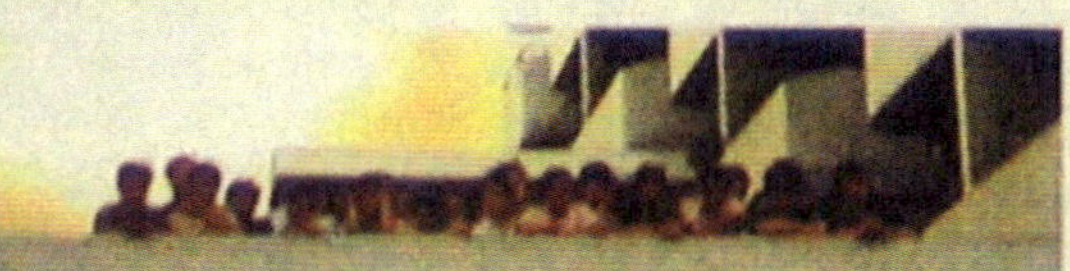

Team "Reality"

Name: A day of work

Idea: A view of a busy office area, although work needs more effort.

Installation: The employees put the bureaus and chairs together to represent the office environment.

Performance: Angel dance and group singing.

Group: 6 people

Leader: Lu Li

Member: Zhang Zhao / Wu Weiqing / Zheng Zhifeng / Chen Liyun / Li Weirao

Occupation: seller, product line worker

Specialty: street dance, ballet, singing

Craft

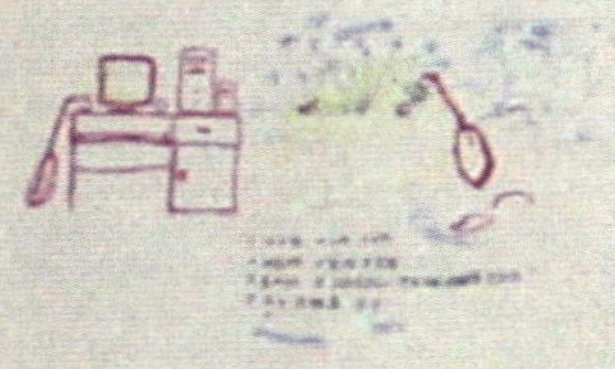

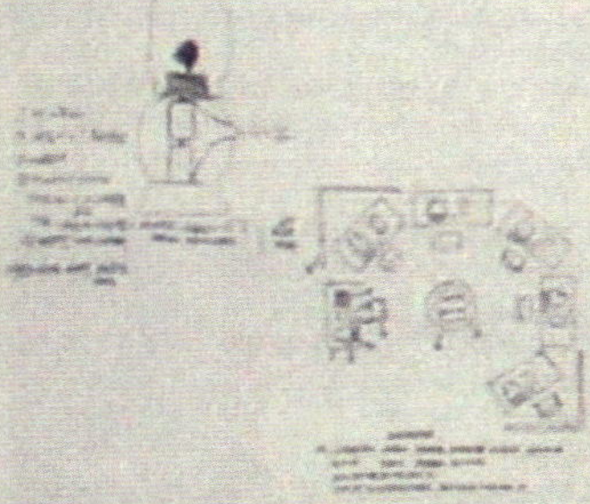

Rehearsal

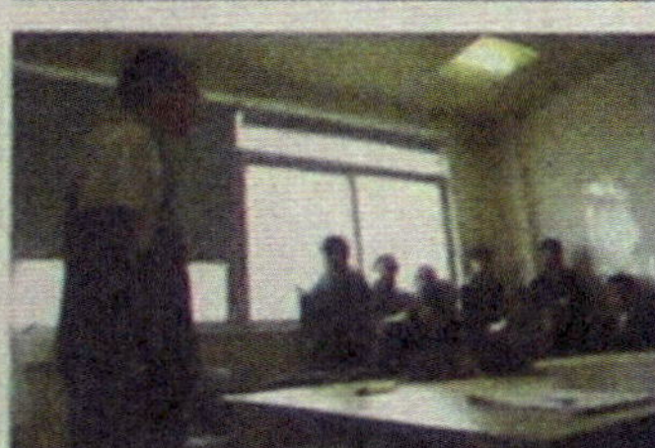

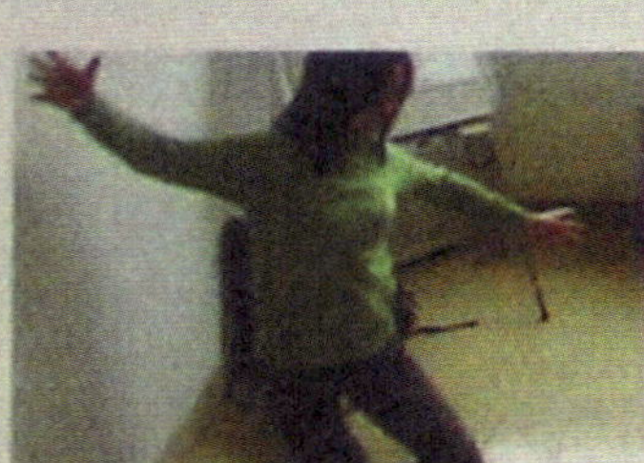

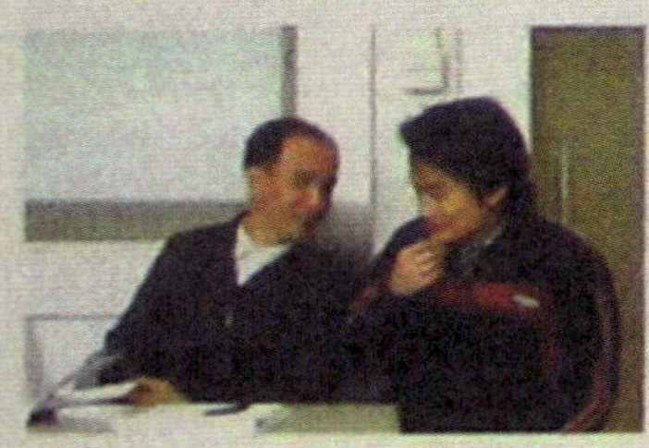

TPM stream-line 02

REALITY

Team "Reality" Members (OSRAM Employees)

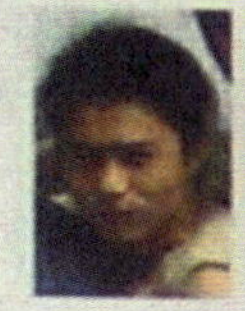
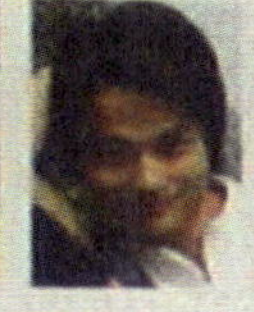
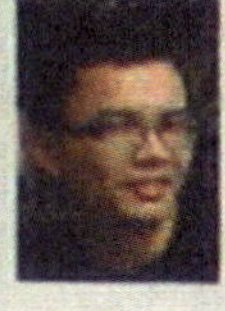
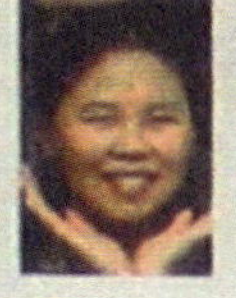
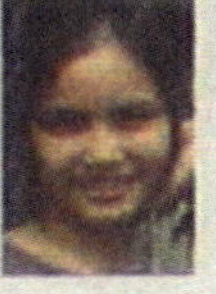
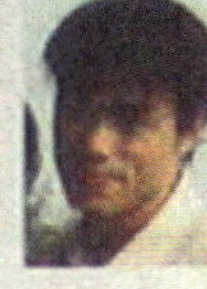
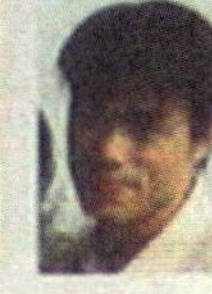

Process

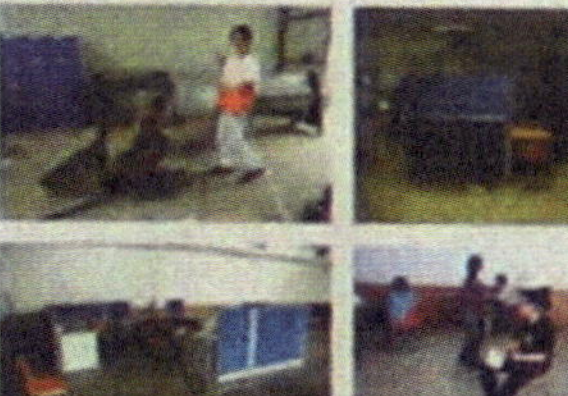
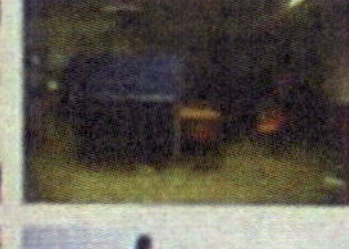
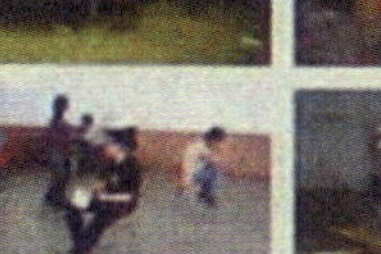
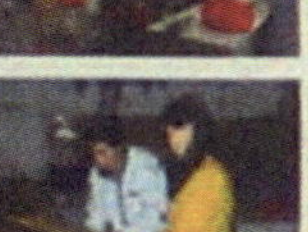
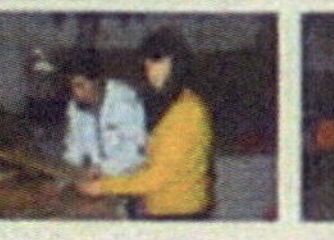
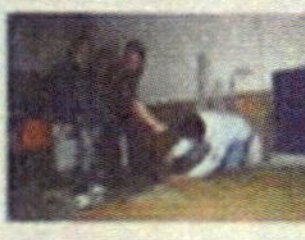

Performance

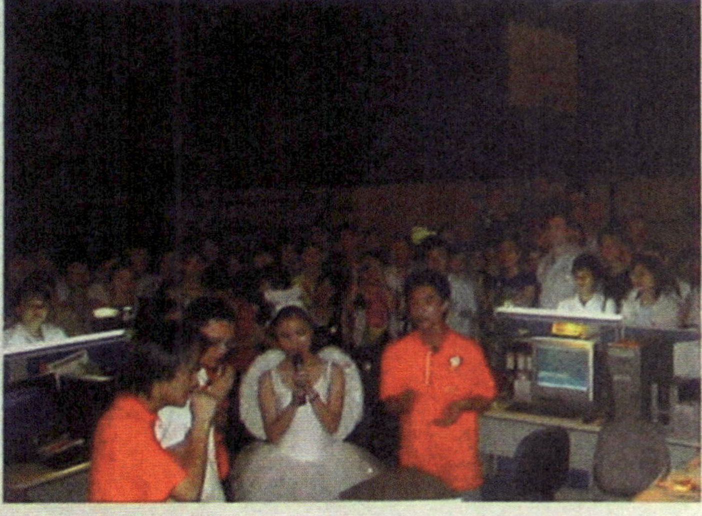

The music drama happened in a quiet office where everyone was busy working. Mrs. Li was chatting with her online friends, only to be caught off-guard by her boss, who decided to punish her. After she begged for a long time, the boss forgave her on condition that she turned in the friend list of her QQ (an IM software). Although reluctant initially, Mrs. Li was persuaded by her colleagues and finally became happy again.

Works

The whole accessory of an office with the workshop employees personal belongings, paper files, photos, DVDs, teacups, toys, sound boxes. And a light box with blue colour circled itself, printed "$", "¥", "€" on its face.

Questionnaire

Zeng Zhifeng, the team "Reality" member, interviewed after the opening day.

1. What do you think of the performances on *What are you doing here?*, April 11th?

The program is nice, but the sound system could be better.

2. What's special in your group's performance?

Ours is diversified, with sketch, dancing and singing.

3. Which is your favourite work or performance? Why?

My favourite is "Keep flying ahead", it's just personal taste.

4. Which topic (Hometown / Reality / Dream / Future / Ideal) would you choose to base your work on next time? Why?

I prefer to sing a song like this time.

5. Which process impresses you most? a). Drafting, b). the making of, c). the performance, d). interview / playing with light bulbs. Why?

My girlfriend is the first choose if she wasn't one of the performers. In another case, I want some friends who respect my show.

6. Given another chance, which form of expression would you choose? Drawing / dancing / singing / sword-playing / yoga / calligraphy / sketch or others? Or would you prefer to be an audience?

I regard her as a person who is close to everybody, persuasive and respectable, also I admire her working style.

7. If you're allowed to bring but one audience to see the opening, whom would you invite?

More forms of expression and more perform appliances.

8. Please describe your feelings about Cao Fei, do you have any advices for this kind of working method?

I do not quite know about the TPM in our department. The new TPM is creative. It stands for team spirit.

9. What do you see as the difference between *What are you doing here?* And other projects of Siemens Arts Program you saw before?

I would like to finish my work firstly than to join it in.

10. Please define the concept of TPM (Team / People / Management) as used in your department. What do you think of the re-defined TPM (Team / People / Motivation)?

I got no new feeling about others.

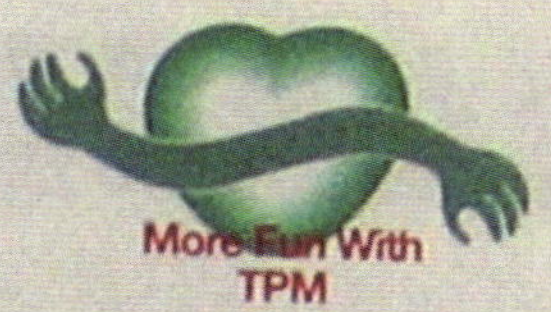

TPM stream-line 03

★ DREAM ★

Team " Dream" Members (OSRAM Employees)

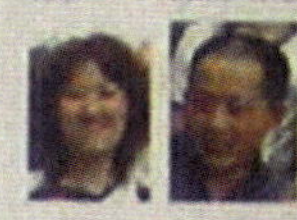
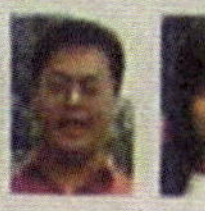
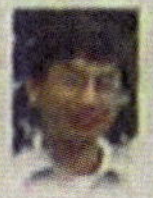
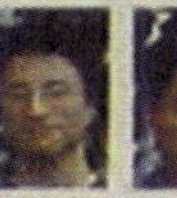
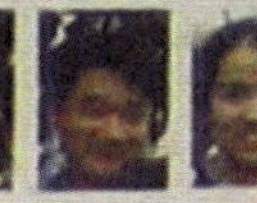
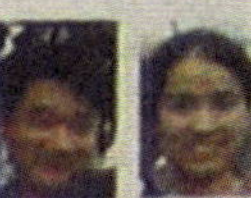

Team "Dream"

Name: Heading towards the dream.
Idea: Walking up the spiral stairs to the heaven of dreams, from there you can reach to your wonderland.
Installation: A staircase mounted on a grass base, spiraling upwards into a mosquito net, which serves as the metaphor of "wonderland".
Performance: Breakdance.
Group: 6 people
Leader: Hou Xiaoxia
Member: Zhang Jingfang / Yang Zhiqiang / Zhang Guoqiang / Yu Huafeng / Huang Xiaoling / Cai Kunming / Huang Yuanbing
Occupation: factory workers, quality checker, product line worker
Specialty: dancing.

Craft

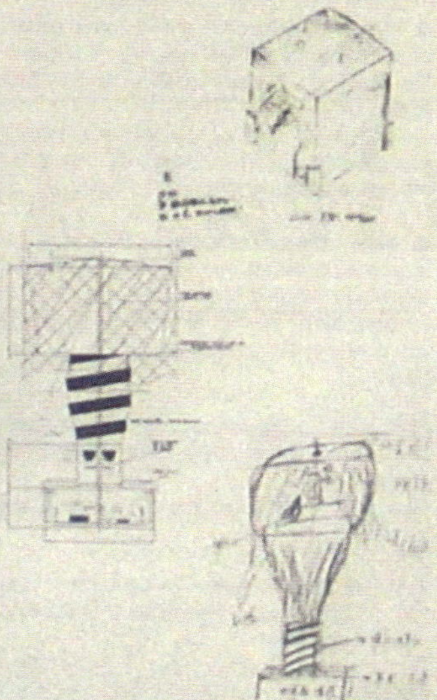

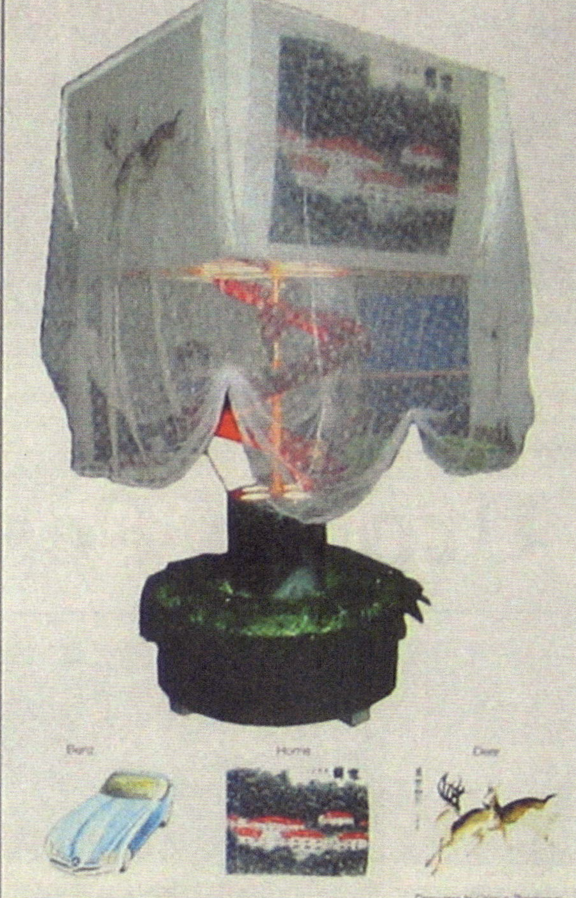

Benz
Home
Deer

Drawing by Yang Zhiqiang

Works

Glass covered the basic of groundsill with lights shine inside, pillar is painted as the landscape far away in the traditional Chinese painting. Stairs circled around with red carpet and toys are on the middle of the stairs. Pictures including the "Benz", "Home", "Deer" were hung on the mosquito net, a mini future house was exhibited at the end of the stairs, with a couple and their belongings-TV, sofa, Hi-fi, bed, flowers and plants inside.

Process

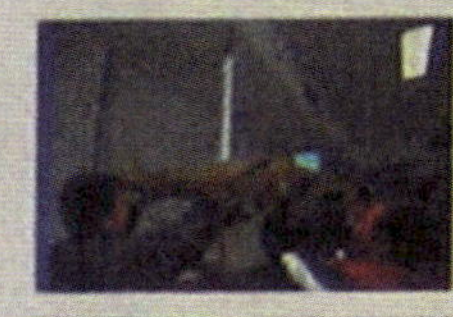
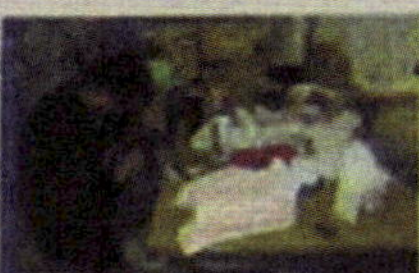
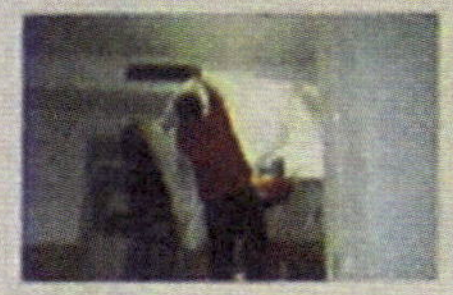
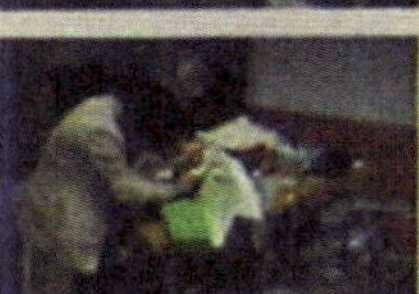
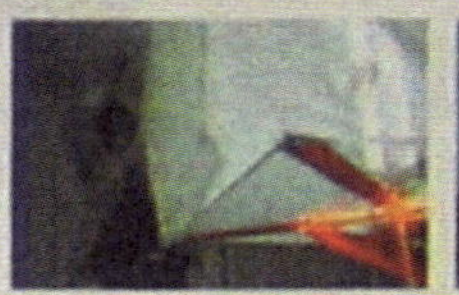
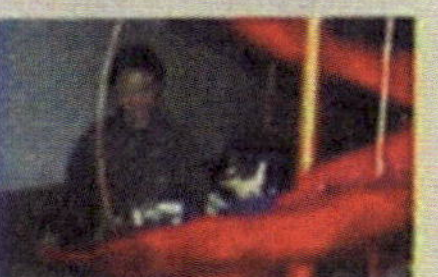

Rehearsal

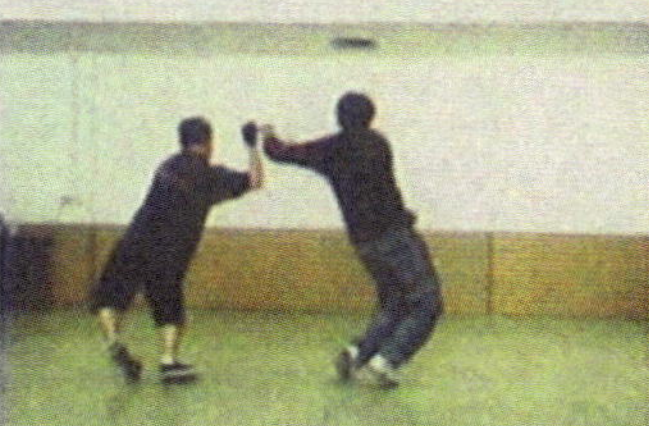
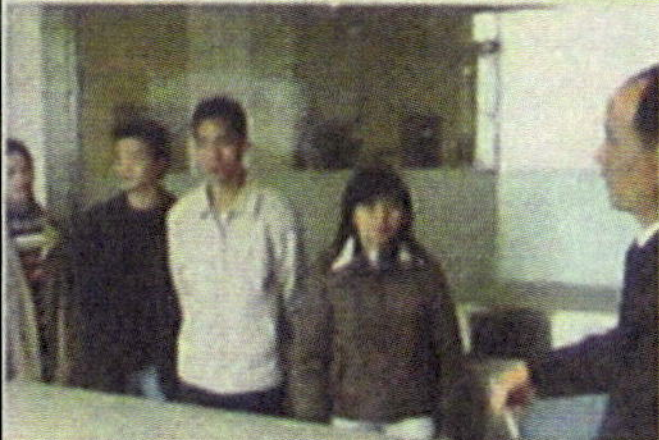
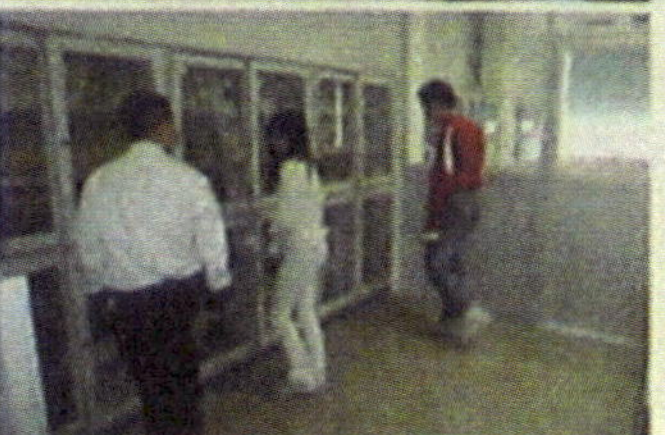

Performance

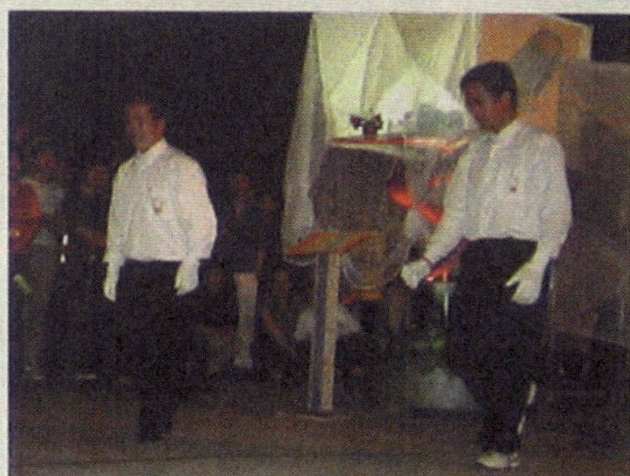

The show took place in the mosquito net. There the dancers stood inside taking a nap dressed in the fashion of white-collar workers. When the music started, the dancers began to perform their break dancing piece called "Walking in the space". They danced towards the audience and made reaction with each other, suddenly a phone rang, the dancer picked it up without stopping the body movement and started bargaining, "50 million?", "40 million is ok." "Deal!" After the negotiation, they shook hands with each other and signed the contract.

Questionnaire

Huang Xiaoling, the team "Dream" member, interviewed after the opening

1. What do you think of the performances on *What are you doing here?* , April 11th?
It is very interesting.

2. What's special in your group's performance?
It's more dreamy and full of imagination.

3. Which is your favourite work or performance? Why?
I would choose my own piece, one always prefers his own stuff, because it involves my own endeavour.

4. Which topic (Hometown / Reality / Dream / Future / Ideal) would you choose to base your work on next time? Why?
I would choose future. It's full of challenge and aspiration.

5. Which process impresses you most? a). Drafting, b). the making of, c). the performance, d). interview / playing with light bulbs. Why?
The performance, because it justified all our previous efforts.

6. Given another chance, which form of expression would you choose? Drawing / dancing / singing / sword-playing / yoga / calligraphy / sketch or others? Or would you prefer to be an audience?
I would choose Sketch.

7. If you're allowed to bring but one audience to see the opening, whom would you invite?
My mother.

8. Please describe your feelings about Cao Fei, do you have any advices for this kind of working method?
She always presents a new kind of sensibility, and full of imagination.

9. What do you see as the difference between *What are you doing here?* and other projects of Siemens Arts Program you saw before?
I haven't seen any of them before.

10. Please define the concept of TPM (Team / People / Management) as used in your department. What do you think of the re-defined TPM (Team / People / Motivation)?
Team-work is powerful.

11.Would you participate if the new TPM is brought into effect? How would you promote and realize the idea?
I would, and I will focus on developing team spirit.

12.Have your impression of your colleagues been refreshed by this project? And how?
Yes, but it's hard to describe.

13.Has your feeling about yourself been refreshed by this project?
Yes, art has become closer to us, and closer to life.

Utopia Daily | ENTERTAINMENT | Page 8

Thursday, Jun 08, 2006 ★ ★ ★ ★ ★ Your Utopia is Ours

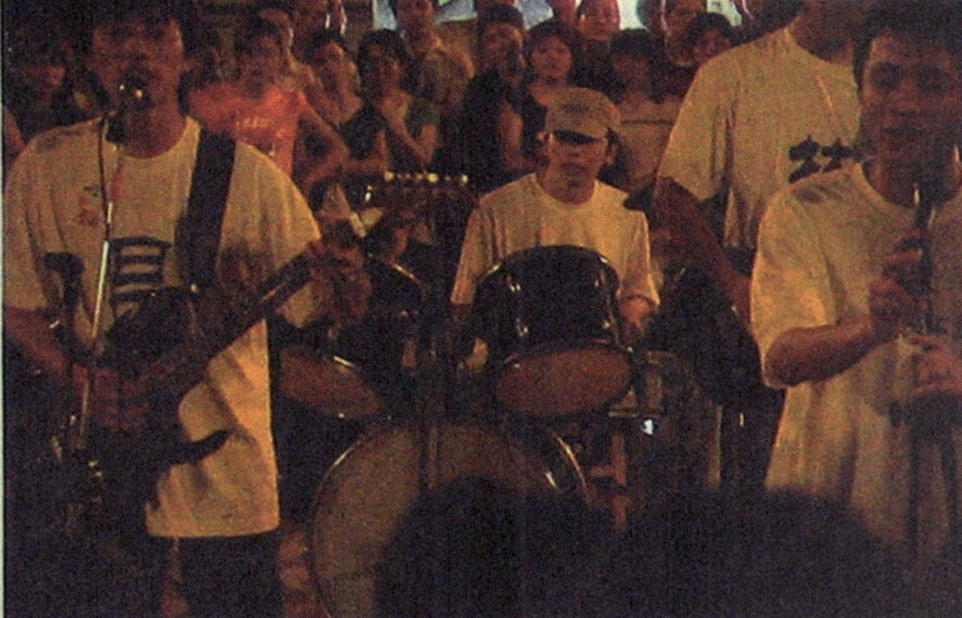

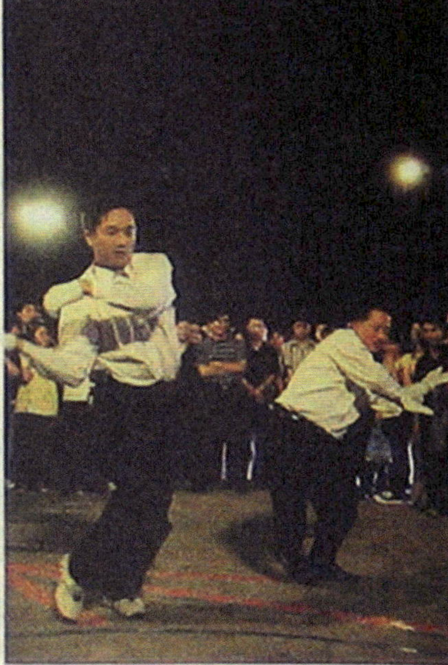

Above: The band from the Future group is performing a rock song - "My future is not a dream" in the middle of the stage, wearing clothes with the song's name in Simplified Chinese. The boy with the character "shi" ("is") on his T-shirt is the lead singer.
Right: Two dancers dancing according to the design of Dream group. Dressed in suits in the fashion of white-collar wokers, they pretended to work while dancing - reading files, using mobile phones, even doing business negotiation.

★ The 1st Utopia Festival ★

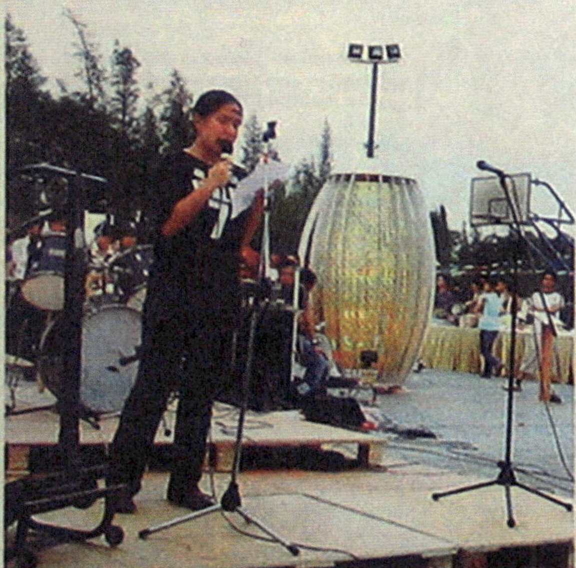

Above: Cao Fei briefing about her Siemens Arts Project What are they doing here? at the beginning of the performance.
Bottom: Zafka playing music on the box sill at the beginning of the open day surrounded by audience.

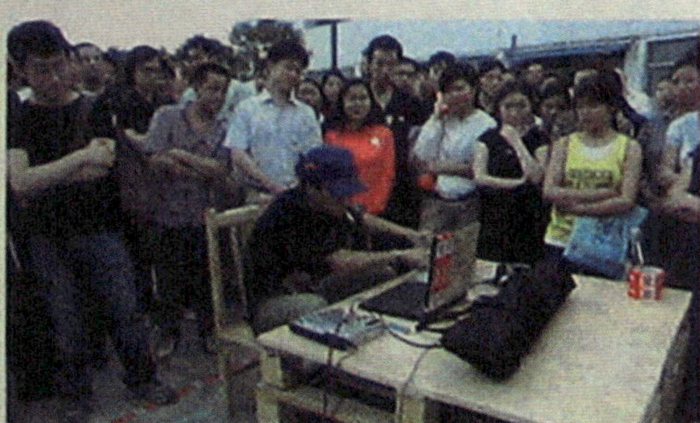

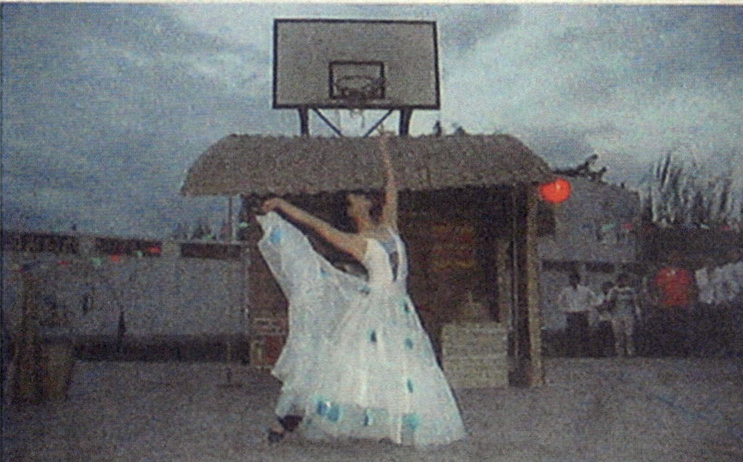

Above: The female peacock dancer in front of the installation by the Hometown group in the music drama.

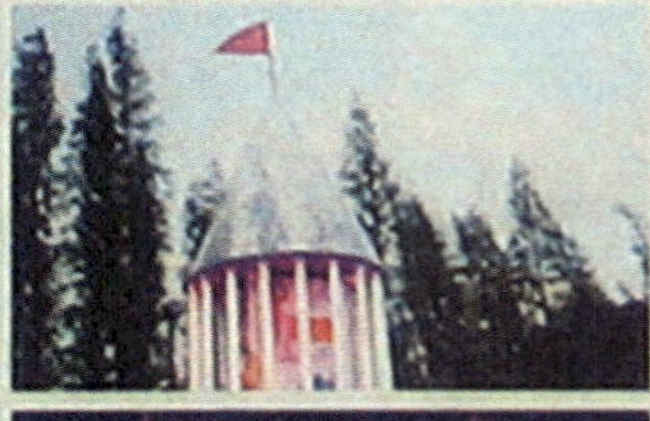

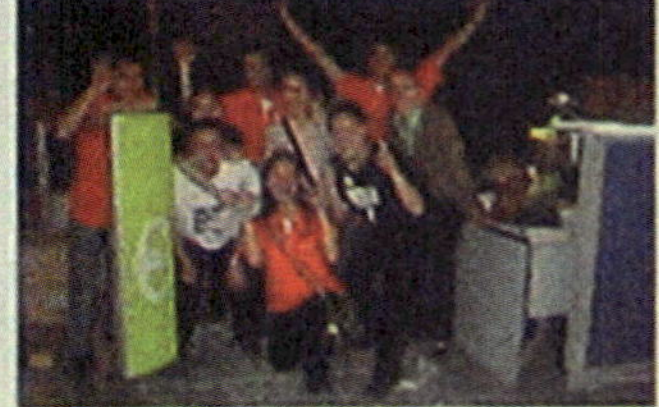

Above: The top red flag of the Ideal group flow in the air.
Bottom: Cao Fei and Christine with the members of Reality group.

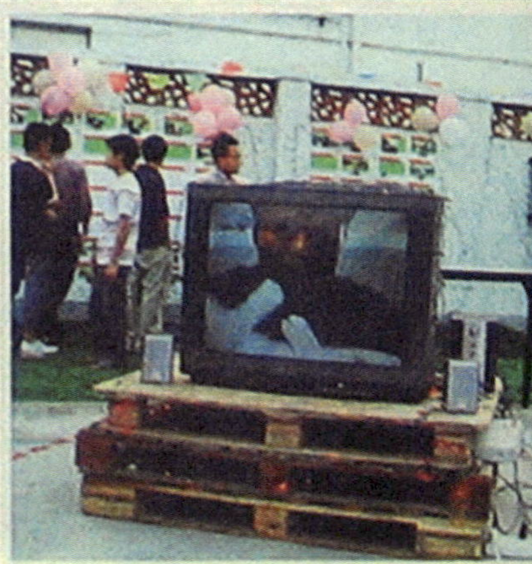

Above: The TV on the box sill was showing Cao Fei's interviews with several Osram employees. It also showed the sound game project by Zafka.

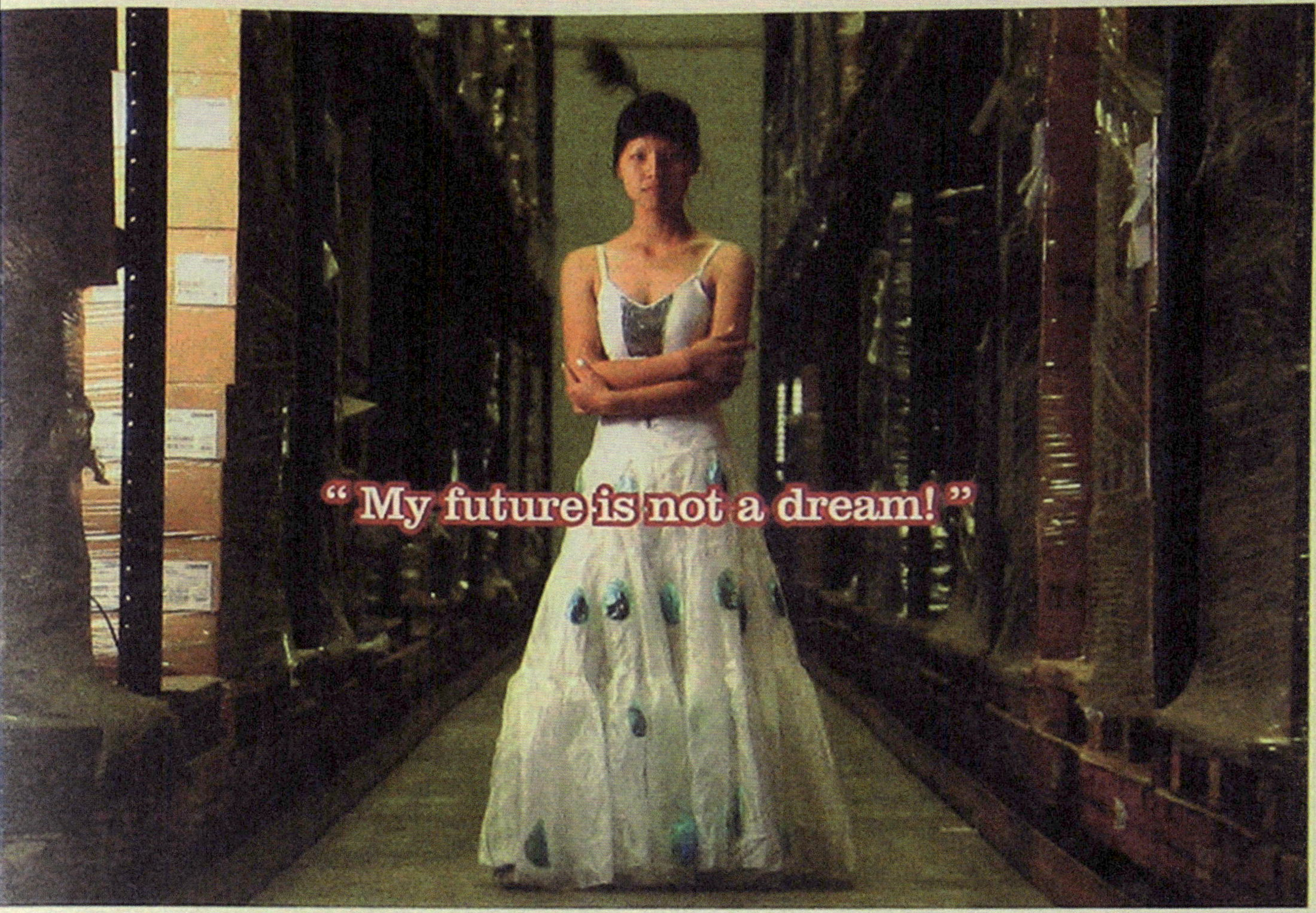

Utopia Daily | CELEBRETY | Page 9

Thursday, Jun 08, 2006 ★★★★★ Your Utopia is Ours

"My future is not a dream!"

Above: The 20-year old Peacock girl worked in the Quality Department is standing between the huge exported goods in the warehouse, with dust and insects circled around her, facing ahead with confidence. After the performance - What are they doing here? in the basketball court of April 11th, Cao Fei went back to take video and photos, she stayed in the Osram factory for one day.

★ Utopia Idol ★

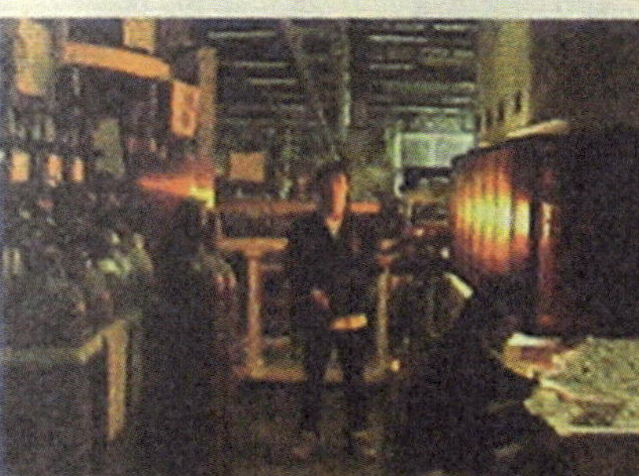

The boy sings in the noisy mechanical area, hot fire illuminates his face.

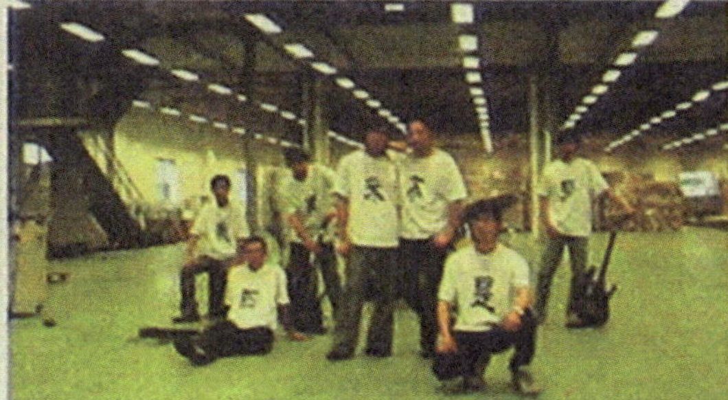

The band performs in the product line, announcing the words "My future is not a dream" which is printed on their white clothes.

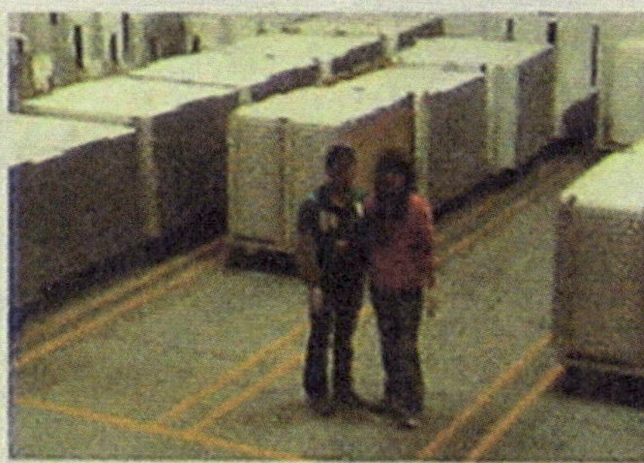

Two girls dress up with pink and green clothes in the piles of lights.

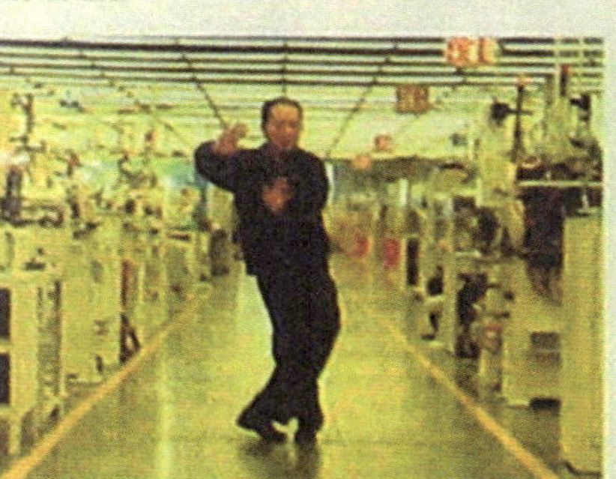

The man weared Osram uniform dance with pop music in the rigid product area.

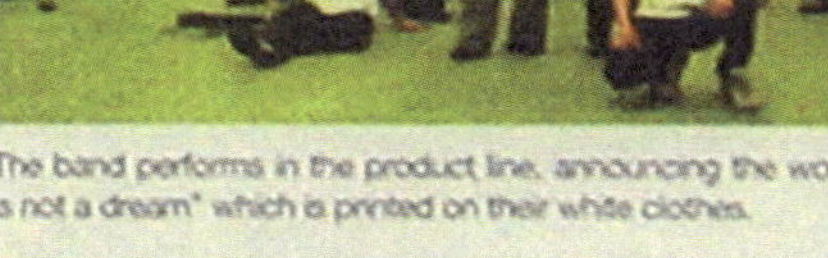

The Coolest Worker

Most of the workers are young, the average age is 25, mostly single. They came from sub-cities and countryside of Guangdong province. Technical staff usually came from inland provinces, marketing and managing staff are mostly local (Guangzhou, Foshan). Senior technical consultants come from either German headquarter or South East Asia (Hong Kong, Taiwan). Workers in the workshops form the main body of the factory, they play active roles on the various production lines. The reason of their leaving hometown is to change their life status, the motivation behind their hard working and enthusiasm towards new skills is the aspiration of an urban lifestyle. They are the most active, most talented, most respectable new generation, in the process of creating wealth, they're also recreating themselves.

Cool: youthful, fashionable, handsome, refined, confident, quiet, unruly, tender, practical, mind-free, idealistic.

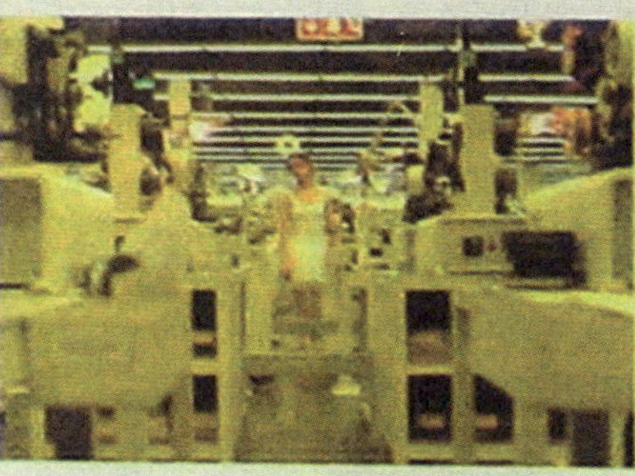

White angle with furry wings and aura is standing in the lifeless, clean and tidy working area.

Utopia Daily

INVESTMENT

Page 10

Thursday, Jun 08, 2006

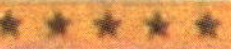

Your Utopia is Ours

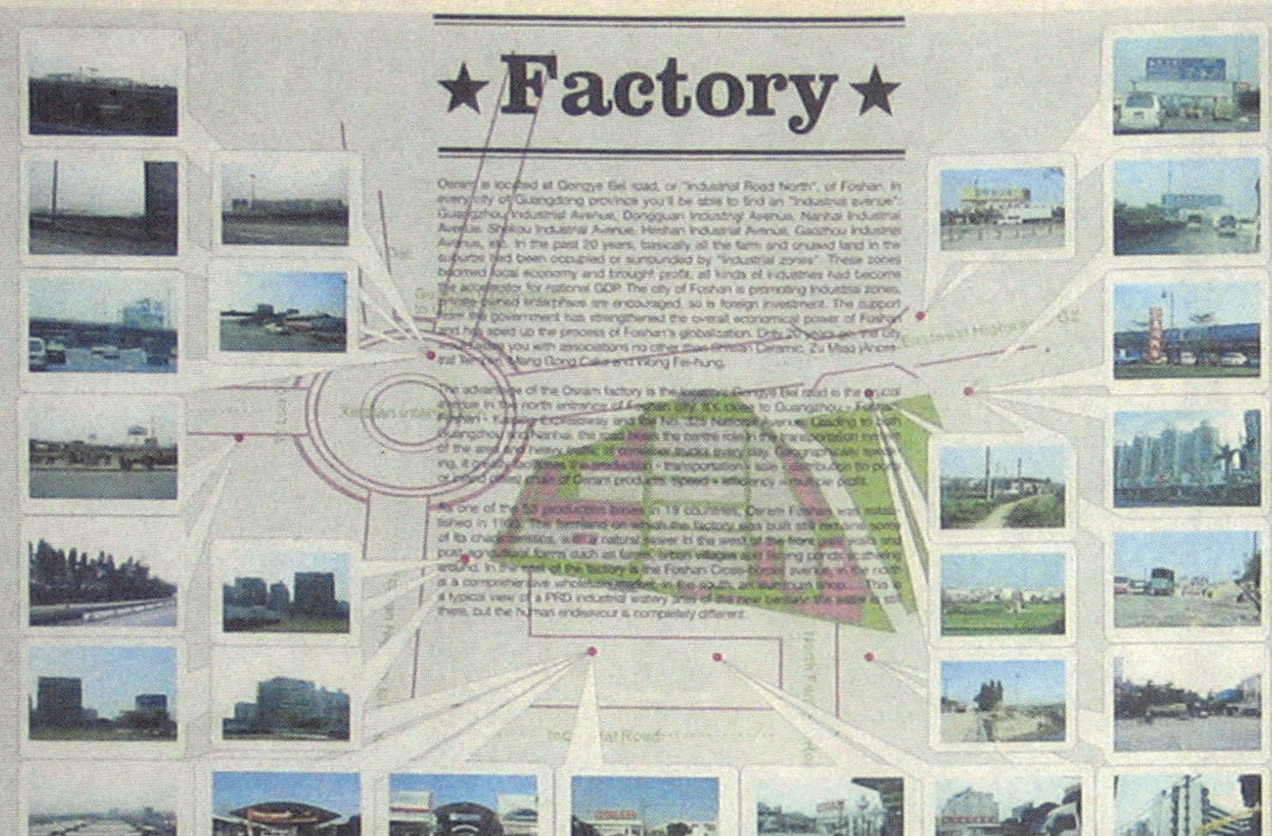

★Factory★

Osram is located at Gongye Bei road, or "Industrial Road North", of Foshan. In every city of Guangdong province you'll be able to find an "industrial avenue": Guangzhou Industrial Avenue, Dongguan Industrial Avenue, Nanhai Industrial Avenue, Shekou Industrial Avenue, Heshan Industrial Avenue, Gaozhou Industrial Avenue, etc. In the past 20 years, basically all the farm and unused land in the suburbs had been occupied or surrounded by "industrial zones". These zones boomed local economy and brought profit, all kinds of industries had become the accelerator for national GDP. The city of Foshan is promoting industrial zones, privately-owned enterprises are encouraged, so is foreign investment. The support from the government has strengthened the overall economical power of Foshan and has sped up the process of Foshan's globalisation. Only 20 years ago the city would provide you with associations no other than Shiwan Ceramic, Zu Miao (Ancestral Temple), Mang Gong Cake and Wong Fei-hung.

The advantage of the Osram factory is the location. Gongye Bei road is the crucial avenue in the north entrance of Foshan city. It is close to Guangzhou - Foshan, Foshan - Kaiping Expressway and the No. 325 National Avenue. Leading to both Guangzhou and Nanhai, the road takes the centre role in the transportation network of the area and heavy traffic of container trucks every day. Geographically speaking, it [illegible] production + transportation + sale + distribution to [illegible] chain of Osram products. Speed + efficiency = multiple profit.

As one of the 53 production bases in 19 countries, Osram Foshan was established in [illegible]. The farmland on which the factory was built still retains some of its characteristics, with a natural sewer in the west of the front yard and post-agricultural forms such as farms, urban villages and fishing ponds scattering around. In the east of the factory is the Foshan Cross-border avenue, in the north is a comprehensive wholesale market, in the south, an aluminium shop.... This is a typical view of a PRD industrial estate [illegible] there, but the human endeavour is completely different.

Factory: Rational Time vs. Sensitive Time

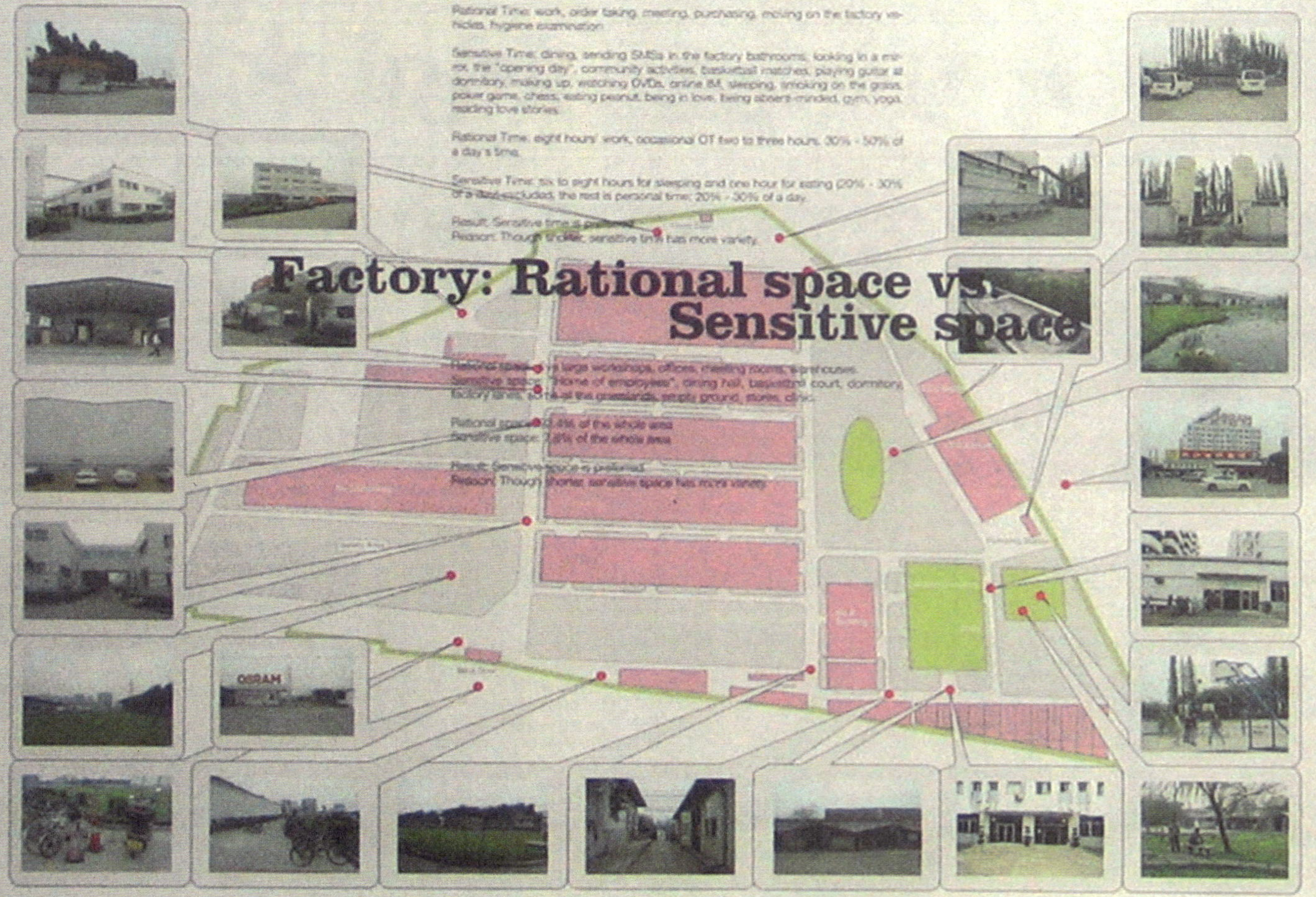

Rational Time: work, order taking, meeting, purchasing, moving on the factory vehicles, hygiene examination

Sensitive Time: dining, sending SMSs in the factory bathrooms, looking in a mirror, the "opening day", community activities, basketball matches, playing guitar at dormitory, making up, watching DVDs, online IM, sleeping, smoking on the grass, poker game, chess, eating peanut, being in love, being absent-minded, gym, yoga, reading love stories

Rational Time: eight hours' work, occasional OT two to three hours. 30% - 50% of a day's time.

Sensitive Time: six to eight hours for sleeping and one hour for eating (20% - 30% of a day excluded), the rest is personal time: 20% - 30% of a day.

Result: Sensitive time is preferred.
Reason: Though shorter, sensitive time has more variety.

Factory: Rational space vs. Sensitive space

Rational space: large workshops, offices, meeting rooms, warehouses
Sensitive space: "Home of employees", dining hall, basketball court, dormitory, factory lanes, [illegible] the grasslands, empty ground, stores, clinic.

Rational space: [illegible] of the whole area
Sensitive space: [illegible] of the whole area

Result: Sensitive space is preferred.
Reason: Though shorter, sensitive space has more variety.

Questionnaire (the first period of research)

Where do you believe you will be if wondering in the factory with your eye closed?
Zhang Zaiqun: Feel like walking on the lawn.
Zhang Zhao: The pond.
Wu Liting: Refectory.
Zuo Jiasheng: Housetop.
Lu Junhua: Falling off.
Wang Pingying: Light workshop.
Deng Snufen: Workshop NO.4.
Alex chen: Factory.
Bai Bing: Office.
Yu Huafeng: It is unsafe to walk without eye.

Could you please describe one scene that can remind you of yesterday.
Wang Xingling: Running in the lawn.
Wu Liting: Happy, worry about nothing.
Wang Yingping: BBQ on weekend.
Yang Xiaogang: It is a flash that hard to recall.
Comme: Having dinner with family members.
Alex chen: Playing around in summer holiday.
Yu Huafeng: It is great that getting light from bulb.
Wang Daiyou: Playing football in jokul.
Deng Yonghai: New years, working wage.

Close again your eye, imagine about the picture after 5 years.
Liang Jianghua: Open a Tea Shop after 5 years.
Zuo Jiasheng: Reading while listening music, then my wife talk to me that there is no money at home.
Lin Jun: Get rid of smoking.
Wang Daiyou: Buying a car for work.
Liu Wen: Hard to imagine, might getting fatter and aged.
Deng Yonghai: Making progress in work.
CandyWang: Long beard.
Vsn: Driving a airplane with Osram lights.

Lets talk about present. Could you mind talking about your expectation about these days?
Wang Xining: Higher salary.
Deng Yonghai: Girls.
Hou Xiaoxia: Super man, super head with super memory.
Li Lan: Two-fold in salary.

What is your goal in this city?
Huang Minxia: Say it out after it become true.
Mai Dongsheng: High quality of life.

What is the largest harvest you've got from the work?
Chen Zhedong: The secret of success.
Li Weirao: I had Learnt to cooperate with others. But I still hard to fawned on the superior.
Yang Xiaogang: Human rights in western countries.

What is the Common topic in factory?
Zuo Jiasheng: Girl friend, people's salary and the future goal.
Lin Jun: Girls.
Wen Zhimin: Money.
Zhang Zhao: Amusement after work.
Lv Li: Family and relationship.
Wang PingYing: How to crack the problem and avoid them.

What is your dream?
Wei Qiurong: I dream of to be a boss that anybody love.
Huang Xiaoling: I want to be an entrepreneur.
Wang Guangen: I want to be a boss who care about environment.
Shun Shiwei: Middle class, Happy mood, Good friends, stable income and health body.
Yu Huafeng: I won't tell until it come true.
Kuang Huijun: Stable life, a happy family, a good job and a MBA certificate

Have you ever think of such an action that crying out to the noise in front of the machine? Or how about other weird behaviors that can release your stress?
Zuo Jiasheng: I want to sing a song.
Shun Dong: Smashing the machine for a long time obsession.
Xie Jun: Never think of that because it is too loud the sound made by the machine.
Li Weirao: Yes, I'd like to. The secret might never be heard by others for it would soon be covered by the mass sound.

What are you thinking about in the minute before and after work?
Li Weirao: Breakfast / Machine sanitation
Zhang Zhao: Sanitation / Sanitation as well
Mai Dongsheng: Work today / Amusement
Yu Huafeng: Card puncher / Can't go home on time without call-back pay
Liu Wen: Card puncher / Card puncher
Dolphin: Start working / Finish working
Xian Xueying: Catch up with the factory bus / Preparing for the dinner

What would you like to do when you are in blue mood.
He Shangwen: Play PC game and win the rival.
Shun Shiwei: I need good mood instead of a blue one.
Hu Chunming: Learn to tolerate anything and comfort myself. I am the lucky one.

Which places you like to escape to?
Shun Shiwei: Want to talk to mermaid.
Wang PingYing: Seaside because it is rare here.
Yang Xiaogang: Fresh air the space is of boundless.
Yu Huafeng: Surfing, in the sun.
Lv Li: The sea, the severe waves and gust.
Wang Daiyou: Home settled by the seaside.
Liu Wen: I have never been there before.

Let's talk about the topic of worship. Who is your idol?
Chen Zhedong: EINSTEIN. He didn't care what he had got but care what he had created.
Shun Shiwei: Zhou Enlai. Because he knew everything.
Li Weirao: Worship wisdom, fortune and good luck. Healthy brings happiness.
Zhang Zaiqun: Chairmen Mao. Great man.
Zhang Zhao: Everyone. We know different things so everyone is your teacher.
Mai Dongsheng: Beckham.
Liang Jianghua: Myself. We can do things better if we trust ourselves.
Lv Junhua: Li Jiacheng. Genius and courageous.

Have you ever been to other places after working in OSRAM?
Li Weirao: No,short of money.
Zhu Shiqiao: Shenzhen Pleasantville.
Zhang Zhao: Yes! He yuan water power plant. Dongguan Hu Men Tai Ping square.
Er Dongsheng: Shenzhen and Guangzhou.
Yu Huafeng: Sheng chuan dao sea scenery.

What is your fear?
Zhu Shiqiao: Lost peace.
Zhang Zhao: I fear no money!!! It is hard to travel around without money.
Li Zhongmi: Occupational disease.
Yu Huafeng: I Fear nothing.
Lin Guohao: Falling down from high place.
Andy Ye: Talking to the boss here.
Hu Chunming: I had spent too much that can't be understood, only fruitless hard working. Safety of my family and relatives is the best happiness to me.

Osram as A Sample

In this art project supported by Siemens, we take the Osram factory as a sample to deal with the following issues: how can these immigrant workers, who represent the global competitive strength of China, obtain a new experience, new norm and new meaning which are radically different from the one they had back in rural hometowns? How can we consequently observe the way they activate their own utopia, through which we can further explain how the permeating globalization can cause great social changes not only in the PRD area, but also in the whole China.

Their utopia is also our utopia, it's also utopia of more people who have hope for the future......let's hope that utopia is not just an illusion, that it will be realized one day.

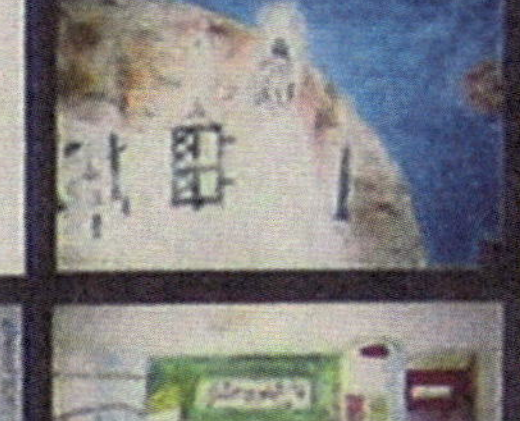

Drawing by employees

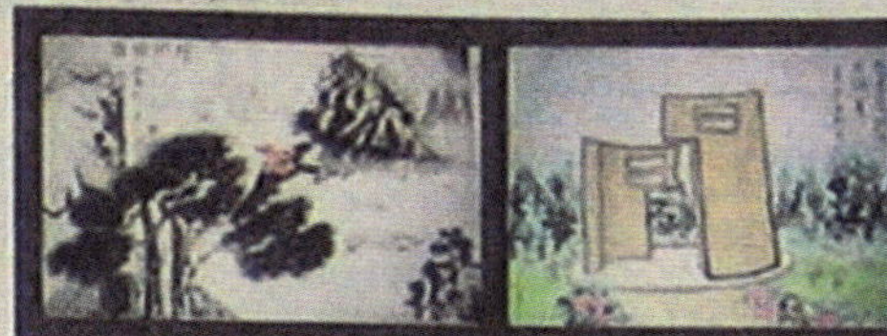

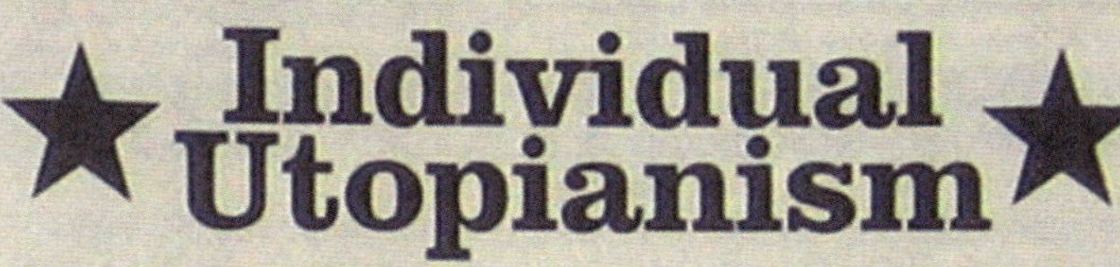

★ Individual Utopianism ★

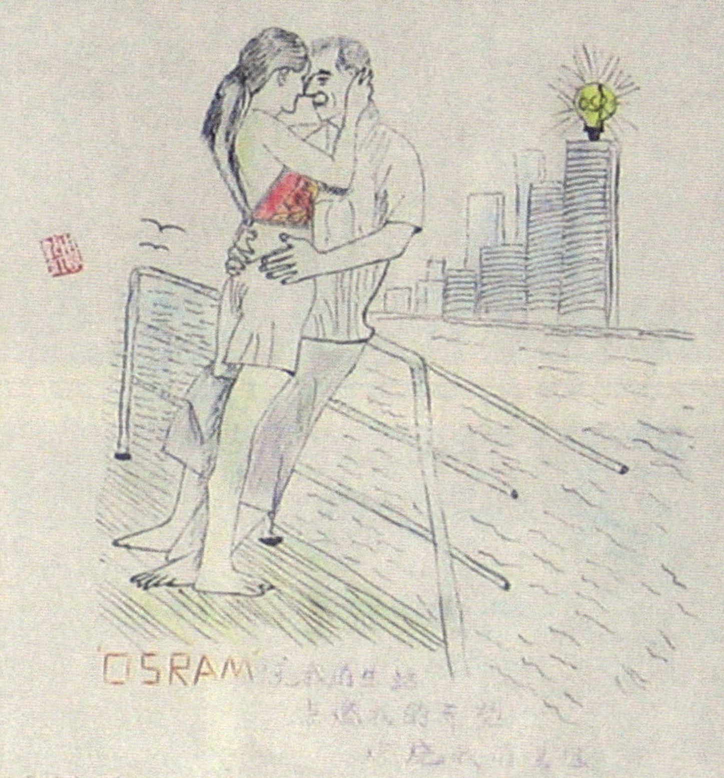

Drawing by employee

Please choose different grade you are satisfy with the following project:

01.economic income(86 people)
so-so 59%, unsatisfied 38%, satisfied 16%, perfect 0%

02.What would you likely do when you are homesick? (95 people)
phone call 77%,
back to work 14%,
confide in colleague 5%,
others 3%,
write a letter 1%

03.The reason why you leave your hometown(85 people)
seek opportunity 55%,
intend to learn technic 24%,
earn more 9%,
yearn towards city life 8%,
vacancy at home 4%

04.Would you tell me the reasons you come to OSRAM?(38 people)
want to change the working site 56%,
others 36%,
the need of assignment 8%,
interest in China 0%

05.Do you hum songs on the way to work?(78 people)
no 55%, yes 45%

06.Could you draw the OSRAM logo at once?(83 people)
Yes 98%, No 2%

07.Do you feel secure living in this city?(57 people)
Yes 56%, No 44%

08.Do you imagine crying out toward the machine? Or want to take some unreasonable behavior?(35 people)
never 74%, yes 26%

09.Have you ever dream about the working scene of your daily life?(94 people)
Sometimes 63%, never 25%, frequently12%

10.Do you like your uniform(43 people)
dislike 58%, like 30%, just so-so 12%

11.Do you pay your attention to news and OSRAM?(89 people)
Yes 94%, no 6%

12.Where do you choose to get away from work? (90 people)
seaside 72%, forest 10%, high hill 8%, others 6%, bar 4%

13.How do you know about PRD?
(45 people)
A bit 69%, no 31%

14.What is your feeling everyday when you wake up? (73 people)
longing 67%, blank 18%, satisfied14%, other 1%

15.working environment(95 people)
so-so 47%, unsatisfied about 32%, satisfied 20%, perfect 1%

16.Does your (girlfriend/wife or husband) is working in OSRAM as well?
If she/he is not, would you expect her/him together in?(90 people)
No 50%, Yes 50%

17.Developing chance(96 people)
so-so 47%, unsatisfied 28%, satisfied 23%, perfect 2%

18.Have you ever homesick(94 people)
sometimes(54%),frequently(35%),never(11%)

19.What is your attitude about youself in the future? (92 people)
longing 73%, worry 15%, never think about that 12%

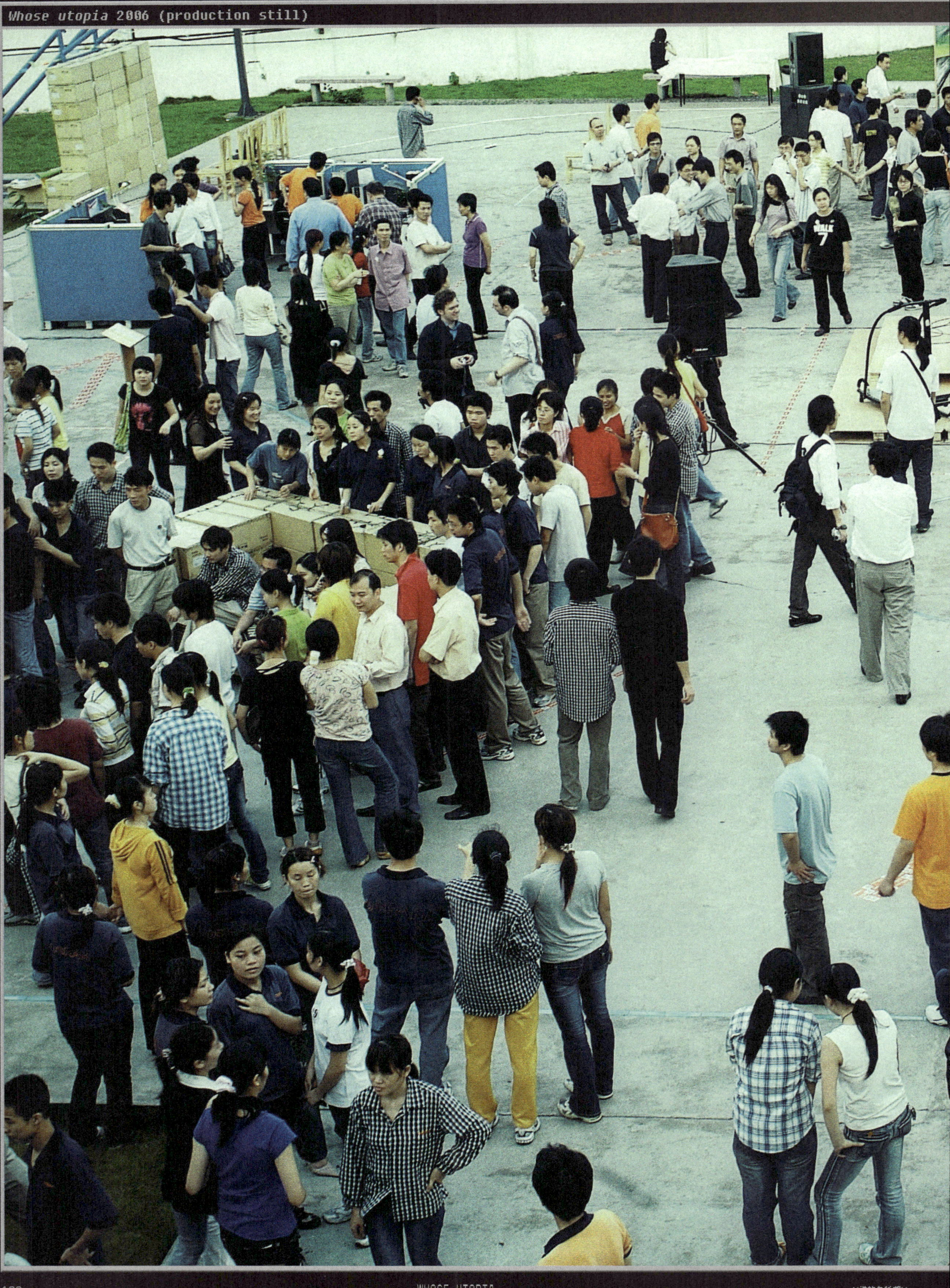

Whose utopia 2006 (production still)

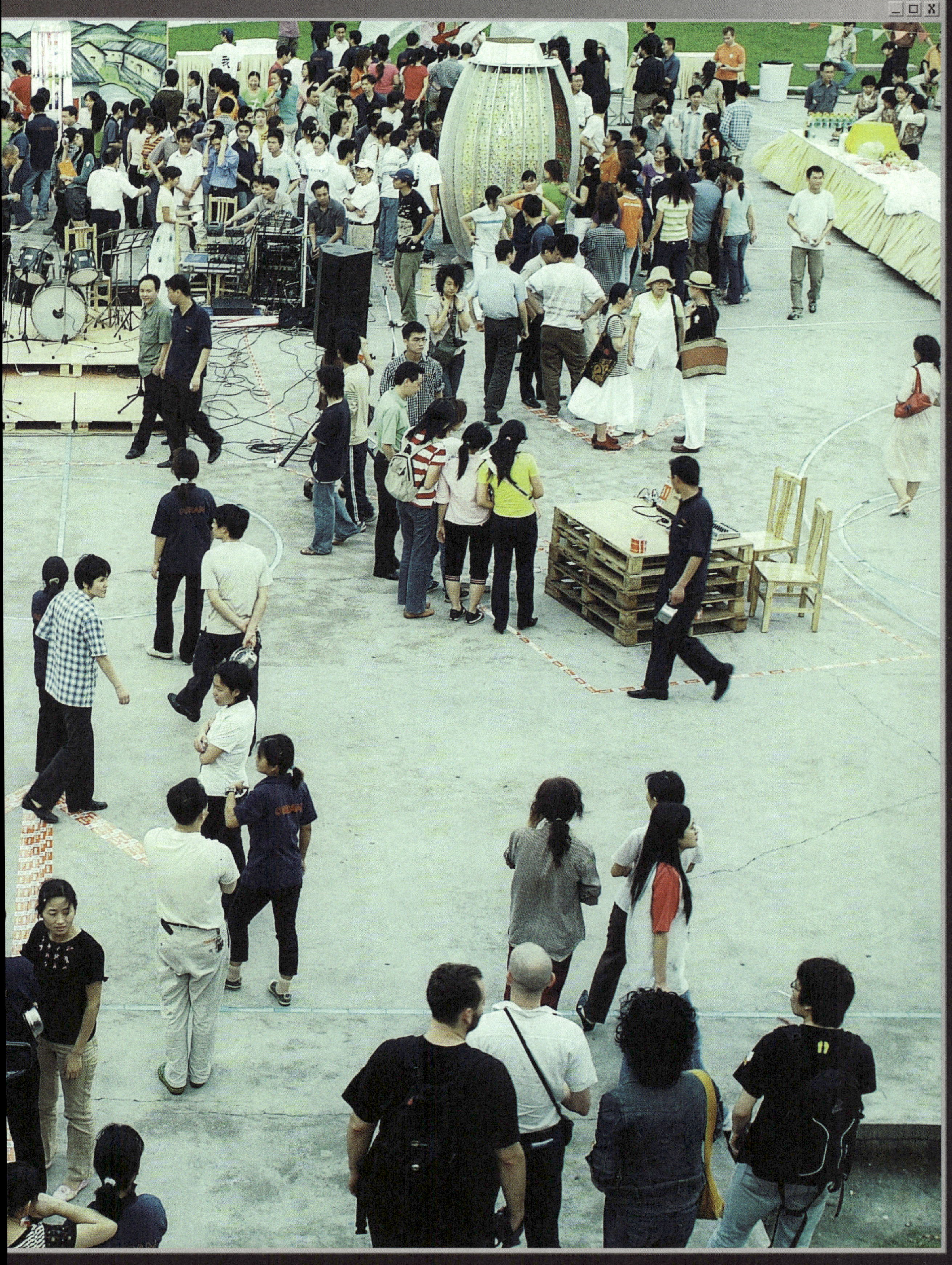

1 RMB CITY: A SECOND LIFE CITY PLANNING 人民城寨：第二人生城市计划 2007

2 I.MIRROR 我·镜 2007

3 LIVE IN RMB CITY 人民城寨的生活 2009

4 TONIGHT LIVE INTERVIEW WITH CHINA TRACY (SLCN.TV) "今夜现场"节目采访中国·翠西 2009

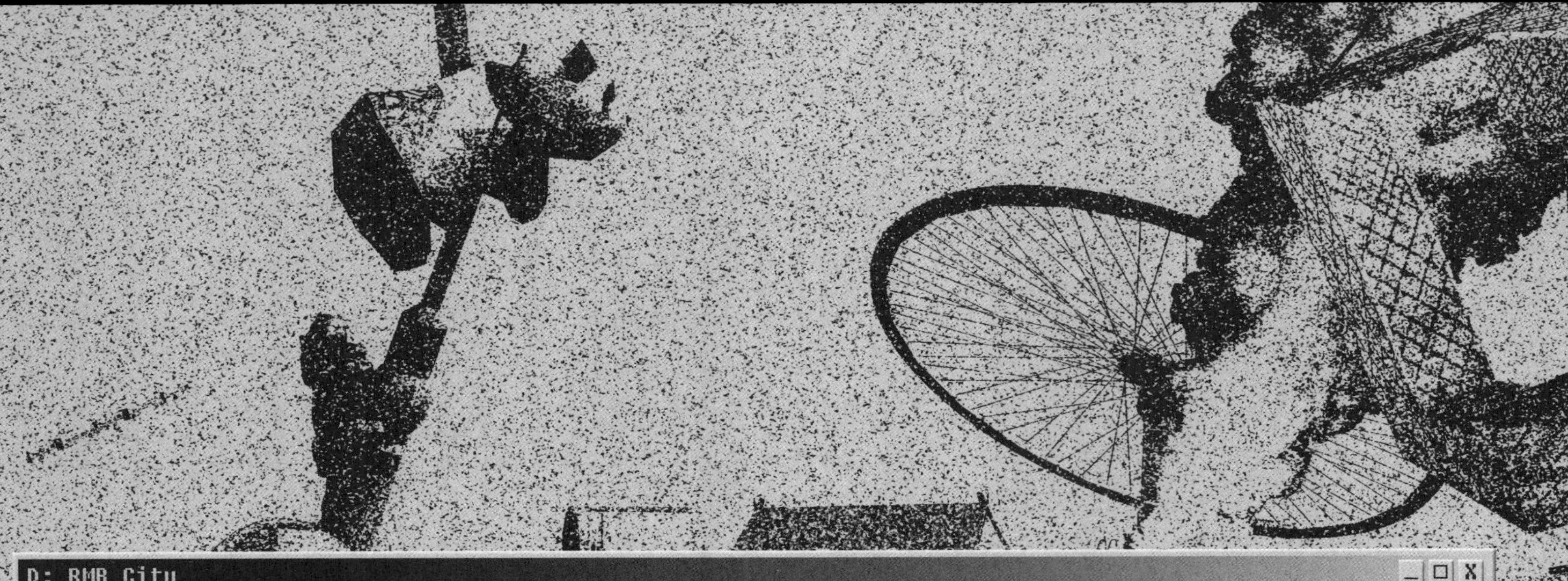

D: RMB City

RMB City was a virtual Chinese metropolis constructed on Second Life, the once-popular, still functional, online platform where users interact in communal environments. Between 2007 and 2011, Cao Fei – and a team of coders and programmers across Beijing and the Philippines – constructed a digital city replete with a running economy, a manifesto and a mayor. Cao offered an exploded vision of China's rapacious boom-and-bust real-estate development. Familiar landmarks appeared on the skyline, warped through vaporwave glitch. Statues of Chairman Mao Zedong floated next to Beijing's recently built Olympic Stadium, now a rusted structure sinking into a digital sea. Presiding over the city was Cao's avatar China Tracy – cyber-mother, cyber-lover, cyber-boss – who oversaw various parties, feng shui sessions and auctions of digital real estate to real-life buyers. Operational as a live gaming environment, *RMB City* was a pioneering work of net art, a prophetic project anticipating the all-virtual forms of social interaction that have since become everyday. Today the work exists as a digital ruin accessed through an archived fly-through of the original city and a series of videos.

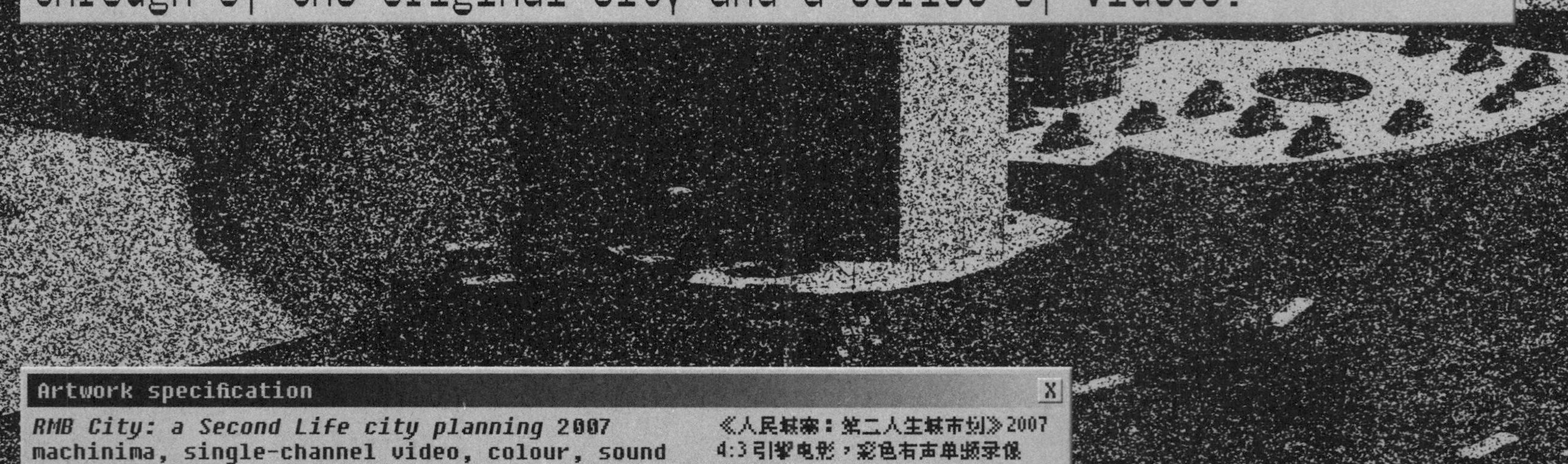

Artwork specification

RMB City: a Second Life city planning 2007
machinima, single-channel video, colour, sound
5:57 min, 4:3

《人民城寨：第二人生城市规划》2007
4:3 引擎电影，彩色有声单频录像
5分57秒

RMB CITY: A SECOND LIFE CITY PLANNING 人民城寨：第二人生城市计划

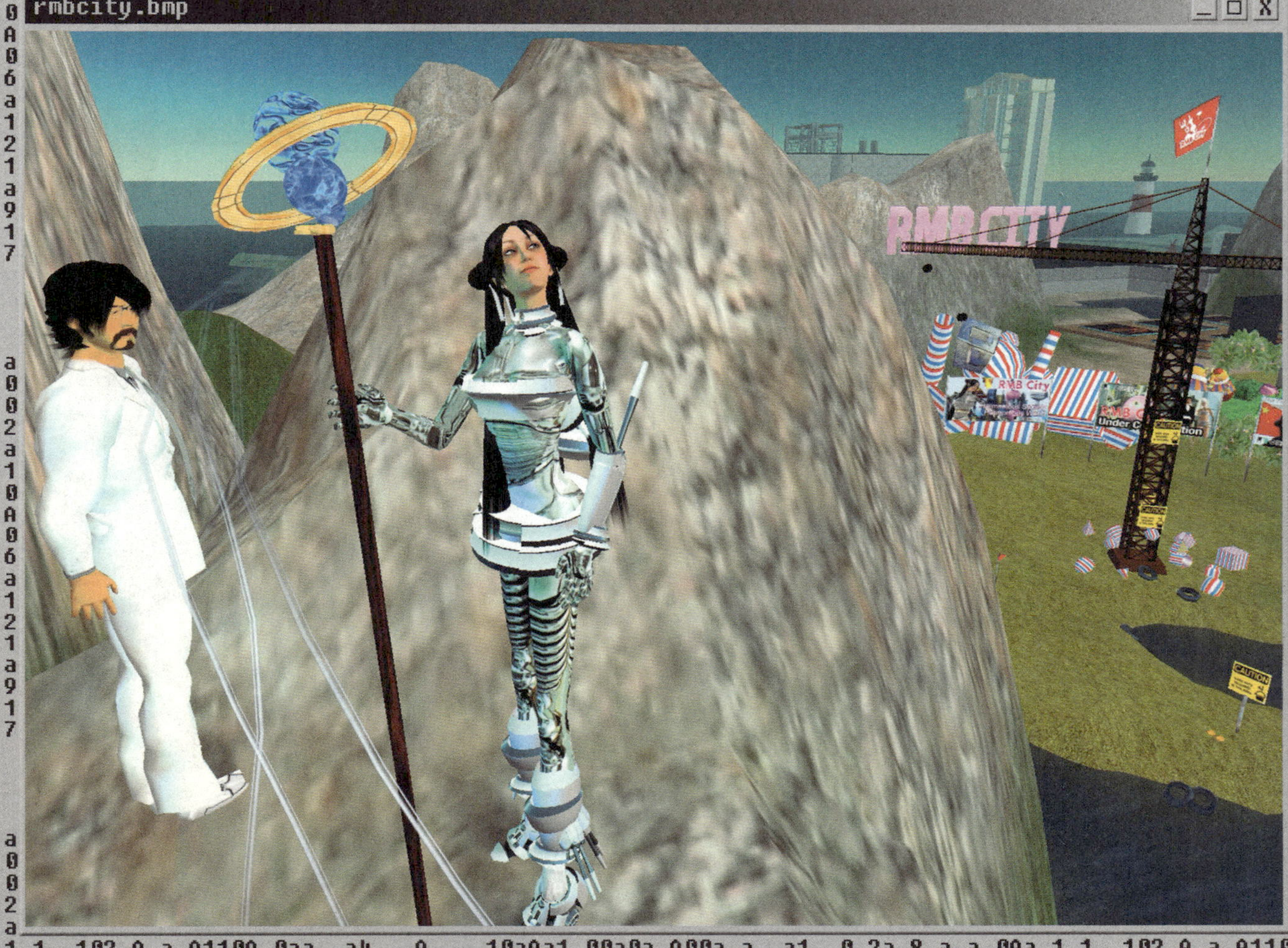

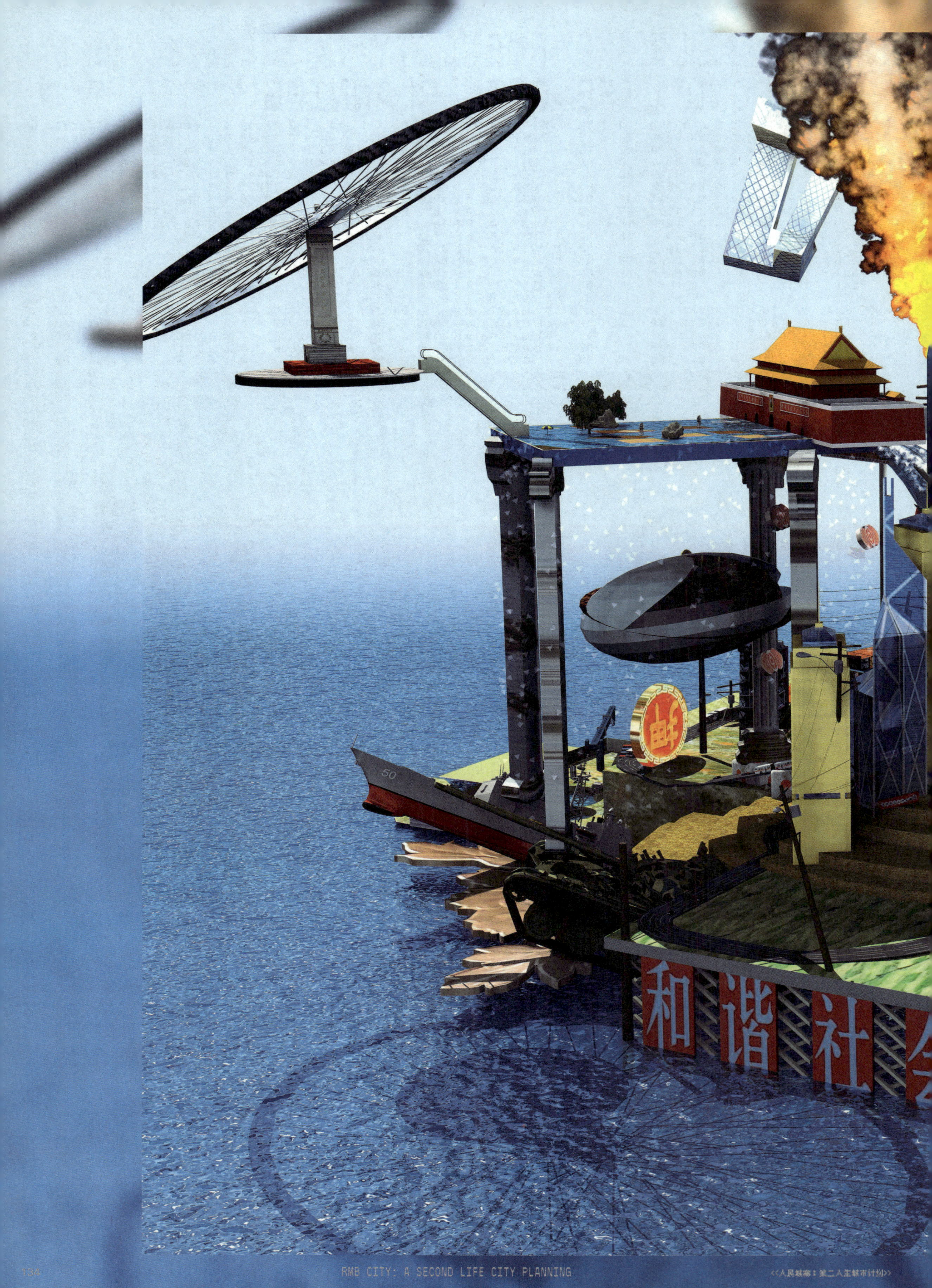
50
和谐社

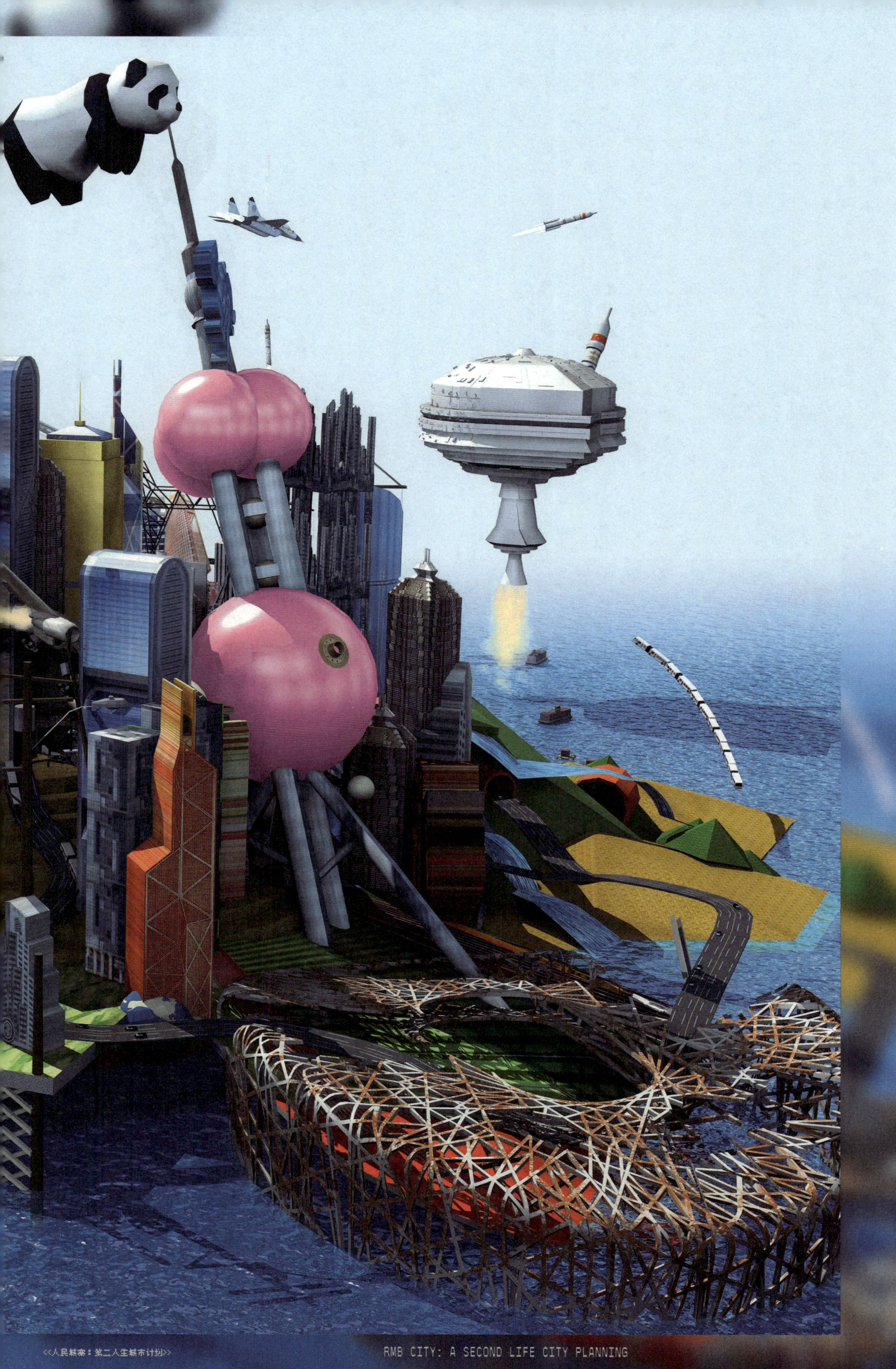

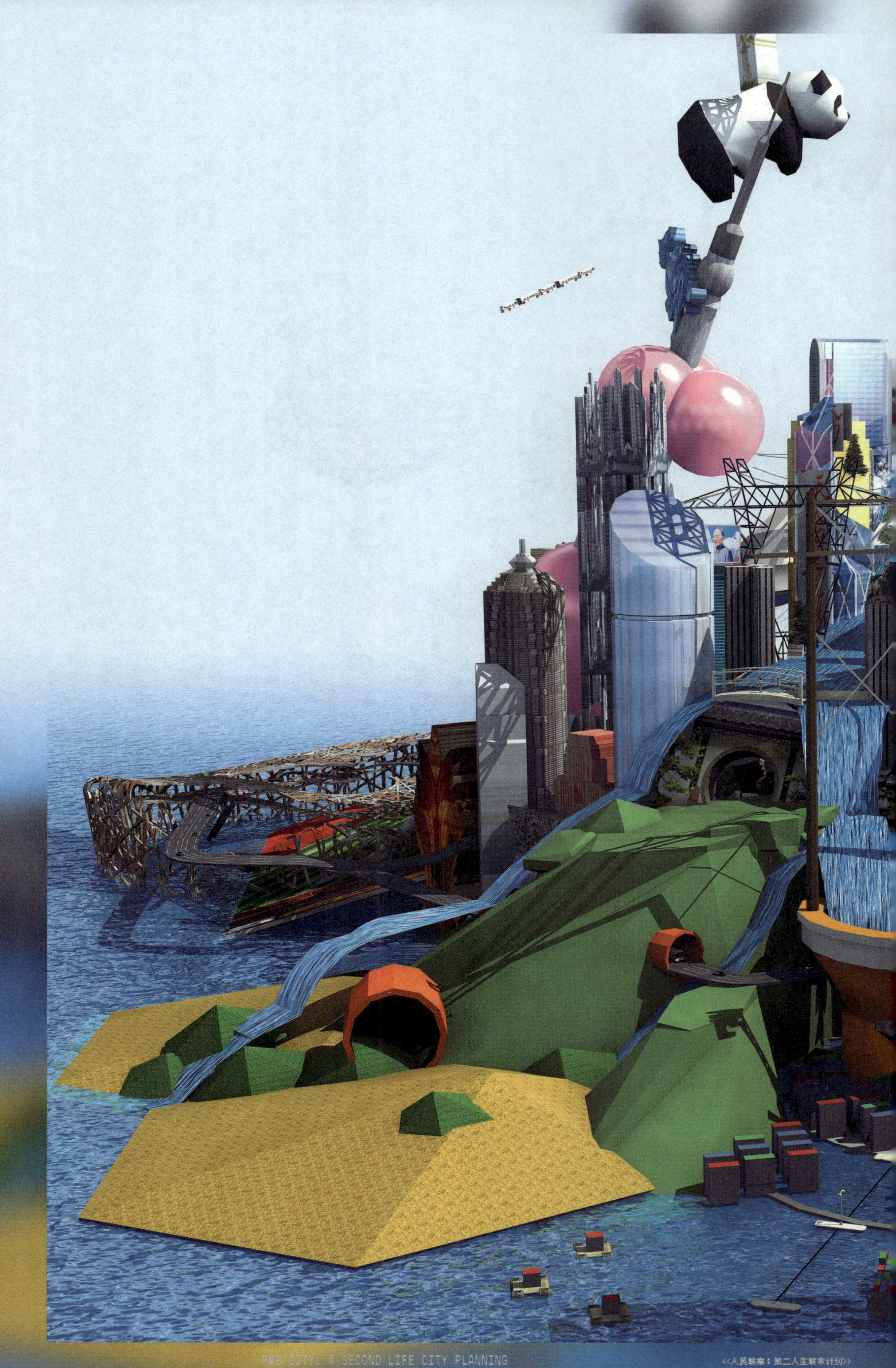

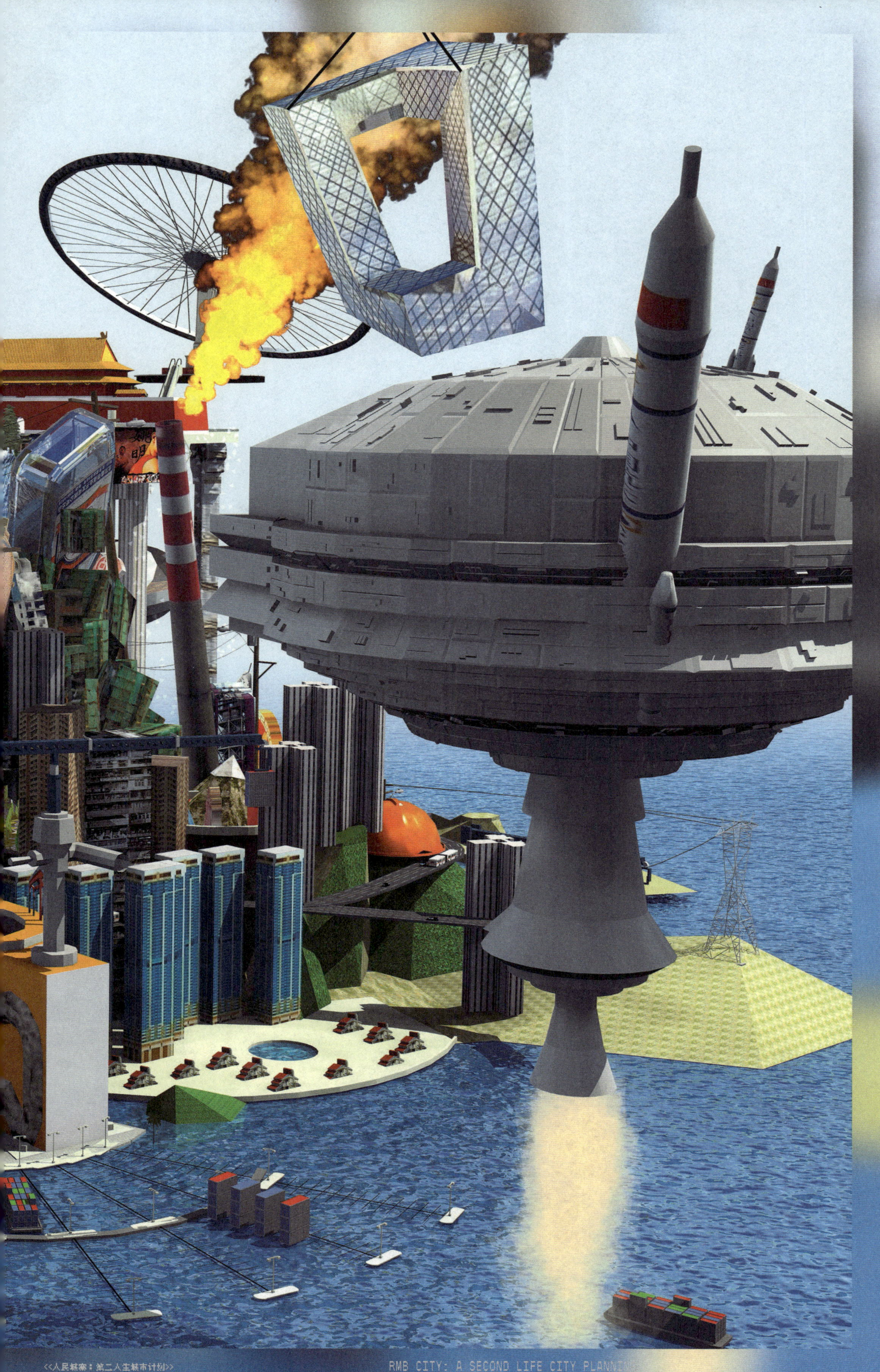

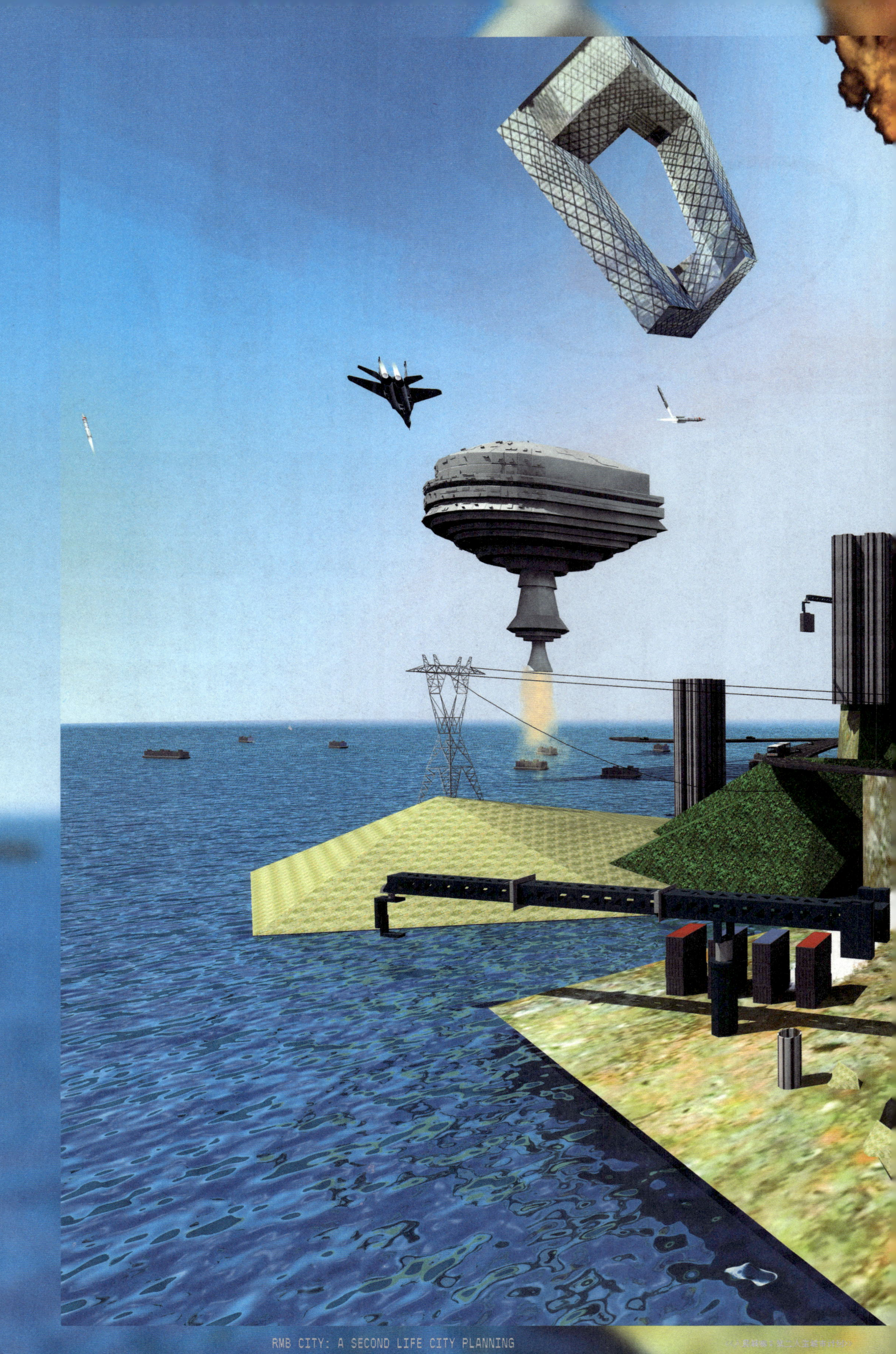

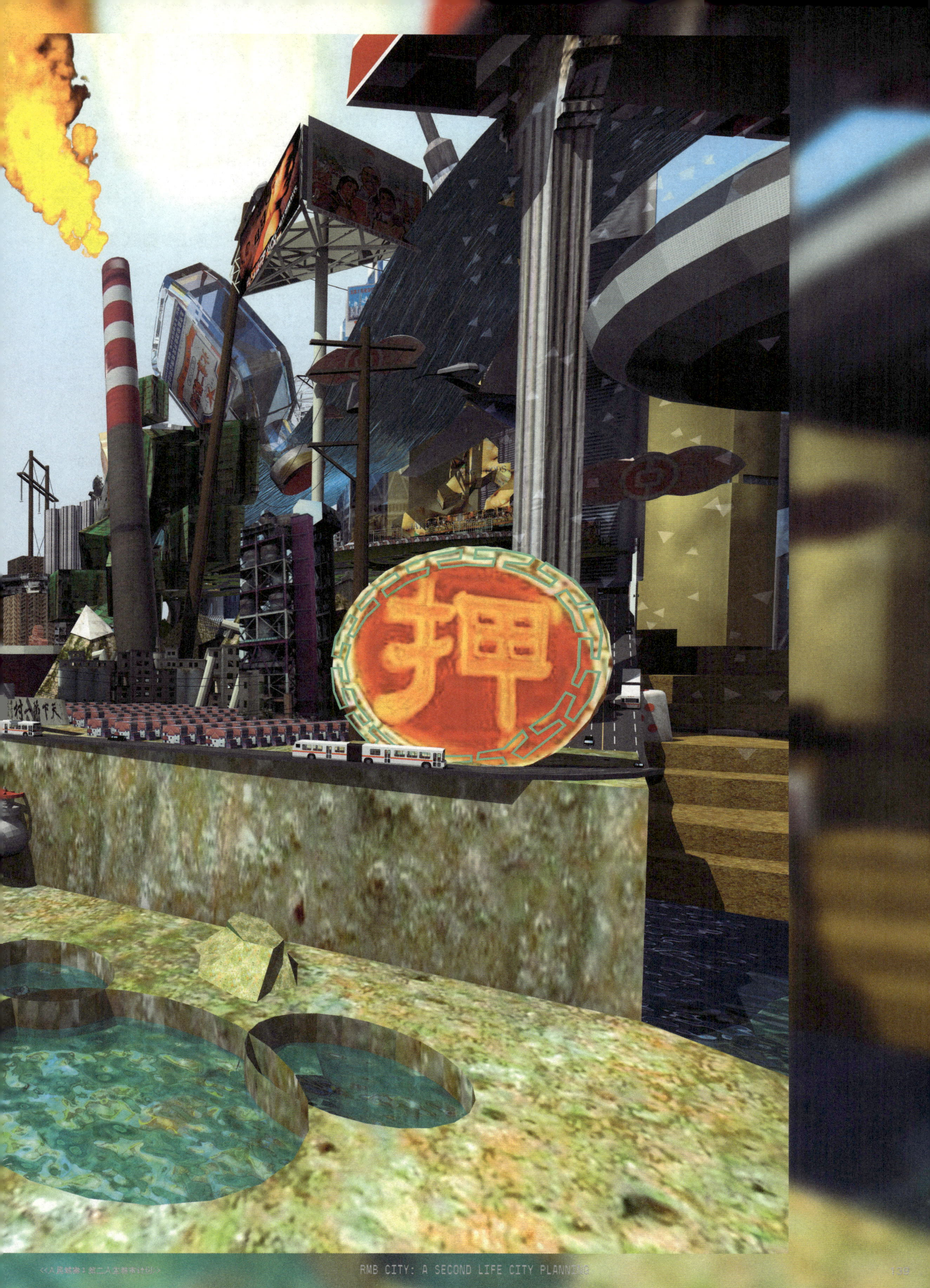

"人民城寨" 城市宣言

"人民城寨" 城市宣言，第二人生计划
两个幽灵，虚拟的幽灵，在一个轻盈的城市上空飞翔。为了对这个幽灵进行神圣的围剿，旧世界的一切，人和看得见的风景、信仰和预言、规则和智慧，都联合起来了。

现在是RMB CITY向全世界公开说明自己的观点、自己的目的、自己的意图并且拿自己的宣言来告诉人们：这是一座从一开始你就无法从你记忆中抹去的城市。

一、我们

RMB CITY 是一个形容词，一个失重的梦，一些偶然的巧合。当我一只脚跨进虚拟世界悬浮的大气层里，等待着向最柔软的土地降落，你在粉色的结晶体里向我招手，而我另一只脚还残留在现实世界那块冰凉的地板上。

心神不定的你，来这里和我一起奔跑吧，我们未曾拥有的不是很远，这个城市会告诉我们应该思索的东西，也会讲述我们不同的故事，无论过去、现在、还是将来。

二、谜城

"它是由各种例外、障碍、矛盾、不合逻辑与自相矛盾与冲突构成的。" ——马可.波罗

RMB CITY不是一个虚像之城，它既没有还原今天的全部也没有唤起我们对过去的怀念。这是一面从局部开始反光的镜子，我们能看到自己从哪里来，可以发现某些"联系"填充了我们现实和虚拟过渡间的空白，而这些"联系"的线索在这里都又被混乱了，丰富了，润色了，它又自然重组了一些新的秩序，生发了奇异的智慧。

支离破碎的白夜映着城市上空的海，烟囱喷出刺破云端的火焰灼烧着那面火红的旗，通天梯朝着太阳颤抖地运行，飞弹射入不可返回的轨迹，河流越过宫殿的秘密涵道渐渐温暖了两岸的建筑，林中连绵的村庄与寂寞的骑士擦肩而过，天使和疯子在坍塌的楼宇和被遗弃的田垄间决斗，堤坝码头那里的精明商人忙碌起来，一个蜗居女人在摩天大楼间盘旋沉思，善良的野兽得到了渴望的爱情…

我们试图寻觅这座城市的秘密，在虚拟的阴影下寻觅自己。我们看得见这座城市罕见的辉煌，沸腾的色彩，我们能通过意识呼吸到那里自由的空气，甚至感受到湿度，还有爱的能力。

三、虚实

"世界的核心是空虚，在宇宙里移动的事物的原则就是虚无空间，现存的一切围绕着不存在而构成…" ——帕尔西法尔

如果：我们看得见的和触摸到的是实，我们呼吸着的和能感受的是虚，我们的声音是实，我们的记忆是虚，财富是实，贫穷是虚，满足是实，忧郁是虚，怨恨是实，爱恋是虚，聚集是实，智慧是虚，统治是实，忍受是虚，生存是实，死亡是虚，大地是实，天空是虚… 那么，从现在起RMB CITY里所有关于虚实的对立都不再成立。

从真实世界的黄昏下出逃吧，试图把所有关于对真实的讨论放在虚拟的光年中让其颠倒过来，与虚拟垂直或者平行，或用虚拟刺穿现实的防护，这次，真实是一个战败者，尽管他曾经是个战无不胜的英雄。

四、世界

塔罗牌上描绘着的"世界"是一个周围有圆圈防护的城市。

而我们的世界是用"透明"和"想象"制造出来的，它可能真的不存在，哪怕现在存在着，将来也不会存在，它在我们访问它后结束，在我们再次抵达时开始。如此反复地出逃和潜入，终于，我们分享到了世界的全部。

"你可曾见过跟这座城市相似的城市吗？"忽必烈对马克.波罗发问。

"没有，陛下" 马可回答，"我从未想到会有这样的城市。"

RMB CITY就是这样的一个城，欢迎你的登陆。

RMB CITY MANIFESTO

(RMB – TO BE REMEMBER)
"IS THIS YOUR CITY?" ASKED THE YOUNG MAN. THE ANGEL ANSWERED: "IT'S YOURS." THE CASTLE OF CROSSED DESTINIES, ITALO CALVINO.

TWO SPECTERS ARE HOVERING OVER A CITY OF LIGHTNESS–VIRTUAL SPECTERS. IN THE NAME OF THE HOLY WAR AGAINST THEM, EVERYTHING FROM THE OLD WORLD UNITED–HUMAN BEINGS, LANDSCAPE, FAITH AND PROPHECIES, RULES AND WISDOM.

NOW, IT'S TIME FOR RMB CITY TO MAKE THE DECLARATION TO THE WORLD ABOUT ITS VIEW, ITS PURPOSE AND ITS INTENTION. IT'S TIME TO MANIFEST TO PEOPLE: THIS IS A CITY THAT YOU CAN'T WIPE OUT FROM YOUR MEMORY.

1. US

RMB CITY IS AN ADJECTIVE, A LOOSE DREAM AND SOME RANDOM COINCIDENCES. YOU WAVE TO ME IN THE PINK CRYSTAL WHEN I'M ABOUT TO LAND ON THE SOFTEST OF ALL EARTH, ONE FOOT IN THE VIRTUAL ATMOSPHERE, AND ONE STILL REMAINS ON THE COLD, HARD FLOOR OF MY REAL LIFE.

COME RUN WITH ME, YOU DISTURBED BEING. THOSE WE DESIRE ARE NOT FAR AWAY, THE CITY IS GOING TO TELL US WHAT TO THINK AND THE DIFFERENT VERSIONS OF OUR STORIES, IN THE PAST, THE PRESENT, AND THE FUTURE.

2. MIRRORING CITY

"IT IS A CITY MADE ONLY OF EXCEPTIONS, EXCLUSIONS, INCONGRUITIES, CONTRADICTIONS." MARCO POLO

RMB CITY IS NOT A CITY OF MAGICAL MIRROR, IT DOESN'T RESTORE THE FULL PRESENT, NOR DOES IT RECALL OUR REMINISCENCE OF THE PAST. IT'S A MIRROR THAT PARTIALLY REFLECTS; WE SEE WHERE WE WERE COMING FROM, DISCOVER SOME OF THE "CONNECTIONS" THAT FILL THE PALE ZONE BETWEEN THE REAL AND THE VIRTUAL, THE CLUES OF WHICH GET DISTURBED, ENRICHED, AND POLISHED. NEW ORDERS ARE BORN, SO ARE NEW, STRANGE WISDOM.

THE SEA ABOVE THE CITY IS REFLECTED ON THE SHATTERING WHITE NIGHT; FIRE FROM THE CHIMNEY POKES THROUGH THE CLOUD, BURNING THE FLAG RED; SKY-ELEVATOR IS ASCENDING TOWARDS THE SUN, TREMBLING; A MISSILE FLIES A TRAJECTORY OF NO RETURN; THE RIVER FLOWS THROUGH THE SECRET TUNNEL IN THE PALACE AND WARMS UP THE BUILDINGS ALONG ITS BANKS; A LONELY KNIGHT STROLLS ACROSS THE STRETCHED-OUT VILLAGES; ANGELS AND MADMEN ARE HAVING A DUEL AMONG THE RUINS OF COLLAPSED BUILDINGS AND THE ABANDONED FIELDS; THE ASTUTE BUSINESSMEN ARE BUSYING ON THE CONTAINER DOCK; A BATWOMAN IS CONTEMPLATING IN THE AIR BETWEEN SKYSCRAPERS; THE KIND BEAST HAS ITS DESIRE FOR LOVE REALIZED...

WE ARE TRYING TO UNCOVER THE SECRETS OF THIS CITY, AND TO DISCOVER OURSELVES IN THE SHADOW OF VIRTUALITY. WE CAN SEE THE CITY'S RARE MOMENT OF SUBLIMITY AND ITS BOILING COLORS, WE CAN BREATHE ITS FREE AIR THROUGH OUR CONSCIOUSNESS, WE CAN EVEN FEEL THE HUMIDITY, AND THE POWER OF LOVE.

3. VIRTUAL / REAL

"THE CORE OF THE WORLD IS EMPTINESS, THE RULE OF THE MOVING THINGS AND OBJECTS IN THE UNIVERSE IS EMPTY SPACE, THOSE WHICH EXIST REVOLVE AROUND NON-EXISTENCE ..." PARSIFAL

IF: WHAT WE SEE AND TOUCH ARE REAL, WHAT WE BREATHE AND FEEL ARE VIRTUAL; OUR VOICE IS REAL, OUR MEMORY IS VIRTUAL; FORTUNE IS REAL, POVERTY IS VIRTUAL; FULFILLMENT IS REAL, SADNESS IS VIRTUAL; RESENTMENT IS REAL, AFFECTION IS VIRTUAL; FOOLISHNESS IS REAL, WISDOM IS VIRTUAL; REIGNING IS REAL, ENDURANCE IS VIRTUAL; LIVING IS REAL, DYING IS VIRTUAL; THE LAND IS REAL, THE SKY IS VIRTUAL ...THEN, FROM THIS MOMENT ON, LET ALL THE VIRTUAL-REAL CONFLICTS VANISH IN RMB CITY.

FLEE FROM THE TWILIGHT OF THE REAL WORLD, TRY REVERSING ALL THE DISCUSSIONS ABOUT REALNESS BY SHIFTING THEM INTO THE VIRTUAL LIGHT YEAR. BE VERTICAL AGAINST OR PARALLEL TO THE VIRTUAL, STAB THROUGH THE PROTECTION OF REALITY WITH THE SWORD OF VIRTUALNESS. THIS TIME, THE ONCE-INVINCIBLE REAL IS THE DEFEATED ONE.

4. THE WORLD

"THE WORLD" DEPICTED ON THE TAROT IS A CITY WITH ROUND BARRIER.

OUR WORLD, HOWEVER, IS CONSTRUCTED WITH "TRANSPARENCY" AND "IMAGINATION", DOES IT EXIST? IT MAY NOT BE. EVEN IF IT EXISTS NOW, IT WON'T IN THE FUTURE. IT COULD END AFTER OUR VISIT, AND START OVER AGAIN WHEN WE RETURN. EVENTUALLY, AFTER NUMEROUS FLEEING AND SNEAKING IN, WE WILL HAVE THE EXPERIENCE OF THE WHOLE WORLD.

"DID YOU EVER HAPPEN TO SEE A CITY RESEMBLING THIS ONE?" KUBLAI KHAN ASKED MARCO POLO. "NO, SIRE," MARCO ANSWERED, "I SHOULD NEVER HAVE IMAGINED A CITY LIKE THIS COULD EXIST."

RMB CITY IS SUCH A CITY, YOU ARE SINCERELY WELCOMED.

TRANSLATION: LAWRENCE LI
FIRST PUBLISHED ONLINE AS PART OF *RMB CITY*, 26 MAY 2009

Inventory 资料库 – ✕

File Create Sort

Type here to search

All Items | Recent Items

▼ RMB City 人民城寨

▶ Profile 身份
Cyber Citizen: China Tracy 数字公民：中国·翠西

▶ Search 探究
Second Life: Uncertain Reality, Uncertain Virtuality
第二人生：不确定的现实与不确定的虚拟

▶ View 视图
Here Comes Vitual Reality: A Neo Existential Manifesto
虚拟实境来临：一份存在主义新宣言

▶ World 世界
Cyber Epic—*i.Mirror*, Chinese Pavilion, 52nd Venice Biennale
电子史诗《我/镜》，第52届威尼斯双年展中国馆

▶ Attitude 姿态
Manifesto of RMB City 人民城寨宣言

▶ Construction 营建
RMB City–Online Urbanization 人民城寨 – 非物质的城市化

▶ Landmark 地标
Map of RMB City 城寨图谱

▼ Cameras 景观
City and Sky 城市与天空
City and Signs 城市与标志
City and Memory 城市与记忆
City and Desire 城市与愿望
City and Trade 城市与贸易

▶ Chat 对话
The Weight of the Unbearable Lightness in Reality
不可承受之轻在现实中的重量

▶ Buy ¥L 投资
RMB City Development Instruction 人民城寨—发展指南

▶ Recent Items 当前项
RMB City: The Sales Instruction of Spacial Units in Second Life
人民城寨虚拟单元出售列表

▶ Notecard 手记
The Second Life of Cao Fei 曹斐的第二人生

▶ Quit 离线

Profile

2nd Life | Web | Interests | Picks | Classified | 1st Life | My Notes

Name: China Tracy

Photo:

Born: 1/6/2007

Account: Resident
Payment info used

Partner: ?

Groups:
Member of #joiito
Member of Anti Sarko+LePen
Member of Golden Girls of SL
Member of Not Possible IRL
Member of SL Beijing
Member of SL Dream Team
Member of PhotoArt Gallery
Member of Video Game Legends
Member of Videobloggers
Member of Virtual Italian People
Member of White Cube Gallery Guests

About: (500 chars)
From China, Named Tracy.

Give item: Drop inventory item here.

☑ Publish on the web ?

OK | Cancel

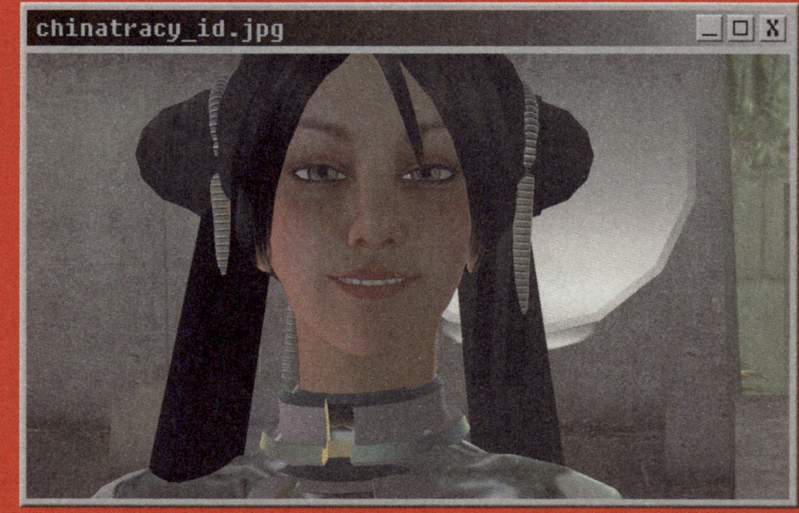

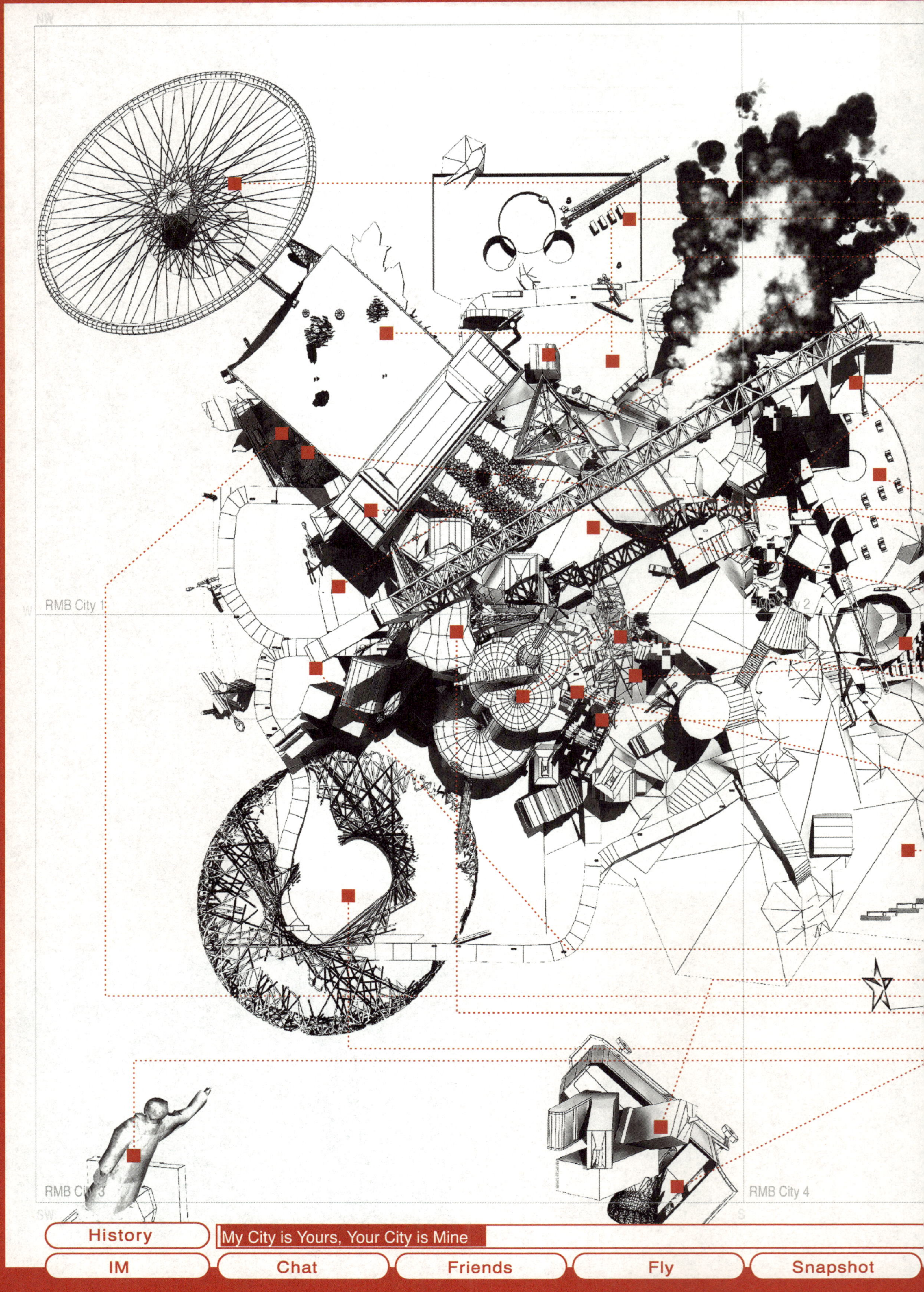

NW
N
W
RMB City 1
RMB City 2
RMB City 3
RMB City 4
SW
S
History
My City is Yours, Your City is Mine
IM
Chat
Friends
Fly
Snapshot

RMB City 城寨图谱

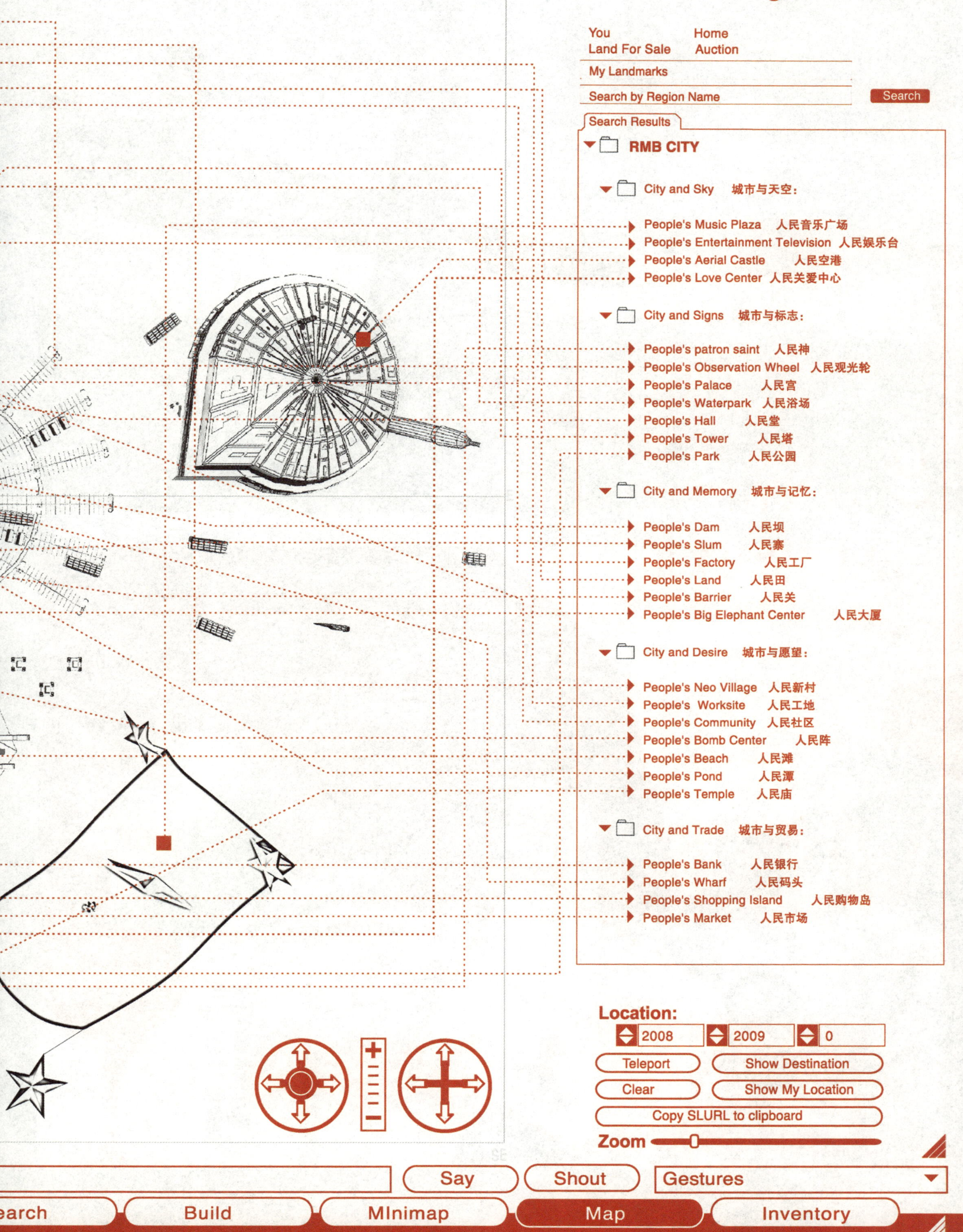

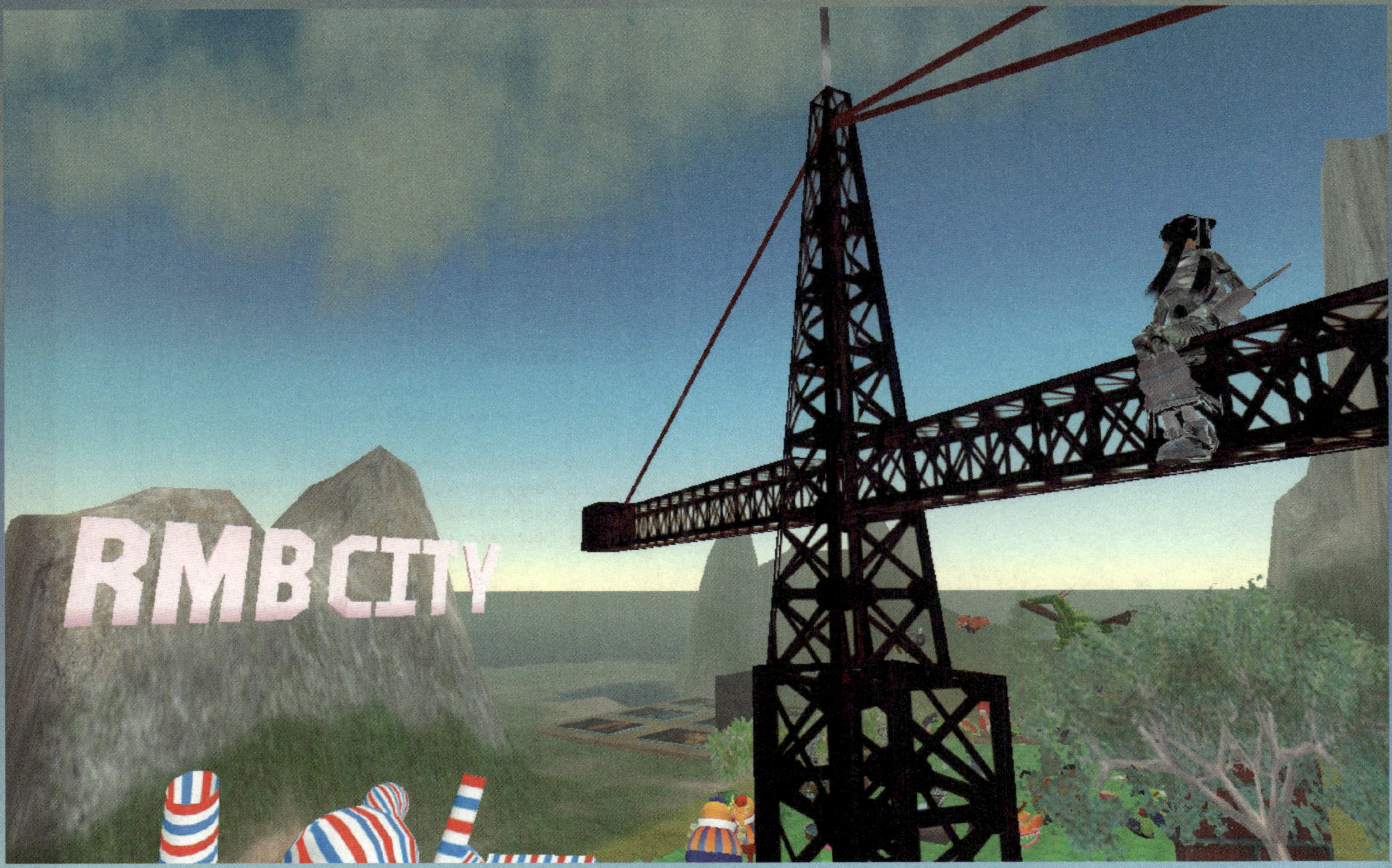
RMB CITY

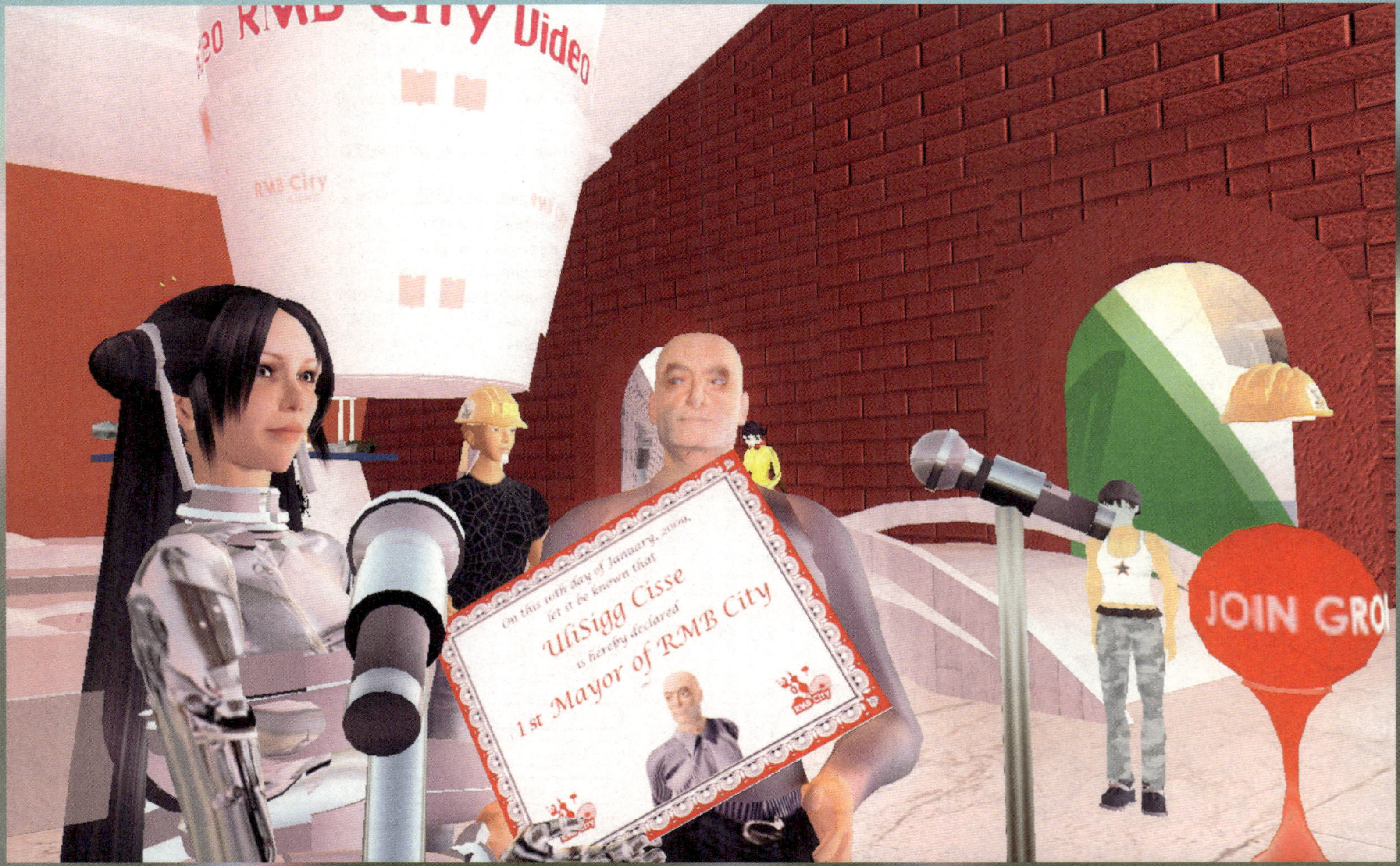
RMB City Video
On this 10th day of January, 2008,
let it be known that
UliSigg Cisse
is hereby declared
1 st Mayor of RMB City
JOIN GRO

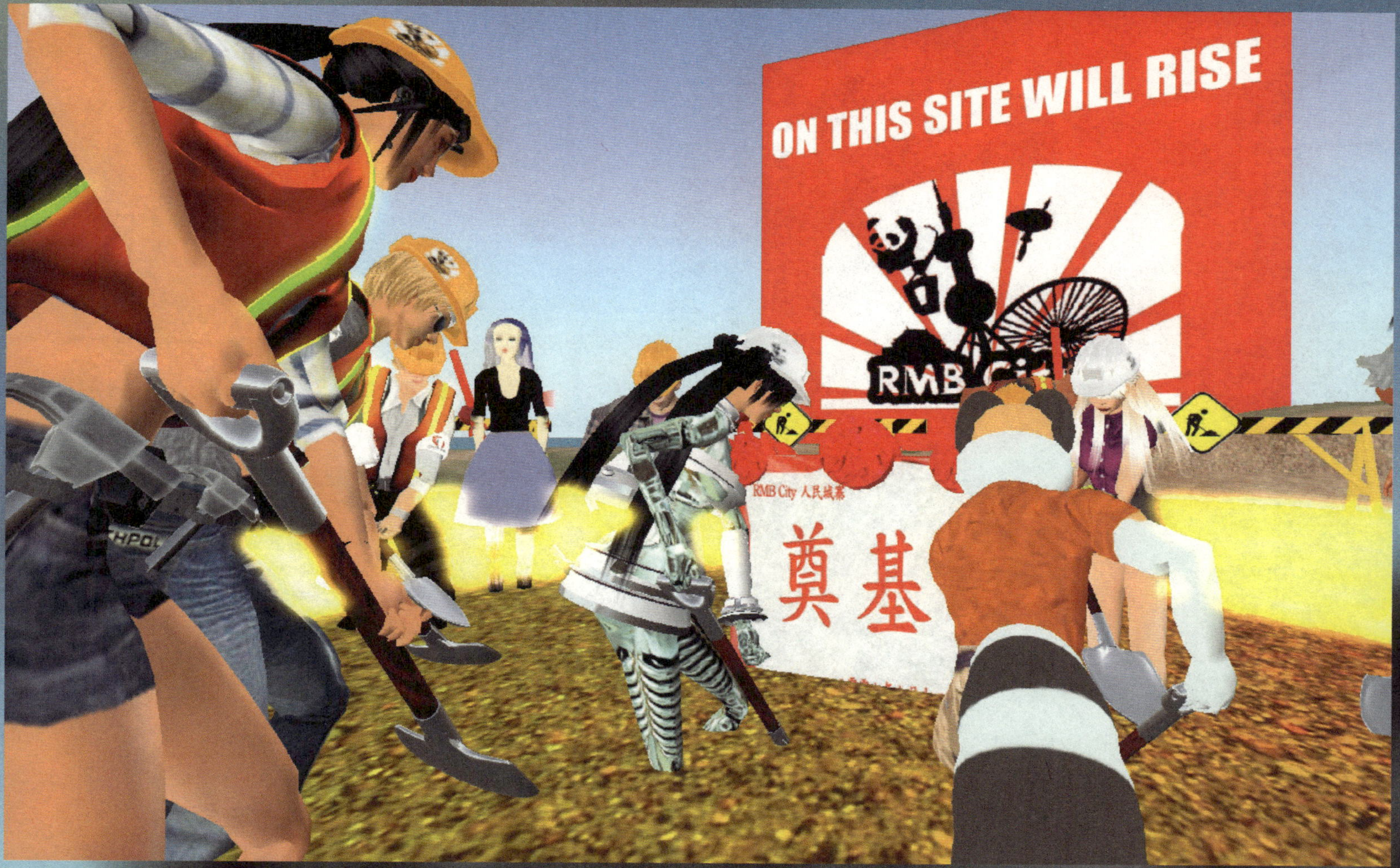
ON THIS SITE WILL RISE
RMB City 人民城寨
奠基

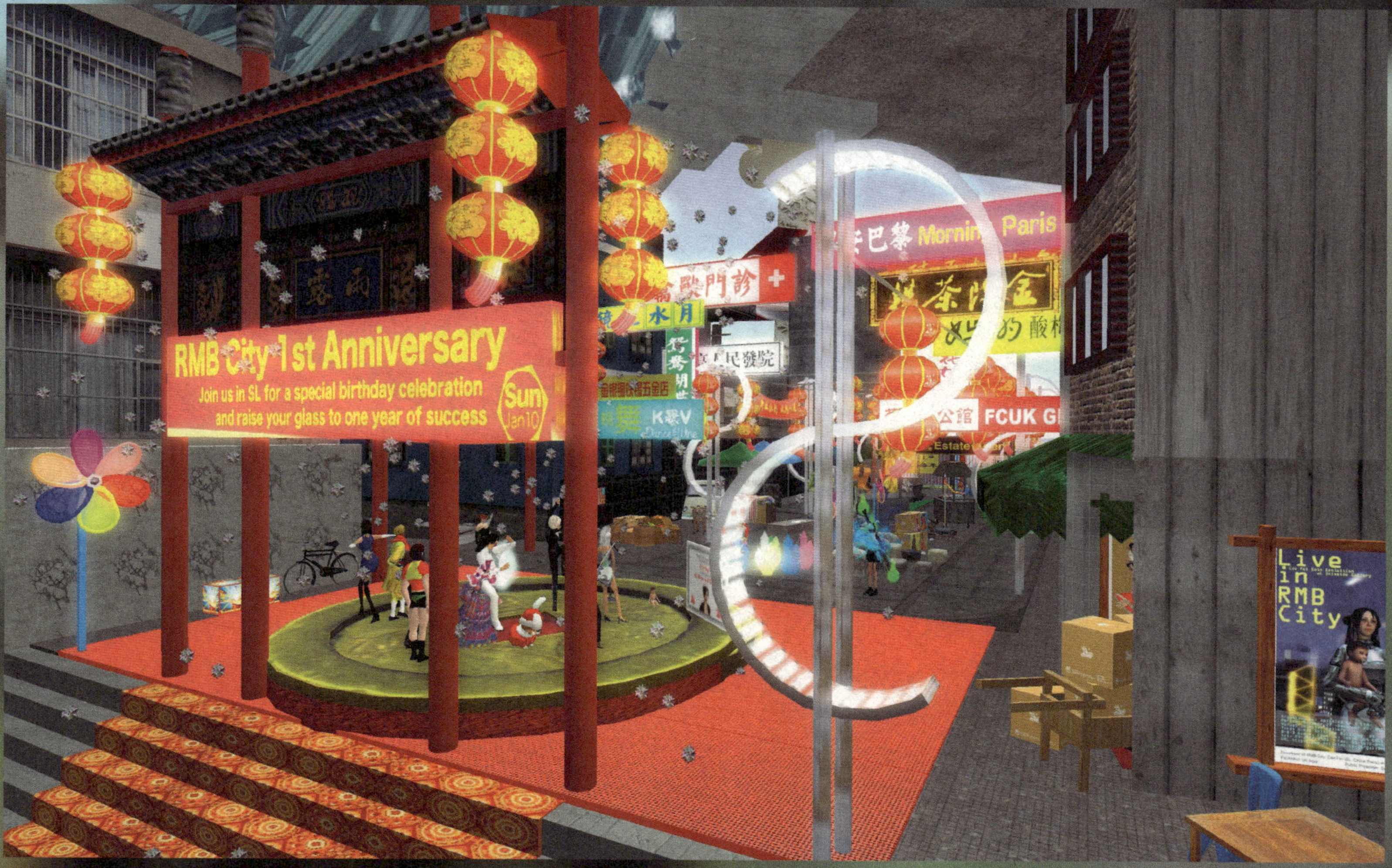
RMB City 1st Anniversary
Join us in SL for a special birthday celebration
and raise your glass to one year of success
Sun
Jan10
FCUK
Live in RMB City

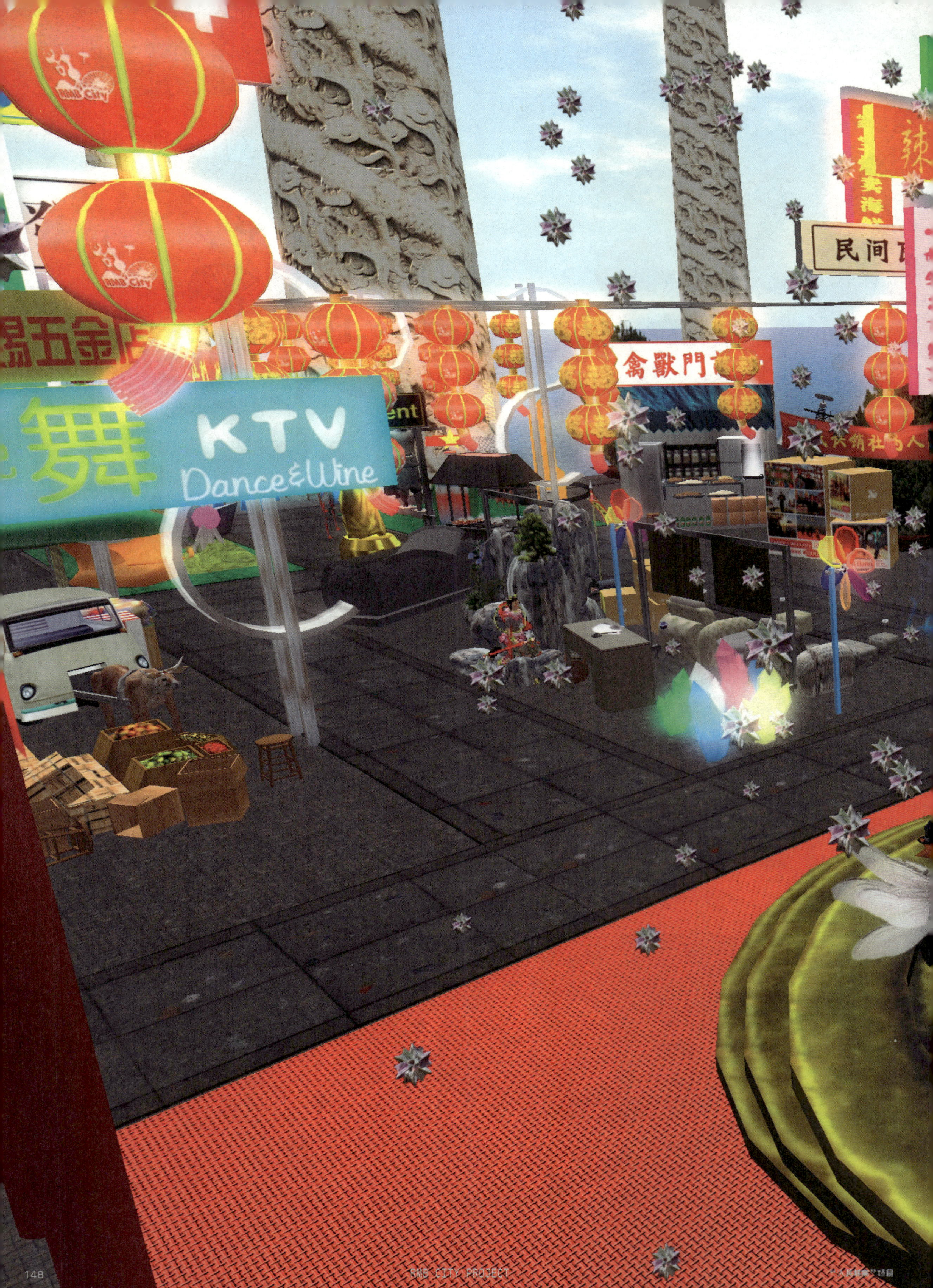
KTV
Dance&Wine
禽獸門
民间

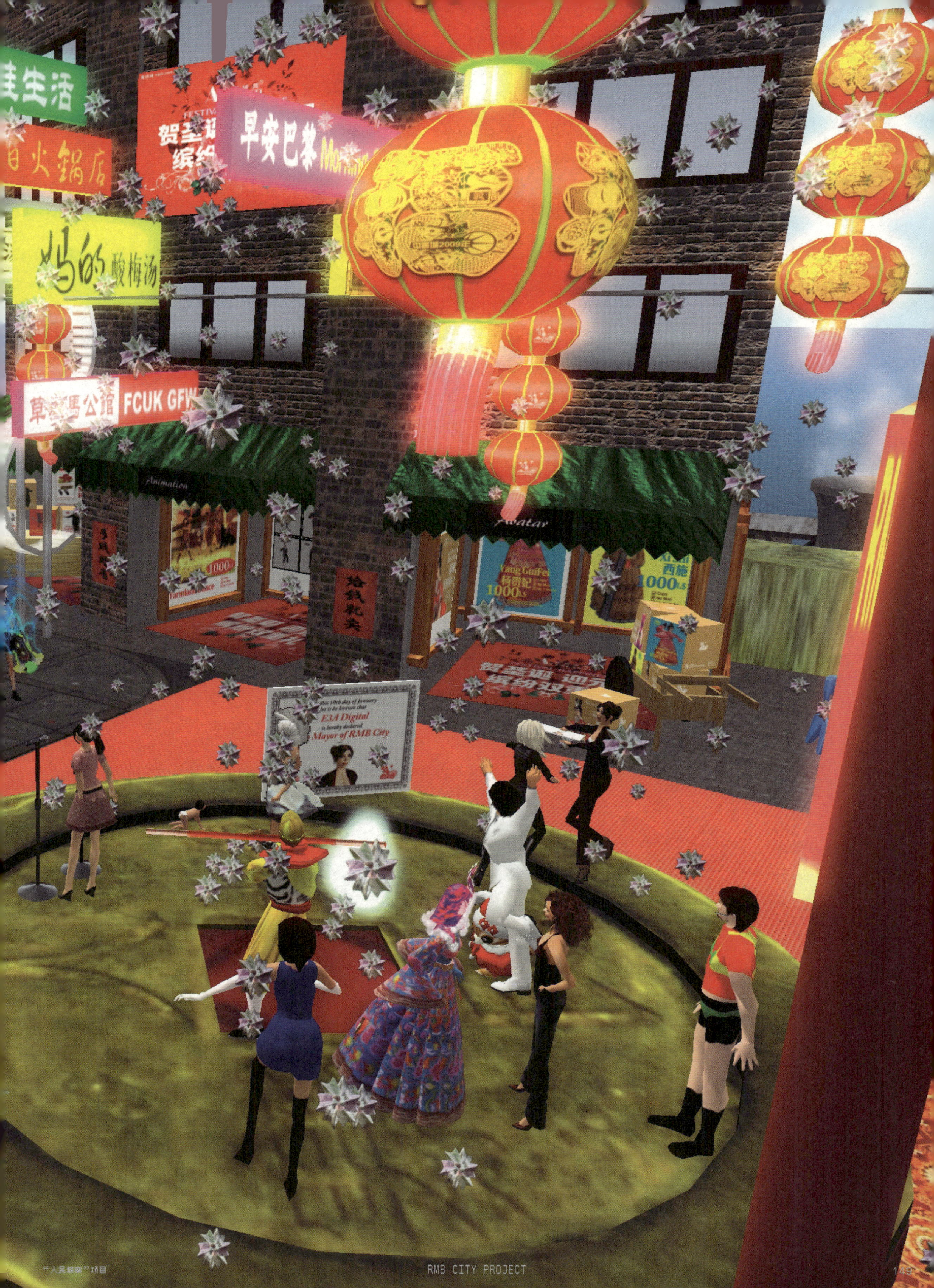
早安巴黎
FCUK GFW
酸梅汤
Avatar
Yang GuiFei
杨贵妃
西施
EXA Digital
Mayor of RMB City

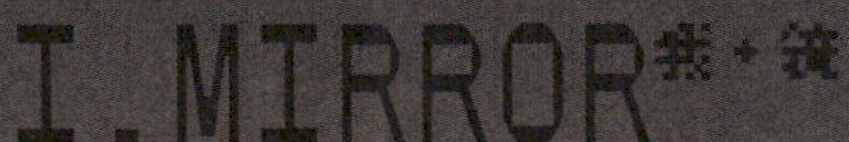

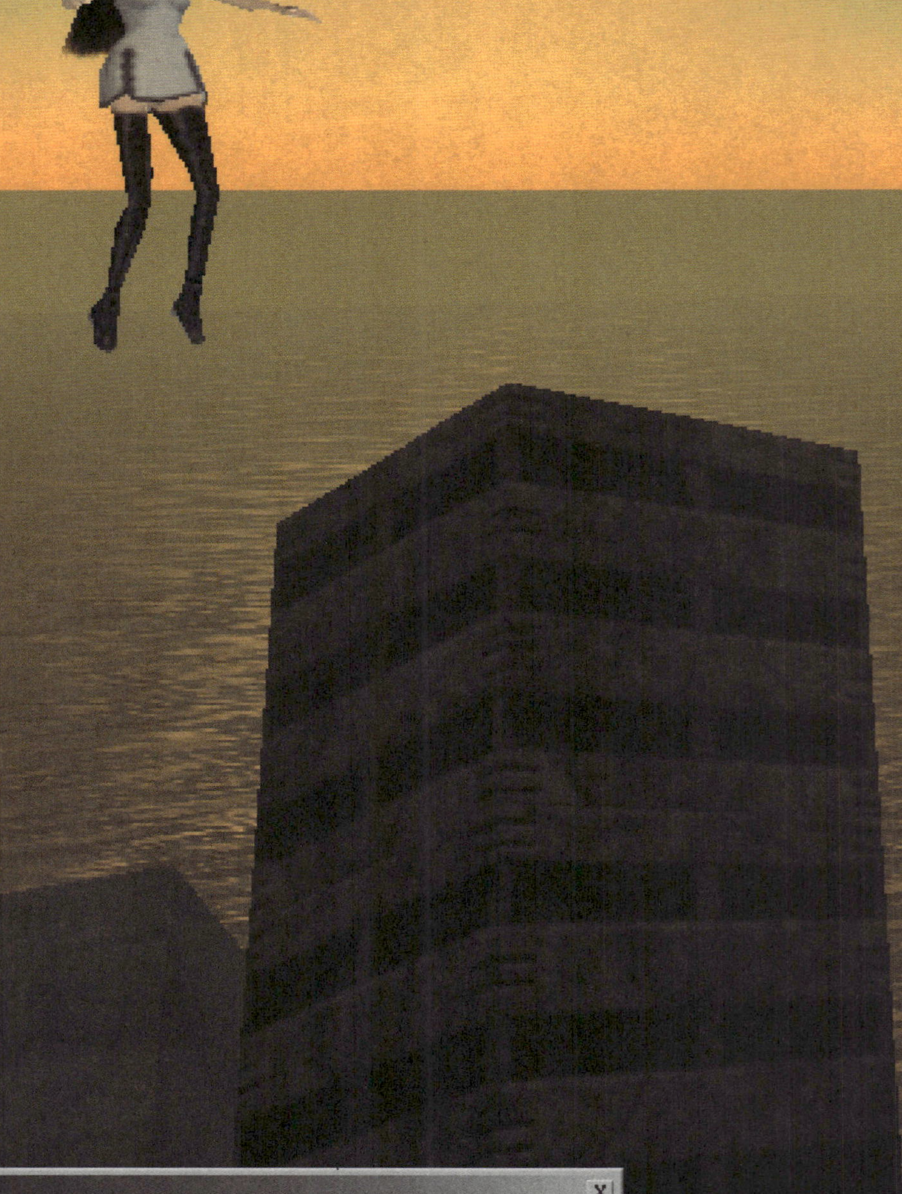

Artwork specification

i.Mirror 2007
machinima, single-channel video, colour, sound
28 min, 4:3

《我+镜》2007
4:3 引擎电影，
彩色有声单频录像 28分

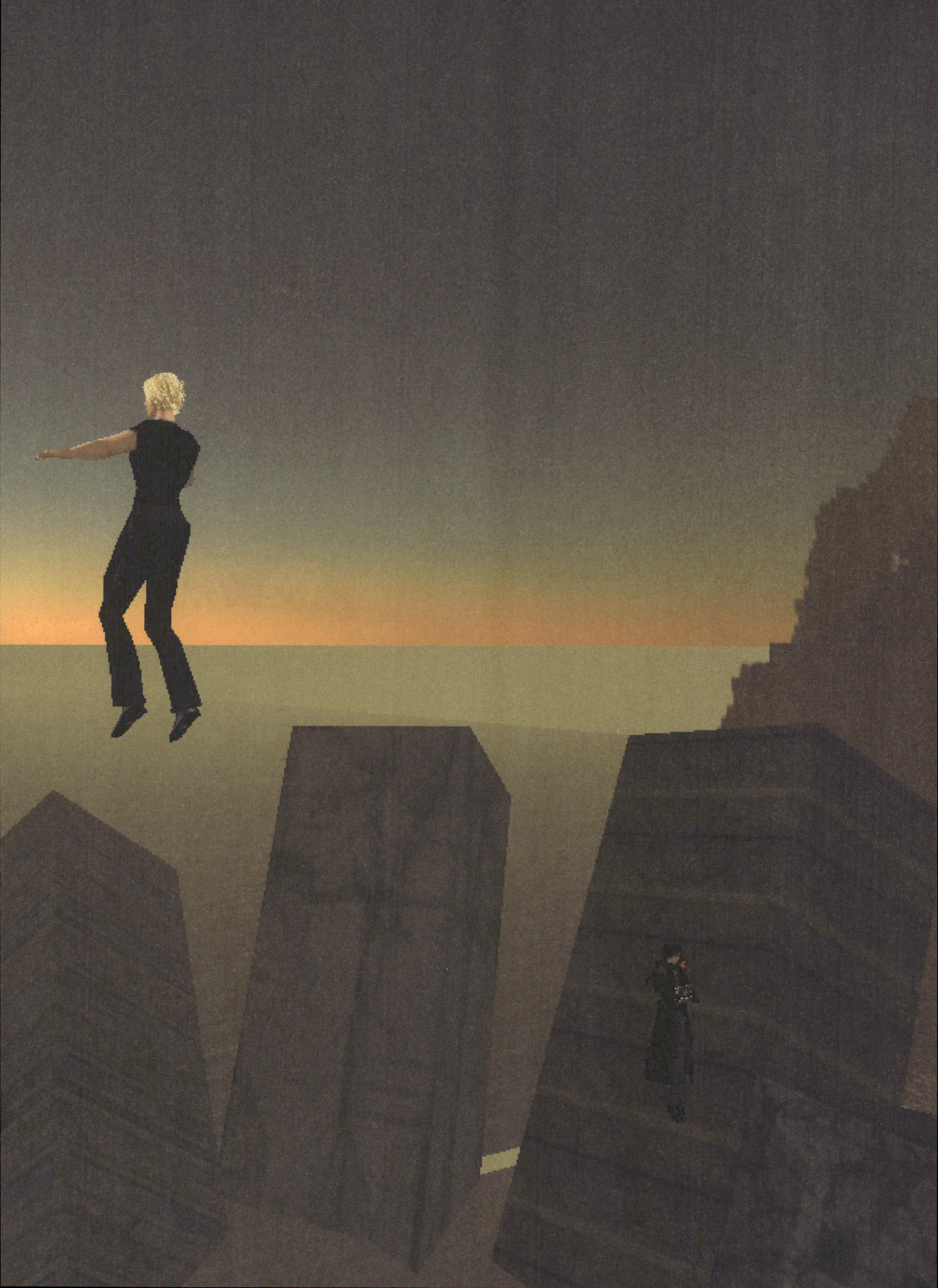

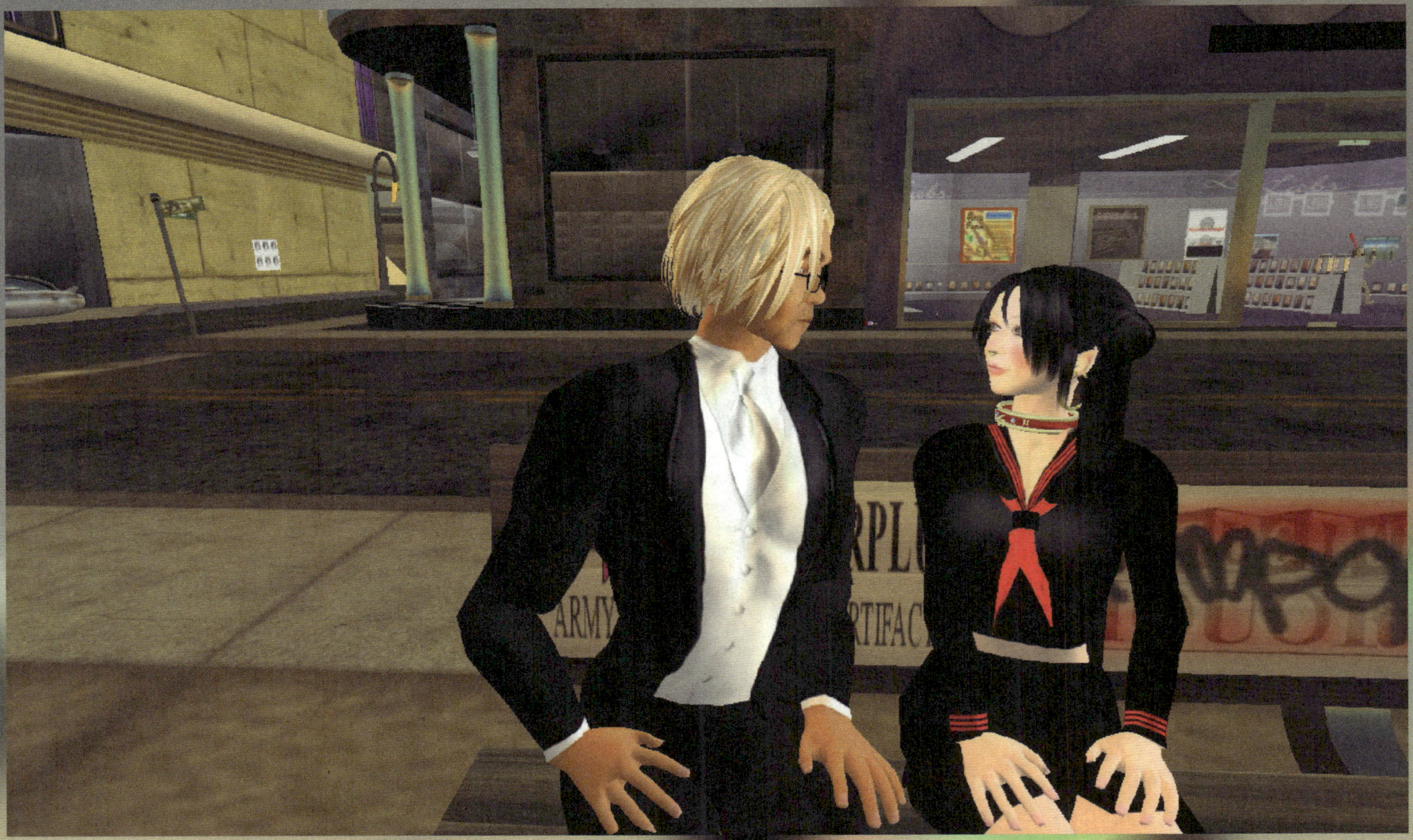
ARMY
RTIFAC

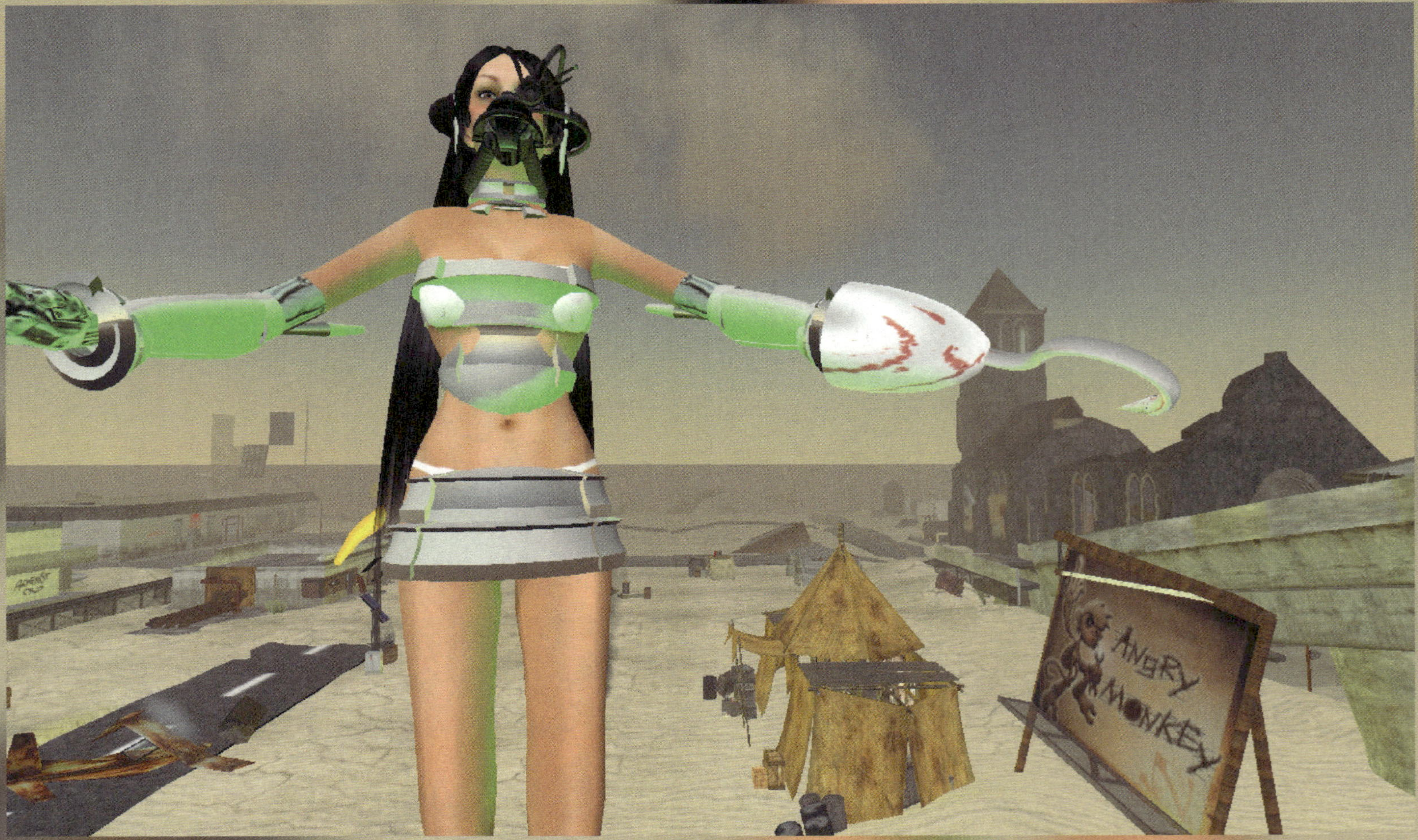
ANGRY
MONKEY

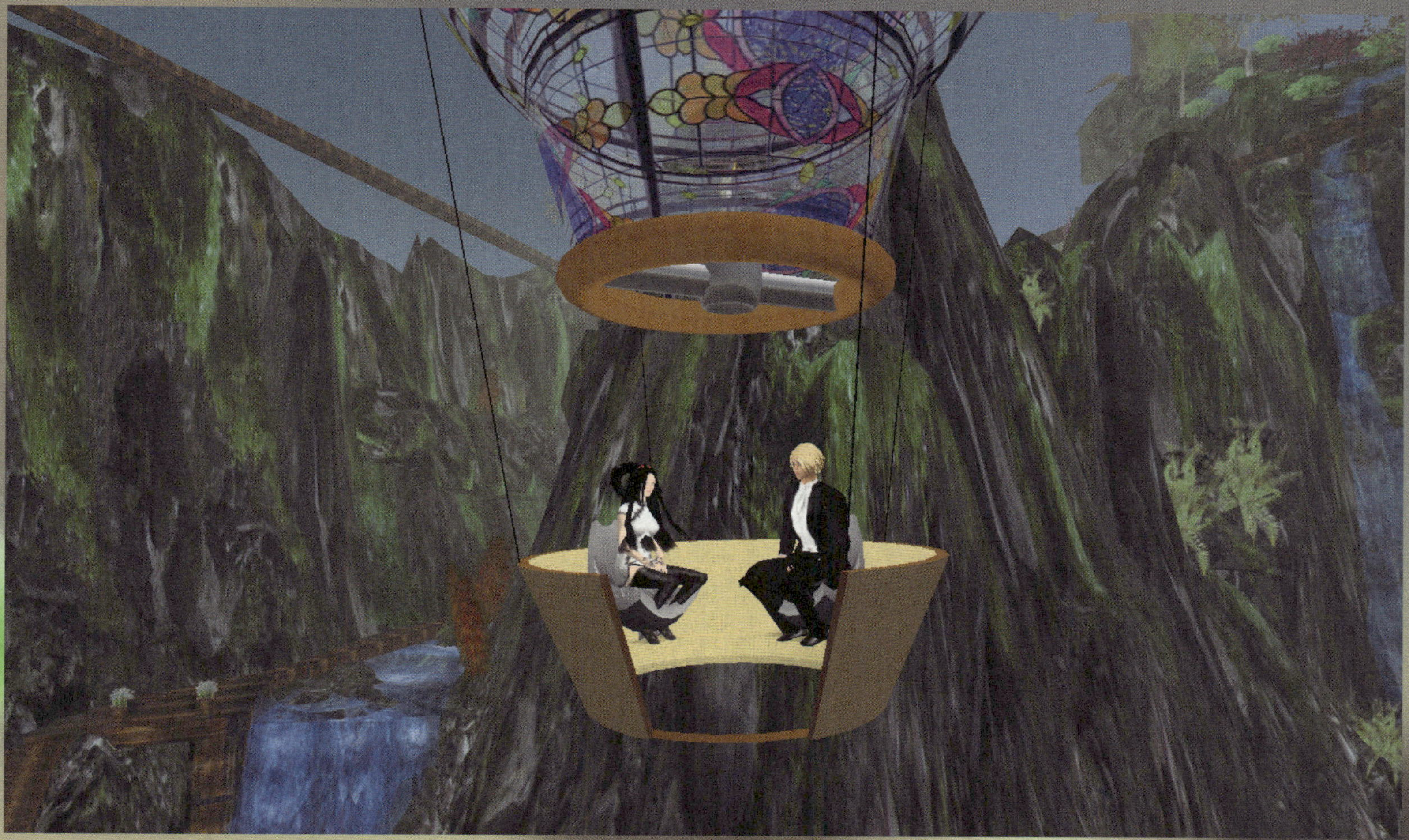

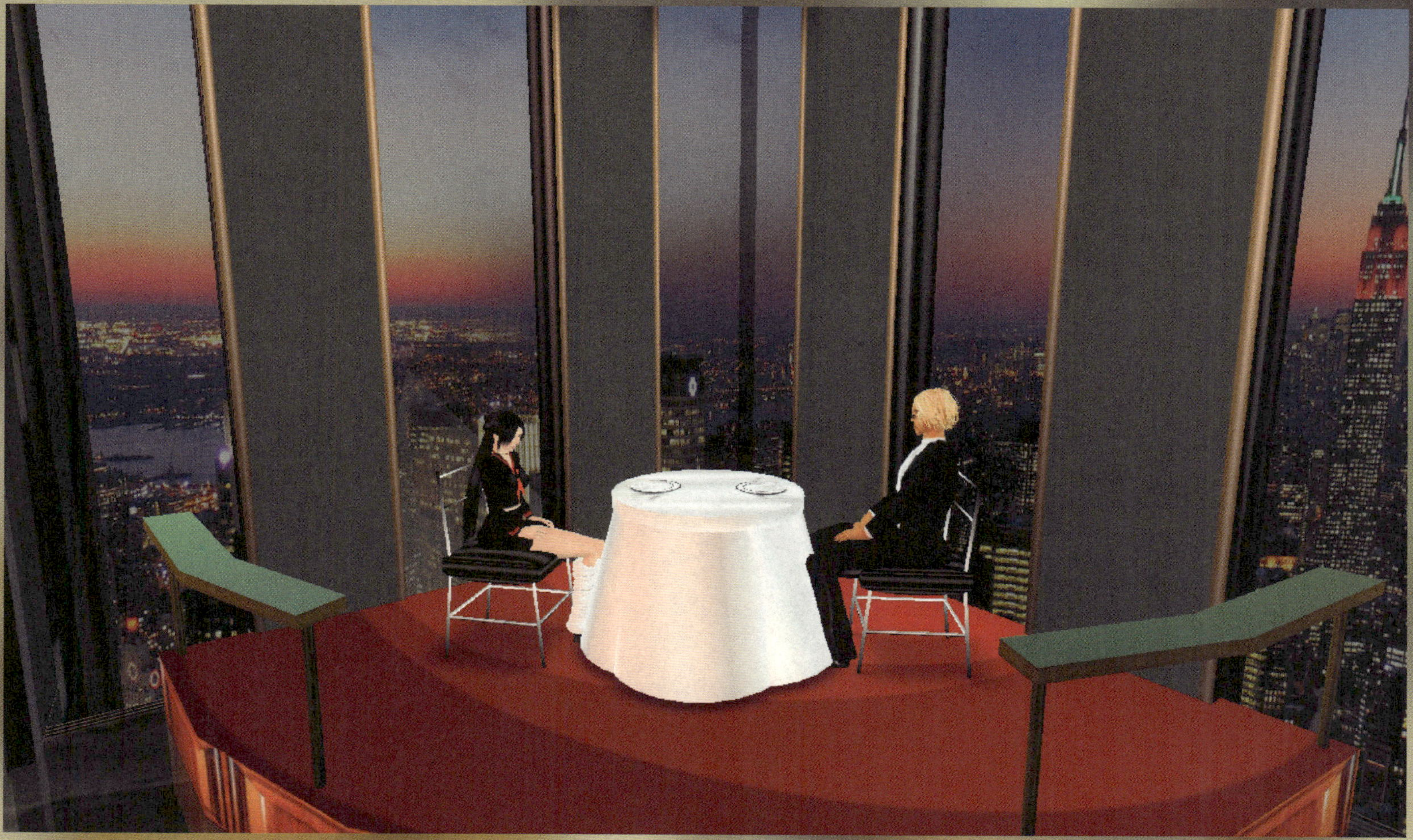

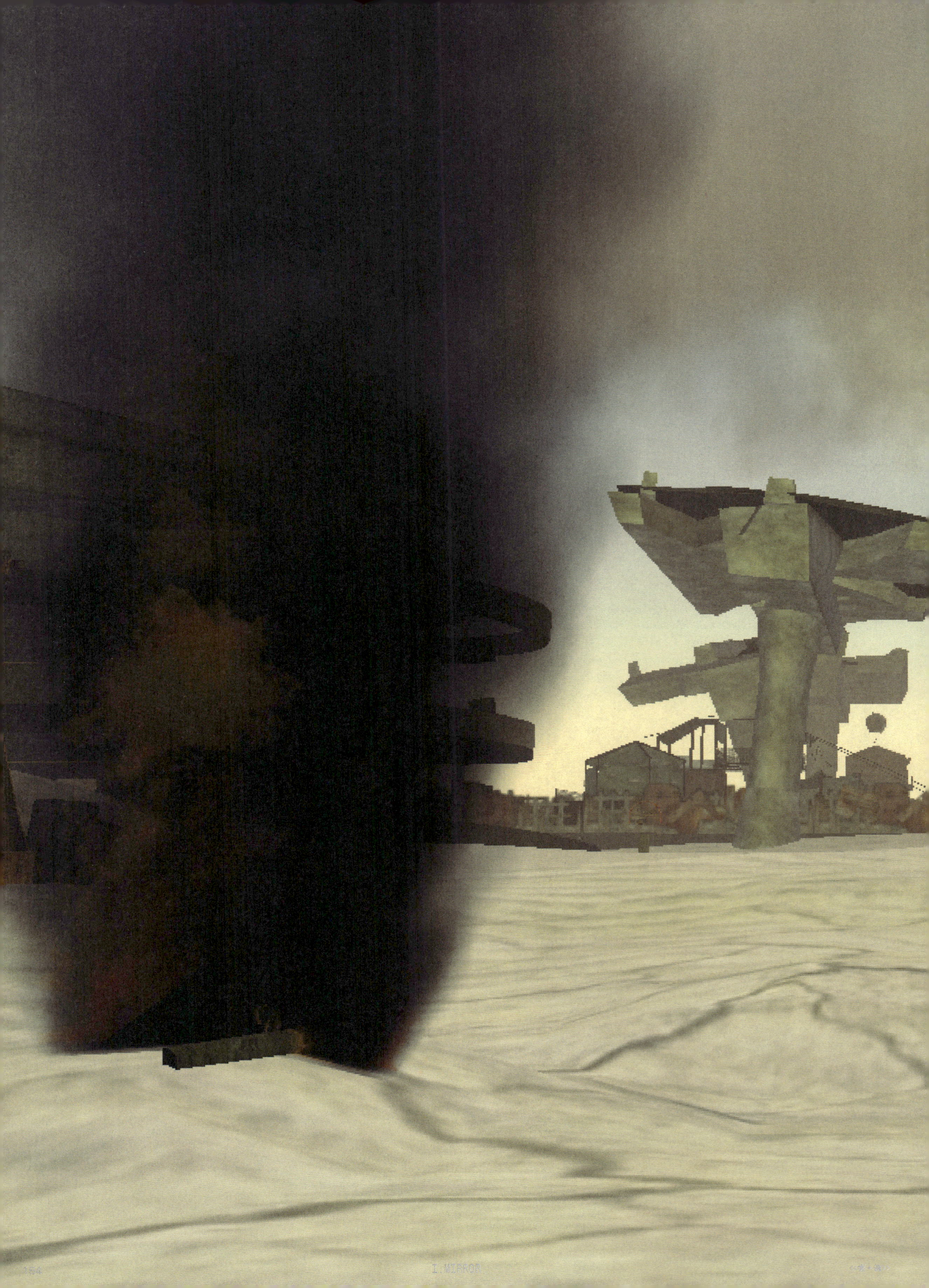

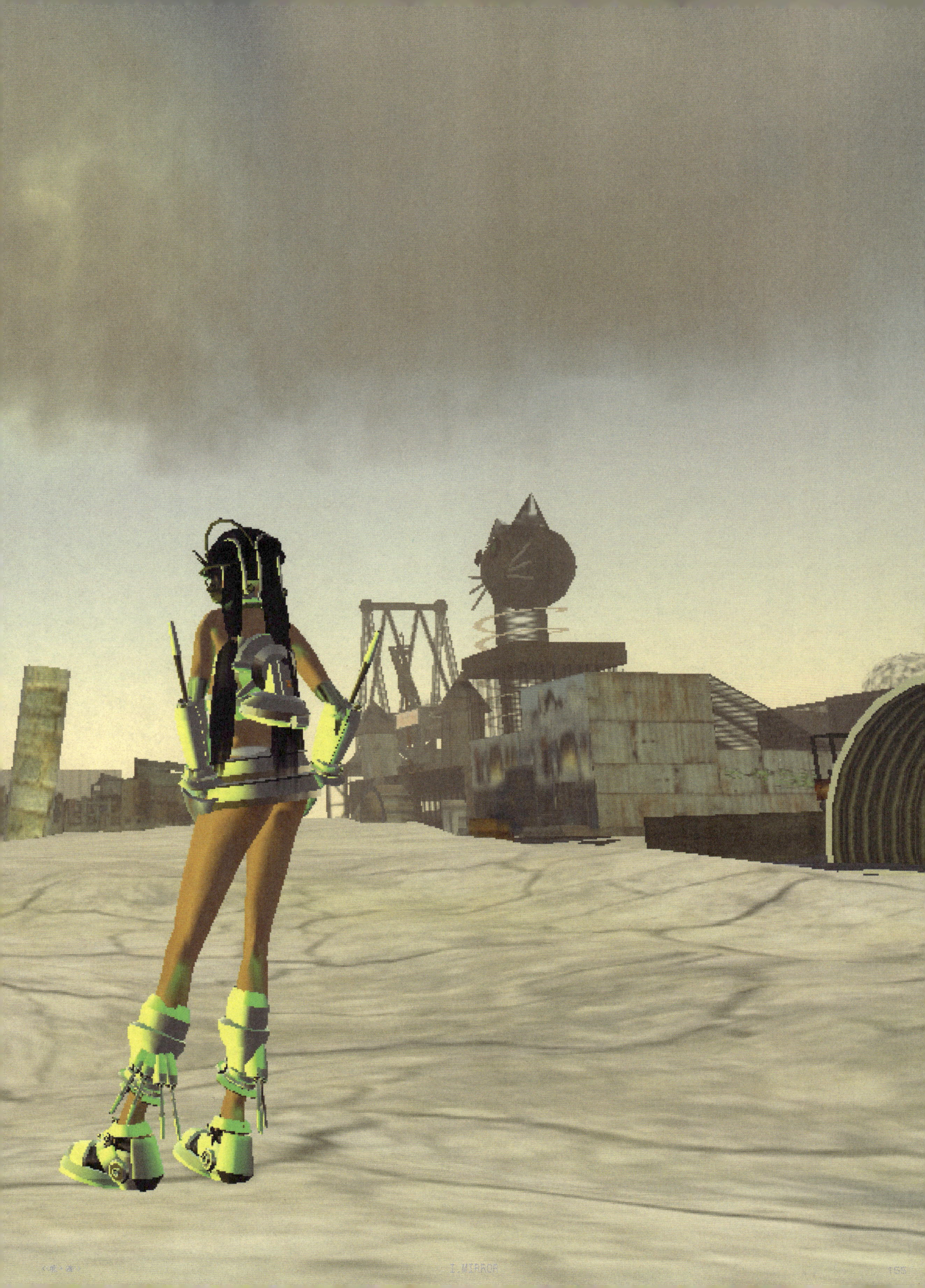

LIVE IN RMB CITY 人民城寨的生活

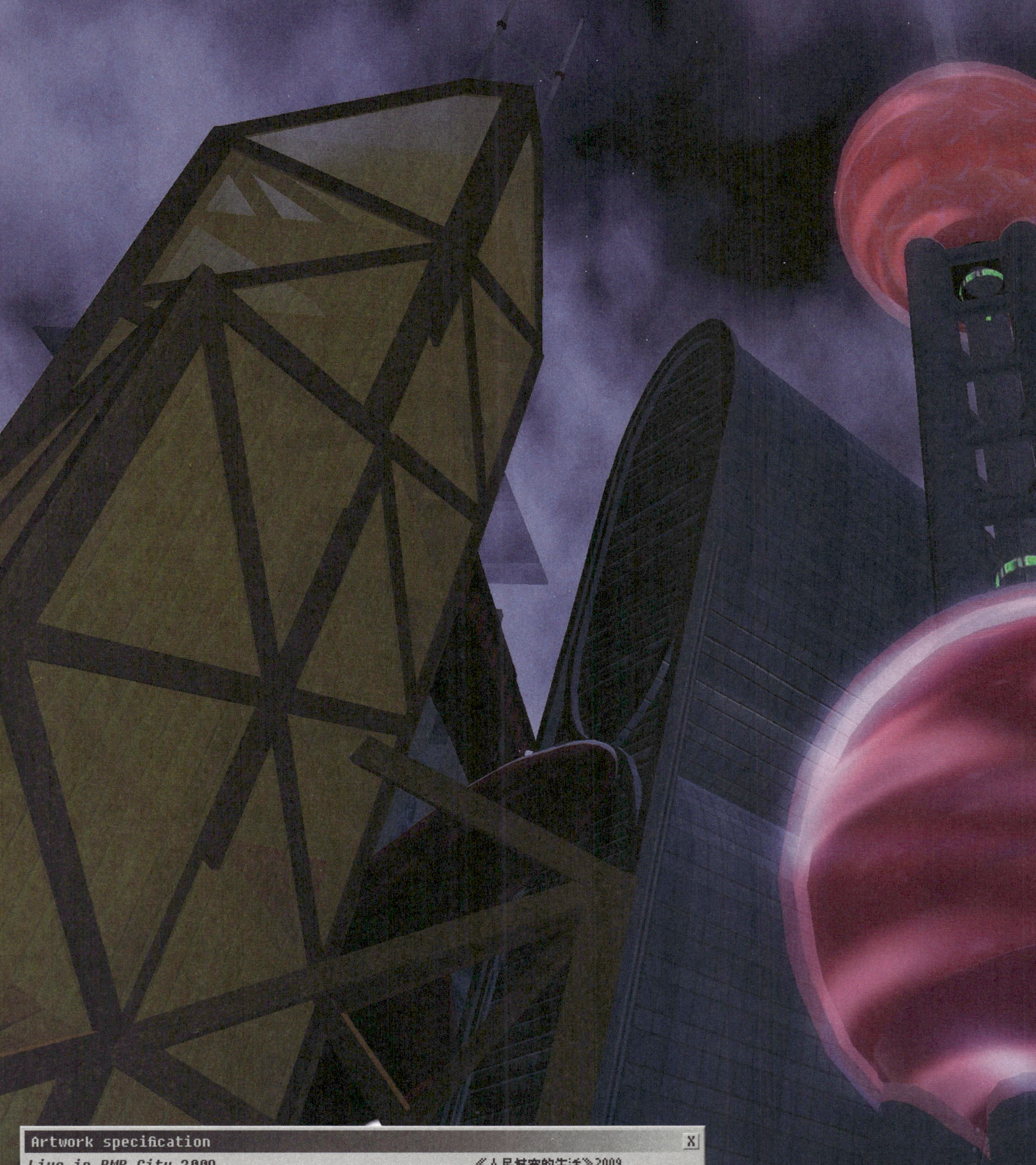

Artwork specification

Live in RMB City 2009
machinima, single-channel video, colour, sound
24:05 min, 5:4

《人民城寨的生活》2009
5:4引擎电影，彩色有声单频录像
24分5秒

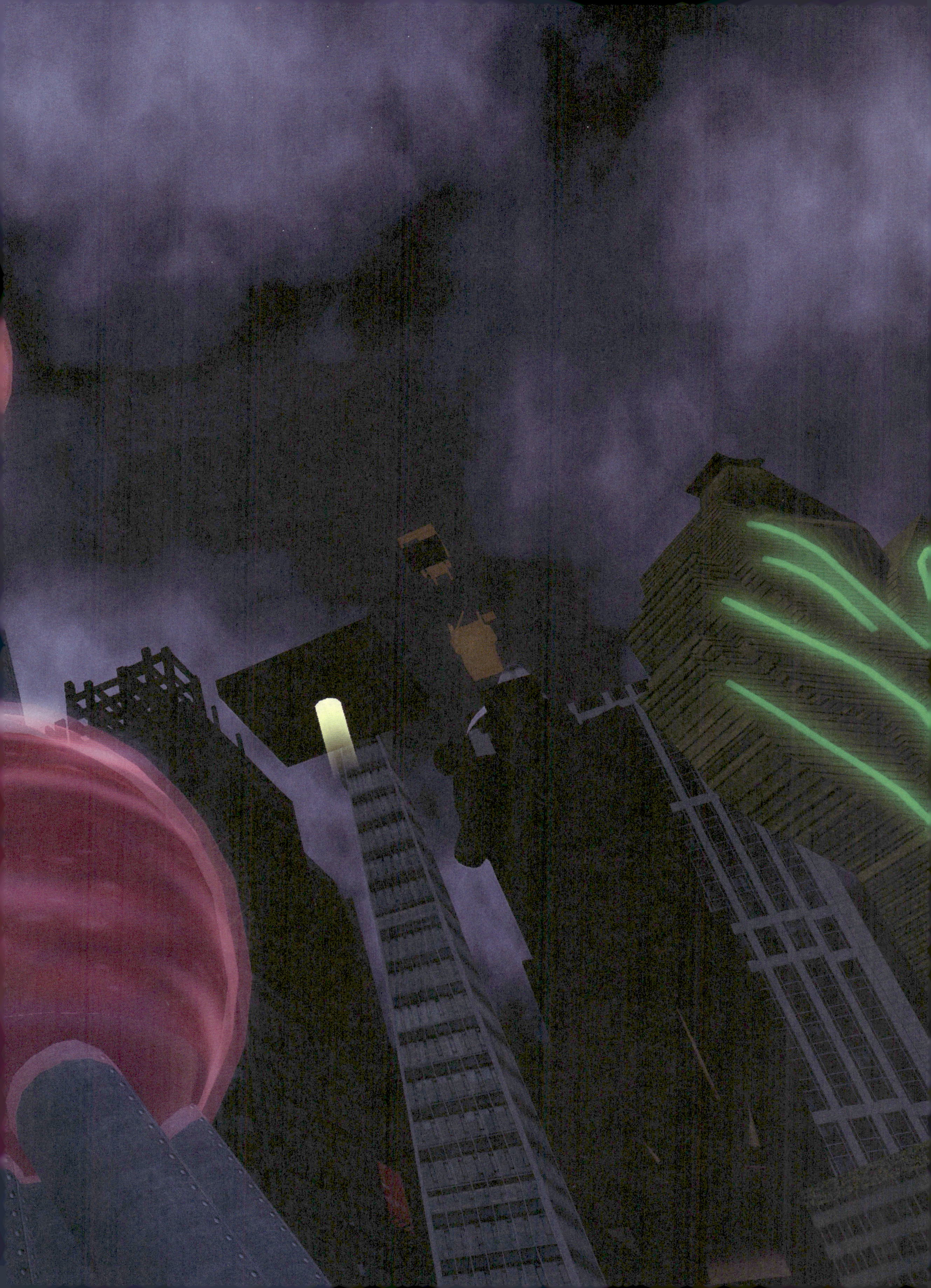

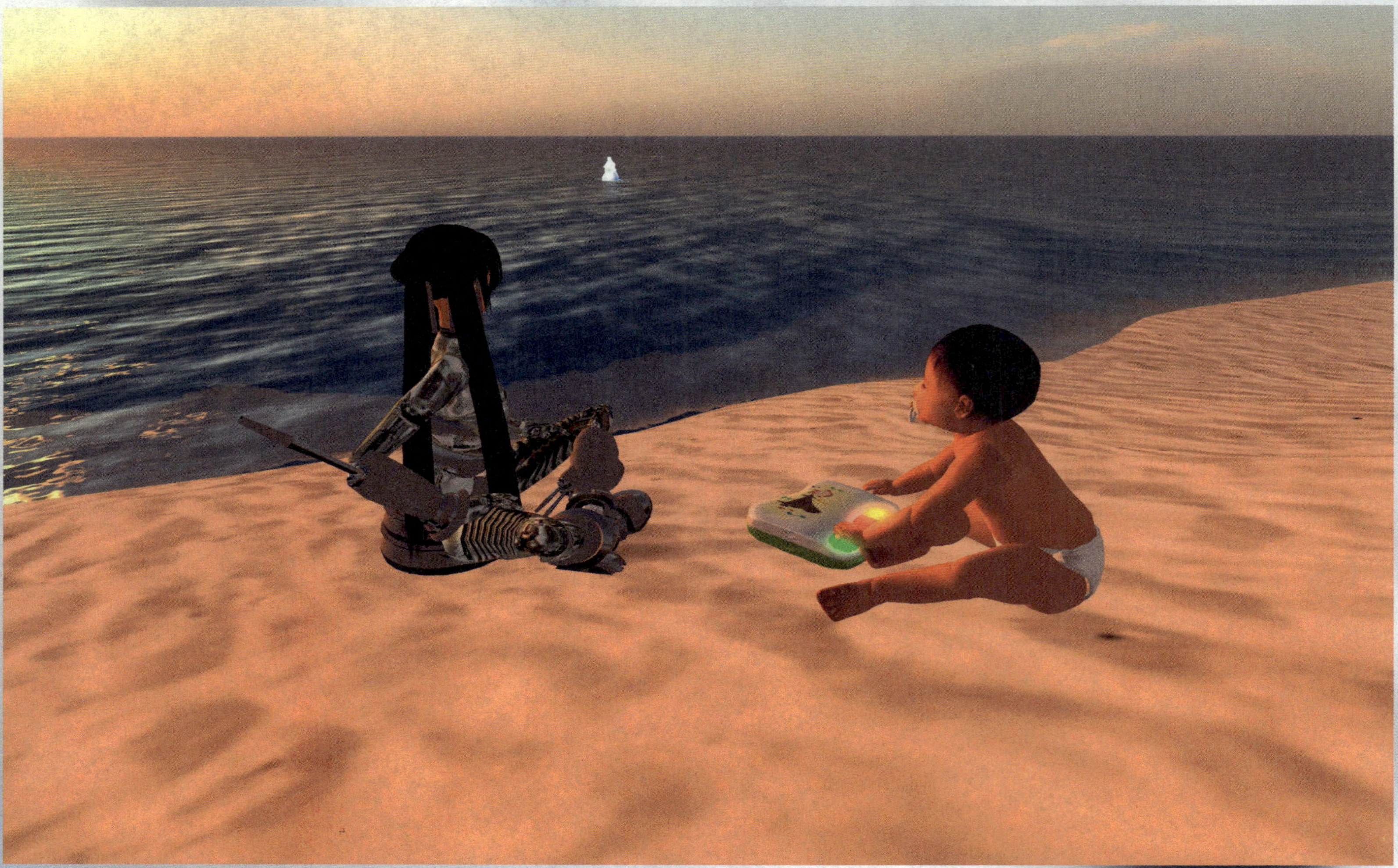

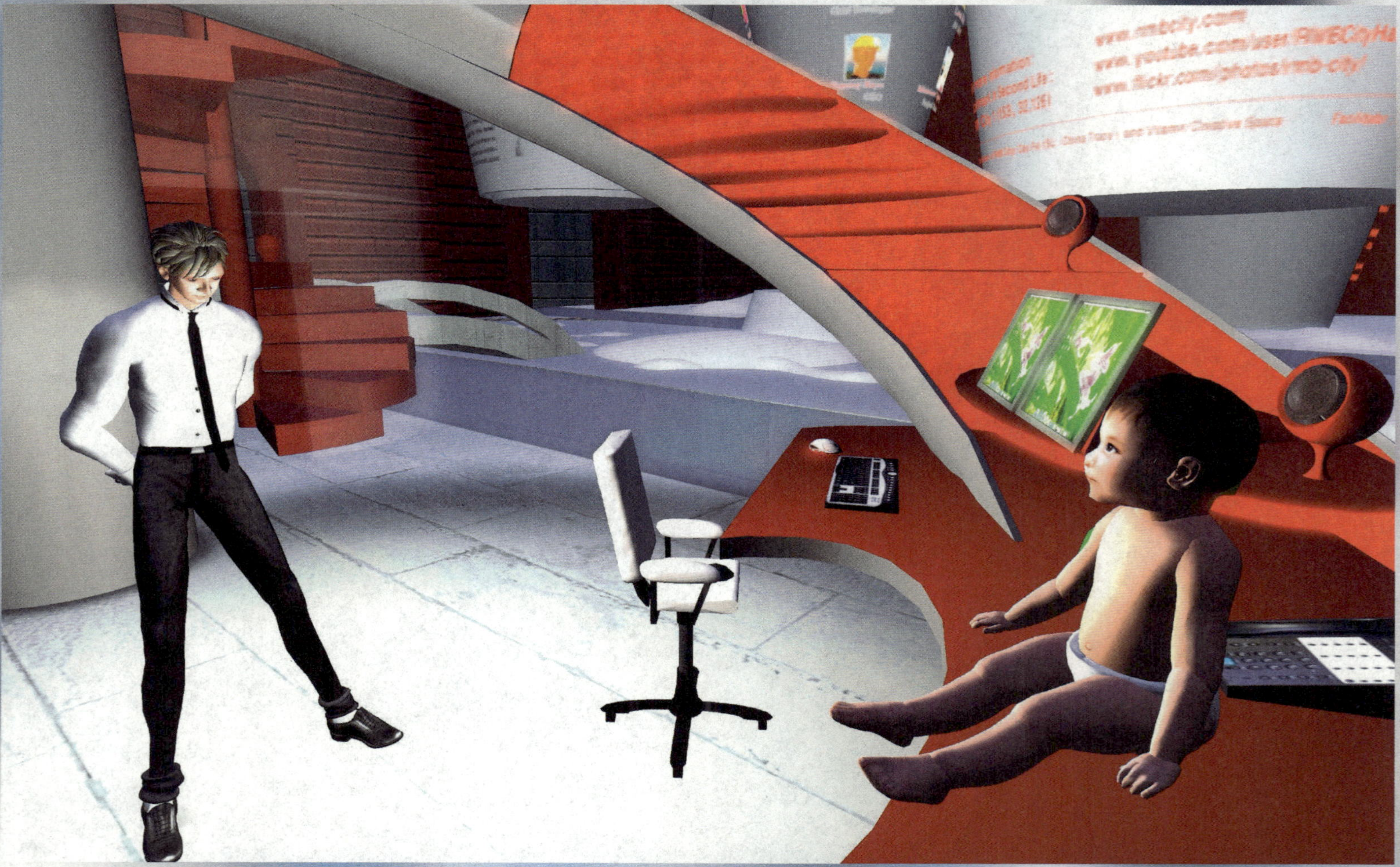

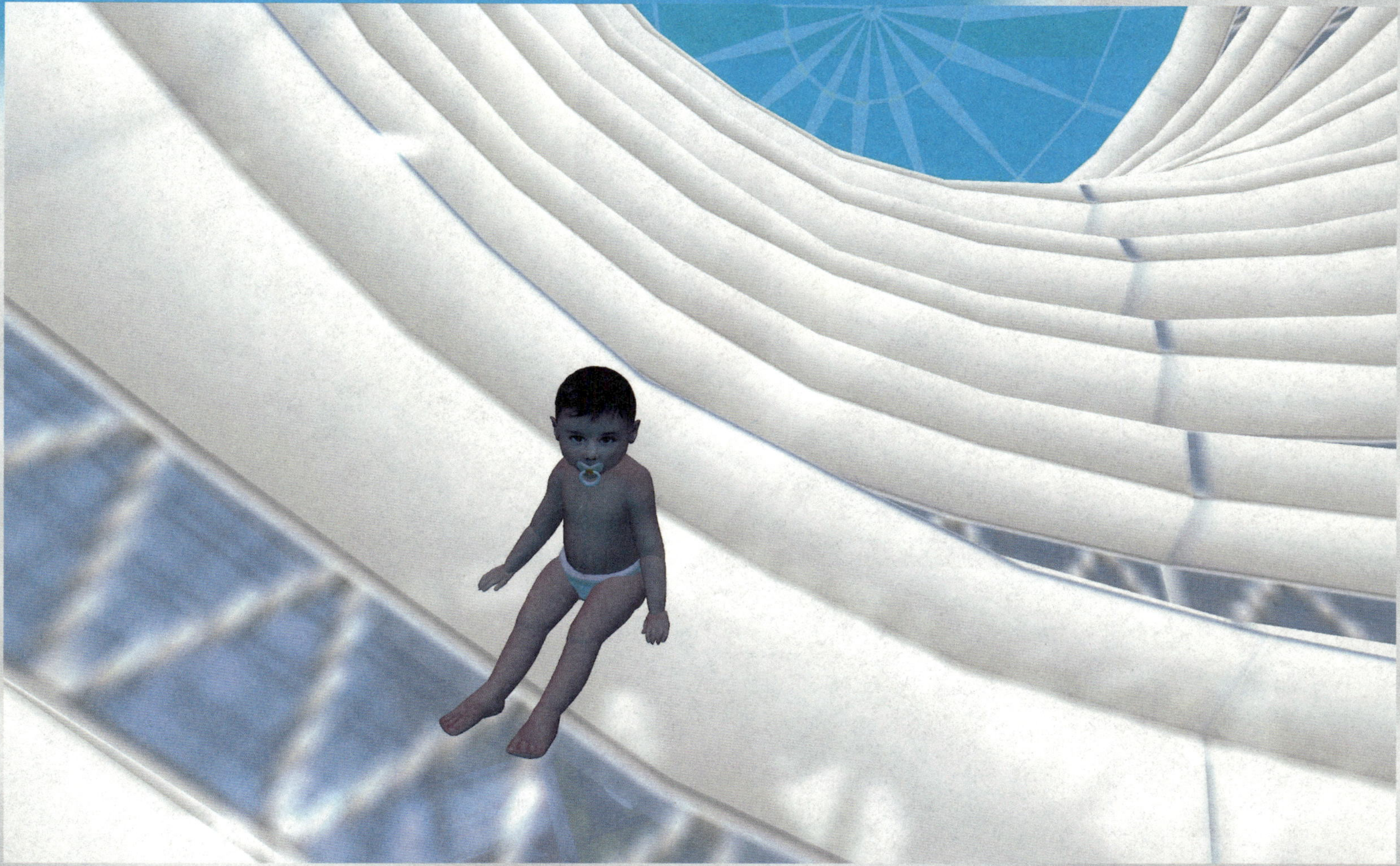

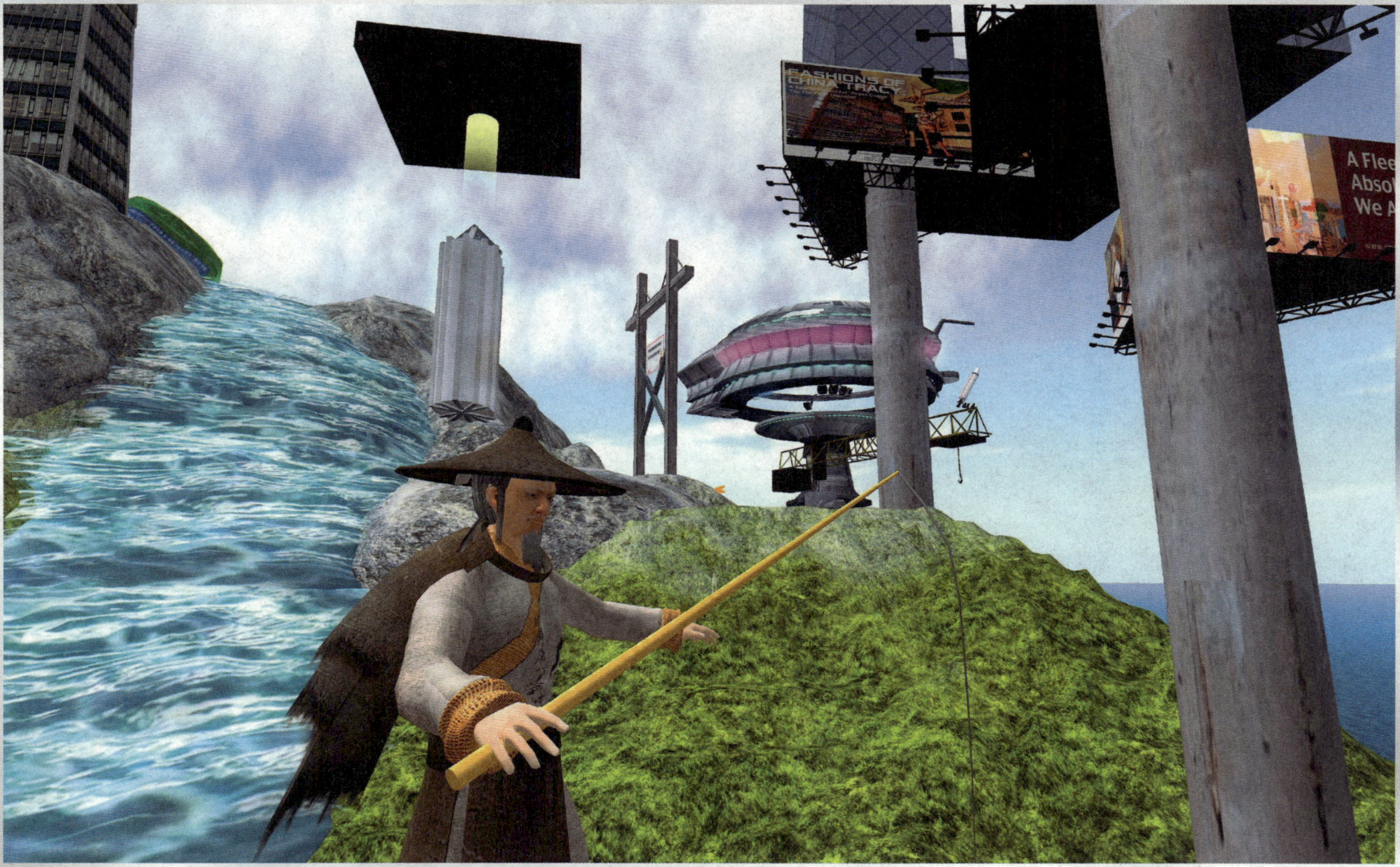
FASHIONS OF CHINA TRACY
A Flee
Abso
We A

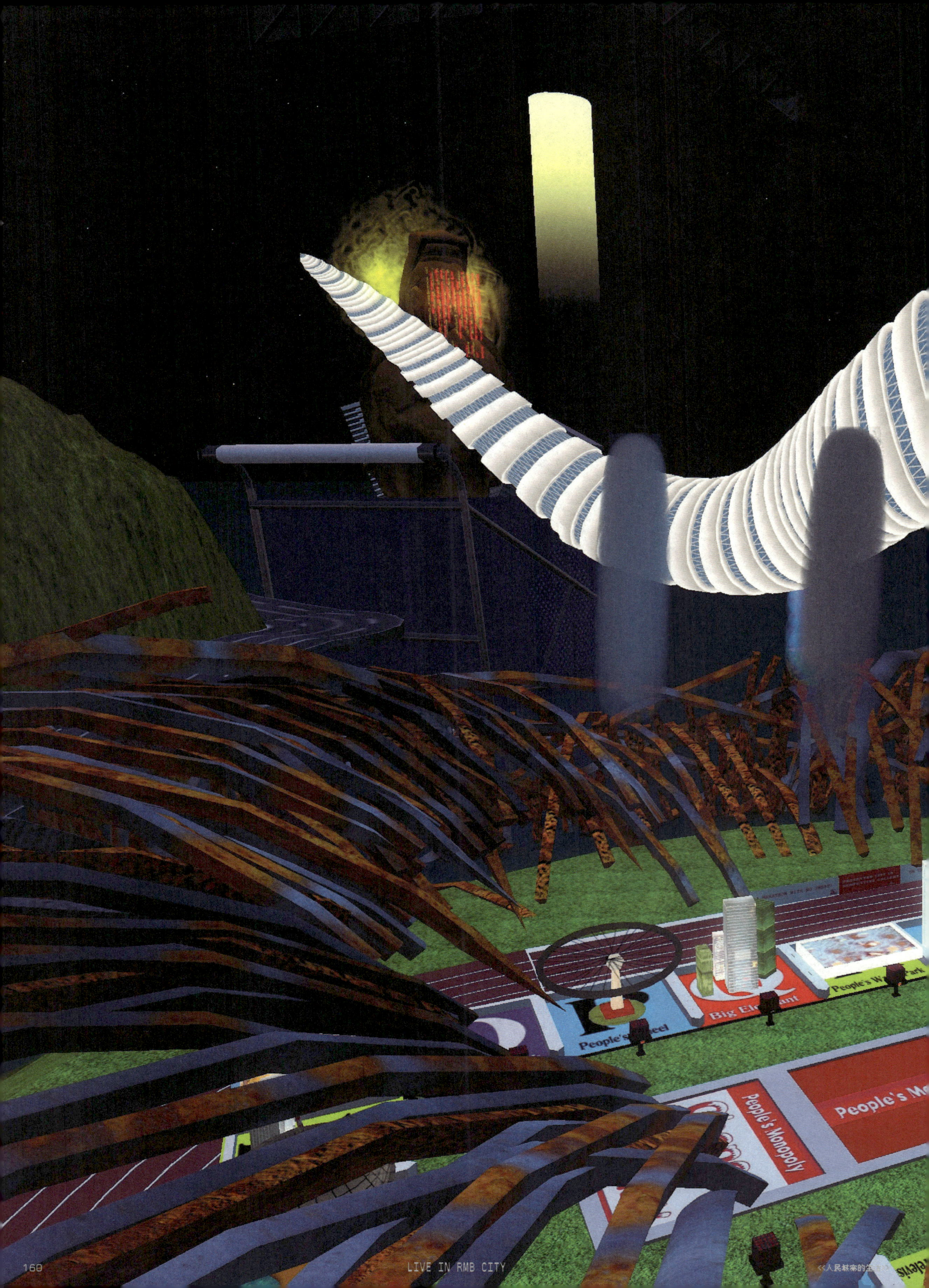
People's Monopoly

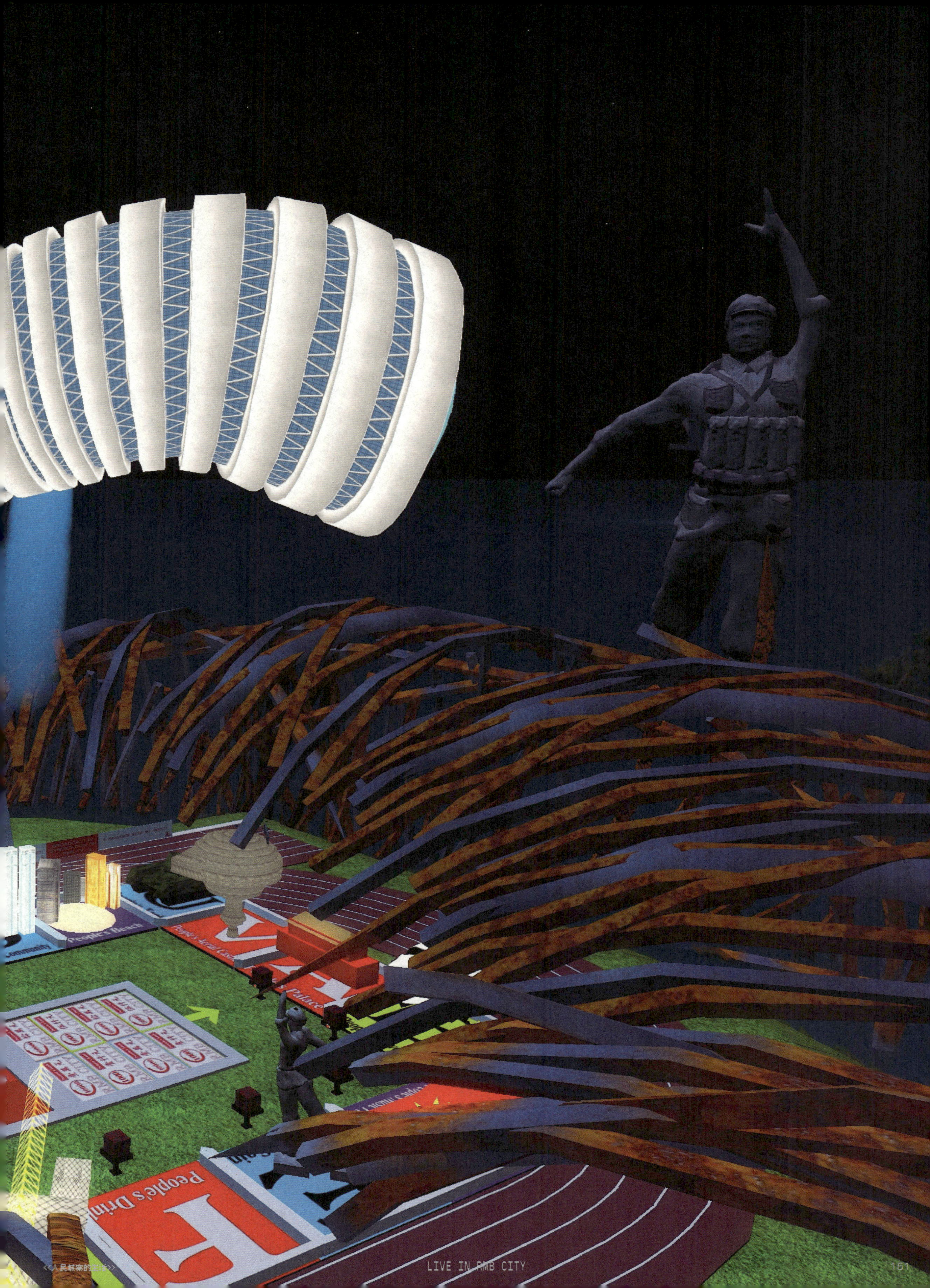
People's Beach
Community
Palace

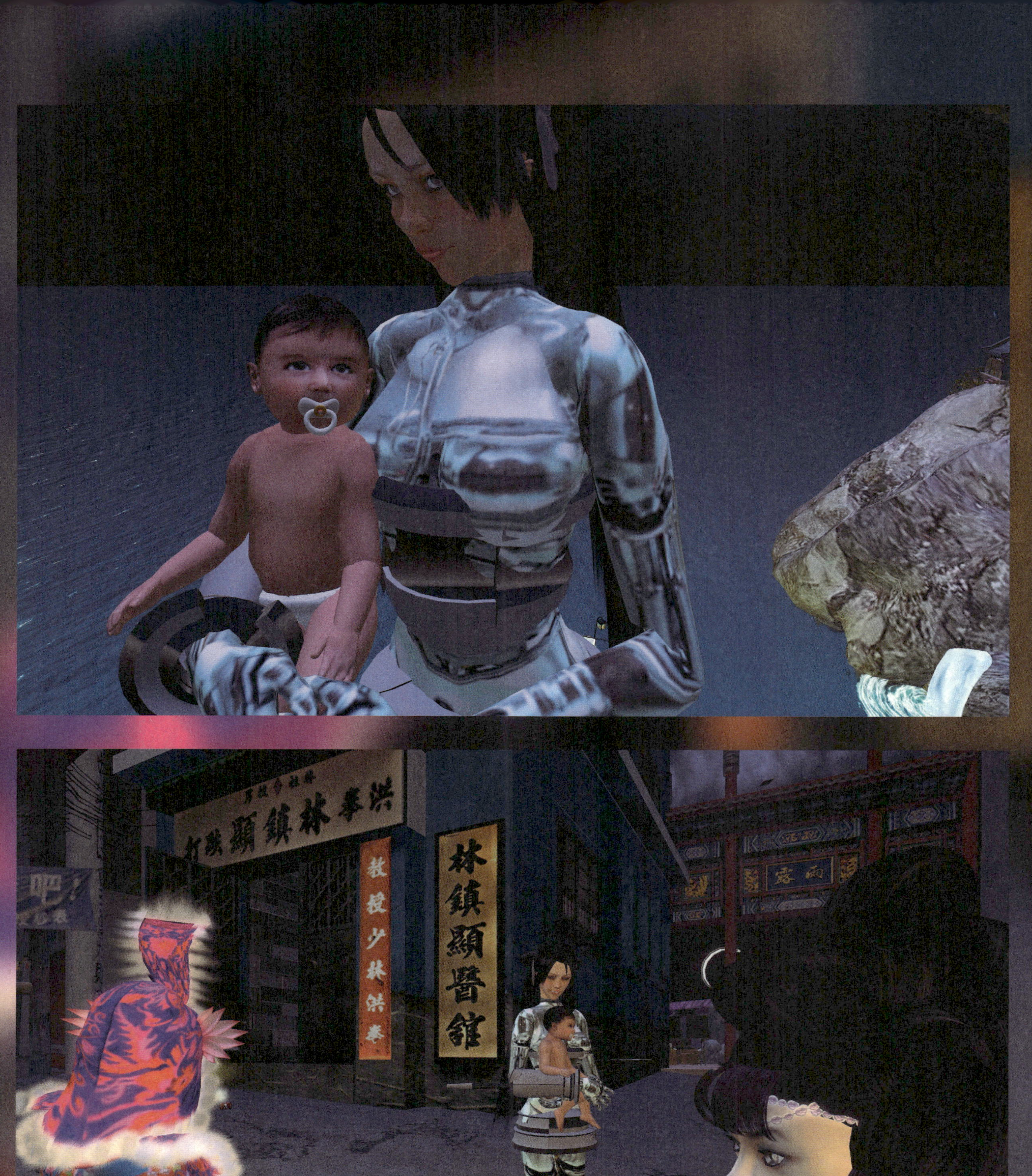
洪拳林鎮顯跌打
教授少林洪拳
林鎮顯醫館

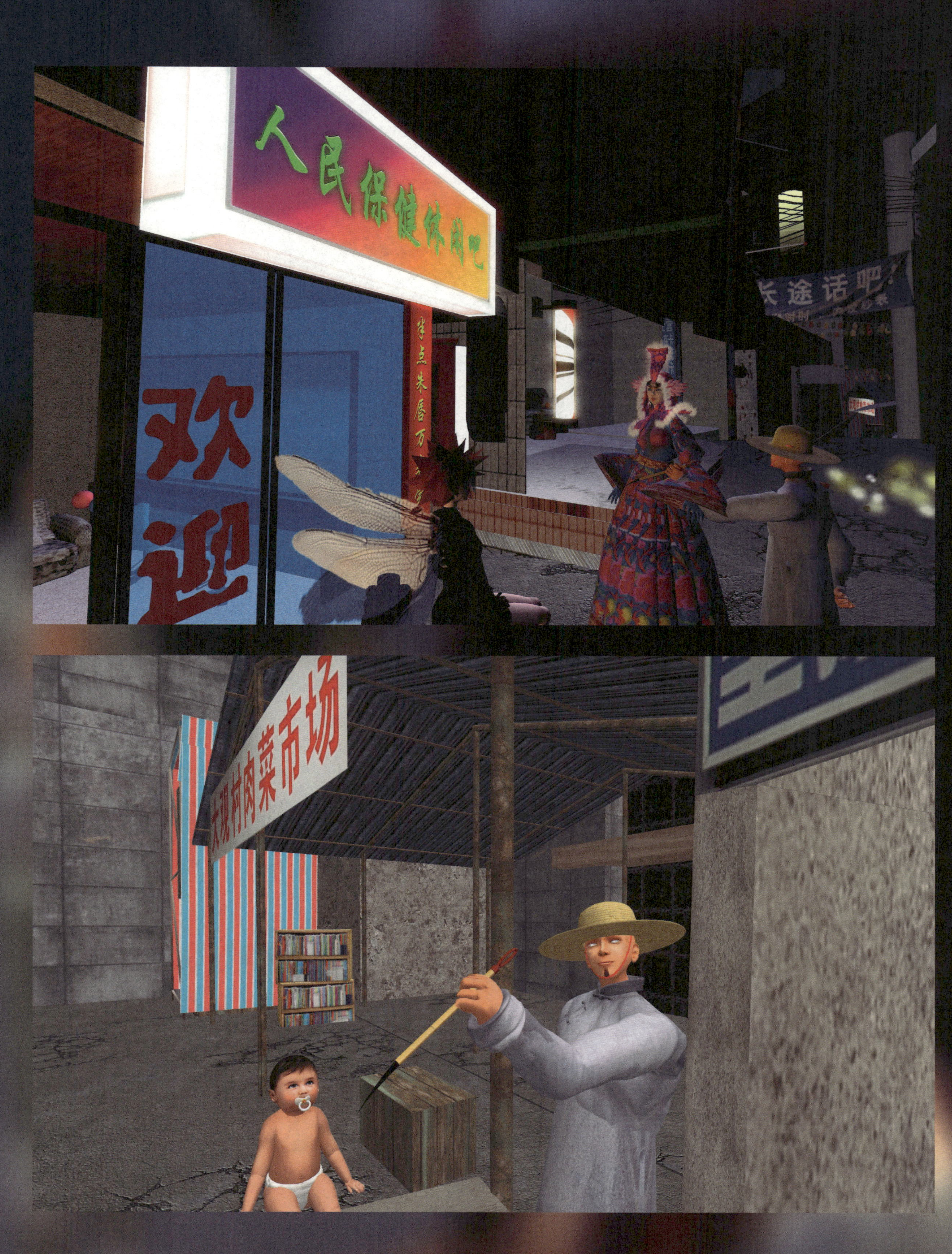
人民保健休闲吧
欢迎
长途话吧!
大观村肉菜市场

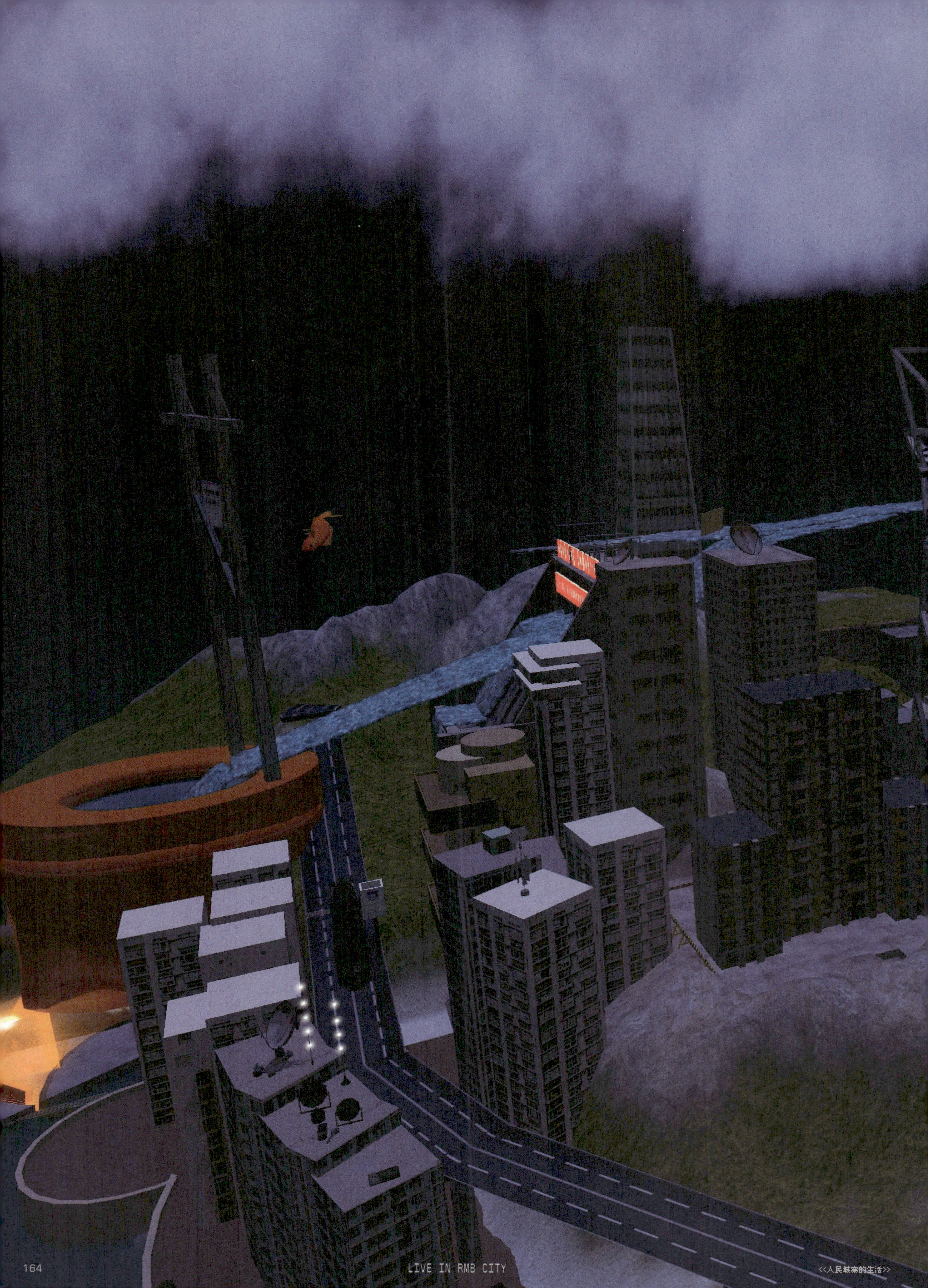

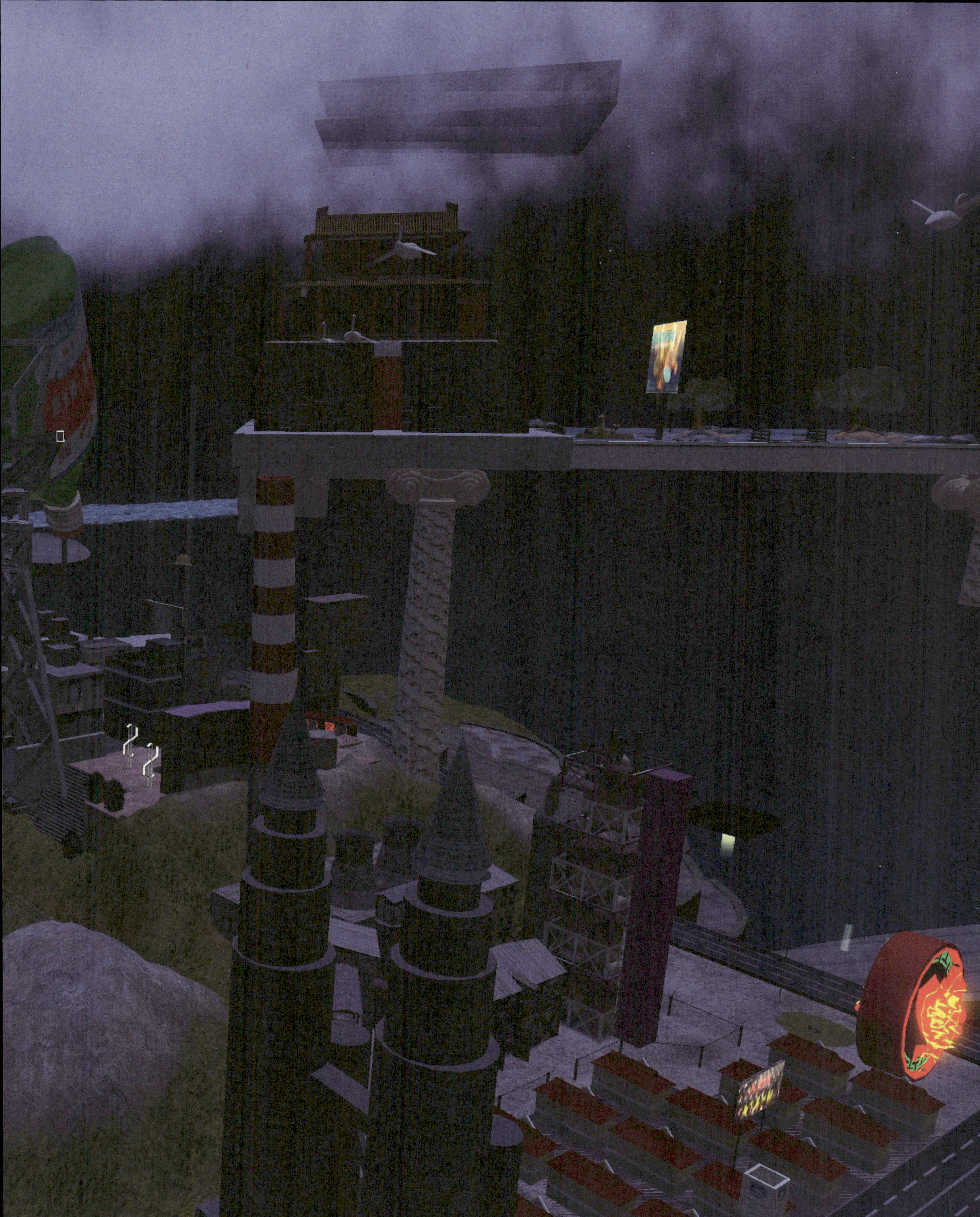

TONIGHT LIVE INTERVIEW WITH CHINA TRACY (SLCN.TV) “今夜现场”节目采访中国·翠西

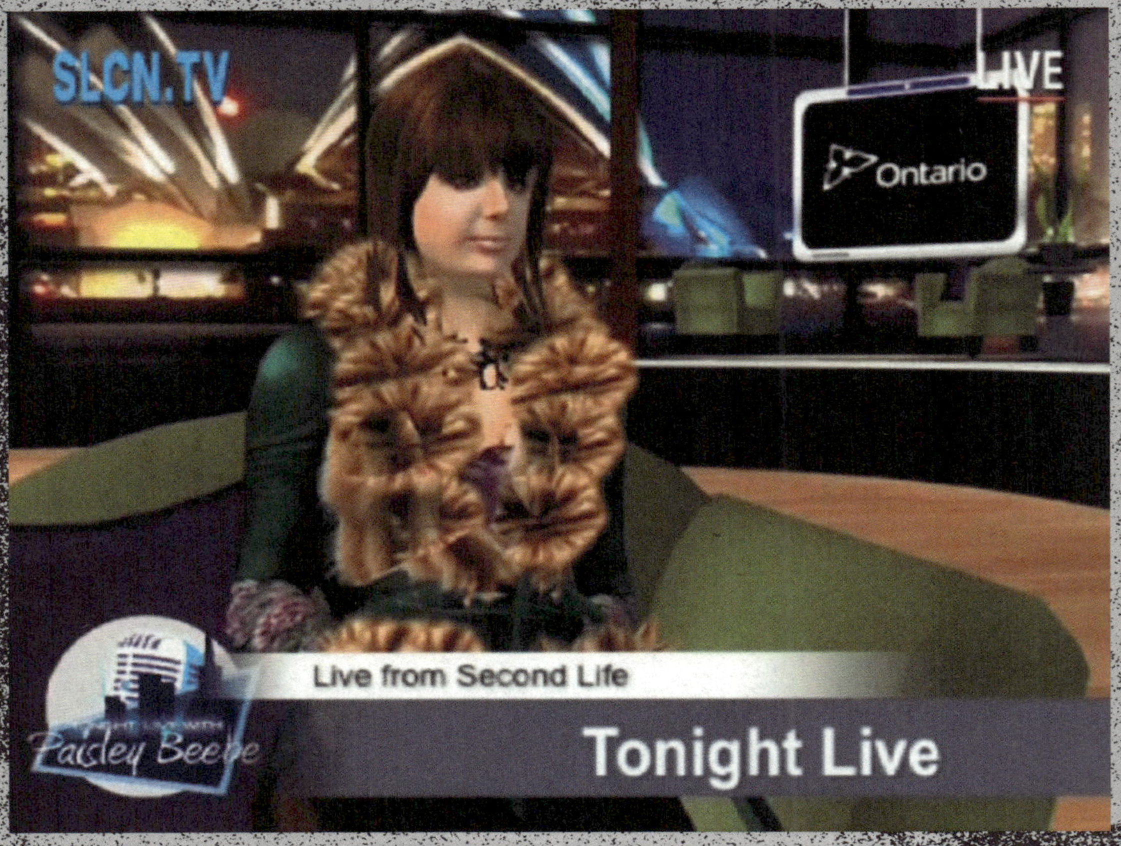

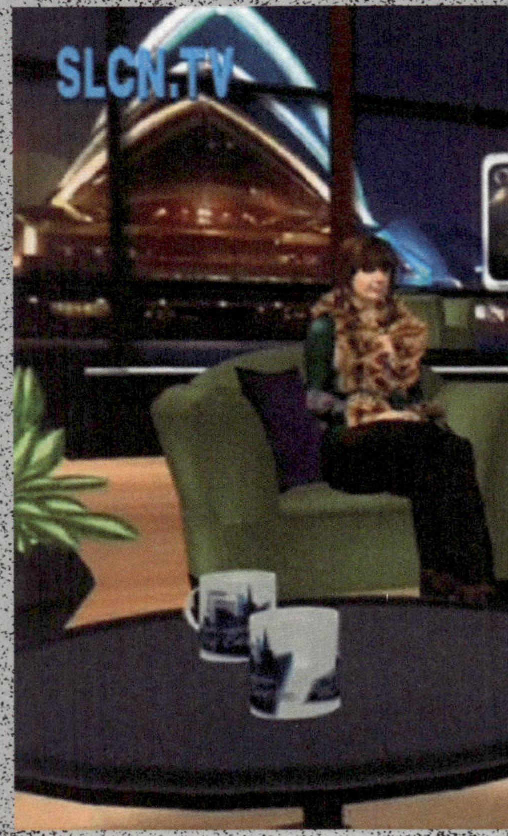

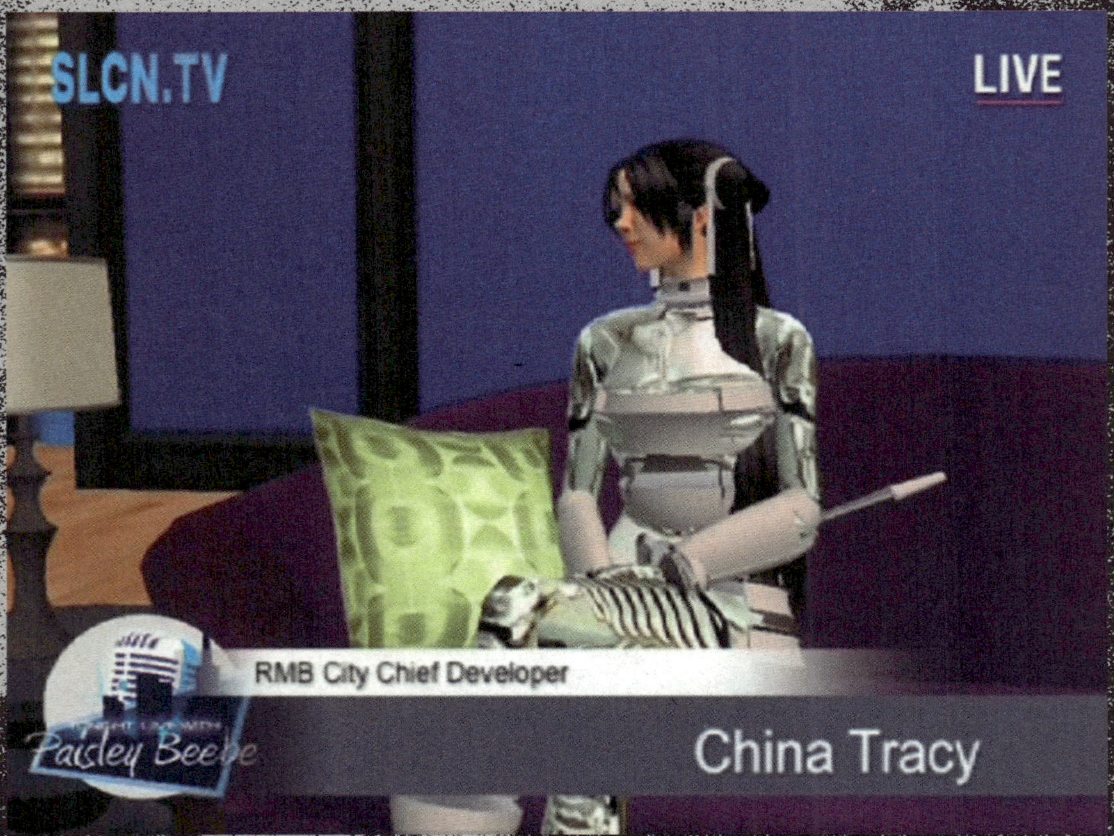

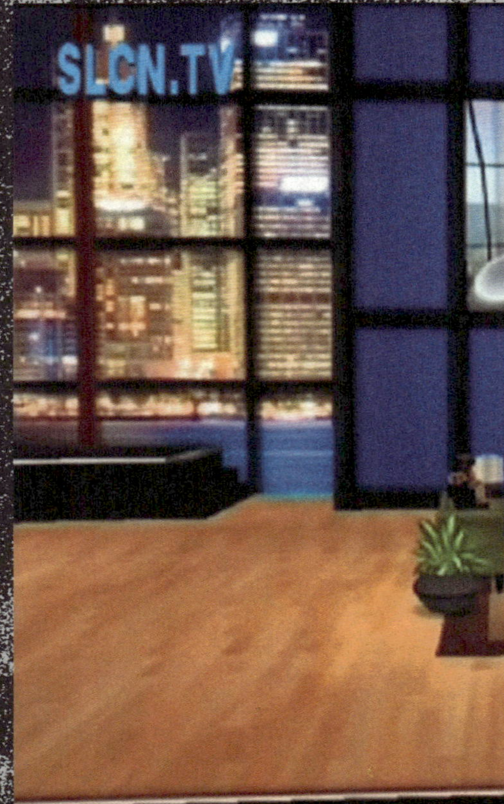

Artwork specification

Tonight Live interview with China Tracy (SLCN.TV) 2009
single-channel digital video, colour, sound
13:04 min, 4:3

《“今夜现场”节目采访中国·翠西》2009
4:3 彩色有声单频影像
13分4秒

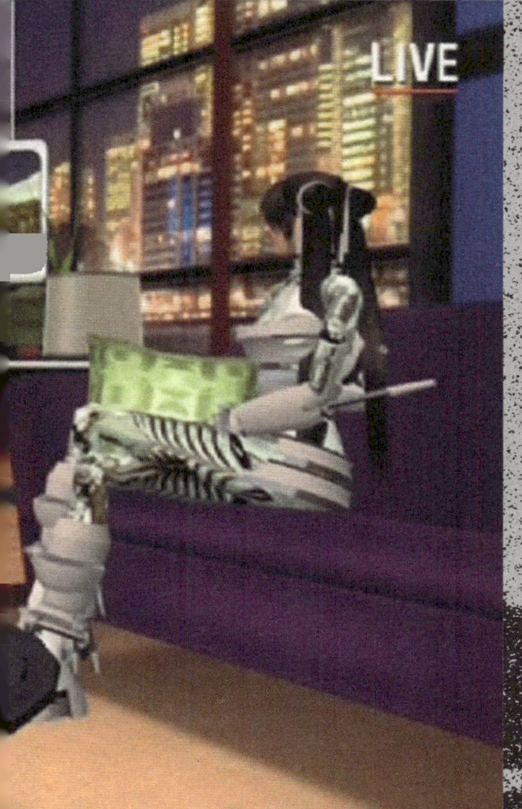

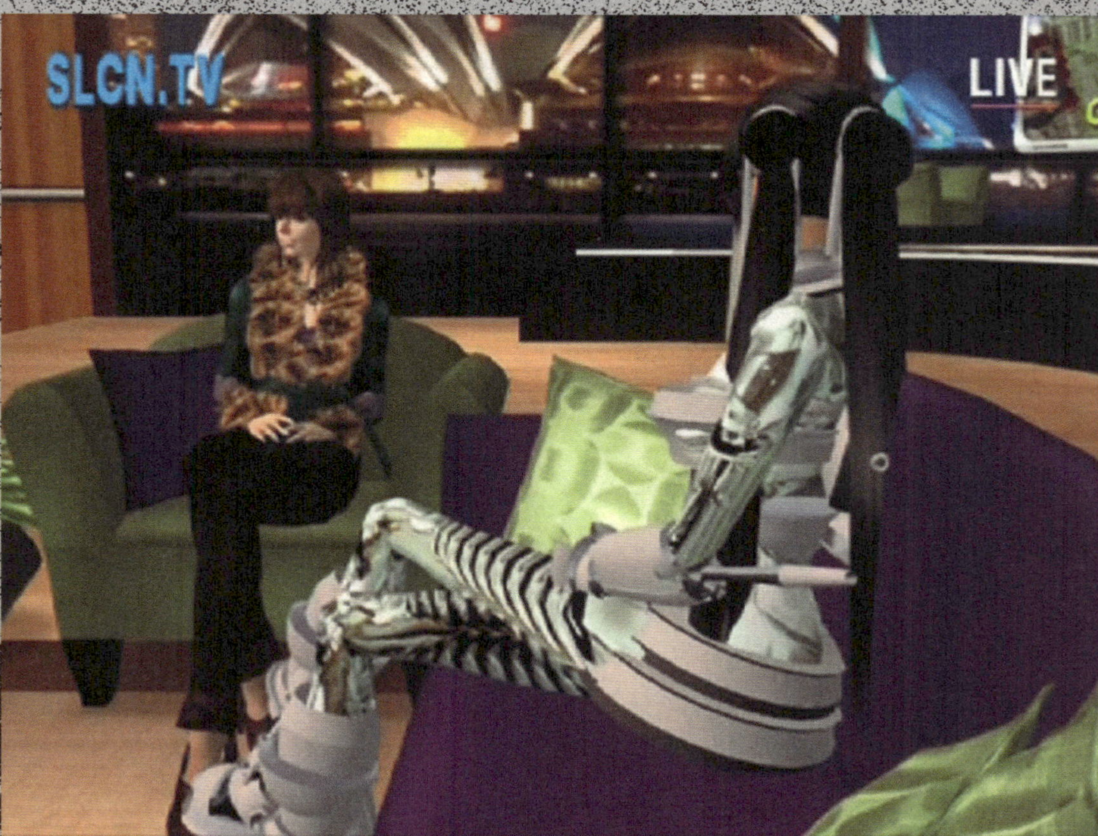

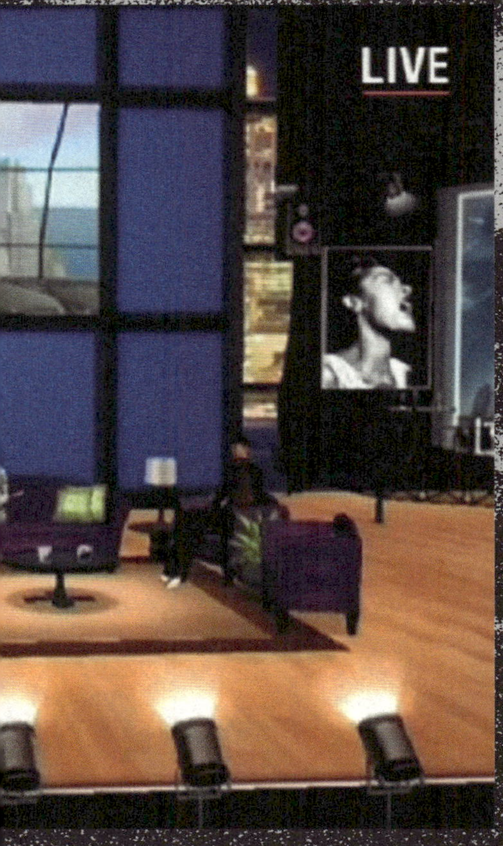

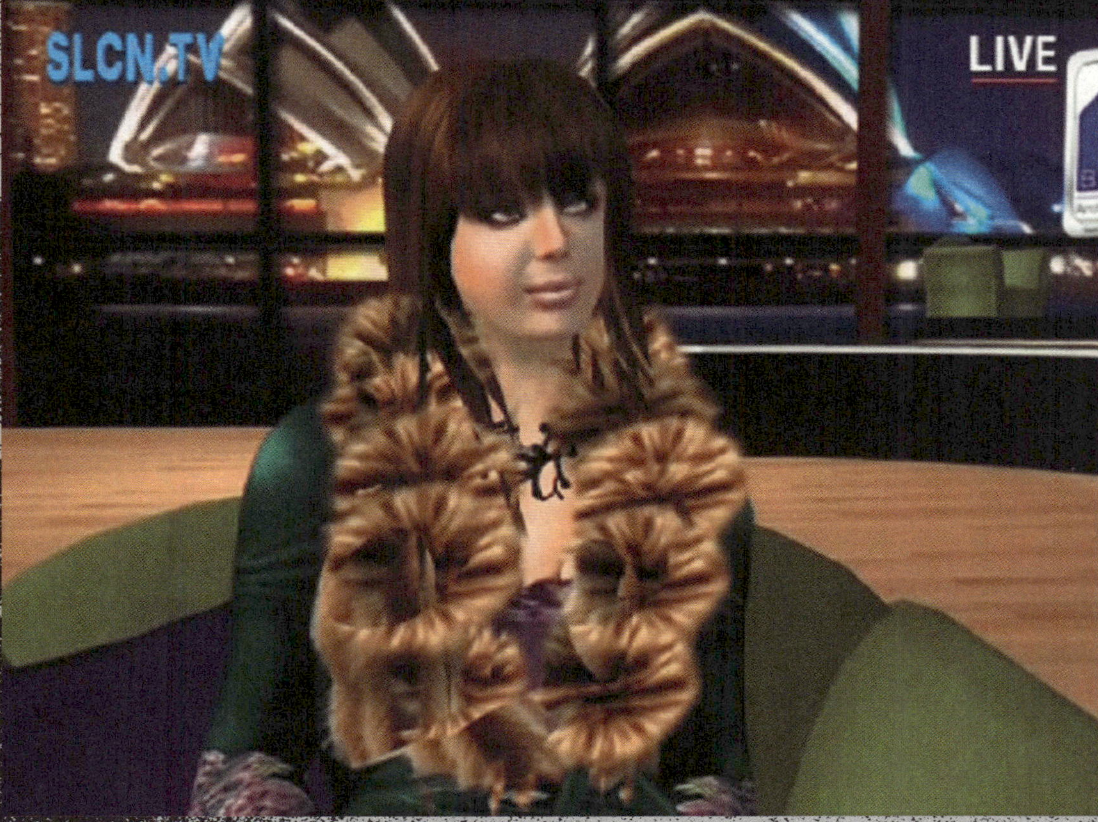

China Tracy

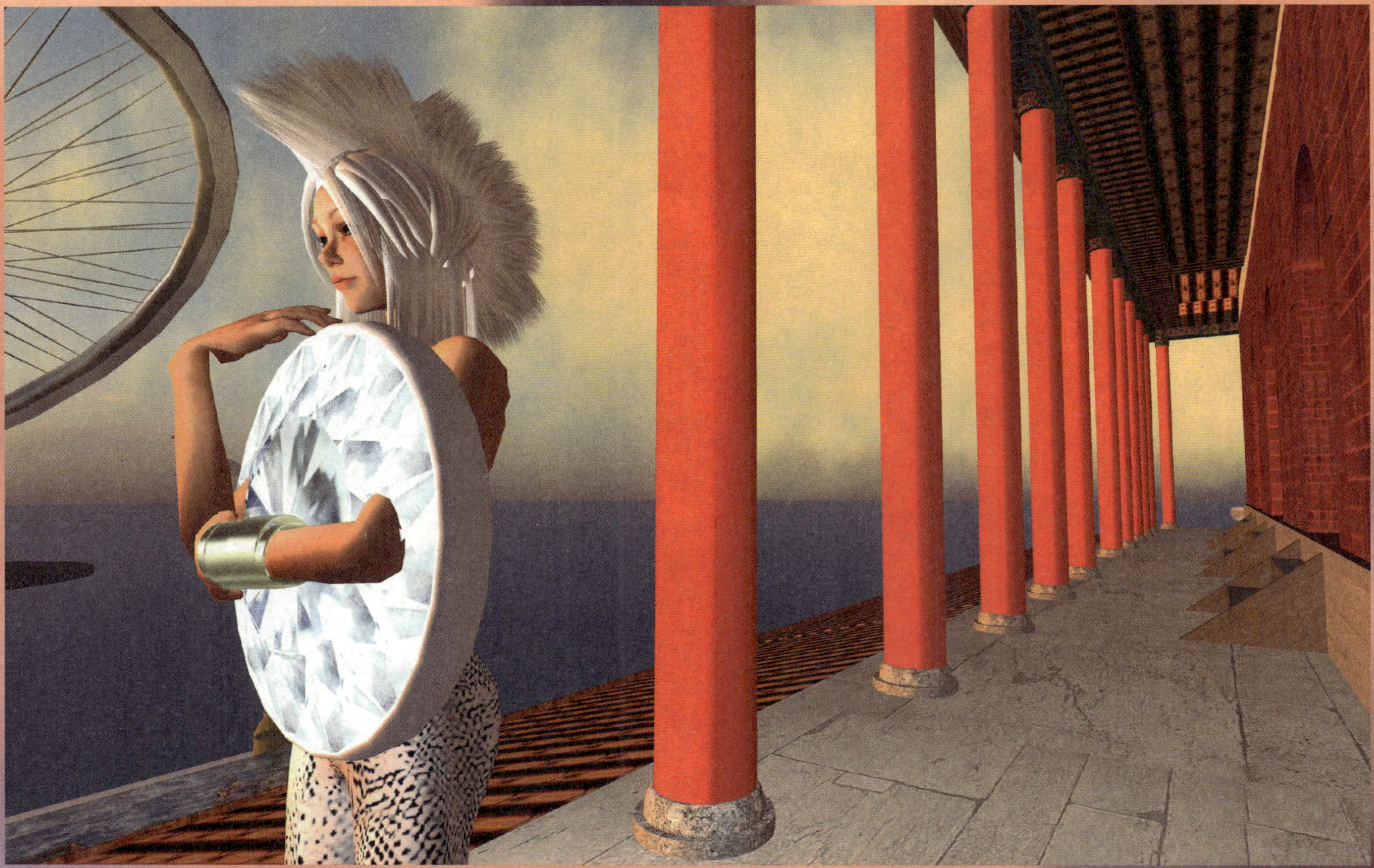

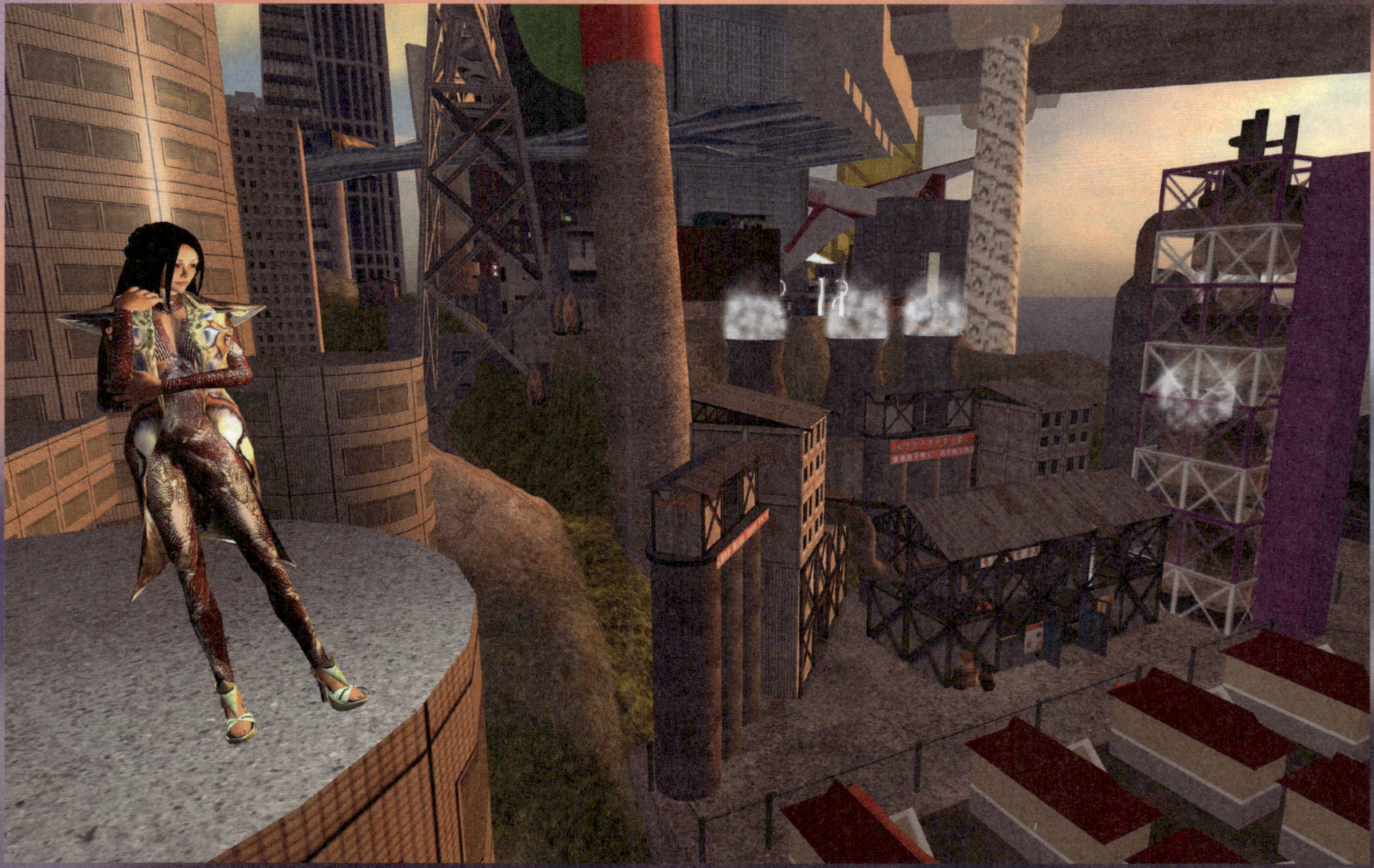

RMB City: the fashions of China Tracy 02–05
2009, inkjet prints on paper, 30 x 50 cm

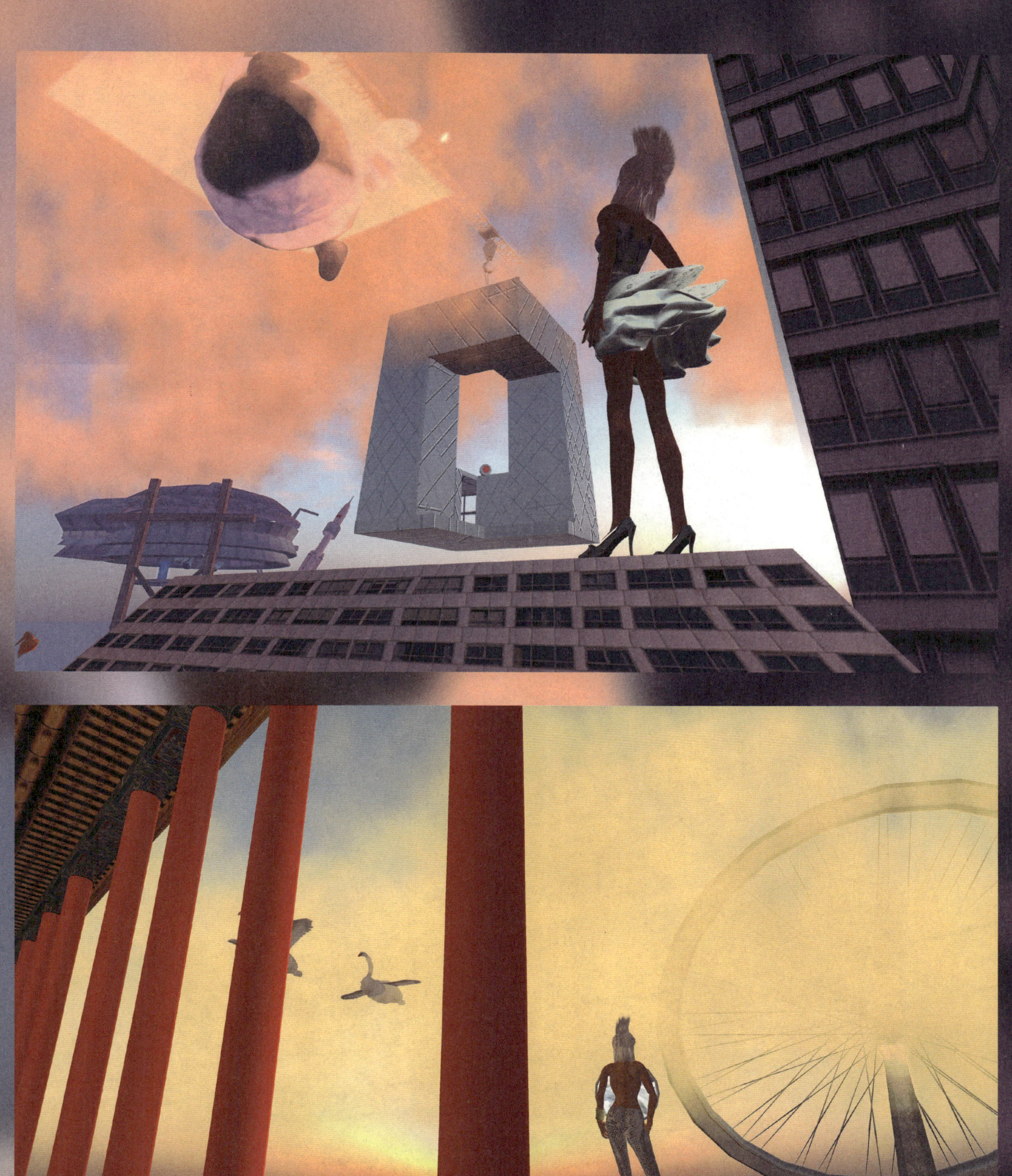

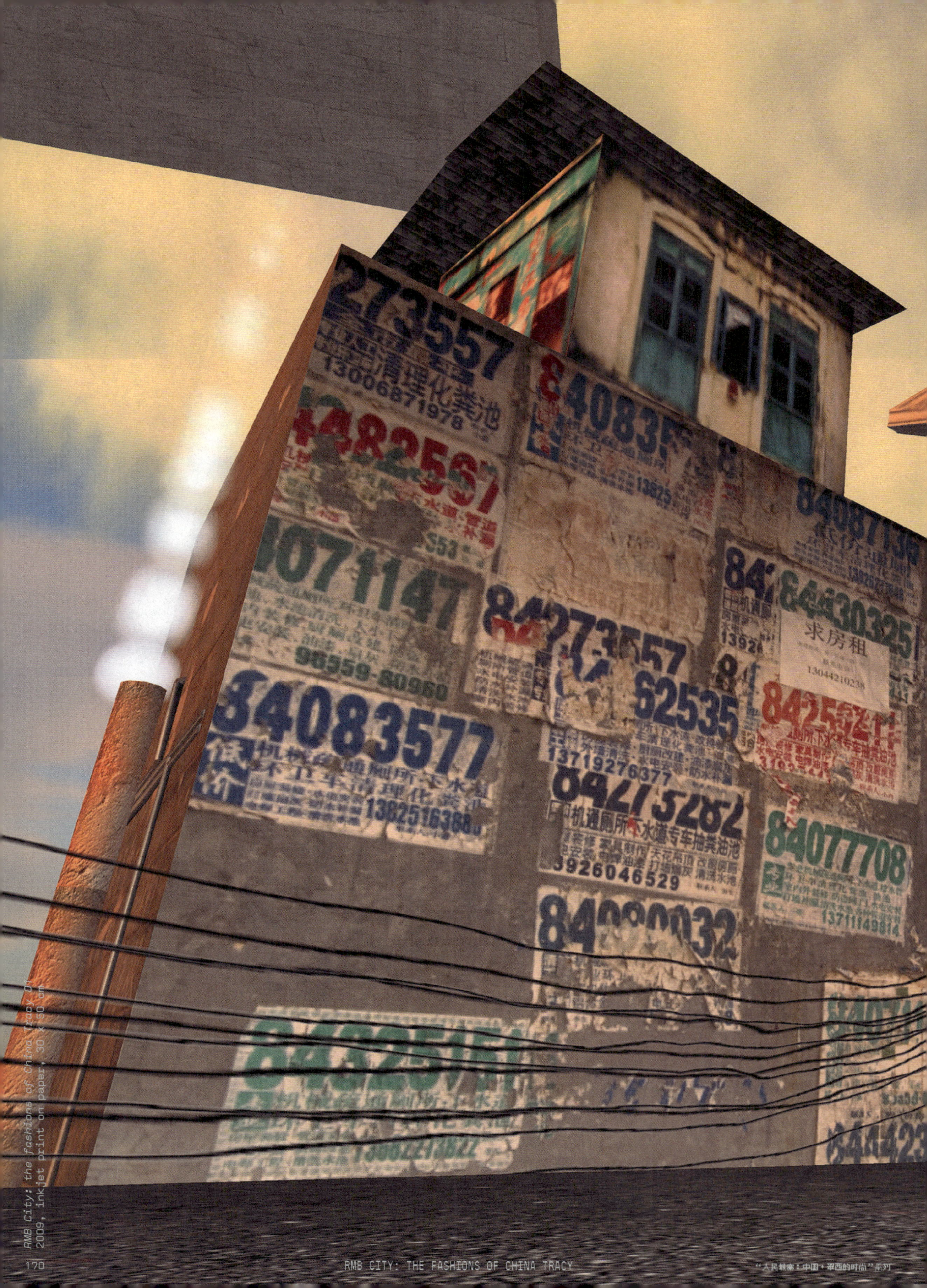

RMB City: the fashions of China Tracy 01
2009, inkjet print on paper, 30 x 50 cm

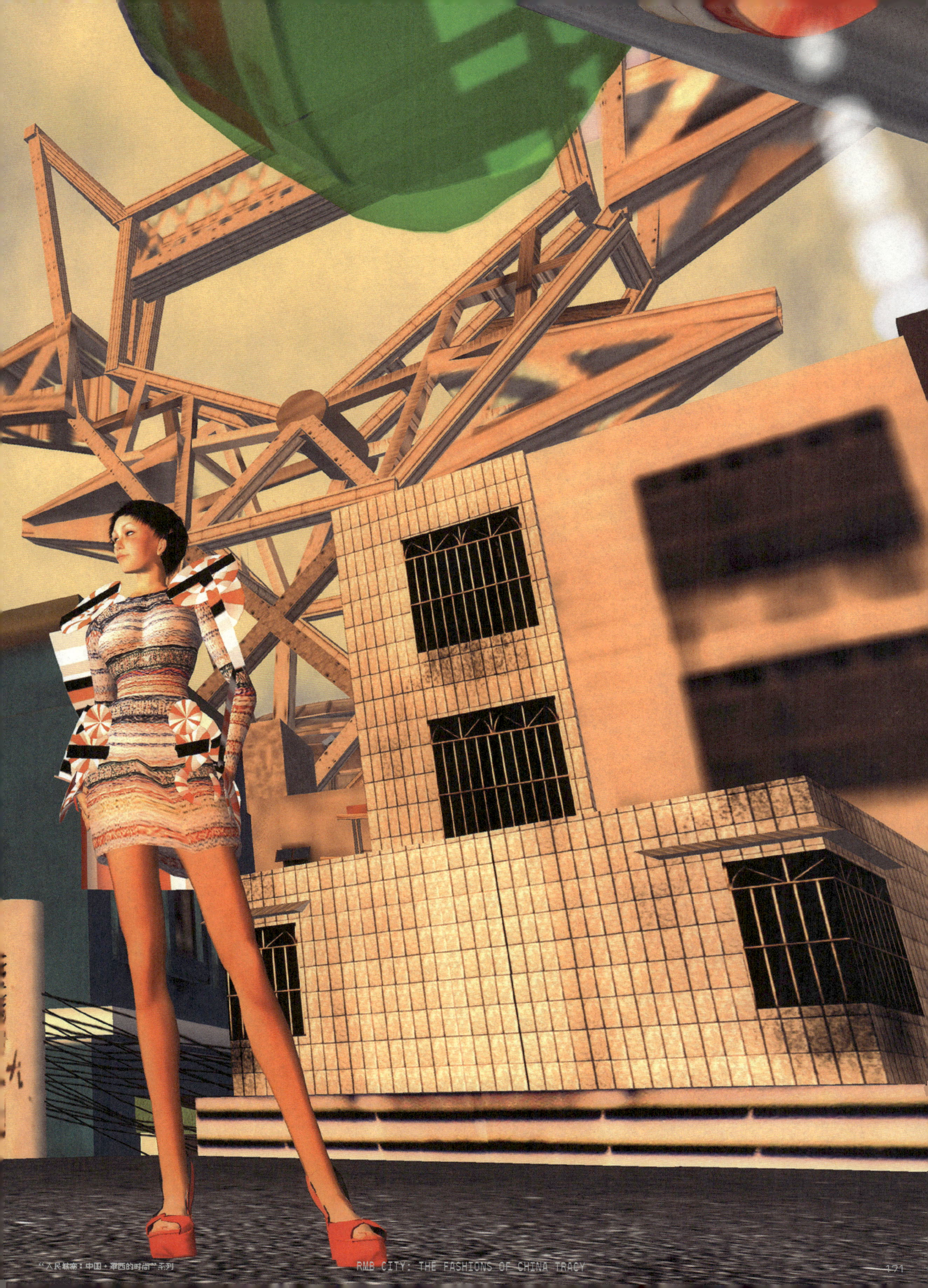

"人民城市：中国・翠西的时尚"系列

RMB CITY: THE FASHIONS OF CHINA TRACY

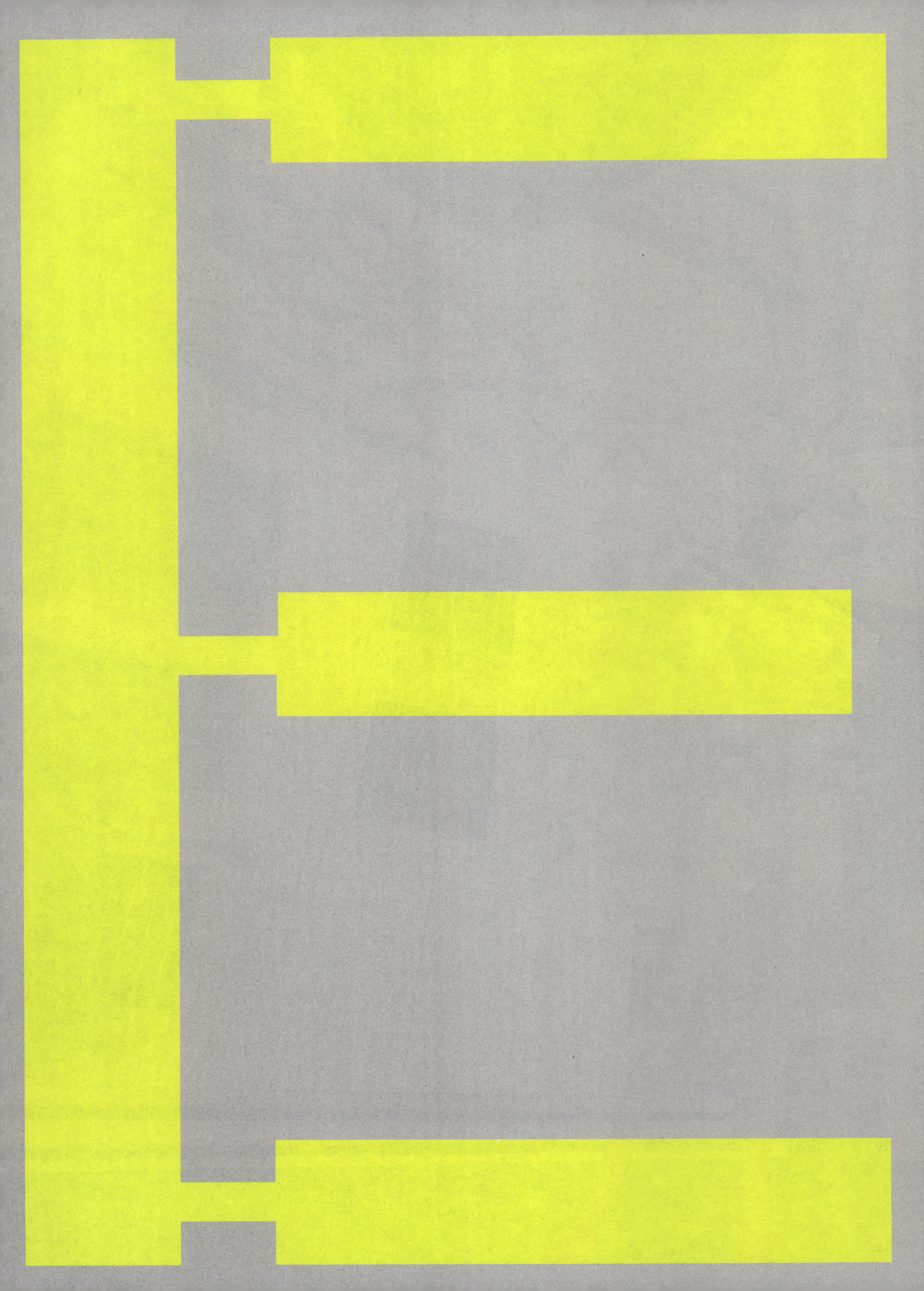

EAST WIND

2011

东风

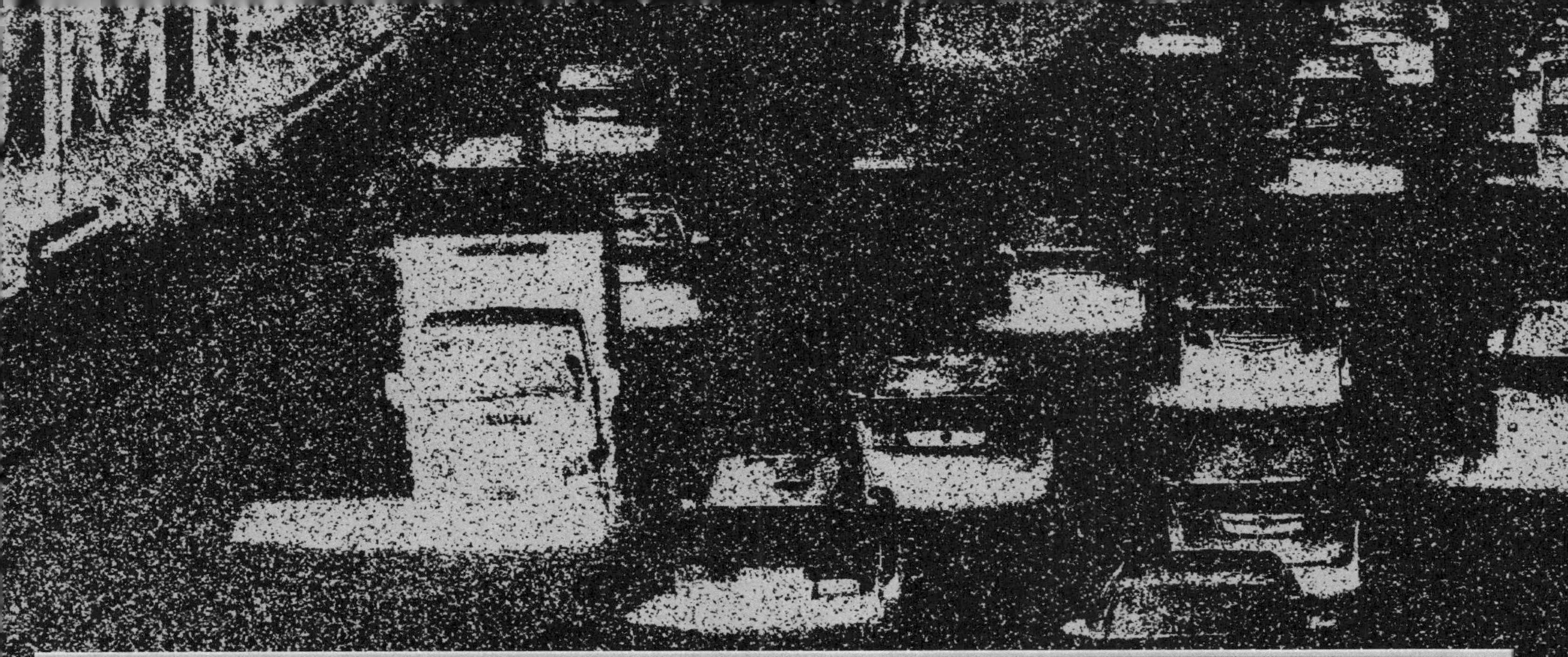

E: East wind

A dinky dump truck with the face of Thomas the Tank Engine rides around Beijing's ring roads, transporting construction rubble to the outskirts of the city. The work's title references Mao Zedong's famous declaration that the 'East wind' would prevail over the 'West wind', a statement associated with the communist leader's 'Third front' strategy that sought to protect China from invasion by Western powers. The 'East wind' (Dongfeng 东风) automobile company was founded in 1969 as part of this campaign. By giving the truck a facelift – with the beneficent facade of a popular British cartoon – Cao Fei drolly gestures towards contemporary China's shifting relationship to the West in an era of globalised consumerism. In Cao's words, 'the film is as much about Chinese appropriation of Western culture as it is about Western hegemony'.[1]

[1] Christen Cornell, 'Teasing consumerism: profile, artist Cao Fei', *realtime*, 105, Oct–Nov 2011, realtimearts.net/article/105/10472, accessed 2 Feb 2024.

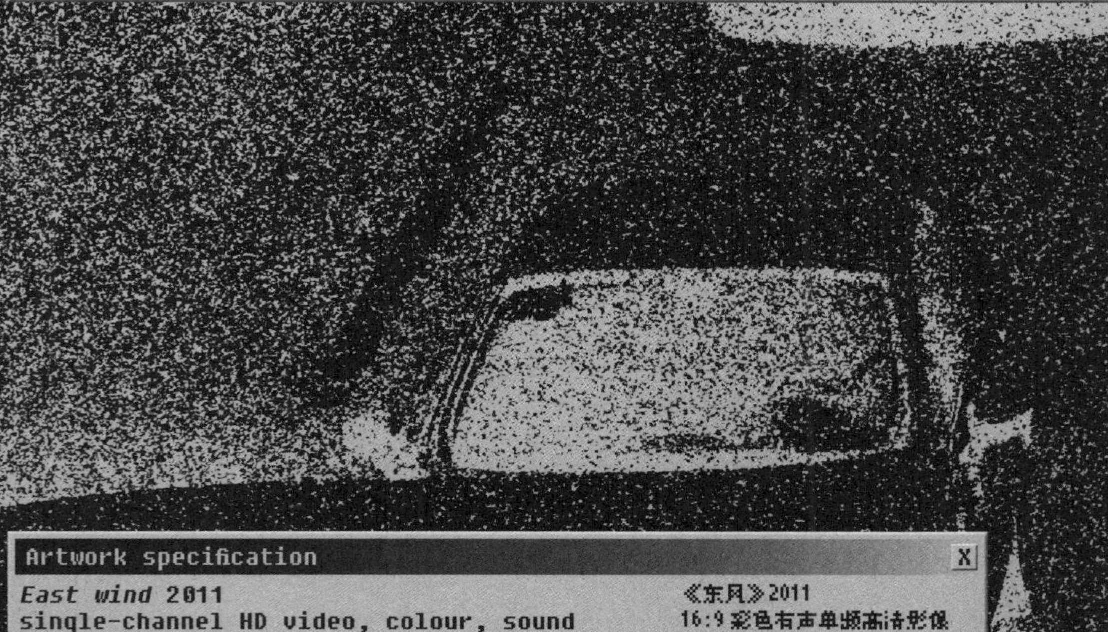

Artwork specification

East wind 2011
single-channel HD video, colour, sound
11:14 min, 16:9

《东风》2011
16:9 彩色有声单频高清影像
11分14秒

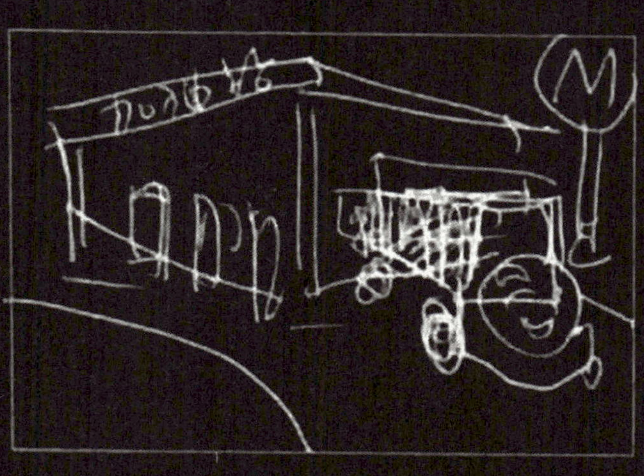

加油站（出发）

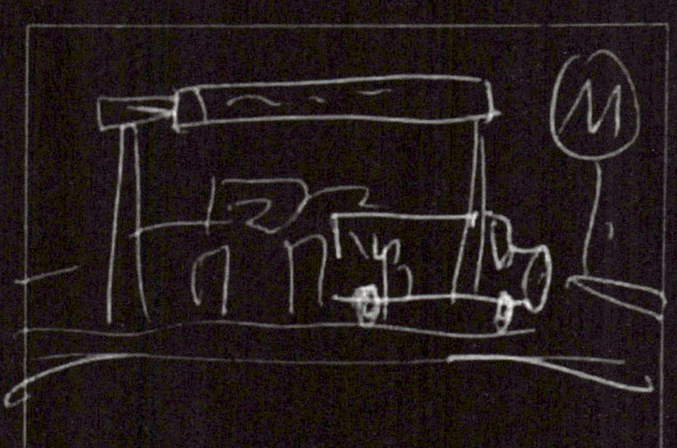

加油站·马路对面

eastwindprod.jpg

小便（中午）

停车（废墟）

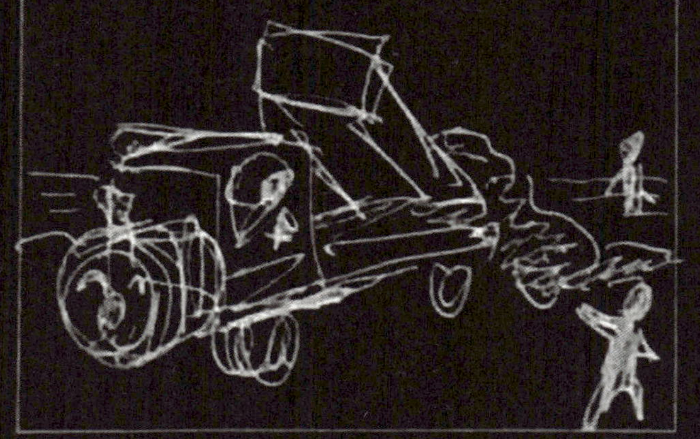

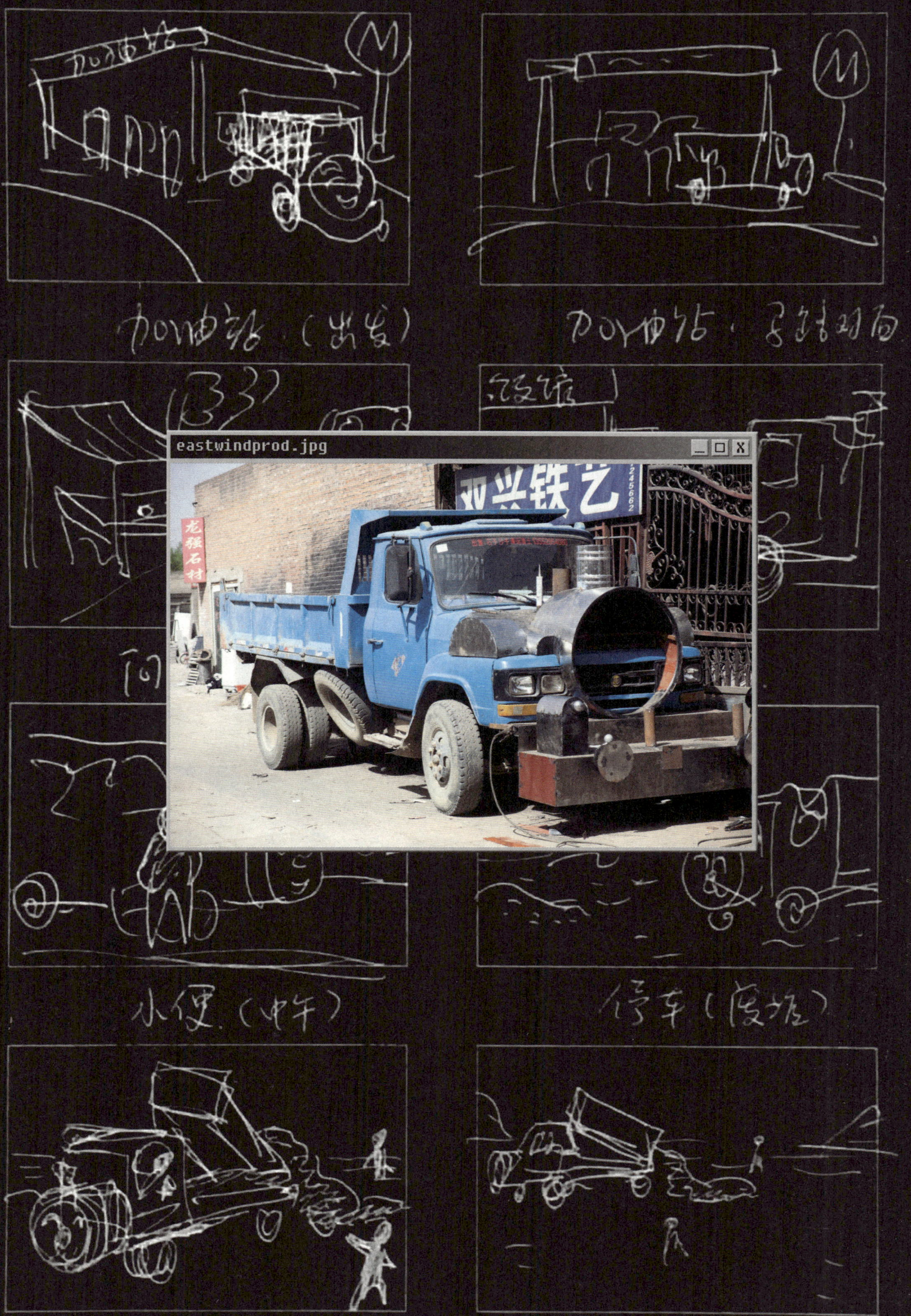

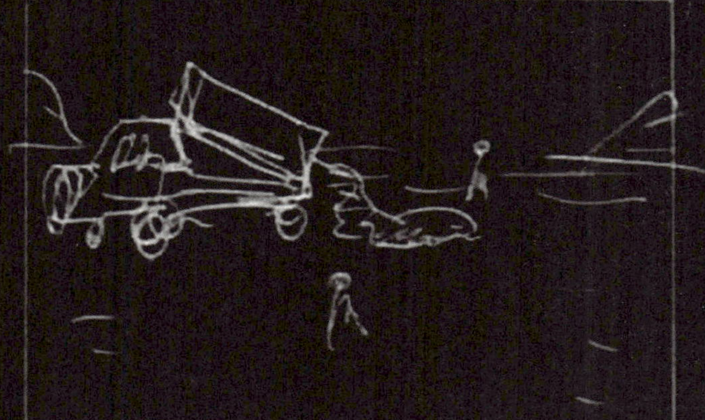

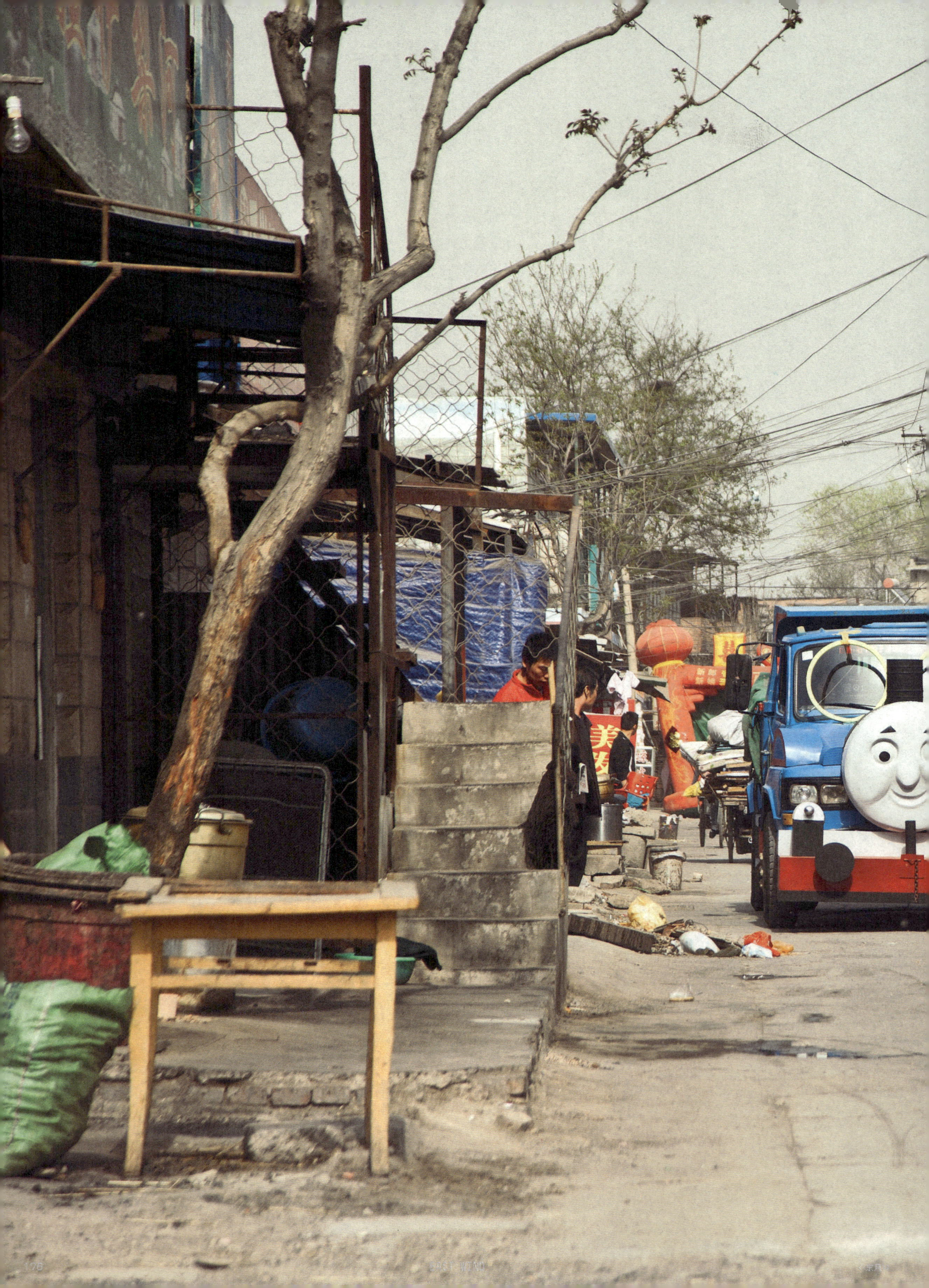
美

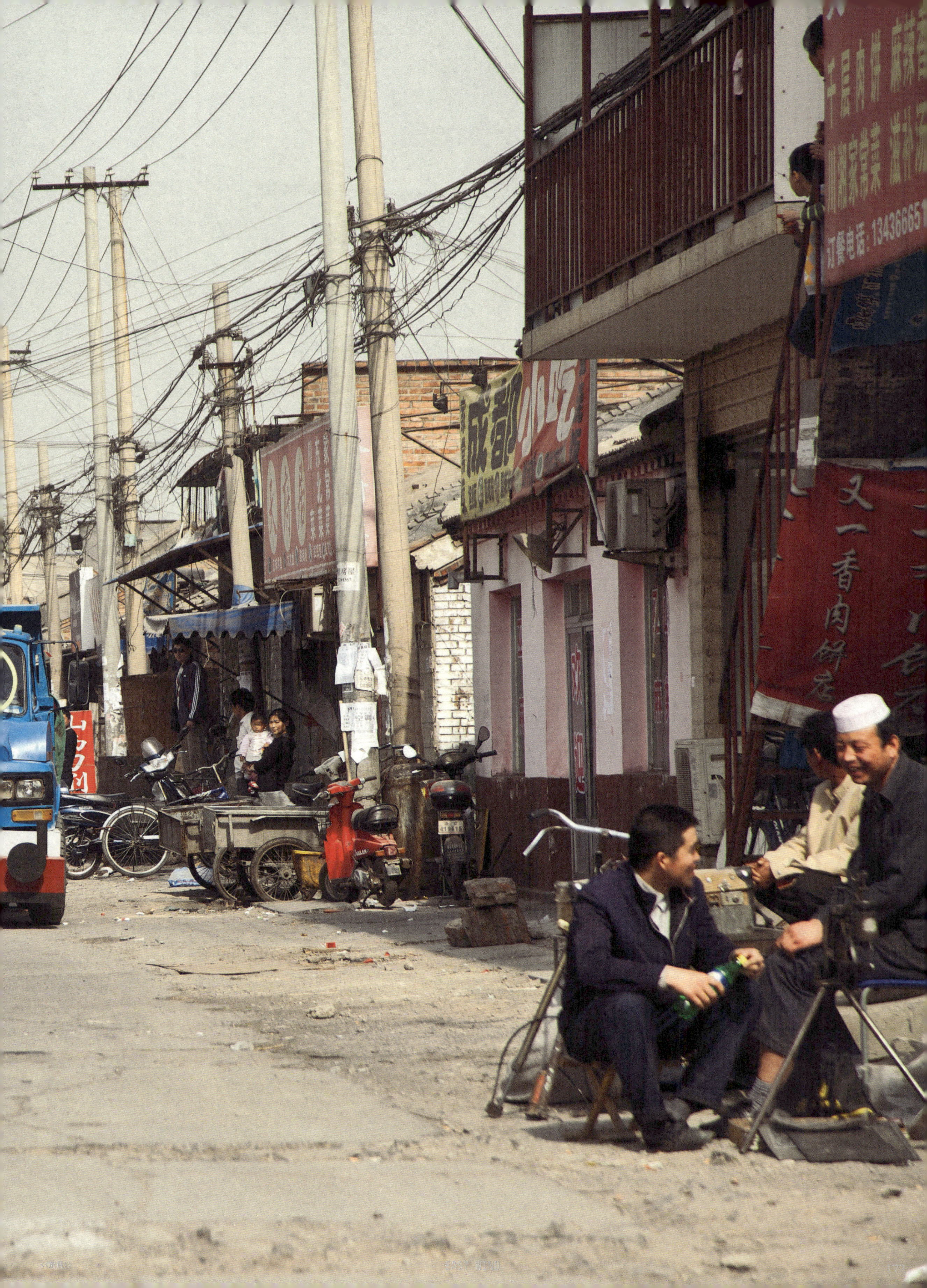
成都小吃
又一香肉饼店

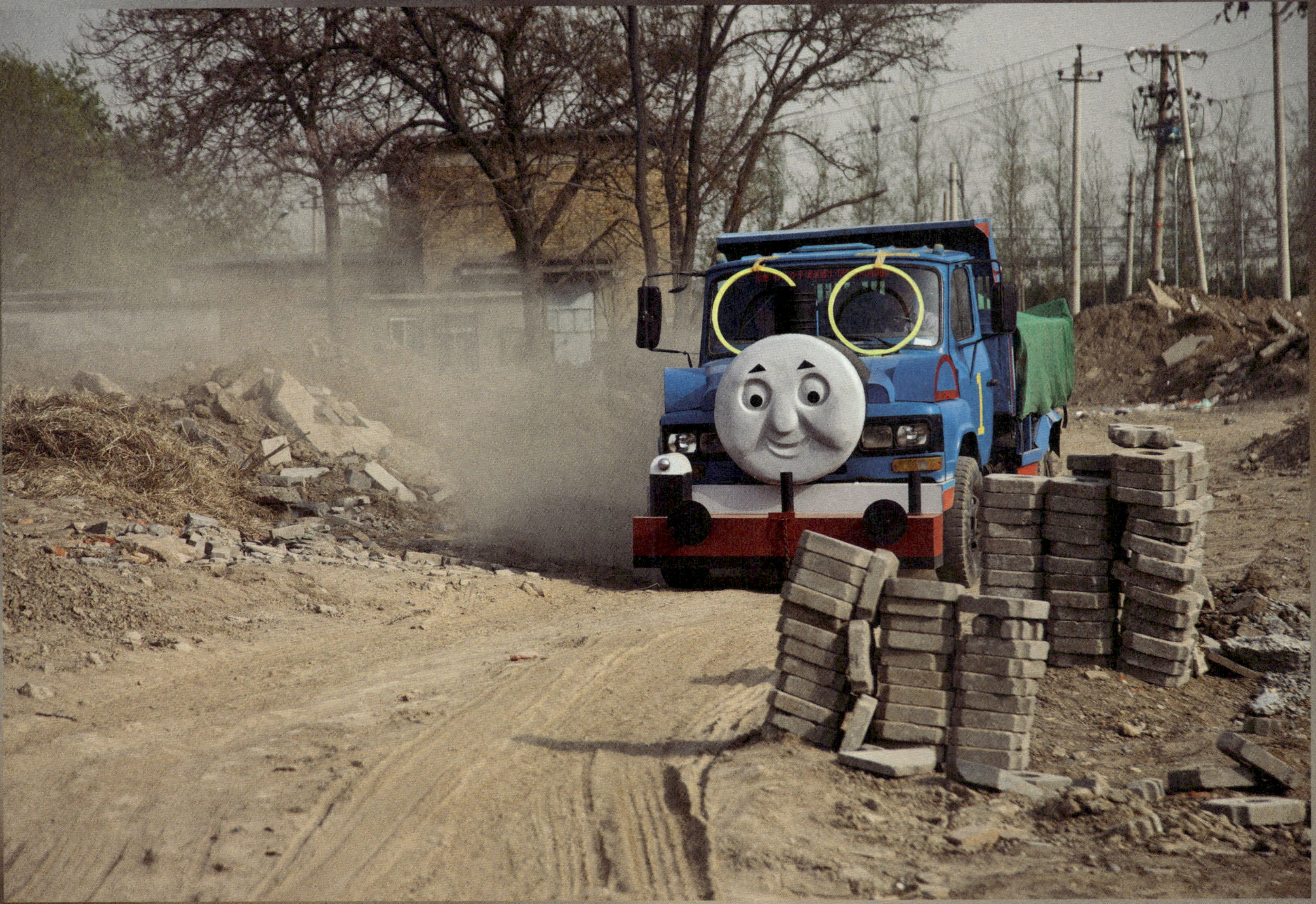

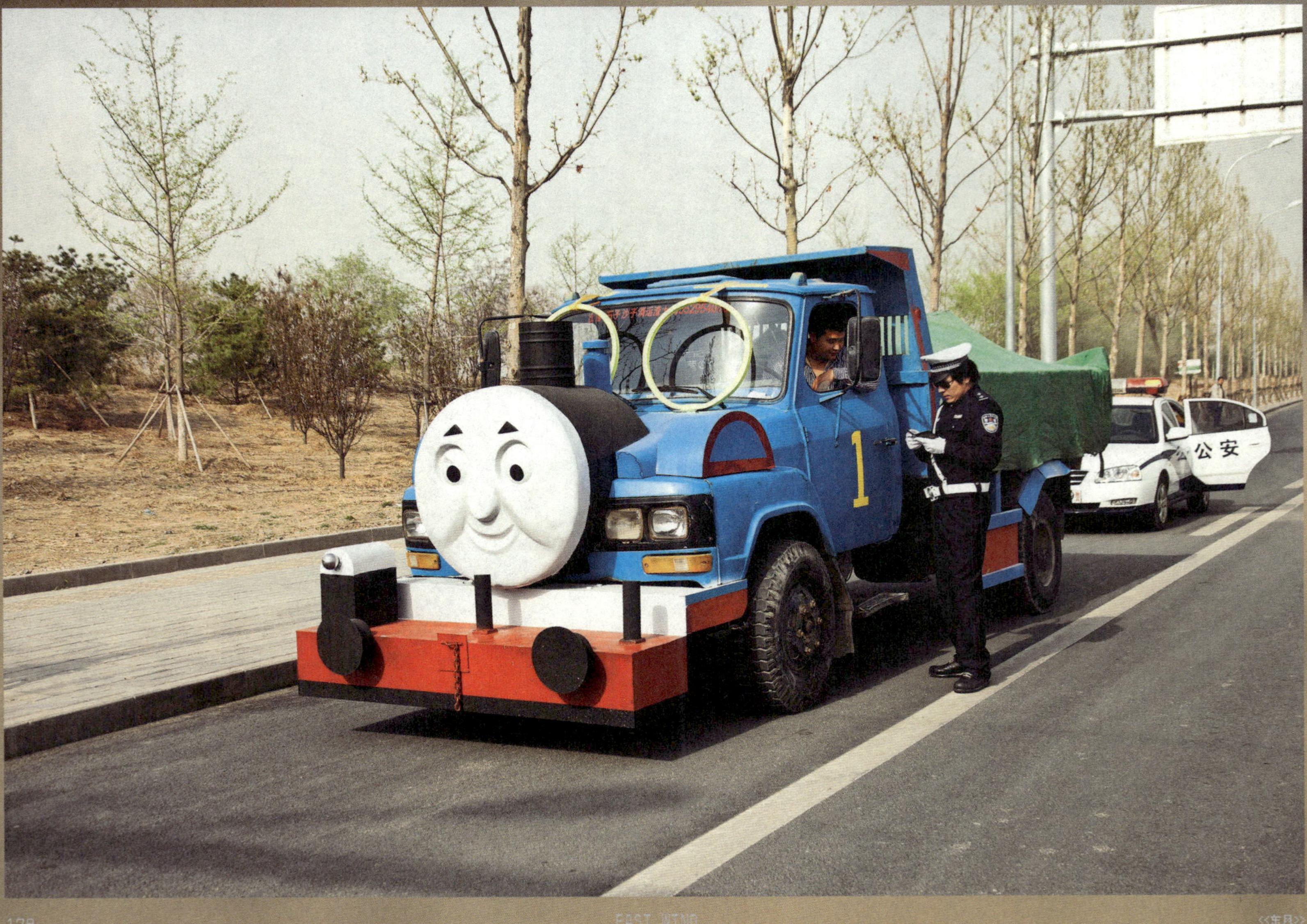

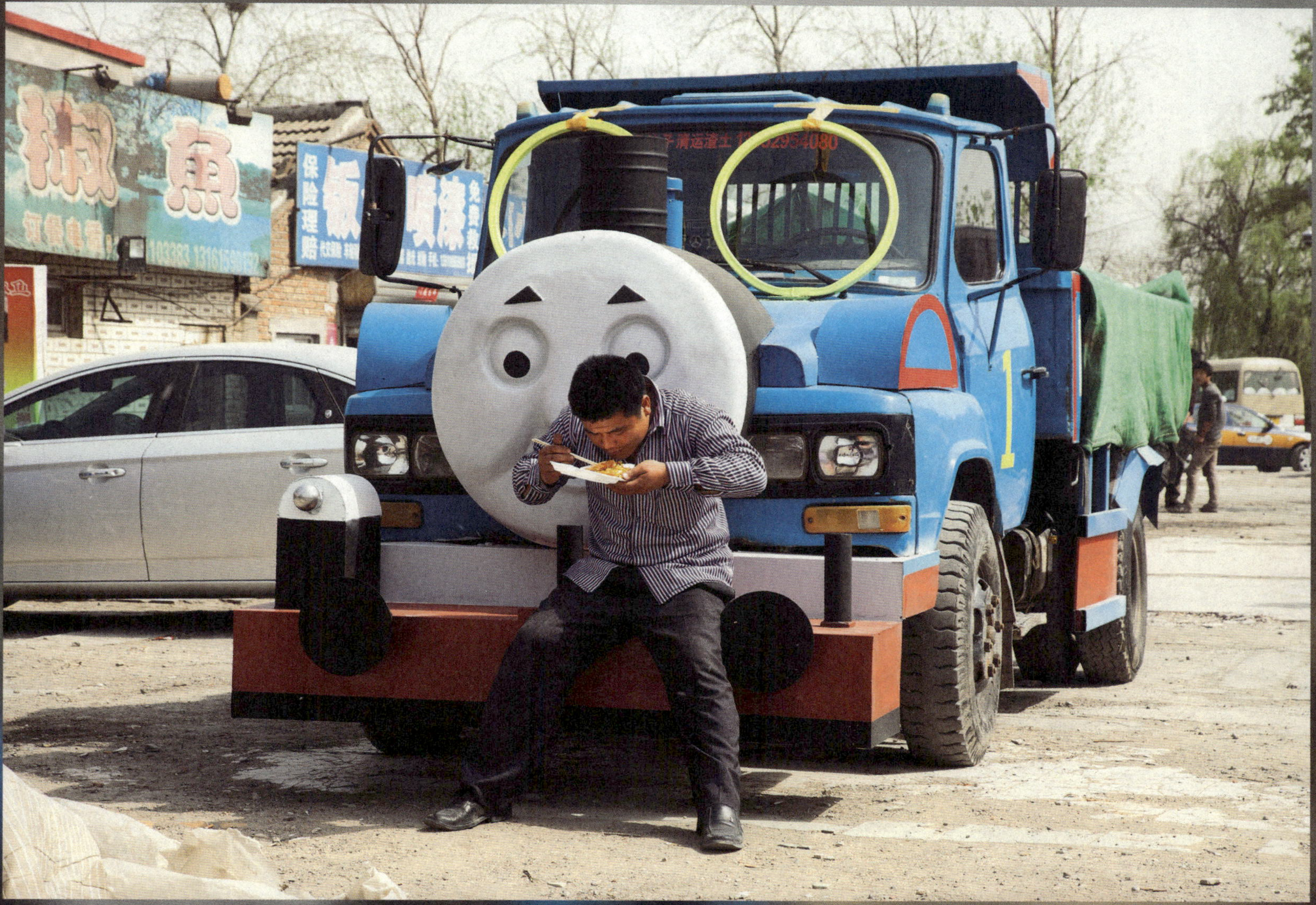

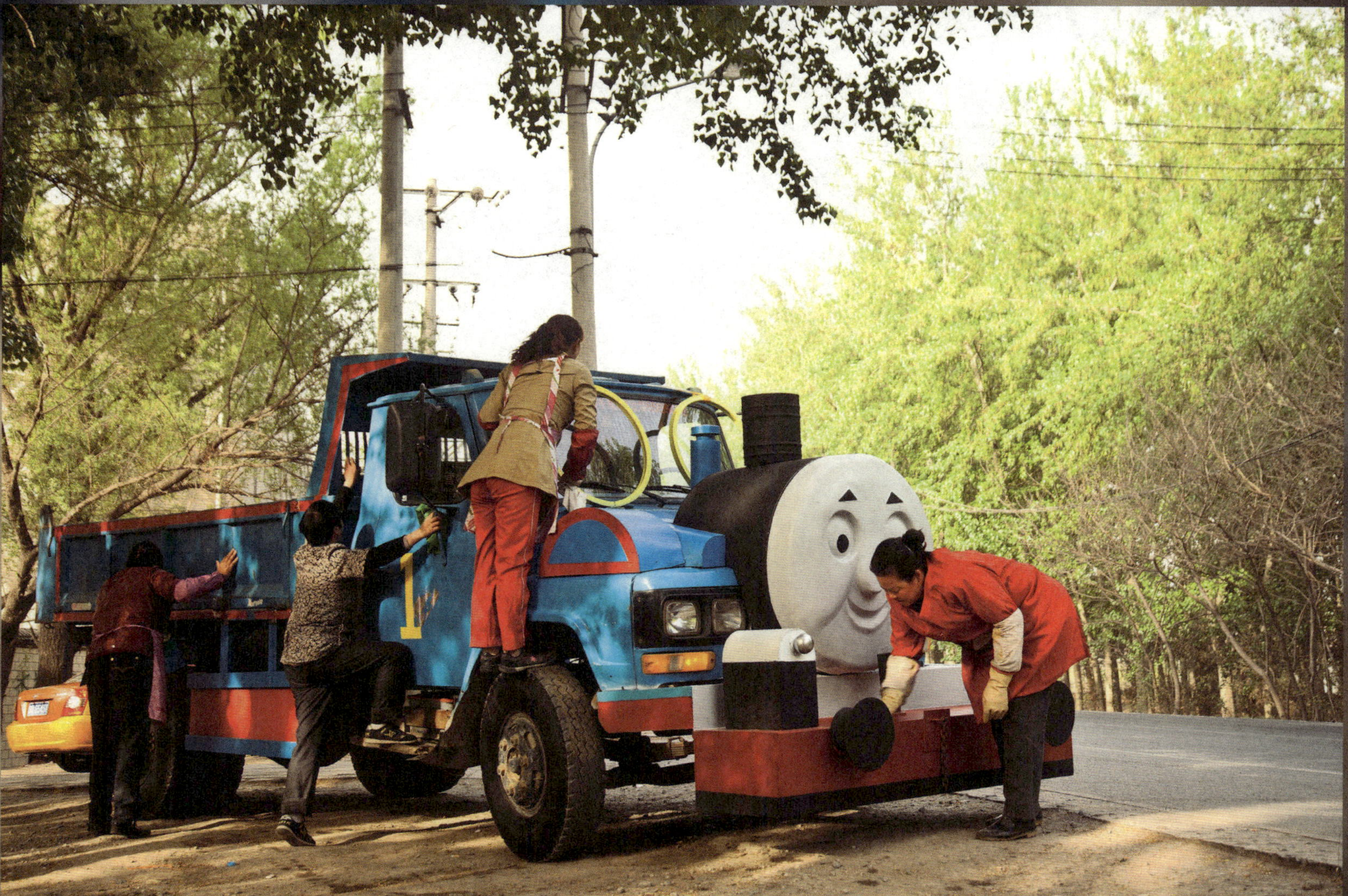

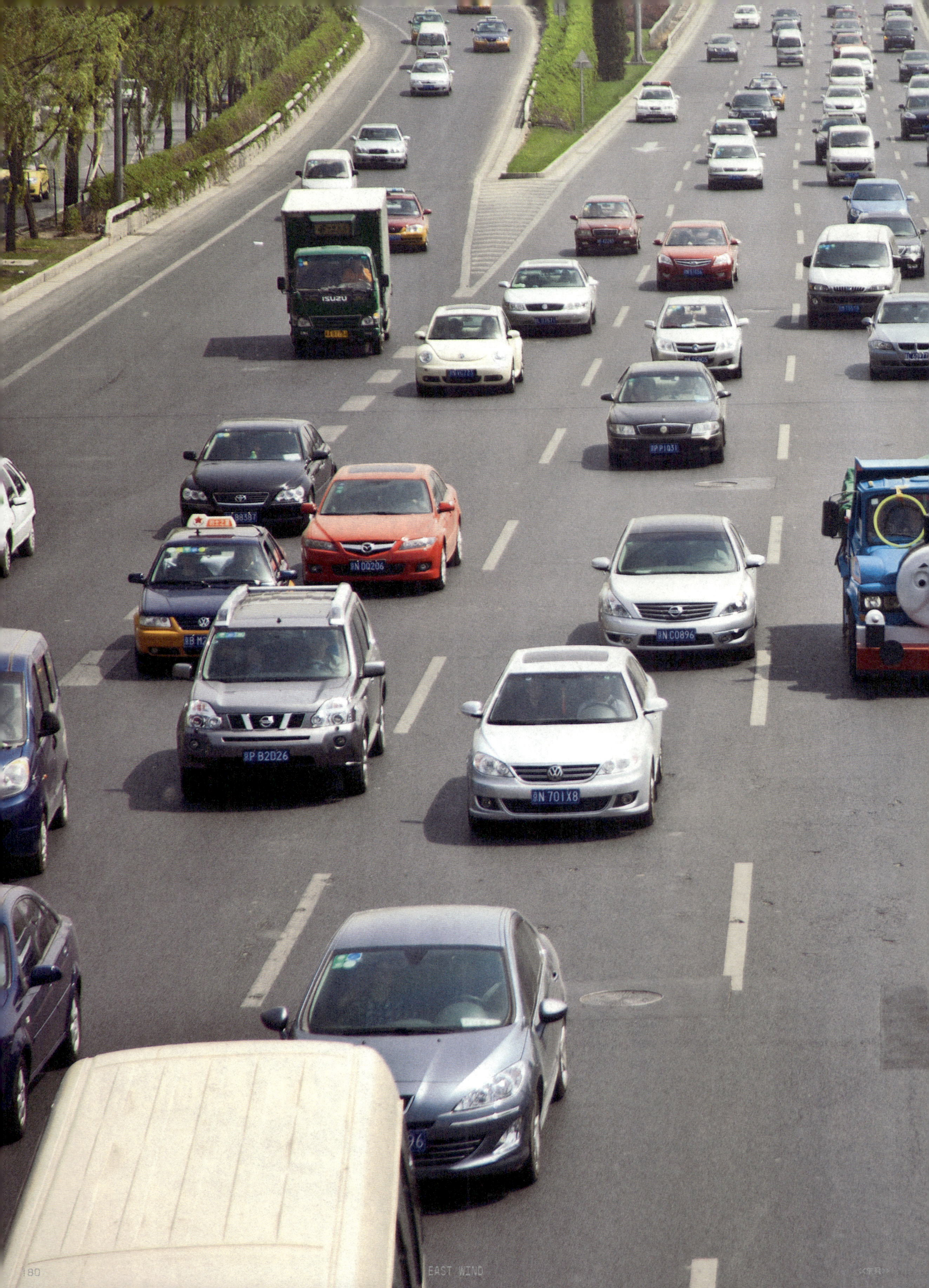

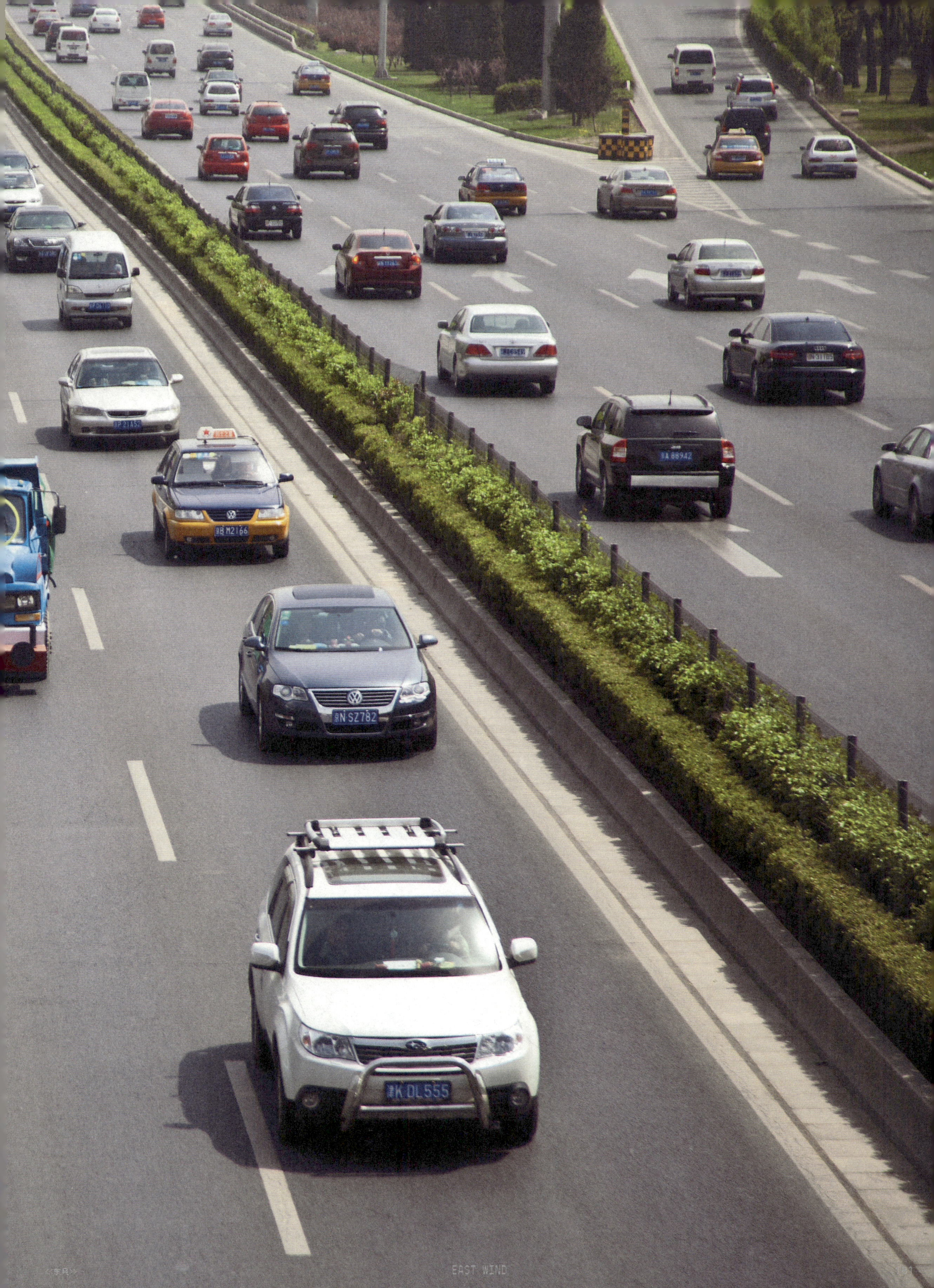

C:/dongfeng

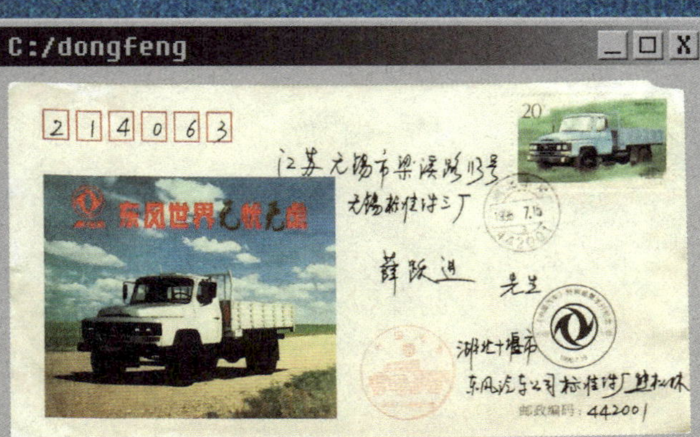

Dongfeng Motor Corporation stamped envelope

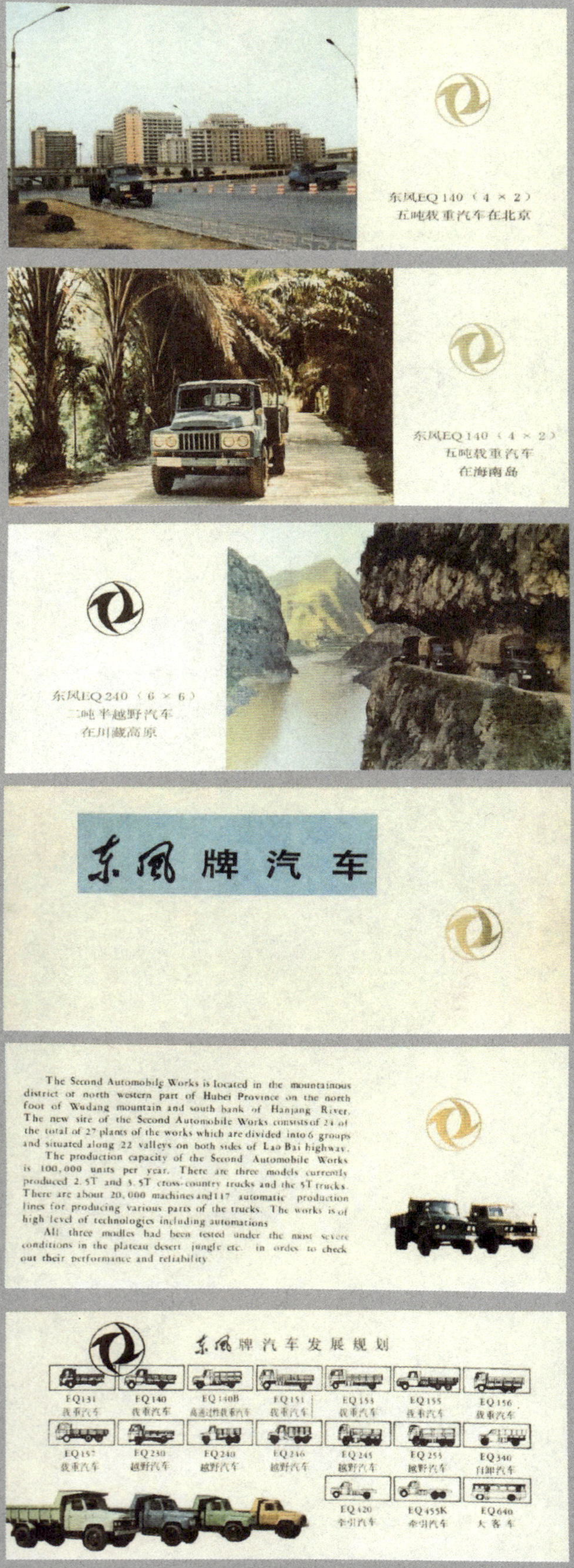

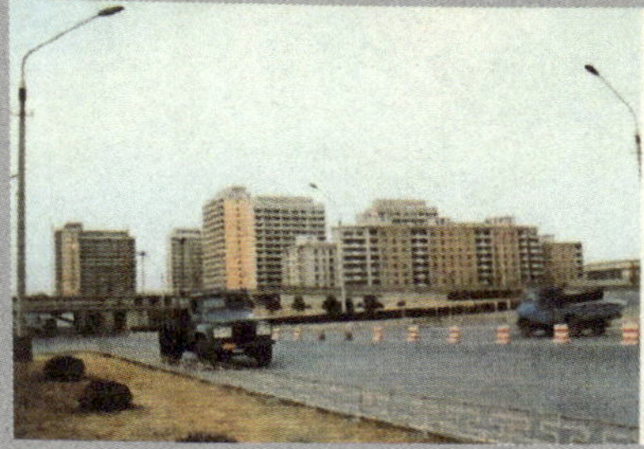

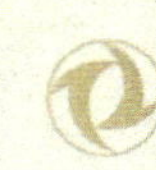

东风EQ 140 （4 × 2）
五吨载重汽车在北京

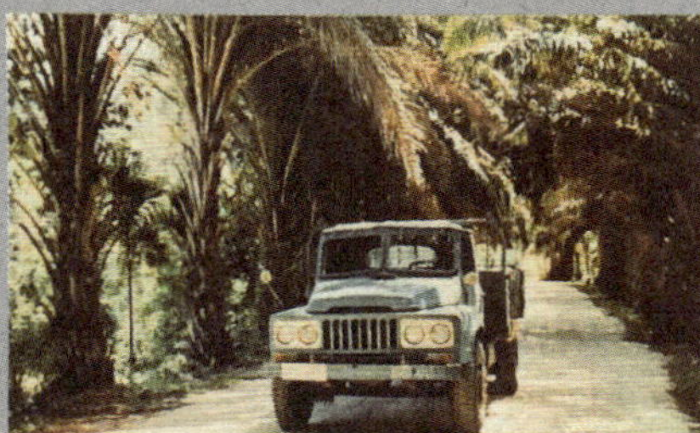

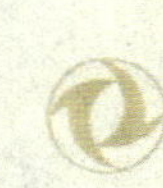

东风EQ 140 （4 × 2）
五吨载重汽车
在海南岛

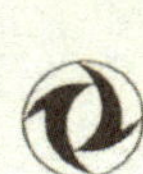

东风EQ 240 （6 × 6）
二吨半越野汽车
在川藏高原

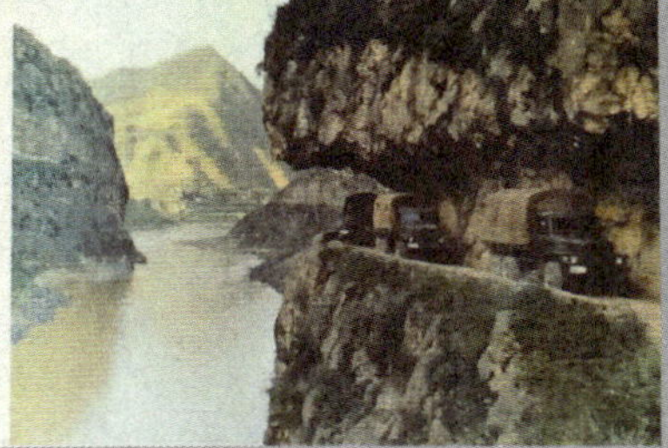

东风牌汽车

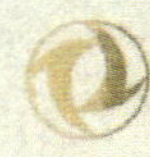

The Second Automobile Works is located in the mountainous district of north western part of Hubei Province on the north foot of Wudang mountain and south bank of Hanjang River. The new site of the Second Automobile Works consists of 24 of the total of 27 plants of the works which are divided into 6 groups and situated along 22 valleys on both sides of Lao Bai highway.

The production capacity of the Second Automobile Works is 100,000 units per year. There are three models currently produced 2.5T and 3.5T cross-country trucks and the 5T trucks. There are about 20,000 machines and 117 automatic production lines for producing various parts of the trucks. The works is of high level of technologies including automations

All three modles had been tested under the most severe conditions in the plateau desert jungle etc. in ordes to check out their performance and reliability

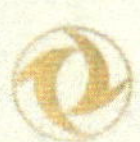

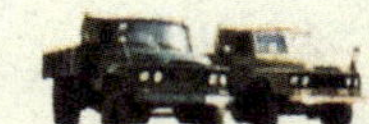

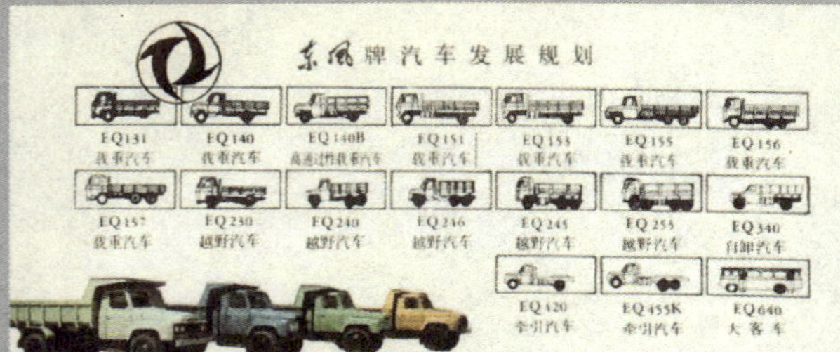

Dongfeng Motor Corporation postcards

Background: Dongfeng Motor Corporation photograph

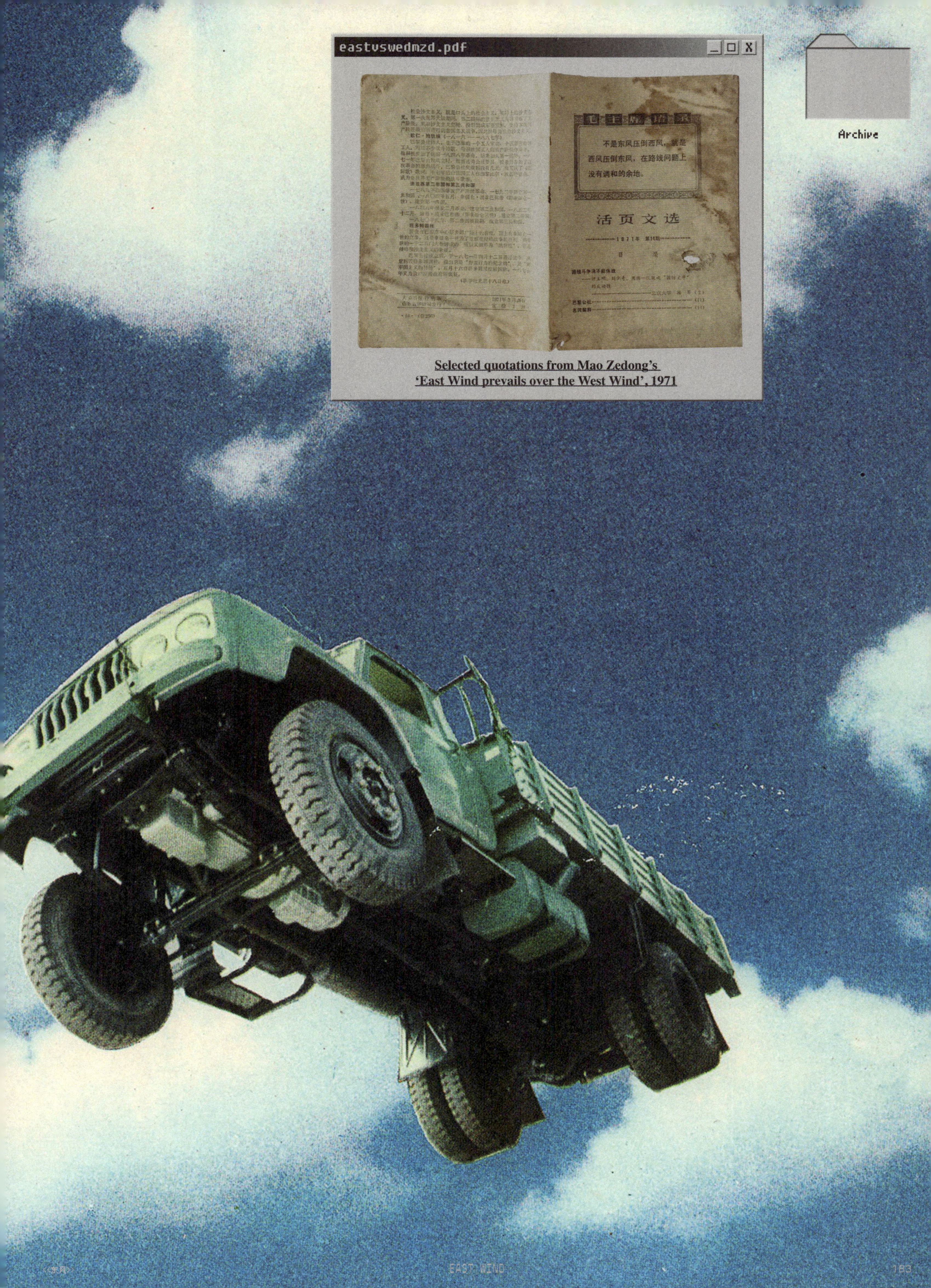
eastvswedmzd.pdf
Archive
毛主席语录
不是东风压倒西风，就是西风压倒东风，在路线问题上没有调和的余地。
活页文选
1971年 第14期
目 录
巴黎公社
名词解释
Selected quotations from Mao Zedong's
'East Wind prevails over the West Wind', 1971

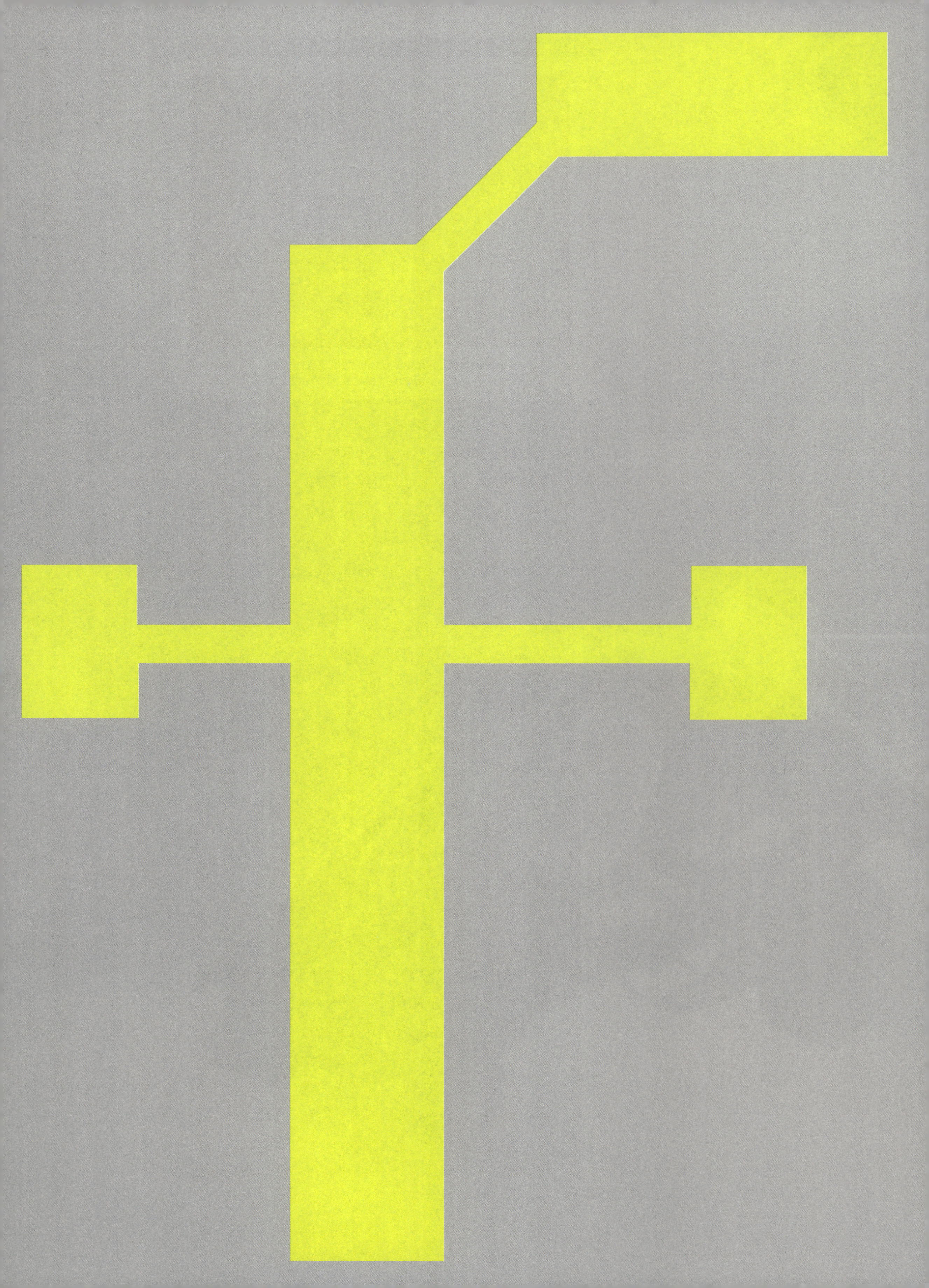

LA TOWN 2014

F: La Town

A mysterious cityscape fashioned from tiny handmade dioramas. Two narrators ponder the fate of this abandoned metropolis, surveying its empty casinos and derailed trains. Citing Alain Resnais' classic film *Hiroshima mon amour* 1959 and Italo Calvino's book *Invisible cities* 1972 as influences, Cao conjures a mood of post-apocalyptic devastation. Unlike earlier works exploring the concrete forces shaping the contemporary city (automation, industrialisation, consumerism), *La Town* is a mood piece, a 'feeling-scape'. What happens when the city stops its sprawl? When calamity turns day to night, cloaking everything in ash, like a modern-day Pompeii. Cao has often turned to scale models of cities to distil urban complexity. Where *RMB City* captured the unruly expansion of China's property bubble, this miniature world is frozen in time. The yellow scallop of Shell oil and gas flickers wanly next to burnt-out bowsers. Cao's neon metropolis has turned into a noir ruin.

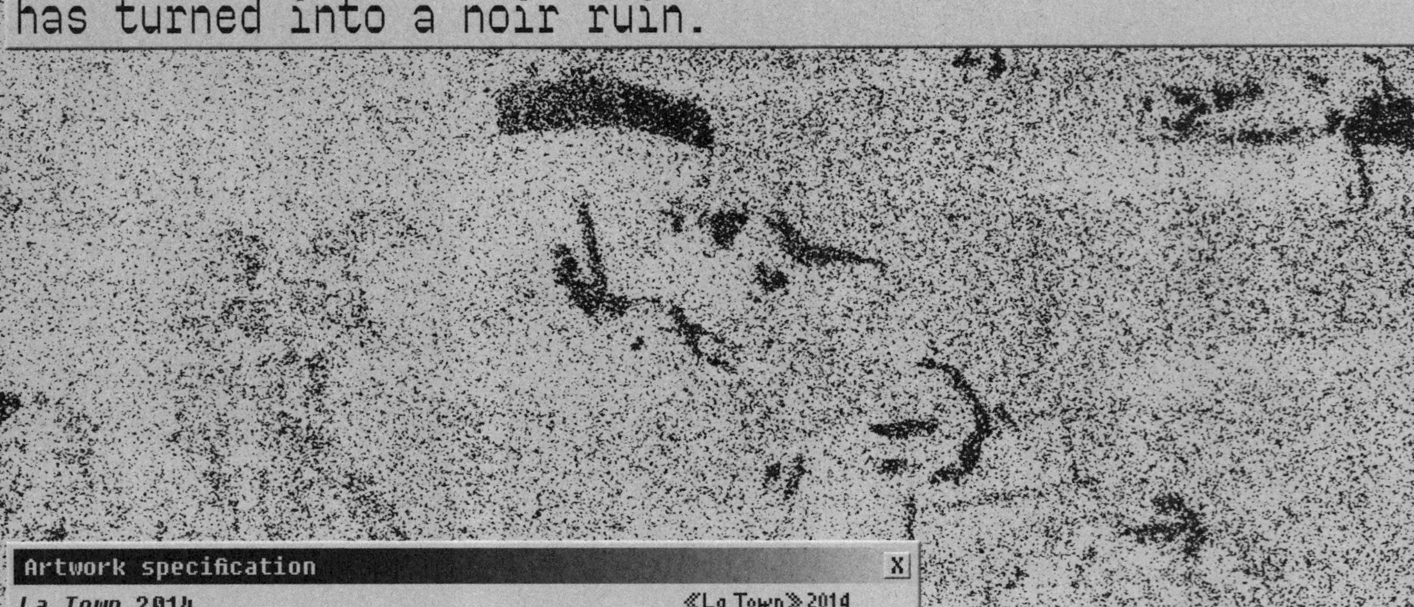

Artwork specification

La Town 2014
single-channel HD video, colour, sound
42:14 min, 16:9

《La Town》2014
16:9 彩色有声单频影像
42分14秒

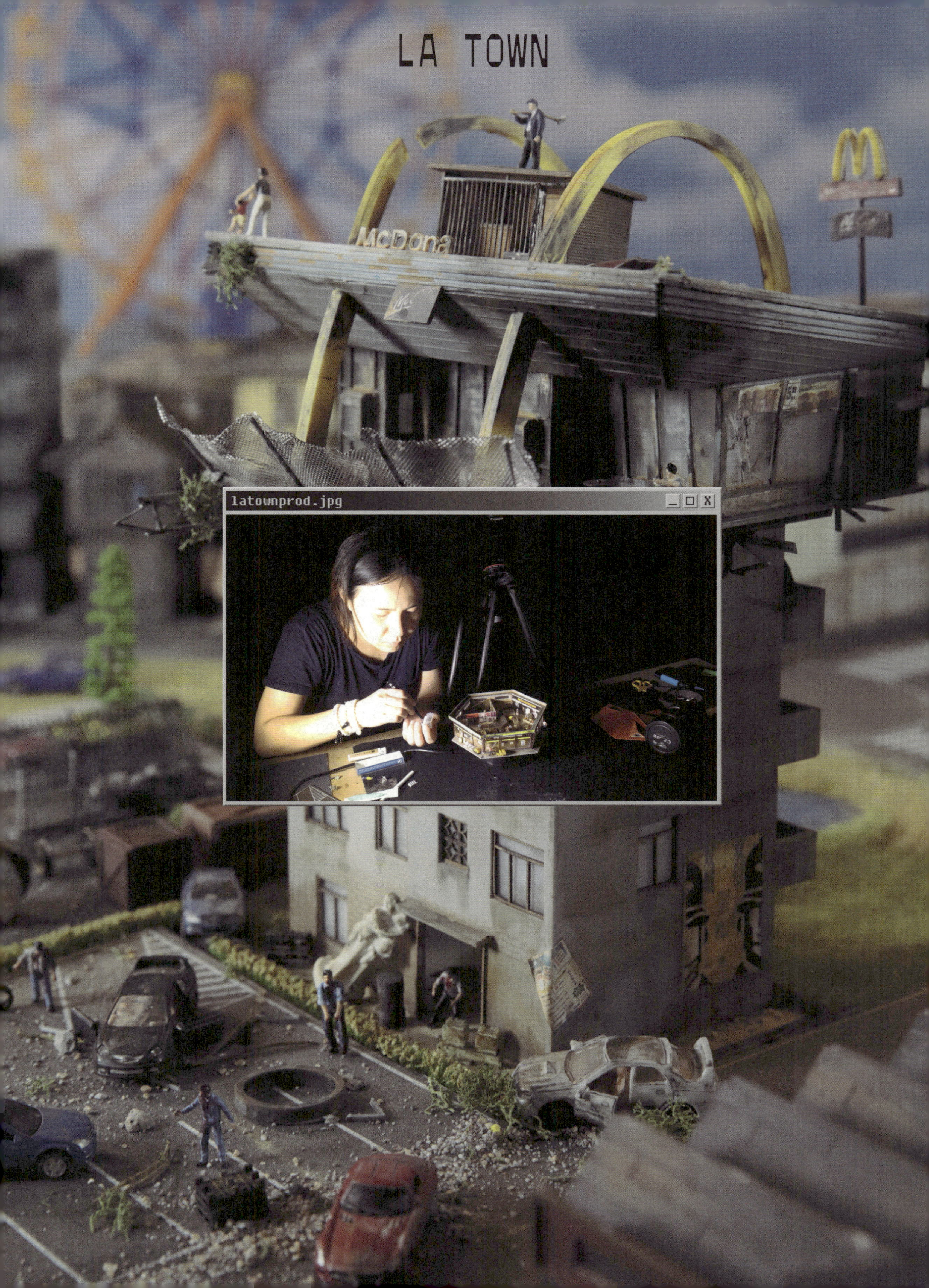
LA TOWN
latownprod.jpg
McDona

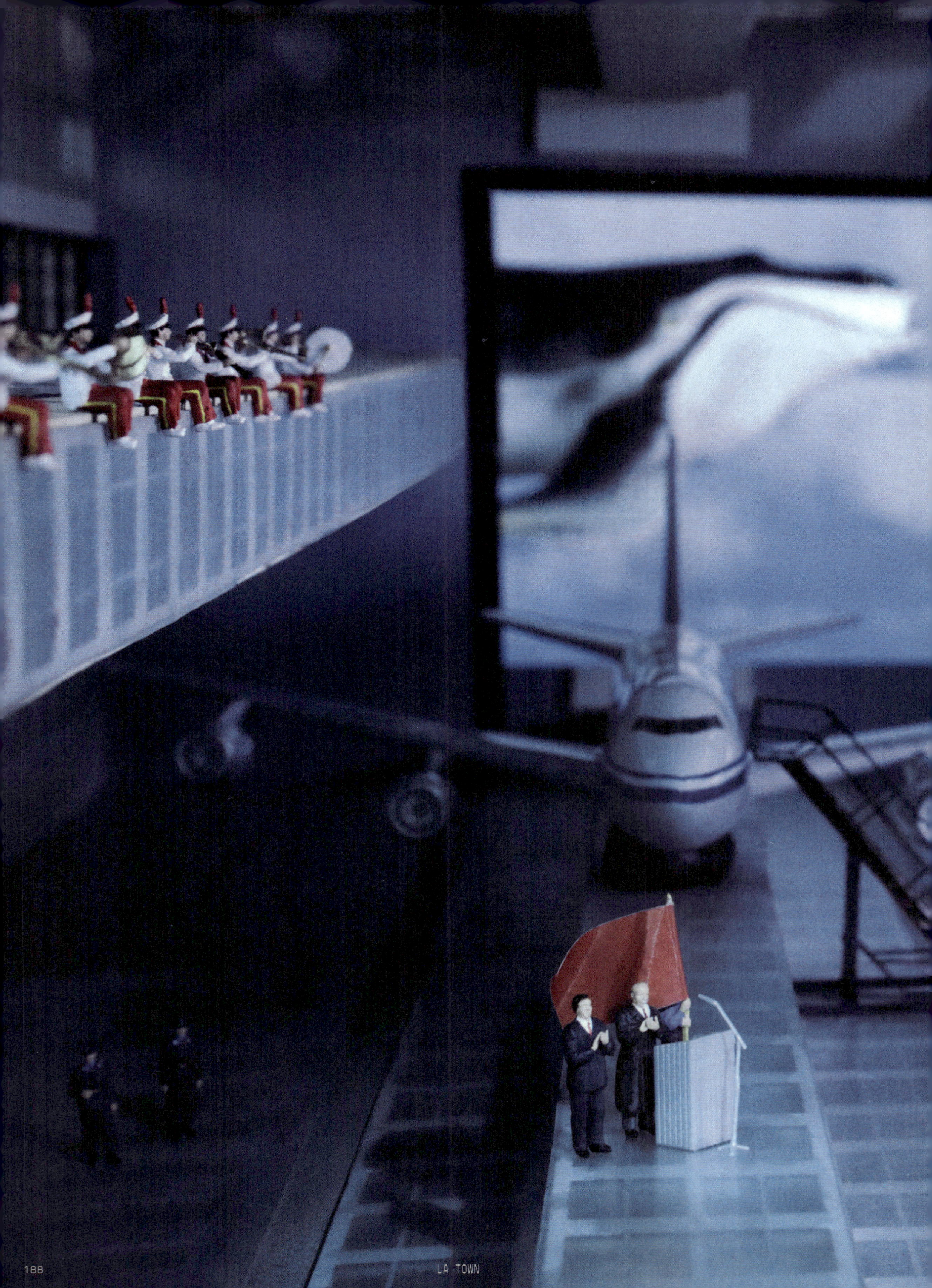

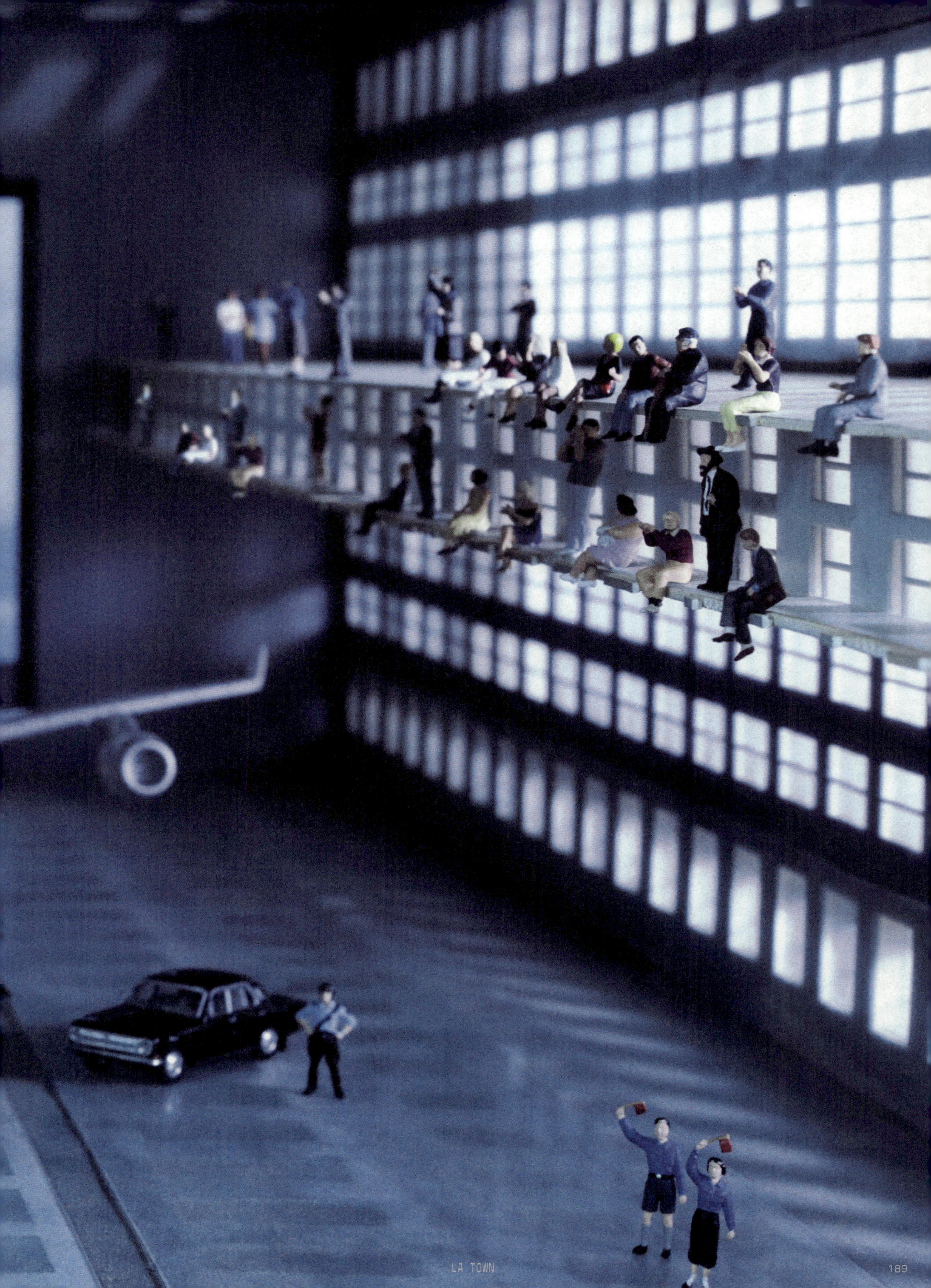

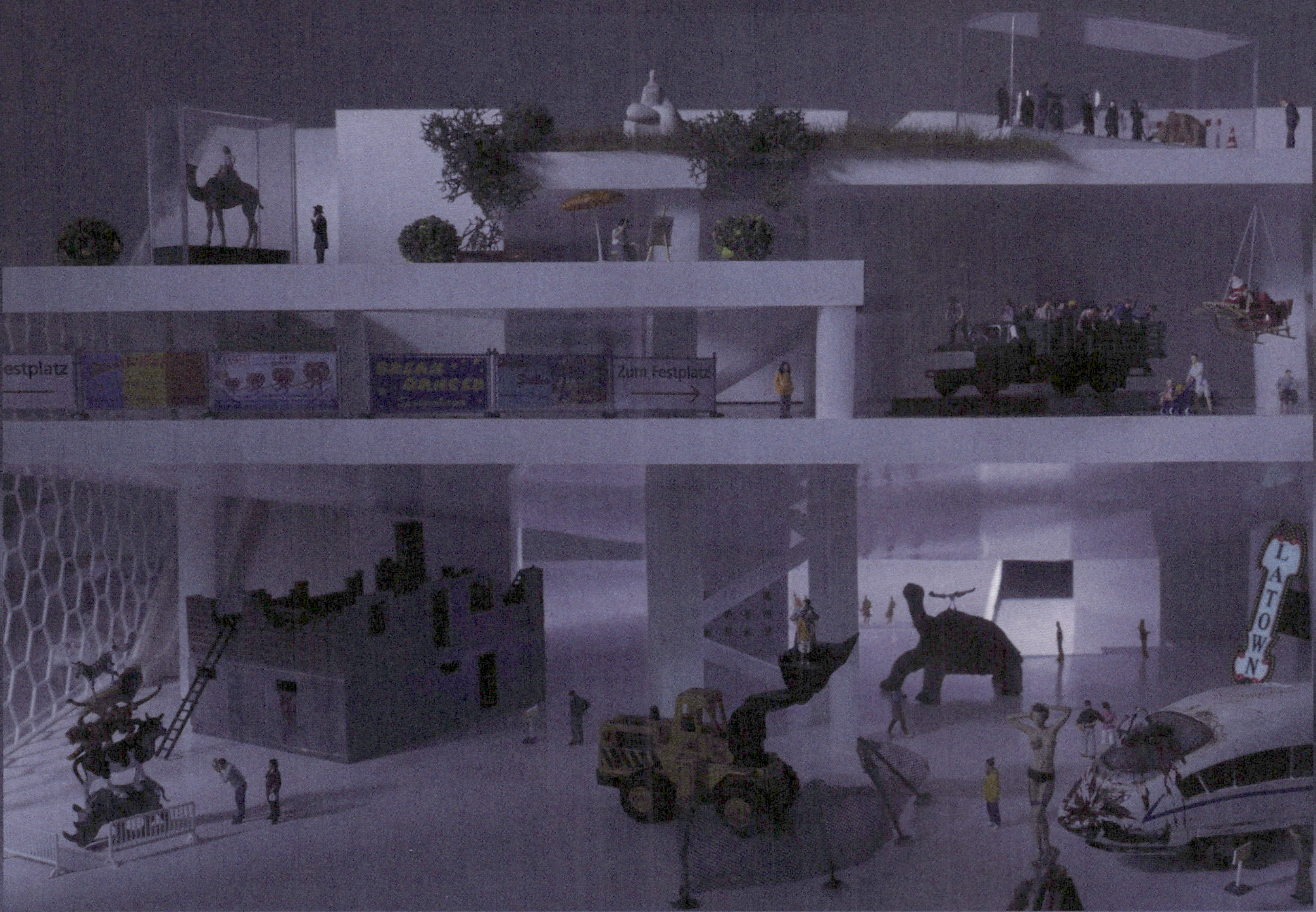

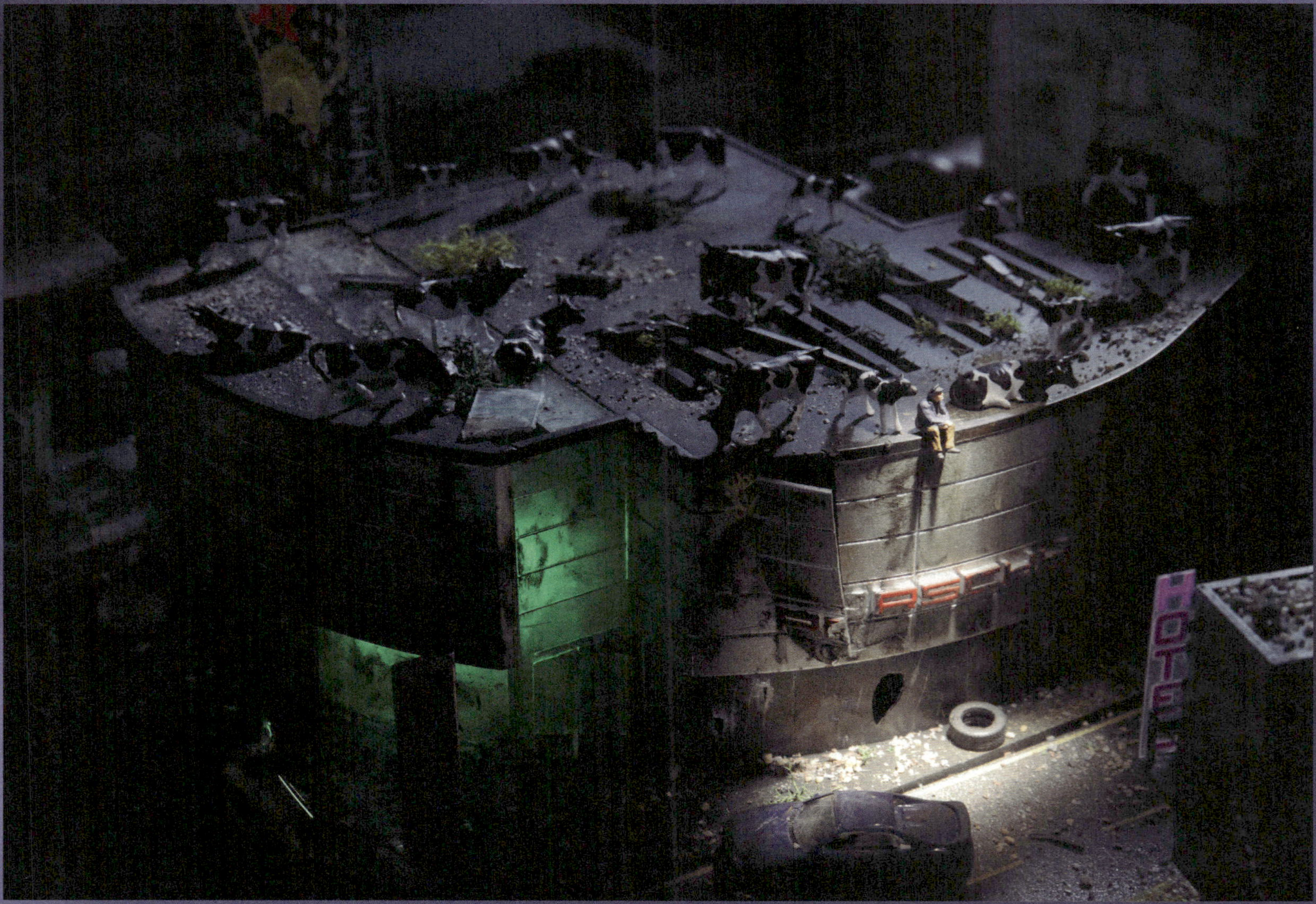

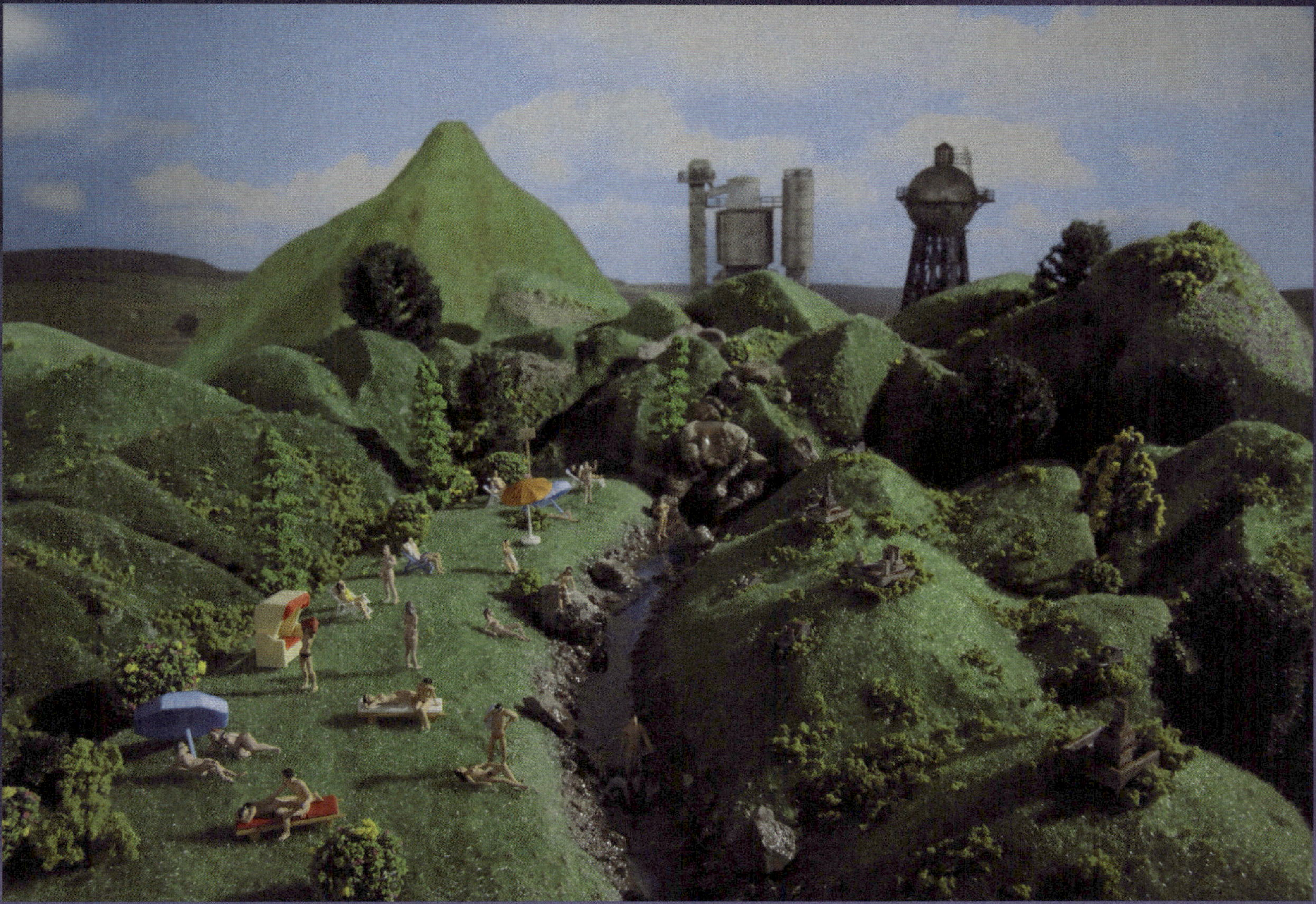

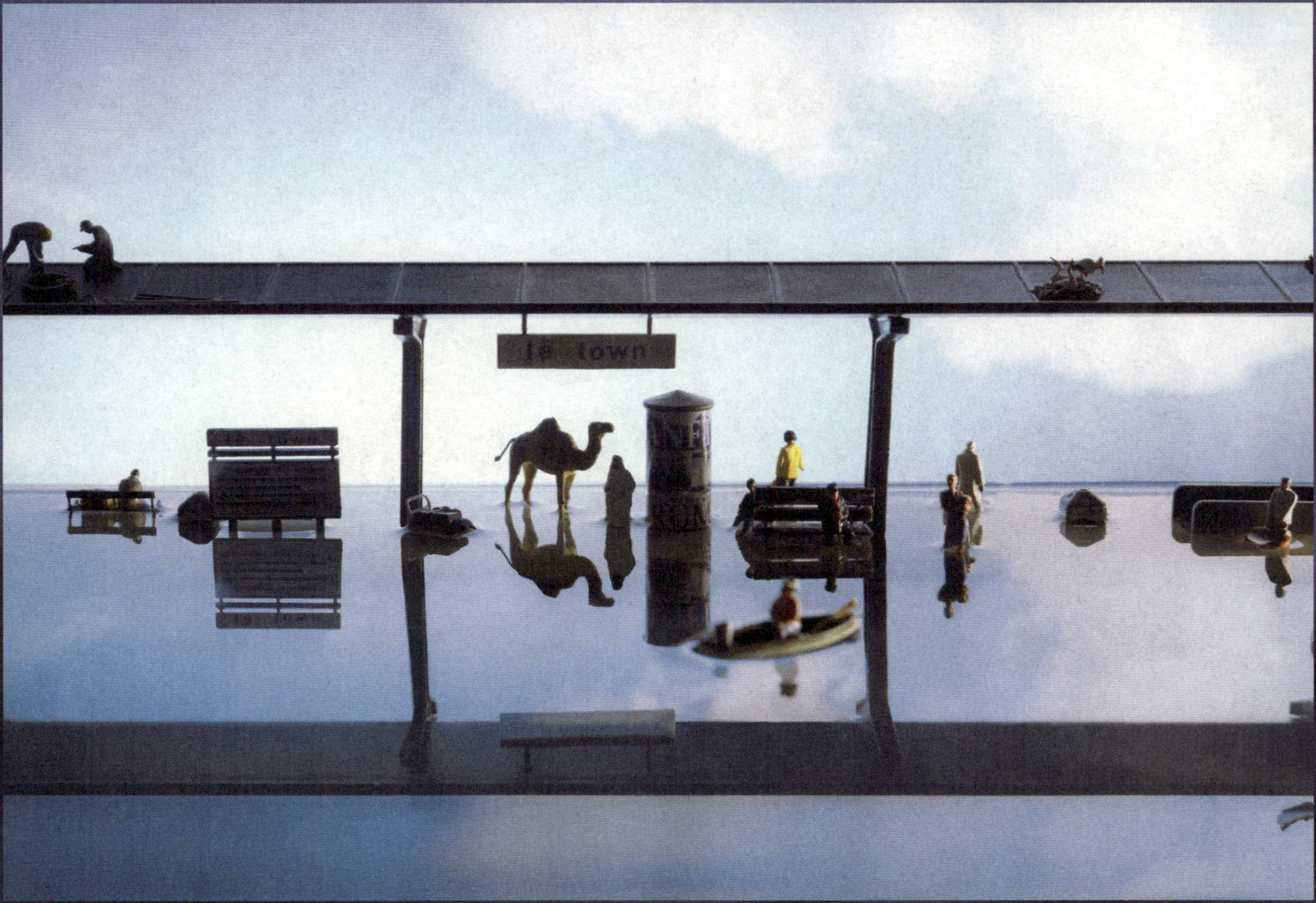

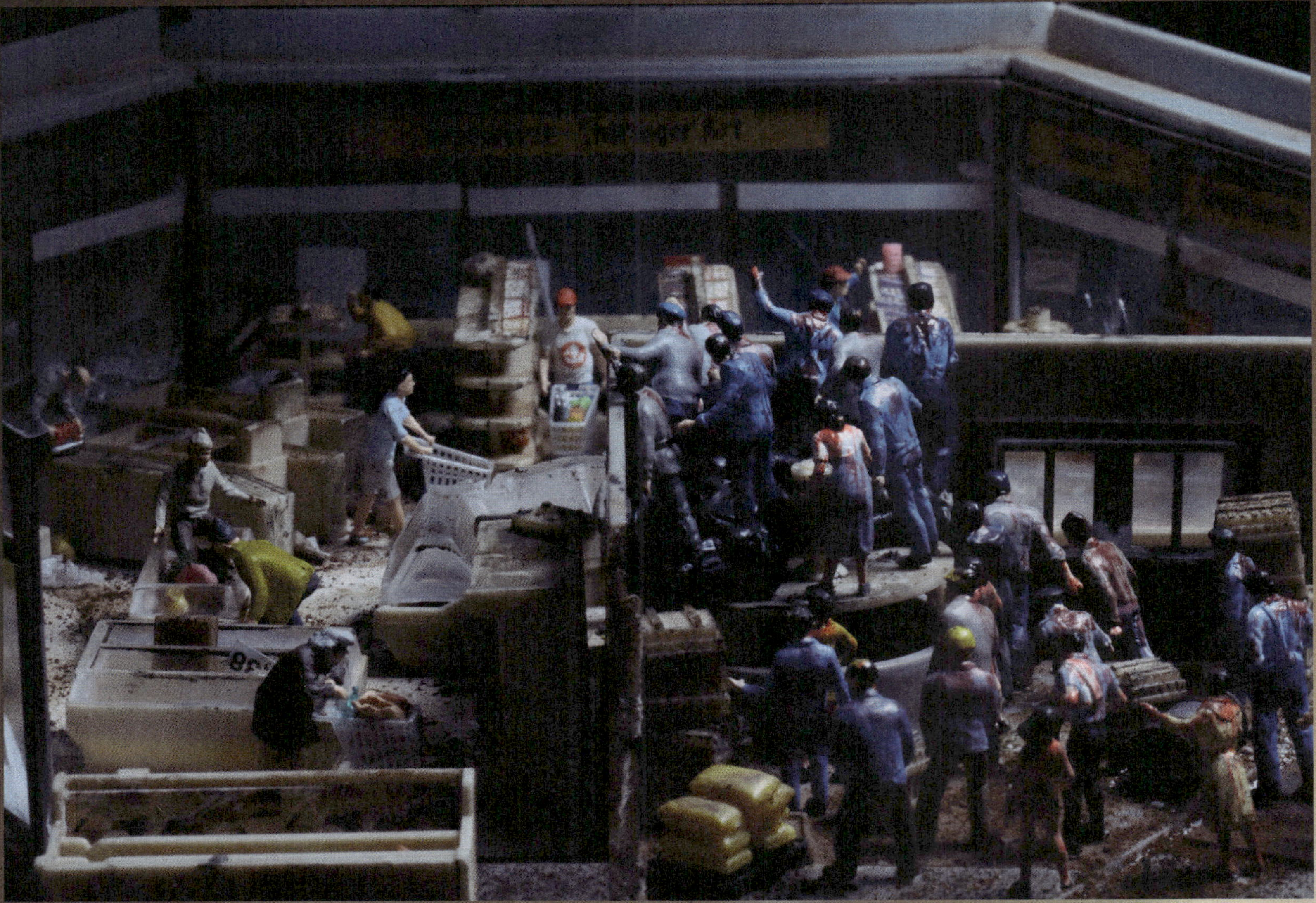

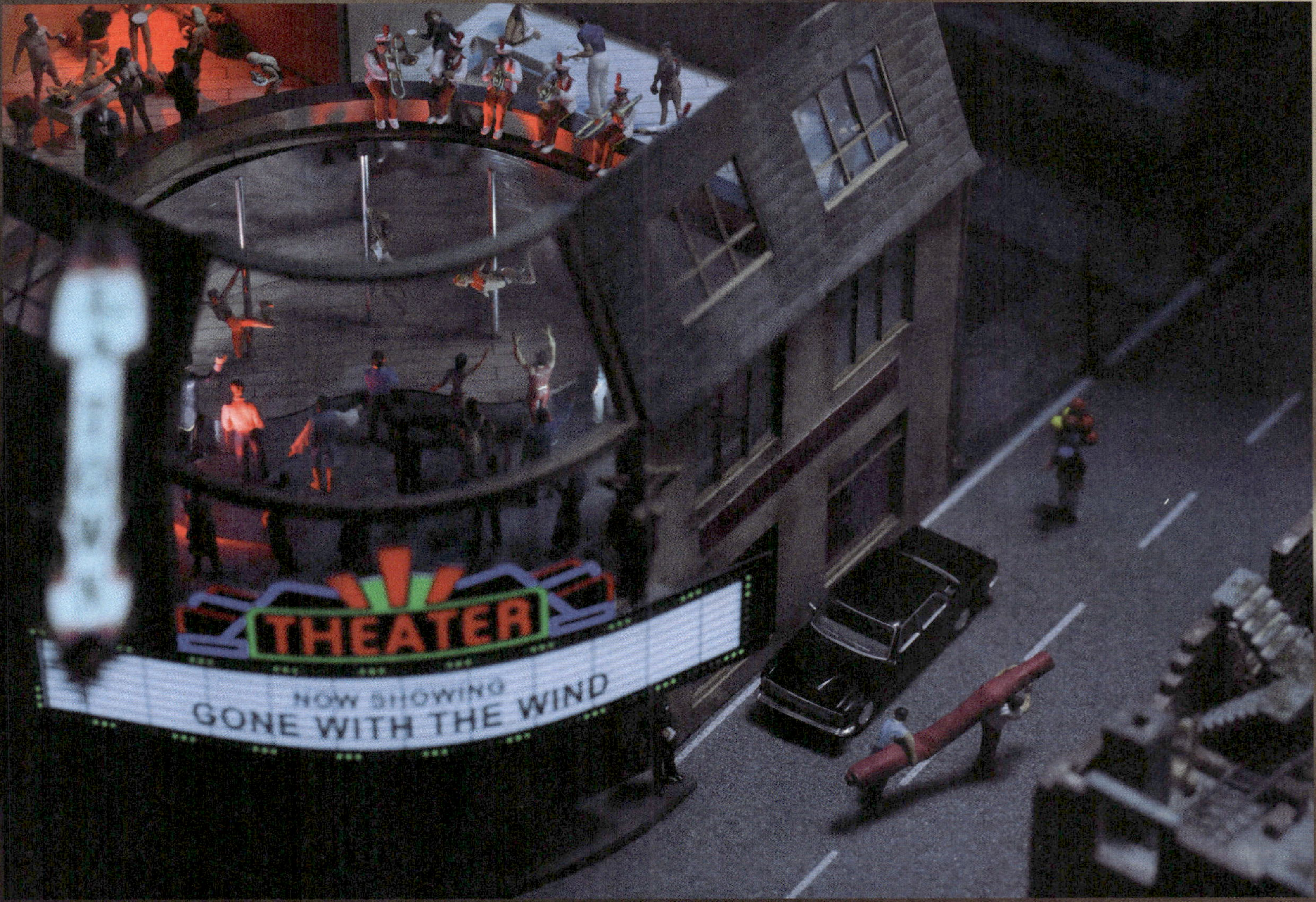
THEATER
NOW SHOWING
GONE WITH THE WIND

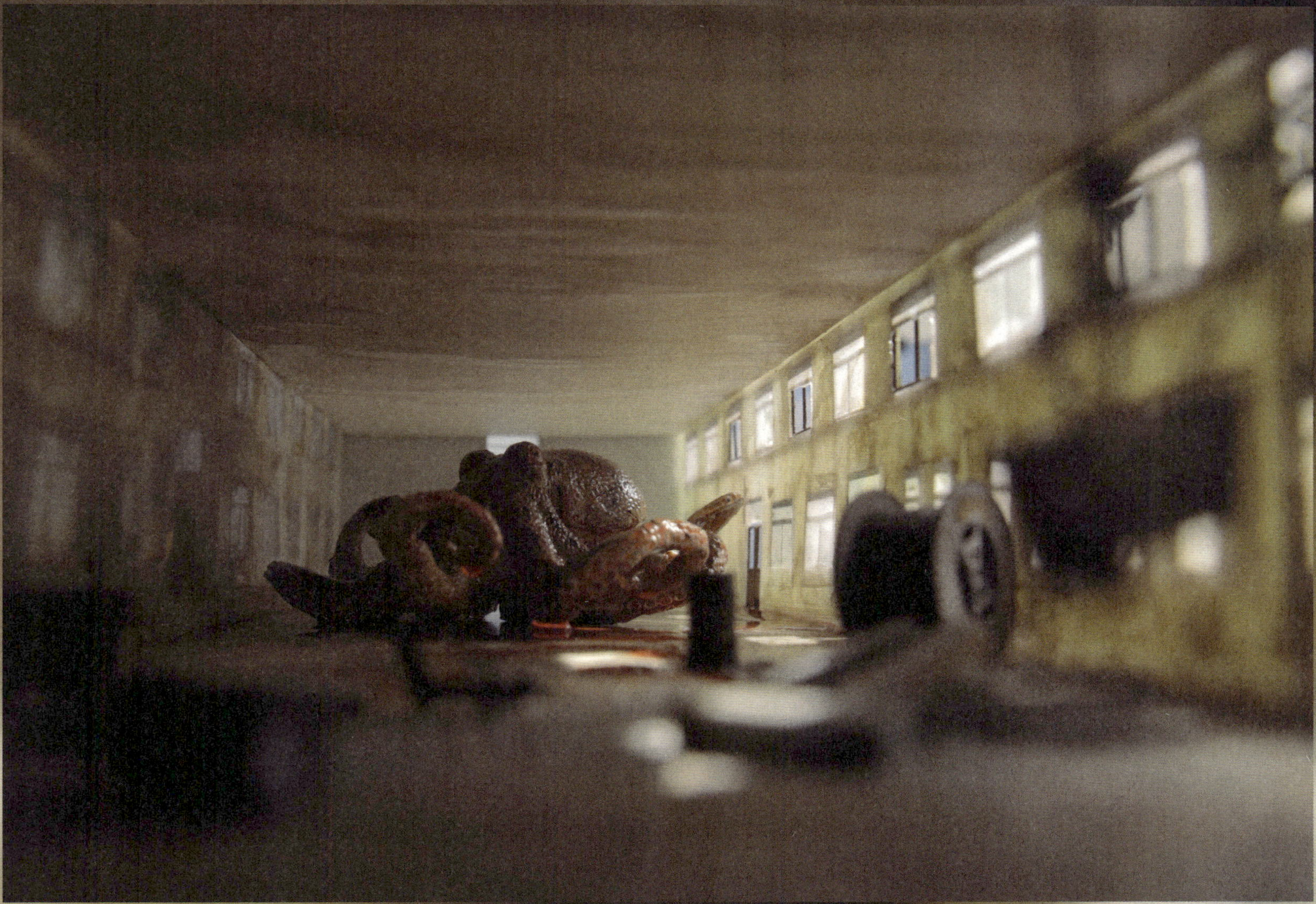

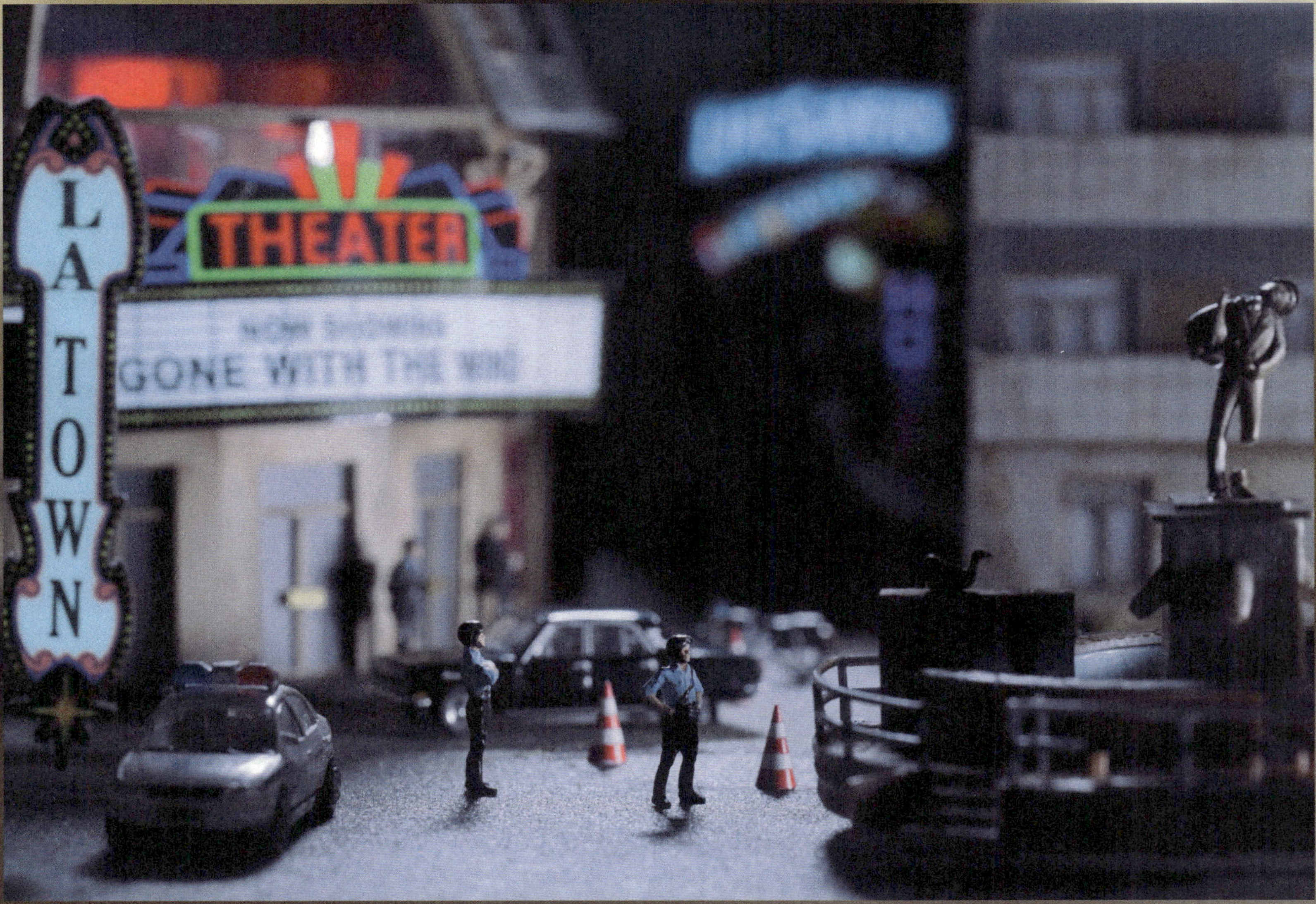
LA TOWN
THEATER
GONE WITH

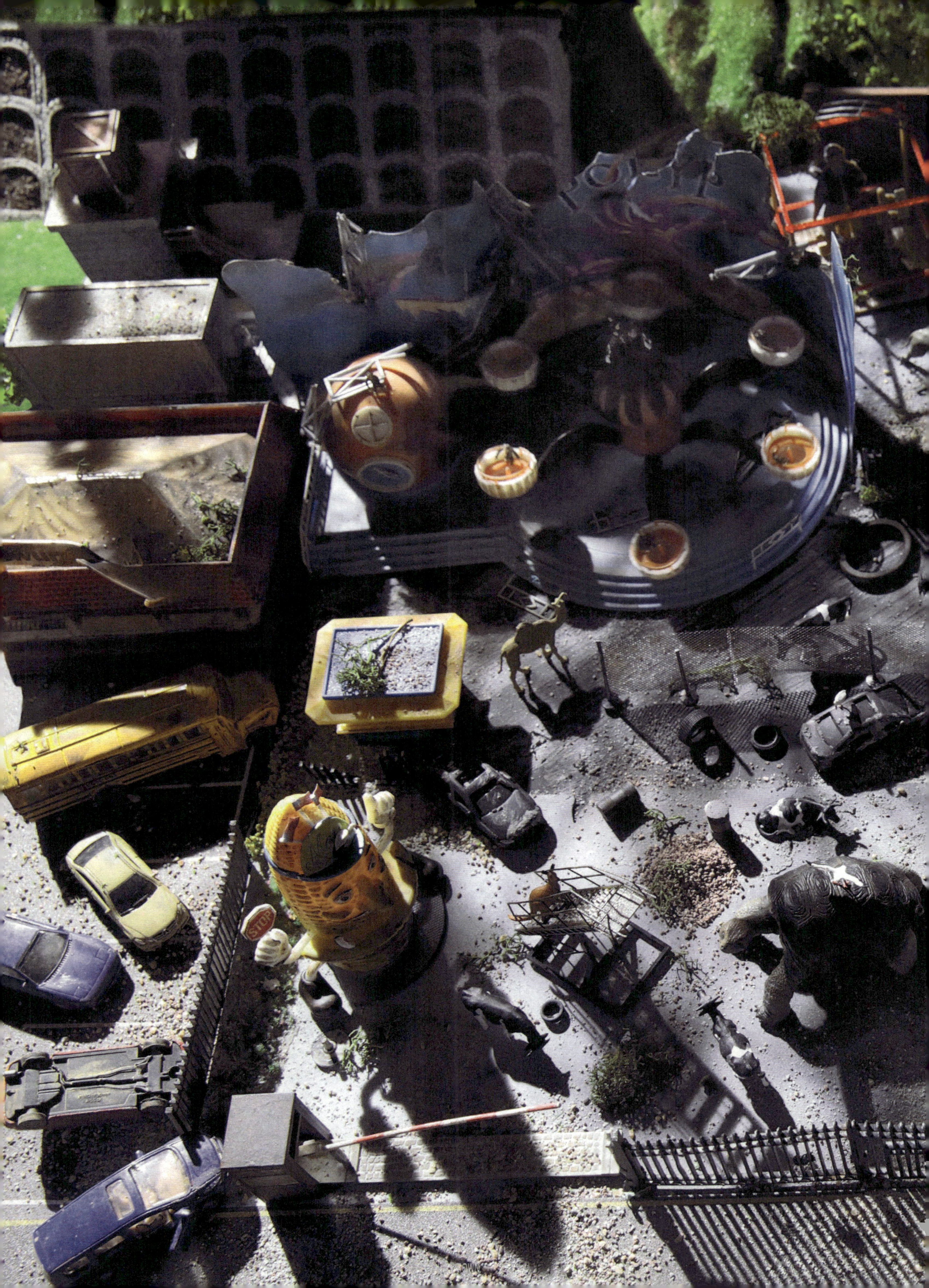
STOP

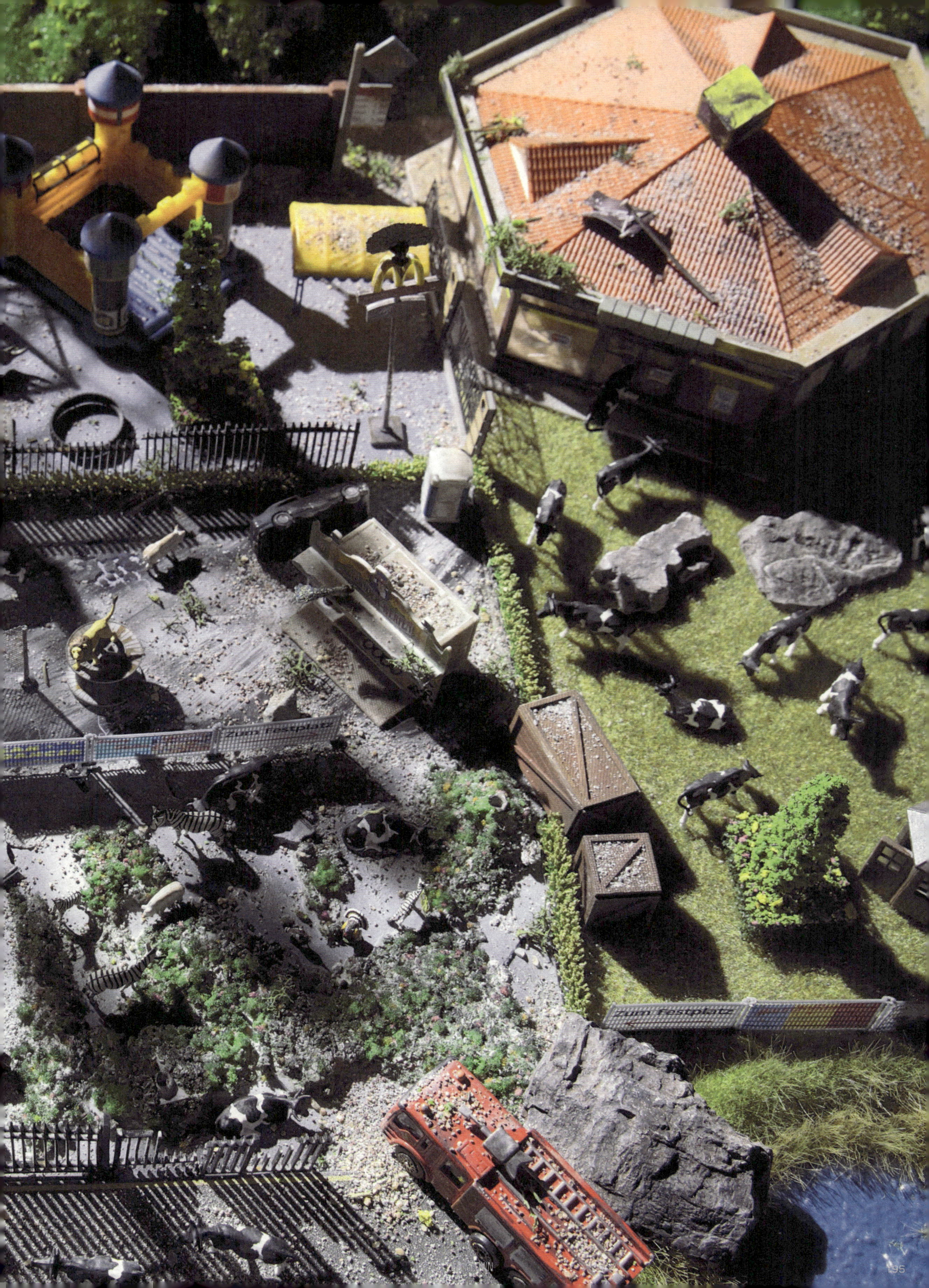
Zum Festplatz
Zum Festplatz

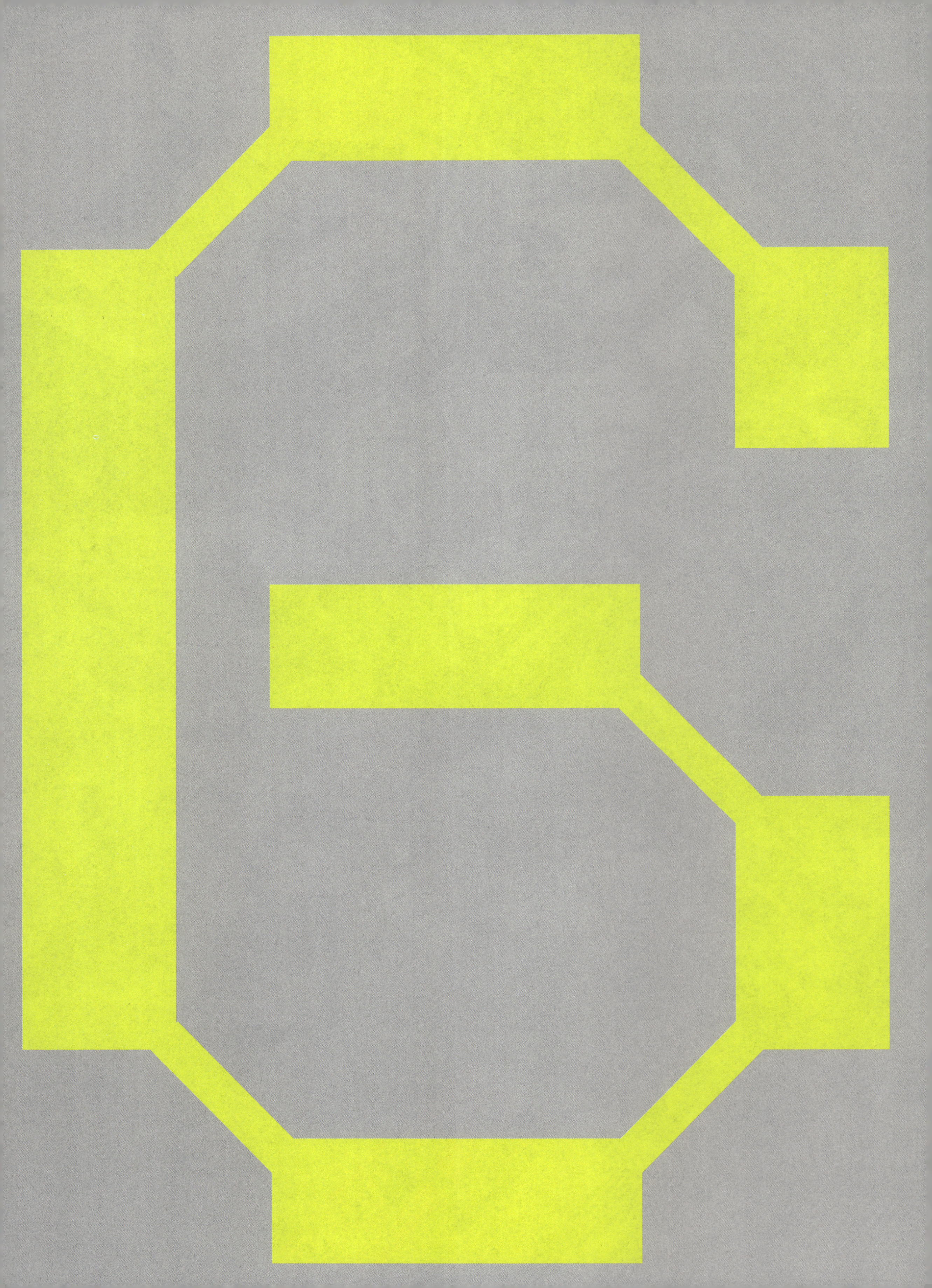

ASIA ONE

2018

亚洲一号

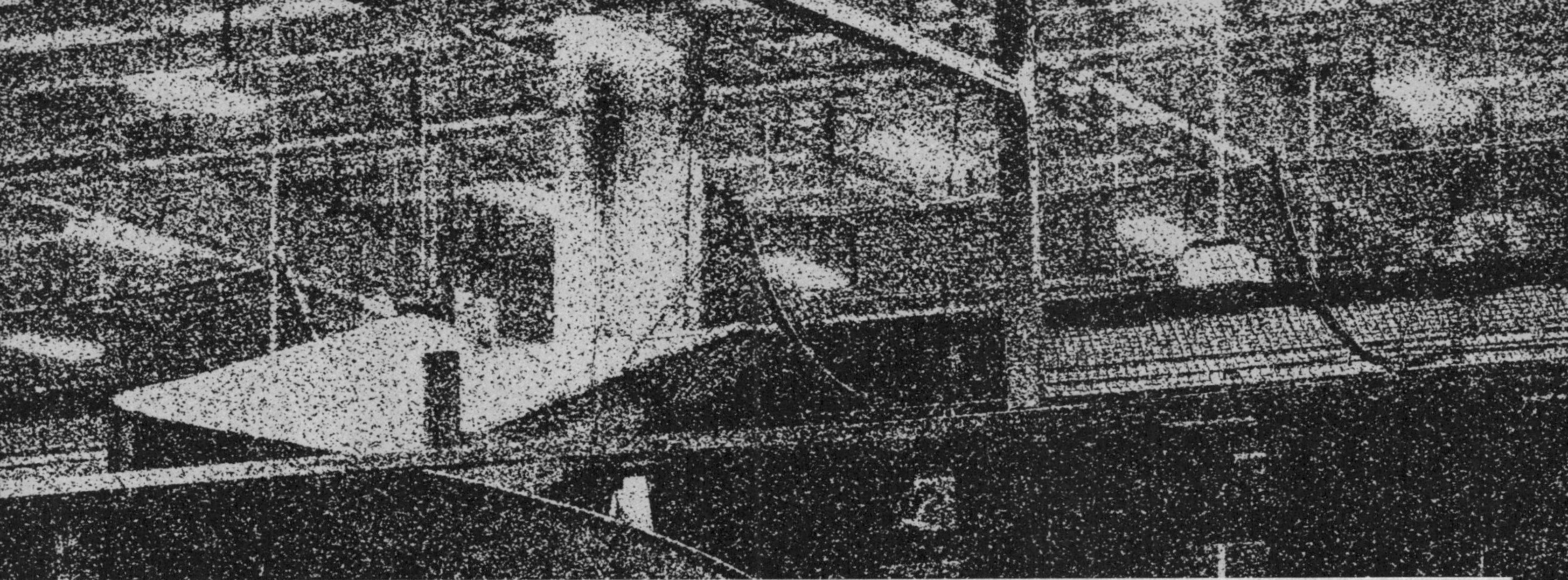

G: Asia one

Add to cart! Down roll the groceries and children's toys. Proceed to checkout. Payment successful! Rice cookers and vitamins are packed, labelled and stacked, ready for distribution. *Asia one* considers China's evolution from a low-tech manufacturing hub to a world leader in 'smart' logistics and AI. This ambitious feature film was shot at the world's first fully automated distribution centre in Kunshan, Jiangsu province. Two lonely employees orbit each other in the gigantic sorting facility where robots oversee production lines whirring with cheap consumables. At first, the two workers struggle to connect, alienated souls in a dystopia of surveillance and machine-sharp efficiency. But soon, the conveyor belt glitches. The pair rebel. The film's space-time continuum ruptures. A troupe of workers, dressed to evoke the characters of Cultural Revolution-era model operas, dance to disco under a banner that reads: 'Humans and machines, hand in hand'. It's a retro fantasy. A promise that machines will serve the interests of workers, easing their burdens.

Artwork specification

Asia one 2018
single-channel HD video, colour, sound
63:21 min, 2.35:1
Commissioned by the Solomon R. Guggenheim Museum, New York, for The Robert H.N. Ho Family Foundation Chinese Initiative

《亚洲一号》2018
2.35:1彩色有声单频高清影像
63分21秒
作品由纽约所罗门·R·古根海姆美术馆为何鸿毅家族基金会中国艺术计划委任创作

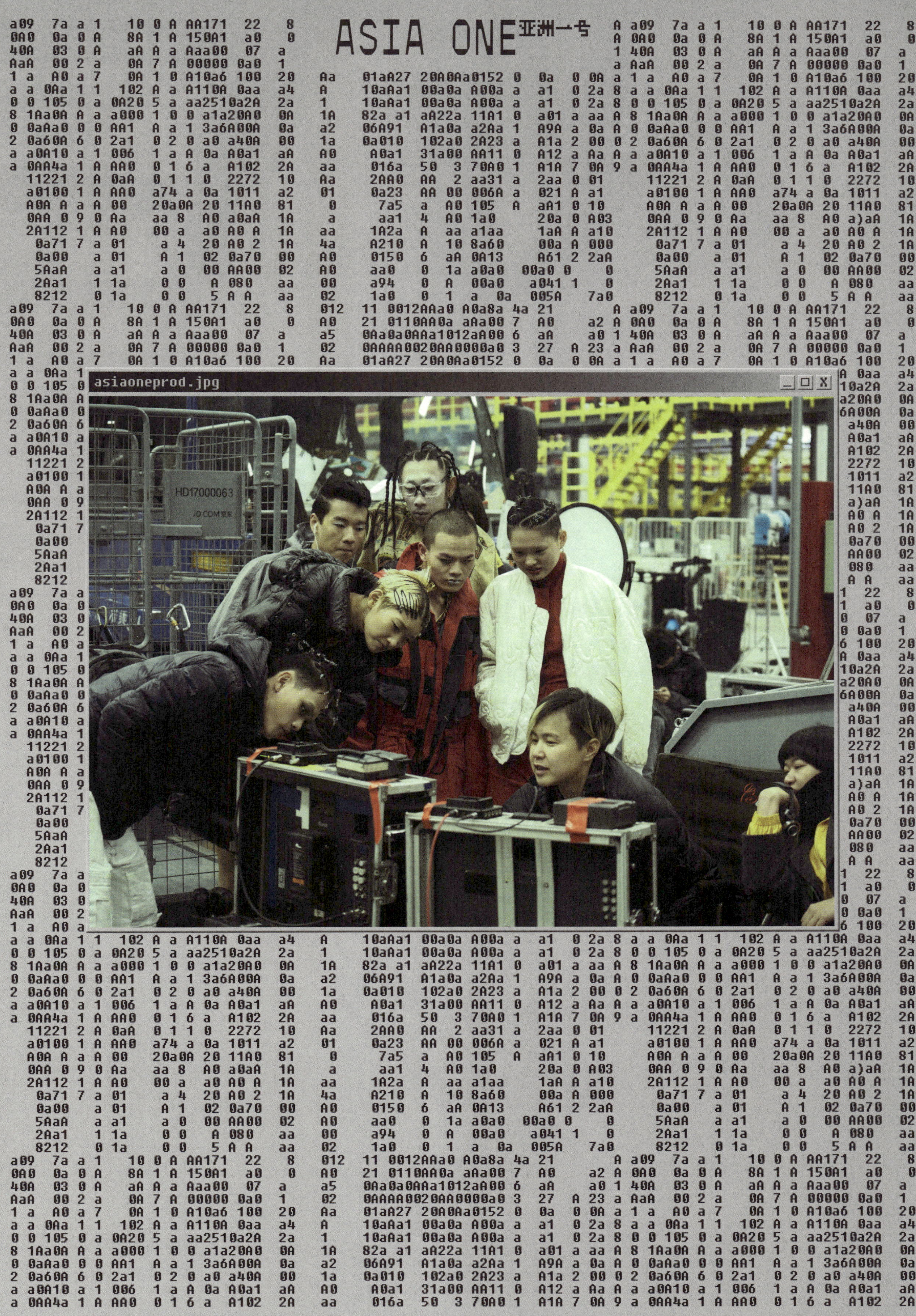
ASIA ONE 亚洲一号
asiaoneprod.jpg
HD17000063
JD.COM 京东

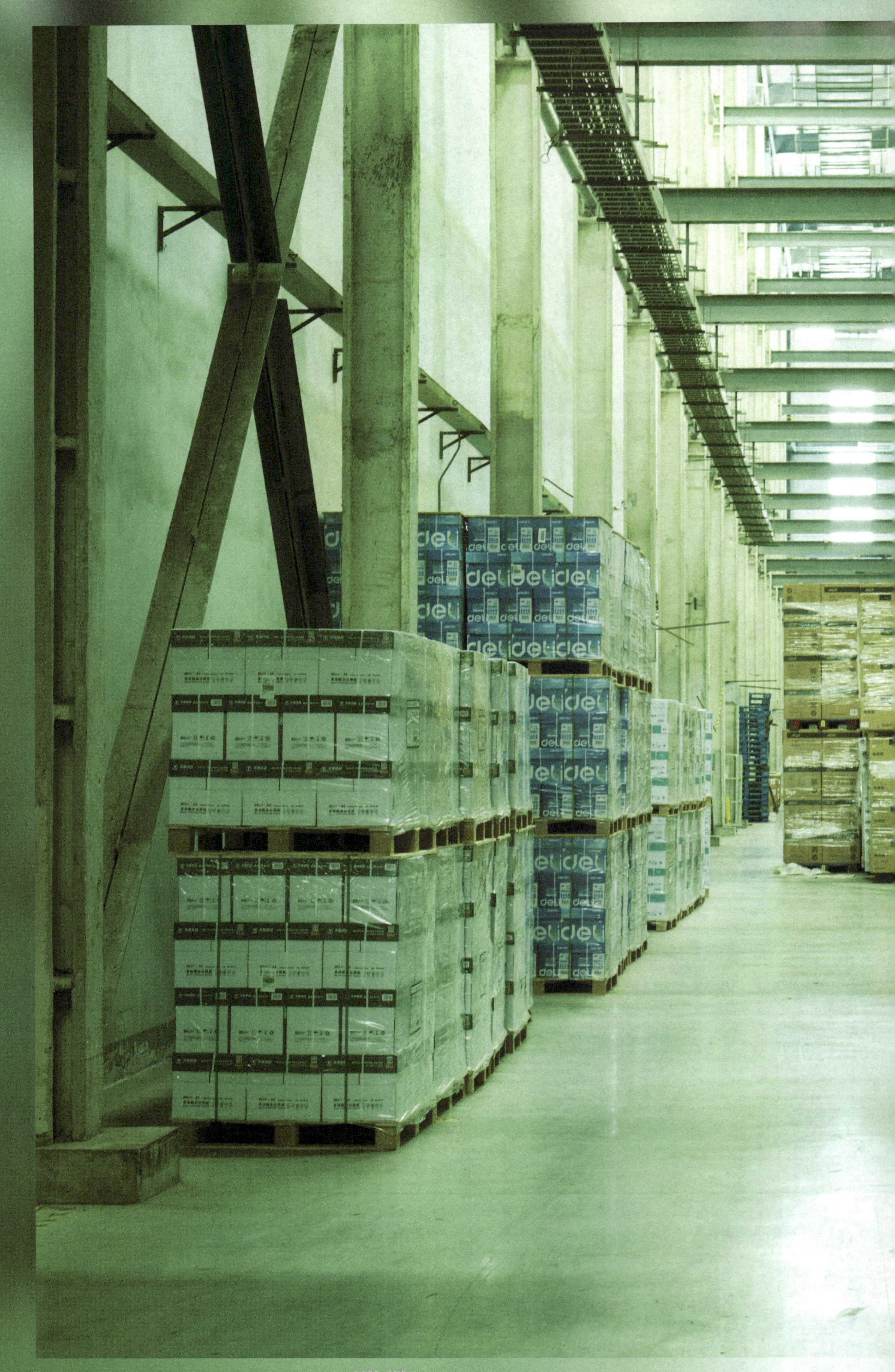
deli

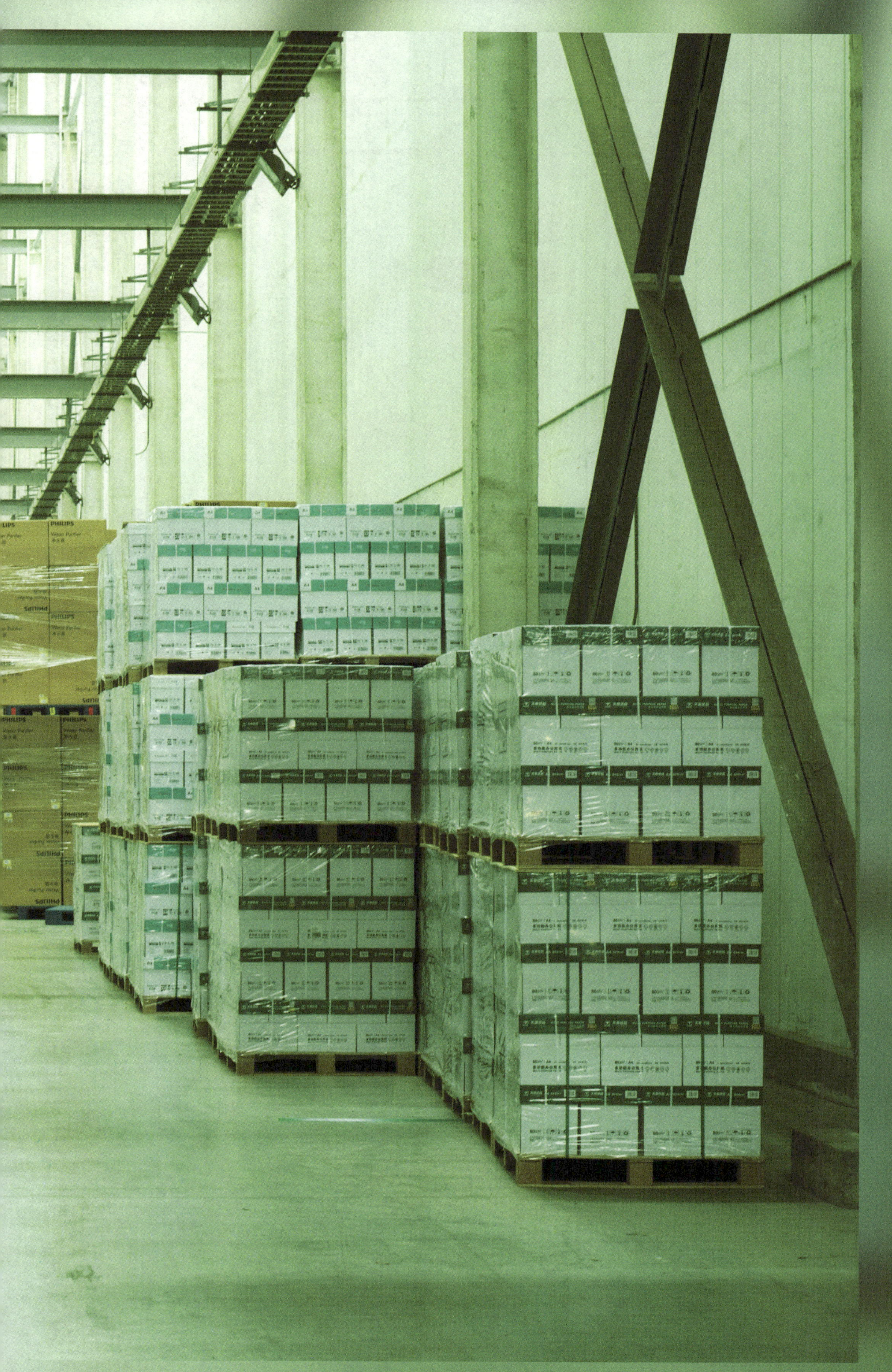

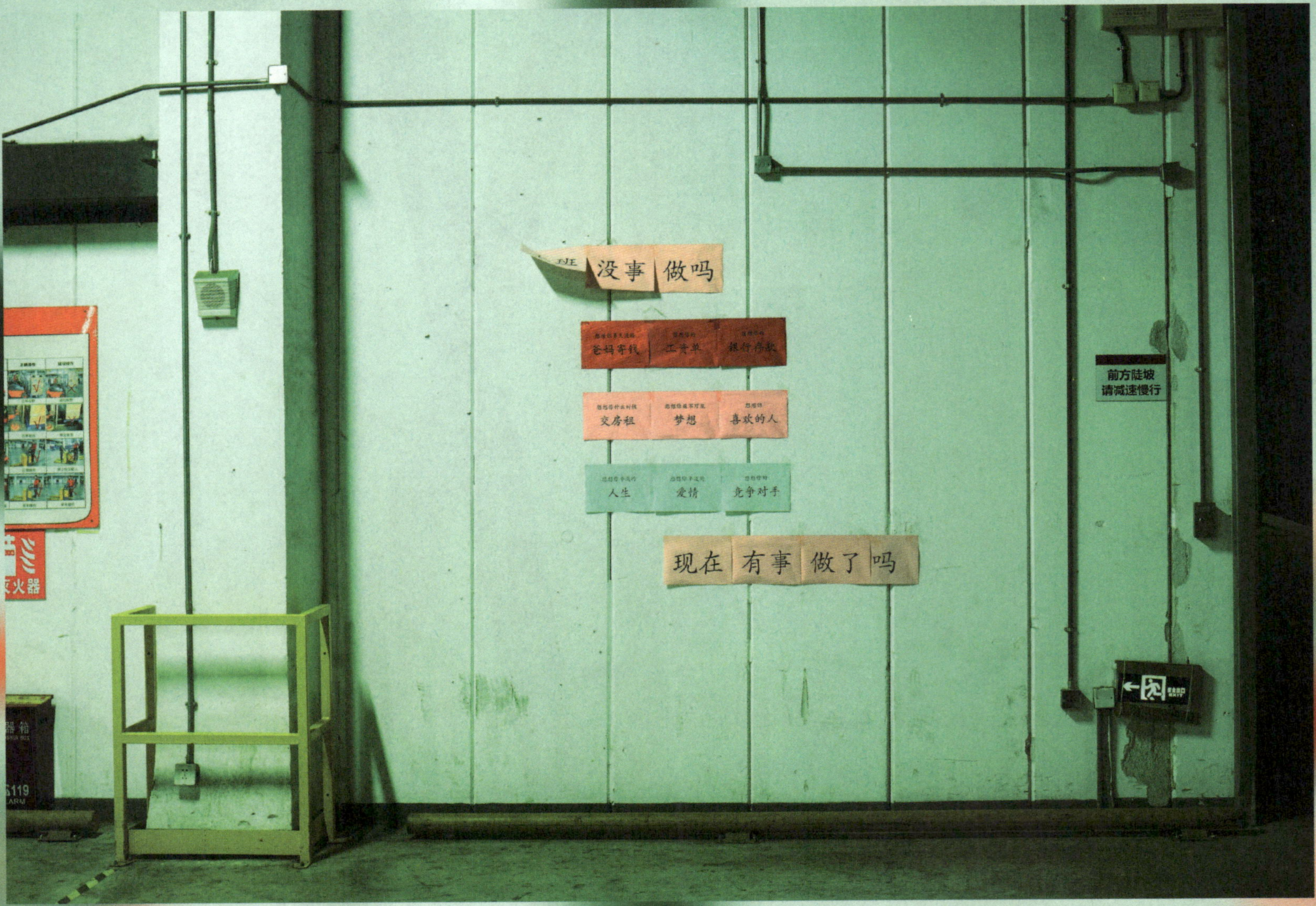
没事 做吗
爸妈寄钱
工资单
银行存款
交房租
梦想
喜欢的人
人生
爱情
竞争对手
现在 有事 做了吗
前方陡坡
请减速慢行

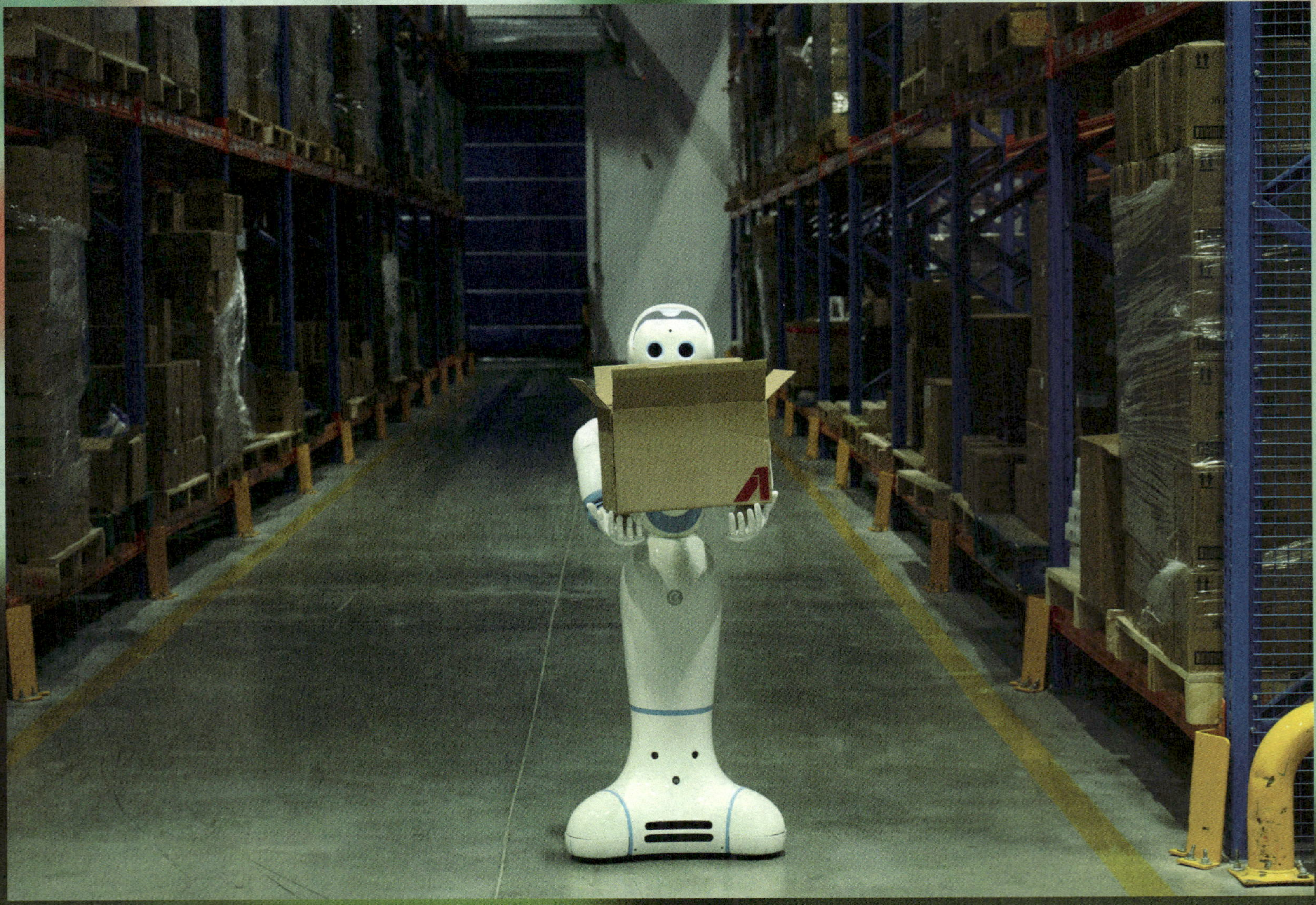

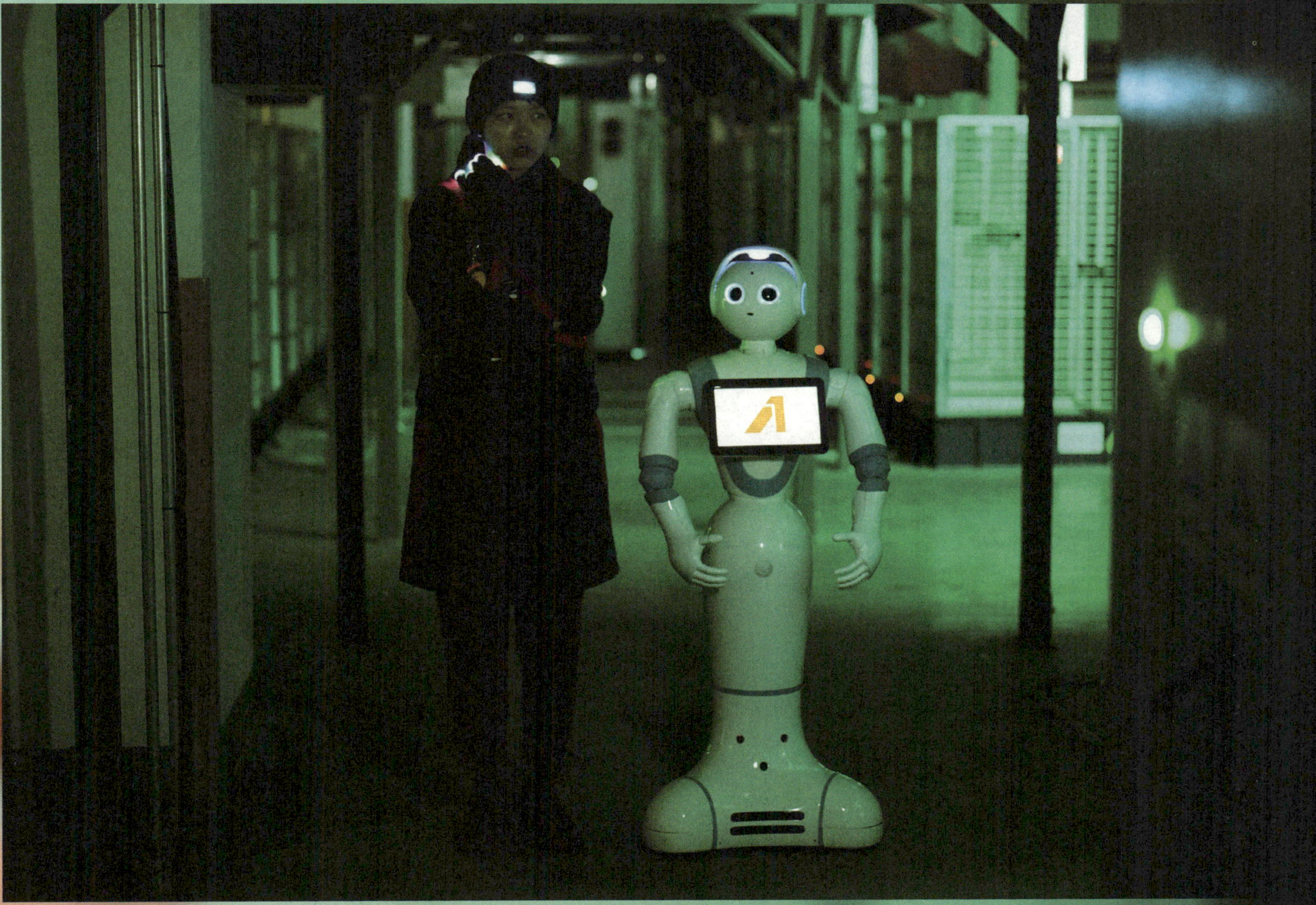

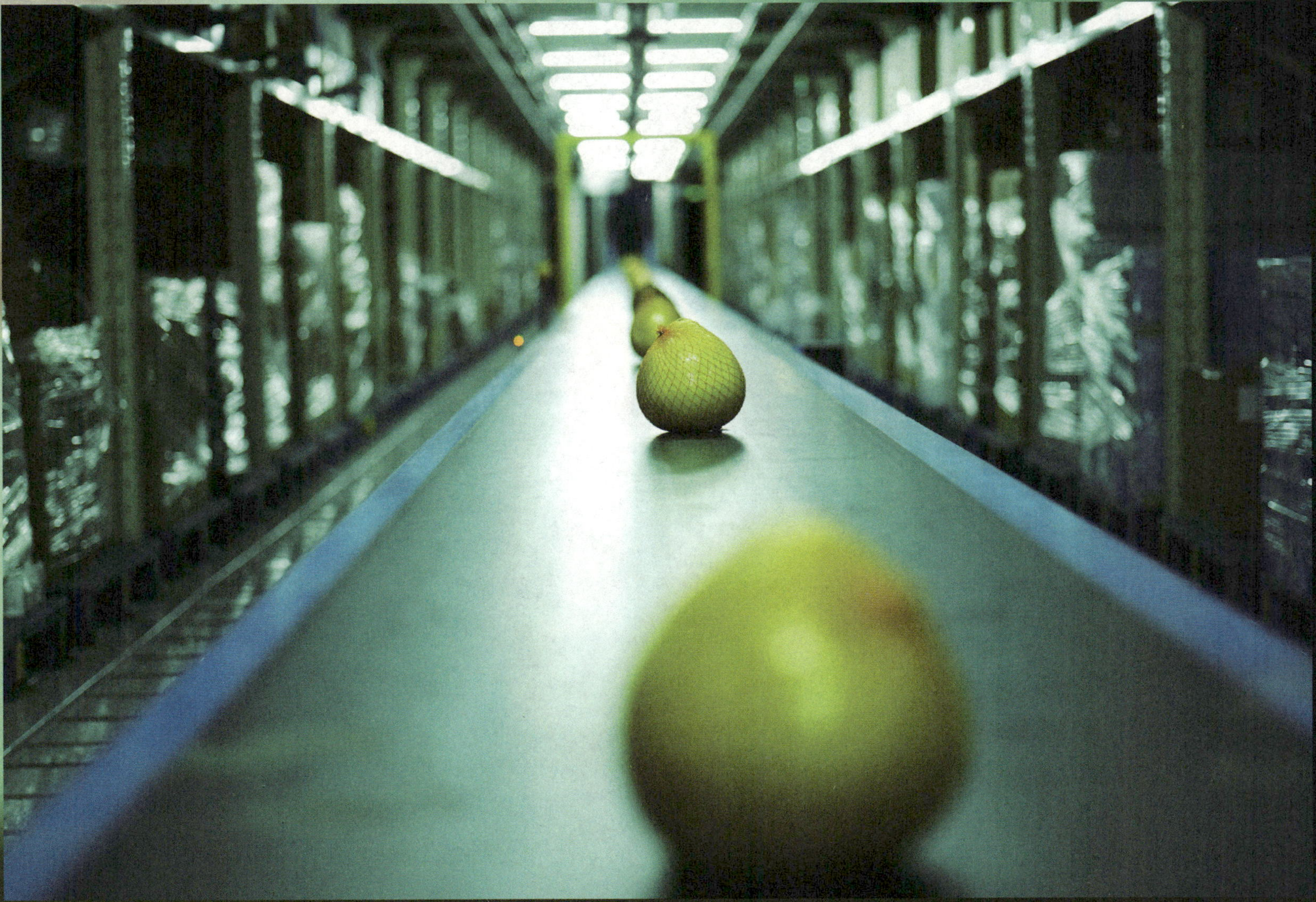

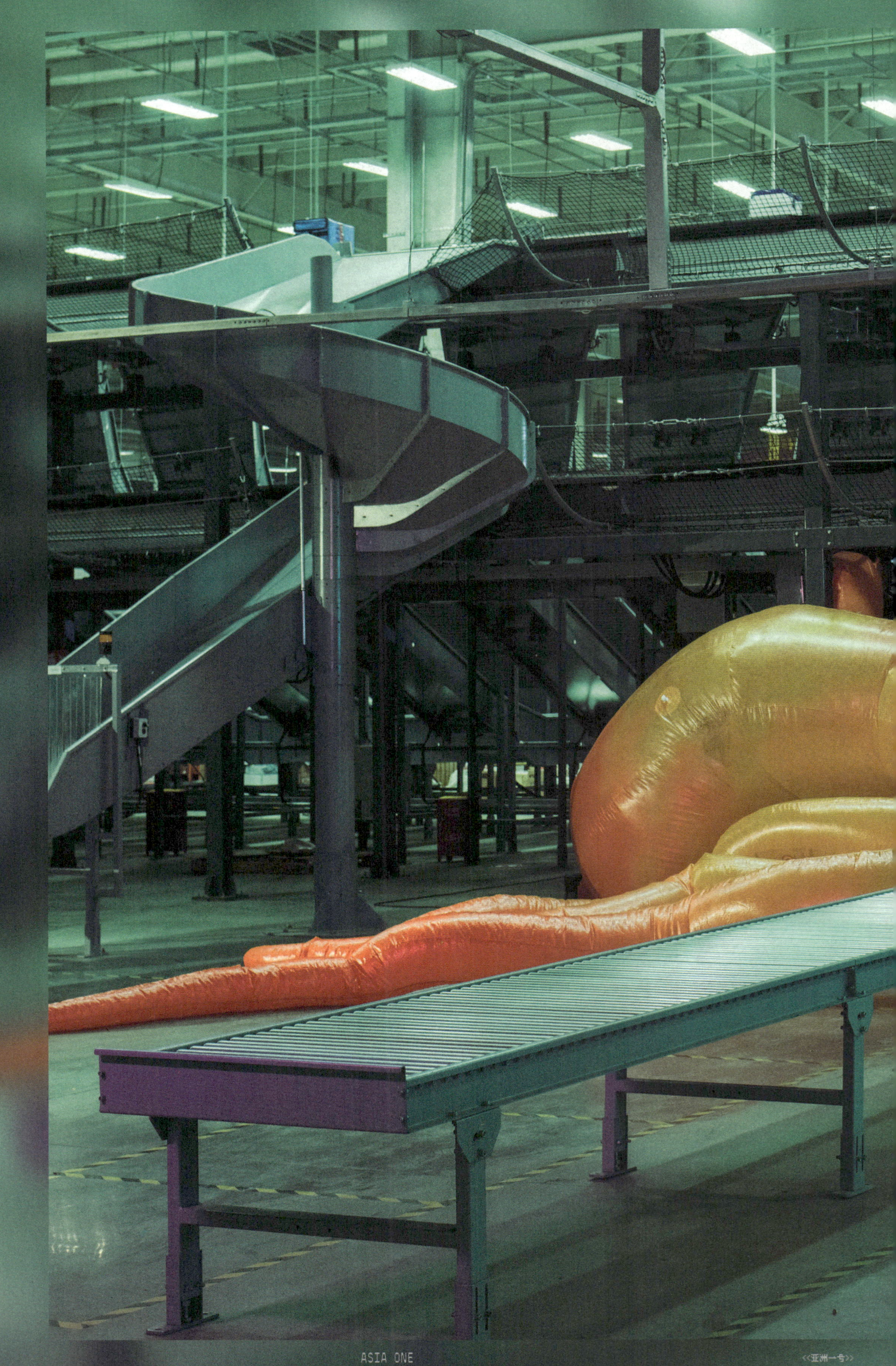

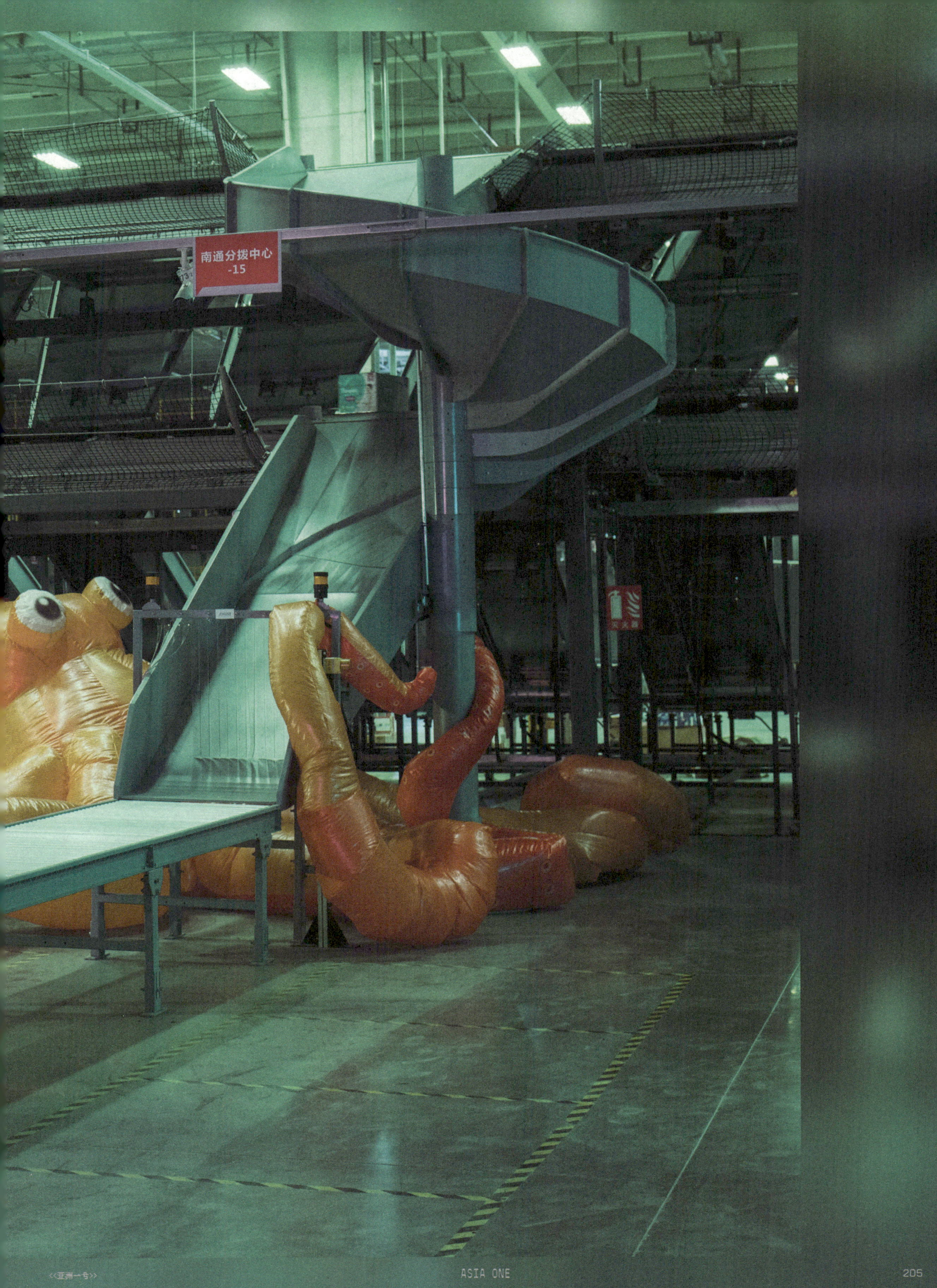
南通分拨中心
-15

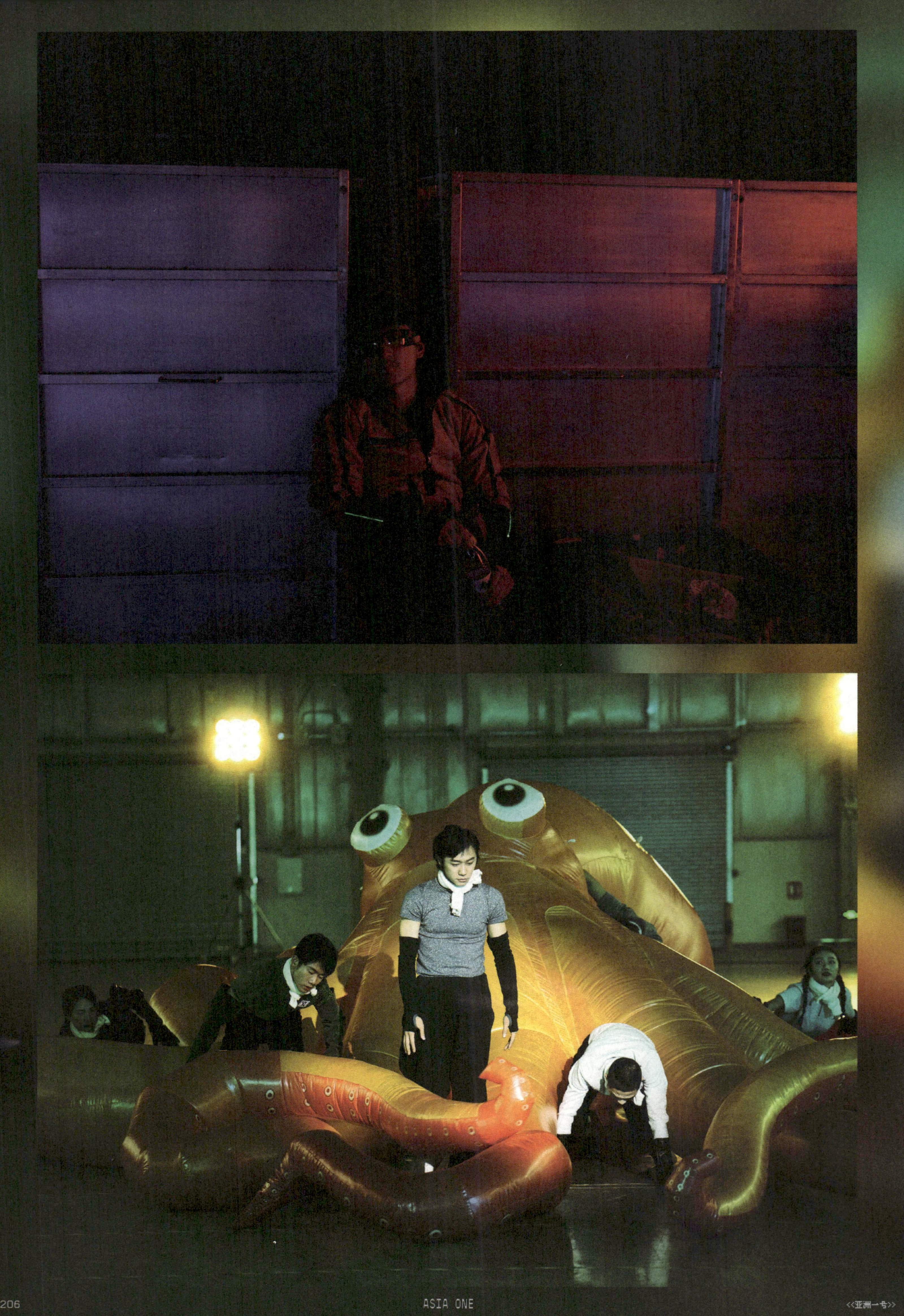

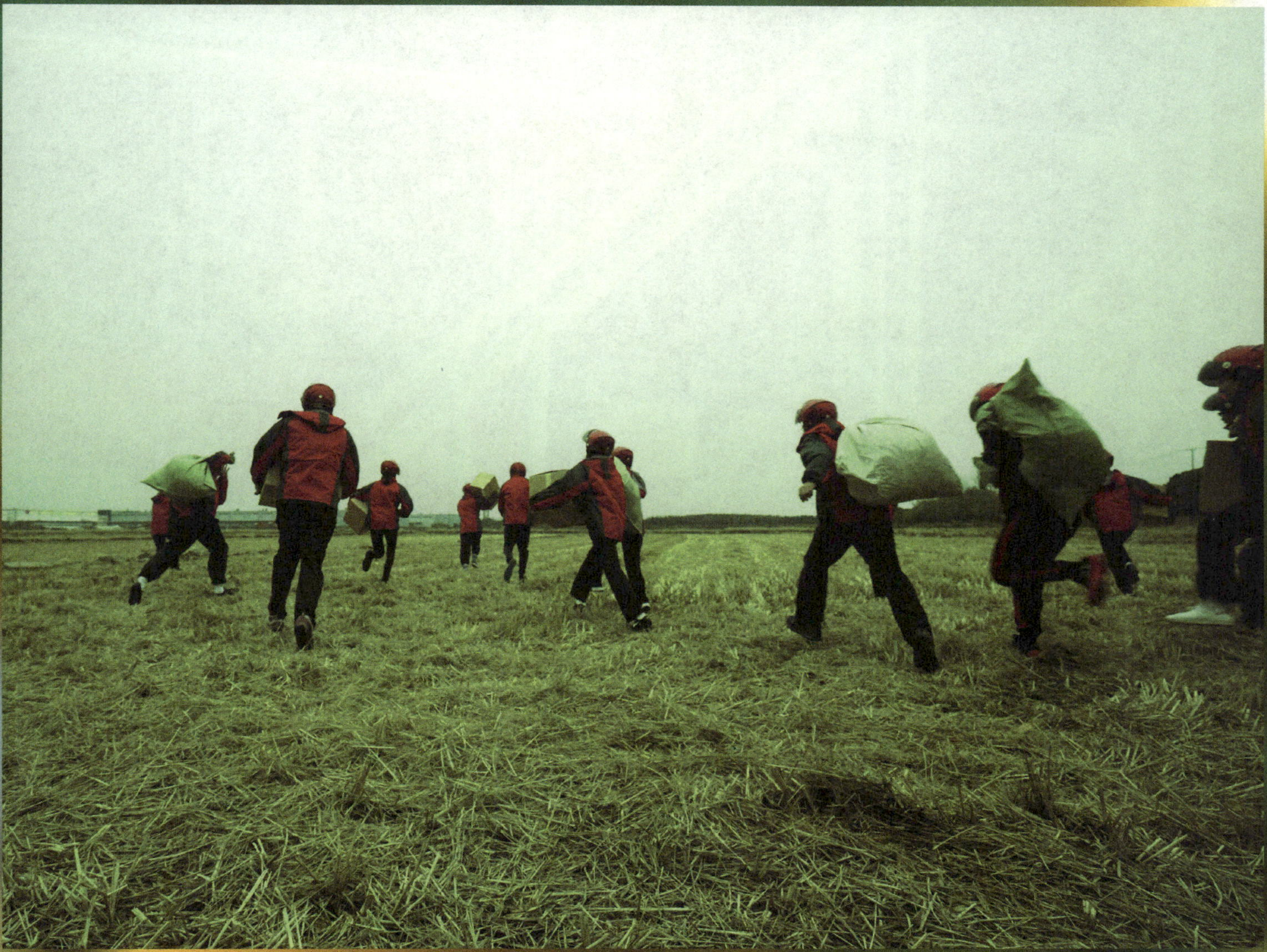

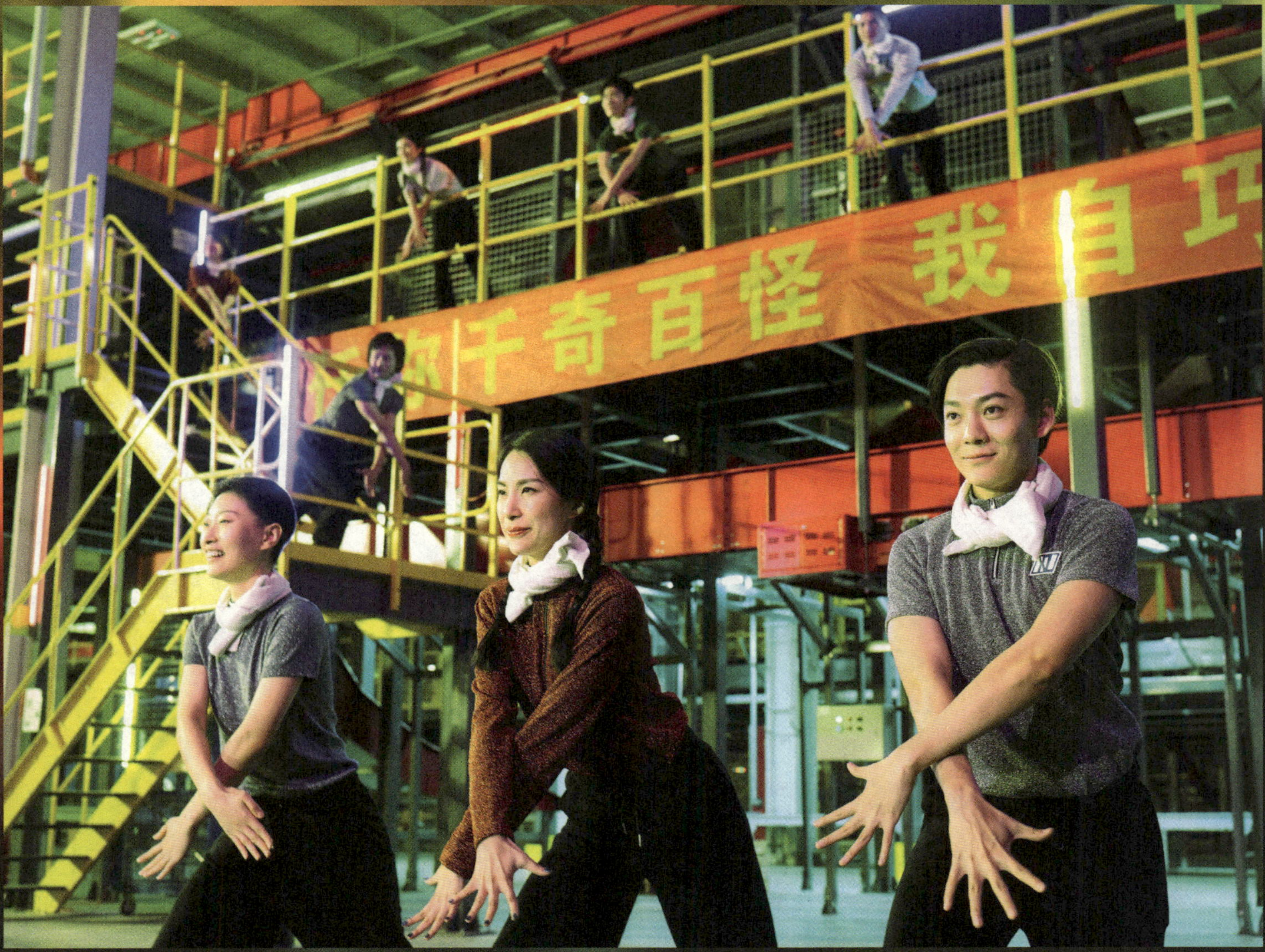

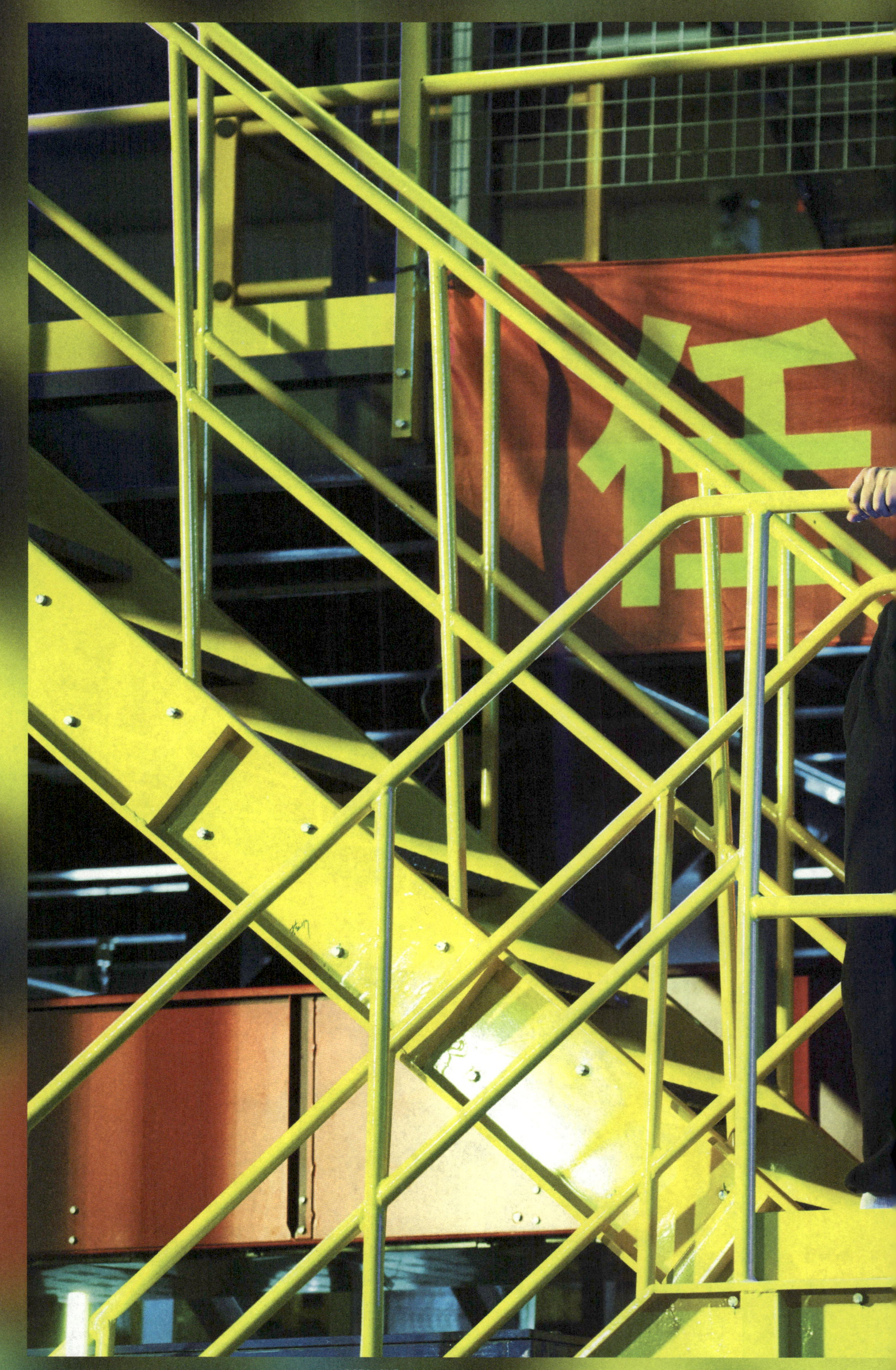

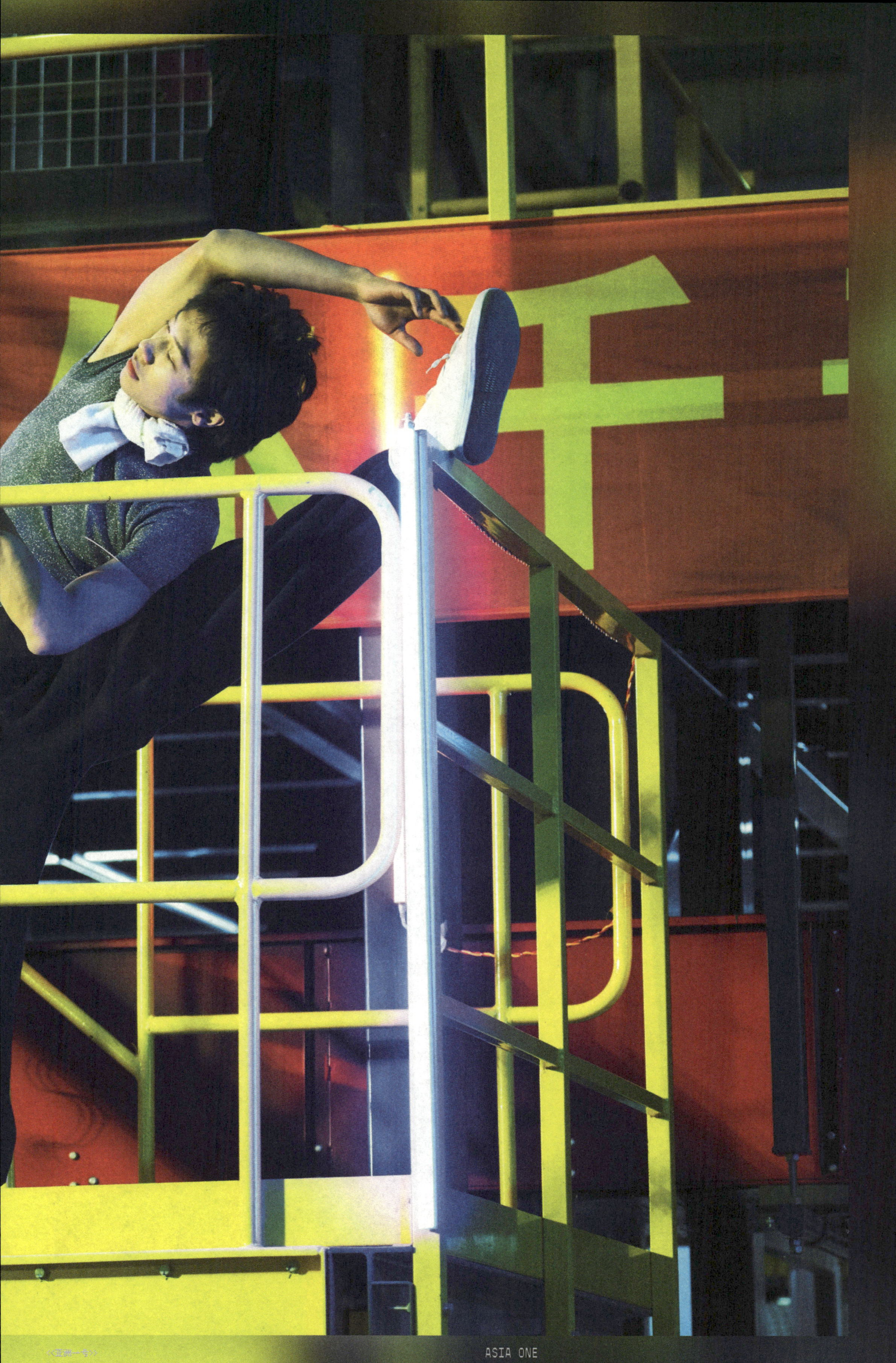

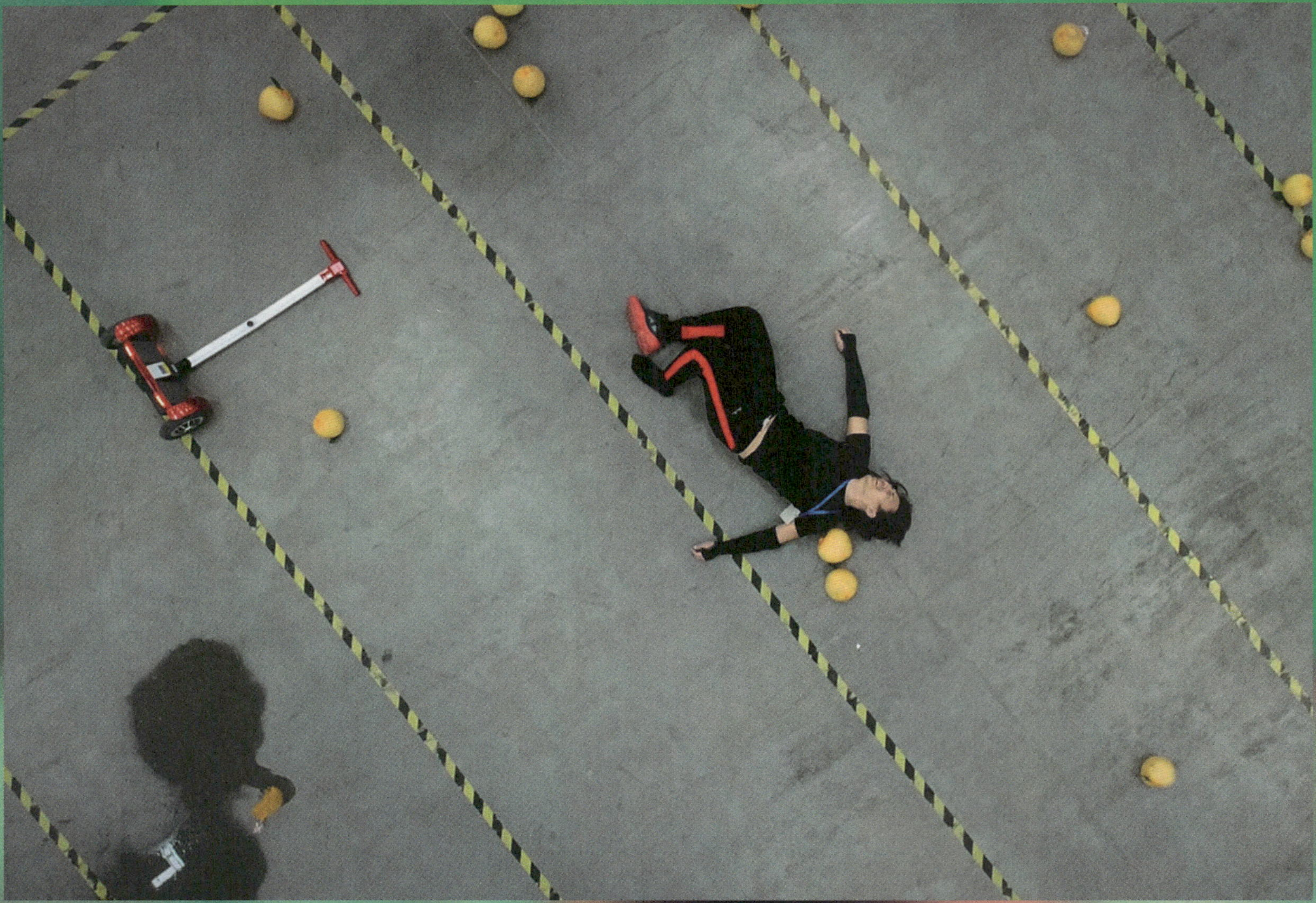

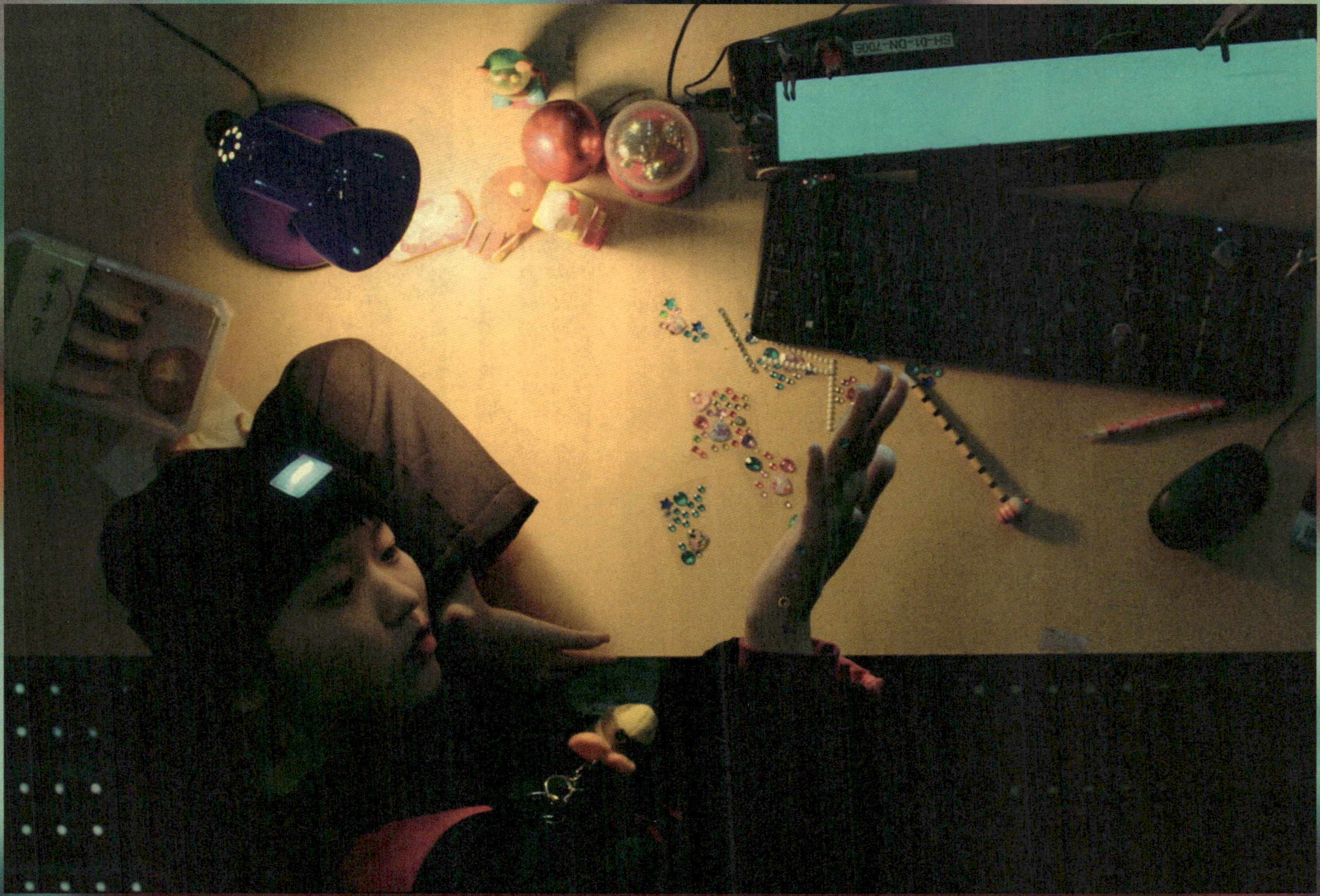

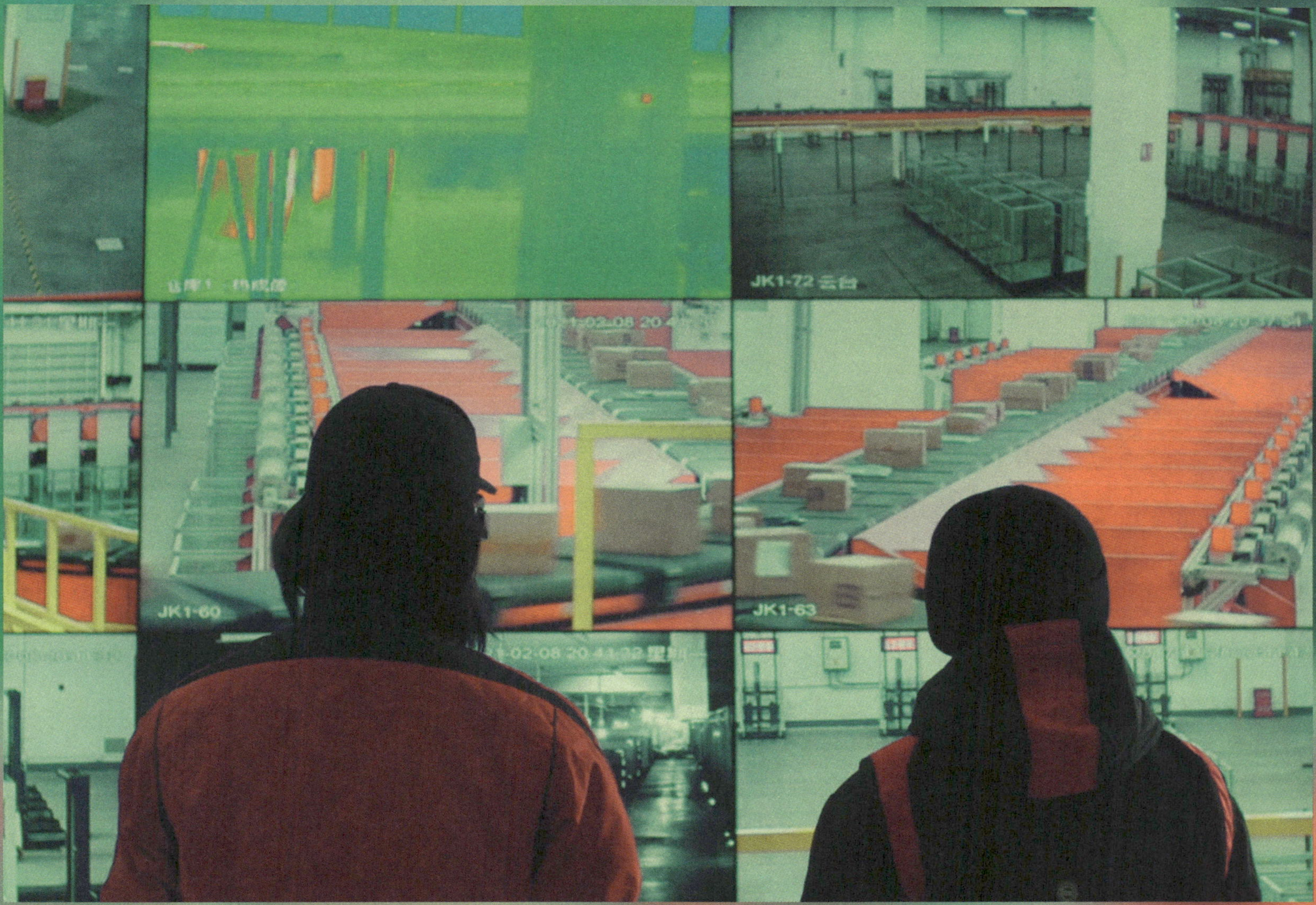

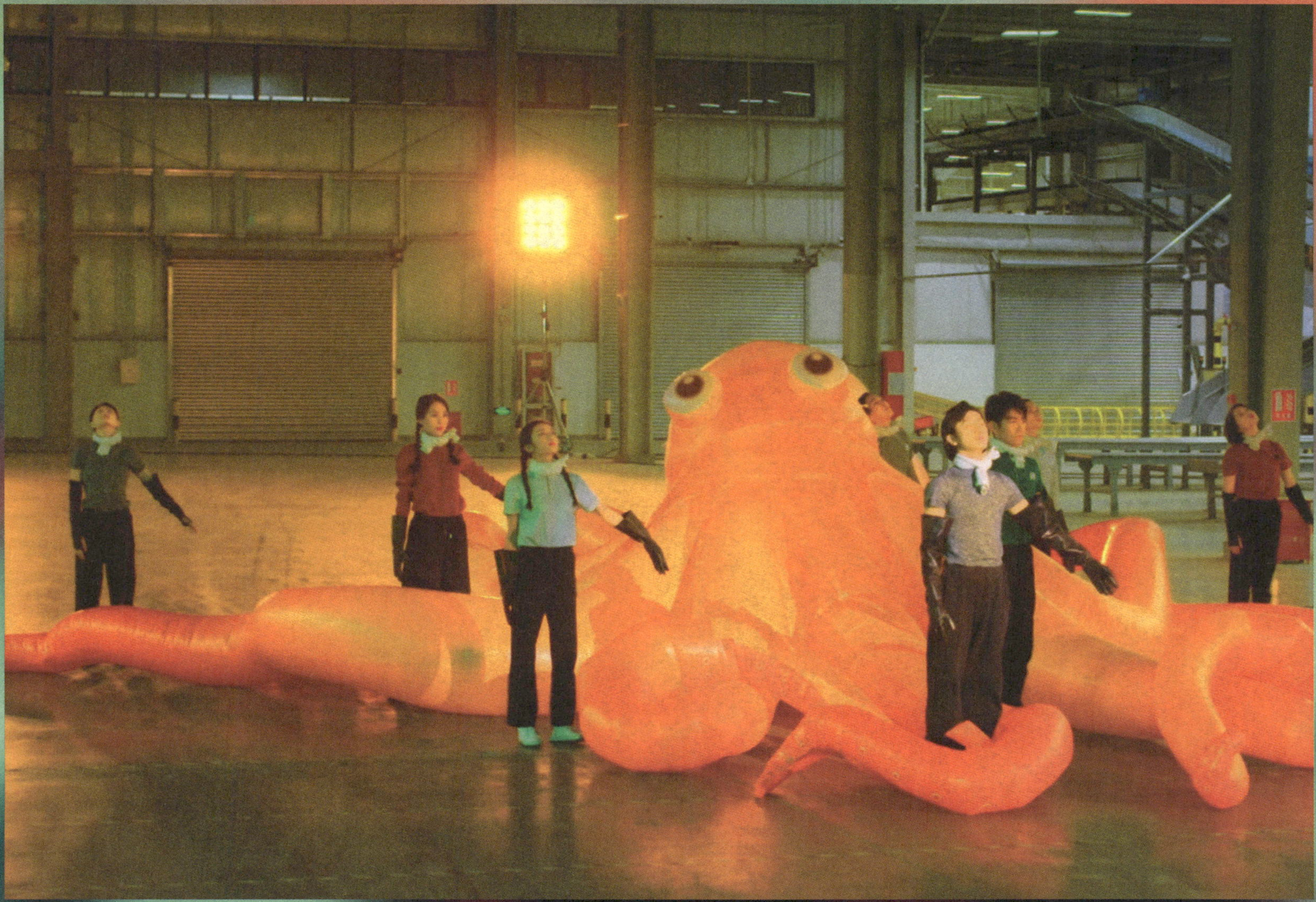

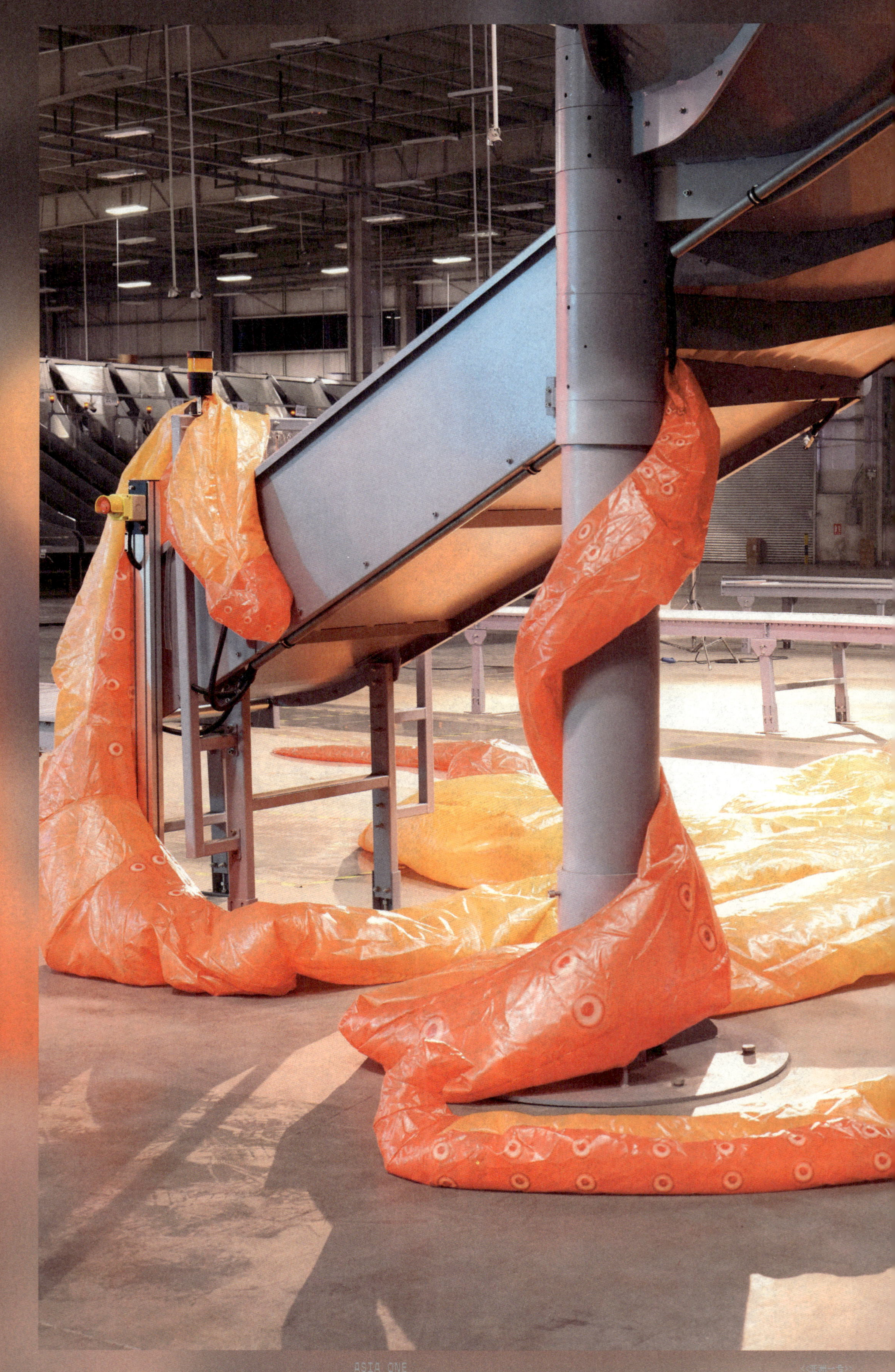

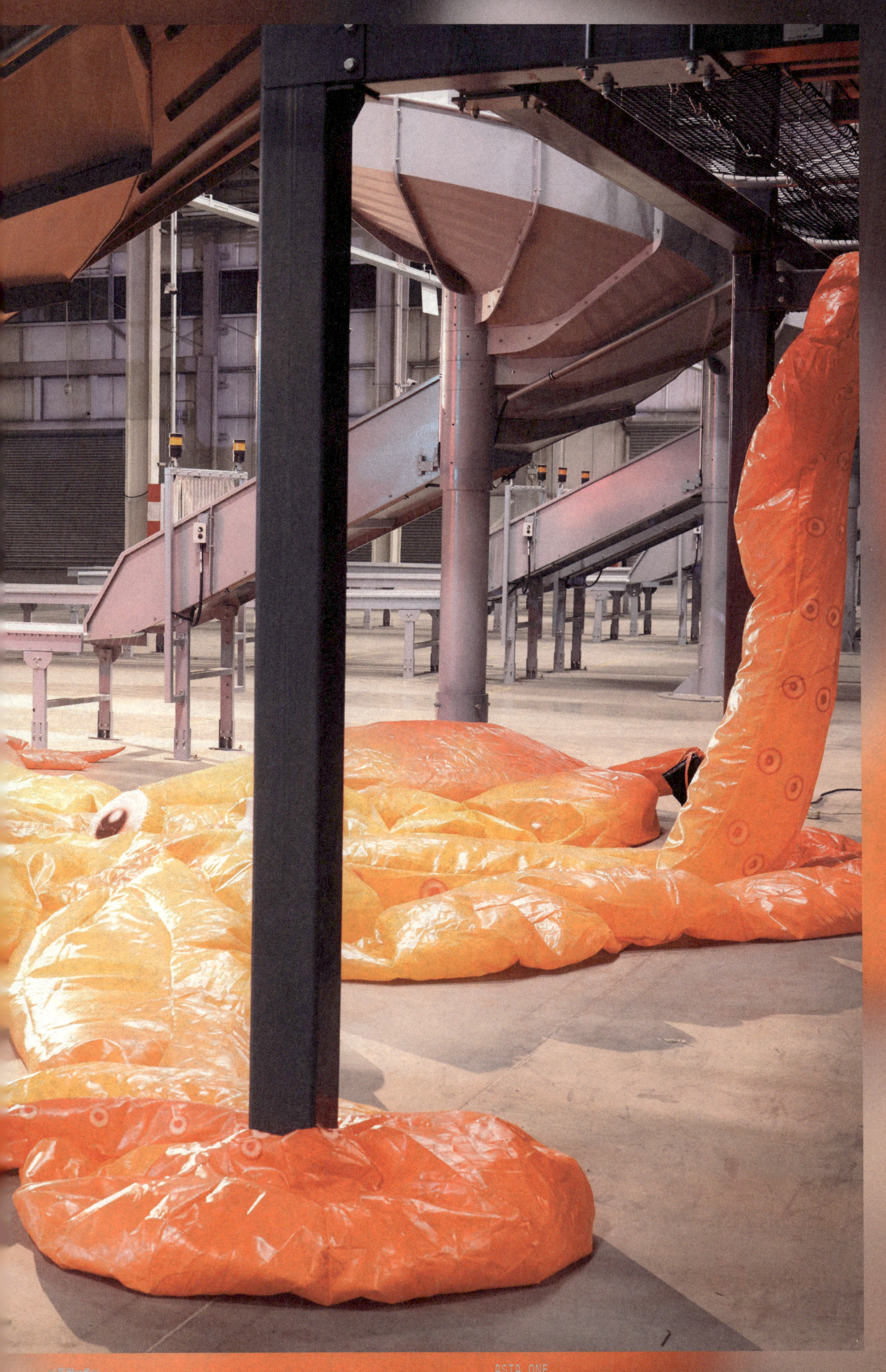

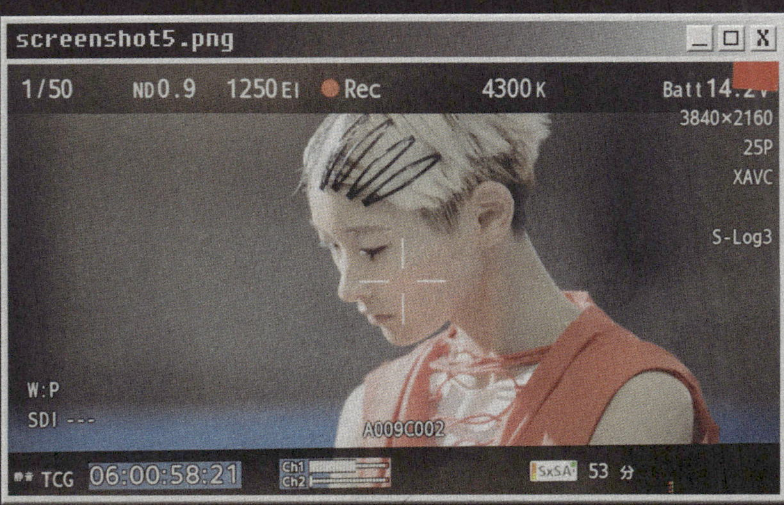

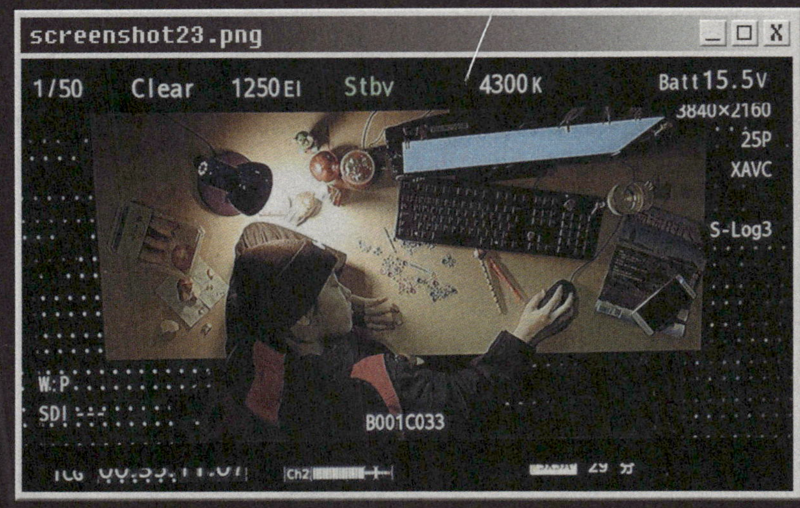

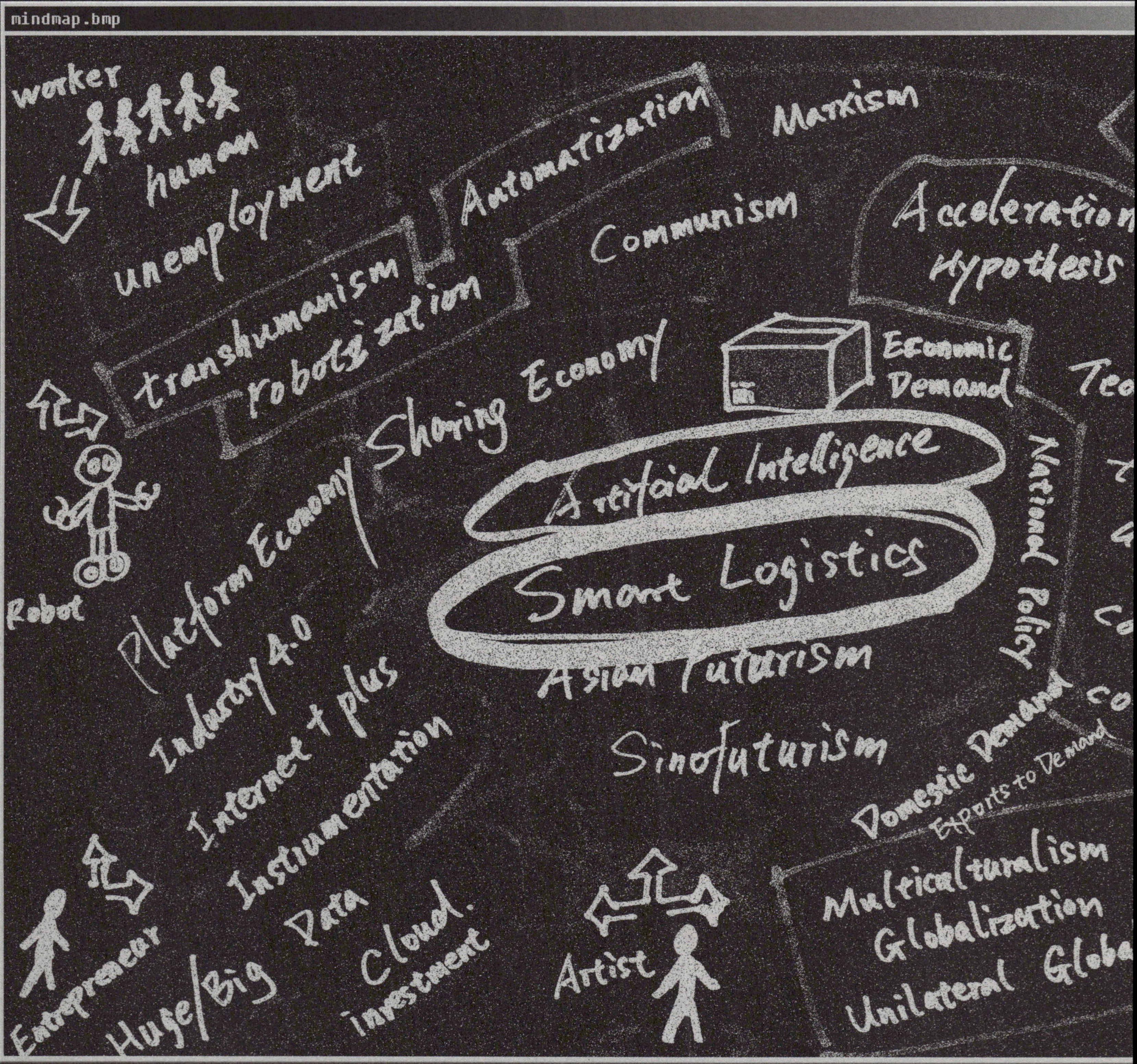

mindmap.bmp

worker
human
unemployment
Automatization
Marxism
Communism
Acceleration Hypothesis
transhumanism
robotization
Sharing Economy
Economic Demand
Robot
Platform Economy
Artifcial Intelligence
Smart Logistics
National Policy
Industry 4.0
Internet + plus
Asian Futurism
Sinofuturism
Instiumentation
Domestic Demand
Exports to Demand
Multiculturalism
Globalization
Unilateral Globa
Entrepreneur
Huge/Big Data
Cloud. investment
Artist

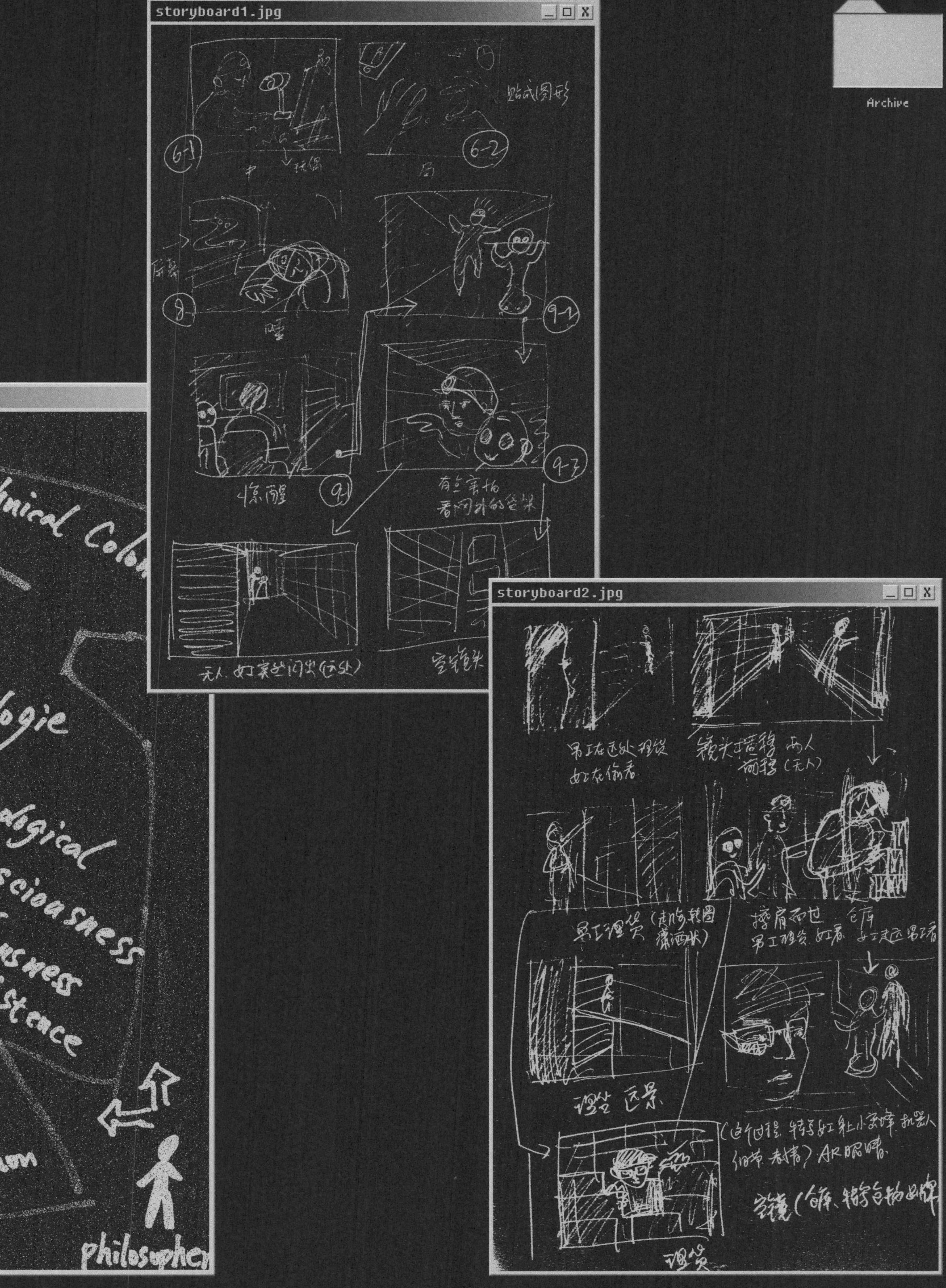

storyboard1.jpg
Archive
惊醒
storyboard2.jpg
理货 远景
philosopher

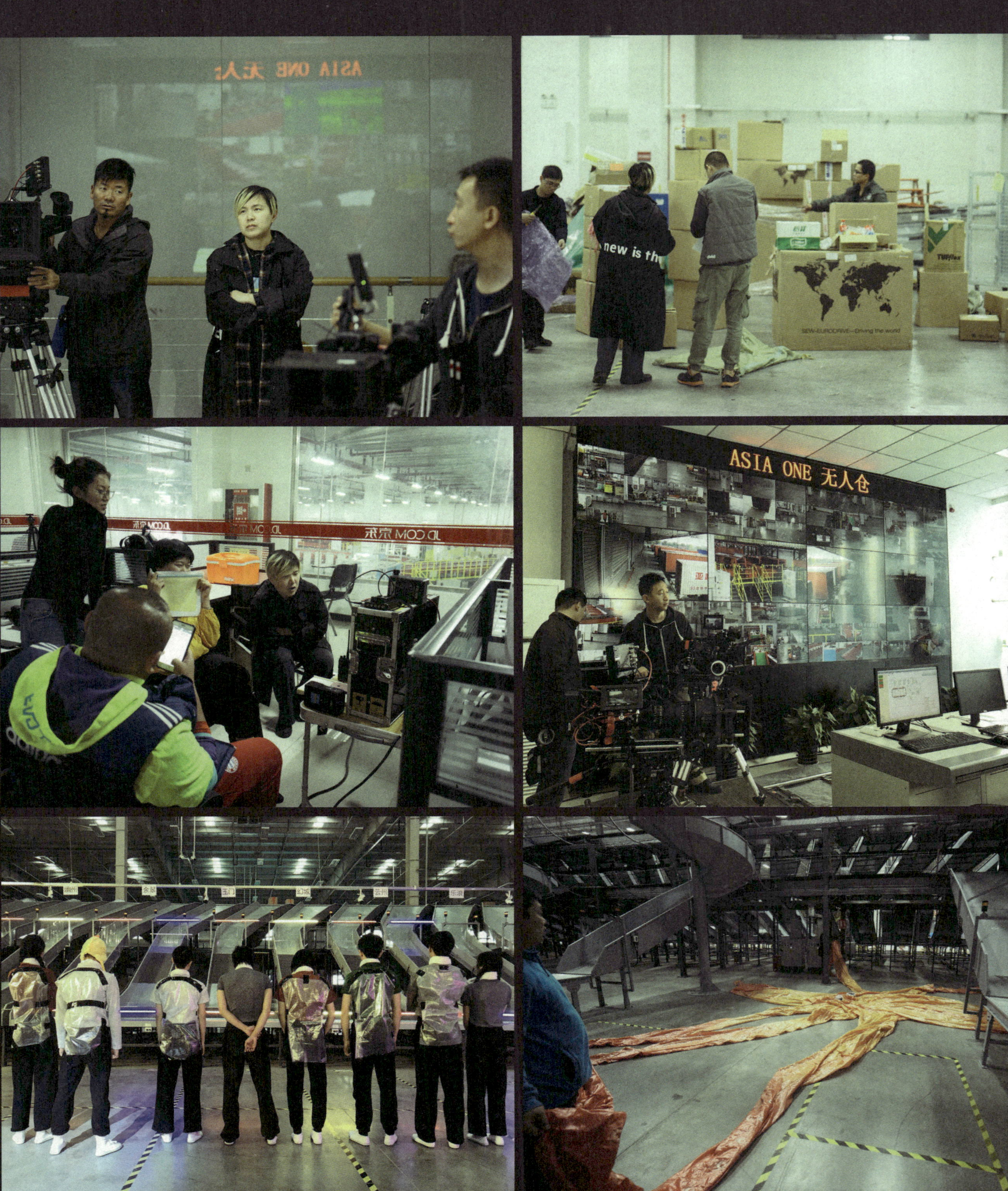
ASIA ONE 无人仓
new is th

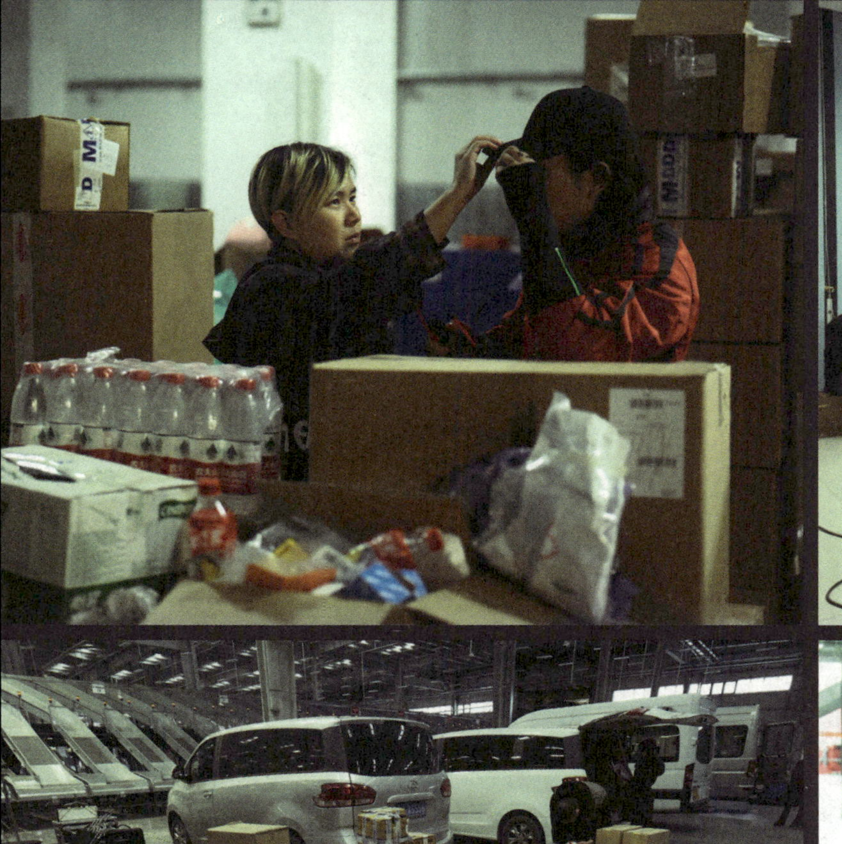
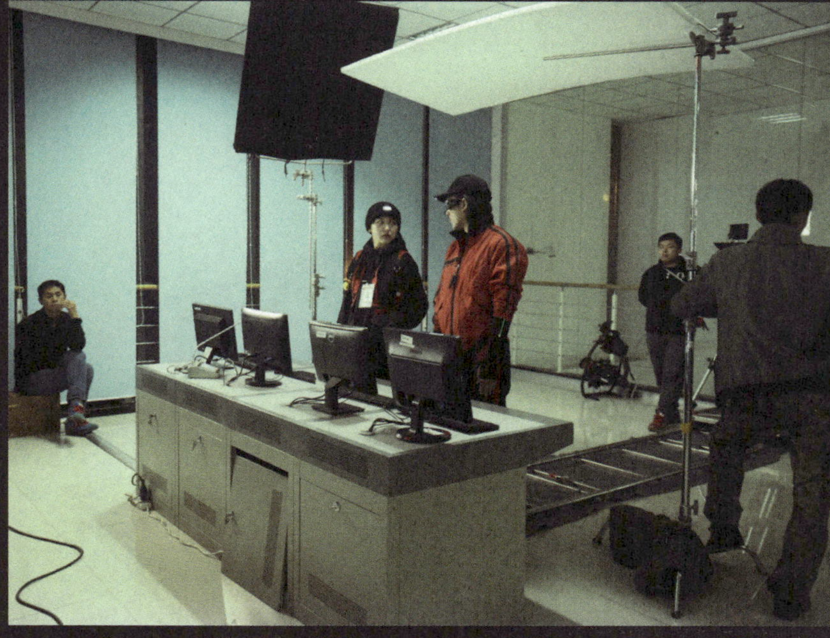
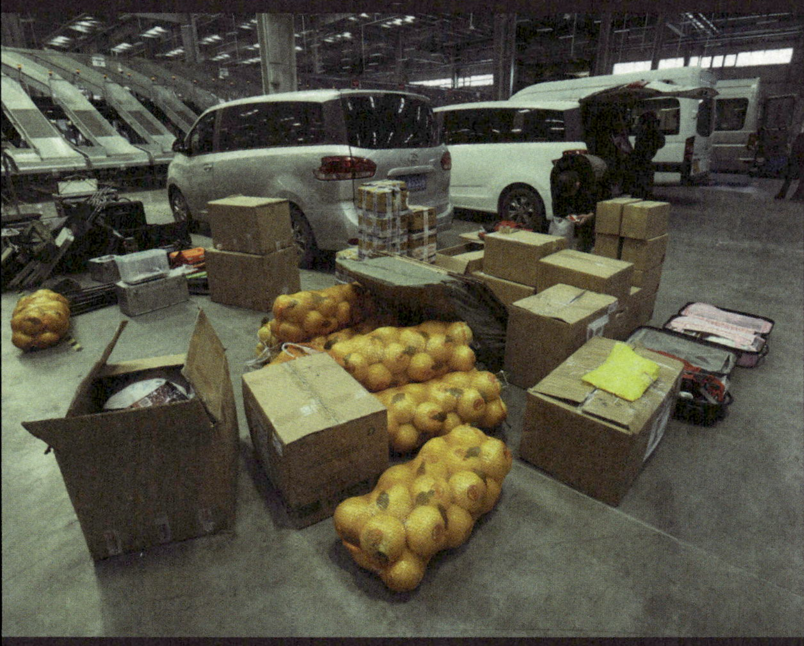
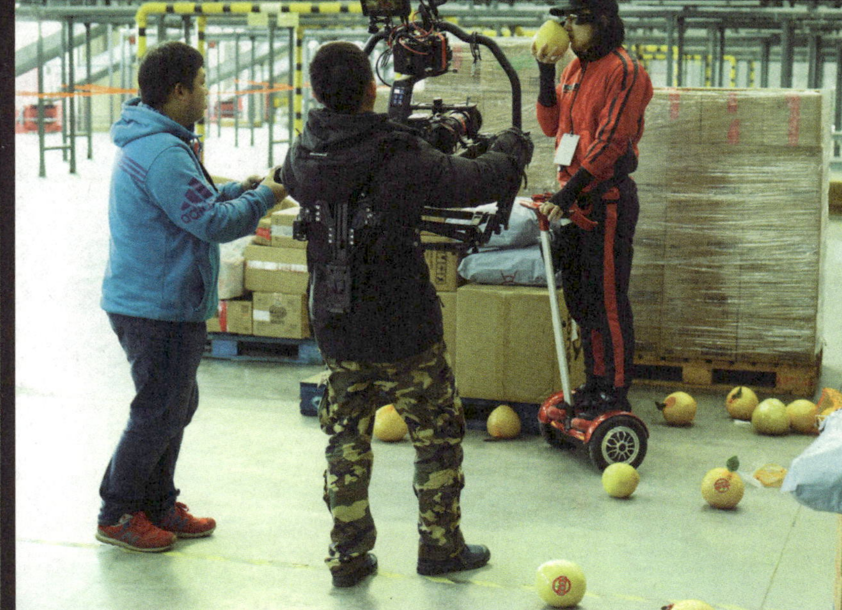
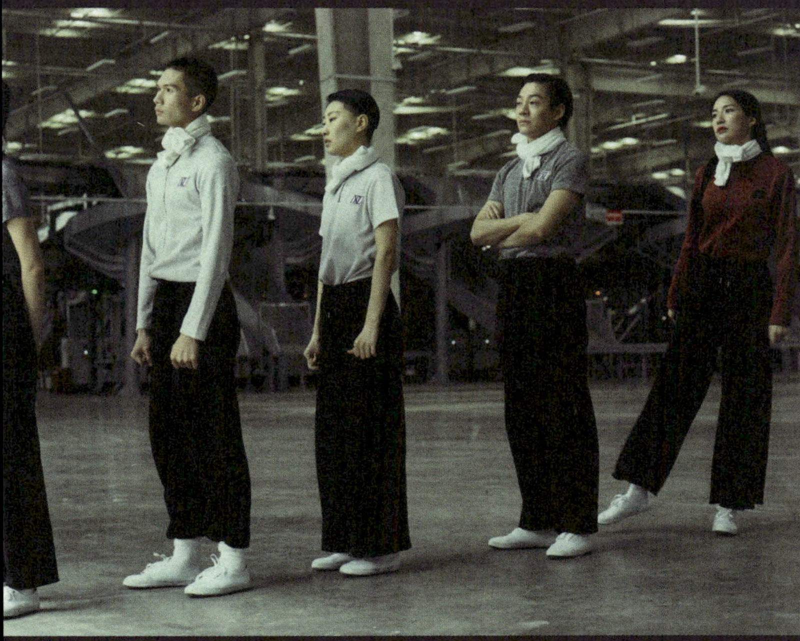
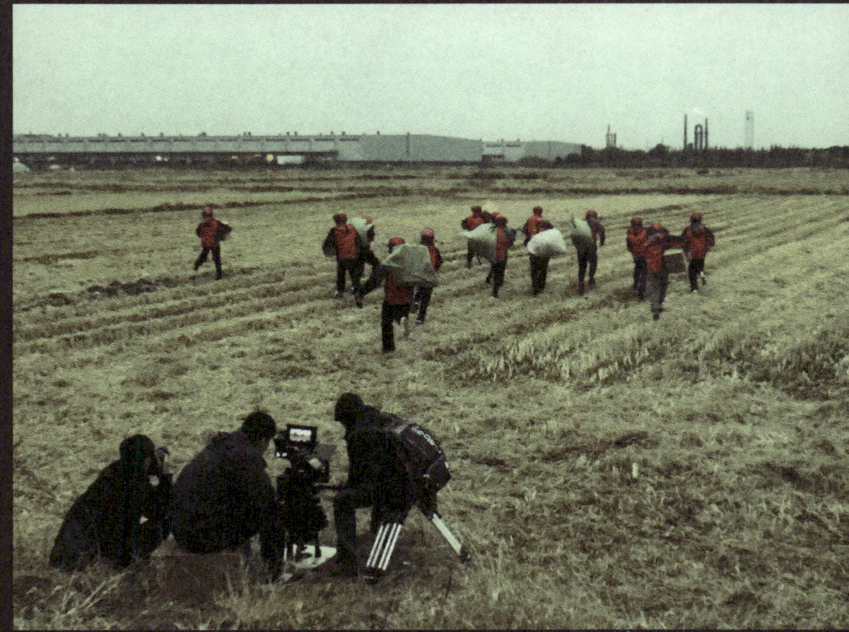

Production Stills

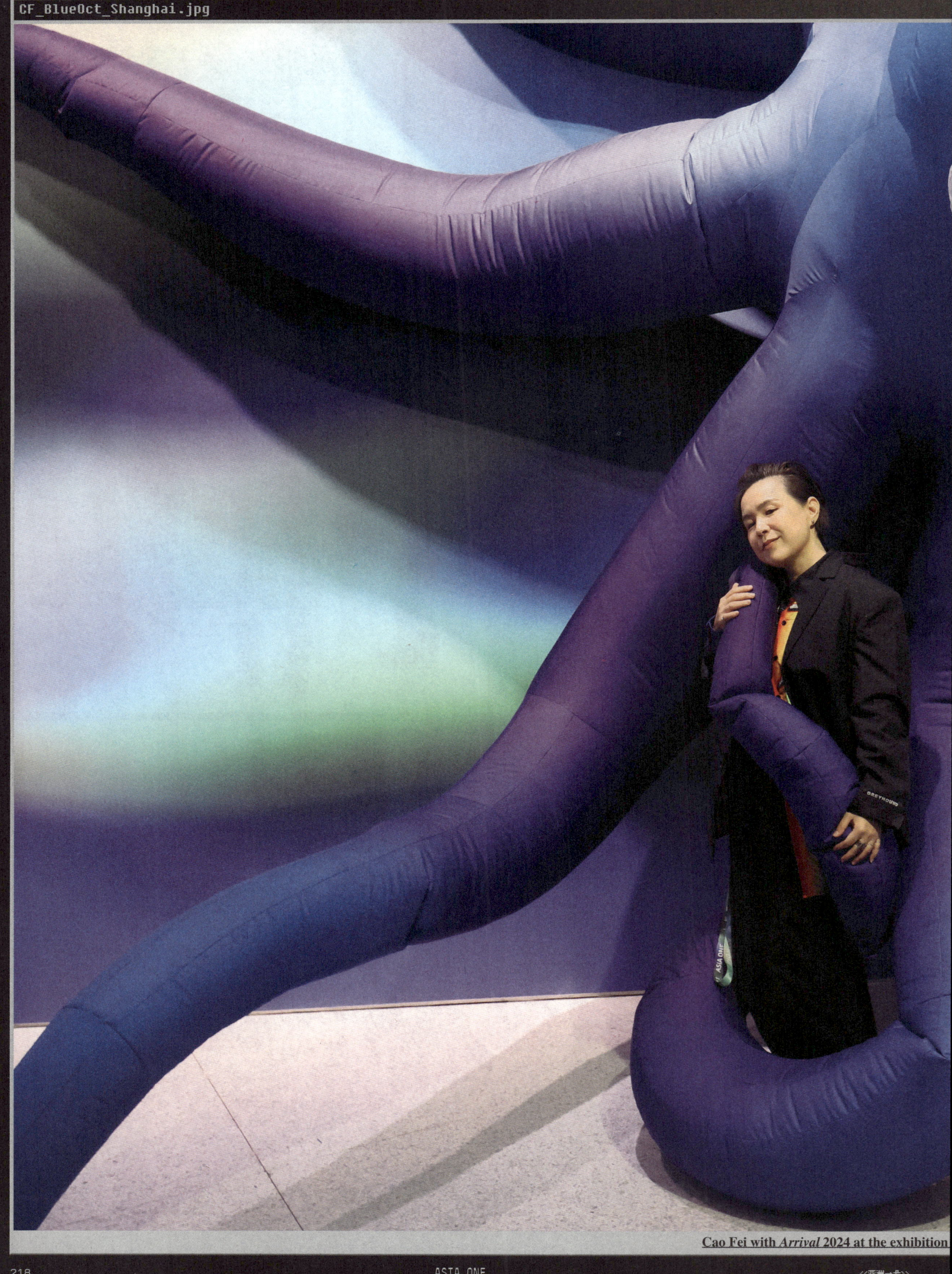

Cao Fei with *Arrival* 2024 at the exhibition

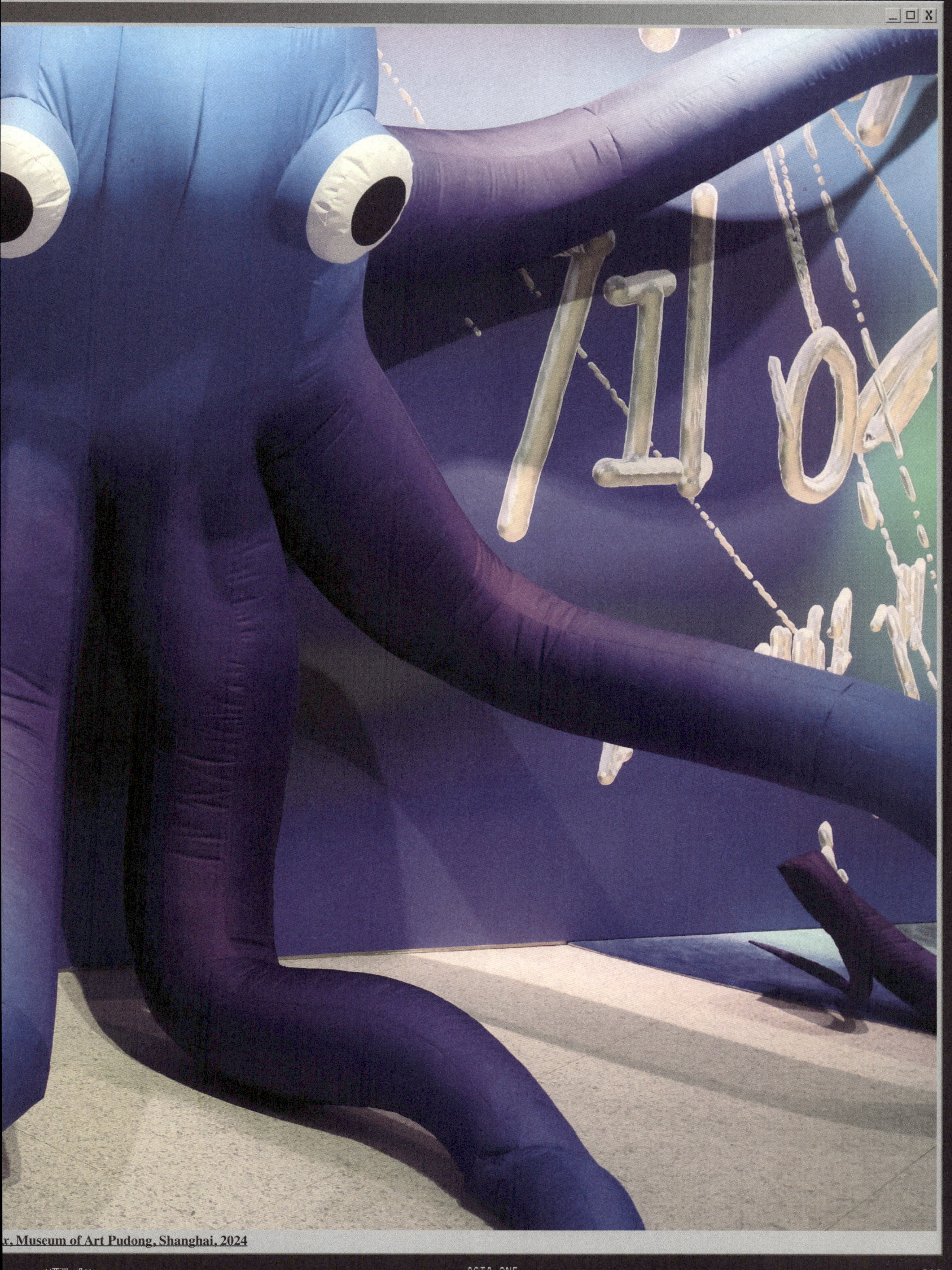

x, Museum of Art Pudong, Shanghai, 2024

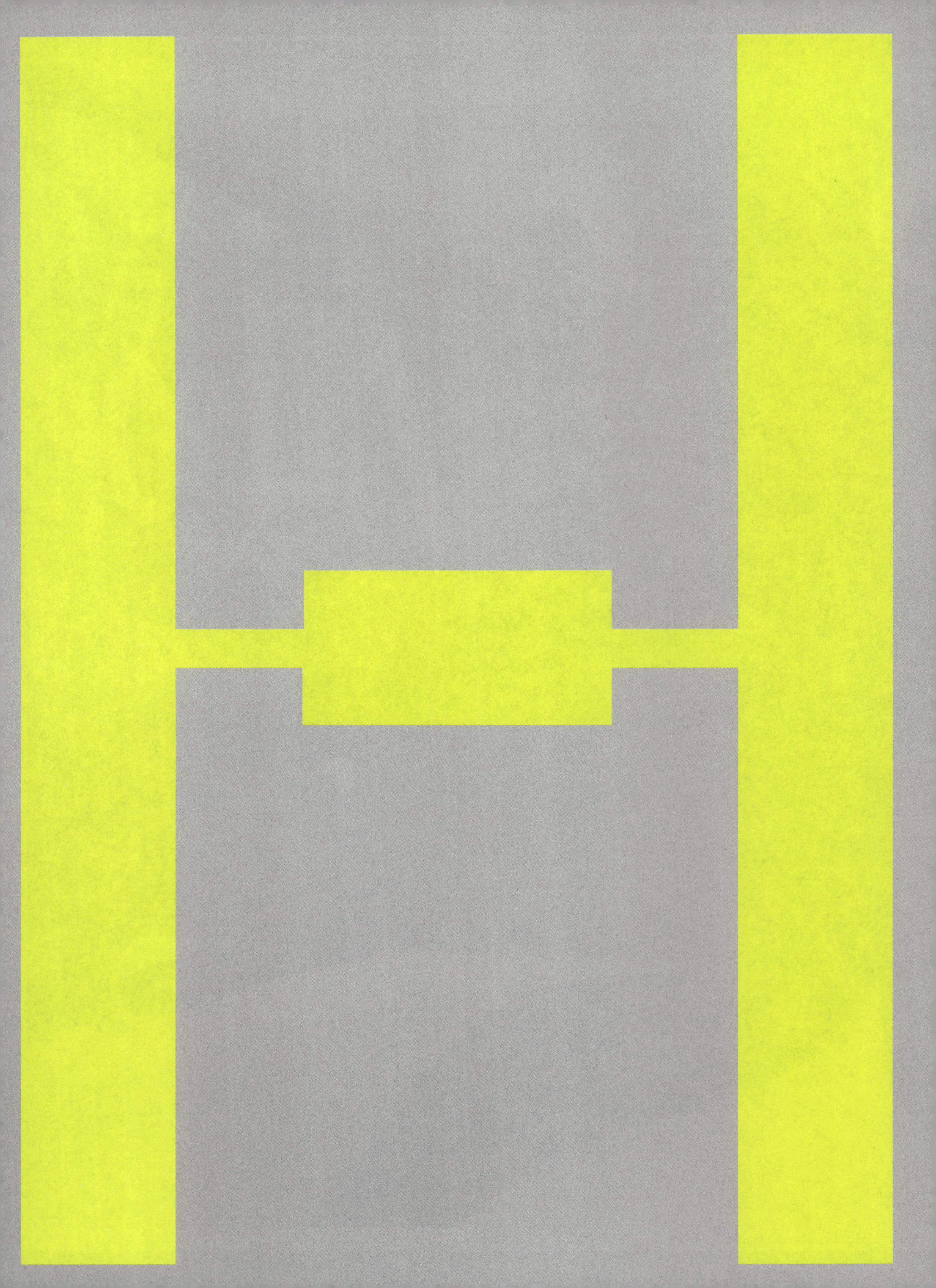

1:1

1:1

2018

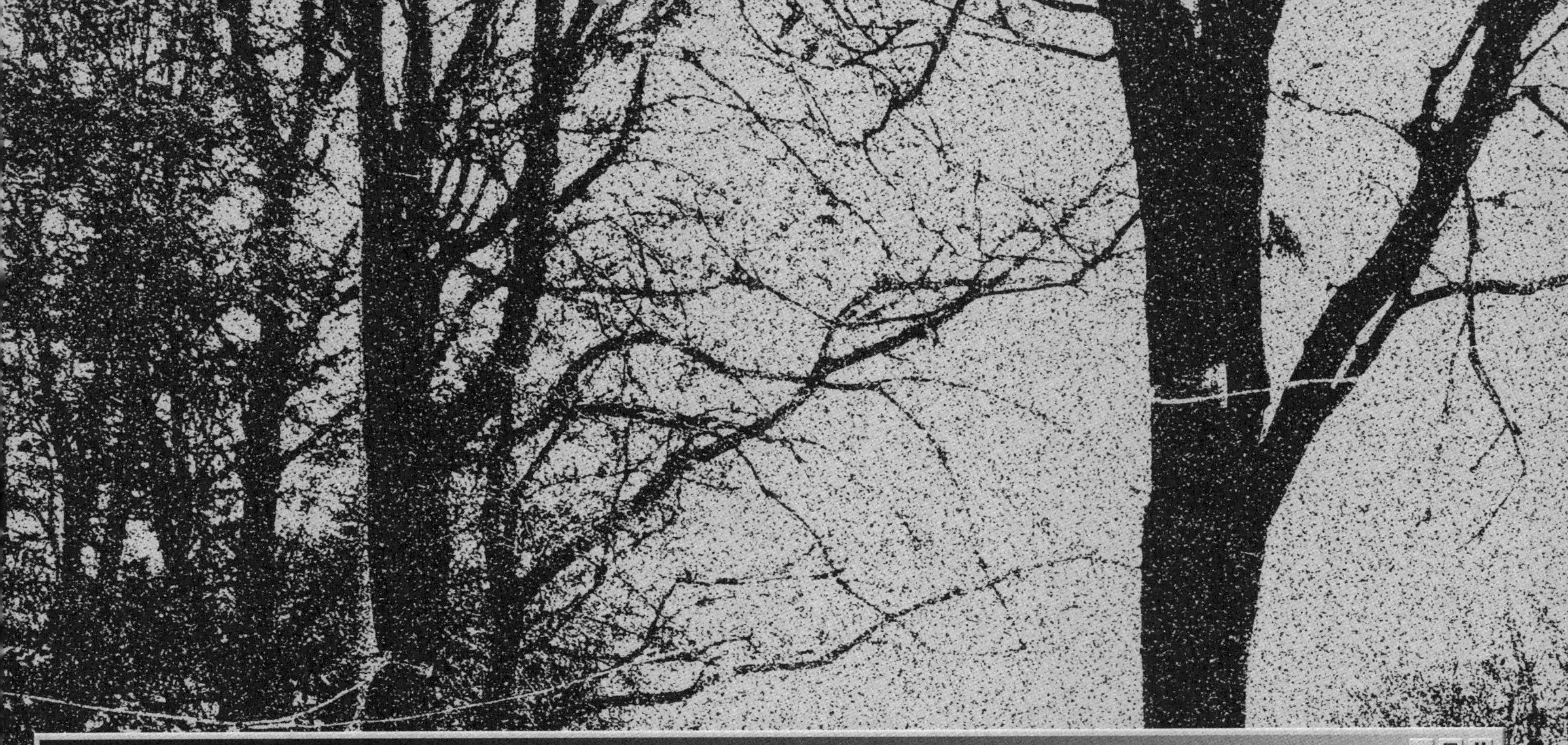

H: 11:11

11:11 shows that behind the 'magic' of big e-commerce, front-line grunt work remains and new forms of precarity prevail. The work refers to 11 November (aka 'Double 11'), the world's largest online shopping day, and records the relentless operations at the Jingdong Logistic company (JD.com) and its distribution centres scattered throughout Beijing. Cao Fei follows and interviews delivery workers who transport all manner of goods to every corner of Beijing, from high-rise skyscrapers to old houses in the courtyards of the inner city that can only be accessed by motorised tricycles. This journey highlights the stark contrast between the working conditions endured by the employees and the frantic consumerism driving demand for their services.

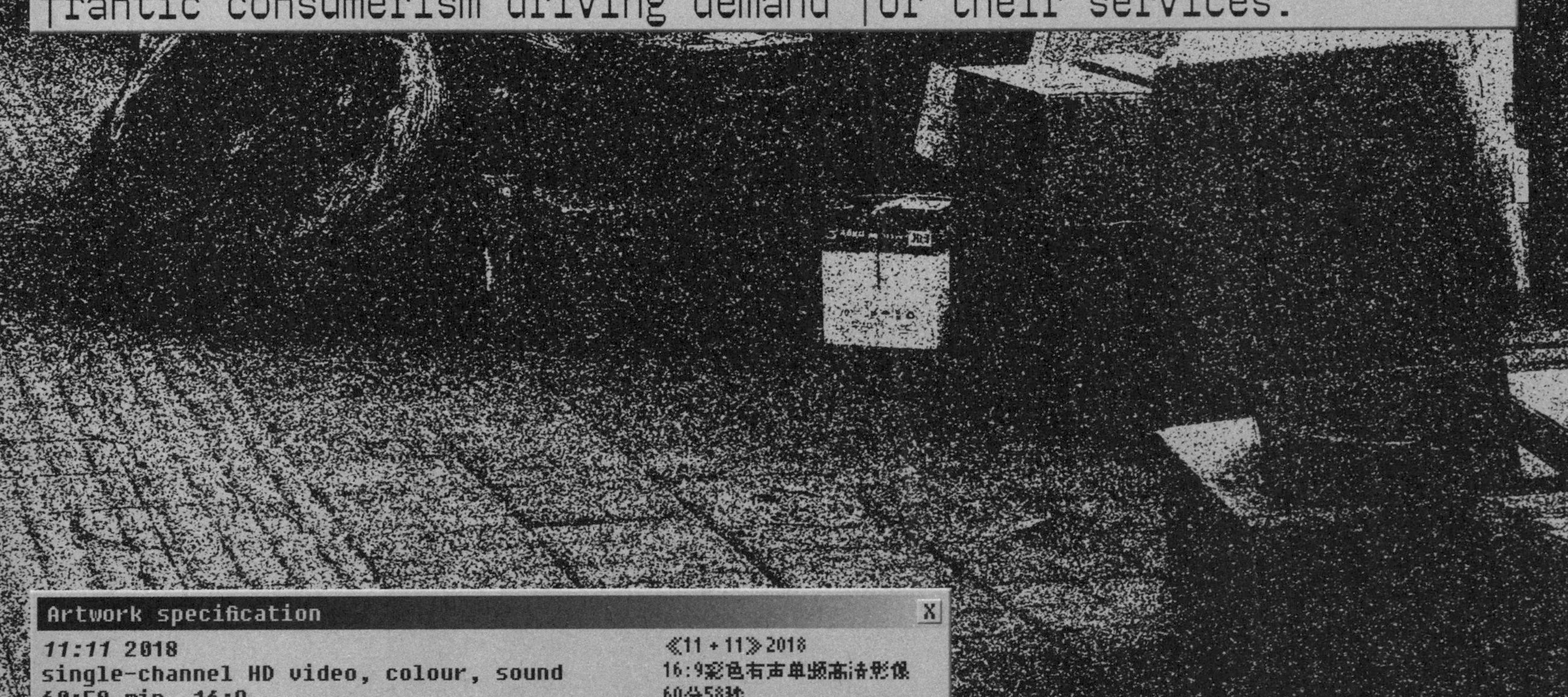

Artwork specification

11:11 2018
single-channel HD video, colour, sound
60:58 min, 16:9

《11・11》2018
16:9彩色有声单频高清影像
60分58秒

11:11

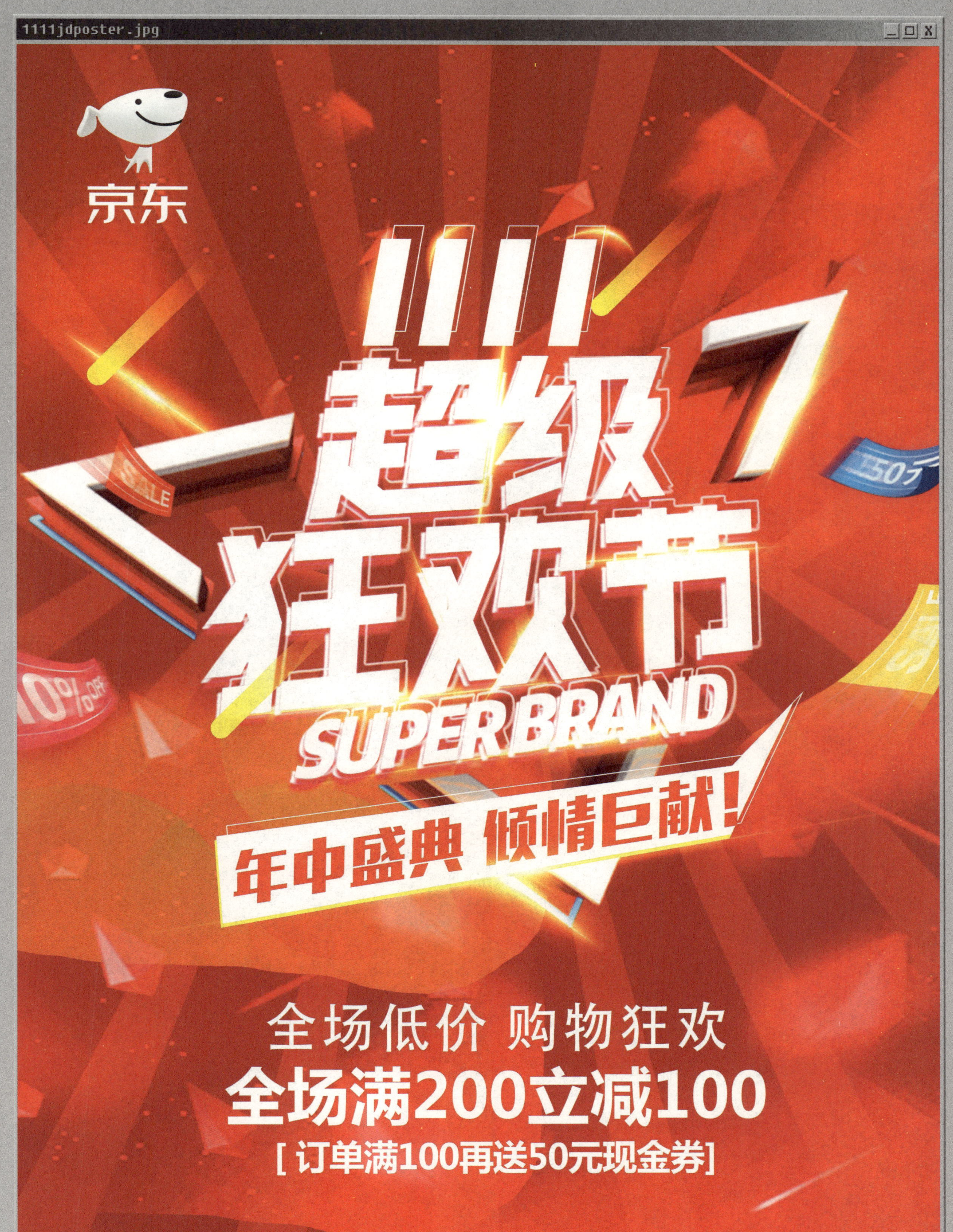

1111jdposter.jpg
京东
1111
超级
狂欢节
SUPER BRAND
年中盛典 倾情巨献!
全场低价 购物狂欢
全场满200立减100
[订单满100再送50元现金券]

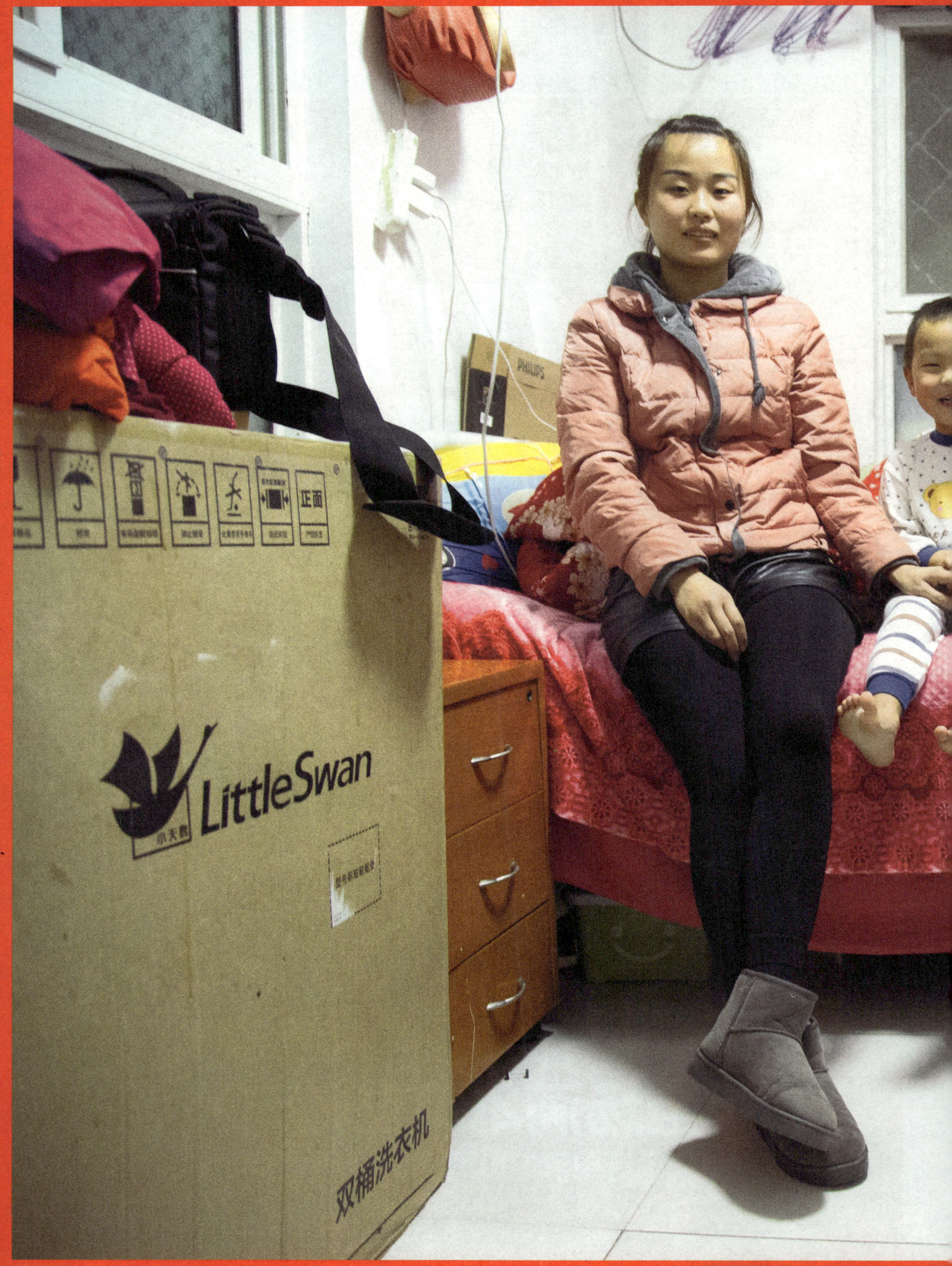
正面
LittleSwan
双桶洗衣机

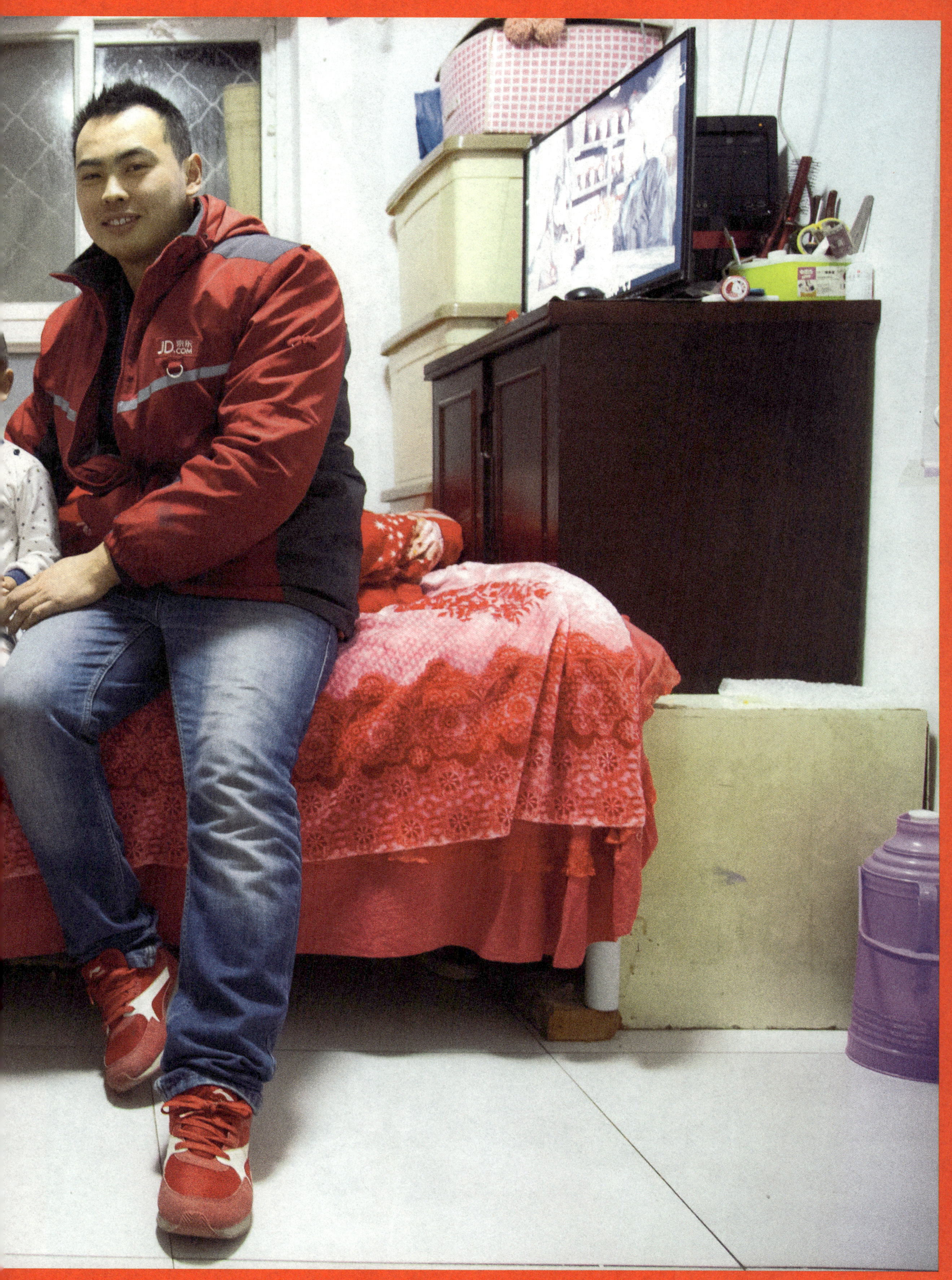

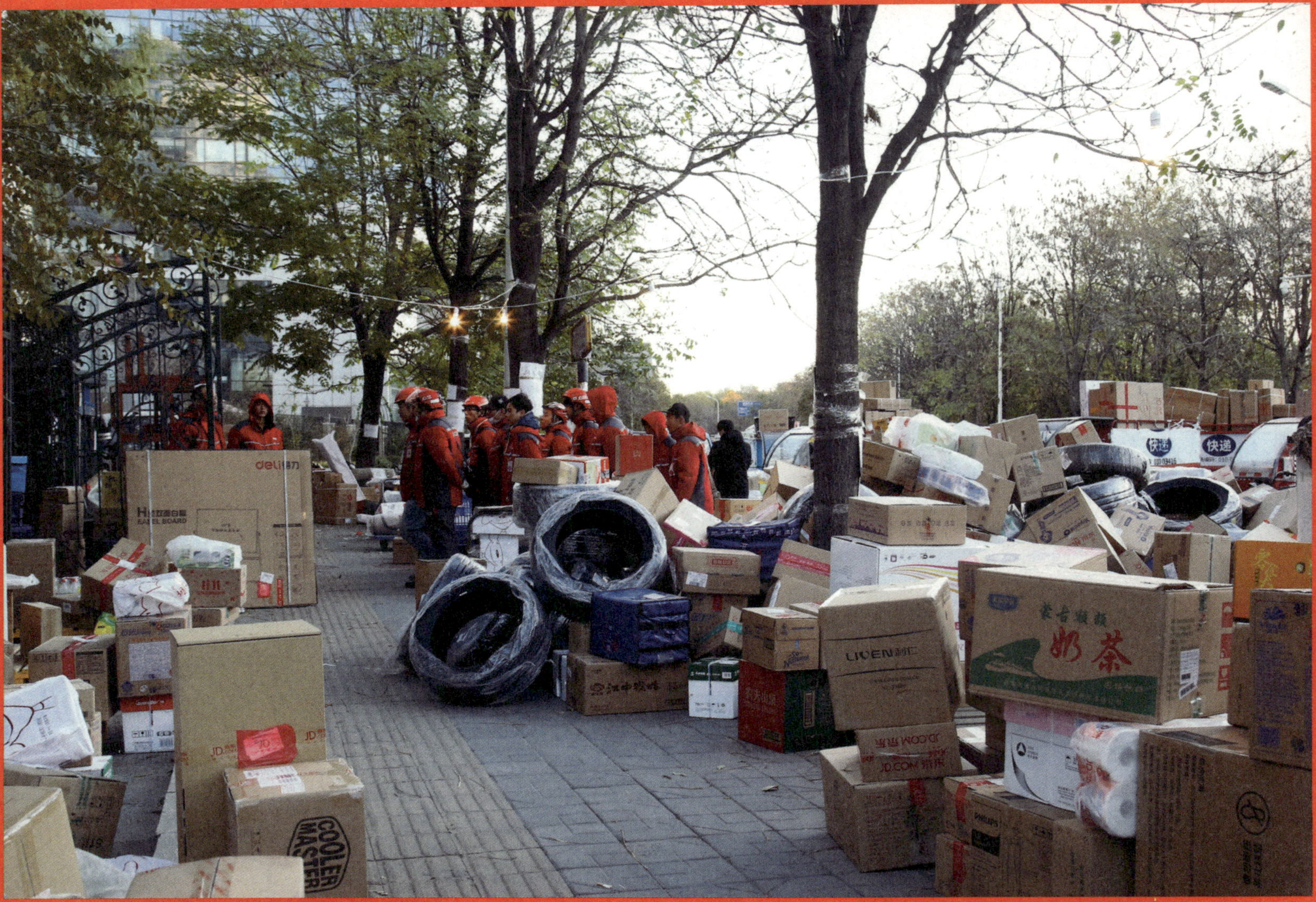
deli
奶茶
COOLER MASTER
快递

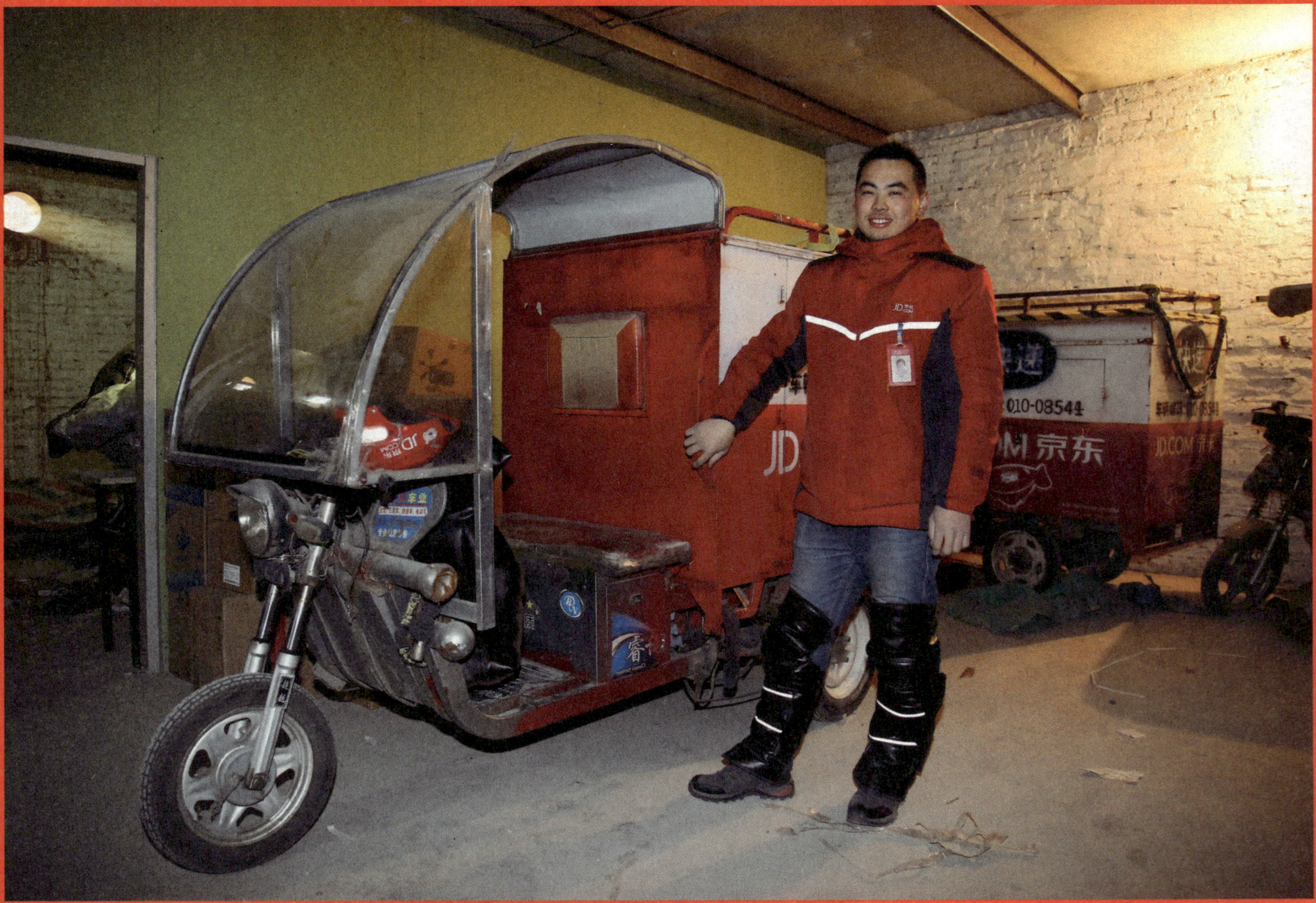
JD
010-08544
京东

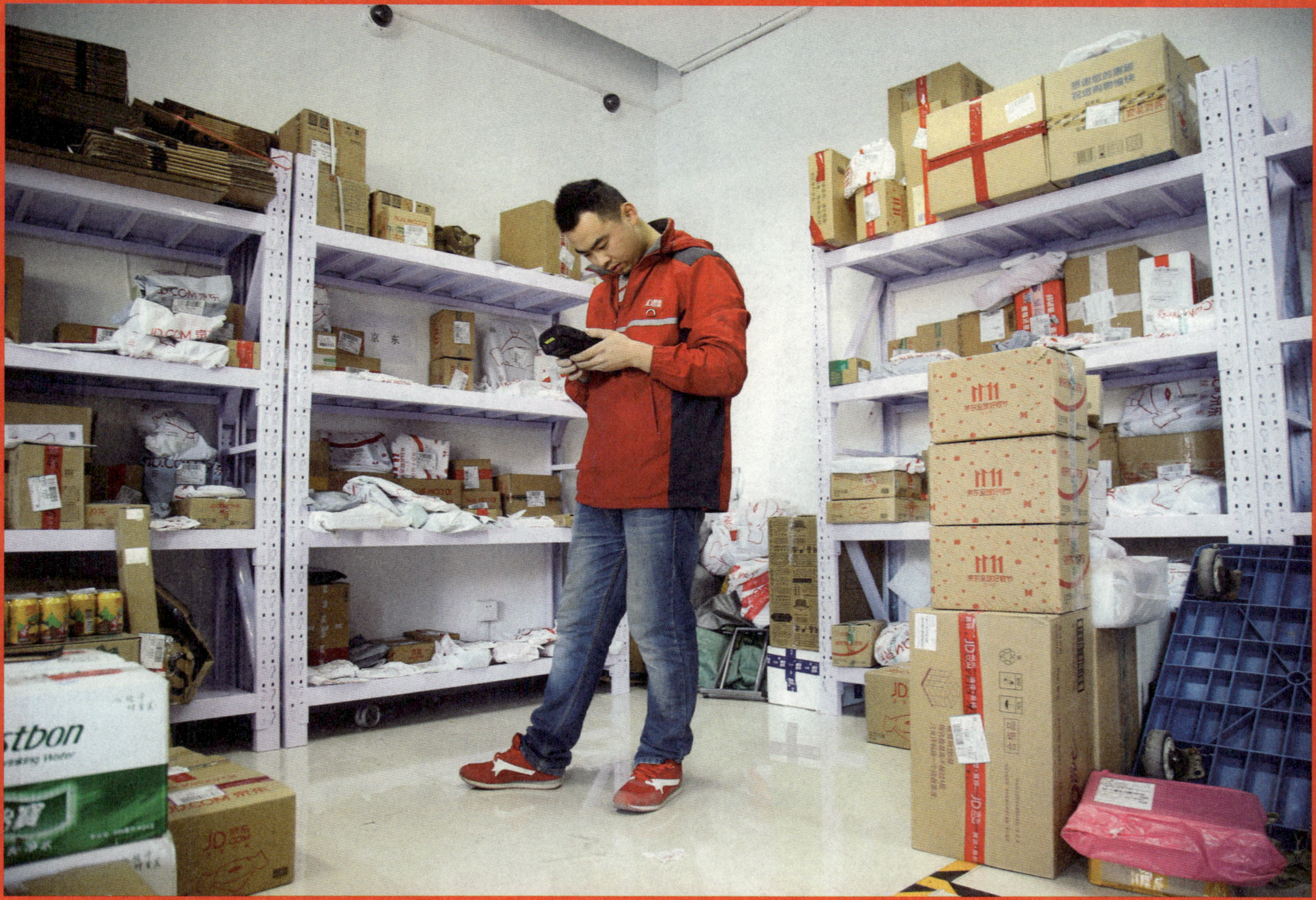

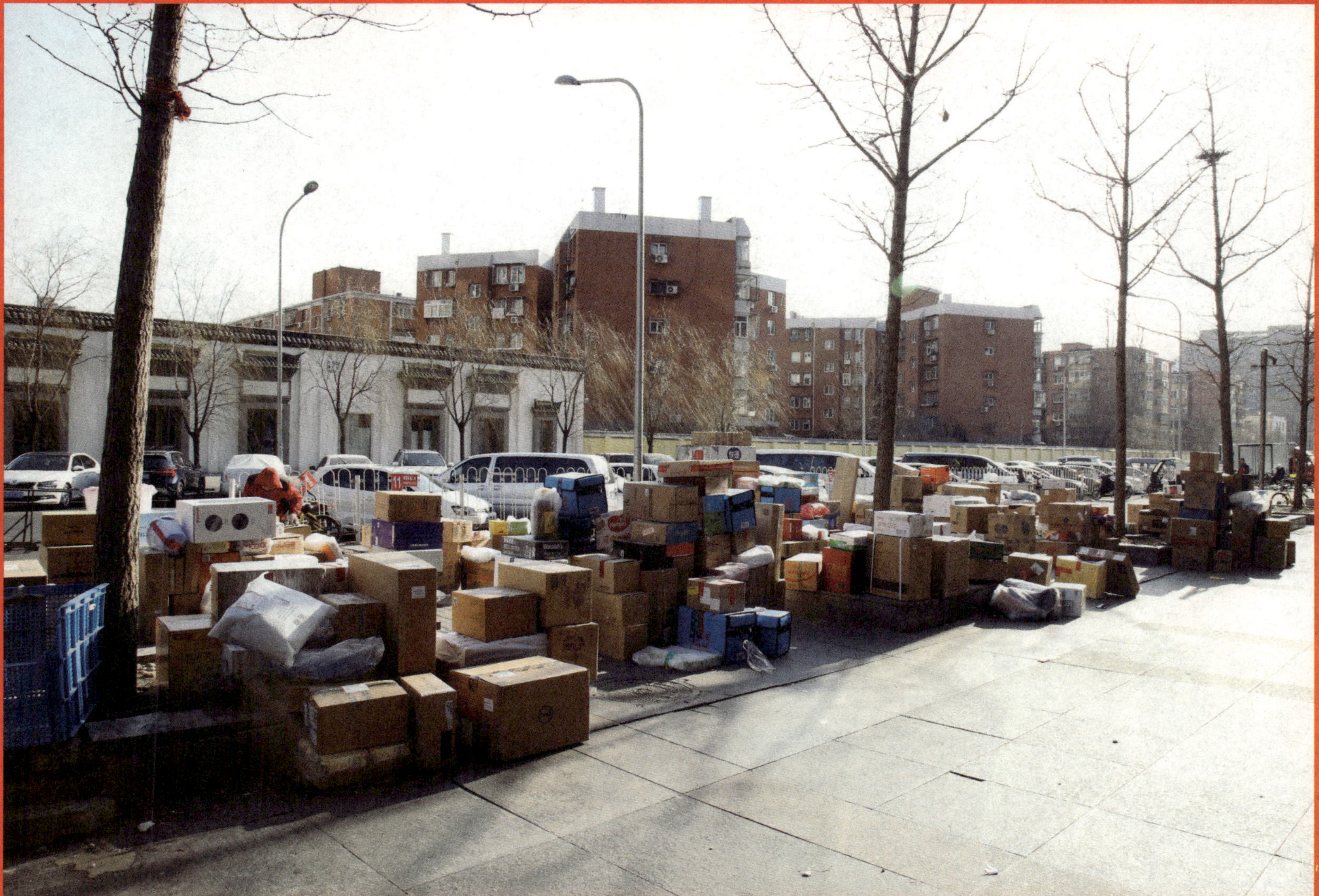

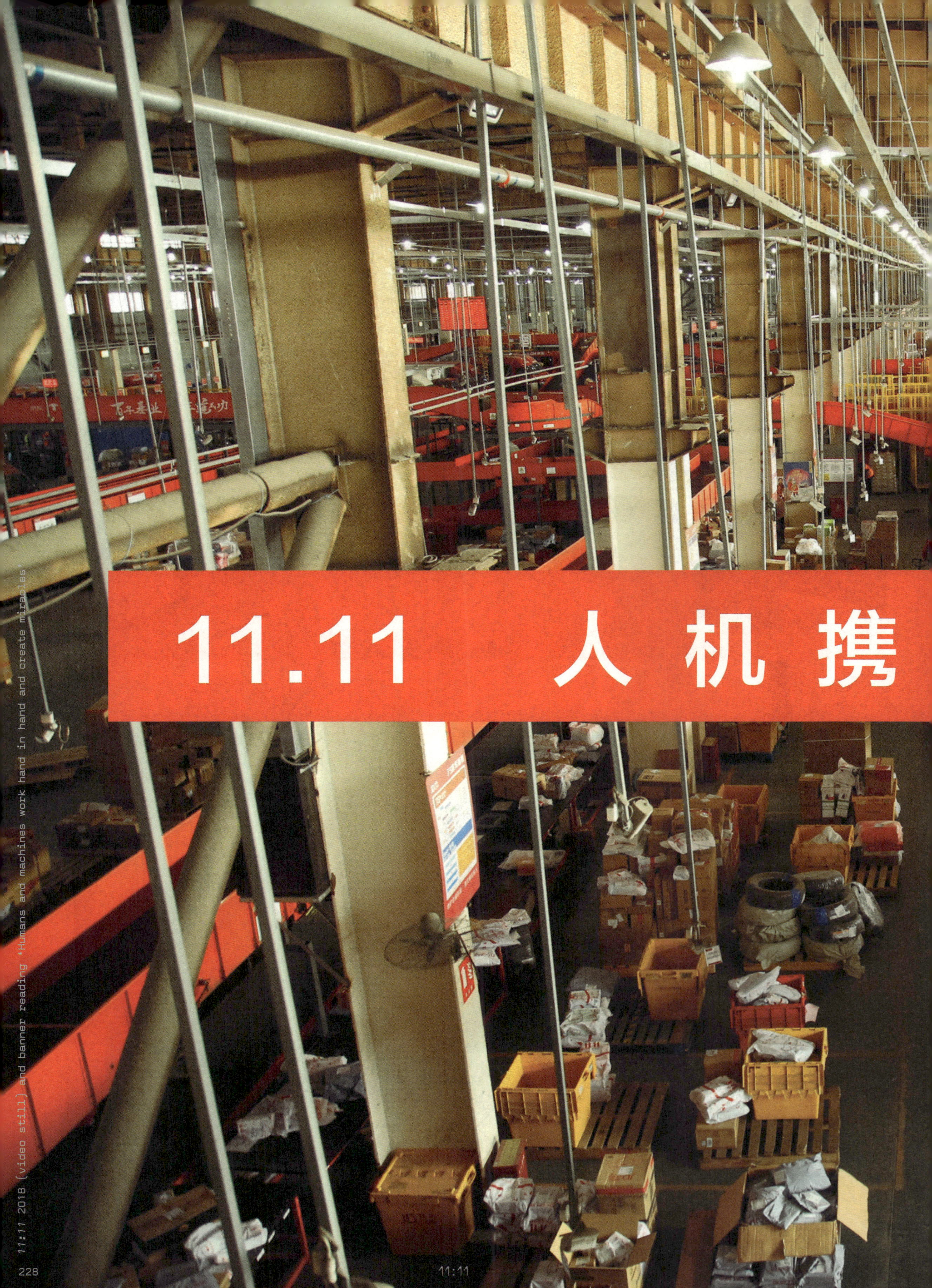

11:11 2018 (video still) and banner reading 'Humans and machines work hand in hand and create miracles'

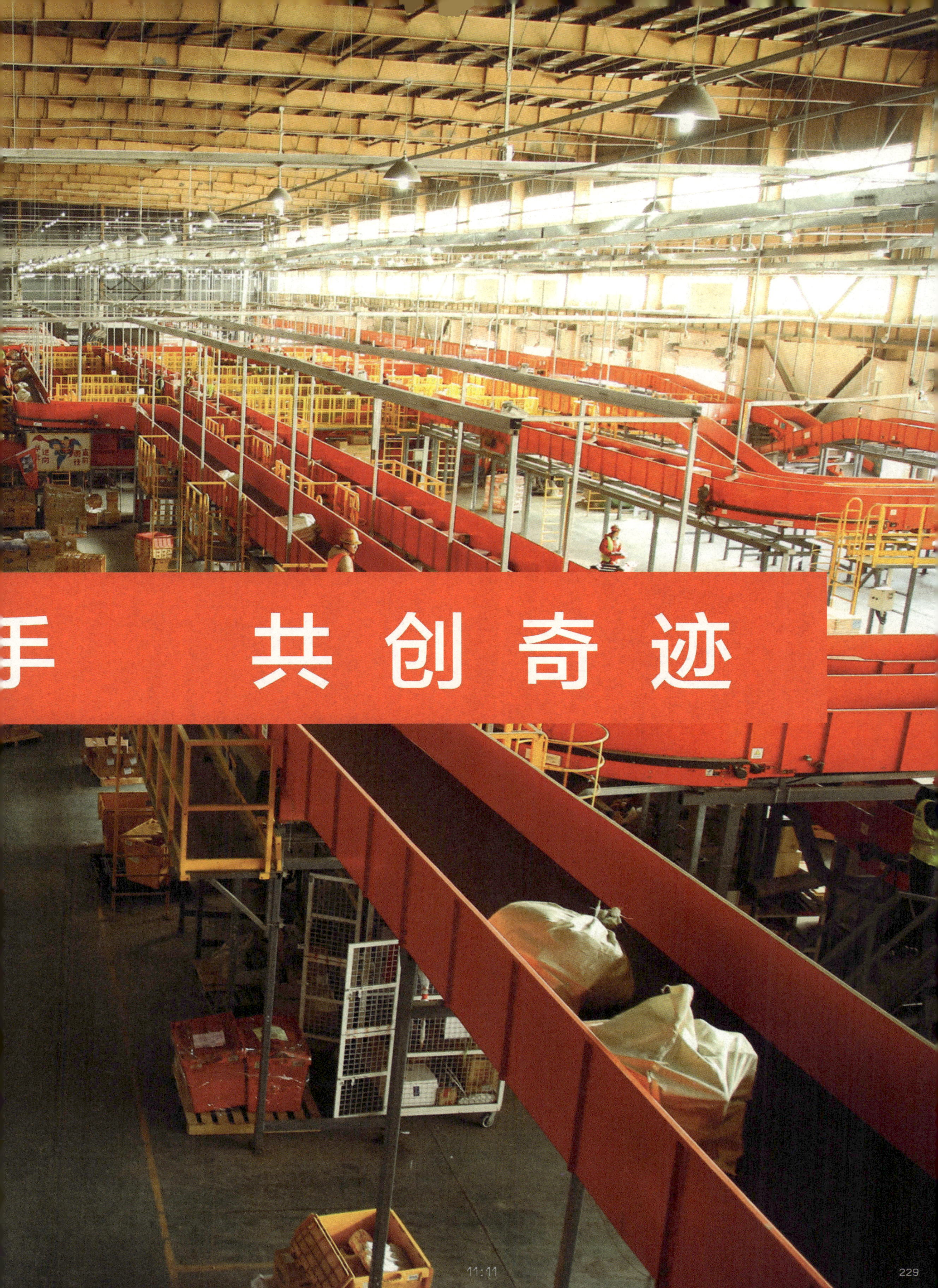
手　　共创奇迹

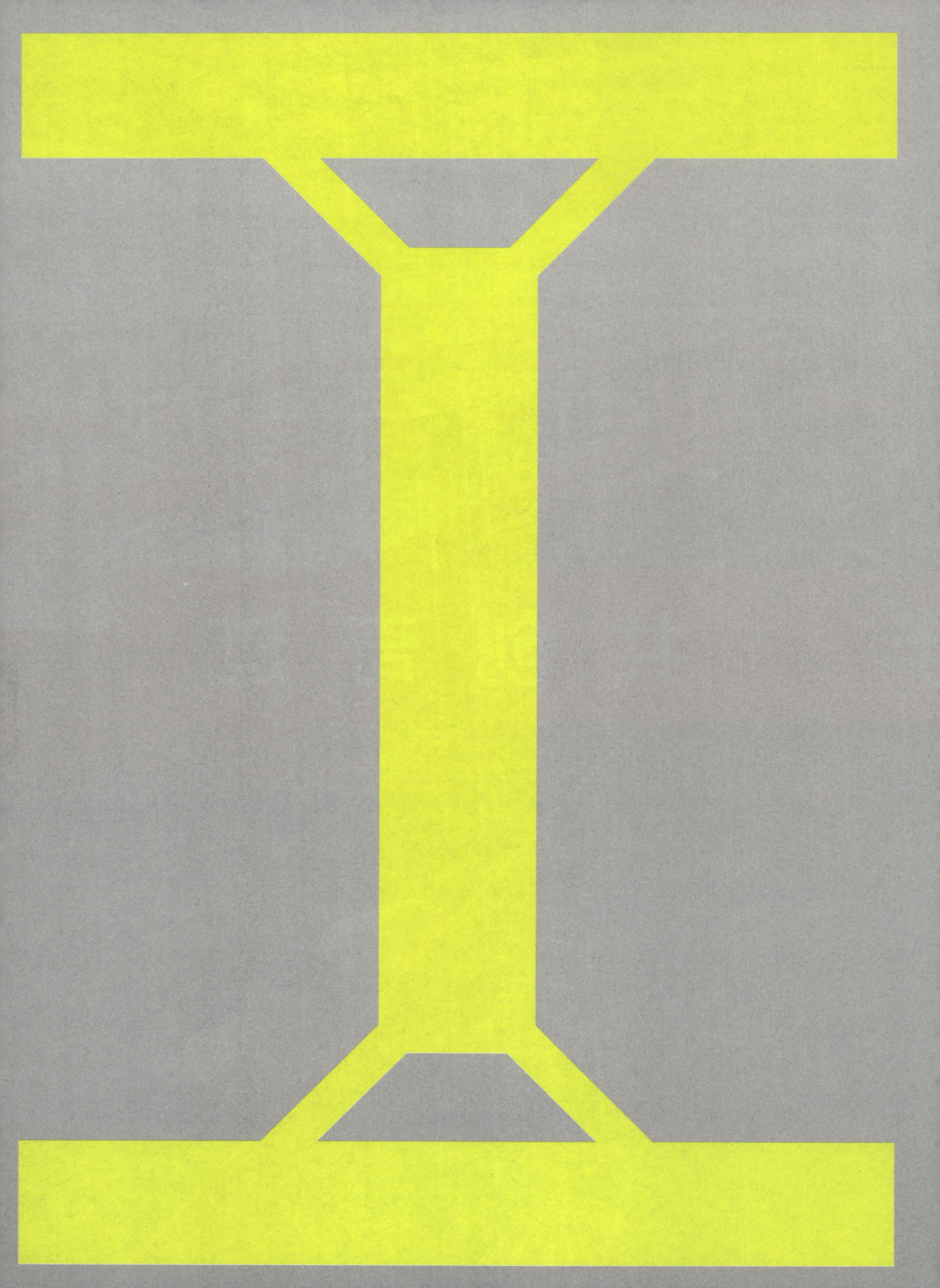

1 HONGXIA

2019 红霞

2 NOVA

2019 新星

3 THE ETERNAL WAVE

2020

永不消失的电波

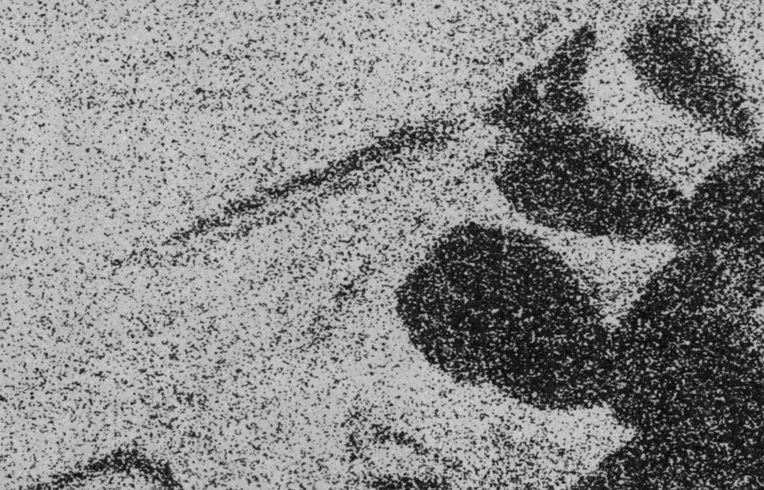

I[1-3]: Hongxia / Nova / The eternal wave

Cao Fei describes this project as an attempt to 'destroy linear time'.[1] The five-year artistic research endeavour – part media archaeology, part social history, part sci-fi fabulation – centres on the Hongxia (Red Dawn) Theatre, a cinema for workers in Beijing's north-eastern Jiuxianqiao district. Cao occupied the space as an artist studio from 2015 to 2020. In the documentary *Hongxia* 2019, Cao looks backward, capturing employees' memories of the Hongxia's role as a neighbourhood social space. In the feature film *Nova* 2019, she looks forward, crafting the sci-fi tale of a computer scientist whose son gets stuck in a wormhole. And in the VR work *The eternal wave* 2020, temporalities collapse, allowing audiences to revisit a perfectly 3D-scanned interior of the Hongxia that plays a 1958 thriller of the same name, director Wang Ping's tale of an underground communist radio transmitter. Cao retrieves neglected narratives and forgotten utopian dreams from China's technological past to spin speculative visions of the future. 'Maybe I want to escape the timeline, you know? And just swim across it. Maybe we can bring unrealised hopes and unrealised disappointments from the past into the future, making it real again'.[2]

1. Günseli Yalcinkaya, 'Artist Cao Fei uses Soviet sci-fi to explode time and space as we know it', *Dazed*, 10 Mar 2020, dazeddigital.com/art-photography/article/48301/1/artist-cao-fei-blueprints-soviet-sci-fi-to-explode-time-and-space-as-we-know-it, accessed 2 Feb 2024.
2. Yalcinkaya 2020.

HONGXIA 红霞

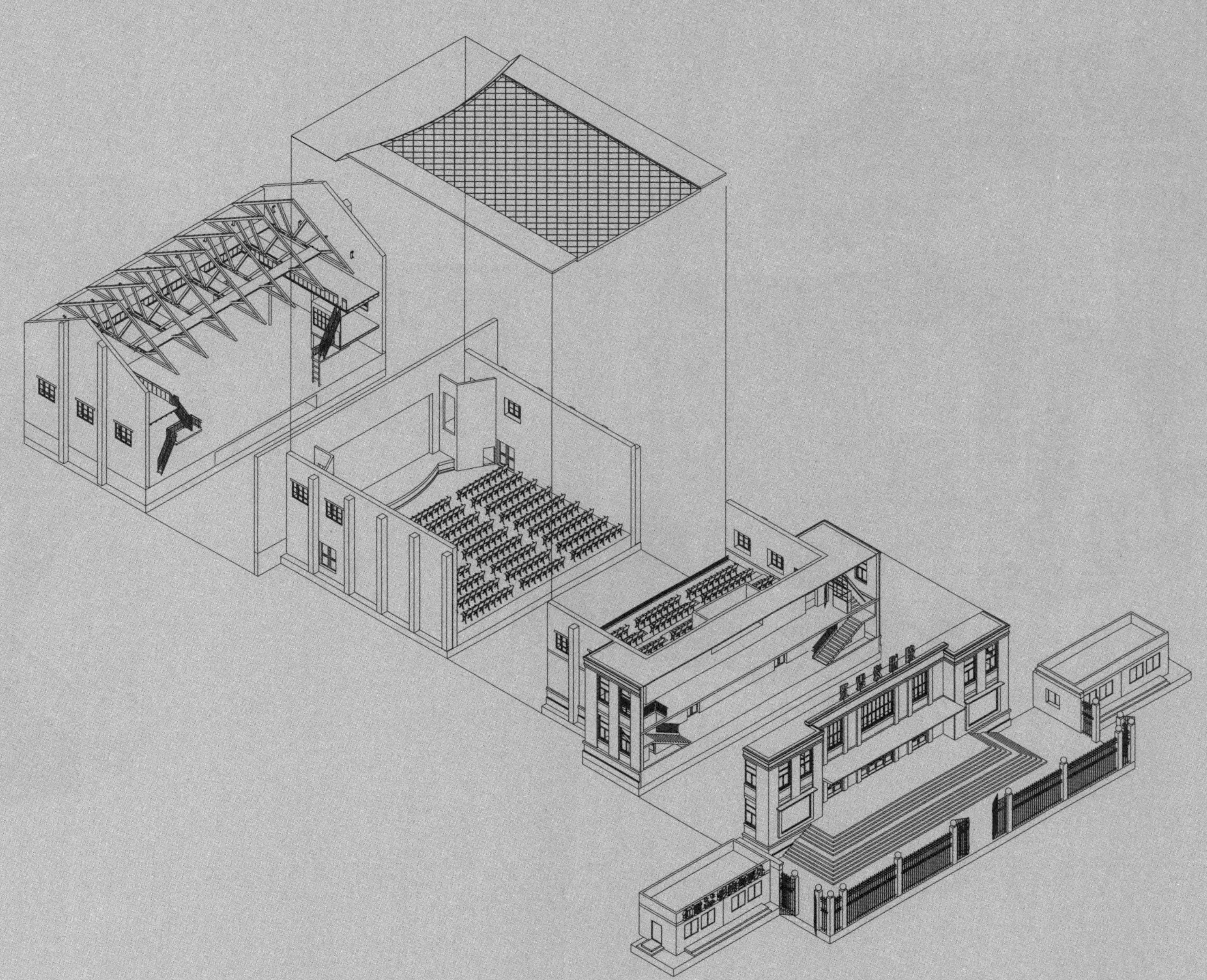

Axial image of Hongxia Theatre building, covering an area of approximately 1653 square metres. Image: FIELD, 2019

Artwork specification X

Hongxia 2019
single-channel HD video, colour, sound
56:56 min, 16:9

《红霞》 2019
16:9彩色有声单频高清影像
56分56秒

3D scan of Hongxia Theatre

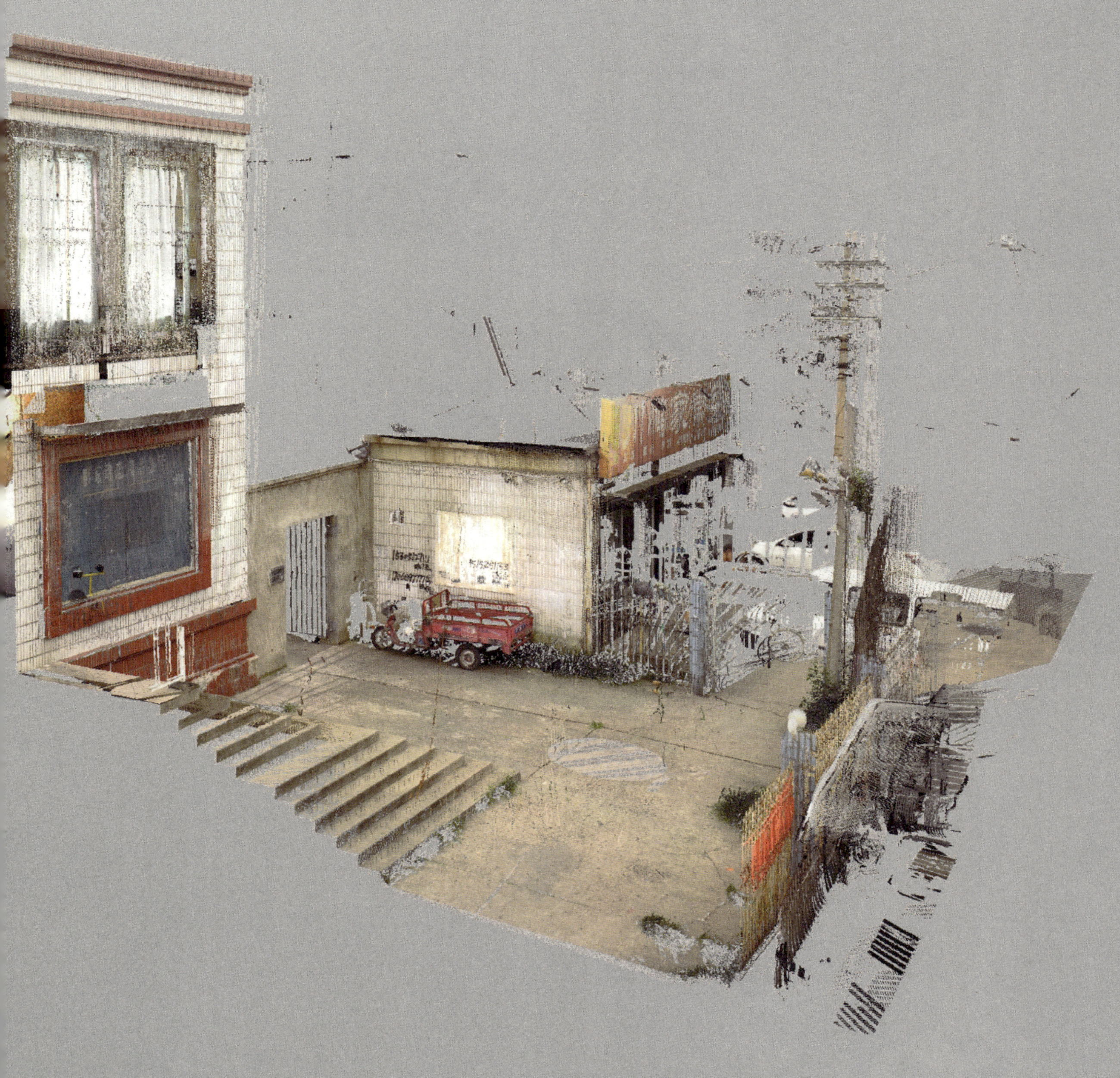

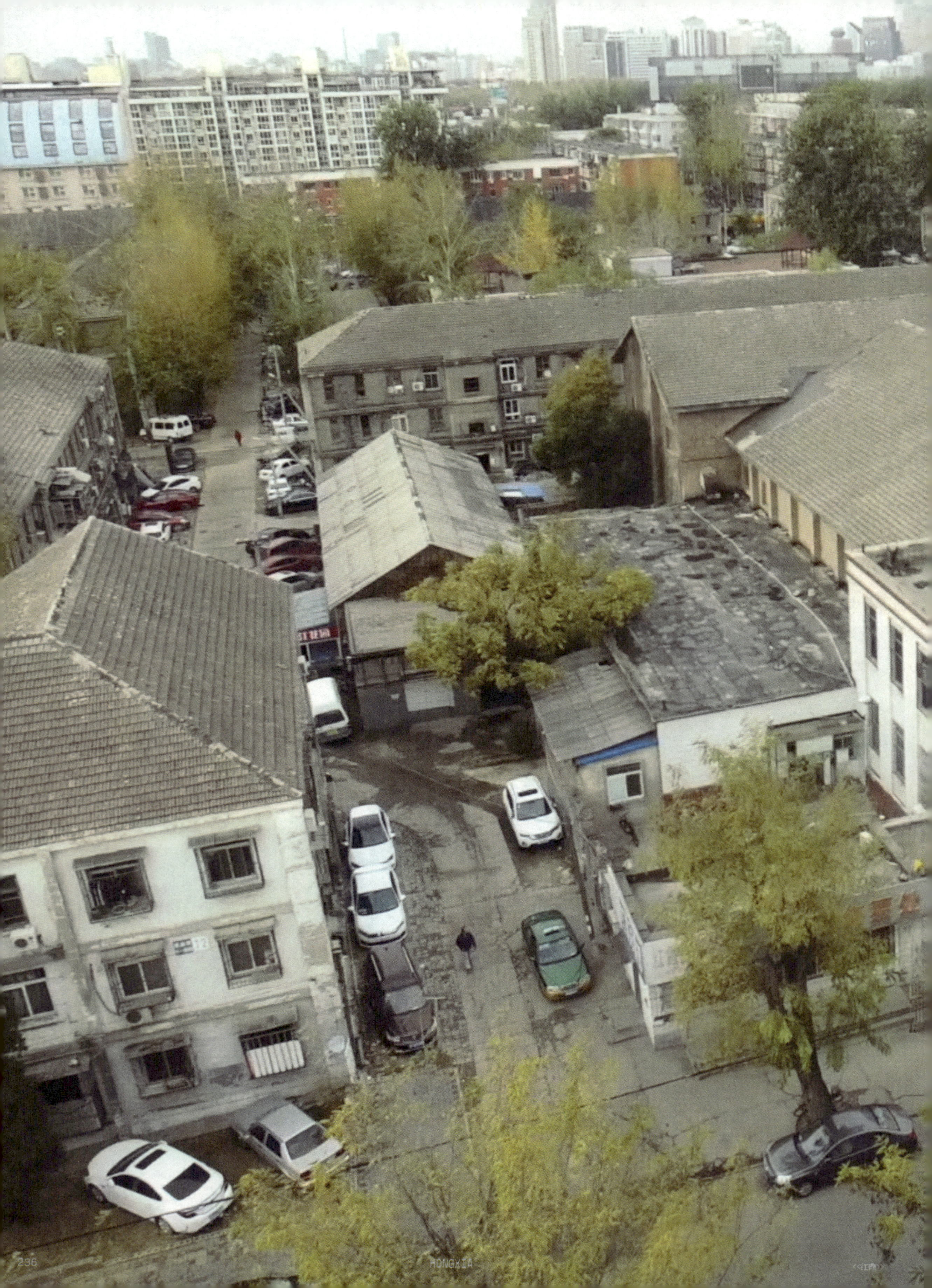

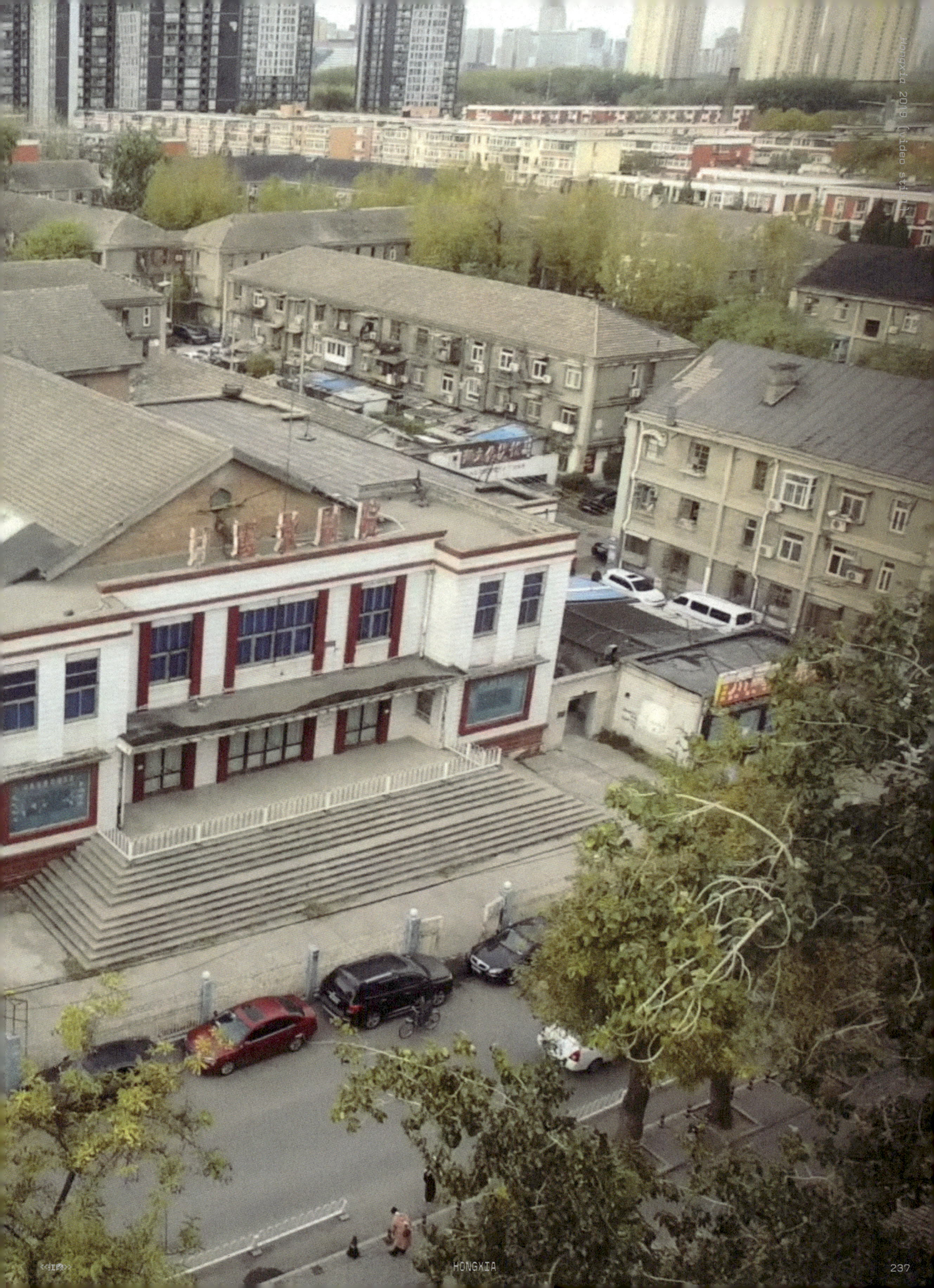

Hongxia 2019 (video still)

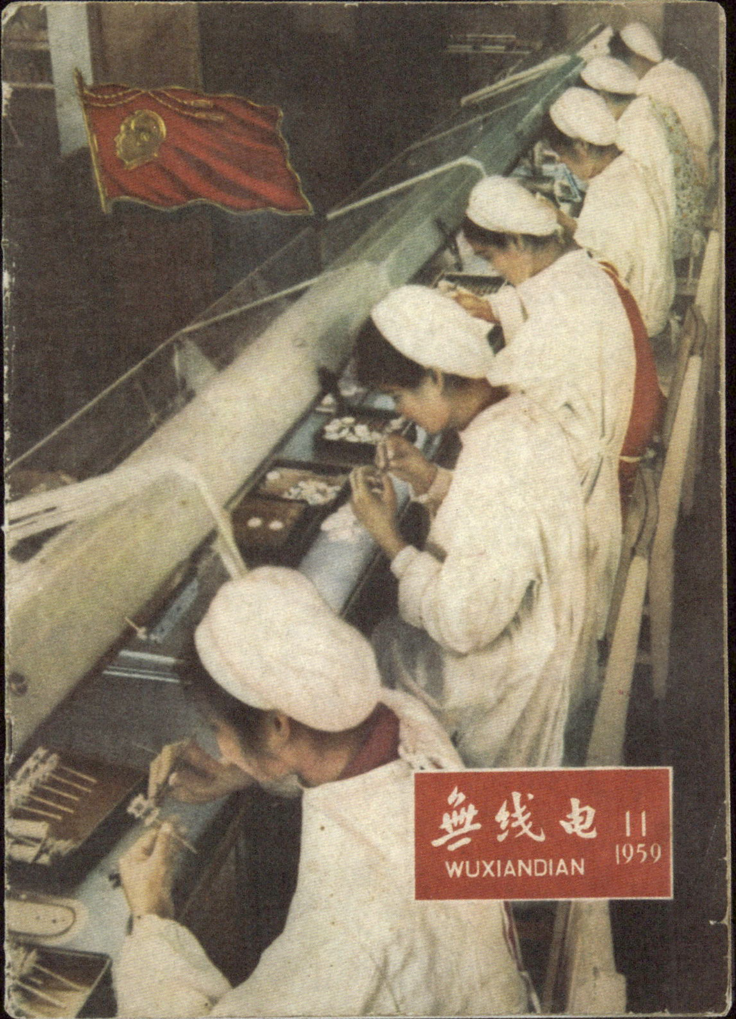

The directly heated tube workshop at Beijing state-owned Electron Tube Factory (Factory 774), chosen as a leading collective in the wireless electronics industry at the 1959 Qunying Conference. Front cover of *Wireless Electronics*, no 11, Posts and Telecom Press, Beijing, 1959.

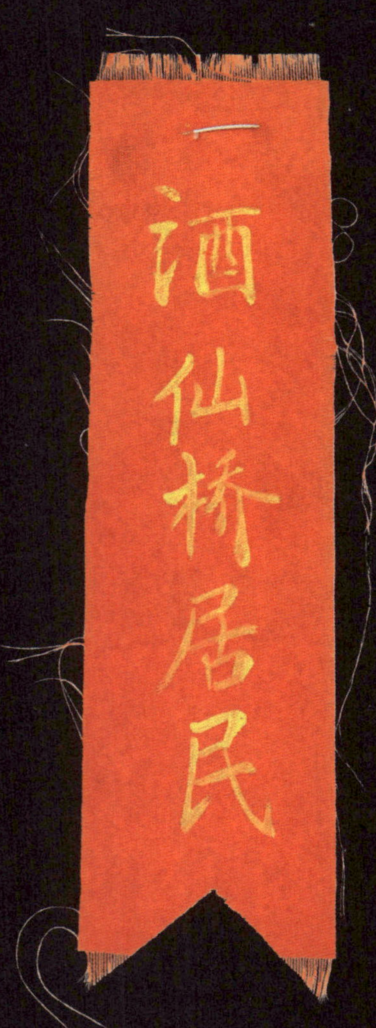

Jiuxianqiao Resident Elector's ribbon, 2000s, found inside Hongxia Theatre, 2016

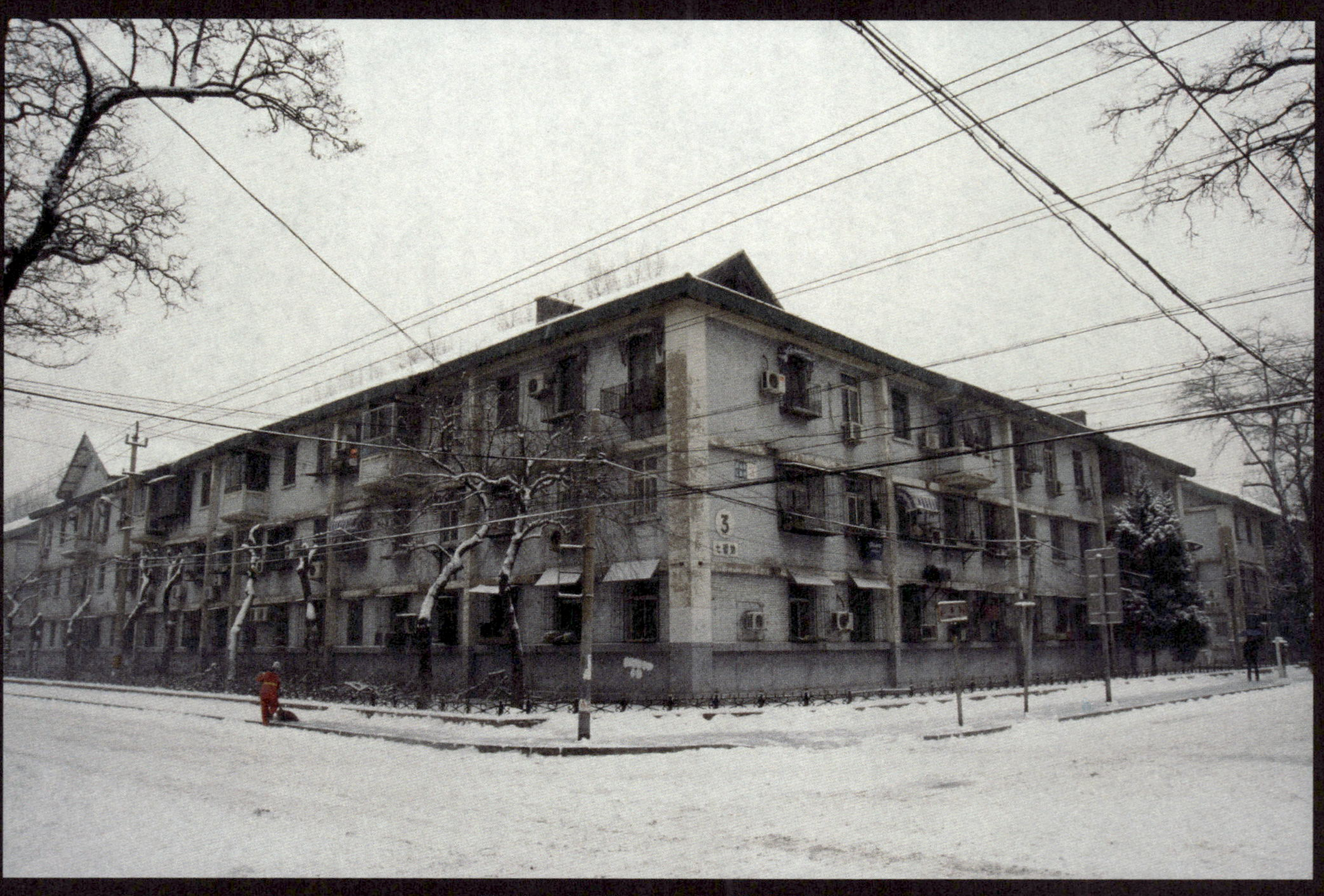

Jiuxianqiao Community No 7, 2010

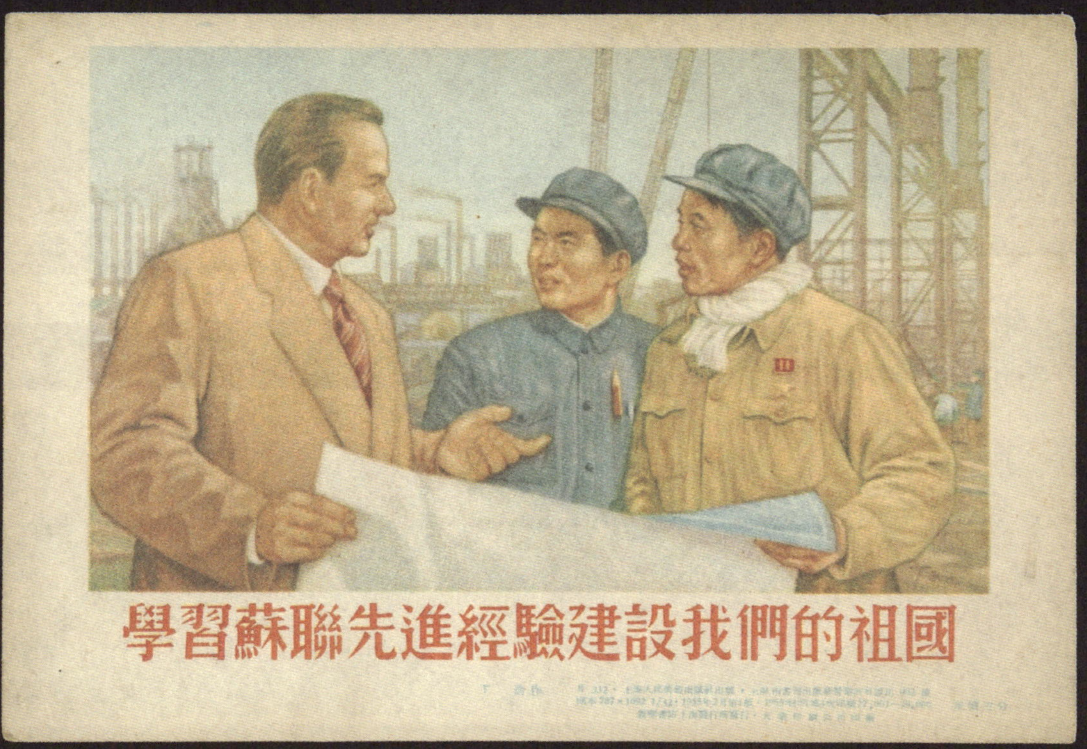

Ding Hao, *Learning from the Soviet Union's advanced experiences to build our motherland*, Shanghai People's Publishing House and Xinhua Bookstore Shanghai Publishing, Shanghai, 1955

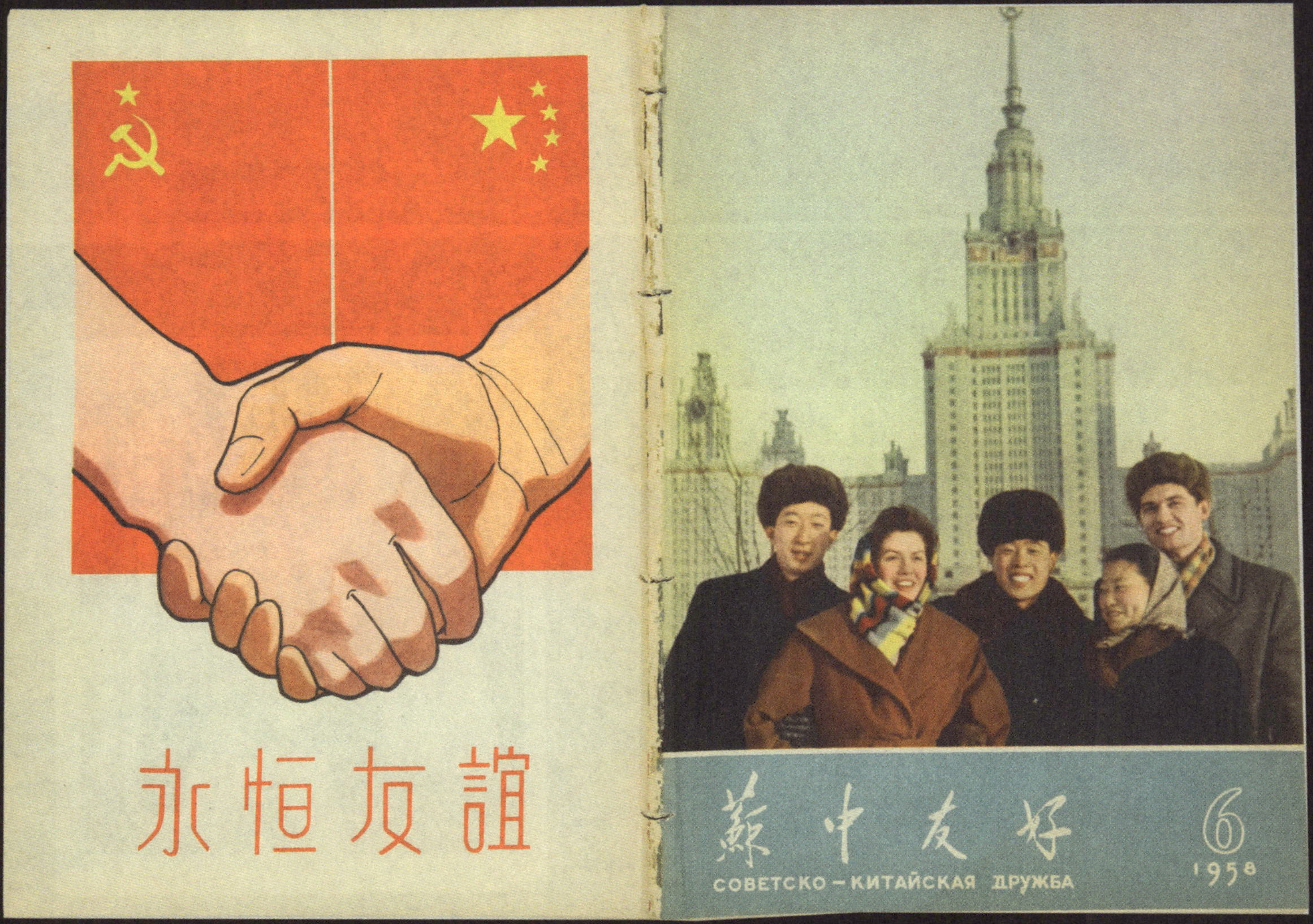

永恒友誼

蘇中友好

СОВЕТСКО–КИТАЙСКАЯ ДРУЖБА

6

1958

Soviet China Friendship, no 6, 1958, Soviet-China Friendship association

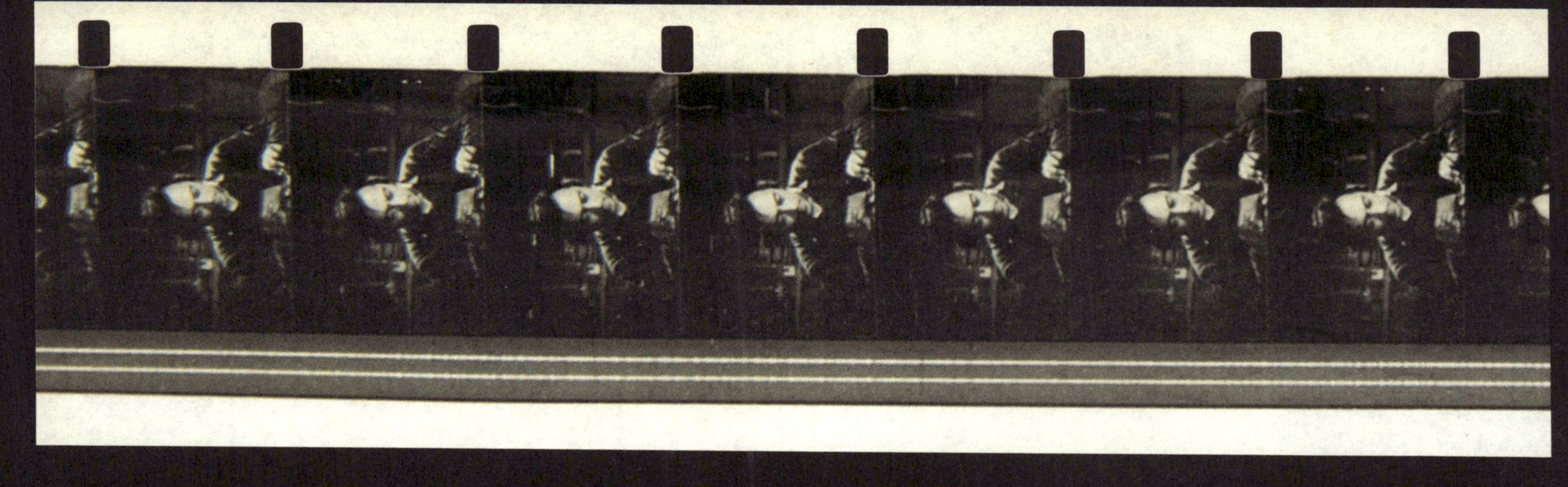

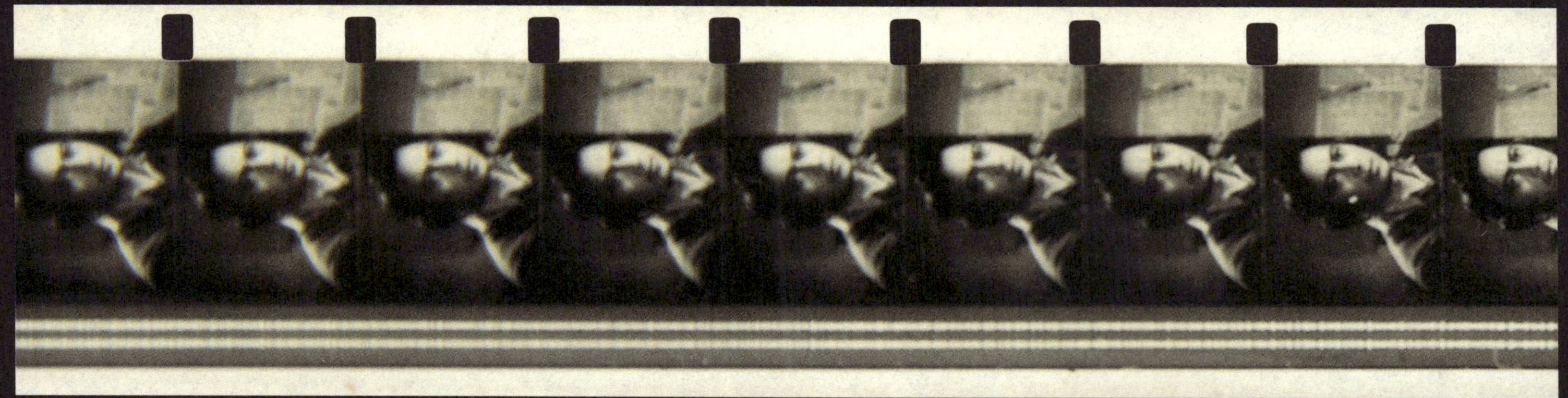

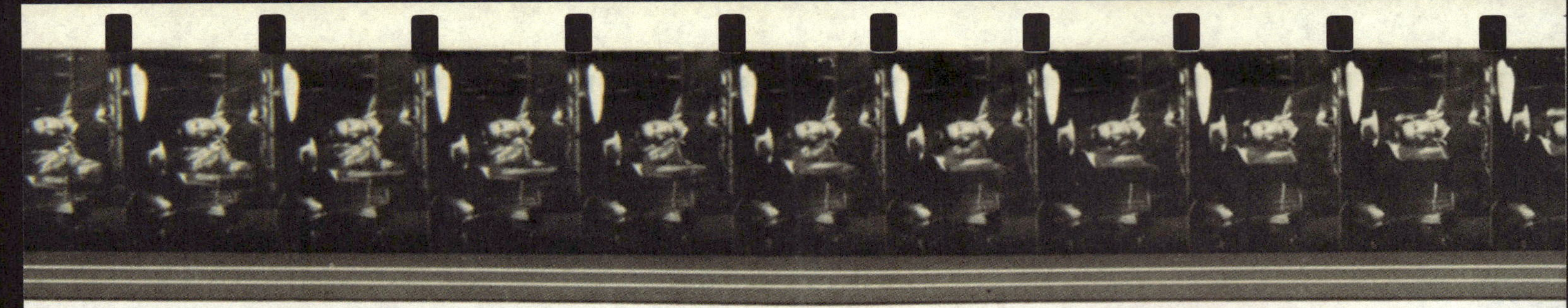

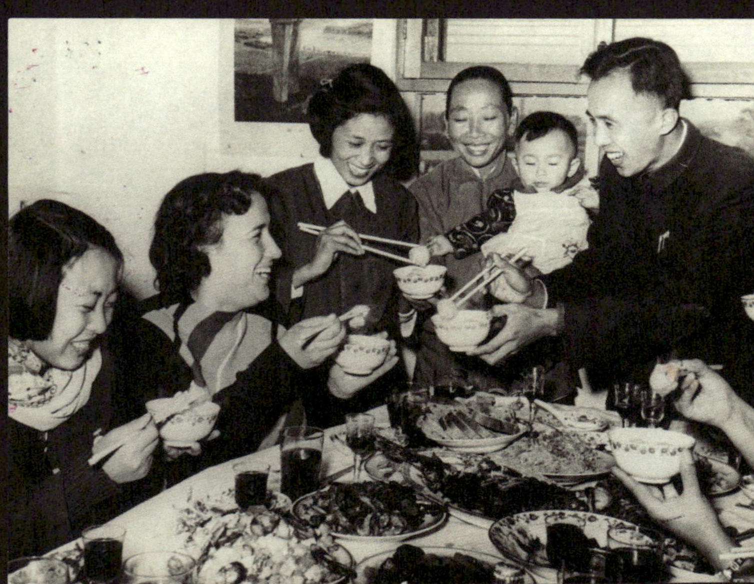

Mao Huixiang (far right), director of the component assembly workshop at Beijing state-owned Wired Electronics Factory (Factory 738), invites Soviet expert to his home to celebrate Spring Lantern Festival, 1957

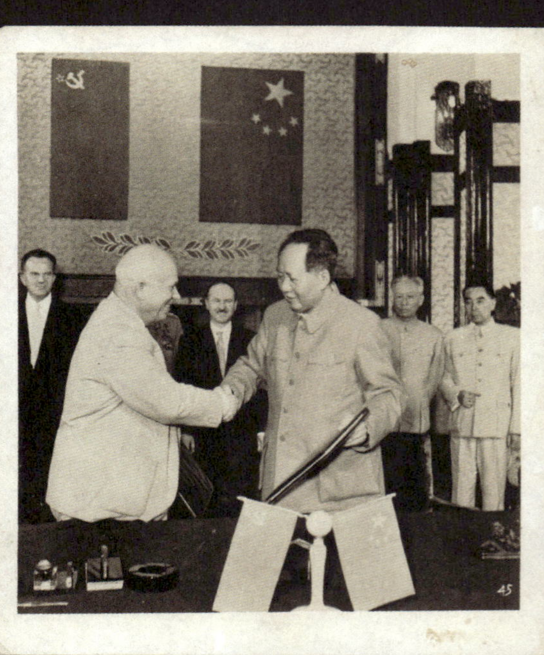

Chairman Mao and Nikita Sergeyevich Khrushchev after signing a joint communique of their meeting, 31 July 1958

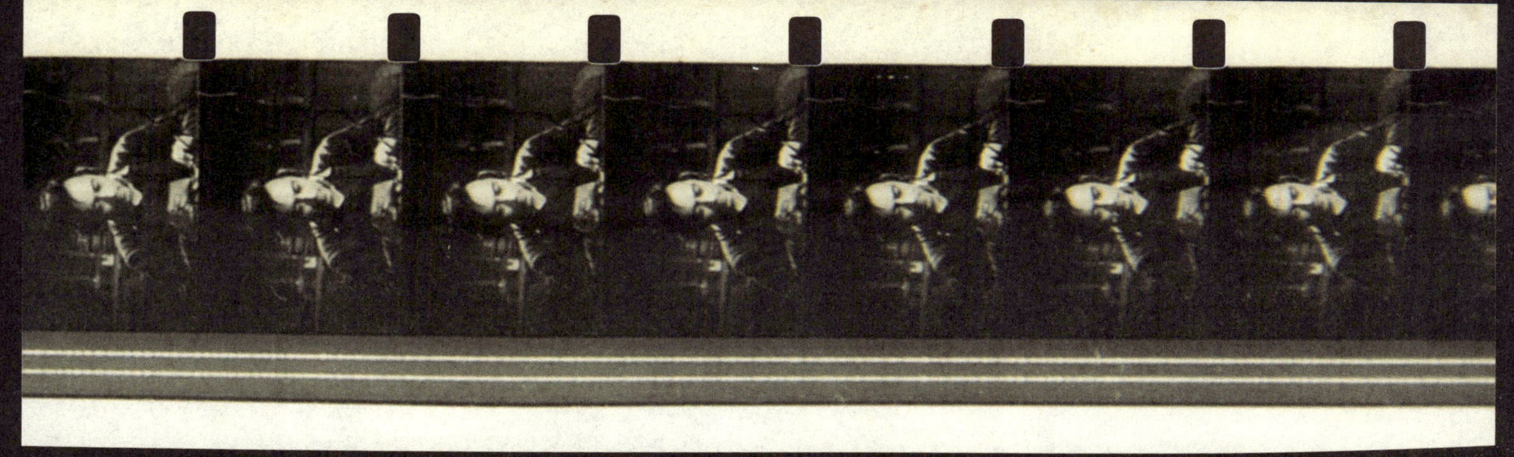

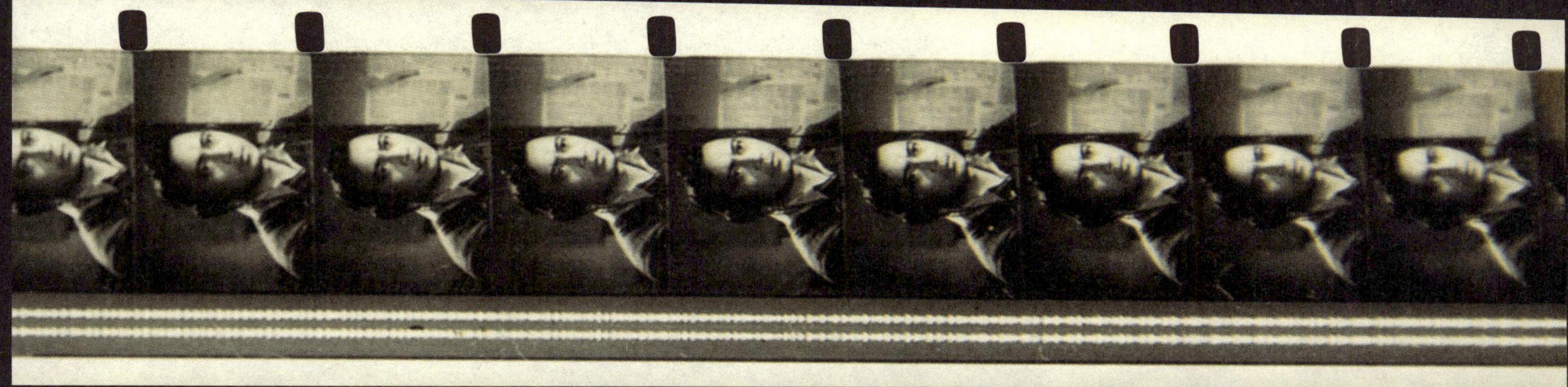

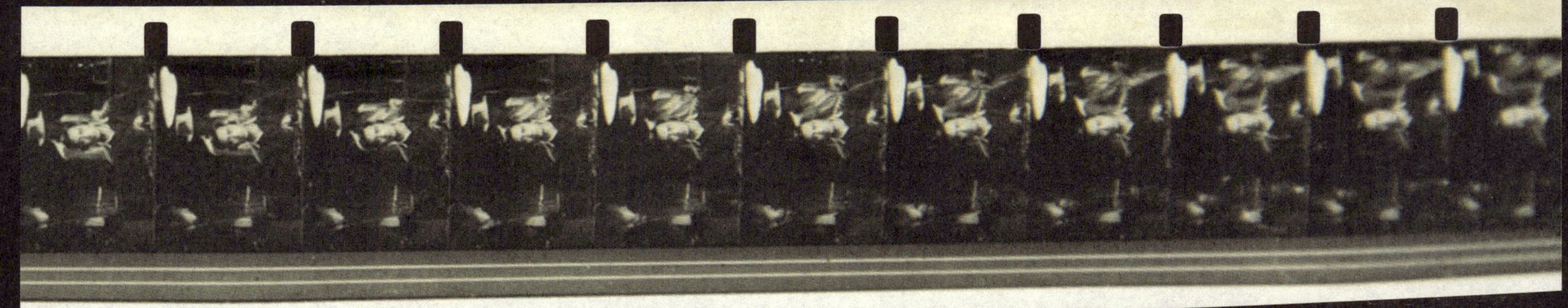

Sections of 16mm film from *The eternal wave*, produced by the People's Liberation Army Bayi Film Studio, 1958

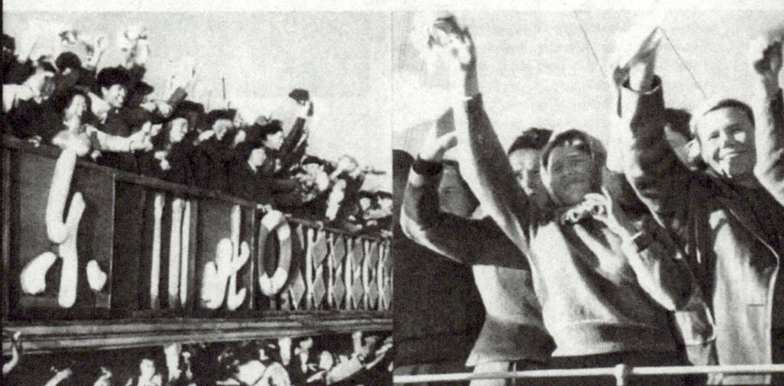

Picture accompanying the article 'Friendship cannot be destroyed' from *Down the new Tsars! Soviet revisionists' anti-China atrocities in Heilung and Wusuli rivers*, Beijing Foreign Languages Press, Beijing, 1969

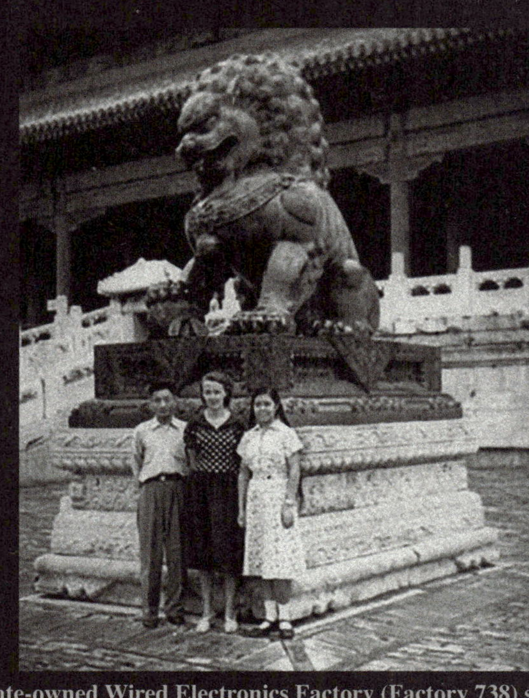

Beijing state-owned Wired Electronics Factory (Factory 738) staff member Zhang Shuyu accompanies Soviet expert Antonova on a visit to the Forbidden City, 1950s

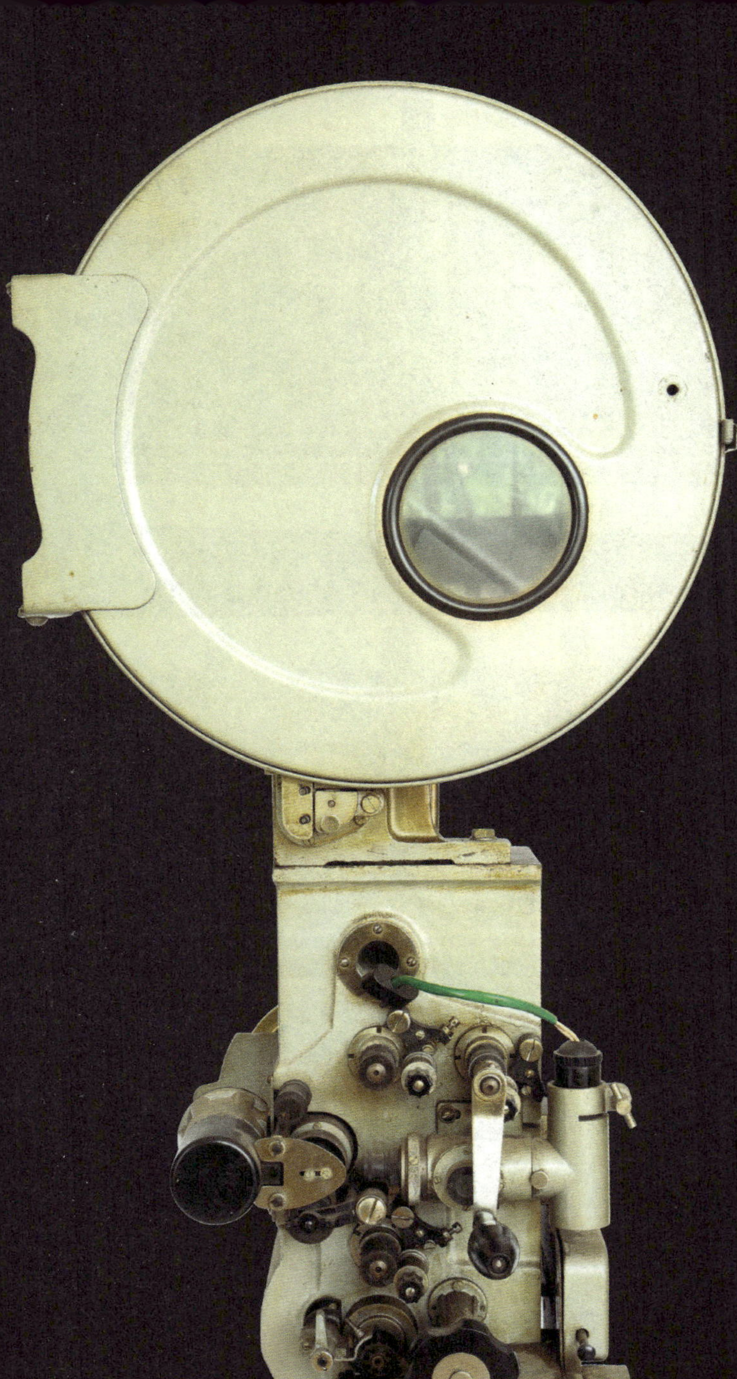

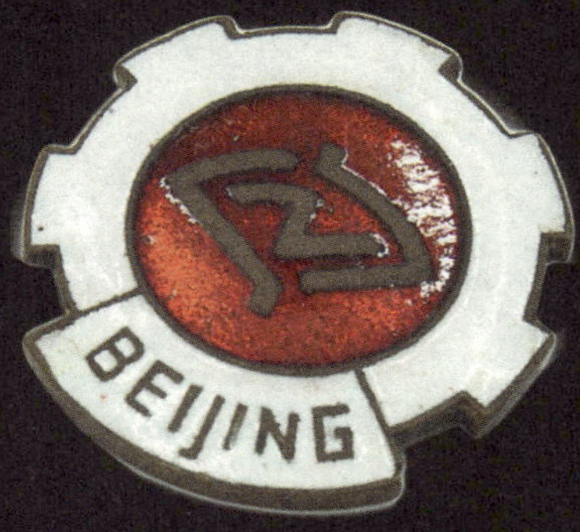

Beijing state-owned Wired Electronics Factory emblem badge, 1950s

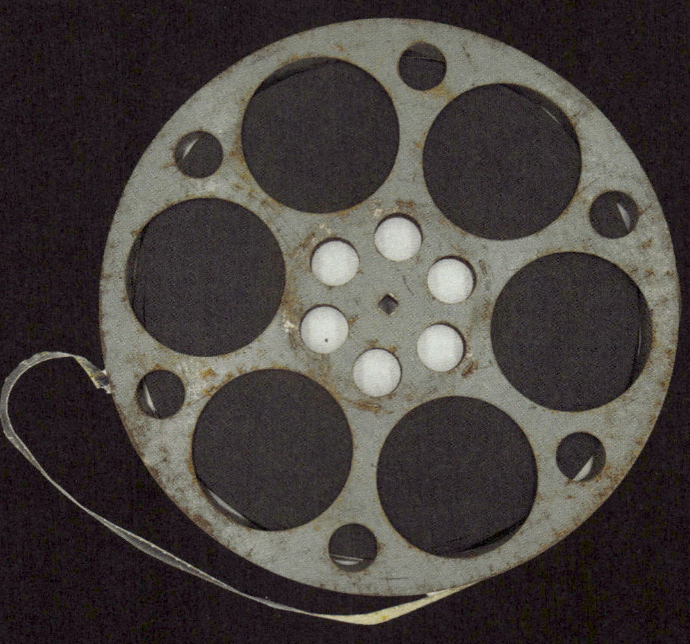

16mm black-and-white film reel of *The eternal wave*,
produced by the People's Liberation Army Bayi Film Studio, 1958

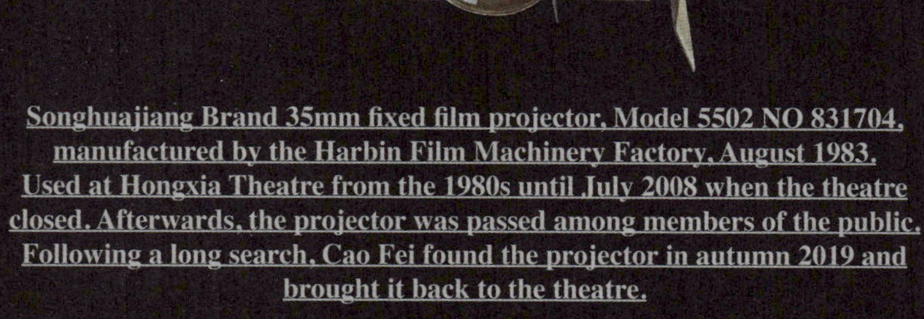

Songhuajiang Brand 35mm fixed film projector, Model 5502 NO 831704, manufactured by the Harbin Film Machinery Factory, August 1983. Used at Hongxia Theatre from the 1980s until July 2008 when the theatre closed. Afterwards, the projector was passed among members of the public. Following a long search, Cao Fei found the projector in autumn 2019 and brought it back to the theatre.

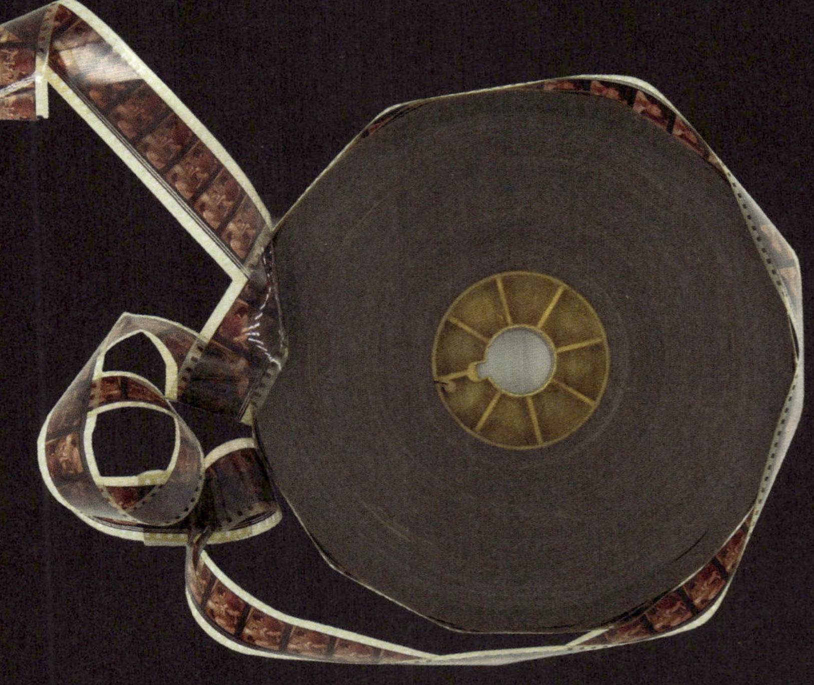

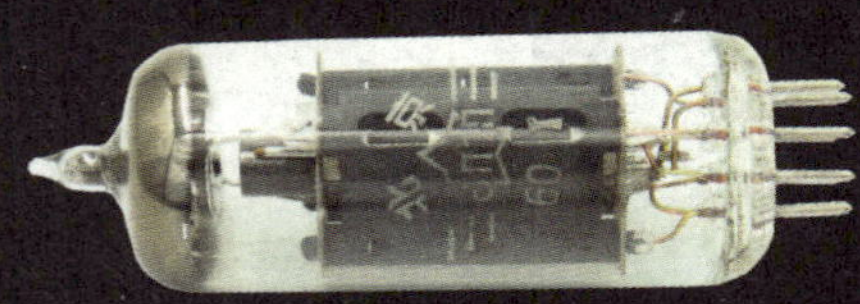

A 'Beijing Brand' electron tube,
produced by the Beijing state-owned Electronic Tube Factory, 1967

35mm colour film reel of *The sea prisoner*, directed by Li Wenhua, released by Hubei Film Studio, 1981. Found backstage at Hongxia Theatre, 2016.

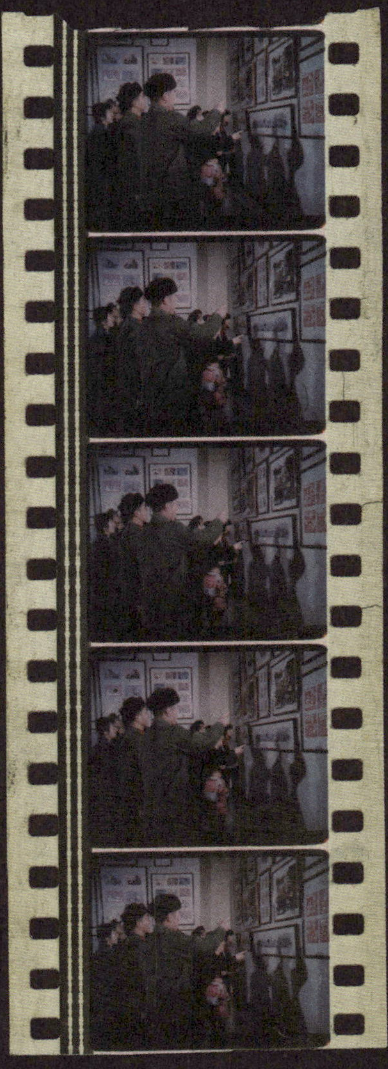

Fragment of 35mm colour film,
found in the projector used at Hongxia Theatre,
title and date unknown

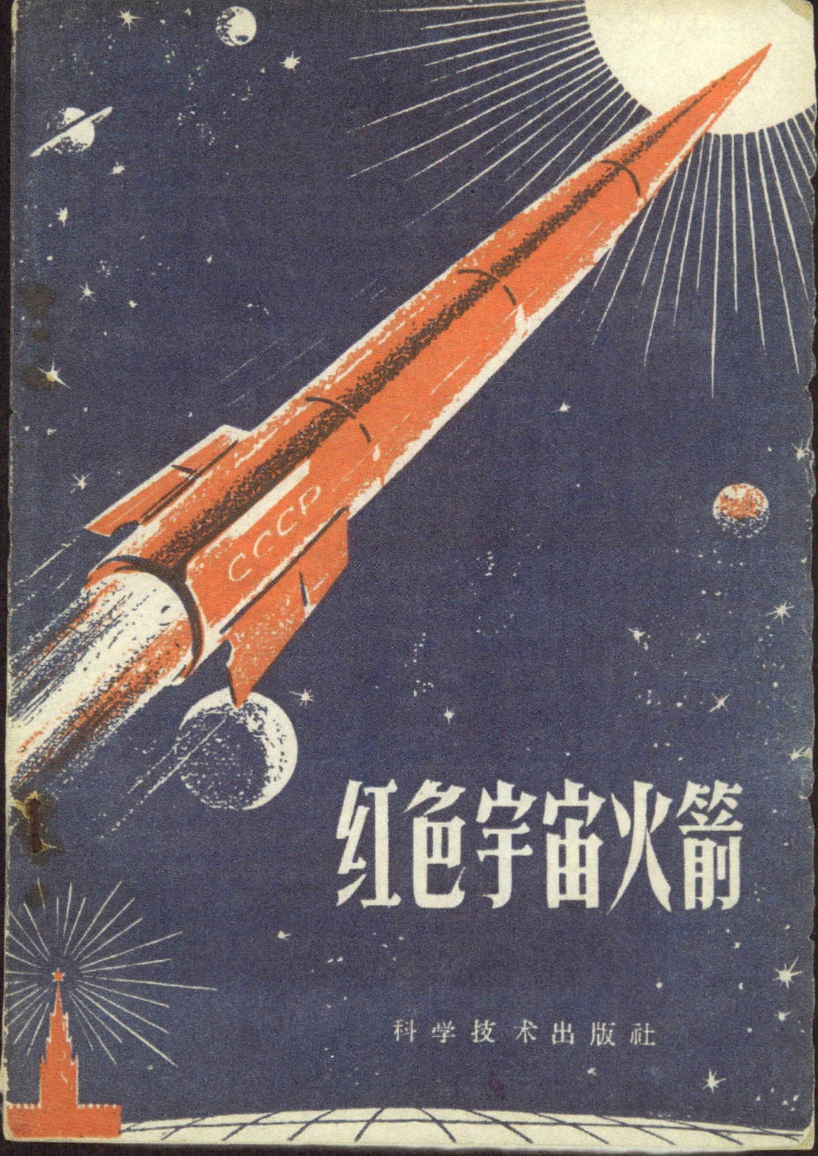

Cosmic red rocket, propaganda material for the Soviet Union's successful launch of the first rocket to leave Earth's orbit, 1959, edited and published by Science and Technology Press, Beijing, 1959

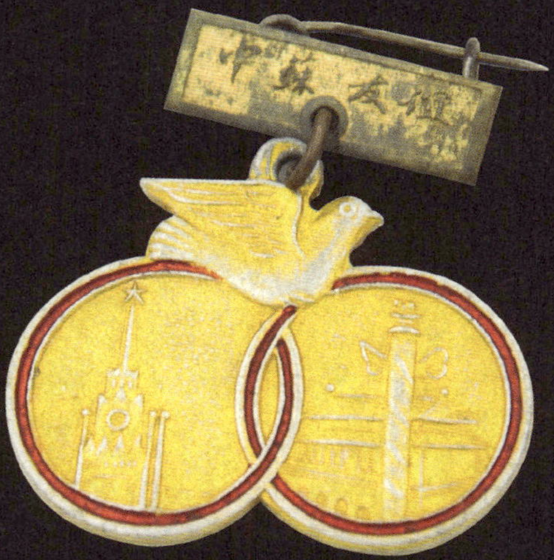

Sino-Soviet friendship pin, 1950s

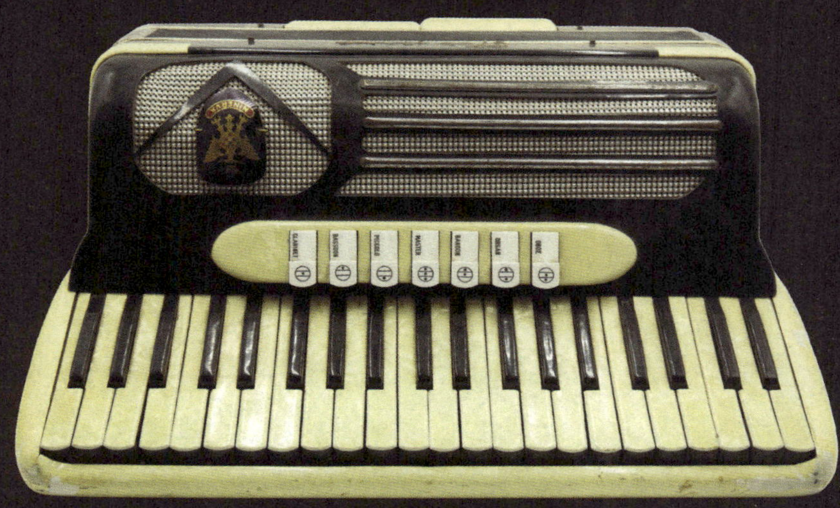

Accordion left behind by Soviet experts at the Central Laboratory of the Beijing North China Optoelectronics Technology Research Institute, 1950s

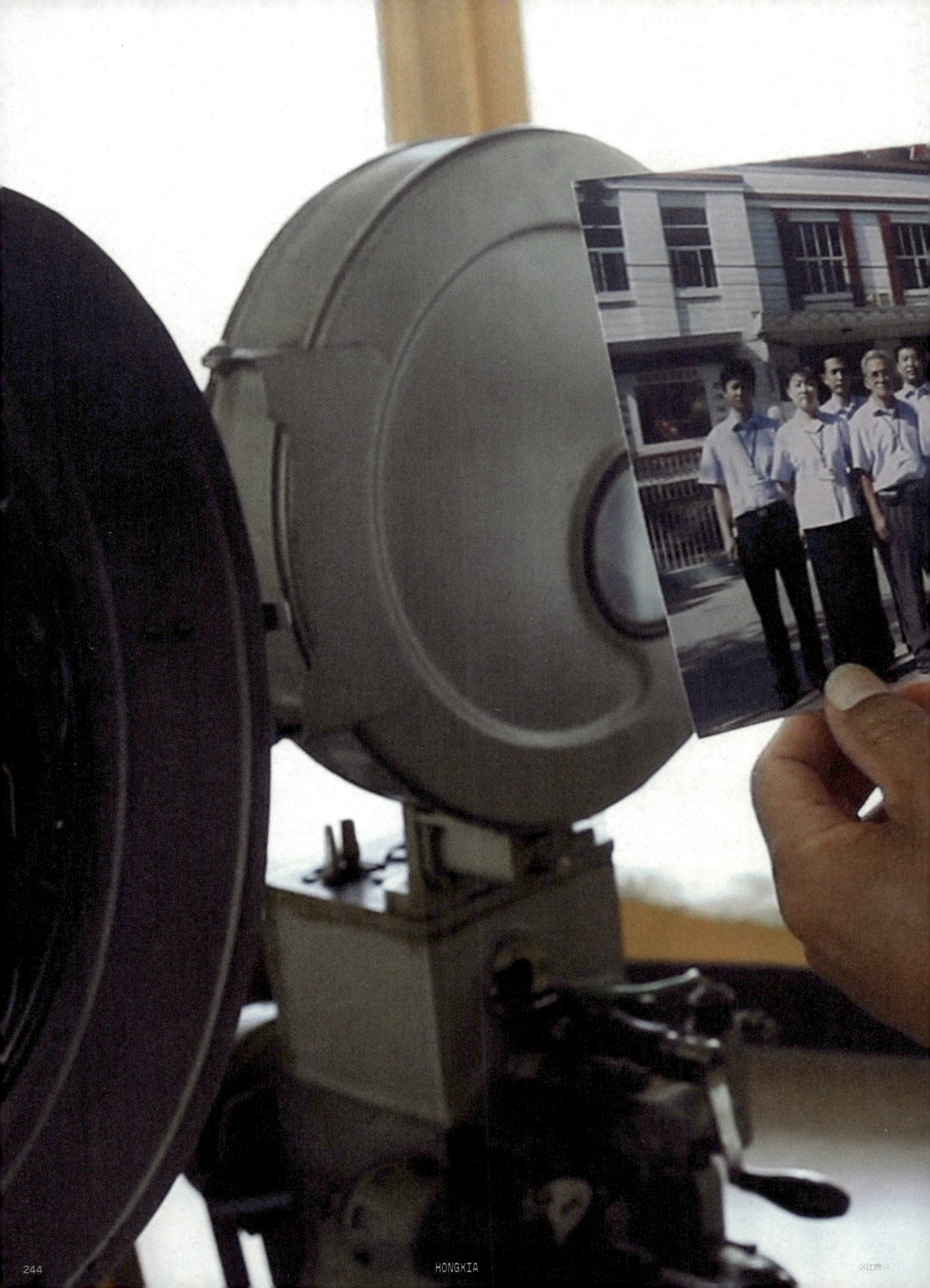

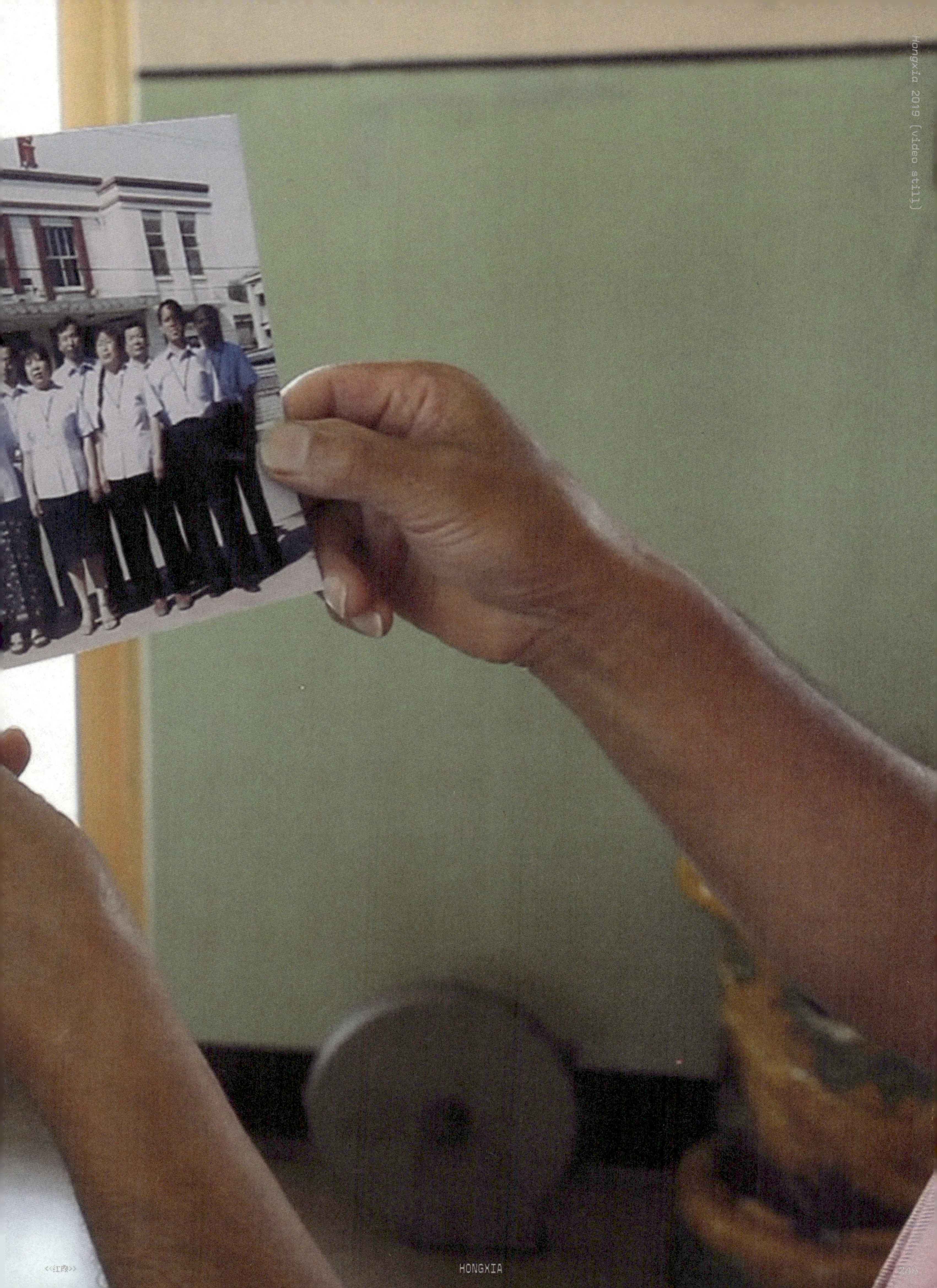

Hongxia 2019 (video still)

Artwork specification X

Nova 2019
single-channel HD video, colour, sound
97:13 min, 2.35:1

《新星》 2019
2.35:1彩色有声单频高清影像
97分13秒

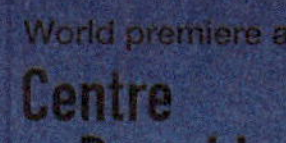

A FILM BY CAO FEI

STARRING
WANG JIAYI

NO 新星 VA

2019

Written and Directed by CAO FEI
Actor: ANAÏS MARTANE YAN NAN LIM SUN YUN ZHAO JINGCHENG Director of Photography: YANG GUANG ZHANG LIMING
Line Producer: OUYANG WEIWEI Curator: YUNG MA Assistant Curator: LOÏC LE GALL Production Manager: XU ZHENGYUE Stylist: HUANG YILEI
Music Composer: DYLAN EBRAHIMIAN Foley Recording Studio: MASSIVE SQUARE AUDIO WORKSHOP
Poster Design: SUN XIAOXI Production: CAO FEI STUDIO Supported by: ZENG ZIMO Distributor: VITAMIN CREATIVE SPACE

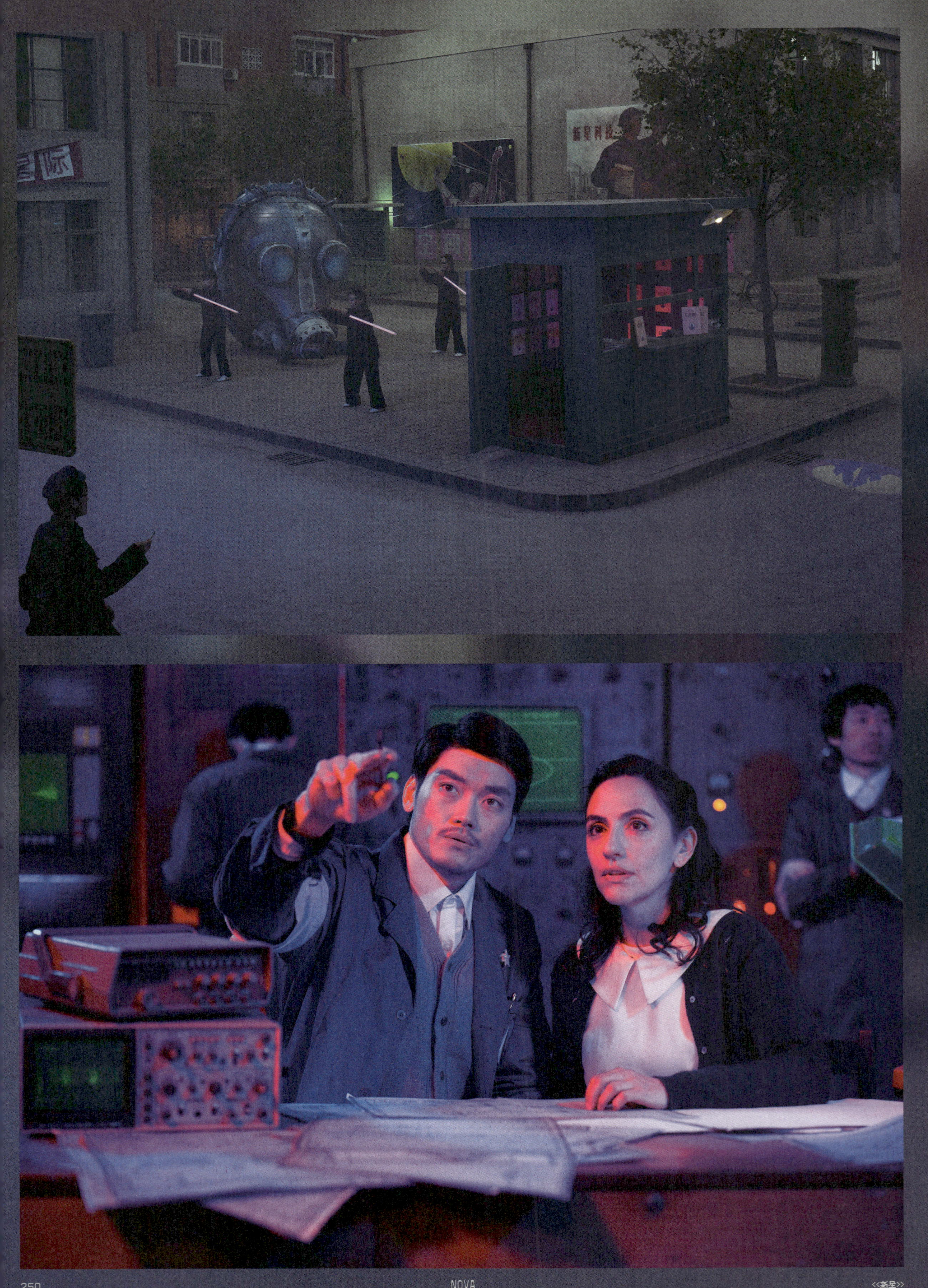
星际
新星科技

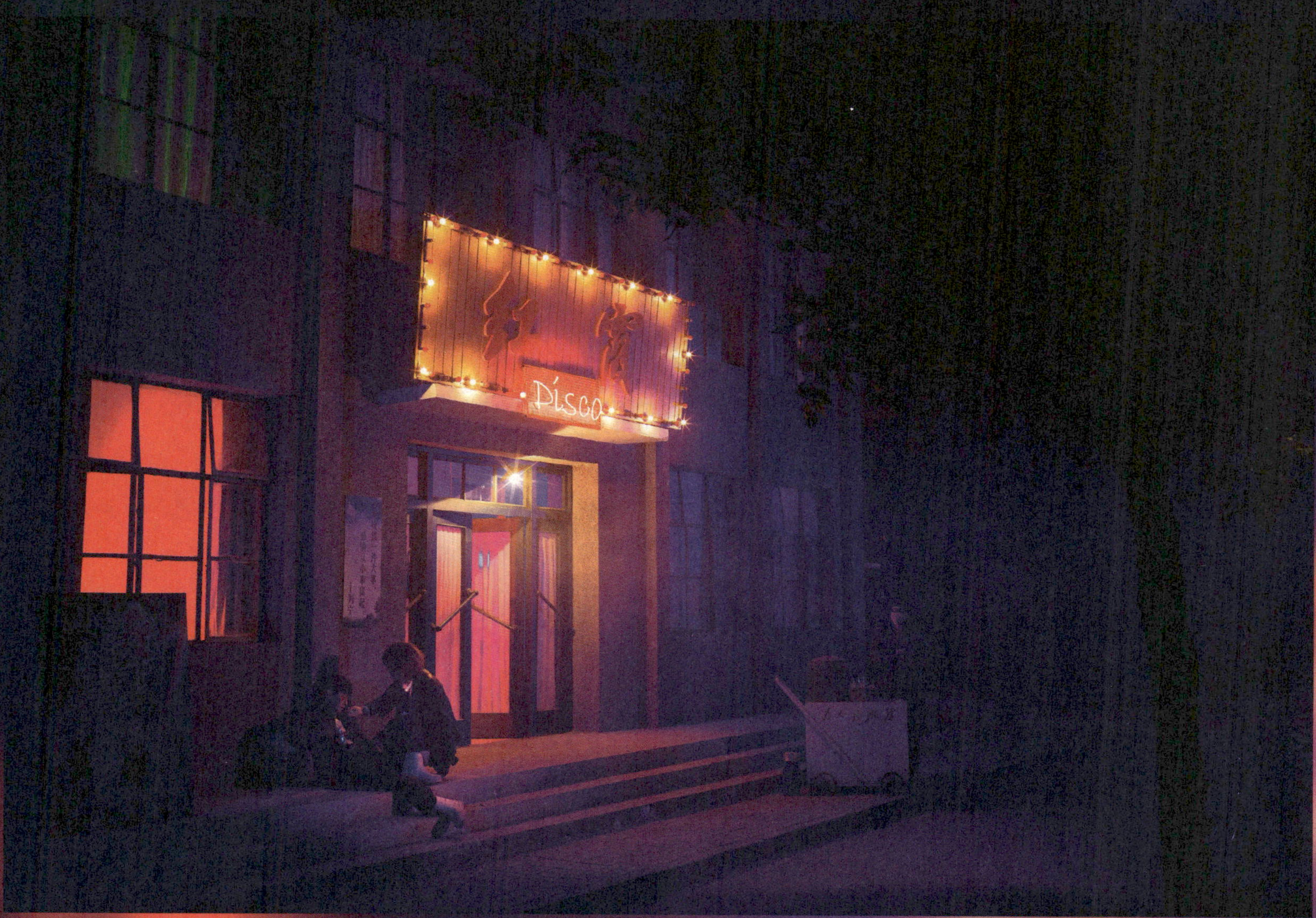

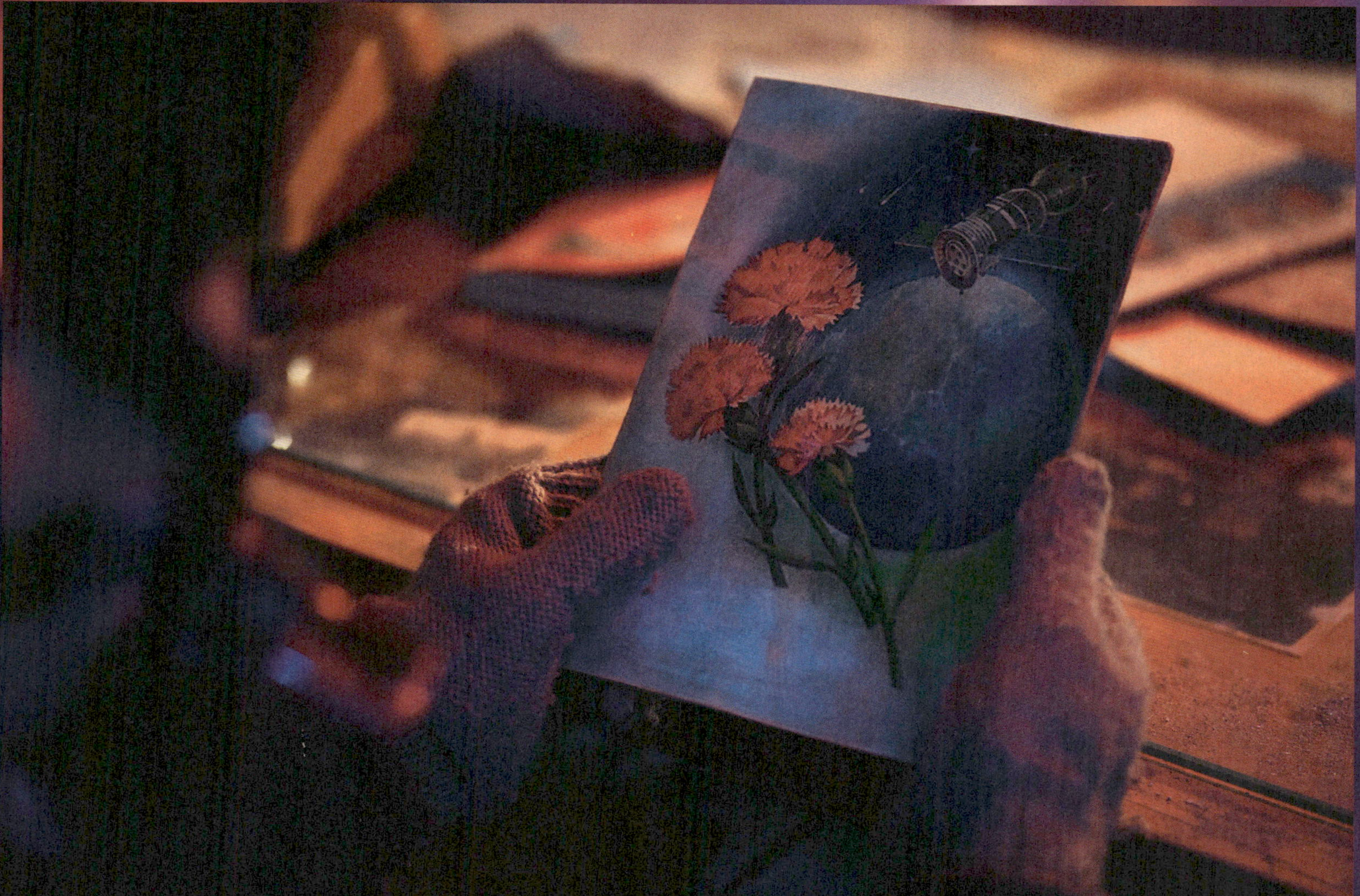

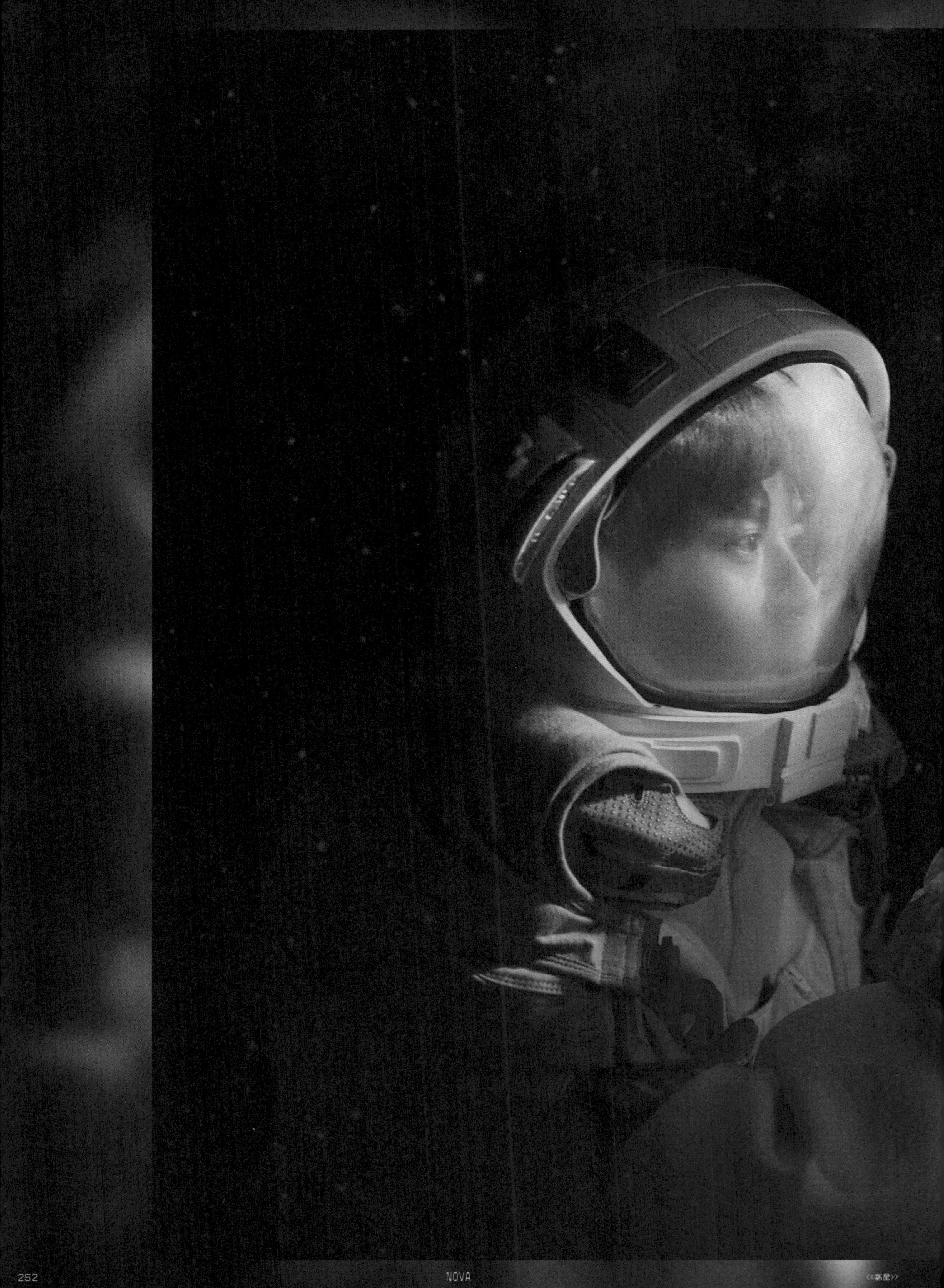

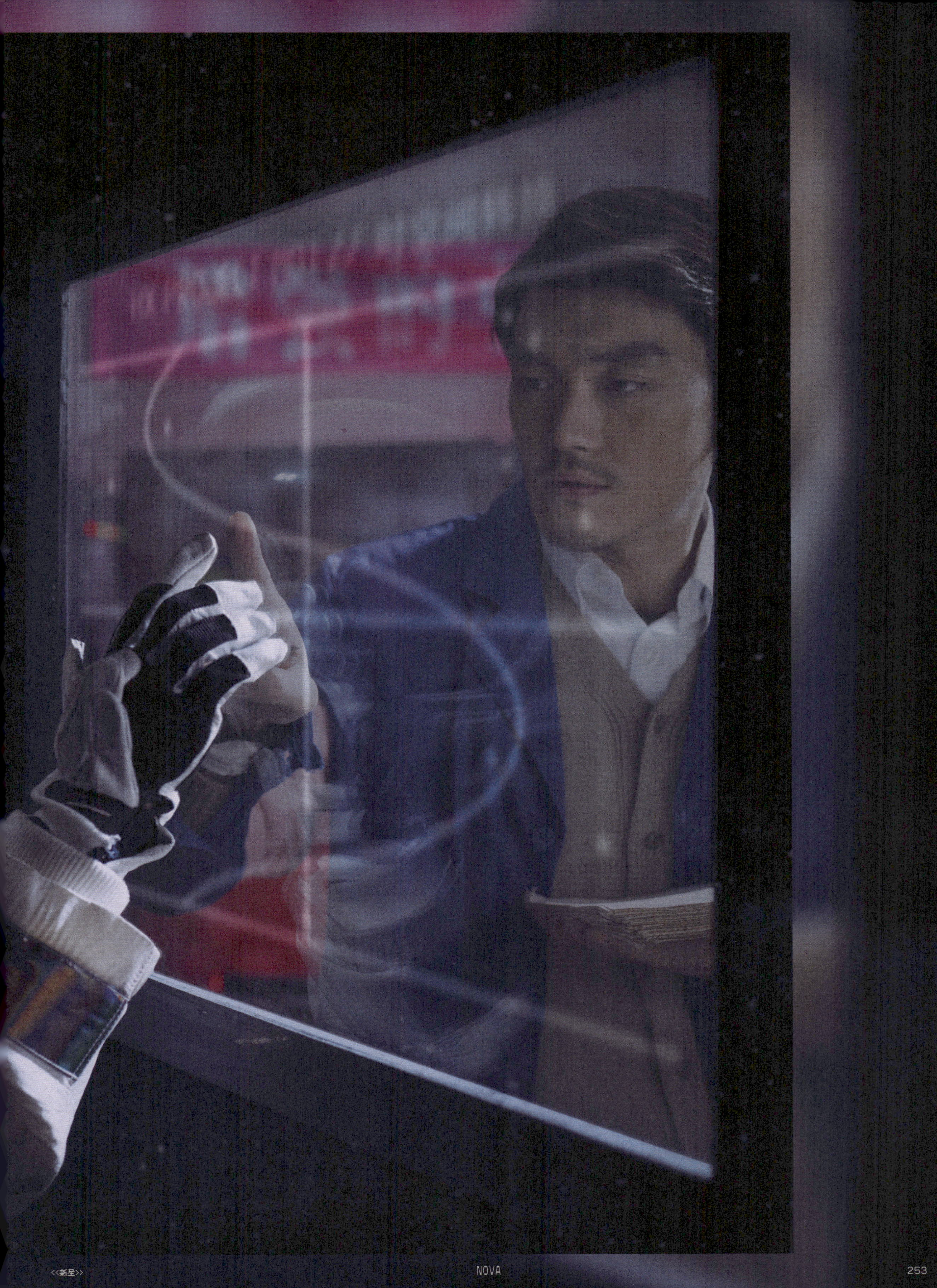

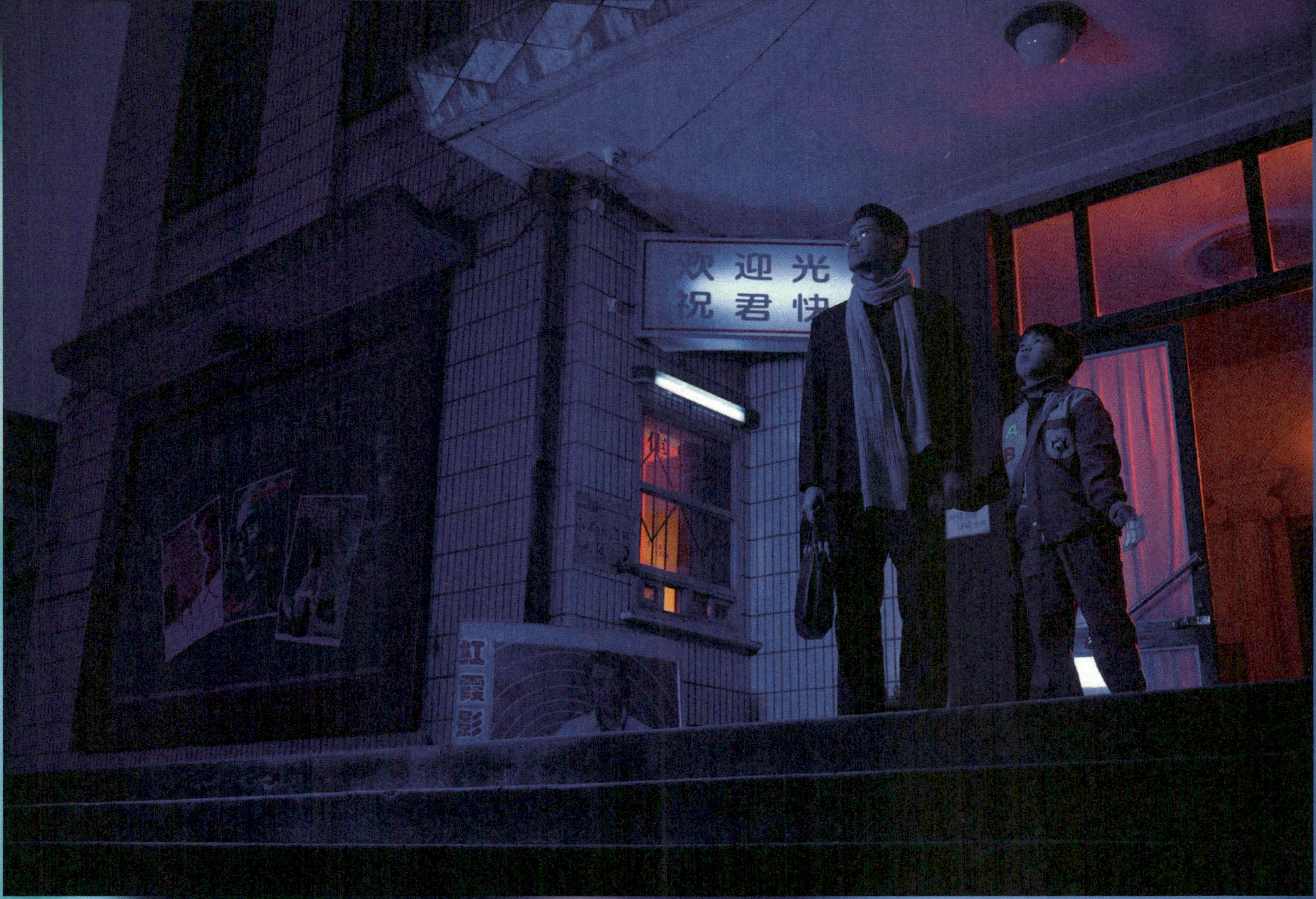

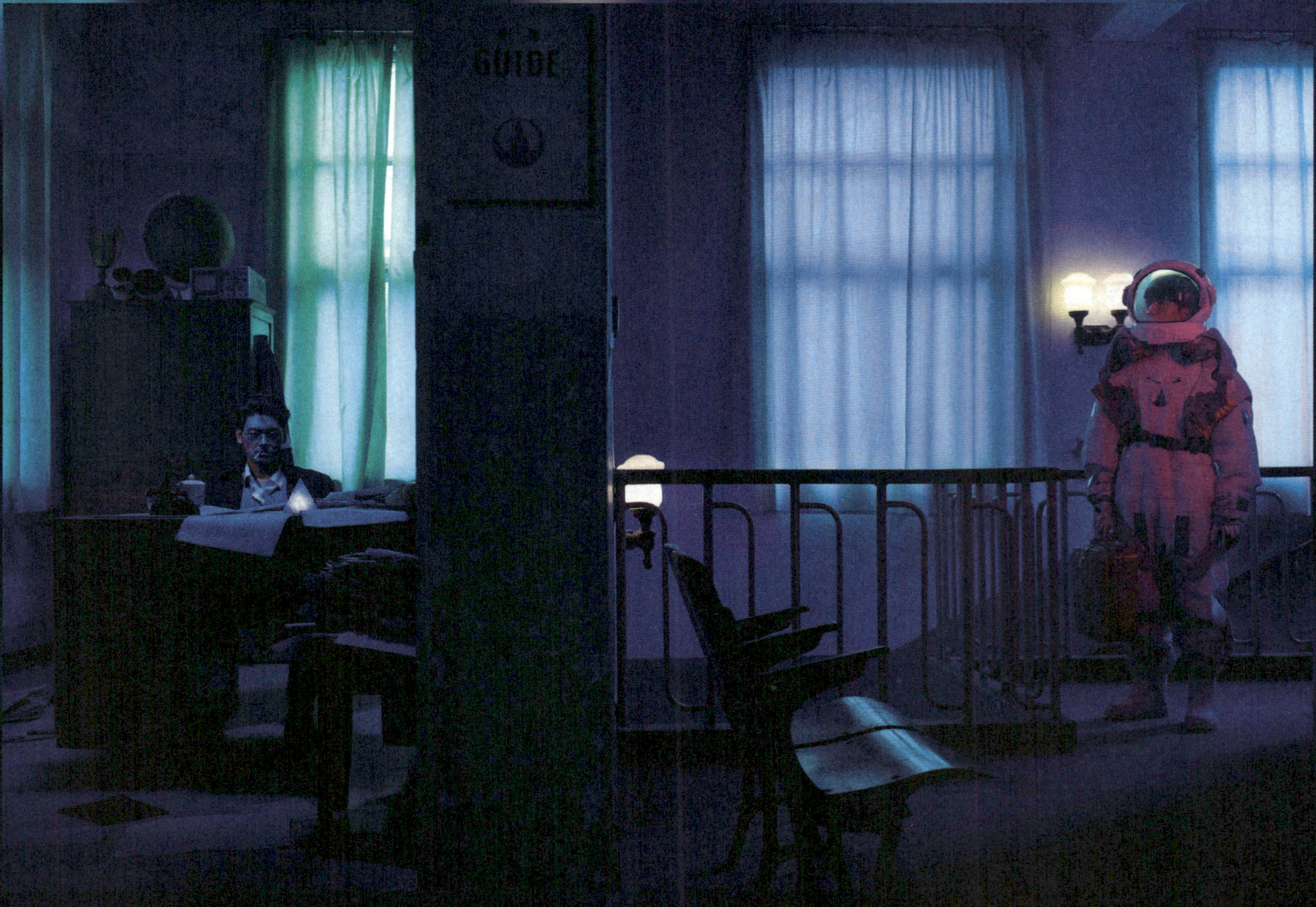

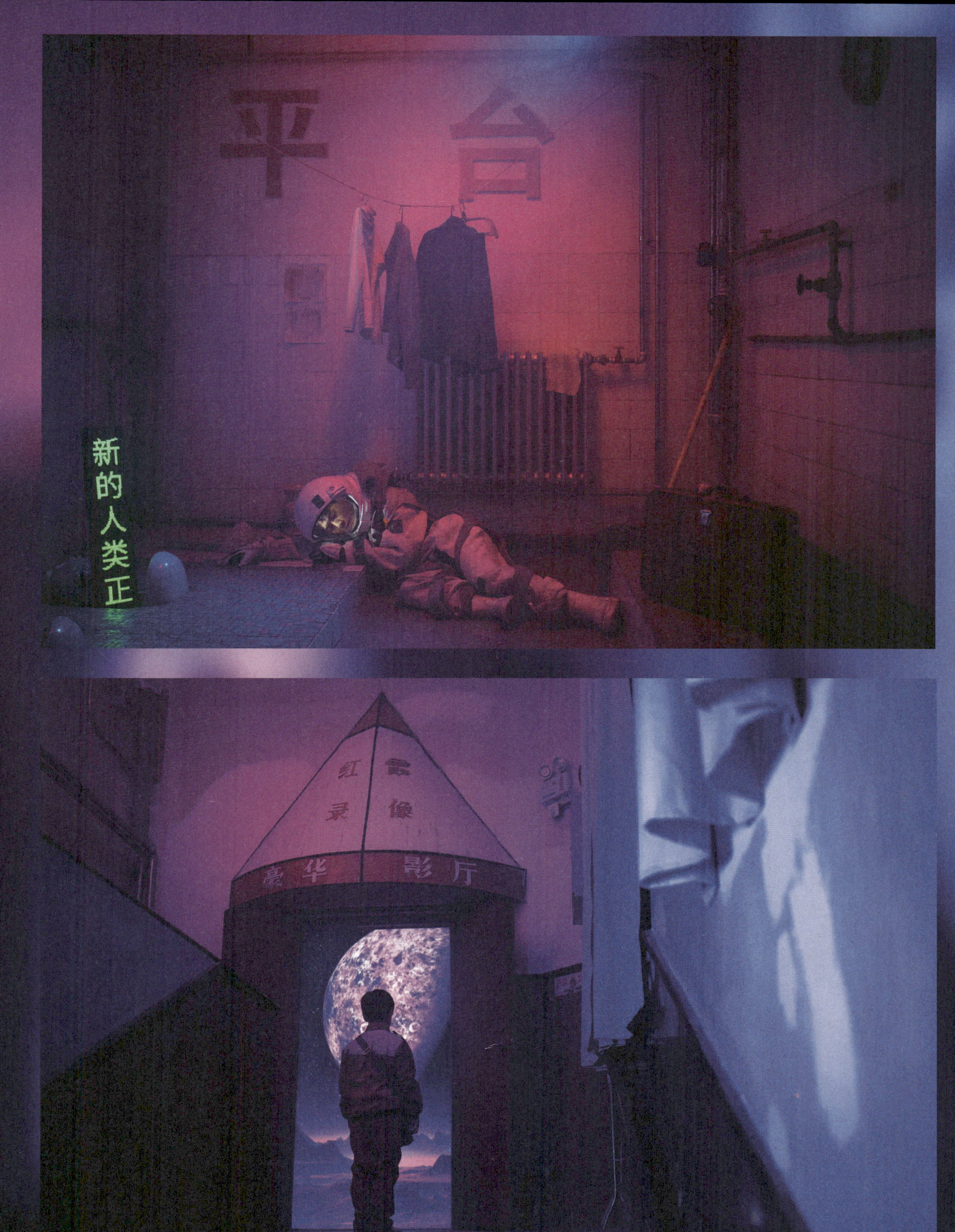
平台
新的人类正
红
录像
豪华影厅

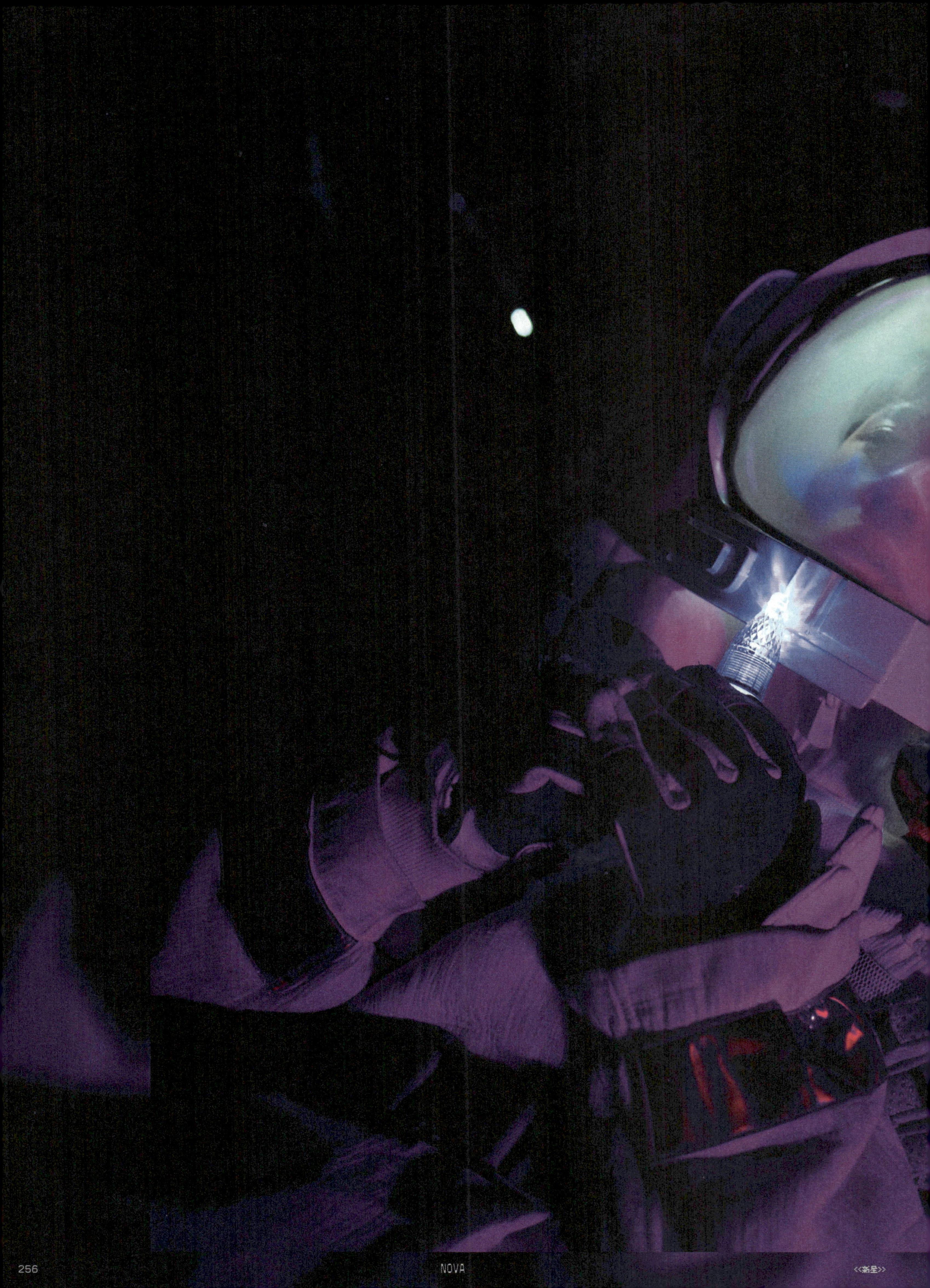

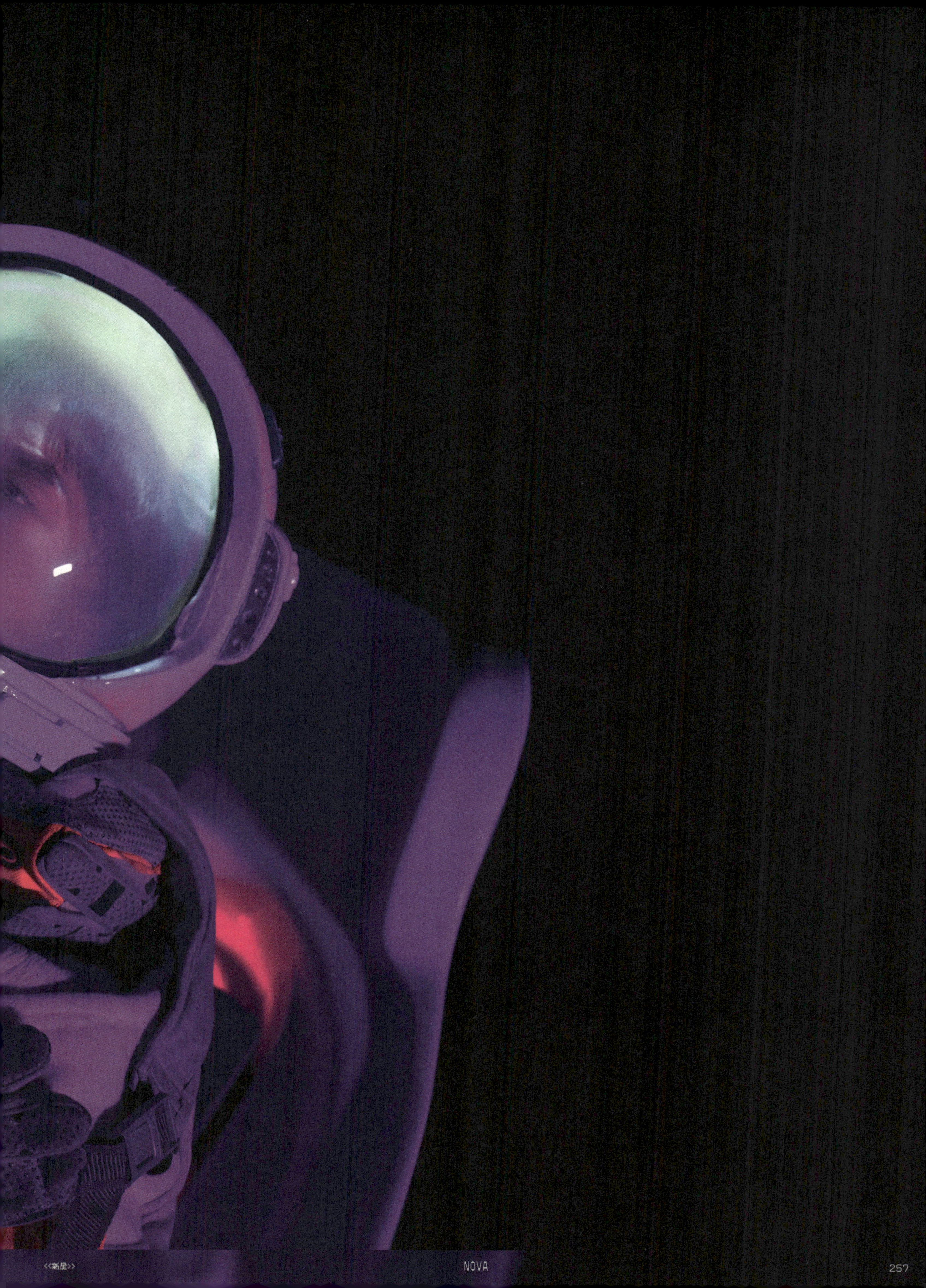

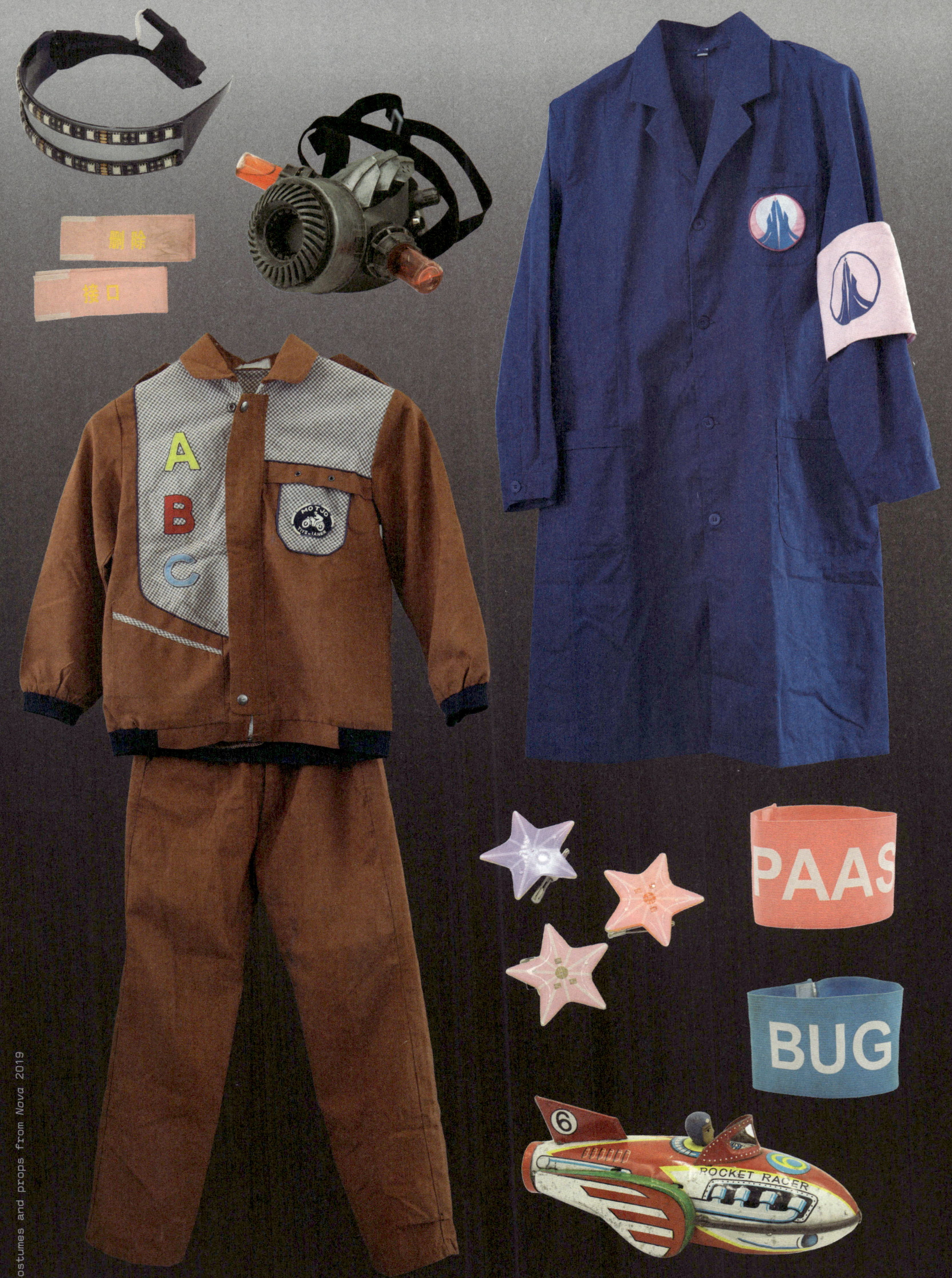

Costumes and props from *Nova* 2019

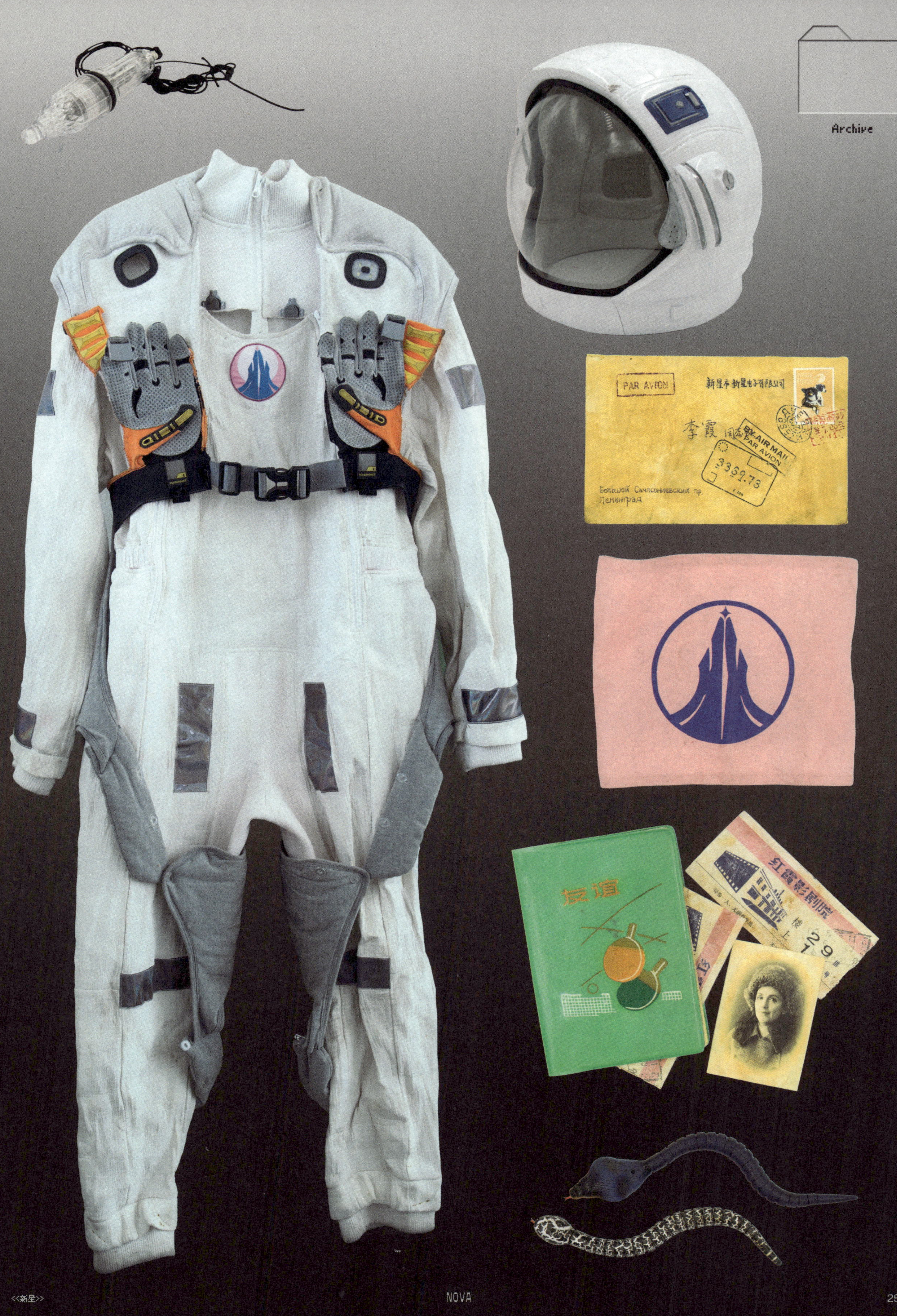
Archive
PAR AVION
新星市新星电子有限公司
李霞
BY AIR MAIL
PAR AVION
3369.73
Большой Самсониевский пр.
Ленинград
友谊
红霞影剧院
楼上
29

THE ETERNAL WAVE 永不消失的电波

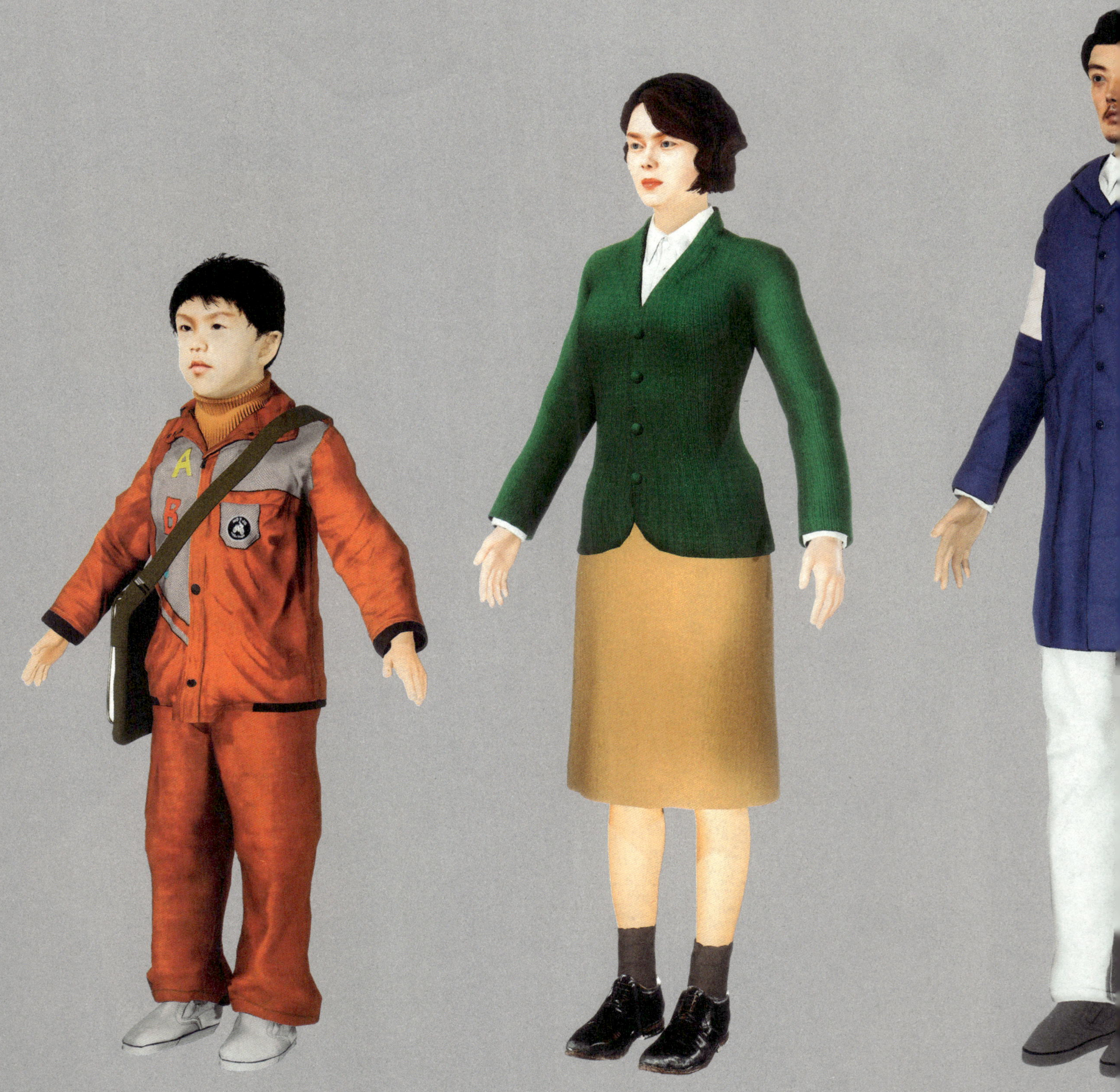

Artwork specification X

The eternal wave 2020
virtual reality, produced in collaboration with Acute Art

《永不消失的电波》2020
虚拟现实 作品与Acute Art联合制作

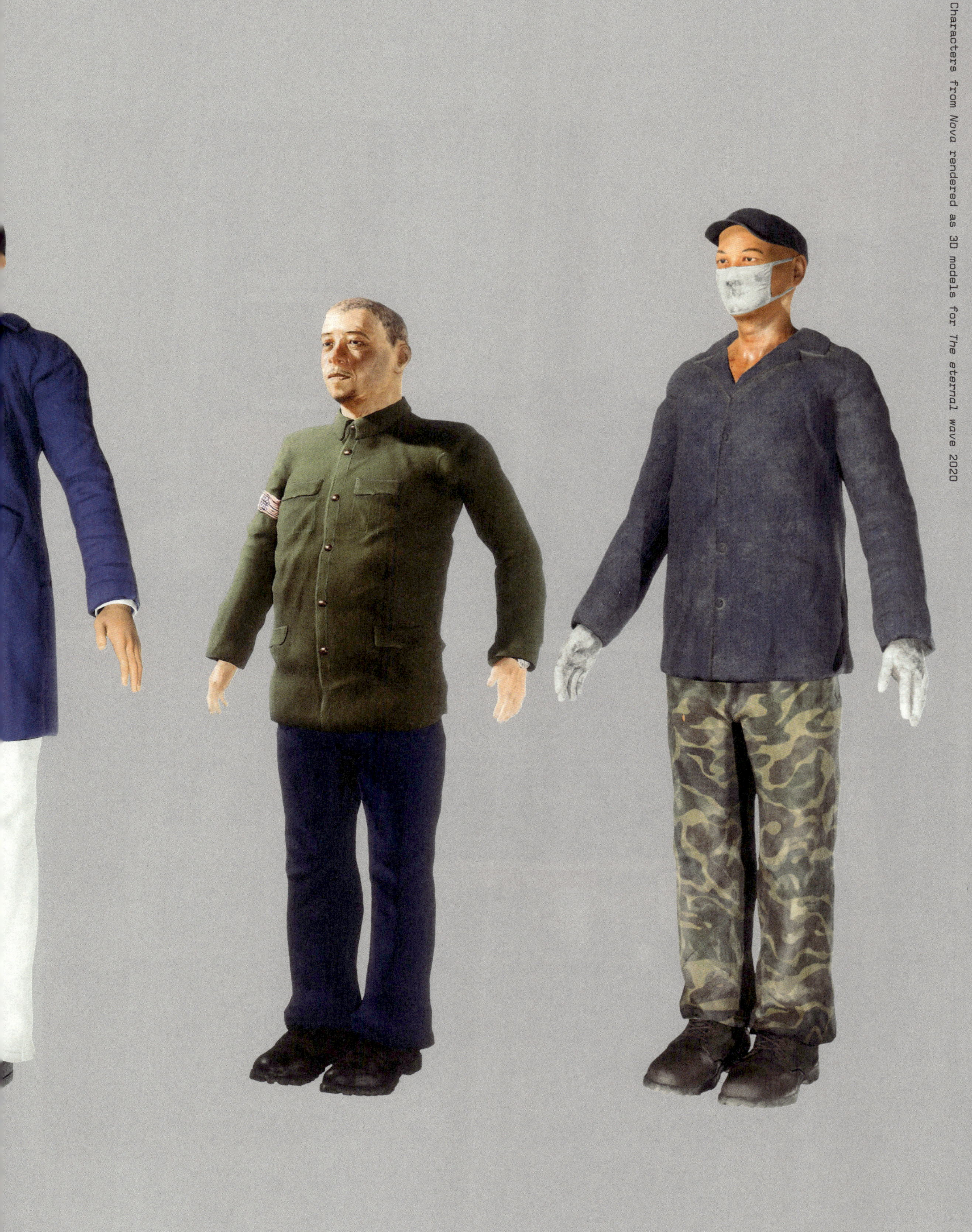

Characters from *Nova* rendered as 3D models for *The eternal wave* 2020

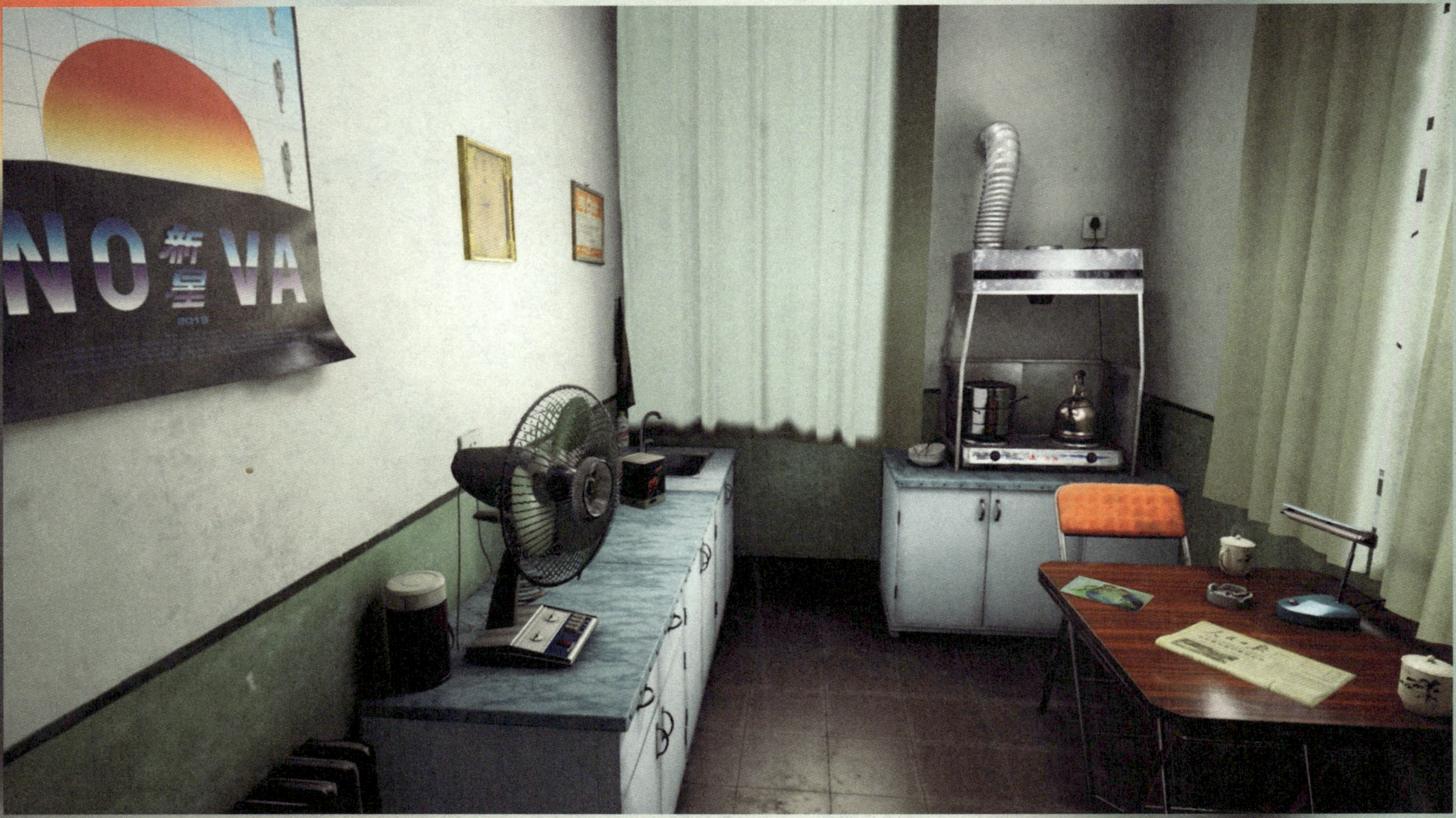
NO 新星 VA
2019

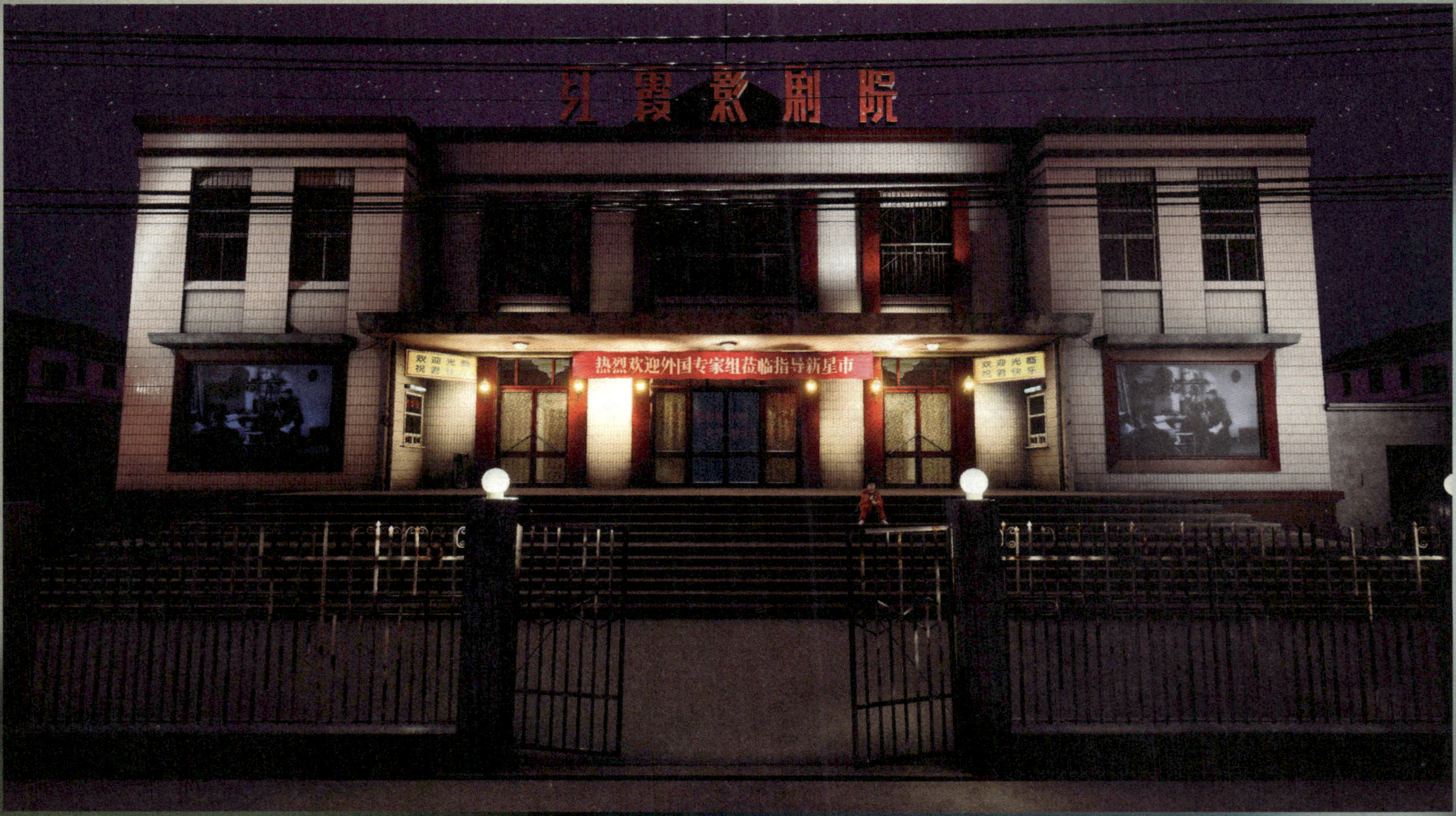
红霞影剧院
热烈欢迎外国专家组莅临指导新星市
欢迎光临
祝君快乐

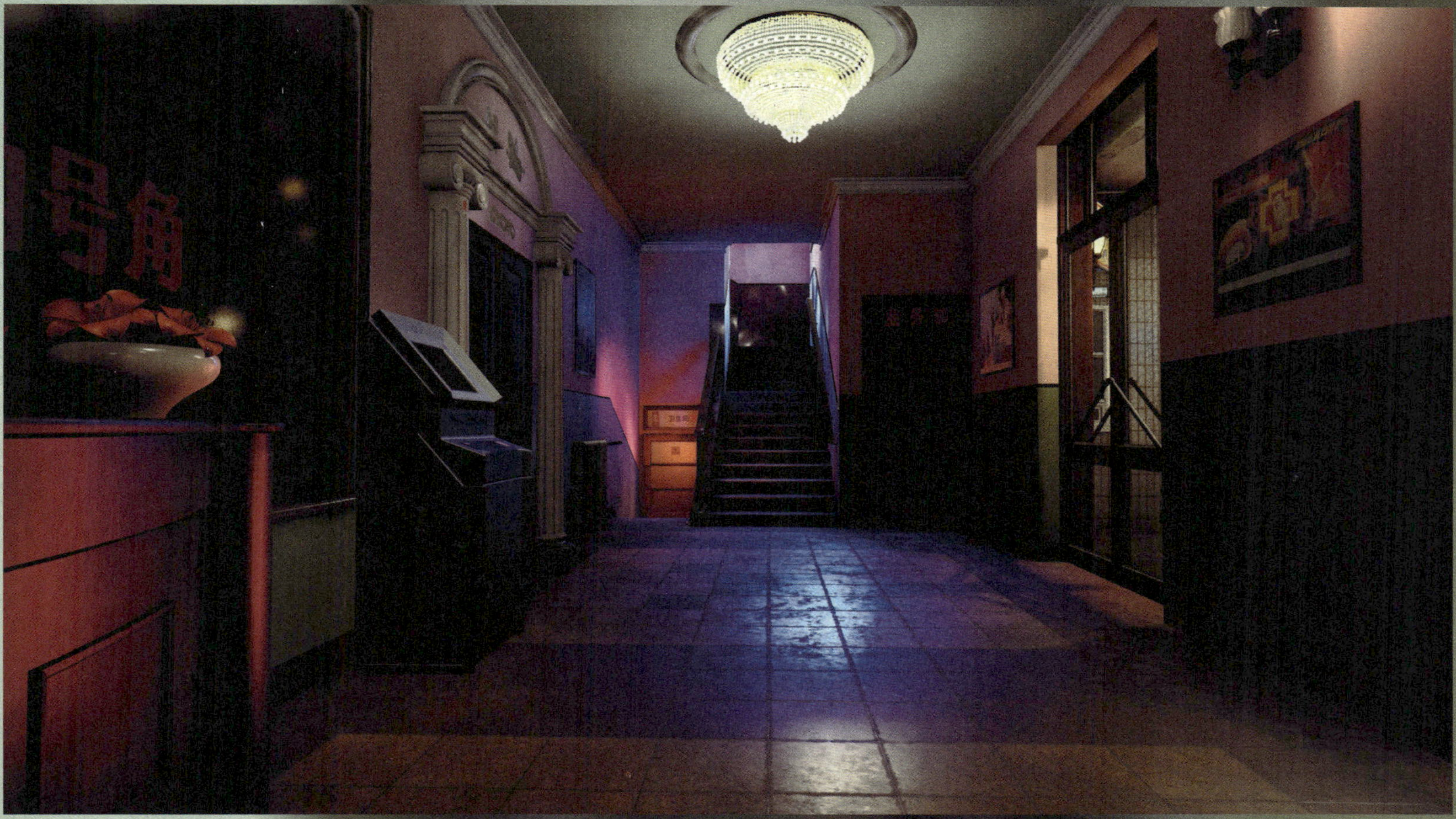

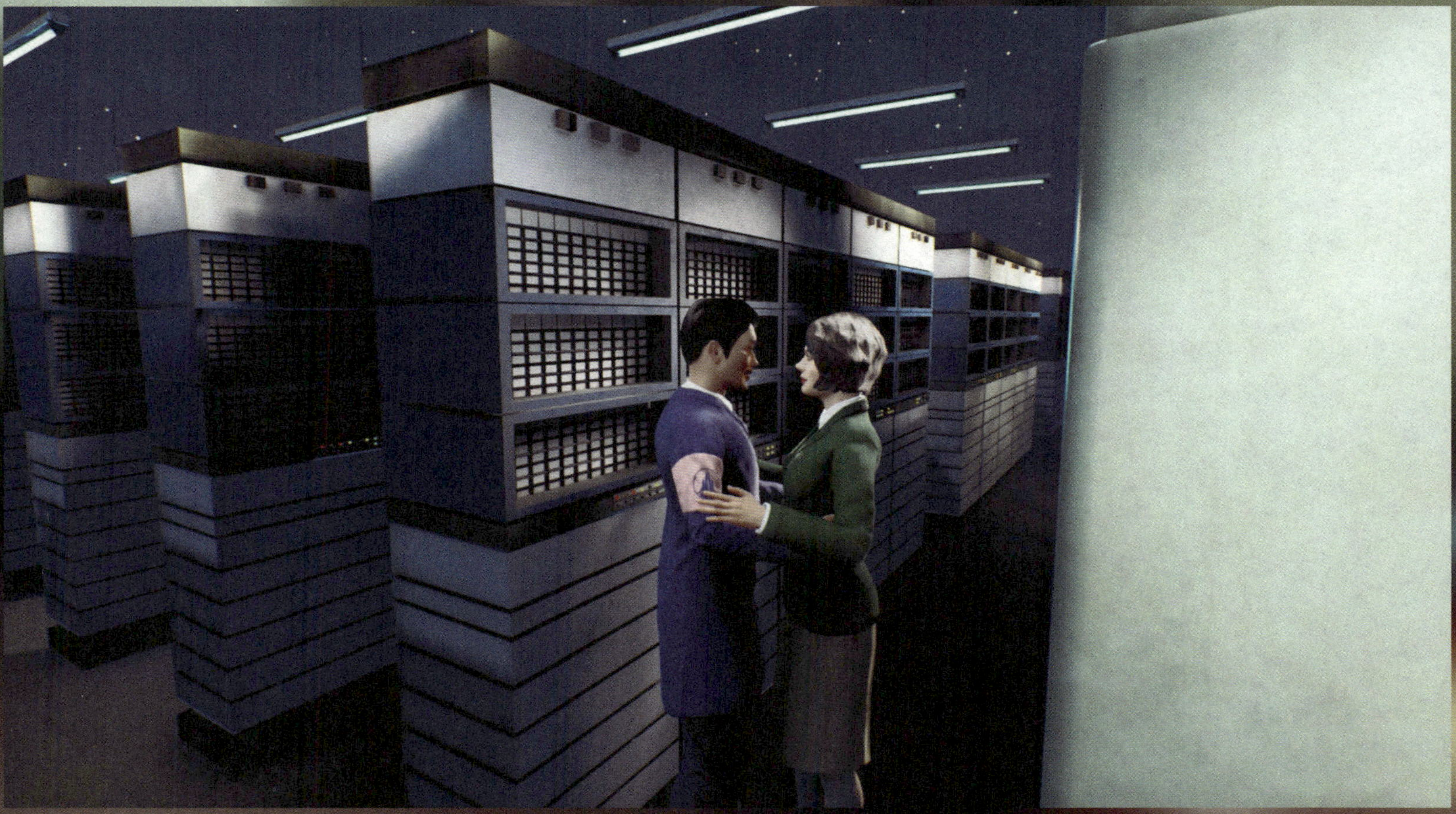

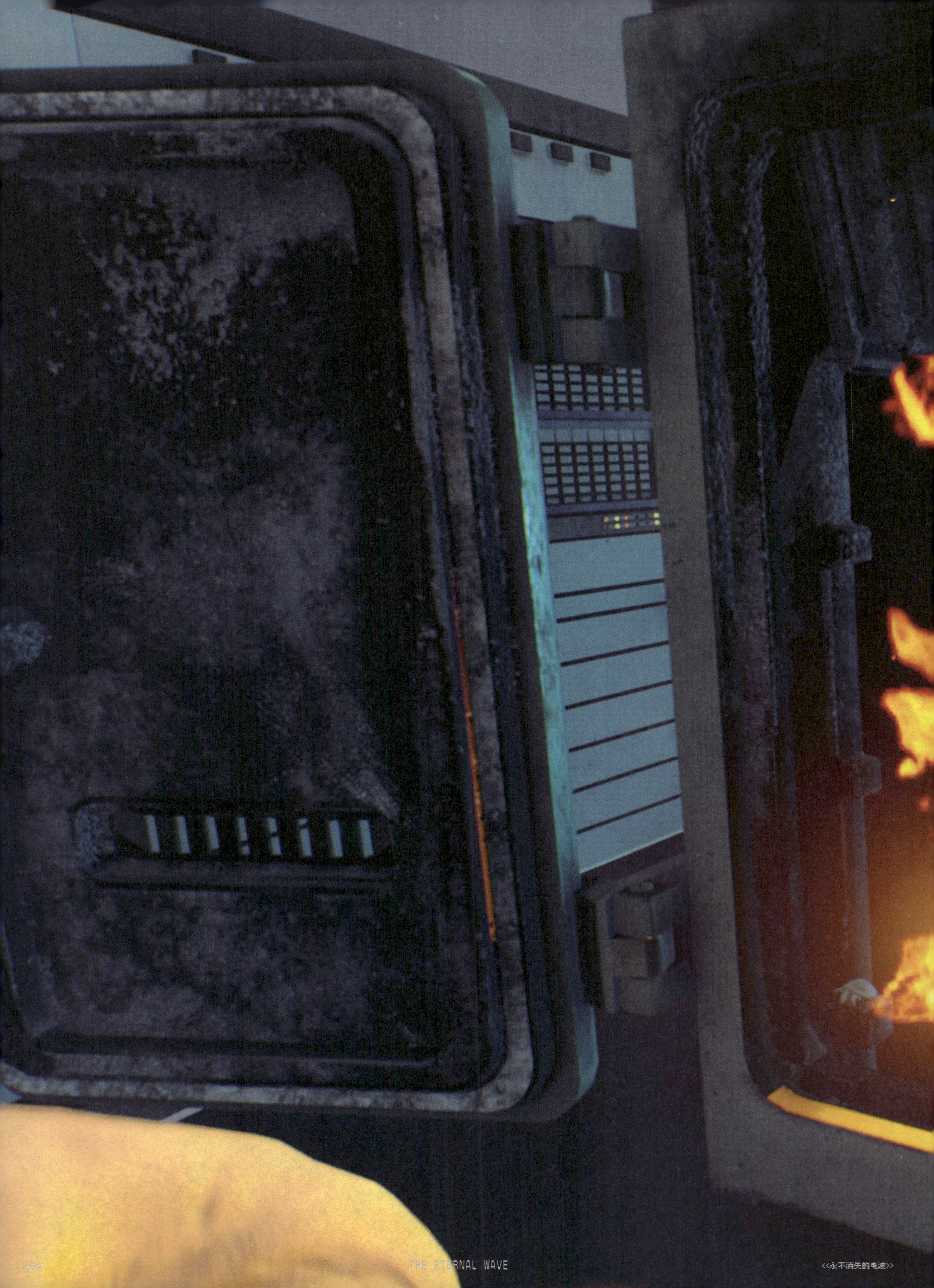

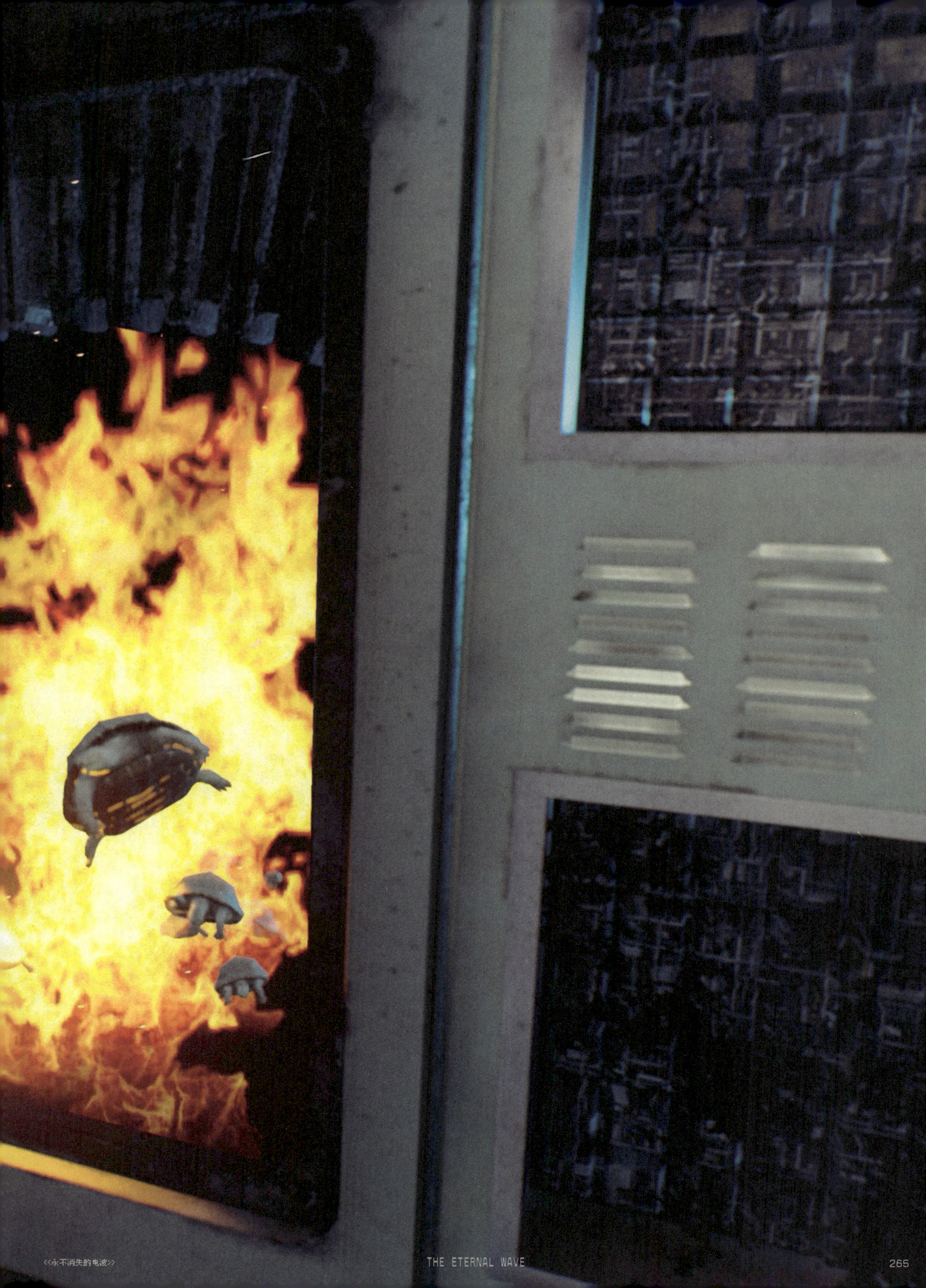

1 02 2022

2 DUOTOPIA VOL 1 2022

多托邦 第一期

3 DUOTOPIA VOL 2 2024

多托邦 第二期

4 META-MENTARY 2022

元纪录

J[1-4]: Oz / Duotopia vol 1 / Duotopia vol 2 / Meta-mentary

An androgynous form with bionic tentacles hovers above a digital skyline, a wizened cyber-pioneer beholding the latest iteration of the metaverse. Cao Fei created her newest avatar, Oz, within Yuanbang Mega City, a metaverse platform developed by the Chinese tech giants Meta Media and Baidu. For Cao, cyberspace has never been a separate realm of abstract zeroes and ones. From her earliest works to today, the 'physical' and the 'virtual' are not opposed but rather 'two trajectories constantly in flux – often indistinguishably close, sometimes intersecting'.[1] Where the digital architectural forms of *Duotopia* spin against pixelated cloudscapes, the documentary *Meta-mentary* is shot from the ground up. Filmed on phones, this vox-pop documentary captures everyday peoples' views on the hyped virtual reality platform. 'I'd probably try to leave', a passer-by tells Cao when asked what he'd do if he found himself in the metaverse.

(1) Klaus Biesenbach (ed), 'Cao Fei in conversation with Klaus Biesenbach,' *Kaleidoscope Asia*, no 3, spring/summer 2016, pp 138–43.

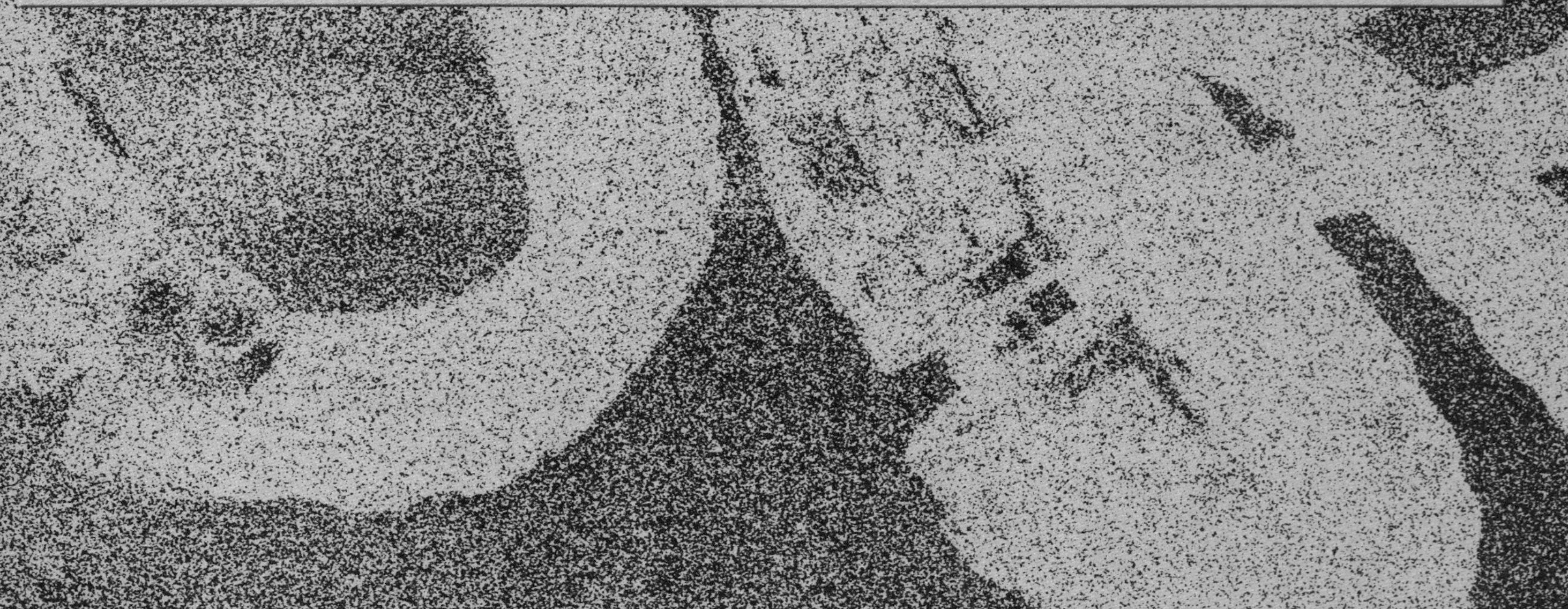

OZ

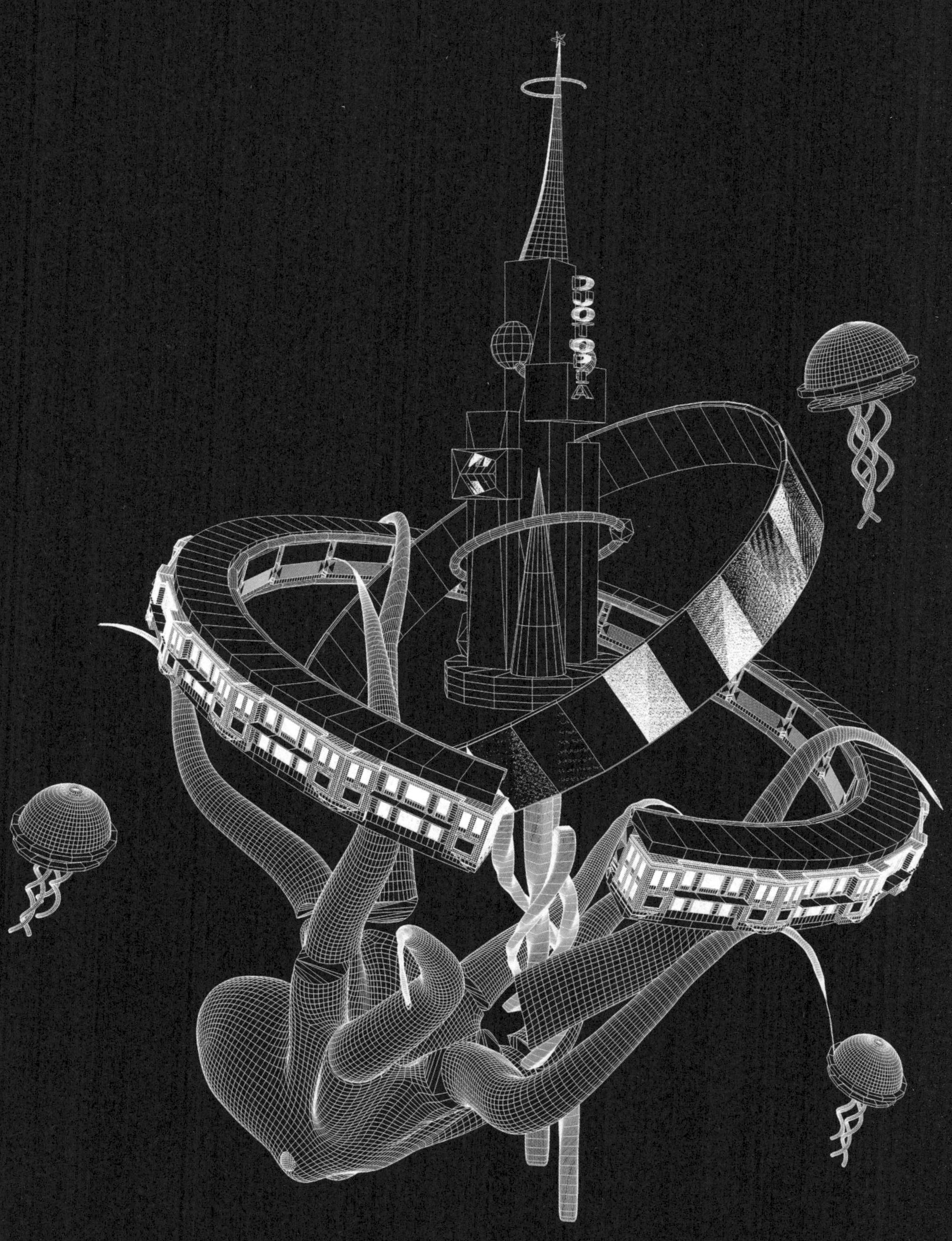

Artwork specification

Oz 2022
dual-screen digital video, colour, sound
1:36 min, 9:16
Music: Ma Haiping

《Oz》2022
9:16彩色有声双屏数字影像
1分36秒
音乐：马海平

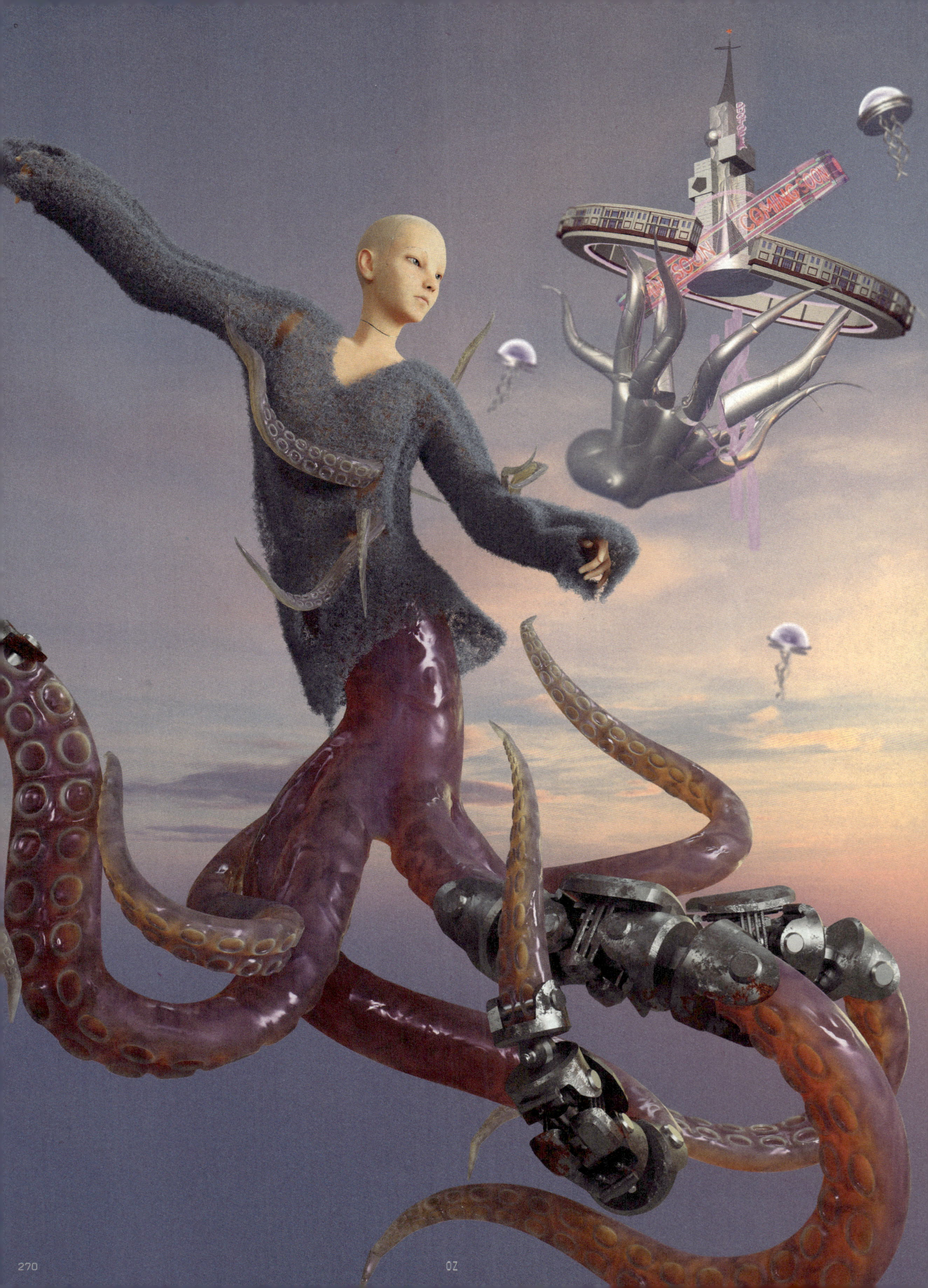
COMING SOON

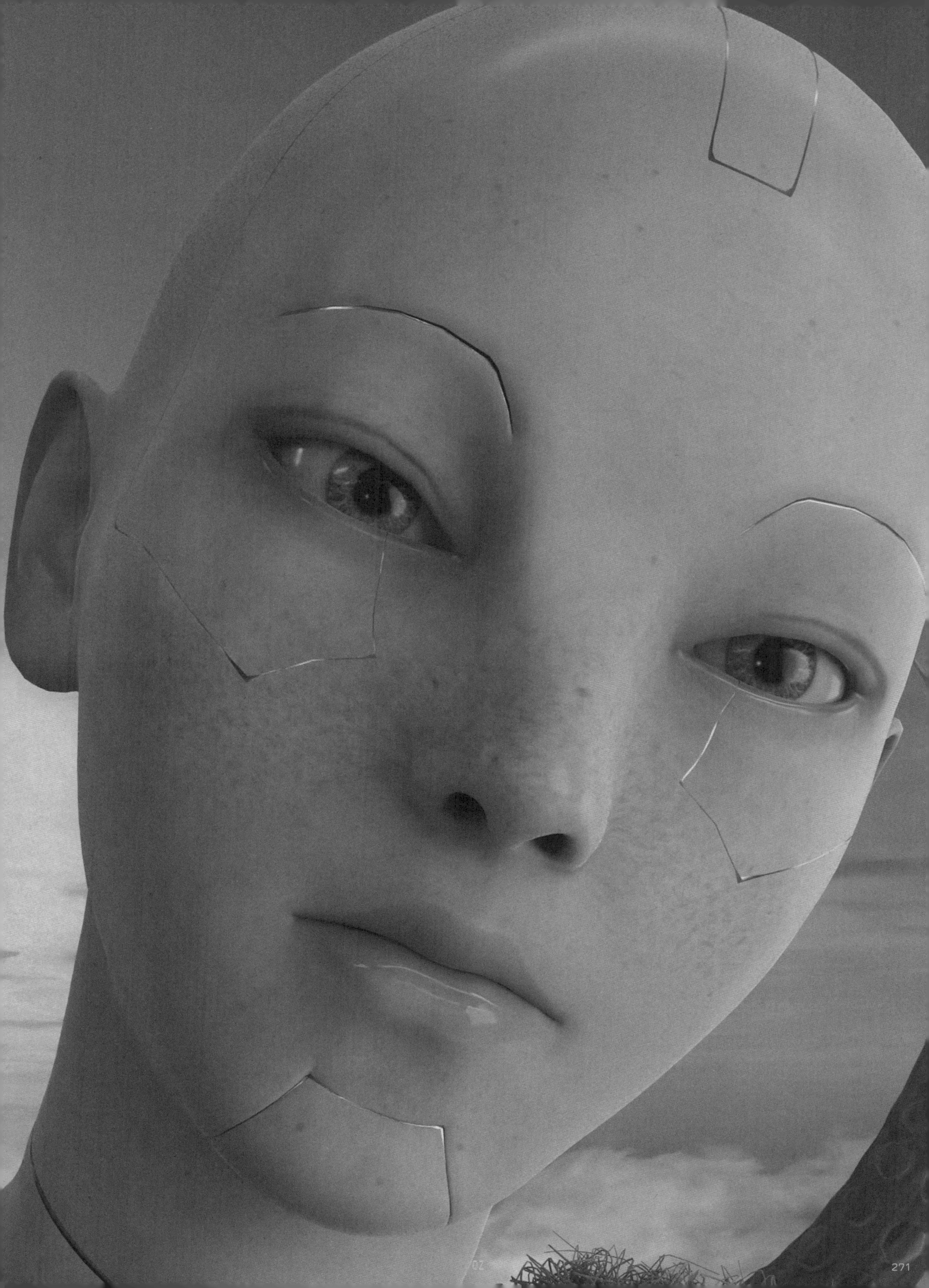

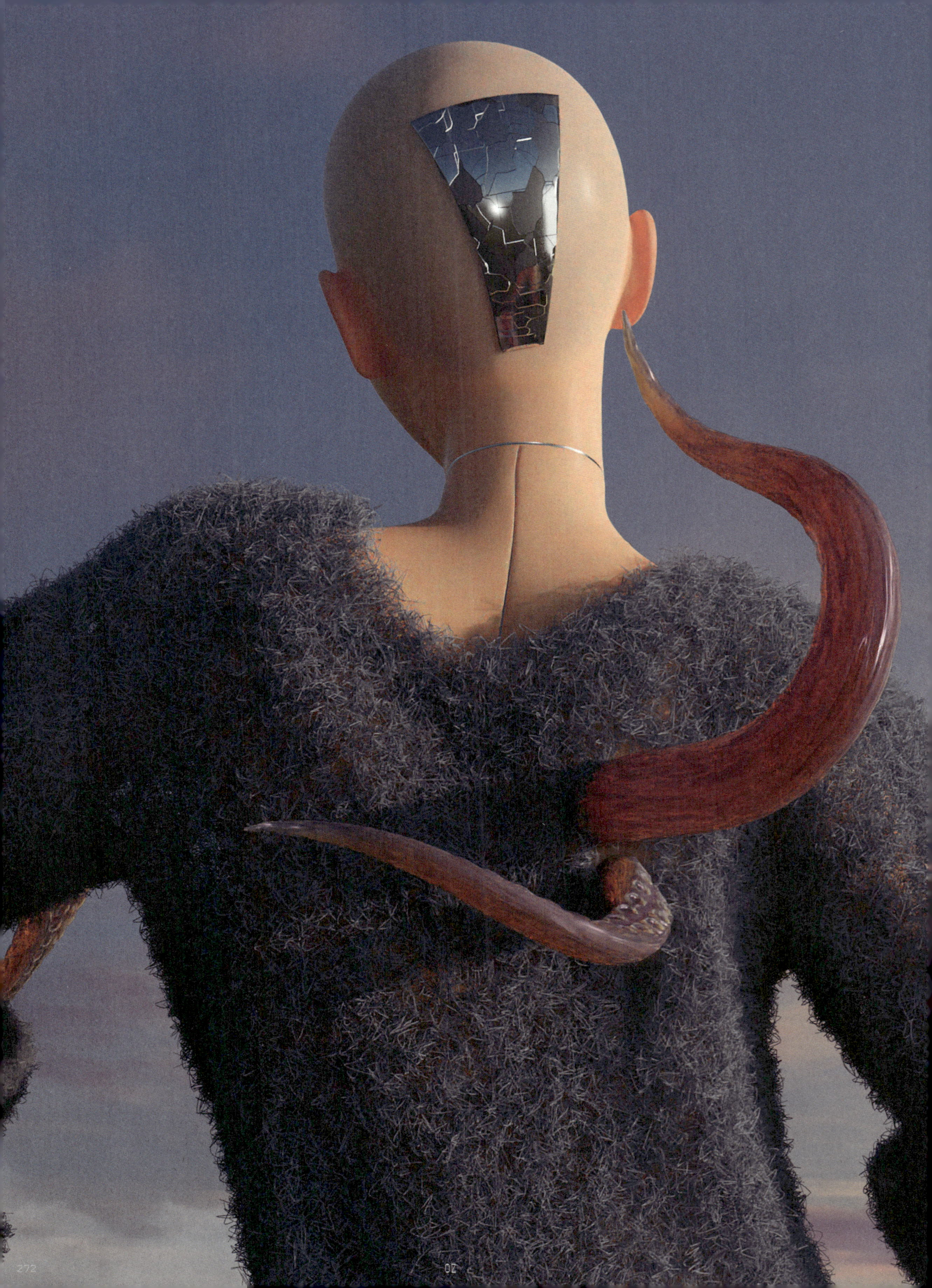

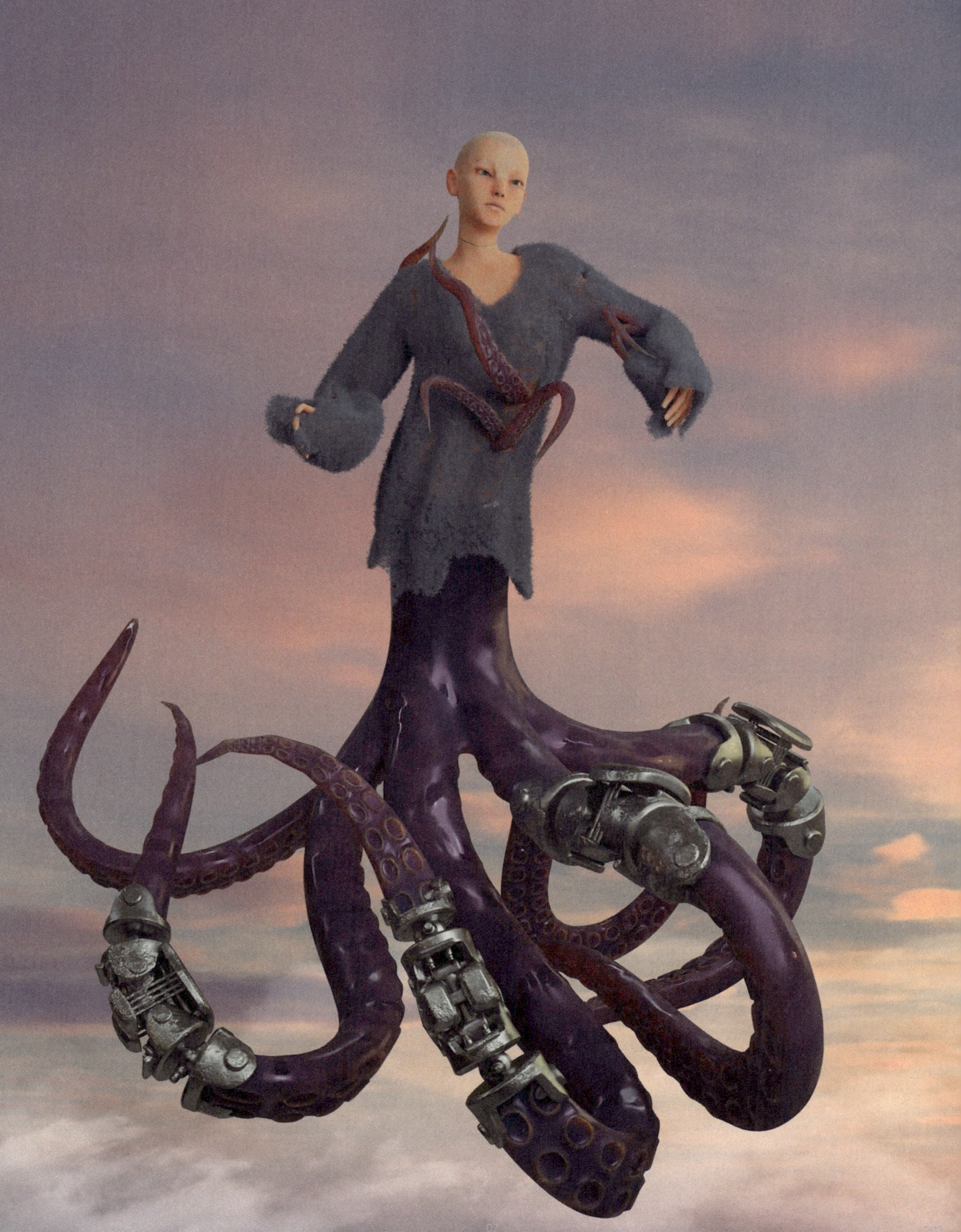

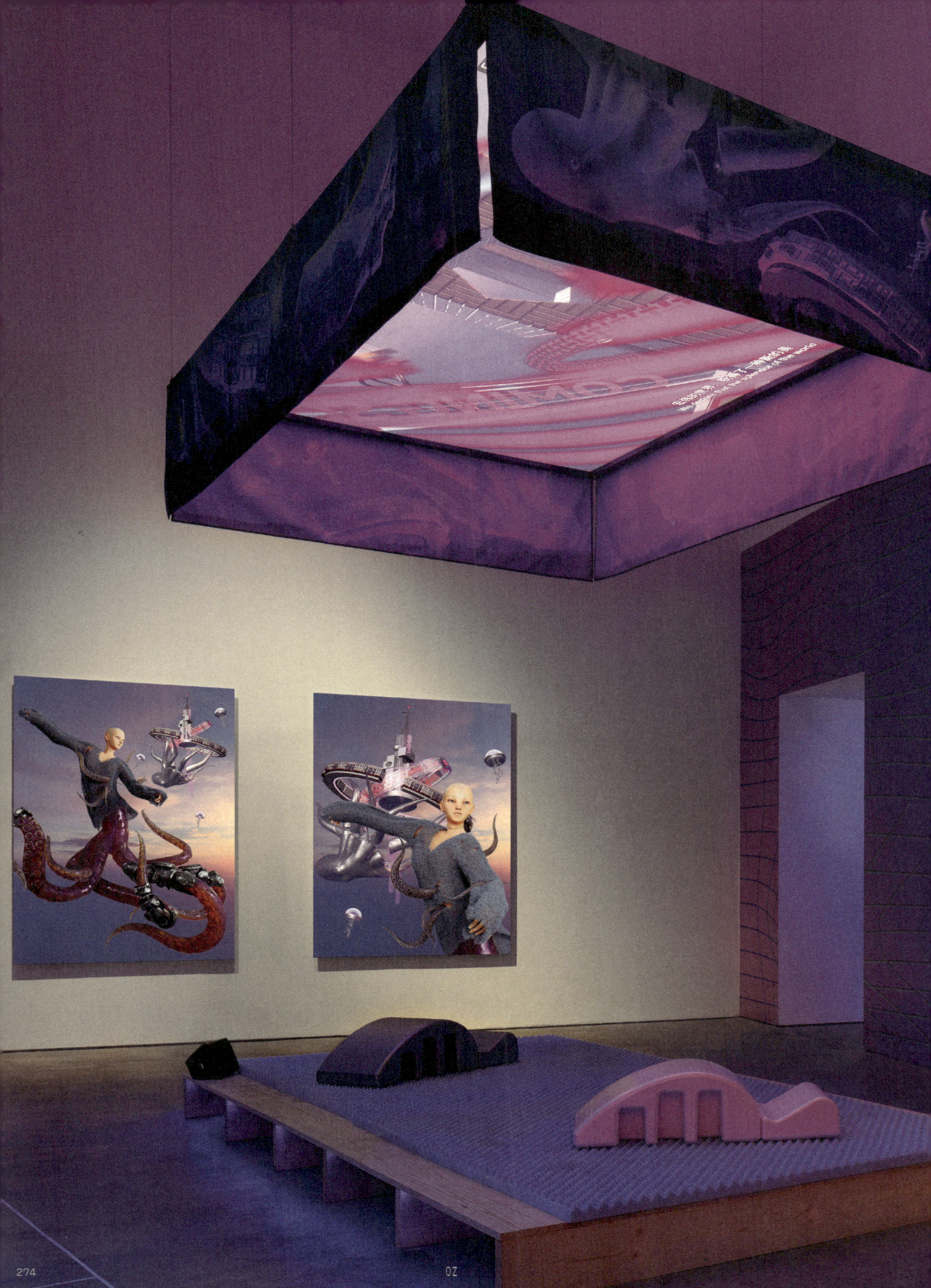

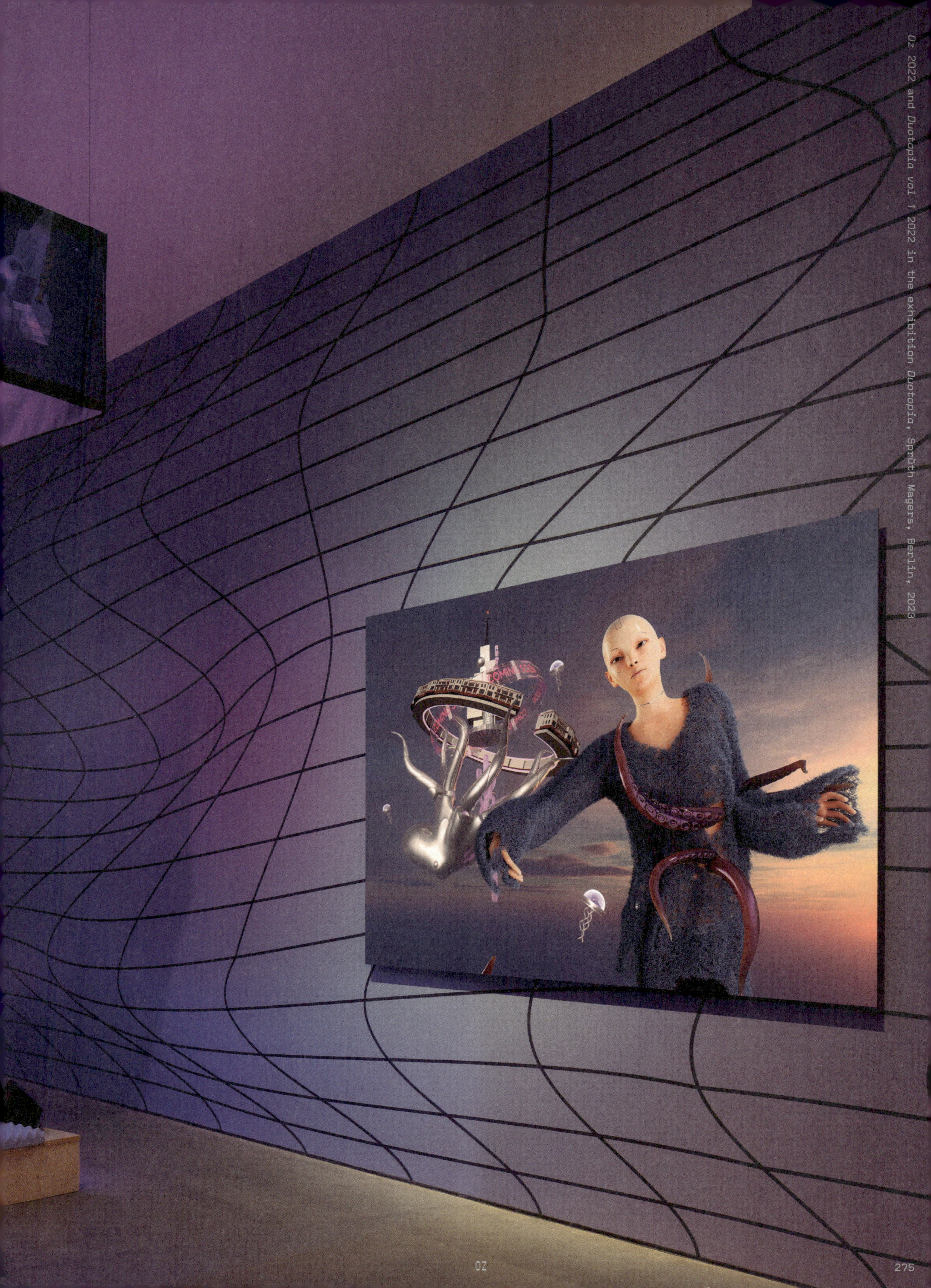

Oz 2022 and *Duotopia vol 1* 2022 in the exhibition *Duotopia*, Sprüth Magers, Berlin, 2023

DUOTOPIA VOL 1 多托邦 第一期

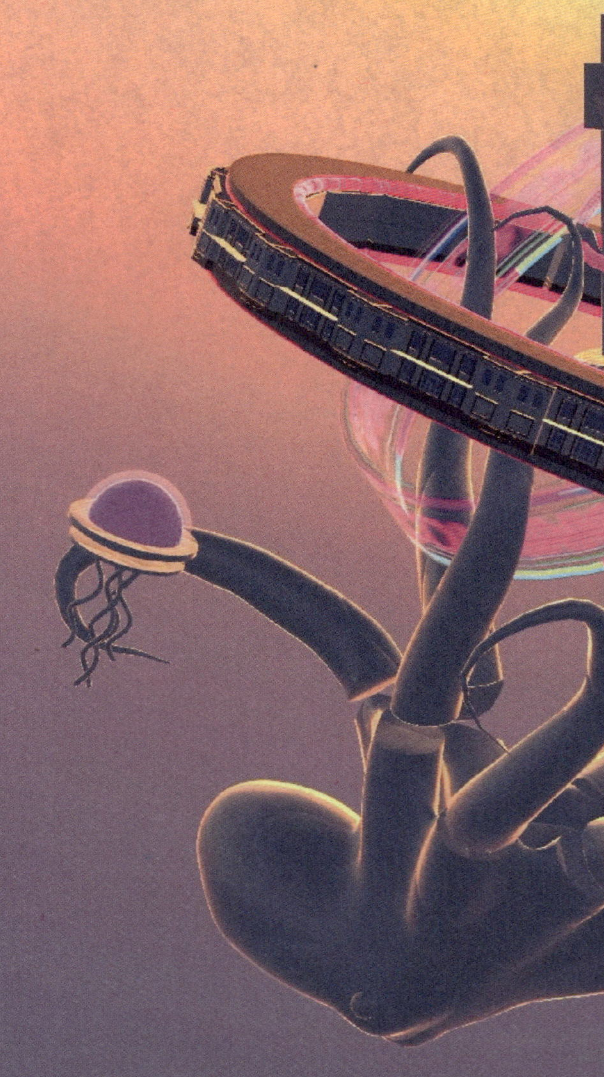

Artwork specification

Duotopia vol 1 2022
3D-rendered video, colour, sound
2:40 min, 16:9
Music: Ma Haiping
Commissioned by Meta City

《多托邦》第一期 2022
16:9 彩色有声三维渲染数字影像
2分40秒
音乐：马海平
作品由元邦委托创作

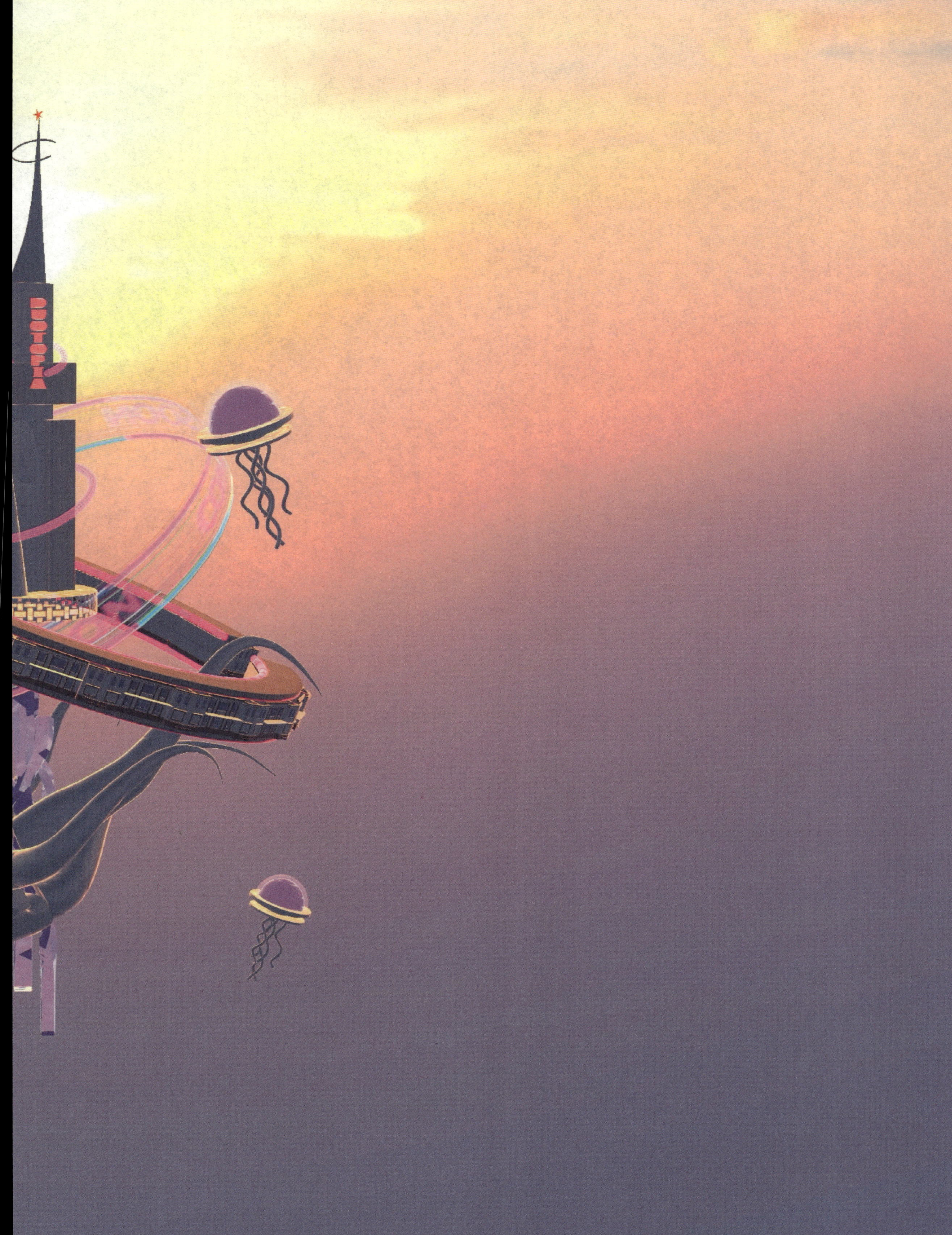
DUOTOPIA

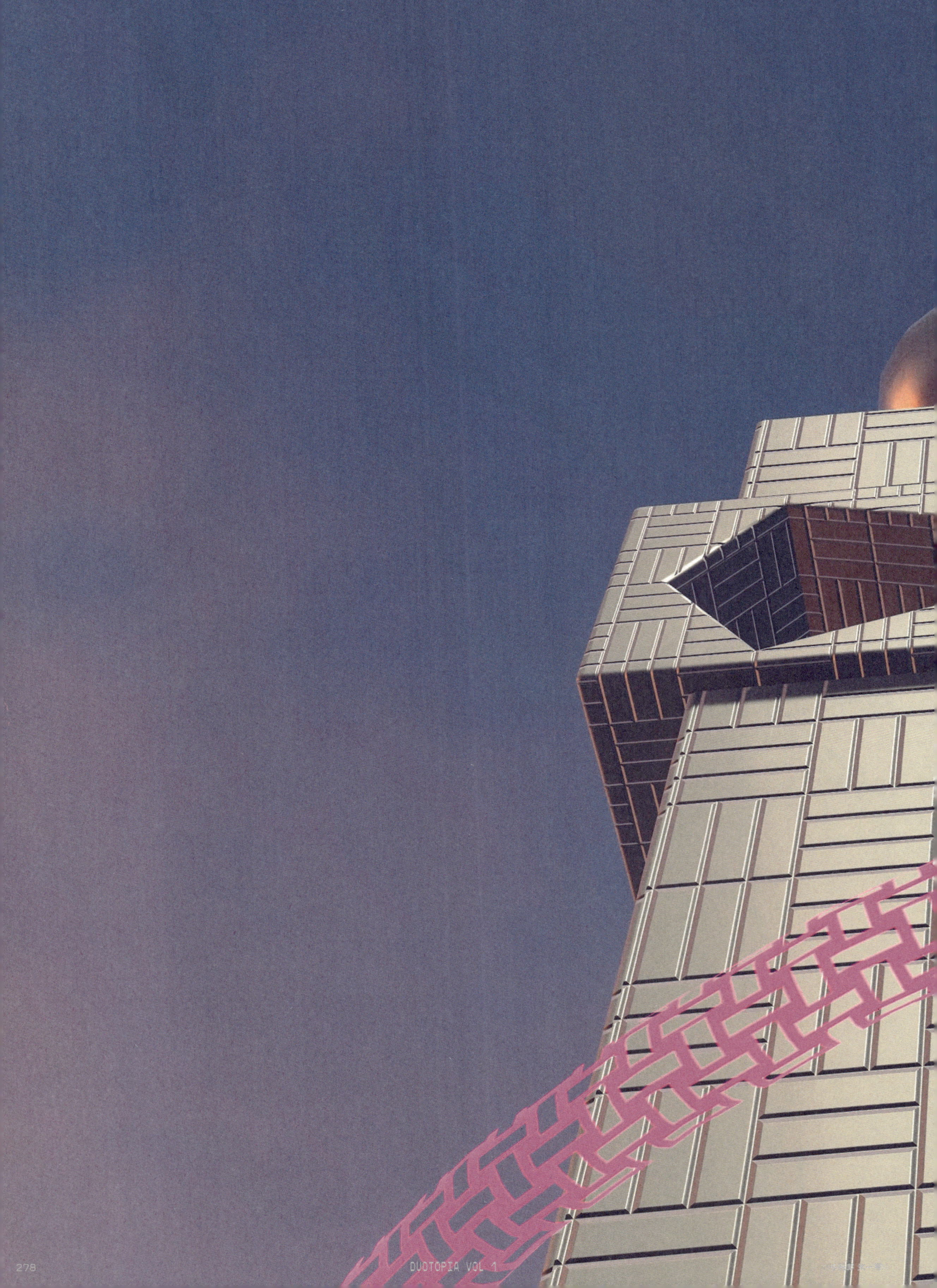

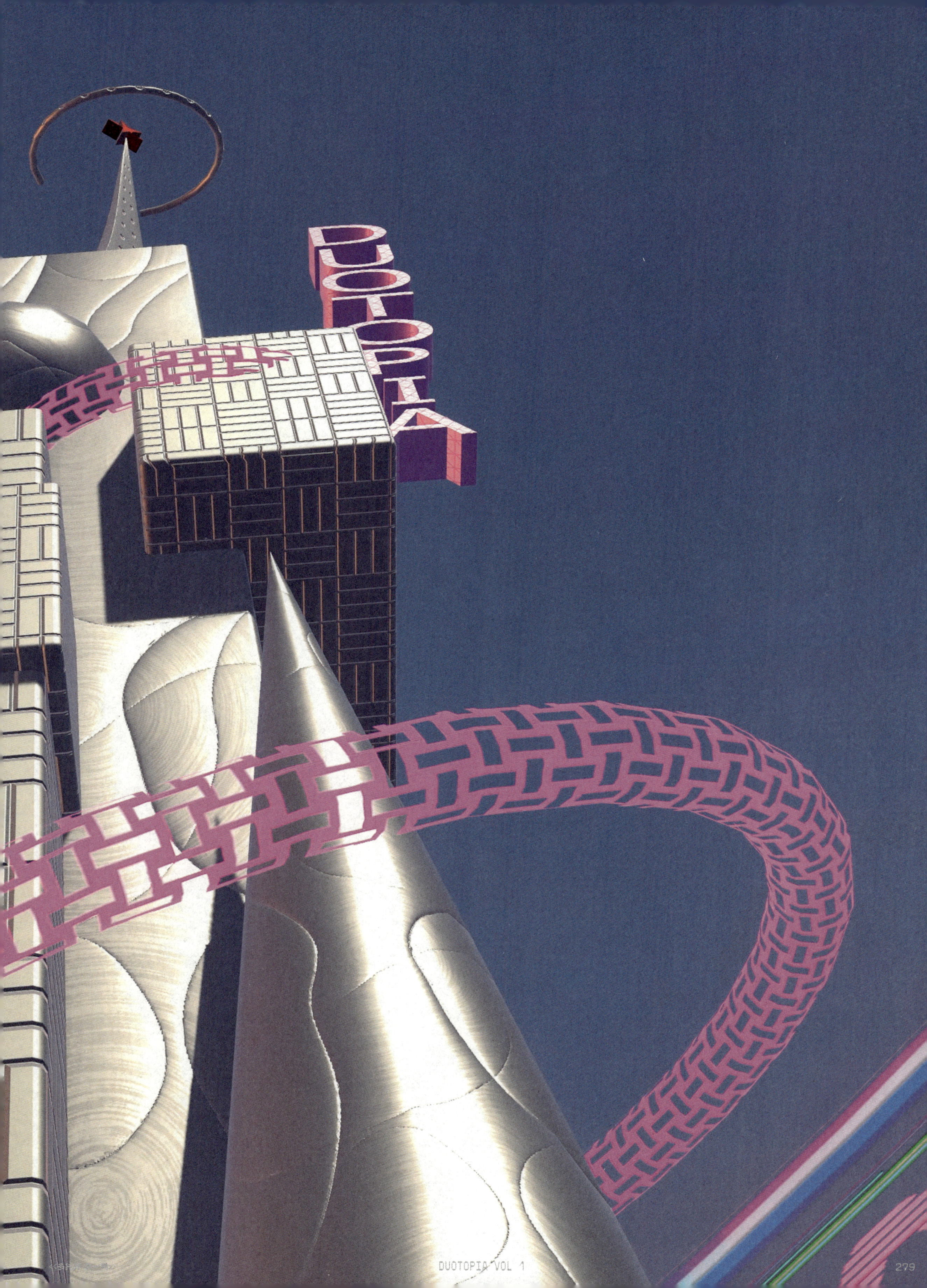
DUOTOPIA

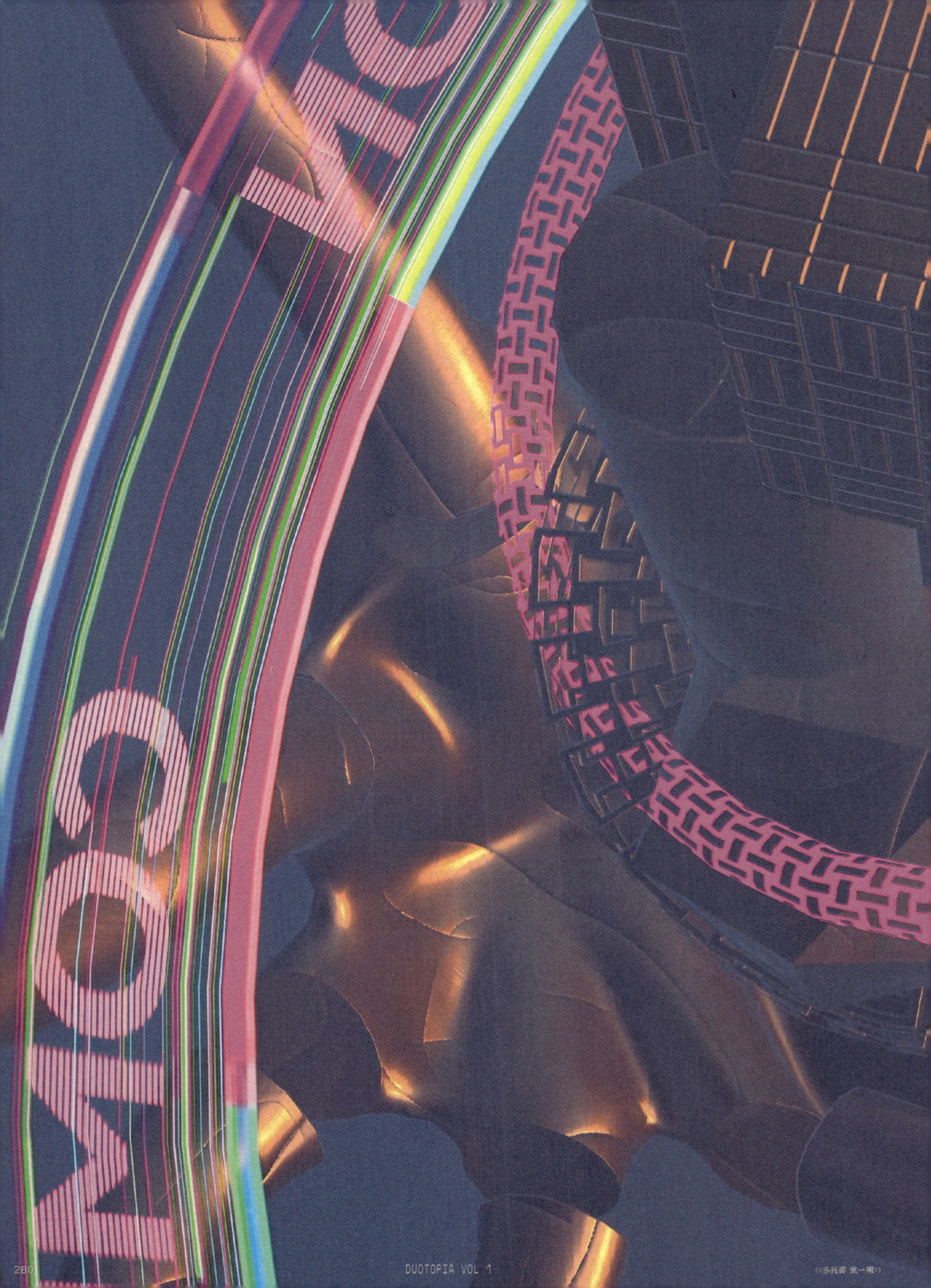

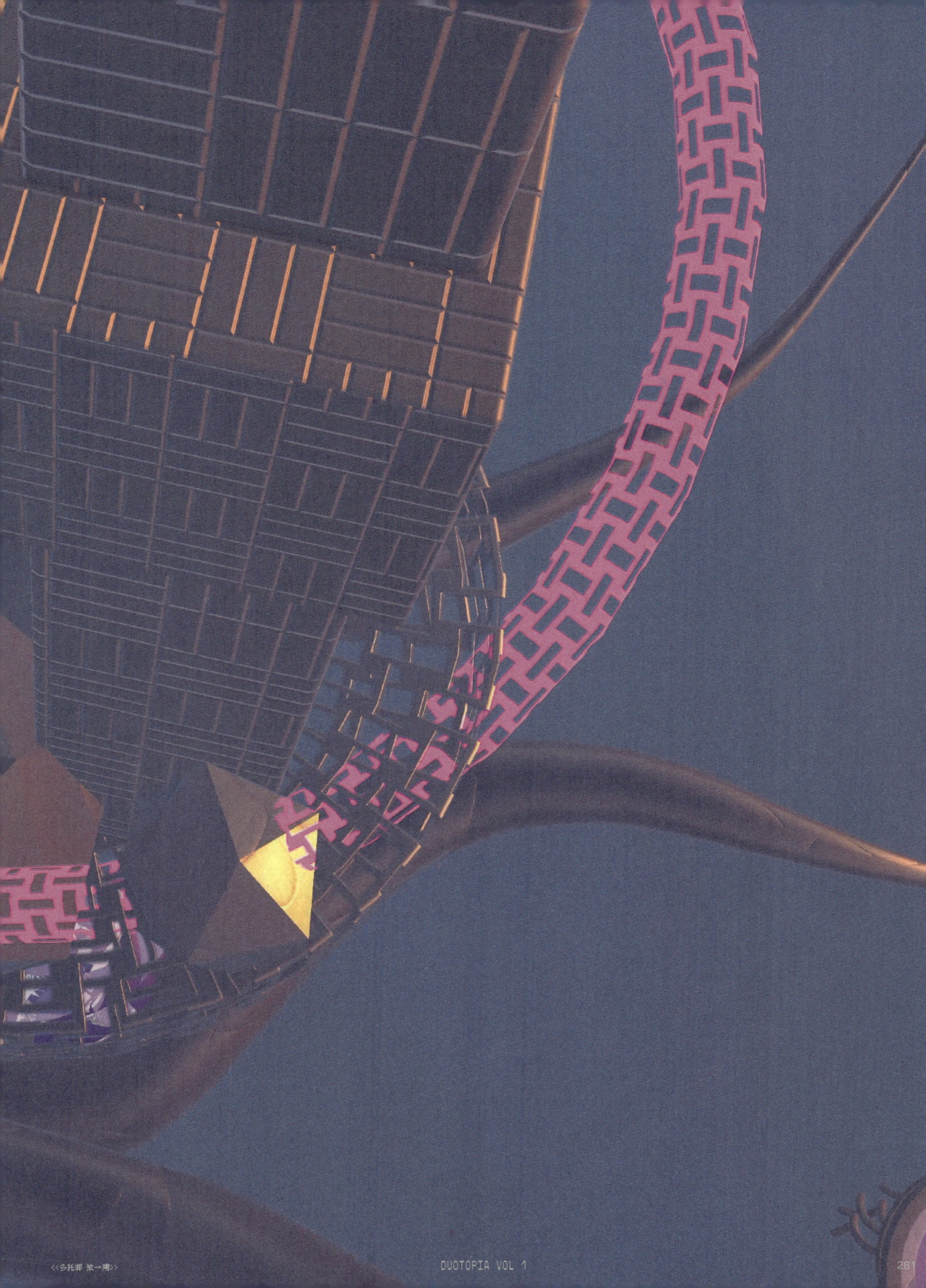

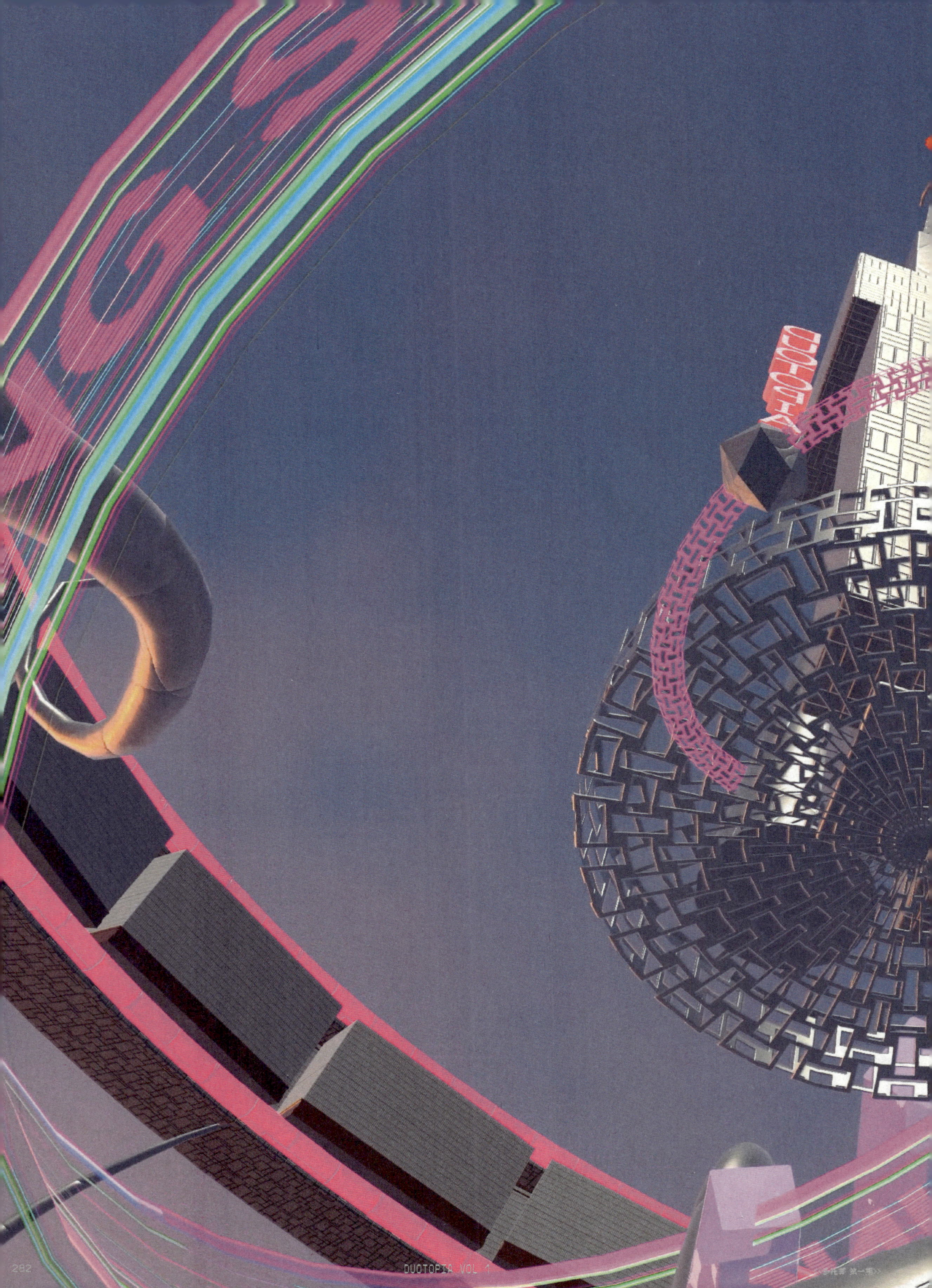
DUOTOPIA

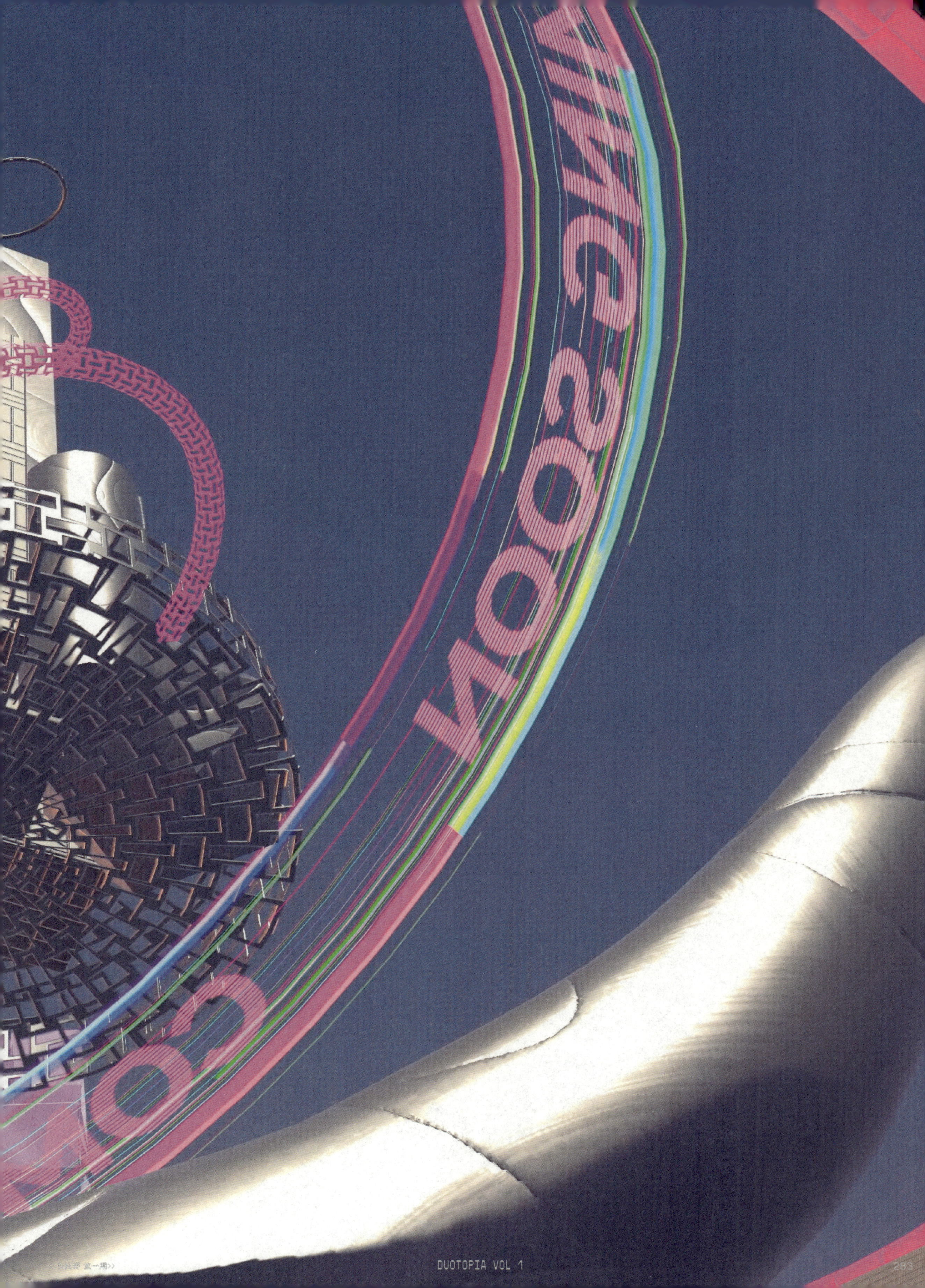

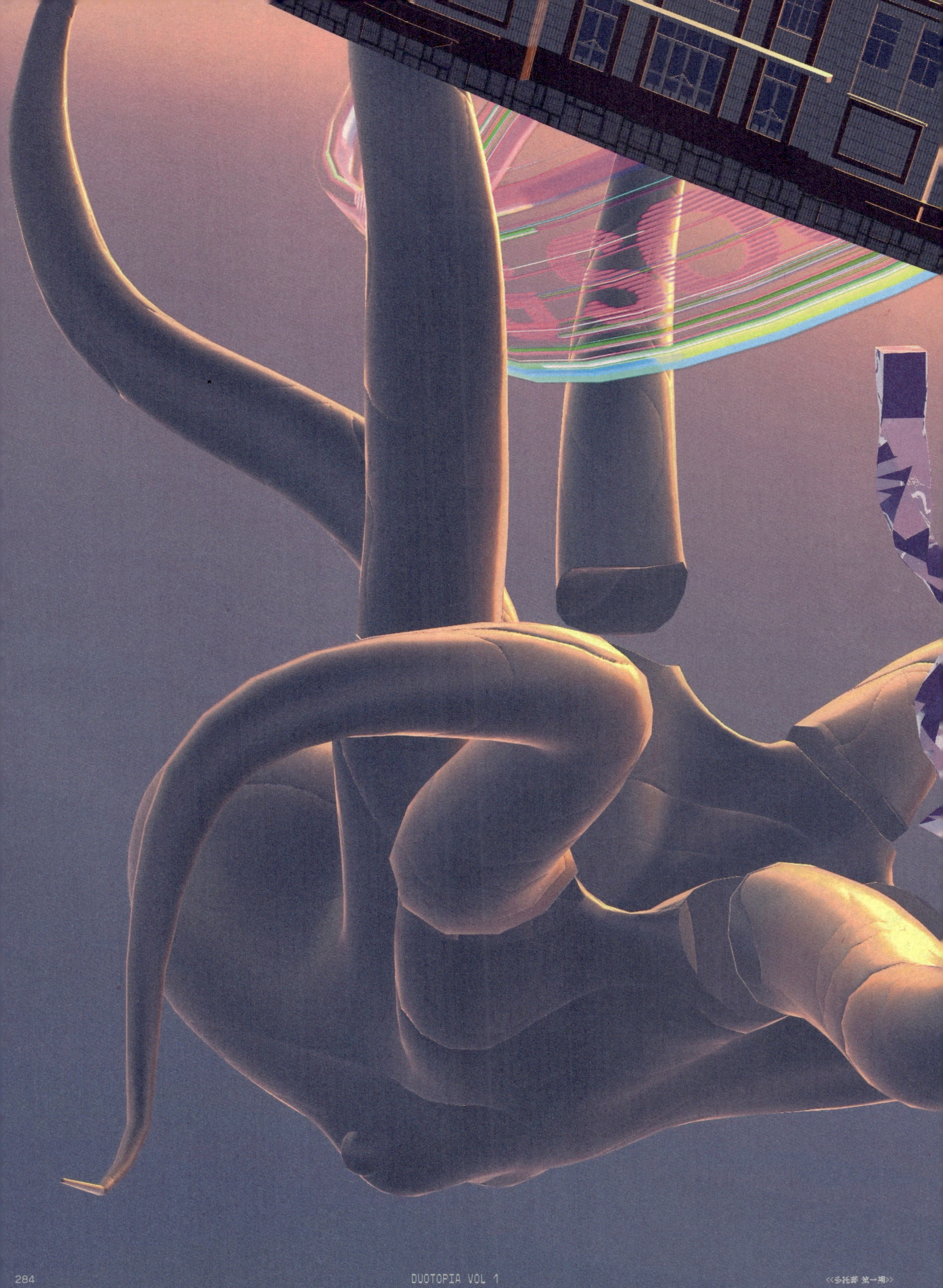

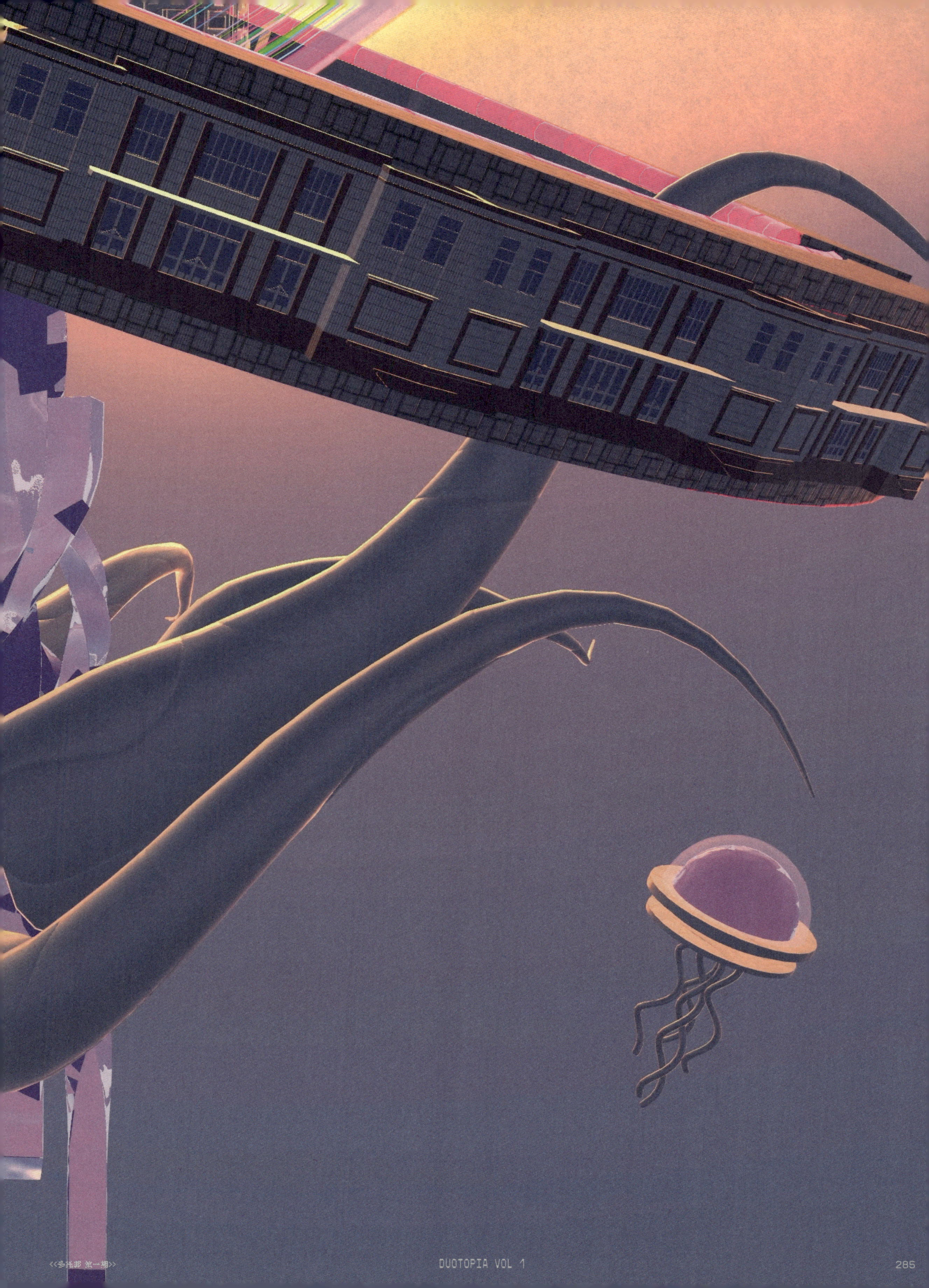

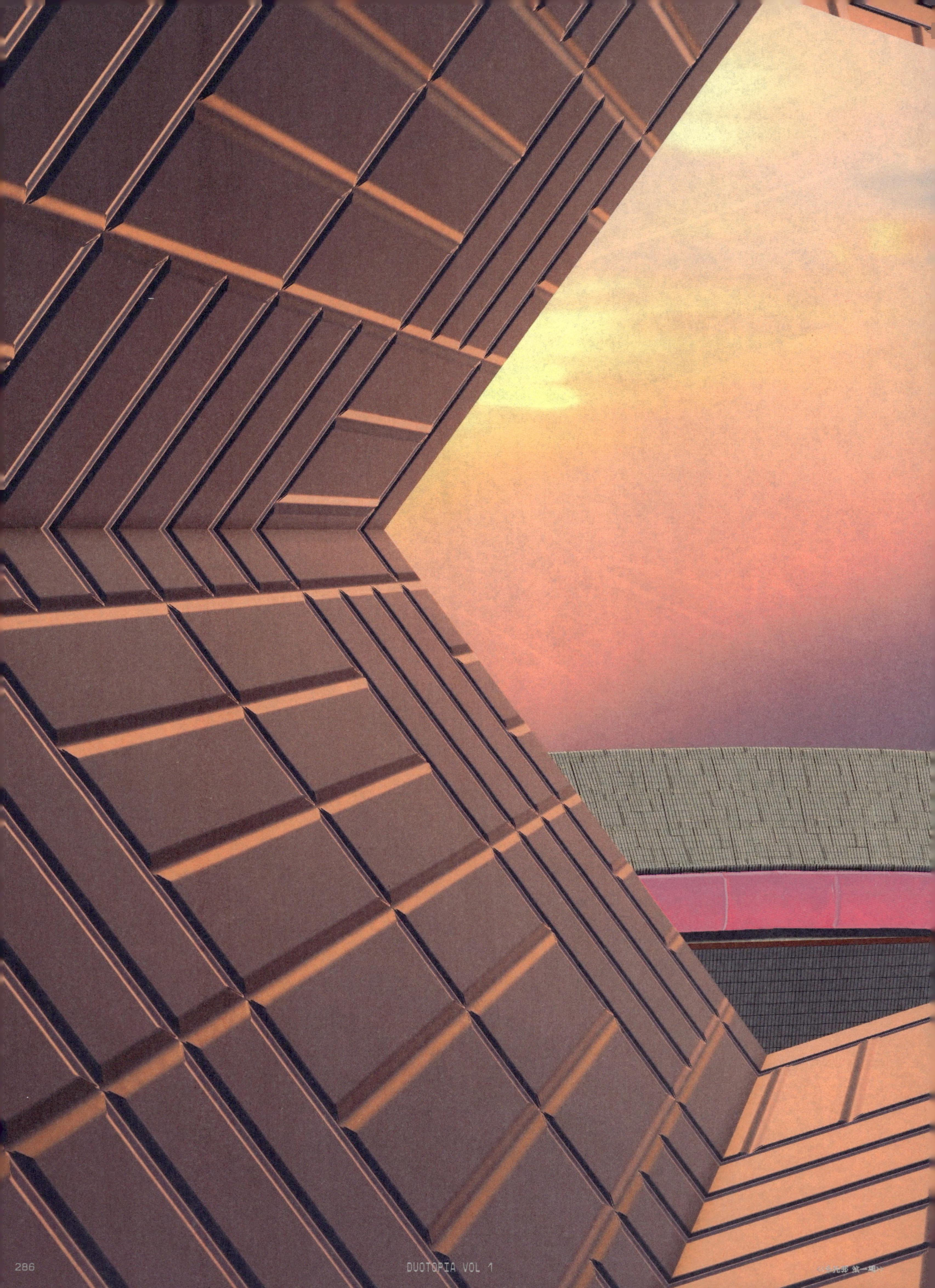

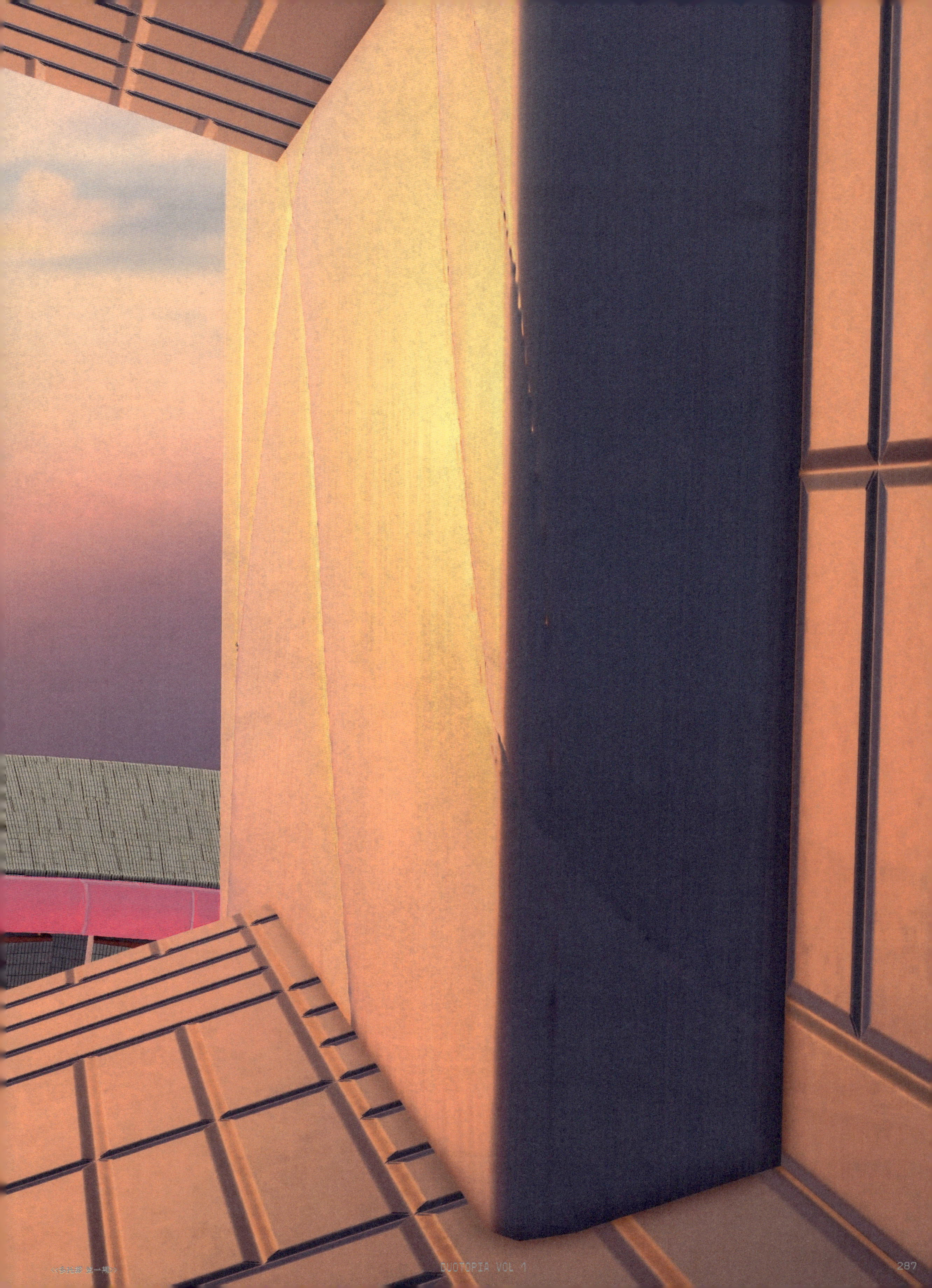

DUOTOPIA VOL 2 多托邦 第二期

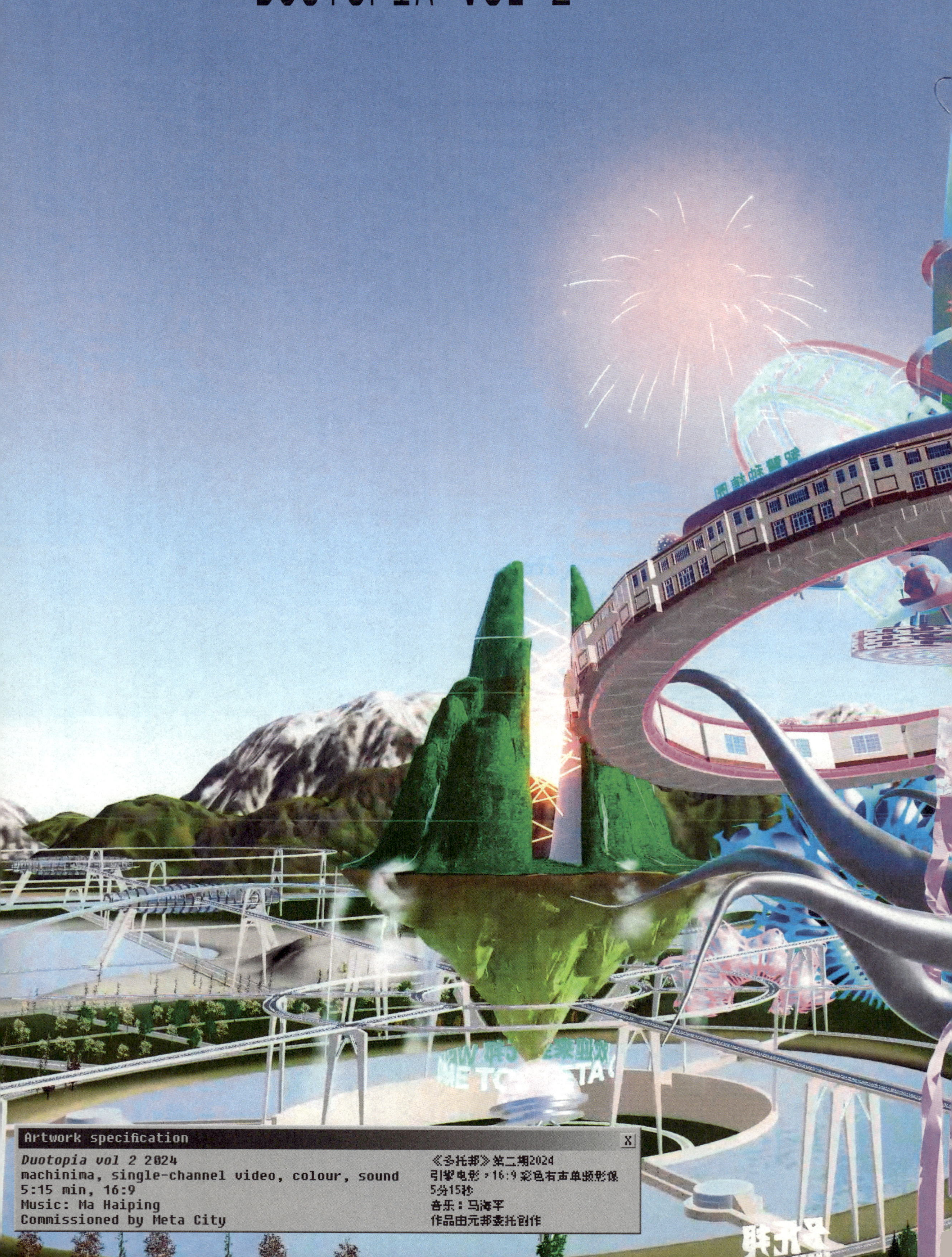

Artwork specification

Duotopia vol 2 2024
machinima, single-channel video, colour, sound
5:15 min, 16:9
Music: Ma Haiping
Commissioned by Meta City

《多托邦》第二期2024
引擎电影，16:9 彩色有声单频影像
5分15秒
音乐：马海平
作品由元邦委托创作

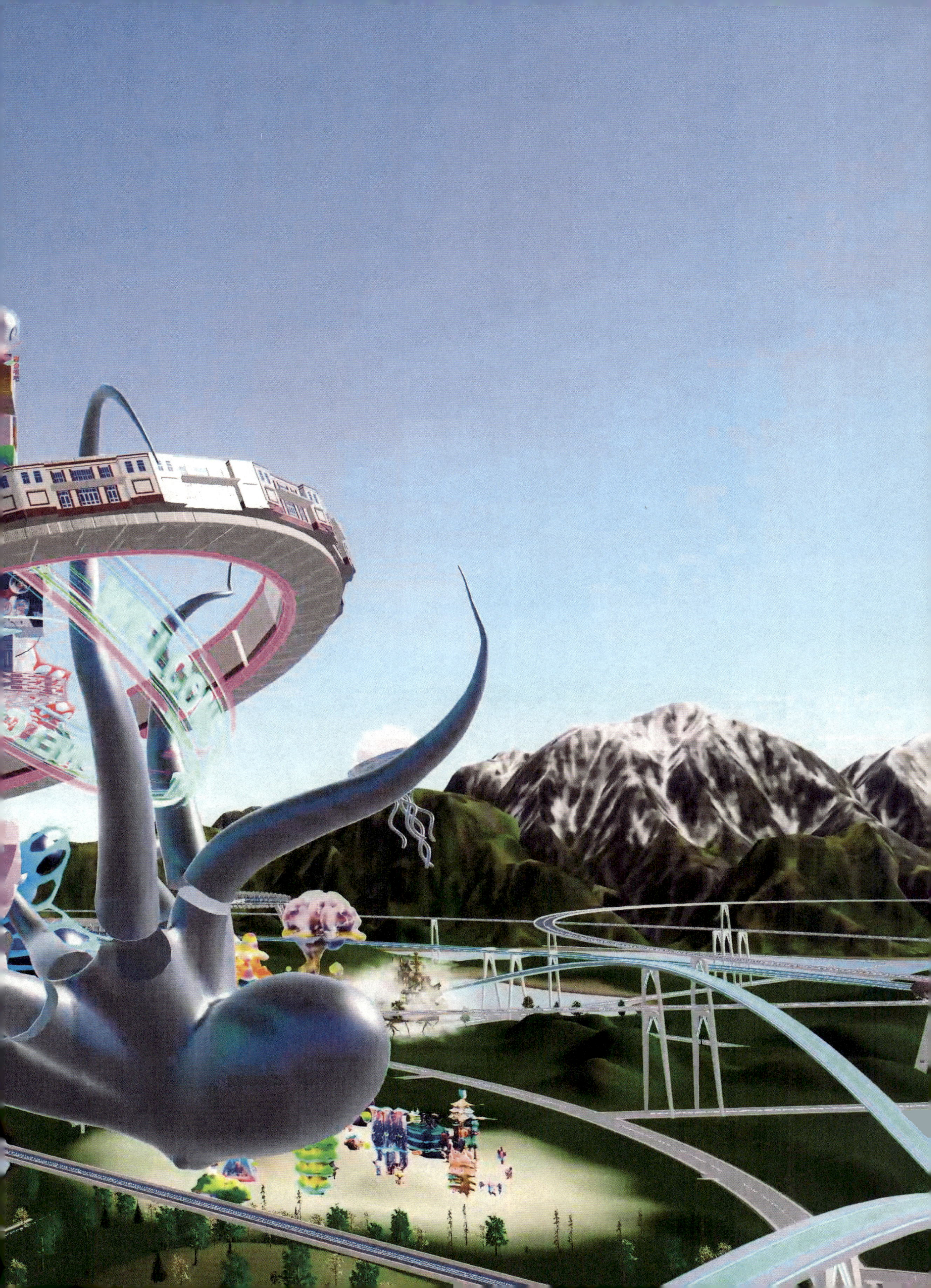

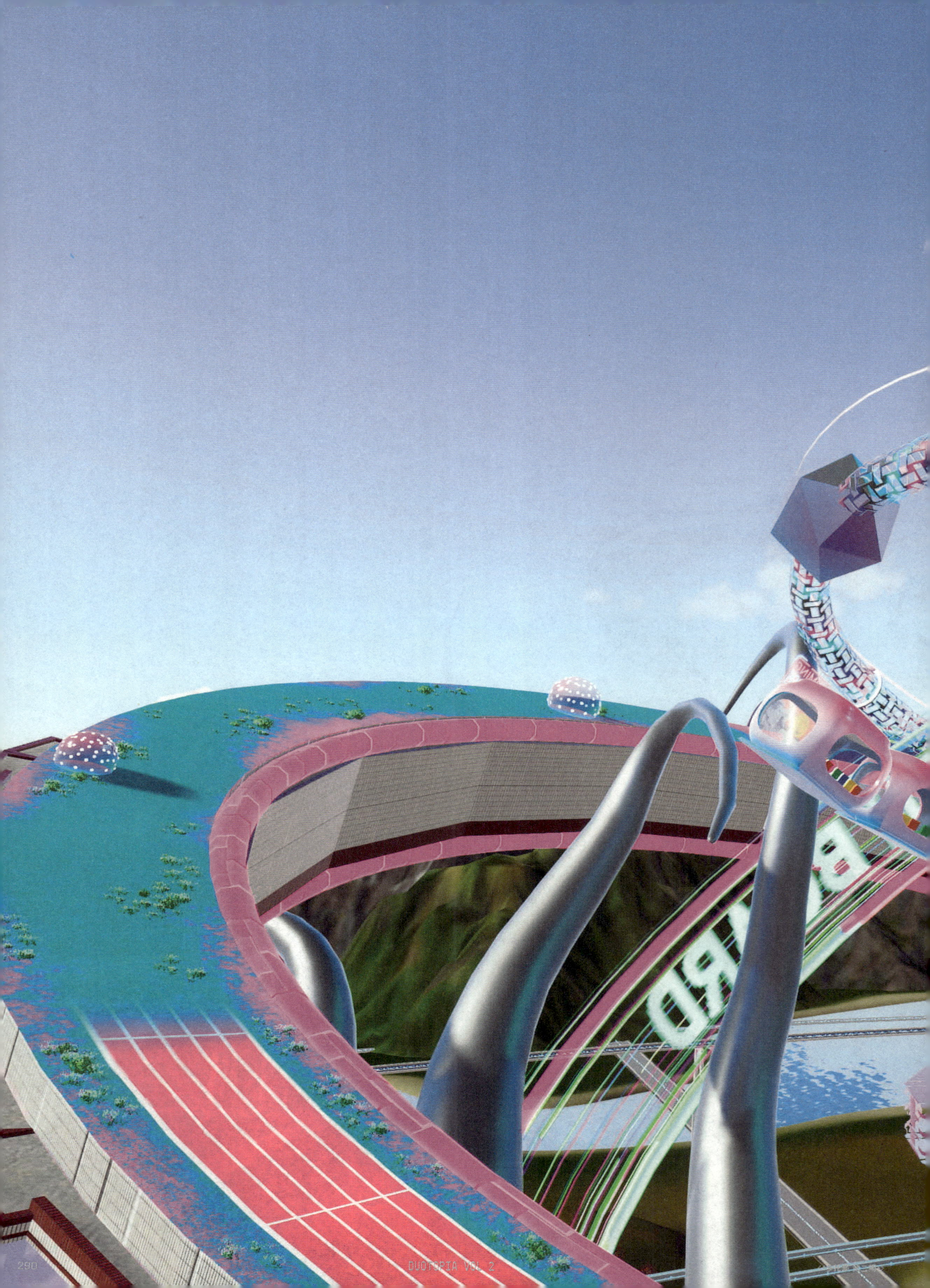

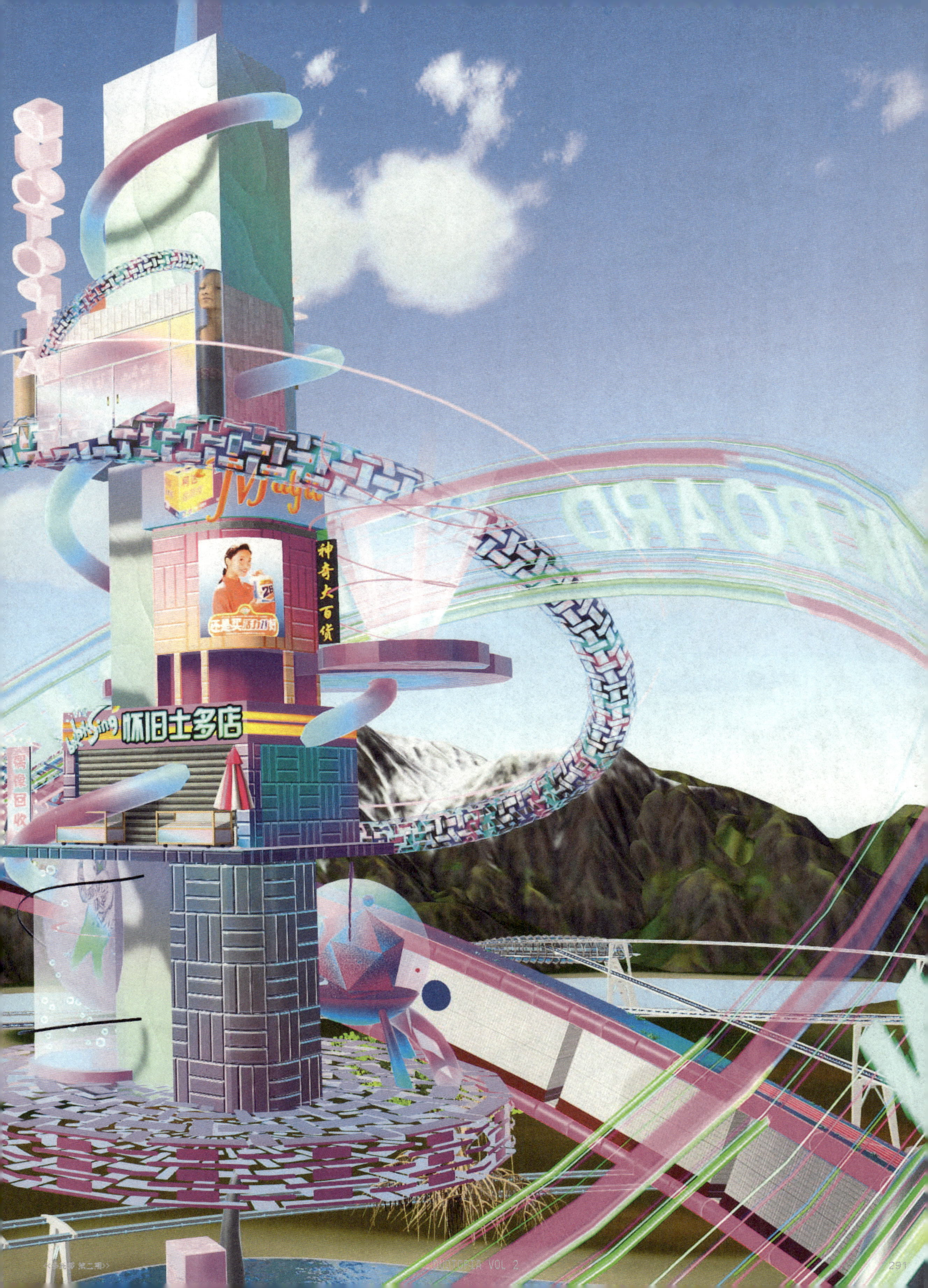
神奇大百货
怀旧士多店
ROAD

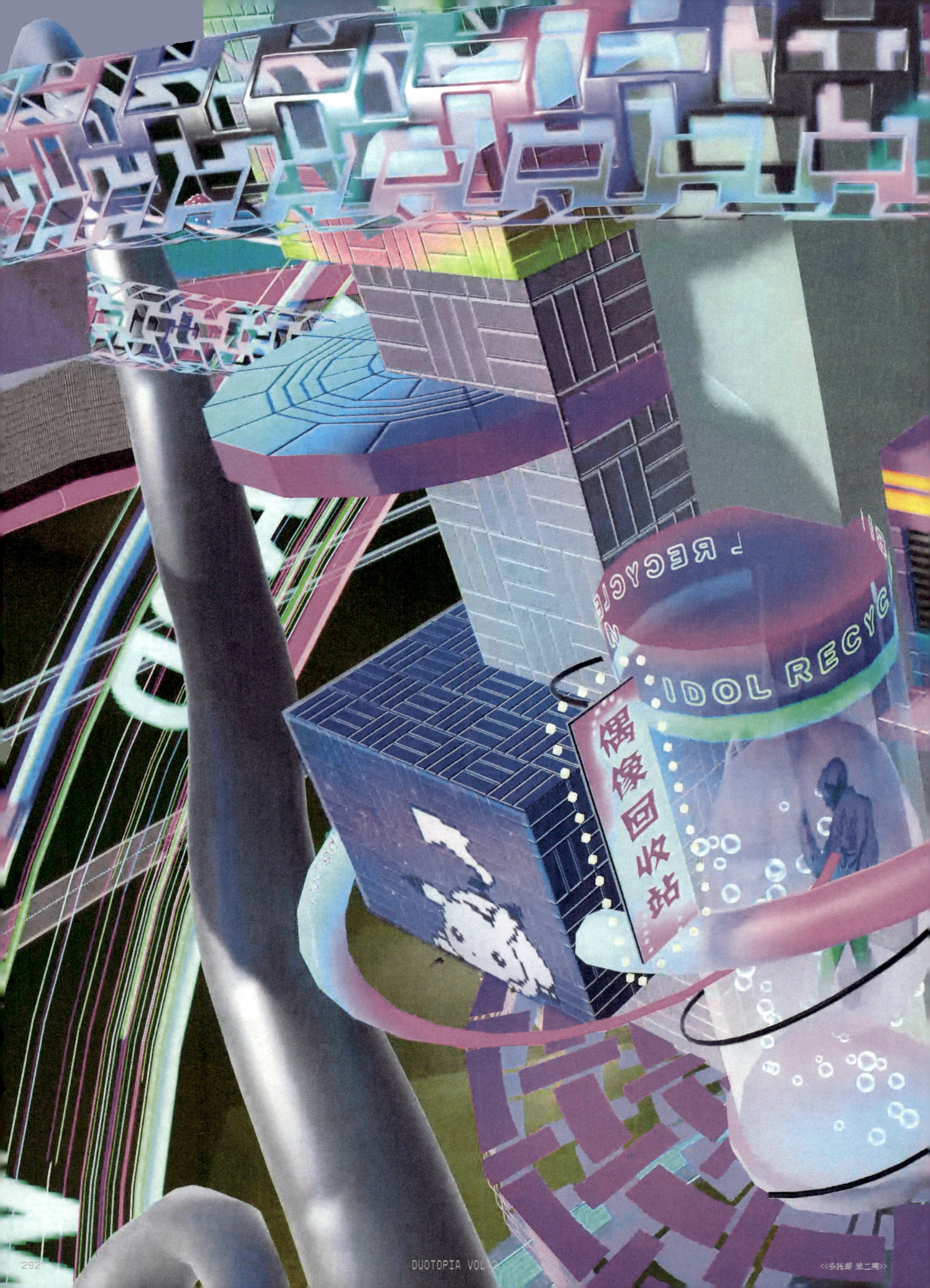
RECYCLE
IDOL RECYC
偶像回收站

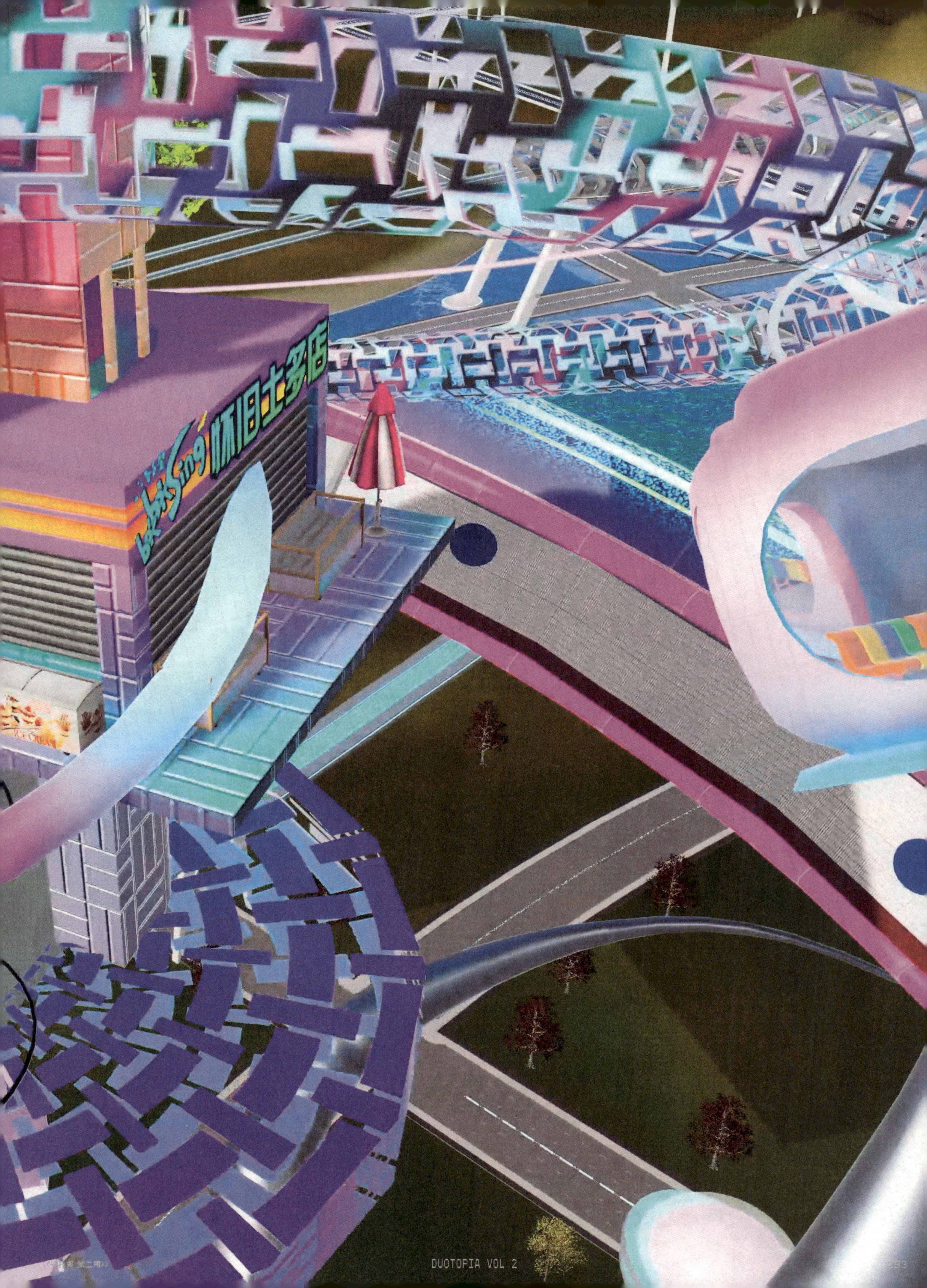
怀旧士多店

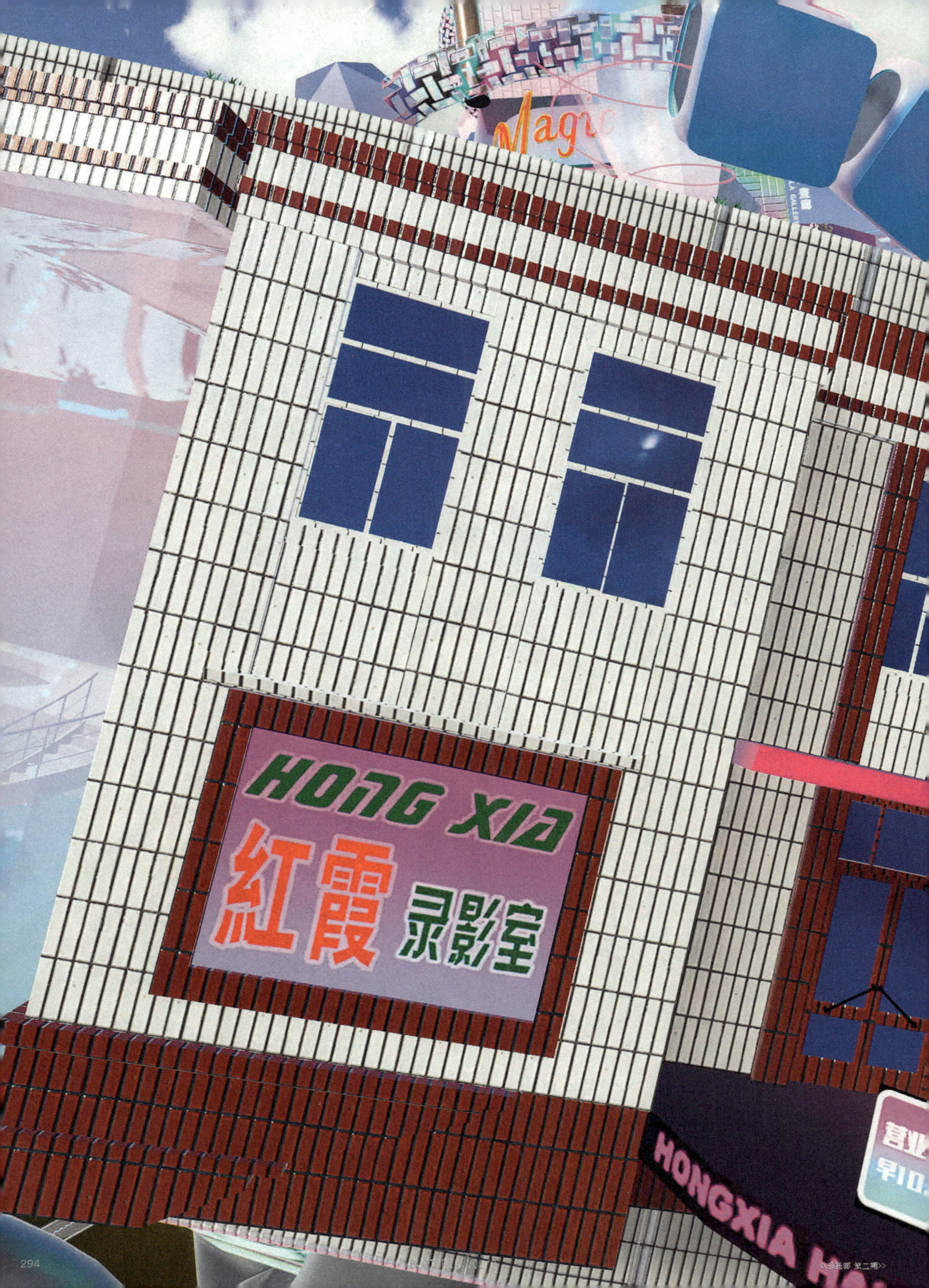
HONG XIA
紅霞
录影室
HONGXIA

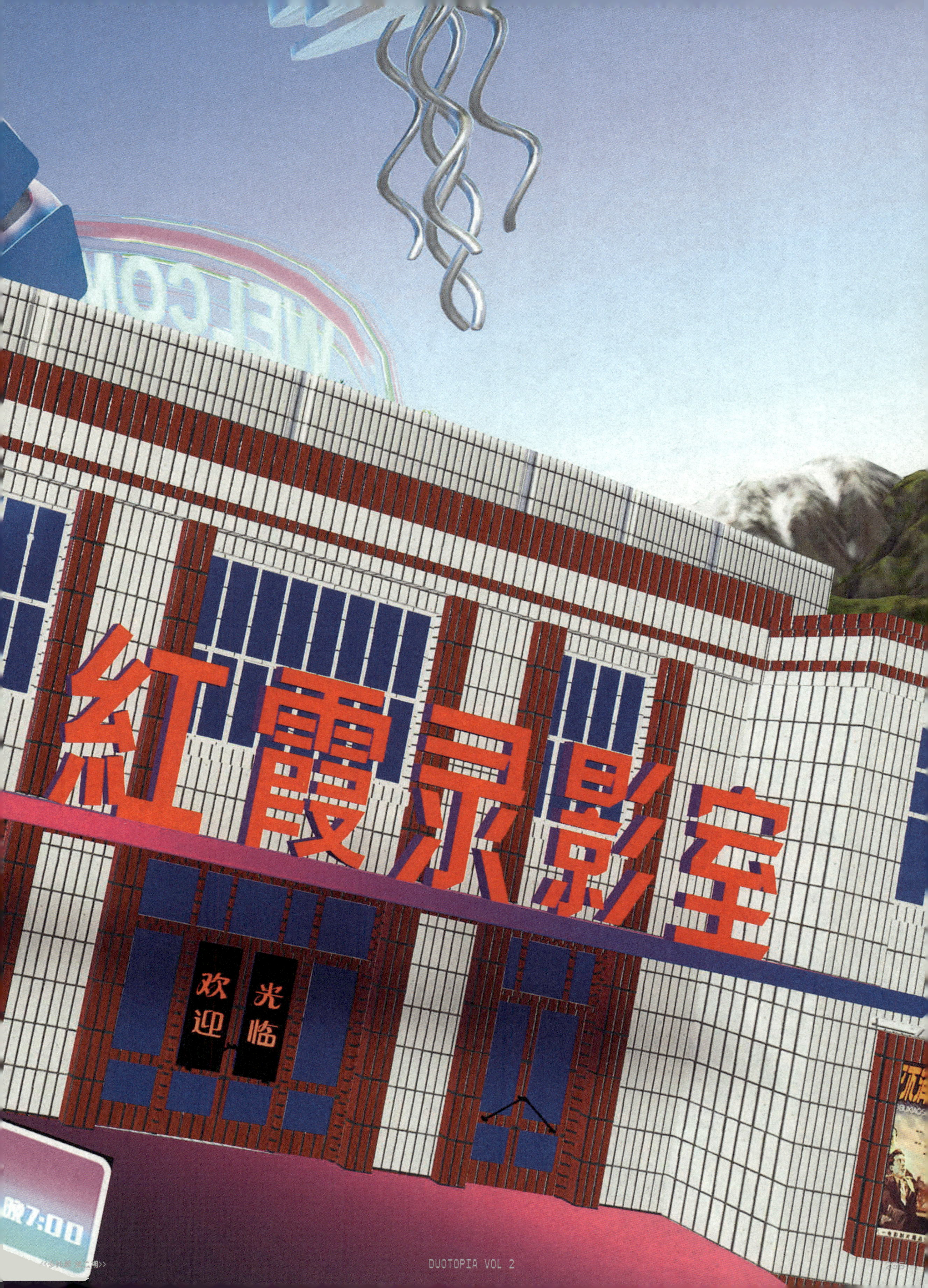
紅霞录影室
欢迎
光临
7:00

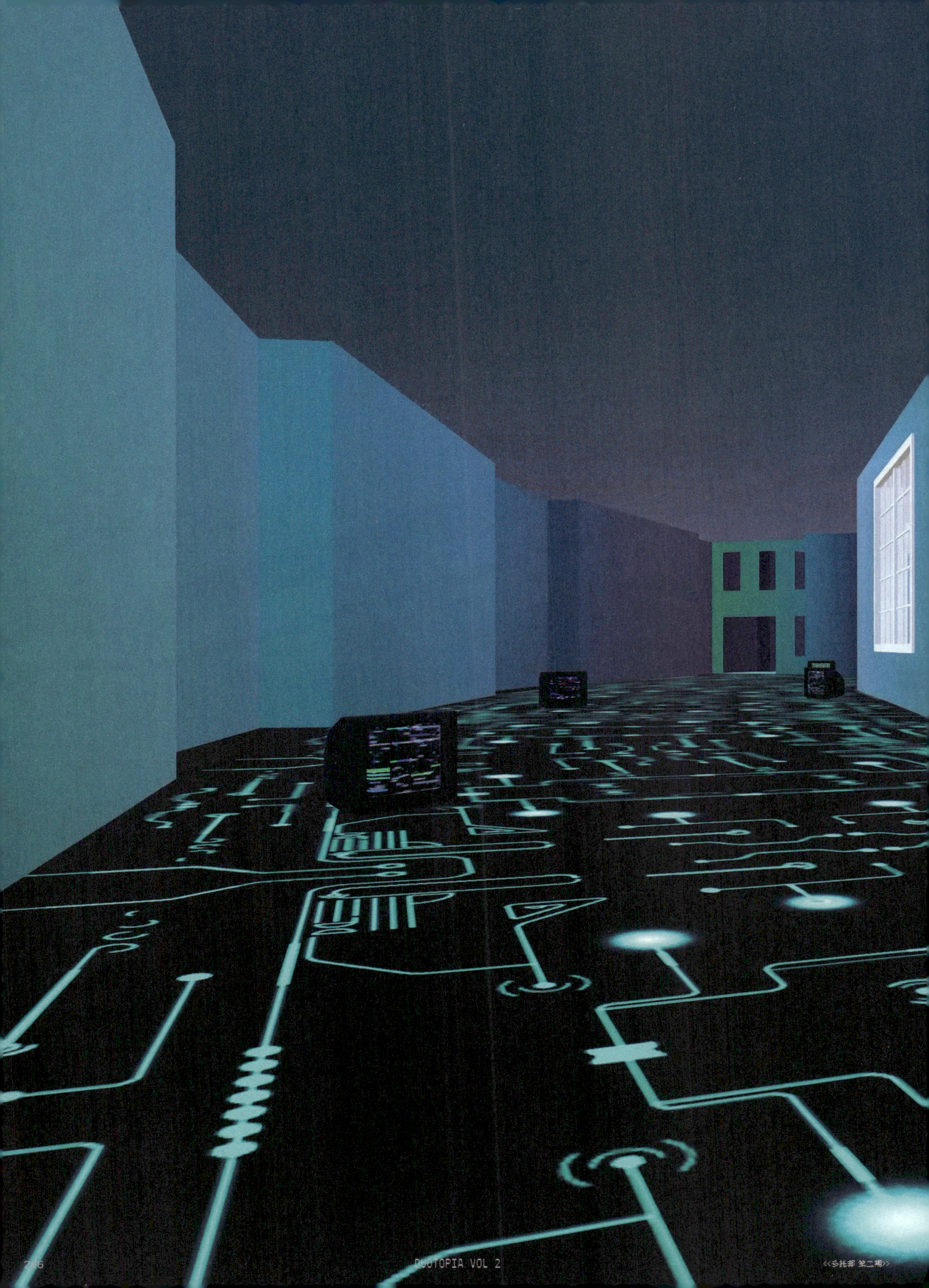

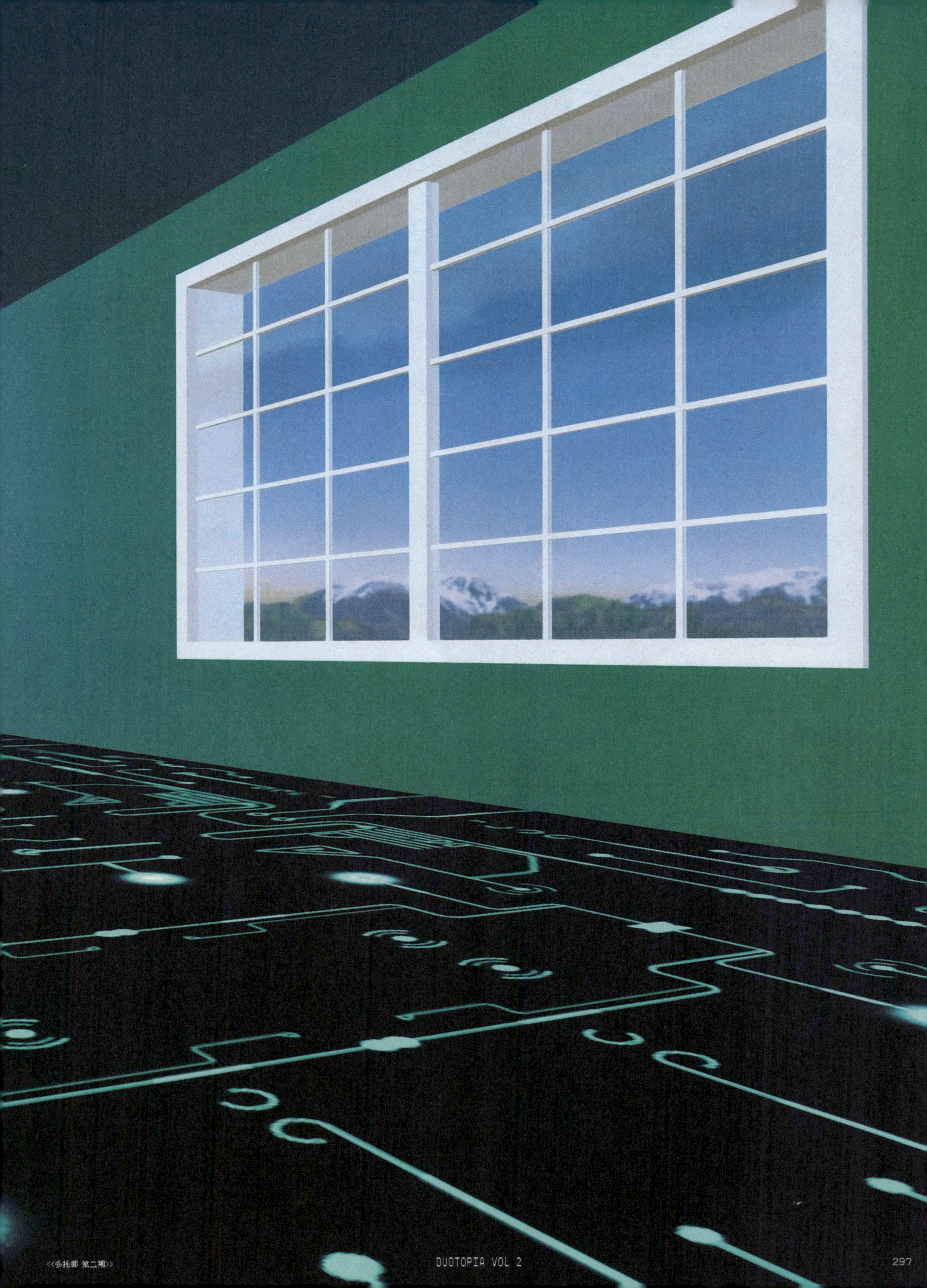

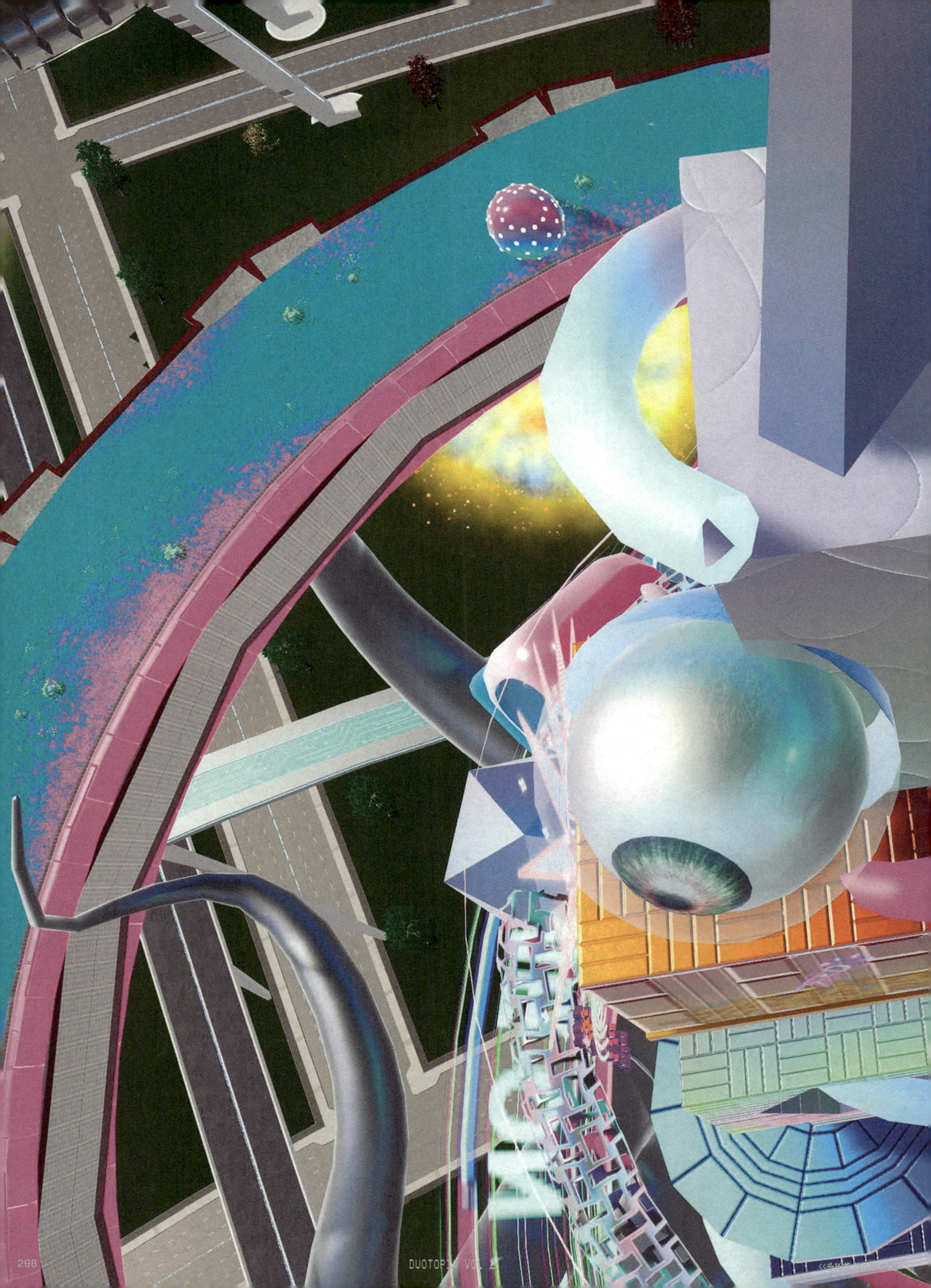

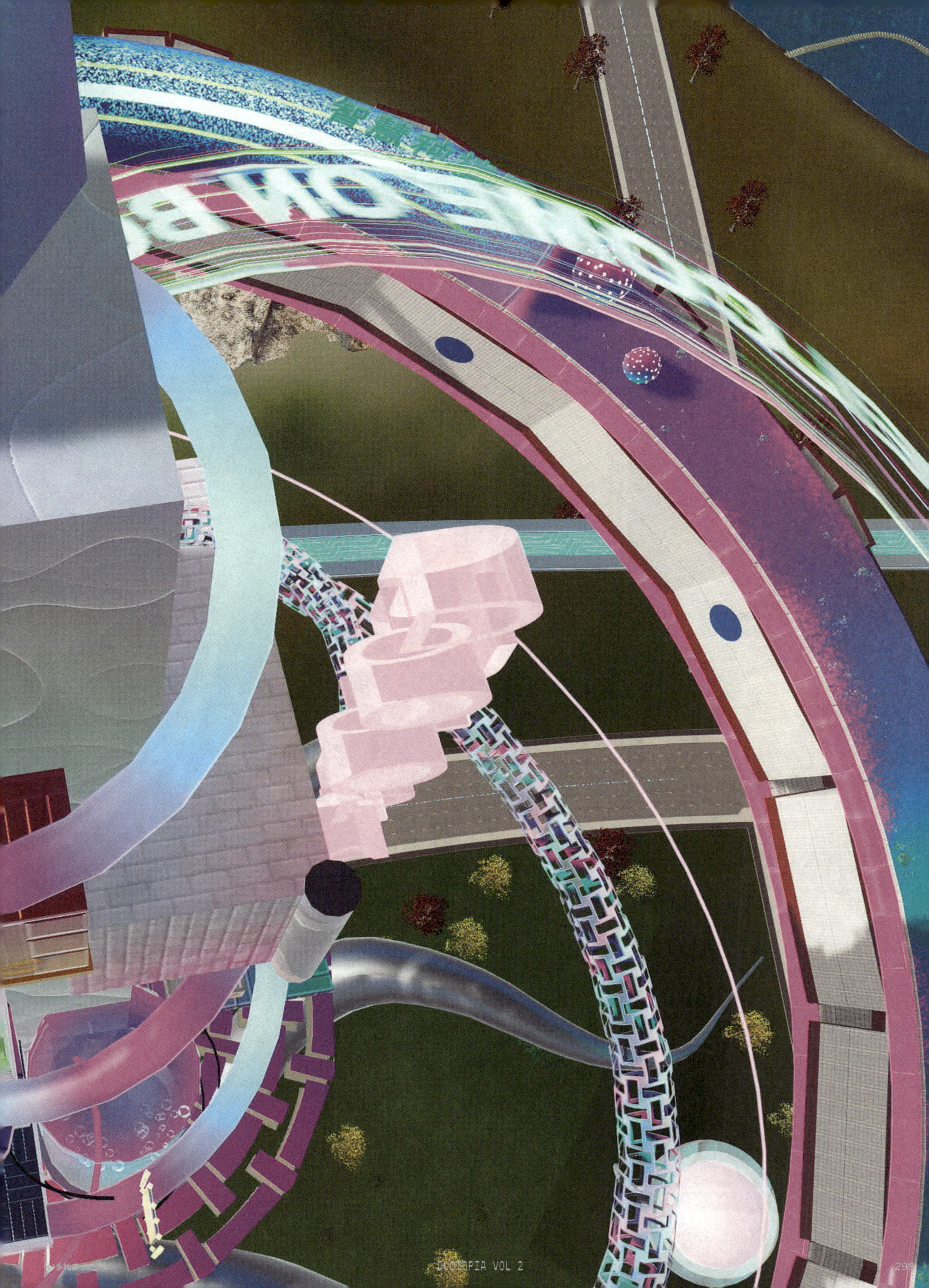

META-MENTARY元纪录

meta-mentary_still_01.png

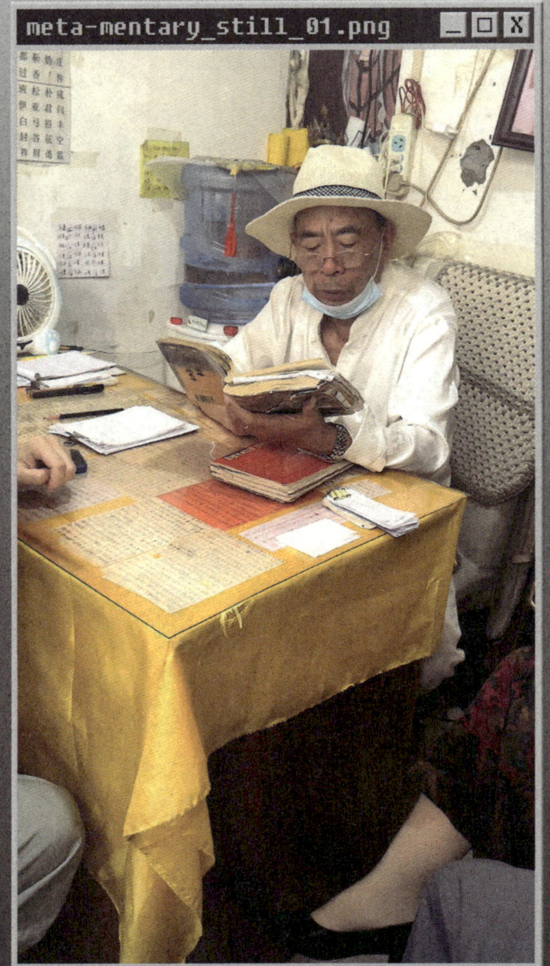

meta-mentary_still_02.png

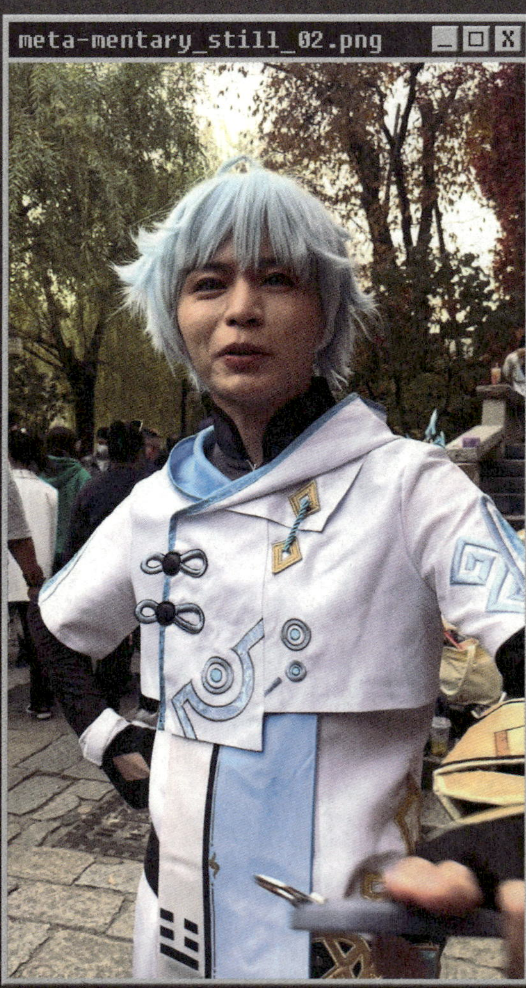

meta-mentary_still_03.png

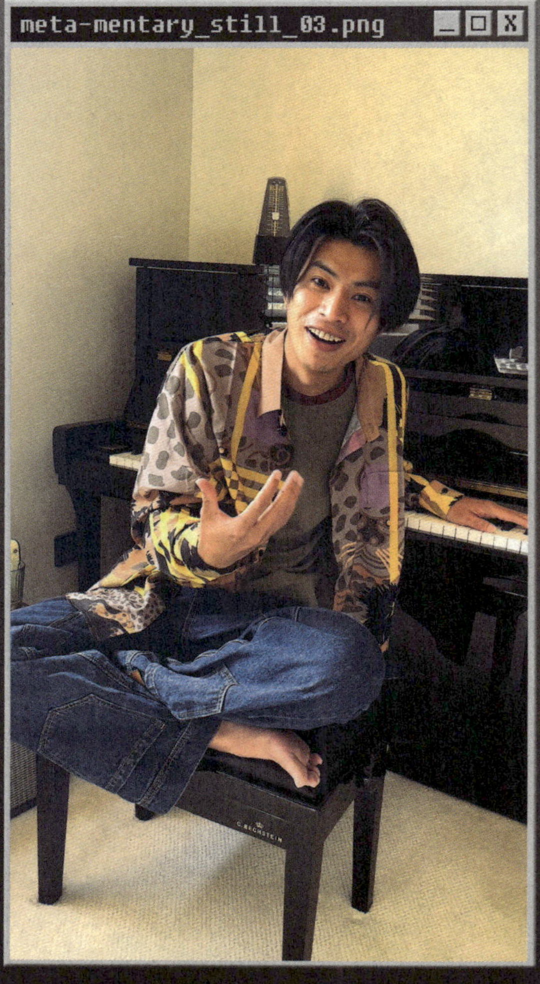

meta-mentary_still_04.png

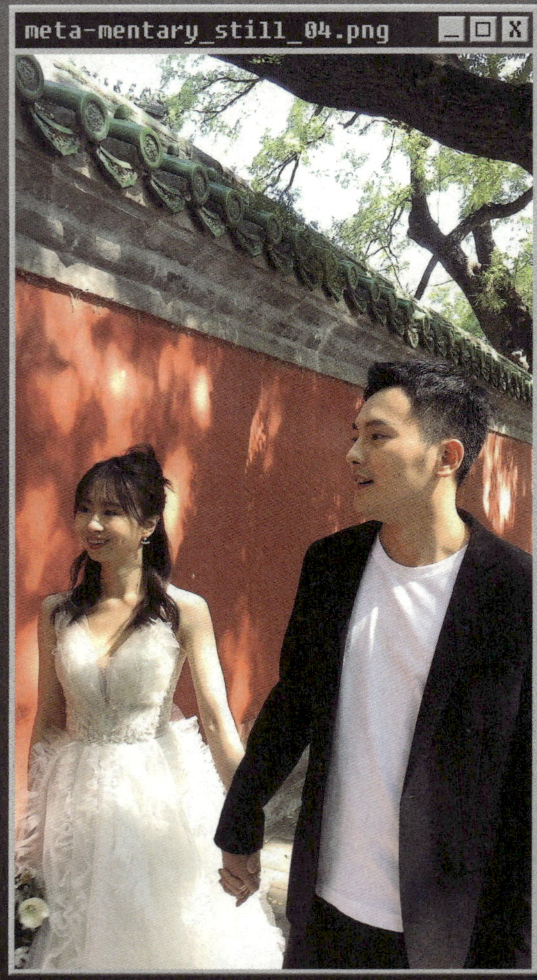

Artwork specification

Meta-mentary 2022
single-channel HD video, colour, sound
28:17 min, 9:16

《元纪录》2022
9:16 彩色有声单频高清影像
28分17秒

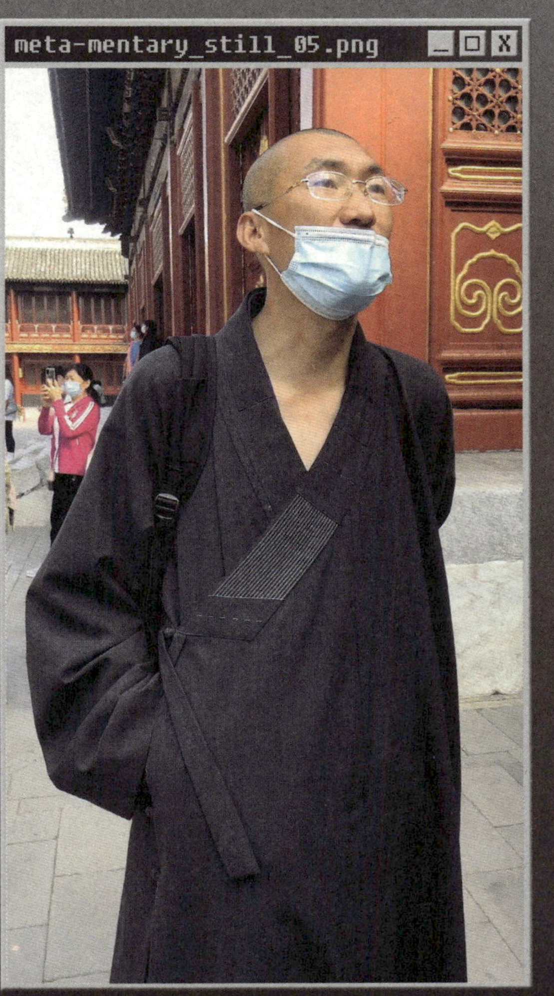
meta-mentary_still_05.png

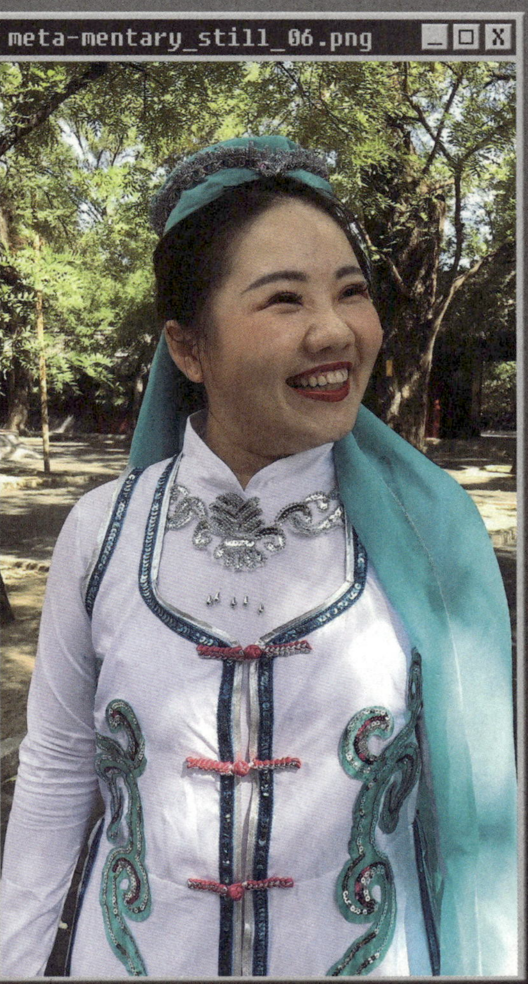
meta-mentary_still_06.png

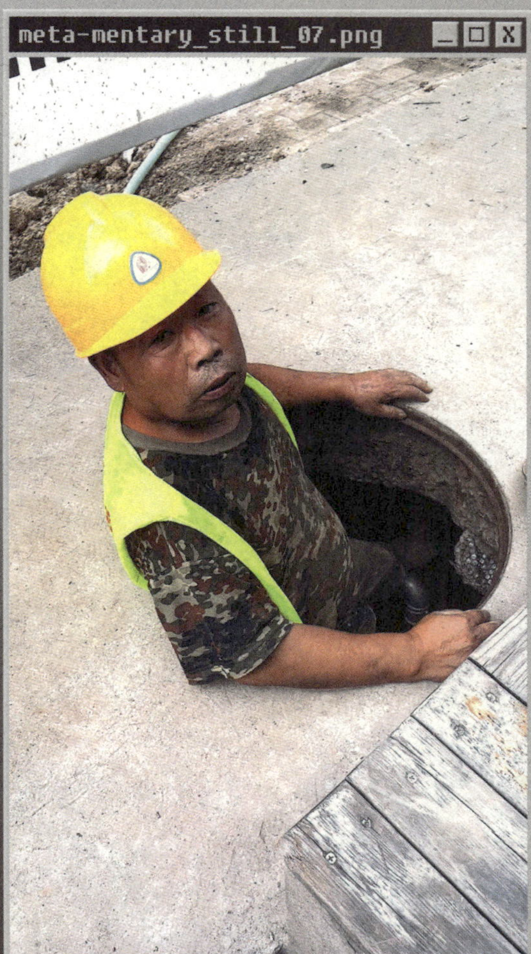
meta-mentary_still_07.png

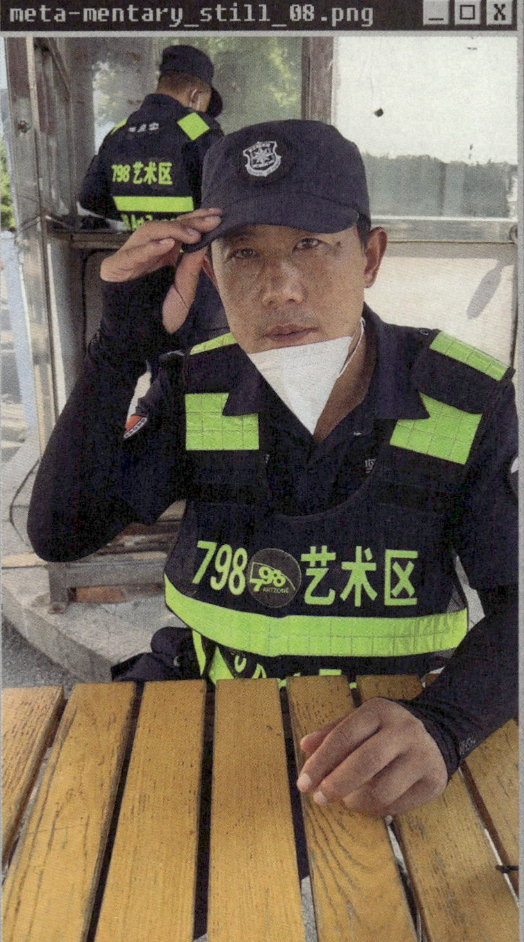
meta-mentary_still_08.png
798 艺术区

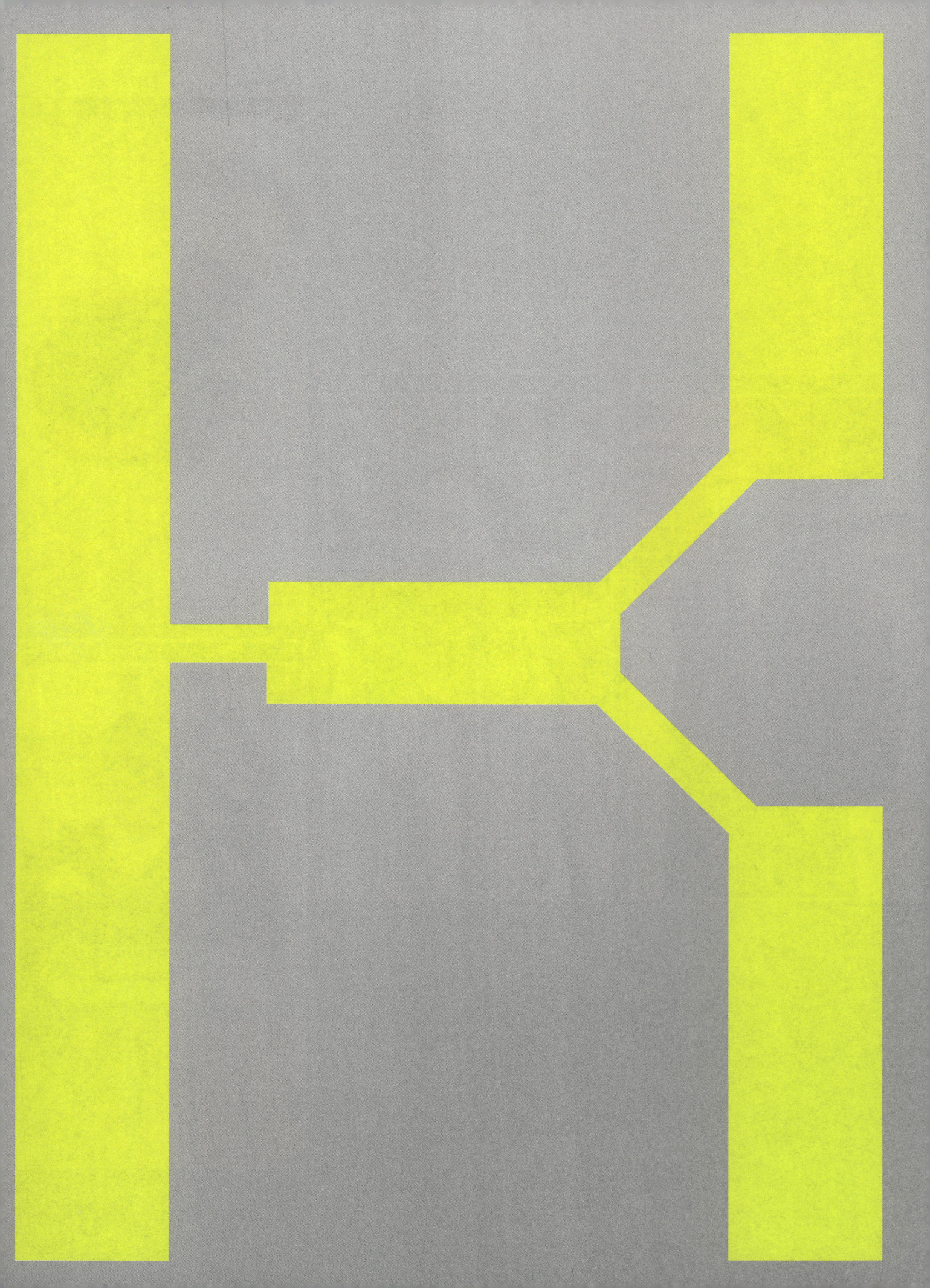

THE GOLDEN WATTLE

2024

相 思 木

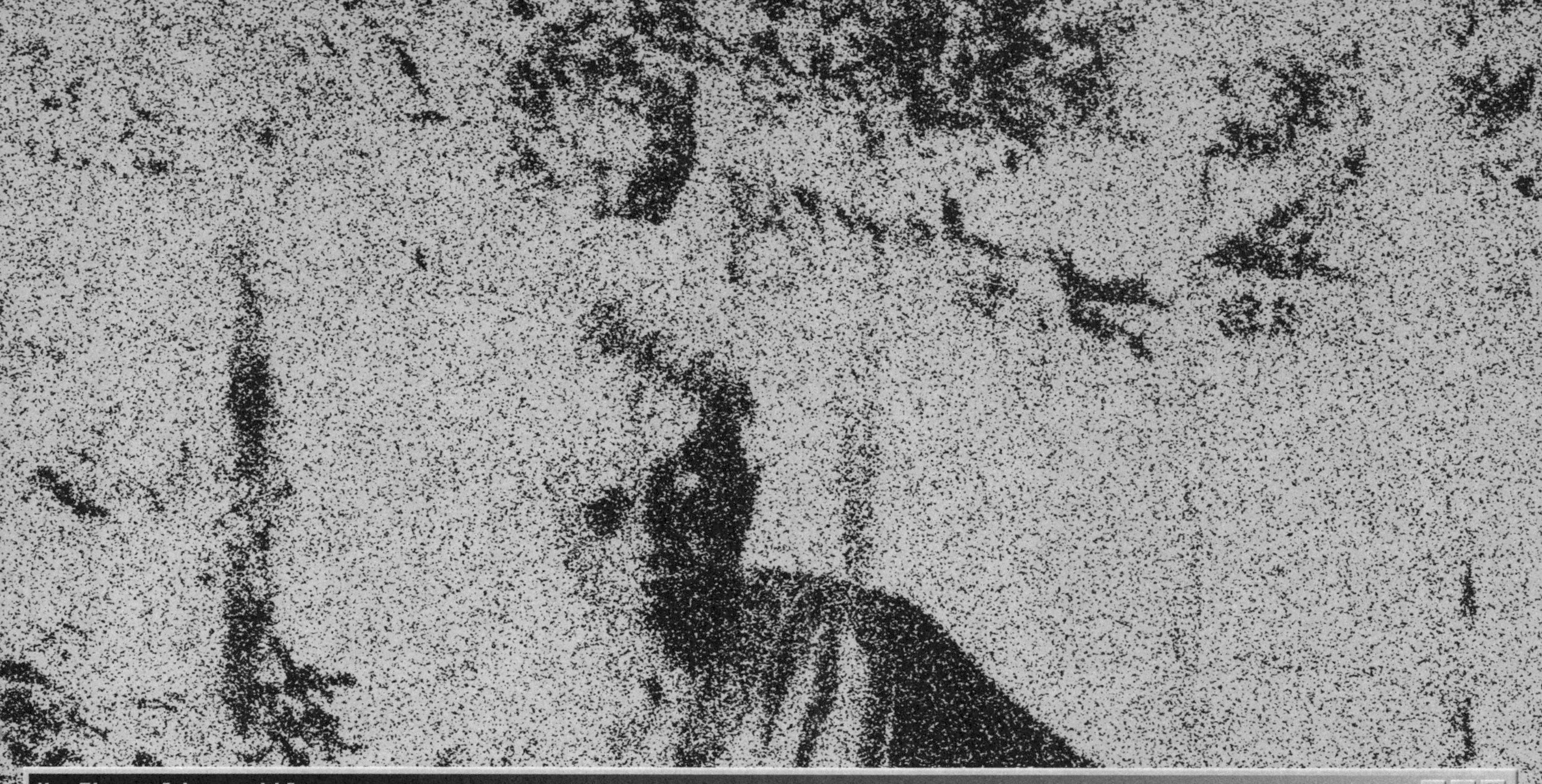

K: The golden wattle

In this new commission, Cao Fei creates a shrine-like memorial to her late sister Cao Xiaoyun (1971–2022), an artist who migrated from Guangzhou to Sydney in the late 1990s. The work takes its name from a watercolour by Xiaoyun, who had a particular fondness for the golden wattle (*Acacia pycnantha*), Australia's national flower. This deeply personal project takes the form of an exhibition within an exhibition, presenting Xiaoyun's paintings from her time in the city, alongside family photos, personal items and a documentary. *The golden wattle* embodies the profound yearning felt by Cao Xiaoyun's family and friends.

Artwork specification

The golden wattle 2024 《相思木》2024
mixed media installation 综合媒介装置
dimensions variable 尺寸可变

THE GOLDEN WATTLE 相思木

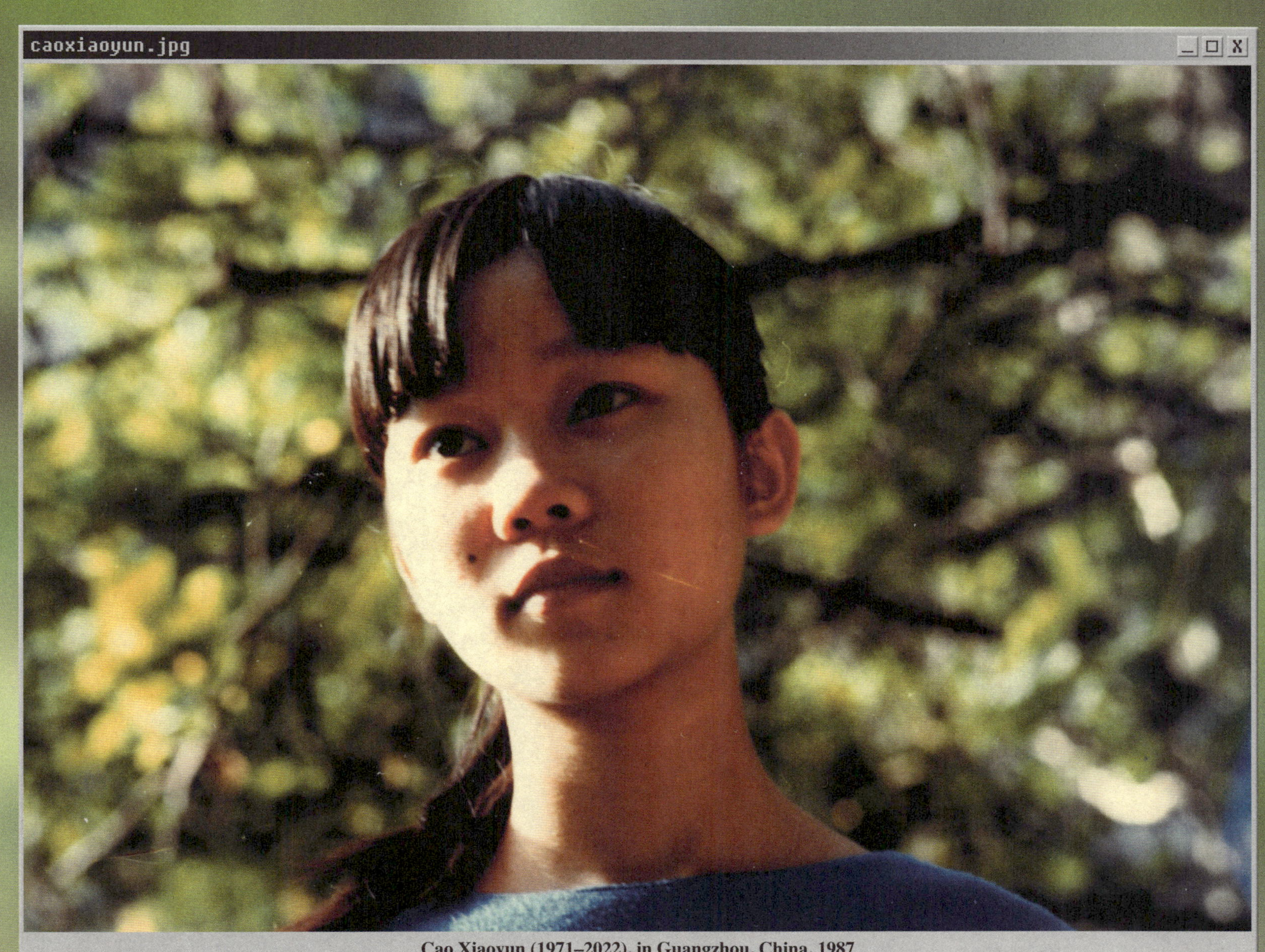

Cao Xiaoyun (1971–2022), in Guangzhou, China, 1987

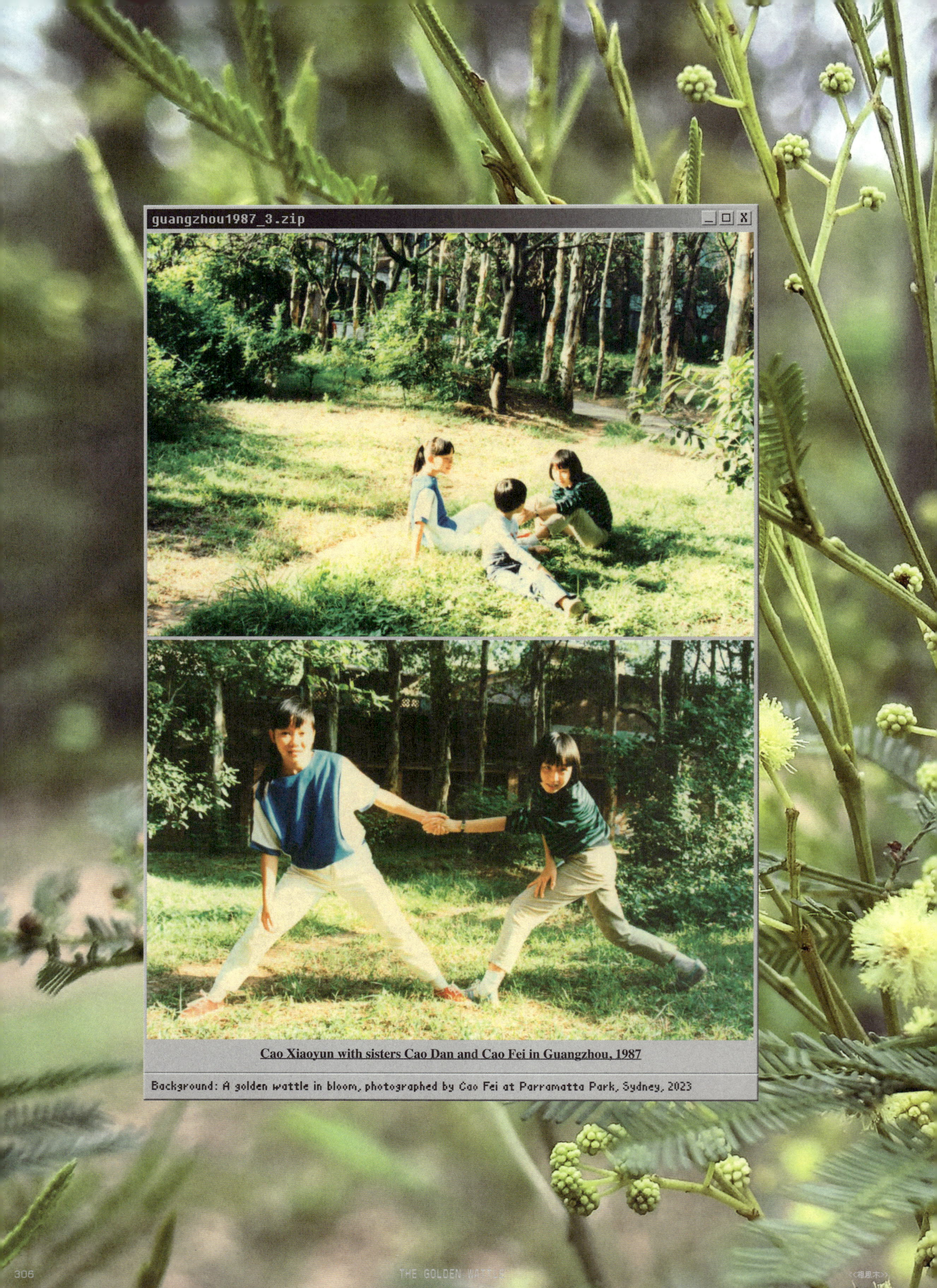

Cao Xiaoyun with sisters Cao Dan and Cao Fei in Guangzhou, 1987

Background: A golden wattle in bloom, photographed by Cao Fei at Parramatta Park, Sydney, 2023

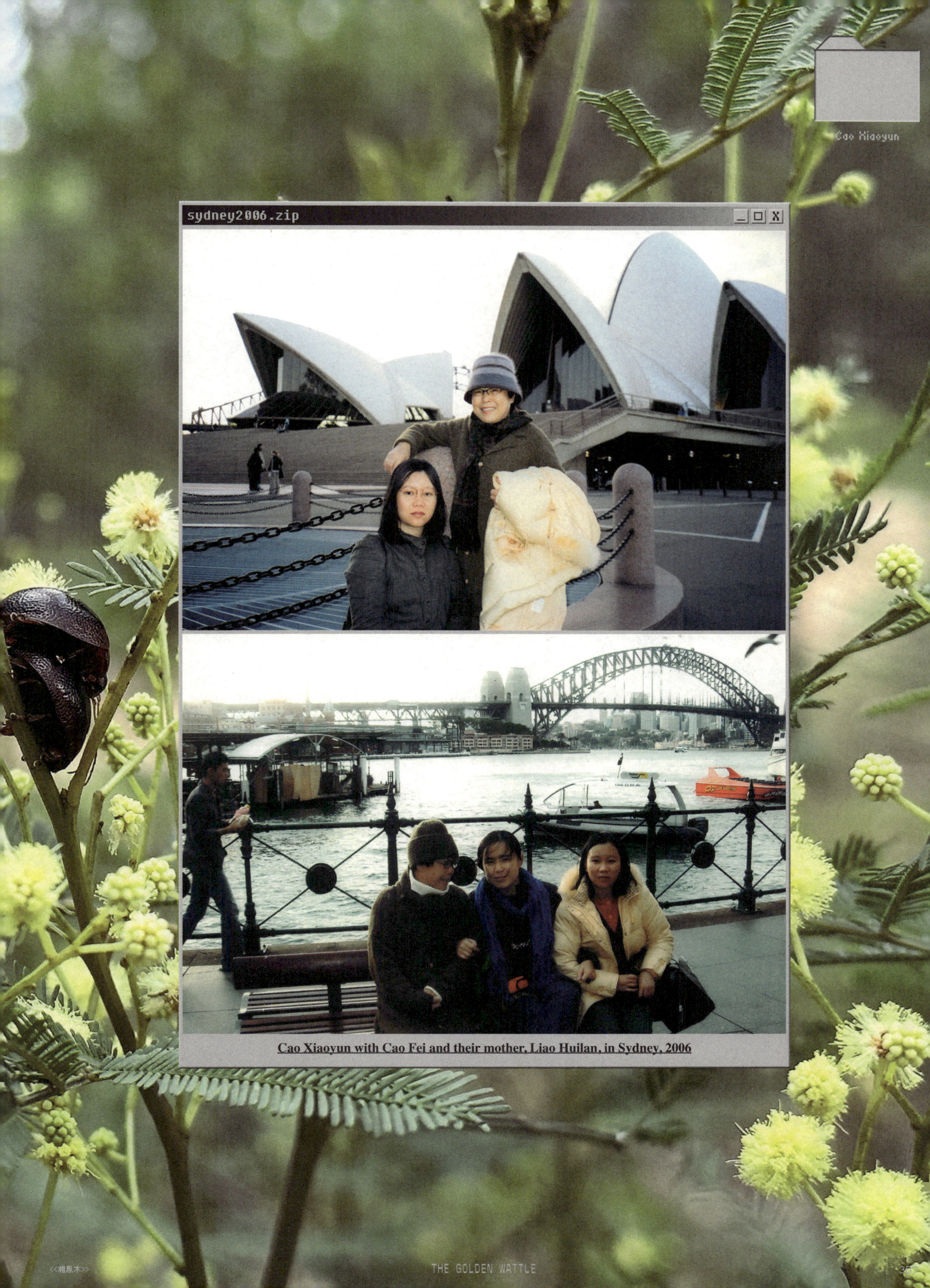

Cao Xiaoyun with Cao Fei and their mother, Liao Huilan, in Sydney, 2006

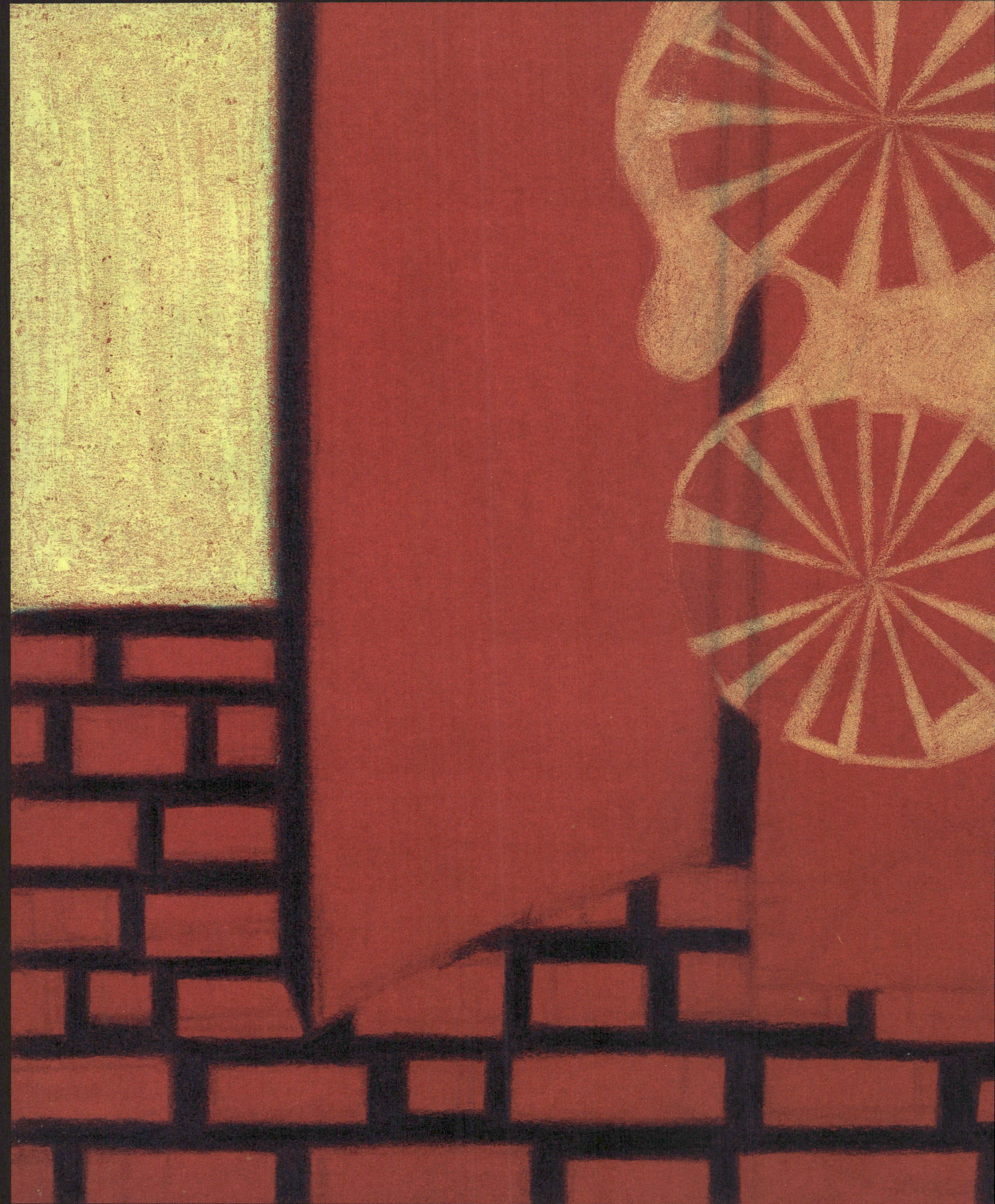

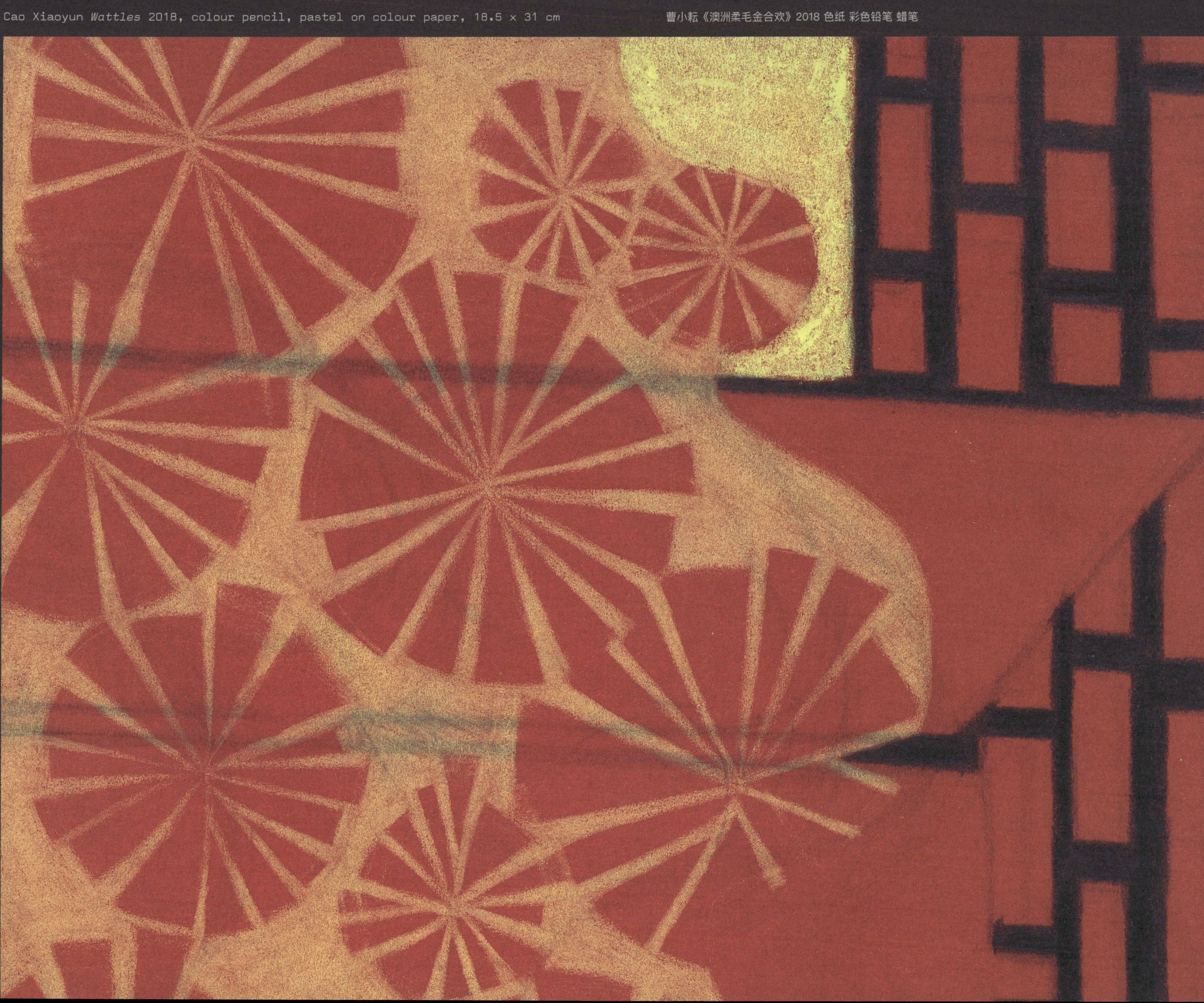

Cao Xiaoyun *Wattles* 2018, colour pencil, pastel on colour paper, 18.5 × 31 cm

曹小耘《澳洲柔毛金合欢》2018 色纸 彩色铅笔 蜡笔

曹小耘《姐妹》2019 纸本 彩色铅笔

Cao Xiaoyun *Sisters* 2019, colour pencil on paper, 29.5 x 21 cm

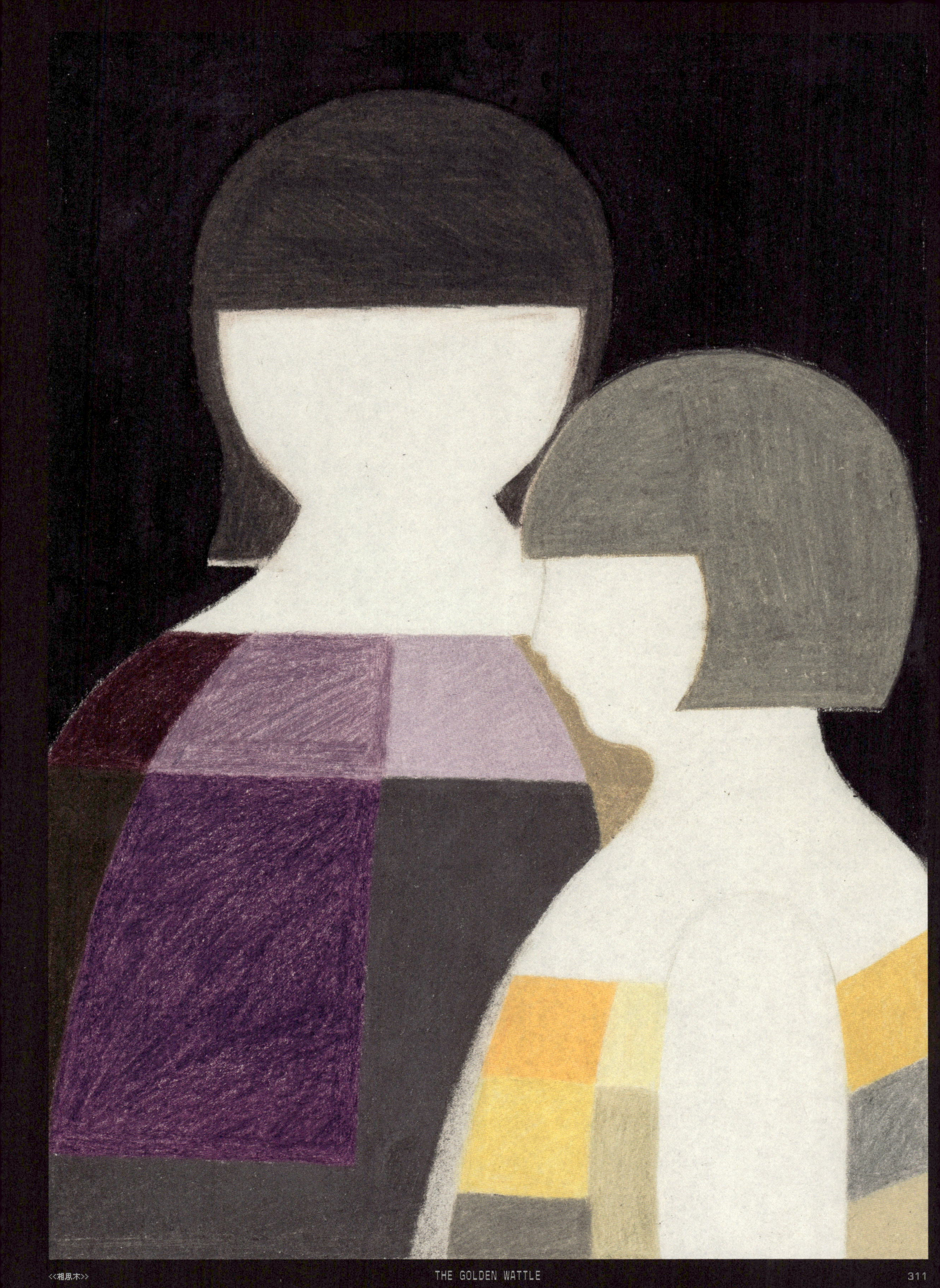

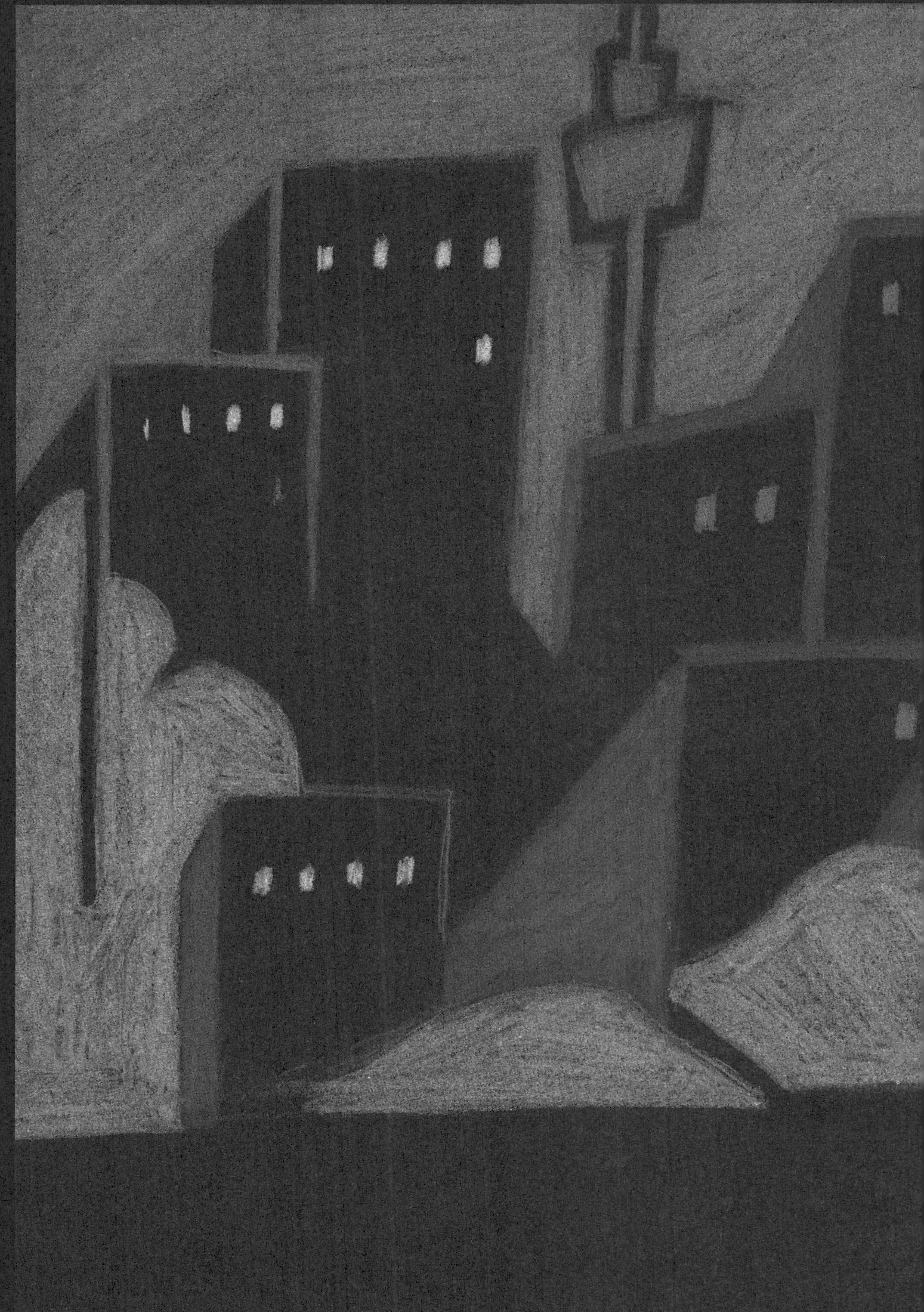

曹小耘《悉尼印象-2》2022 色纸 彩色铅笔 蜡笔

Cao Xiaoyun *Impressions of Sydney-2* 2022, colour pencil, pastel on colour paper, 29.7 × 21 cm

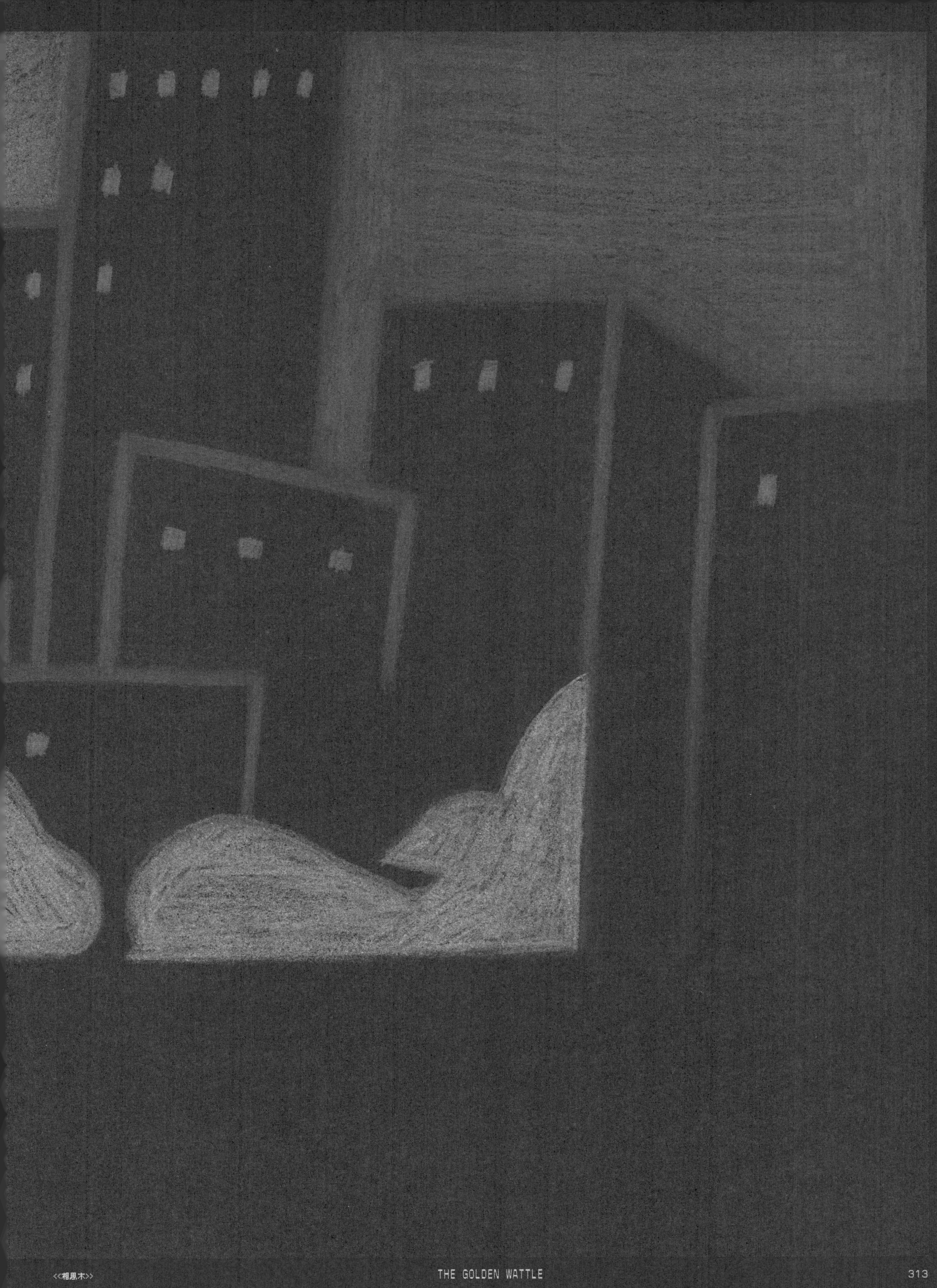

LIST OF EXHIBITED WORKS

UNLESS OTHERWISE INDICATED, ALL WORKS ARE SOLELY BY CAO FEI.

COURTESY OF THE ARTIST, VITAMIN CREATIVE SPACE AND SPRÜTH MAGERS

WORKS ARE LISTED IN CHRONOLOGICAL ORDER, THEN ALPHABETICAL ORDER FOR EACH YEAR.

Cao Fei 曹斐
China b1978

TIME-BASED ART 时基艺术

Imbalance 257 1999
single-channel video,
colour, sound
25:41 min, 4:3

《失调 257》1999
4:3 彩色有声单频影像
25分41秒

Rabid dogs 2002
single-channel video,
colour, sound
8:52 min, 5:4

《狗》2002
5:4 彩色有声单频影像
8分52秒

Hip hop: Guangzhou 2003
single-channel video,
colour, sound
3:28 min, 5:4

《嘻哈：广州》2003
5:4 彩色有声单频影像
3分28秒

Cao Fei and Ou Ning
San Yuan Li 2003
single-channel video,
black and white, sound
40:2 min, 4:3

曹斐、欧宁
《三元里》2003
4:3 黑白有声单频影像
40分2秒

Cosplayers 2004
single-channel video,
colour, sound
9:12 min, 4:3

《角色》2004
4:3 彩色有声单频影像
9分12秒

Hip hop: Fukuoka 2005
single-channel video,
colour, sound
7:40 min, 5:4

《嘻哈：福冈》2005
5:4 彩色有声单频影像
7分40秒

Hip hop: New York 2006
single-channel video,
colour, sound
5:14 min, 5:4

《嘻哈：纽约》2006
5:4 彩色有声单频影像
5分14秒

Whose utopia 2006
single-channel video,
colour, sound
20:20 min, 5:4

《谁的乌托邦》2006
5:4 彩色有声单频影像
20分20秒

i.Mirror 2007
machinima, single-channel
video, colour, sound
28 min, 4:3

《我·镜》2007
4:3 引擎电影，彩色有声单频录像
28分

RMB City: a Second Life city planning 2007
machinima, single-channel
video, colour, sound
5:57 min, 4:3

《人民城寨：第二人生城市计划》2007
4:3 引擎电影，彩色有声单频录像
5分57秒

Live in RMB City 2009
machinima, single-channel
video, colour, sound
24:05 min, 5:4

《人民城寨的生活》2009
5:4 引擎电影，彩色有声单频录像
24分05秒

Tonight Live interview with China Tracy (SLCN.TV) 2009
single-channel video,
colour, sound
13:04 min, 4:3

《"今夜现场"节目采访中国·翠西》2009
4:3彩色有声单频录像
13分04秒

East wind 2011
single-channel HD video,
colour, sound
11:14 min, 16:9

《东风》2011
16:9 彩色有声单频高清影像
11分14秒

La Town 2014
single-channel HD video,
colour, sound
42:14 min, 16:9

《La Town》2014
16:9 彩色有声单频影像
42分14秒

Asia one 2018
single-channel HD video,
colour, sound
63:21 min, 2.35:1
Commissioned by the Solomon R. Guggenheim Museum, New York, for The Robert H.N. Ho Family Foundation Chinese Initiative

《亚洲一号》2018
2.35:1彩色有声单频高清影像
63分21秒
作品由纽约所罗门·R·古根海姆美术馆为何鸿毅家族基金会中国艺术计划委任创作

11:11 2018
single-channel HD video,
colour, sound
60:58 min, 16:9

《11·11》2018
16:9彩色有声单频高清影像
60分58秒

Hongxia 2019
single-channel HD video,
colour, sound
56:56 min, 16:9

《红霞》2019
16:9彩色有声单频高清影像
56分56秒

Nova 2019
single-channel HD video,
colour, sound
97:13 min, 2.35:1

《新星》2019
2.35:1彩色有声单频高清影像
97分13秒

The eternal wave 2020
virtual reality, produced in collaboration with Acute Art

《永不消失的电波》2020
虚拟现实 作品与Acute Art联合制作

Duotopia vol 1 2022
3D-rendered video,
colour, sound
2:40 min, 16:9
Music: Ma Haiping
Commissioned by Meta City

《多托邦》第一期 2022
16:9 彩色有声三维渲染数字影像
2分40秒
音乐：马海平
作品由元都委托创作

Meta-mentary 2022
single-channel HD video,
colour, sound
28:17 min, 9:16

《元纪录》 2022
9:16 彩色有声单频高清影像
28分17秒

Oz 2022
dual-screen digital video,
colour, sound
1:36 min, 9:16
Music: Ma Haiping

《Oz》2022
9:16彩色有声双屏数字影像
1分36秒
音乐：马海平

An elegy to Hongxia 2023
single-channel HD video,
colour, sound
5:59 min, 16:9

《红霞献曲》 2023
16:9 彩色有声单频高清影像
5分59秒

Postscript of Hongxia 2023
single-channel HD video,
colour, sound
5:26 min, 16:9

《红霞后记》2023
16:9 彩色有声单频高清影像
5分26秒

Duotopia vol 2 2024
machinima, single-channel
video, colour, sound
5:15 min, 16:9
Music: Ma Haiping
Commissioned by Meta City

《多托邦》第二期2024
引擎电影，16:9 彩色有声单频影像
5分15秒
音乐：马海平
作品由元都委托创作

Super delivery 2024
single-player side-scrolling game installation, arcade cabinet, interactive software, desktop computer, arcade joystick, audio system

《超级快递》2024
单机横版游戏装置，游戏机柜，交互程序，台式电脑，街机游戏摇杆，音响

The golden wattle 2024
mixed media installation
dimensions variable
Commissioned by the Art Gallery of New South Wales

《相思木》2024
综合媒介装置
尺寸可变
受新南威尔士艺术博物馆委托创作

Hip hop: Sydney 2024
three-channel digital video,
colour, sound
work in progress
at time of publication
Commissioned by the Art Gallery of New South Wales

《嘻哈：悉尼》2024
彩色有声三频影像
图录出版时仍在制作中
受新南威尔士艺术博物馆委托创作

PHOTOGRAPHS 图片

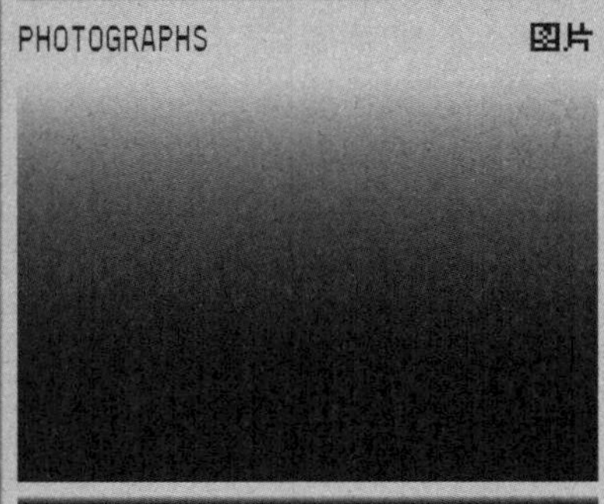

From the *Cosplayers* series 2004
“角色”系列摄影 2004

City watcher
inkjet print on paper
75 × 100 cm

《城市守望者》
纸本艺术微喷
75 × 100 cm

From the *My future is not a dream* series 2006
“我的未来不是梦”系列摄影 2006

My future is not a dream 05
inkjet print on paper
120 × 150 cm

《我的未来不是梦 05》
纸本艺术微喷
120 × 150 cm

My future is not a dream 06
inkjet print on paper
120 × 150 cm

《我的未来不是梦 06》
纸本艺术微喷
120 × 150 cm

From the *Un-Cosplayers* series 2006
“非角色”系列摄影 2006

Bunny's world
inkjet print on paper
90 × 120 cm

《奔尼的世界》
纸本艺术微喷
90 × 120 cm

Hello! Kitty
inkjet print on paper
90 × 120 cm

《你好！凯蒂》
纸本艺术微喷
90 × 120 cm

Old Wukongs
inkjet print on paper
90 × 120 cm

《老悟空》
纸本艺术微喷
90 × 120 cm

From the *RMB City* series 2007
“人民城寨：‘第二人生’城市规划”系列摄影 2007

China Tracy and China Sun 01
inkjet print on paper
70 × 118 cm

《中国+翠西 和 中国+山 01》
纸本艺术微喷
70 × 118 cm

RMB City: a Second Life city planning 05
inkjet print on paper
120 × 160 cm

《人民城寨：第二人生城市规划 05》
纸本艺术微喷
120 × 160 cm

From the *RMB City: the fashions of China Tracy* series 2009
“人民城寨：中国+翠西的时尚”系列摄影 2009

RMB City: the fashions of China Tracy 01
inkjet print on paper
30 x 50 cm

《人民城寨：中国+翠西的时尚 01》
纸本艺术微喷
30 × 50 cm

RMB City: the fashions of China Tracy 02
inkjet print on paper
30 x 50 cm

《人民城寨：中国+翠西的时尚 02》
纸本艺术微喷
30 × 50 cm

RMB City: the fashions of China Tracy 03
inkjet print on paper
30 x 50 cm

《人民城寨：中国+翠西的时尚 03》
纸本艺术微喷
30 × 50 cm

RMB City: the fashions of China Tracy 04
inkjet print on paper
30 x 50 cm

《人民城寨：中国+翠西的时尚 04》
纸本艺术微喷
30 × 50 cm

RMB City: the fashions of China Tracy 05
inkjet print on paper
30 x 50 cm

《人民城寨：中国+翠西的时尚 05》
纸本艺术微喷
30 × 50 cm

From the *Haze and fog* series 2013
“霾”系列摄影 2013

Haze and fog 04
inkjet print on paper
70 × 105 cm

《霾04》
纸本艺术微喷
70 × 105 cm

Haze and fog 09
inkjet print on paper
70 × 105 cm

《霾09》
纸本艺术微喷
70 × 105 cm

From the *La Town* series 2014
“La Town”系列摄影 2014

La Town: Train Station
inkjet print on paper
70 × 130 cm

《La Town:车站》
纸本艺术微喷
70 × 130 cm

La Town: Center Plaza
inkjet print on paper
80 x 120 cm

《La Town:中心广场》
纸本艺术微喷
80 × 120 cm

La Town: 13 White Street
inkjet print on paper
80 x 120 cm

《La Town:白街13》
纸本艺术微喷
80 × 120 cm

From the *Asia one* series 2018
“亚洲一号”系列摄影 2018

Asia one 01
inkjet print on paper
90 x 135 cm

《亚洲一号 01》
纸本艺术微喷
90 × 135 cm

Asia one 02
inkjet print on paper
90 x 135 cm

《亚洲一号 02》
纸本艺术微喷
90 × 135 cm

From the *Hongxia Theatre* series 2019
“红霞影剧院”系列摄影 2019

Hongxia Theatre 01
inkjet print on paper
105 × 150 cm

《红霞影剧院 01》
纸本艺术微喷
105 × 150 cm

Hongxia Theatre 02
inkjet print on paper
70 × 100 cm

《红霞影剧院 02》
纸本艺术微喷
70 × 100 cm

Hongxia Theatre 03
inkjet print on paper
70 × 100 cm

《红霞影剧院 03》
纸本艺术微喷
70 × 100 cm

Hongxia Theatre 04
inkjet print on paper
70 × 100 cm

《红霞影剧院 04》
纸本艺术微喷
70 × 100 cm

Hongxia Theatre 05
inkjet print on paper
70 × 100 cm

《红霞影剧院 05》
纸本艺术微喷
70 × 100 cm

From the *Nova* series 2019
“新星”系列摄影 2019

Nova 01
inkjet print on paper
105 × 150 cm

《新星 01》
纸本艺术微喷
105 × 150 cm

Nova 11
inkjet print on paper
110 × 150 cm

《新星 11》
纸本艺术微喷
110 × 150 cm

Nova 13
inkjet print on paper
110 × 150 cm

《新星 13》
纸本艺术微喷
110 × 150 cm

Nova 17
inkjet print on paper
110 × 150 cm

《新星 17》
纸本艺术微喷
110 × 150 cm

From the *Oz* series 2023
“Oz” 系列 2023

Oz 05
inkjet print on paper
145 x 200 cm

《Oz - 05》
纸本艺术微喷
145 × 200 cm

Acknowledgements

WE WOULD LIKE TO EXTEND OUR THANKS TO THE ART GALLERY'S DIRECTOR, MICHAEL BRAND, WHO INITIATED THE FIRST MEETINGS WITH CAO FEI TO DISCUSS THE POSSIBILITY OF PRESENTING A MAJOR SOLO EXHIBITION OF HER WORK IN SYDNEY. WE FEEL PRIVILEGED TO HAVE WORKED WITH THIS INTERNATIONALLY RENOWNED ARTIST OVER THE PAST TWO YEARS. OUR GRATITUDE ALSO GOES TO DEPUTY DIRECTOR MAUD PAGE FOR HER UNWAVERING SUPPORT AND VALUABLE ADVICE ALONG THE JOURNEY OF REALISING THIS PROJECT. WE ARE EQUALLY GRATEFUL TO JOHN RICHARDSON, DIRECTOR OF AUDIENCES AND DEVELOPMENT, AND HIS TEAM FOR LEADING A SUCCESSFUL CAMPAIGN TO SECURE FINANCIAL SUPPORT FOR SUCH AN AMBITIOUS ENDEAVOUR.

WORKING WITH CAO FEI AND HER TEAM HAS BEEN AN ENRICHING EXPERIENCE. THEY HAVE GENEROUSLY SHARED THEIR KNOWLEDGE ON THE SELECTED WORKS AND PRESENTATION IDEAS WITH THE ART GALLERY, ESPECIALLY XIONG XU AND SHEN JINGHAO. WE APPRECIATE THE DEDICATED EFFORTS OF WENZHE ZHU AT VITAMIN CREATIVE SPACE FOR PATIENTLY ASSISTING WITH OUR MULTIPLE REQUESTS TO ACCESS VIDEO PREVIEWS. OUR THANKS ALSO GO TO CHARLOTTE LAFONT-HUGO AND GILLES VANDERSTOCKEN OF BEAU ARCHITECTS IN HONG KONG FOR ACCOMMODATING BOTH CURATORIAL AND ARTISTIC REQUESTS IN THEIR EXTRAORDINARY EXHIBITION DESIGN. ADDITIONALLY, WE EXPRESS OUR GRATITUDE TO COLLEAGUES AT SPRÜTH MAGERS FOR THEIR ASSISTANCE AND TO THE PRIVATE COLLECTORS WHO HAVE GENEROUSLY LENT WORKS BY CAO FEI AND CAO XIAOYUN.

THE EXHIBITION COULD NOT HAVE HAPPENED WITHOUT TREMENDOUS CONTRIBUTIONS FROM DEDICATED COLLEAGUES AT THE ART GALLERY ACROSS VARIOUS DEPARTMENTS. WE ARE PARTICULARLY THANKFUL TO THE FOLLOWING INDIVIDUALS FOR THEIR DIRECT ASSISTANCE IN PREPARING THE EXHIBITION: DANIELLE EARP FROM EXHIBITIONS; DESIGNERS JEMIMA WOO, ISSAC HARRISON, KIEN VAN-YOUNG AND ANALIESE CAIRIS FROM THE CREATIVE STUDIO; KATE BECKINGHAM FROM REGISTRATION; LISA MANSFIELD FROM CONSERVATION; MARK TAYLOR FROM AUDIO VISUAL SERVICES; DIANA PANUCCIO FROM PHOTOGRAPHY; MEGAN YOUNG FROM RIGHTS AND IMAGE LICENSING; FORMER COLLEAGUE SAMANTHA LUCK, SARAH MARTIN AND TONIA PINNERI FROM BUSINESS DEVELOPMENT; AND THE INSTALLATION TEAM LED BY MONICA RUDHAR, AMONG MANY OTHER DEDICATED COLLEAGUES WHO HAVE HELPED MAKE THIS PROJECT A SUCCESS.

IN CREATING THIS PUBLICATION, WE HAVE BEEN INSPIRED BY THE ENTHUSIASM AND CREATIVITY OF DESIGNER EVI O. WE THANK HOU HANRU, MICHAEL SUN AND PAO-CHEN TANG FOR THEIR INSIGHTFUL ESSAYS, WHICH HAVE ENHANCED OUR UNDERSTANDING OF CAO FEI'S ARTWORKS AND HER ARTISTIC PRACTICE. WE ARE INDEBTED TO AMY NEWLAND FOR HER CAREFUL EDITING, FAITH CHISHOLM AS MANAGING EDITOR, AND CARA HICKMAN FOR OVERSEEING THE PRODUCTION OF THE CATALOGUE.

FINALLY, WE WOULD LIKE TO THANK KEY COMMUNITY MEMBERS WHOSE GENEROSITY IN SHARING STORIES AND MATERIAL CULTURE FROM SYDNEY'S CBD CHINATOWN HAVE TRANSFORMED THE EXHIBITION. THESE INCLUDE PETER WONG, GEORGE WING KEE, HAYDEN WONG, KEVIN CHANG AND EDDIE MA OF SOUL OF CHINATOWN AND CONNIE AND CATHERINE CHUNG OF THE MARIGOLD. F THE MARIGOLD.

RUBY ARROWSMITH-TODD AND YIN CAO

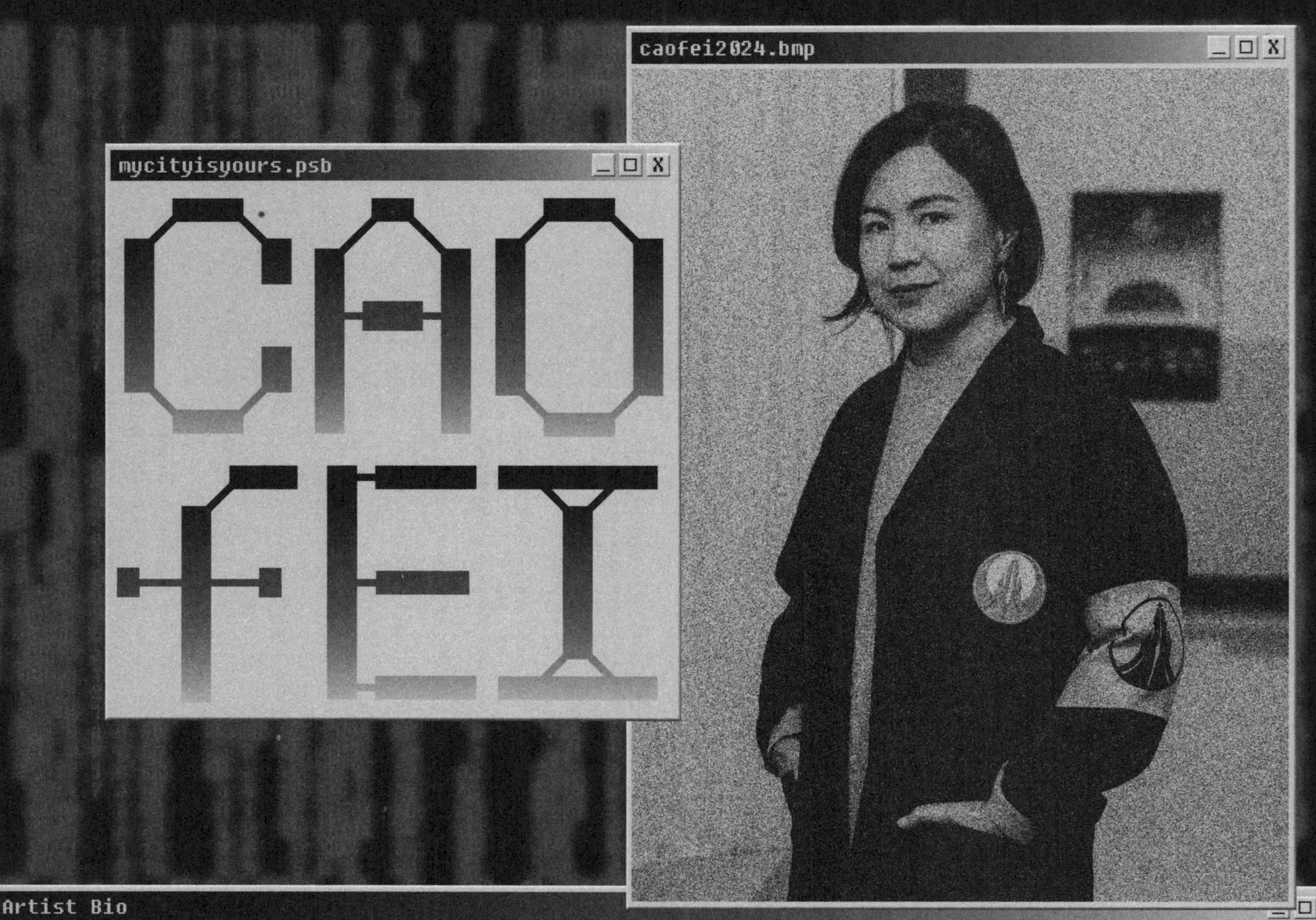

Artist Bio

CAO FEI 曹斐 (B1978, GUANGZHOU) IS AN INTERNATIONALLY RENOWNED CHINESE CONTEMPORARY ARTIST, CURRENTLY LIVING IN BEIJING. SHE MIXES SOCIAL COMMENTARY, POPULAR AESTHETICS, REFERENCES TO SURREALISM, AND DOCUMENTARY CONVENTIONS IN HER FILMS AND INSTALLATIONS. HER WORKS REFLECT ON THE RAPID AND DEVELOPMENTAL CHANGES THAT ARE OCCURRING IN CHINESE SOCIETY TODAY.

CAO'S WORKS HAVE BEEN EXHIBITED AT A NUMBER OF INTERNATIONAL BIENNALES AND TRIENNALES, INCLUDING THE SHANGHAI BIENNALE (2004), THE MOSCOW BIENNALE (2005), THE TAIPEI BIENNIAL (2006), THE 15TH AND 17TH BIENNALE OF SYDNEY (2006 AND 2010), THE ISTANBUL BIENNIAL (2007), THE YOKOHAMA TRIENNALE (2008), THE 50TH, 52ND AND 56TH VENICE BIENNALE (2003, 2007 AND 2015), THE AICHI TRIENNALE (2022), AND SHARJAH BIENNIAL (2023).

CAO'S MAJOR PROJECTS IN RECENT YEARS INCLUDE THE SOLO EXHIBITIONS: *CAO FEI* AT MOMA PS1, NEW YORK (2016); *A HOLLOW IN A WORLD TOO FULL* AT TAI KWUN CONTEMPORARY, HONG KONG (2018); *CAO FEI* AT K21, DÜSSELDORF (2018); *HX* AT CENTRE POMPIDOU, PARIS (2019); *BLUEPRINTS* AT SERPENTINE GALLERIES, LONDON (2020); *CAO FEI: STAGING THE ERA* AT UCCA CENTER FOR CONTEMPORARY ART, BEIJING (2021); *CAO FEI: SUPERNOVA* AT MAXXI, THE NATIONAL MUSEUM OF 21ST CENTURY ARTS, ROME (2021); *ASIA ONE* AT KUNSTHAL CHARLOTTENBORG, COPENHAGEN (2022); *THE FUTURE IS NOT A DREAM* AT PINACOTECA CONTEMPORÂNEA, SÃO PAULO (2023); *AT THE EDGE OF SUPERHUMANITY* AT SCAD MUSEUM OF ART, GEORGIA, USA (2024); *META-MENTARY* AT LENBACHHAUS MUNICH (2024); AND *CAO FEI: TIDAL FLUX* AT THE MUSEUM OR ART PUDONG (2024).

CAO FEI IS THE WINNER OF THE SCAD DEFINE ART (2024) AND DEUTSCHE BÖRSE PHOTOGRAPHY FOUNDATION PRIZE (2021). SHE WAS NOMINATED FOR THE HUGO BOSS PRIZE AND THE FUTURE GENERATION ART PRIZE IN 2010 AND WAS AWARDED THE BEST YOUNG ARTIST AND BEST ARTIST AT THE CHINA CONTEMPORARY ART AWARD (CCAA) IN 2006 AND 2016 RESPECTIVELY. SHE HAS ENTERED *ARTREVIEW*'S POWER 100 LIST OF INFLUENTIAL ARTISTS SIX CONSECUTIVE TIMES SINCE 2018 AND HAS BEEN RANKED WITHIN ITS TOP TEN TWICE. CAO WAS ON THE JURY OF THE SELECTION COMMITTEE FOR THE CURATORSHIP OF THE 8TH BERLIN BIENNALE (2014), THE JURY OF THE BONNEFANTEN AWARD FOR CONTEMPORARY ART (2016), AND THE JURY OF THE HUGO BOSS ASIA ART PRIZE (2019). SHE WAS THE NOMINATOR OF THE ROLLS-ROYCE ART PROGRAM MUSE (2019) AND THE JUROR OF THE CHANEL NEXT PRIZE (2021 AND 2024).

CONTRIBUTORS

Yin Cao.txt

YIN CAO 曹音 IS CURATOR OF CHINESE ART AT THE ART GALLERY OF NEW SOUTH WALES. HER MOST RECENT EXHIBITIONS AND RELATED PUBLICATIONS INCLUDE *HEAVEN AND EARTH IN CHINESE ART: TREASURES FROM THE NATIONAL PALACE MUSEUM, TAIPEI* (AGNSW, 2019), *TANG: TREASURES FROM THE SILK ROAD CAPITAL* (AGNSW, 2016) AND *A SILK ROAD SAGA: THE SARCOPHAGUS OF YUHONG* (AGNSW, 2013). IN PREVIOUS ROLES SHE CO-ORGANISED THE INAUGURAL EXHIBITIONS AT THE ARTHUR M SACKLER MUSEUM OF ART AND ARCHAEOLOGY AT PEKING UNIVERSITY AND THE LEE KONG CHIAN ART MUSEUM AT THE NATIONAL UNIVERSITY OF SINGAPORE. TRAINED AS AN ARCHAEOLOGIST AT PEKING UNIVERSITY, SHE IS A PHD CANDIDATE WITH THE DEPARTMENT OF ANTHROPOLOGY AT HARVARD UNIVERSITY.

Ruby Arrowsmith-Todd.txt

RUBY ARROWSMITH-TODD 曹茹碧 IS CURATOR OF FILM AT THE ART GALLERY OF NEW SOUTH WALES, WHERE SHE HAS CURATED MAJOR CINEMA PROGRAMS AND COMMISSIONED NEW MOVING-IMAGE WORKS BY LOCAL AND INTERNATIONAL ARTISTS. RUBY HAS PUBLISHED WIDELY ON THE CULTURAL HISTORIES OF CINEMA IN AUSTRALIA AND IS GUEST CURATOR AT SYDNEY FILM FESTIVAL, SPECIALISING IN CONTEMPORARY ARTISTS' MOVING IMAGE.

Hou Hanru.txt

HOU HANRU 侯瀚如 IS AN INTERNATIONALLY RENOWNED CRITIC AND CURATOR, AND FORMER ARTISTIC DIRECTOR AT MAXXI, NATIONAL MUSEUM OF 21ST CENTURY ARTS, ROME, ITALY (2013–22). HE WAS PREVIOUSLY DIRECTOR OF EXHIBITIONS AND PUBLIC PROGRAMS AND CHAIR OF EXHIBITION AND MUSEUM STUDIES AT THE SAN FRANCISCO ART INSTITUTE (2006–12) AND HAS CURATED AND CO-CURATED OVER 150 EXHIBITIONS ACROSS THE WORLD, INCLUDING BIENNIALS AND TRIENNIALS IN JOHANNESBURG, VENICE, SHANGHAI, GWANGJU, GUANGZHOU, TIRANA, ISTANBUL, LYON, AUCKLAND AND SHENZHEN. HE HAS BEEN CLOSELY COLLABORATING WITH AND WRITING ON CAO FEI SINCE AROUND 2000, INCLUDING THE SOLO EXHIBITION *CAO FEI: SUPERNOVA* AT MAXXI (2021). HE IS AN ADVISOR TO NUMEROUS INTERNATIONAL INSTITUTIONS AND FREQUENT CONTRIBUTOR TO CONFERENCES, CATALOGUES, PERIODICALS AND BOOKS ON CONTEMPORARY ART, AND HAS BEEN GUEST EDITOR FOR INTERNATIONAL ART JOURNALS INCLUDING *FLASH ART*, *YISHU*, *ART ASIA PACIFIC* AND *LEAP*. A SELECTION OF HIS WRITINGS WAS PUBLISHED AS *ON THE MID-GROUND* IN 2002 (TIMEZONE 8, HONG KONG).

Michael Sun.txt

MICHAEL SUN 孙啟喆 IS A CRITIC, ESSAYIST AND EDITOR FROM CHINA AND AUSTRALIA. HIS WRITING ON FILM, MUSIC AND LITERATURE IS REGULARLY PUBLISHED IN *THE GUARDIAN*, *ESQUIRE*, *THE MONTHLY*, *THE SATURDAY PAPER* AND *ABC ARTS*, AMONG MANY OTHERS. RECENTLY, HE HOSTED *THE GUARDIAN*'S ONLINE CULTURE PODCAST *SAVED FOR LATER*. HE IS A WINNER OF THE NEW CRITIC PRIZE, AWARDED BY AUSTRALIAN LITERARY JOURNAL *KILL YOUR DARLINGS*.

Pao-chen Tang.txt

PAO-CHEN TANG 唐葆真 IS A LECTURER IN FILM STUDIES AT THE UNIVERSITY OF SYDNEY, WITH A PHD FROM THE UNIVERSITY OF CHICAGO. HE IS A SCHOLAR OF TRANSNATIONAL CINEMA AND ENVIRONMENTAL HUMANITIES. HE HAS WRITTEN FOR *SCREEN*, *JOURNAL OF CINEMA AND MEDIA STUDIES* AND *JOURNAL OF CHINESE CINEMAS*, AMONG OTHERS. CURRENT PROJECTS INCLUDE A CO-EDITED VOLUME ON MEDICAL CULTURE IN EAST ASIAN MEDIA AND HIS FIRST BOOK, DEVOTED TO ANIMISM IN CONTEMPORARY CINEMA.